CONTRACTUAL IN

MW01201847

Promises of indemnity are found in many kinds c　　　　　　　　　　, not just contracts of insurance. This book examines the nature and effect of contractual indemnities outside the insurance context. It is the first work to provide a detailed account of the subject in English law.

The book presents a coherent theory of the promise of indemnity while also addressing important practical issues, such as the construction of contractual indemnities. The subject is approached from two perspectives. The foundations are laid by examining general principles applicable to indemnities in various forms. This covers the nature of indemnity promises; general principles of construction; the determination of scope; and the enforcement of indemnities. The approach then moves from the general to the specific, by examining separately particular forms of indemnity. Included among these are indemnities against liability to third parties, and indemnities against default or non-performance by third parties.

The book states English law but it draws upon a considerable amount of material from other common law jurisdictions, including Australia, Canada, New Zealand and Singapore. It will appeal to readers from those countries.

Volume 12 in the series Hart Studies in Private Law

Contractual Indemnities

Wayne Courtney

·HART·
PUBLISHING
OXFORD AND PORTLAND, OREGON
2015

Published in the United Kingdom by Hart Publishing Ltd
16C Worcester Place, Oxford, OX1 2JW
Telephone: +44 (0)1865 517530
Fax: +44 (0)1865 510710
E-mail: mail@hartpub.co.uk
Website: http://www.hartpub.co.uk

Published in North America (US and Canada) by
Hart Publishing
c/o International Specialized Book Services
920 NE 58th Avenue, Suite 300
Portland, OR 97213-3786
USA
Tel: +1 503 287 3093 or toll-free: (1) 800 944 6190
Fax: +1 503 280 8832
E-mail: orders@isbs.com
Website: http://www.isbs.com

Hart Publishing is an imprint of Bloomsbury Publishing plc.

British Library Cataloguing in Publication Data
Data Available

ISBN: 978-1-50990-501-0

Typeset by Hope Services, Abingdon
Printed and bound in Great Britain by
CPI Group (UK) Ltd, Croydon CR0 4YY

Preface

This book draws upon material developed in my doctoral thesis on contractual indemnities, which I completed in 2009. The book retains the essential thesis argument, most evidently in chapters two and five, but its perspective and purpose are different. I have written the book primarily with practitioners in mind, to set out the legal principles applicable to contractual indemnities. The book's long gestation period is largely attributable to that change in emphasis, which entailed much rewriting and the inclusion of a substantial amount of new material. Nonetheless, I hope that the treatment will still appeal to scholars and advanced students of contract law.

My thesis supervisors were Professor John Carter and Professor Greg Tolhurst. I owe them a tremendous debt of gratitude for their steadfast encouragement and support. Undaunted, Professor Carter also read a complete draft of the manuscript for this book and made many insightful comments. Professor Barbara McDonald read an early draft of chapter four and provided advice generally on issues in tort. Other valuable suggestions came from my thesis examiners, Professor Hugh Beale, Professor Malcolm Clarke and Professor John Phillips. I have also benefited from stimulating conversations with, and the odd case reference supplied by, colleagues. I thank, among others, Associate Professor Lee Aitken, Ross Anderson, Ben Curtin, Professor Michael Furmston, Professor Sheelagh McCracken, Dr Eliza Mik, Professor Andrew Stewart, Professor John Stumbles and Dr Rafal Zakrzewski. At various stages I was fortunate to have research assistance from Sydney Law School students Laurence Rouesnel, Jeffrey Tjeuw, Evan Teo and Leona Zhang.

I am grateful to Richard Hart for agreeing to publish the work. The team at Hart Publishing were always accommodating, efficient and organised, making the process of publication an easy one.

Some elements of the analysis contained in the book have previously appeared in articles in the *Lloyd's Maritime and Commercial Law Quarterly* (2011), the *Journal of Contract Law* (2011, volume 27 and 2013, volume 30), and the *Journal of Business Law* (2012).

Several noteworthy decisions have appeared since the text of the hardcover edition was finalised. These are listed below, as it was not possible to incorporate them into the principal text of this paperback edition. The reader should consider them in conjunction with the material at the paragraphs indicated.

ABM Amro Commercial Finance Plc v McGinn [2014] EWHC 1674 (Comm), on the time at which loss under an indemnity crystallises ([9-29], [9-33]), and mitigation of loss ([4-29]).

Capita (Banstead 2011) Ltd v RFIB Group Ltd [2014] EWHC 2197 (Comm), on concurrent causes of loss ([4-22]–[4-25]), and whether an indemnified party can still suffer loss when its liability is satisfied by a gratuitous payment by another ([5-34], [6-23] fn 85).

Durley House Ltd v Firmdale Hotels Plc [2014] EWHC 2608 (Ch), on whether a settlement by the indemnified party eliminates the risk of loss and thus the need for indemnification ([7-30]), and whether the indemnified party can call for payment to itself before discharging a liability ([7-45]–[7-49]).

Heritage Oil and Gas Ltd v Tullow Uganda Ltd [2014] EWCA Civ 1048, on whether an express requirement of notice operates as a condition precedent to the right to indemnity ([5-9], [5-10], [5-16], [5-18] fn 64).

Rathbone Brothers Plc v Novae Corporate Underwriting Ltd [2014] EWCA Civ 1464, on subrogation and the order of precedence of insurance and non-insurance indemnities ([4-39], [4-41], [4-64], [4-74]).

Transocean Drilling UK Ltd v Providence Resources Plc [2014] EWHC 4260 (Comm), on the construction and operation of indemnities as exclusions of liability ([8-5], [8-11]).

Wuhan Guoyu Logistics Group Co Ltd Emporiki Bank of Greece SA [2013] EWCA Civ 1679; [2014] 1 Lloyd's Rep 273, on demand bonds and accounting between parties in the event of overpayment ([9-25]).

Wayne Courtney
1 October 2015

Contents

Contents

Table of Cases

Australia

Canada

New Zealand

Singapore

United Kingdom

Table of Cases

United States of America

Table of Legislation

Statutory Instruments

Table of Conventions, Agreements etc

Part I

Introduction

1

Introduction

Overview

Contractual Indemnities

[1–1] Subject of book. This is a book about contractual promises of indemnity. The expression 'contract of indemnity' is sometimes used to describe a contract in which the only, or only substantial, executory promise of one party is to indemnify another. For the purposes of this book, it is for the most part unnecessary to distinguish between a 'contract' of indemnity and a promise of indemnity that is merely one of many terms in a contract dealing with a larger subject-matter. The principal subject of analysis is a promise of indemnity in a contract rather than a contract of indemnity.

[1–2] What is a contractual indemnity? A promise of indemnity is a promise to protect another against loss from an event or events, or set of circumstances. It is often expressed in terms of a promise to 'save and keep harmless from loss',[1] or to 'secure' against loss.[2] The term 'indemnity' is, however, elastic and may be used more generally to describe any arrangement under which a party is not to suffer loss. A distinction must be drawn between two kinds of 'indemnity' arrangements: first, those in which the essential concern of the undertaking is to protect the promisee exactly against loss; secondly, those in which the essential concern of the undertaking is not of that nature, though the promisee is incidentally or effectively indemnified against a loss.

This book focuses on the former arrangements; these are promises of indemnity in the strict sense. Usage of 'indemnity' in the latter sense is, nonetheless, quite common. It might be said, for example, that A's payment of damages for breach of a contract with B, of an amount equal to B's loss or B's liability to another, indemnifies B;[3] or that A's guarantee to B provides an indemnity to B against default by a third party, C;[4] or that A's promise to B to pay C, a creditor of B, effects an indemnity against B's liability to C.[5]

---

[1] *Victorian WorkCover Authority v Esso Australia Ltd* [2001] HCA 53; (2001) 207 CLR 520, [16] (Gleeson CJ, Gummow, Hayne and Callinan JJ). See also *Sunbird Plaza Pty Ltd v Maloney* (1988) 166 CLR 245, 254 (Mason CJ); *Firma C-Trade SA v Newcastle Protection and Indemnity Association (The Fanti) (No 2)* [1991] 2 AC 1 (HL), 35 (Lord Goff).

[2] *Yeoman Credit Ltd v Latter* [1961] 1 WLR 828 (CA), 834 (Holroyd Pearce LJ); *State Government Insurance Office (Qld) v Brisbane Stevedoring Pty Ltd* (1969) 123 CLR 228, 253 (Walsh J); *Turner v Leda Commercial Properties Pty Ltd* [2002] ACTCA 8; (2002) 171 FLR 245, [34].

[3] cf *Birmingham and District Land Co v London and North Western Railway Co* (1886) 34 Ch D 261 (CA), 276 (Fry LJ); *Addis v Gramophone Co Ltd* [1909] AC 488 (HL), 491 (Lord Loreburn LC); *Wertheim v Chicoutimi Pulp Co* [1911] AC 301 (PC), 307; *Lexmead (Basingstoke) Ltd v Lewis* [1982] AC 225 (HL), 273 (Lord Diplock); *AMEV-UDC Finance Ltd v Austin* (1986) 162 CLR 170, 194 (Mason and Wilson JJ).

[4] *Harburg India Rubber Comb Co v Martin* [1902] 1 KB 778 (CA), 784 (Vaughan Williams LJ); *Bofinger v Kingsway Group Ltd* [2009] HCA 44; (2009) 239 CLR 269, [7].

[5] cf *Wren v Mahony* (1972) 126 CLR 212, 227 (Barwick CJ).

[1–3] Form and structure of contractual indemnities. Contractual promises of indemnity come in a great variety of forms, the best known of which is probably the insurer's promise of indemnity in a contract of indemnity insurance. This book is not, however, concerned with indemnity insurance.[6] Beyond insurance, an indemnity promise that is an express term of a contract is often structured in the following way:

(1) a description of the indemnifier or indemnifiers;
(2) a verb or set of verbs that describe the essential promise, for example, 'to indemnify', 'to save harmless', 'to keep harmless', or 'to make good';
(3) a description of the indemnified party or parties; and
(4) a statement of the scope of protection provided by the indemnity.

An implied indemnity can be conceptualised in a similar manner.

Promises of indemnity can be analysed along two major dimensions. One dimension is the essential method by which the indemnifier will protect the indemnified party against the defined loss. The two usual possibilities are to prevent loss and to compensate for loss.[7] The other dimension concerns the origin and nature of the loss against which protection is given. The archetypal non-insurance indemnity is an indemnity against claims by or liabilities to third parties. Other common forms include an indemnity against the consequences of a third party's non-performance of some obligation owed to the indemnified party, and an indemnity against the consequences of the indemnifier's breach of a contract with the indemnified party.

[1–4] Meaning of particular expressions. As this book focuses upon promises of indemnity, references to 'contractual indemnities' or 'indemnity clauses' or 'indemnity provisions' should be understood accordingly. The term 'contractual indemnity' is intended to include promises of indemnity in simple contracts and in deeds. To distinguish indemnities in insurance contracts from those in other contexts, the latter are described as non-insurance indemnities. The promisor under a promise of indemnity is described as the 'indemnifier' and the promisee as the 'indemnified party'.

Other Indemnities

[1–5] Sources of indemnity. The indemnities considered in this book arise from the agreement of the parties. A promise of indemnity may be an express term in a contract. The existence of a contract of indemnity may be inferred from the surrounding circumstances. A promise of indemnity may take effect as a term implied, on one of the usual bases or by statute, in a larger contract.

Indemnities also arise from sources other than the parties' agreement. Lord Wrenbury explained in *Eastern Shipping Co Ltd v Quah Beng Kee*:[8]

> A right to indemnity generally arises from contract express or implied, but it is not confined to cases of contract. A right to indemnity exists where the relation between the parties is such that either in law or in equity there is an obligation upon the one party to indemnify the other. There

---

[6] See [1–14].
[7] See [2–3].
[8] *Eastern Shipping Co Ltd v Quah Beng Kee* [1924] AC 177 (PC), 182–83.

are, for instance, cases in which the state of circumstances is such that the law attaches a legal or equitable duty to indemnify arising from an assumed promise by a person to do that which, under the circumstances, he ought to do. The right to indemnity need not arise by contract; it may (to give other instances) arise by statute

[1–6] Indemnities arising by operation of general law. Some indemnities arise by operation of the common law independently of contract. One instance is where a party requests another to perform an act of a ministerial nature, which the latter is under a duty to perform, and that act turns out to be injurious to the rights of a third party.[9] Situations in which one party discharges an obligation which properly rests upon another and then seeks recoupment have also been described as cases of indemnity. Some of the cases coincide with a genuinely contractual promise of indemnity, as where a debtor promises to indemnify a guarantor against its liability to the creditor in respect of the debtor's obligations;[10] or where the drawer of a bill of exchange promises to indemnify an accommodation party who accepts the bill against liability on it;[11] or where the assignee of a lease, who assumes possession of the premises, promises to indemnify the assignor against liabilities in relation to the lease.[12] In general, however, these recoupment cases should nowadays be understood as based on principles from the law of unjust enrichment.[13]

Indemnities of equitable origin are varied. A trustee is entitled to resort to the trust assets for reimbursement for expenses and to exonerate itself from liabilities that arise from proper performance of the trust.[14] A similar equitable right has been recognised for receivers, receivers and managers and company administrators appointed by the court,[15] agents who conduct a business for their principal,[16] and executors who carry on the business of the testator.[17] It was established in *Waring v Ward*[18] that the purchaser of the equity of redemption in a property is generally obliged to indemnify the vendor in respect of the liabilities secured by the mortgage.[19] A similar approach developed in relation to assignments of leases. In the absence of a contrary provision in the contract to assign, the assignor

---

[9] See, eg, *Sheffield Corp v Barclay* [1905] AC 392 (HL); *Naviera Mogor SA v Societe Metallurgique de Normandie (The Nogar Marin)* [1988] 1 Lloyd's Rep 412 (CA). See further [4–53].

[10] See [2–24].

[11] See [1–23], [6–10].

[12] cf *Moule v Garrett* (1872) LR 7 Ex 101.

[13] See generally C Mitchell, P Mitchell and S Watterson (eds), *Goff and Jones: The Law of Unjust Enrichment*, 8th edn (London, Sweet & Maxwell, 2011), 504–05, paras 19-16–19-18.

[14] *Worrall v Harford* (1802) 8 Ves Jun 4, 8; 32 ER 250, 252 (Lord Eldon LC); *Octavo Investments Pty Ltd v Knight* (1979) 144 CLR 360, 371 (Stephen, Mason, Aickin and Wilson JJ). A right also exists under the Trustee Act 2000, s 31(1). As to rights directly against a beneficiary who is *sui juris* and absolutely entitled to the trust property, see, eg, *Hardoon v Belilios* [1901] AC 118 (PC).

[15] *Re British Power Traction and Lighting Co Ltd; Halifax Joint Stock Banking Co v British Power Traction and Lighting Co Ltd* [1906] 1 Ch 497 (Ch) (receiver and manager); *Lockwood v White* [2005] VSCA 30; (2005) 11 VR 402, [34] (Winneke P) (company administrator).

[16] *Davis v Hueber* (1923) 31 CLR 583, 588 (Knox CJ and Starke J). Agents also have a general right to indemnity from the principal for whom they act: see [2–23].

[17] *Dowse v Gorton* [1891] AC 190 (HL); *Vacuum Oil Co Pty Ltd v Wiltshire* (1945) 72 CLR 319 (HCA), 325 (Latham CJ), 335–36 (Dixon J).

[18] *Waring v Ward* (1802) 7 Ves Jun 332; 32 ER 136. See also *Simpson v Forrester* (1973) 132 CLR 499. cf *Mills v United Counties Bank Ltd* [1912] 1 Ch 231 (CA) (no indemnity where express indemnity limited).

[19] The obligation is recognised by statute in some Commonwealth jurisdictions: see, eg, Conveyancing Act 1919 (NSW), s 79(1); Real Property Act 1900 (NSW), s 76. See generally *Re Alfred Shaw and Co Ltd, ex p Murphy* (1897) 8 QLJ 70 (SC); *Official Assignee v Jarvis* [1923] NZLR 1009 (CA).

was usually entitled to have included in the instrument of assignment an effective indemnity from the assignee against liability under the lease.[20]

[1–7] Indemnities arising by operation of statute. Indemnities may be created by statute in several ways. An indemnity may be implied by statute as a term in certain classes of contract,[21] in which case the indemnity is properly regarded as contractual. A statute may confer a power upon a court to order a party to pay another a sum which amounts to an indemnity.[22] A right of indemnity may be established directly by statute. There are many such statutory rights of indemnity in various Commonwealth jurisdictions. A common example is the provision for indemnity in the Partnership Acts.[23] It is generally expressed in terms that the firm is to indemnify every partner in respect of payments made and personal liabilities incurred in the ordinary and proper conduct of the business of the firm, or in anything necessarily done to preserve the firm's business or property.

[1–8] Indemnities as an incident of other remedies. An order for indemnity may be included as an element in more general relief granted by a court. Where a contract is rescinded for misrepresentation, the party at fault may be required to indemnify the rescinding party against liabilities, arising out of the subject-matter of the contract, which have been incurred owing to its entry into the contract.[24] An order for indemnity may be made incidentally to an order for specific performance of a contract.[25]

The Concept of Exact Protection

[1–9] Characteristics of indemnity. Indemnity promises do not all possess the same set of characteristics. That is not surprising, given the variety in form, context and the scope of protection. It is more accurate to say that there are various species within the genus of non-insurance contractual indemnity. Particular types of indemnity share more specific characteristics that are absent from others. There should, however, be some essential quality or characteristic that defines a promise as being one of indemnity, and so draws together indemnities in different forms. The overarching theory presented in this book is that there is such an essential characteristic: a promise of indemnity is a promise of exact protection against loss.

---

[20] *Pember v Mathers* (1779) 1 Bro CC 52; 28 ER 979; *Staines v Morris* (1812) 1 V & B 8; 35 ER 4; *Willson v Leonard* (1840) 3 Beav 373; 49 ER 146; *McMahon v Ambrose* [1987] VR 817 (FC), 825 (McGarvie J). cf *Wilkins v Fry* (1816) 1 Mer 244; 35 ER 665; *Re Poole and Clarke's Contract* [1904] 2 Ch 173 (CA). A similar covenant has been implied by statute, see, eg, Land Registration Act 1925, s 24(1)(b); Law of Property Act 1925, s 77(1)(C) (now repealed but unaffected in relation to tenancies prior to 1 January 1996).

[21] See, eg, nn 19–20.

[22] As under contribution statutes: see, eg, Civil Liability (Contribution) Act 1978, s 2(2).

[23] See, eg, Partnership Act 1890, s 24(2); Partnership Act 1892 (NSW), s 24(2).

[24] *Newbigging v Adam* (1886) 34 Ch D 582 (CA) (affd without reference to the point: *Adam v Newbigging* (1888) 13 App Cas 308 (HL)); *Curwen v Yan Yean Land Co Ltd* (1891) 17 VLR 745 (FC); *Speno Rail Maintenance Australia Pty Ltd v Hamersley Iron Pty Ltd* [2000] WASCA 408; (2000) 23 WAR 291, [35]–[40] (Malcolm CJ). cf *Whittington v Seale-Hayne* (1900) 82 LT 49 (Ch). See also Partnership Act 1890, s 41(c) (rescission of partnership contract for fraud or misrepresentation).

[25] *Paine v Hutchinson* (1868) LR 3 Ch App 388 (transfer of shares). This aspect of the decision might be explicable on the basis of a trust, or an implied term or collateral contract of indemnity: see generally [6–11]. cf *Cruse v Paine* (1868) LR 6 Eq 641, 653.

[1–10] Concept of exact protection. The concept of exact protection against loss comprises three elements. The first element concerns the efficacy of protection. A promise of indemnity will, if properly performed, secure the indemnified party against loss. The method by which the indemnifier must protect the indemnified party depends upon the construction of the promise of indemnity. There are two general methods of protection recognised in the cases: avoidance or prevention of loss to the indemnified party, and compensation of the indemnified party for loss it has already sustained.

The second element is the exactness of protection. The indemnified party should not be under-protected nor over-protected in respect of a loss. The requirement of exactness is concerned generally with the benefits received by the indemnified party (whether through the performance of the indemnity or otherwise) in relation to a given loss. The benefit is usually a sum of money. The requirement of exactness is manifested in several respects:

(1) A promise of indemnity is concerned with loss to an indemnified party, not loss to others.[26]

(2) The indemnified party generally has no direct right to recover for a loss unless and until it has actually sustained that loss.[27]

(3) The indemnified party recovers the amount of its actual loss, no more and no less, ascertained in accordance with the terms of the contract. The better view seems to be that, at least where the loss falls within the scope of the indemnity, recovery is not affected by damages principles such as remoteness or mitigation.[28]

(4) In certain circumstances the indemnified party may obtain relief in relation to a prospective, rather than actual, loss. In considering whether to grant relief and determining the form that relief should take, it is relevant to consider:

(a) whether a potential for loss exists; and

(b) whether certain forms of relief create a risk that the indemnified party will be over-compensated.[29]

Where there is no potential for loss, the indemnified party is not entitled to relief.

(5) Account must be taken of benefits obtained or obtainable by the indemnified party that diminish the loss and are not collateral.[30] If those benefits accrue before the indemnifier performs the indemnity, then the amount of the loss to be indemnified is reduced. Upon fully indemnifying the indemnified party, the indemnifier is generally entitled to be subrogated to the indemnified party's rights against others in diminution of the loss. The right of subrogation in this context derives from the nature of the contract of indemnity. It performs two functions: to ensure that ultimate responsibility for loss is transferred to the appropriate party; and to avoid double-recovery by the indemnified party, thus giving effect to the concept of exact protection.

The third element concerns loss. In theory, subject to statute and public policy, an indemnity may protect against all loss whatsoever from any cause. In practice, the indemnifier engages to protect the indemnified party against a limited range of losses. The concept of exact protection must, therefore, be understood by reference to a defined set of losses,

---

[26] See [5–34].
[27] See [5–40], [5–44].
[28] See [5–47]–[5–50].
[29] See [5–69], [5–71]–[5–73].
[30] See [4–37]–[4–43].

known as the scope of the indemnity.[31] In conformity with point (3) above, the scope of the indemnity is determined by construction.

[1–11] Operation as default rule. The concept of exact protection is subject to an important qualification. A contractual promise of indemnity is founded on the express or implied agreement of the parties. The effect of such a promise is, therefore, ultimately one of construction. Both general and specific principles of contractual construction are relevant.[32] The concept of exact protection is thus best understood as a 'default rule' or presumption of intention which may be altered or displaced by the parties. So, in *Morris v Ford Motor Co Ltd*,[33] James LJ explained that it is 'open to the parties to a contract of indemnity to contract on the terms of their choice, and by the terms they choose they can exclude rights which would otherwise attach to the contract'.

Scope and Structure of Book

Scope

[1–12] Aim and approach. The principal aim is to provide a coherent account of the construction and enforcement of promises of indemnity. The treatment of the subject involves both theoretical and practical aspects. Thus, consideration is given to identifying a unifying conception of the promise of indemnity, and also to matters such as whether an indemnifier may be discharged by a variation in the subject-matter of the indemnity. The emphasis on cohesion means that the treatment of theoretical and practical aspects tends towards the general rather than the particular. Most of the analysis is structured by reference to a type or class of indemnity – for example, an indemnity against liability – rather than a specific form of indemnity as may be found in a standard form charterparty, contract for towage services or construction contract.

[1–13] Applicable law. The primary source of material is case law, which reflects the contractual basis of the topic. Statutory intrusions have generally occurred by way of implied terms,[34] or prohibitions or limitations on the use of contractual indemnities in particular contexts.[35] The book purports to state the law in England and Wales. Australian law also provides a rich source of material, so many decisions and statutes from that jurisdiction are considered. The law on contractual indemnities in these jurisdictions is substantially the same. Reference is occasionally made to significant decisions from other common law jurisdictions, such as Canada, New Zealand, Singapore and the United States; and also to Scottish decisions. The law as stated in this book will be relevant to some extent in those jurisdictions.

---

[31] See generally ch 4.
[32] See generally ch 3.
[33] *Morris v Ford Motor Co Ltd* [1973] QB 792 (CA), 812.
[34] See [1–7].
[35] See, eg, Unfair Contract Terms Act 1977, ss 2 and 4; Companies Act 2006, ss 232–35. See further [5–30].

[1–14] Insurance and non-insurance indemnities. This book is concerned almost exclusively with indemnities in contracts outside the field of insurance. There are several reasons for this. Insurance is the subject of far more detailed treatment in cases, textbooks and other academic writings. Non-insurance indemnities may take forms not generally encountered in insurance. Furthermore, while it is often said that indemnity insurance contracts are contracts of indemnity, not all contracts of indemnity possess identical characteristics.[36]

Differences in context affect the construction of contractual indemnities. An indemnity in a non-insurance contract is often just one of many obligations, and may be ancillary to the main object of the contract. The object of the contract generally, or of the indemnity particularly, may be quite different from the object of insurance. The indemnified party generally does not furnish discrete consideration for the promise to indemnify. There may not be the same element of fortuity as is present in insurance. That is, a non-insurance indemnity may be given in contemplation of a loss that is inevitable or likely, the object being to secure the indemnified party against that loss when it materialises. The indemnifier under a non-insurance indemnity may have greater knowledge of the risk, or the occurrence of loss may lie within its control. There is no general duty of disclosure on the part of the indemnified party as exists in insurance.[37] Finally, a non-insurance indemnity may be used as a contractual device to enhance other legal rights of the indemnified party against the indemnifier in relation to a loss.

Principles from the law of insurance can, however, be useful insofar as they offer insight or guidance on the principles that might apply to non-insurance indemnities in the absence of more direct authority. Accordingly, insurance decisions are occasionally referred to throughout this book.

[1–15] Guarantees and indemnities. Guarantees and many forms of contractual indemnity perform a similar function, namely, to transfer or replicate responsibility for a risk that would not otherwise fall upon the promisor according to ordinary legal principles. It is also commonplace for contracts of guarantee to include, as a separate term, an indemnity against the debtor's default or non-performance.[38] To this extent, the law relating to guarantees is considered in this book but it is not intended to be a specialist work on the topic.

[1–16] Other limitations. Although construction of indemnities is considered extensively, this book does not directly address drafting techniques nor does it provide sample precedents. There are several areas of law that are practically important in the enforcement of indemnities: laws relating to insolvency and bankruptcy,[39] set-off, civil procedure and costs, subrogation and contribution. A detailed treatment is unnecessary, though there is some incidental consideration of these matters to the extent that they relate to general characteristics of indemnity.

---

[36] *Bosma v Larsen* [1966] 1 Lloyd's Rep 22 (QB), 27.
[37] cf *Way v Hearn* (1862) 13 CBNS 292; 143 ER 117.
[38] See generally ch 9.
[39] See, eg, W Courtney and JW Carter, 'Debts, Liquidated Sums and the Enforcement of Claims under Guarantees and Indemnities' (2013) 30 *Journal of Contract Law* 70.

Structure

[1–17] Structure of book. The book is divided into three parts and 10 chapters. Its structure reconciles two opposing considerations. As not all forms of indemnity possess identical characteristics, a thorough treatment requires consideration of distinct types of indemnity. Equally, the book is informed by the unifying theoretical perspective that the promise of indemnity is a promise of exact protection.[40] This theoretical framework is developed principally in chapter two and chapter five.

Part one contains the present chapter. Part two contains chapters two to five. The part is concerned with the construction and enforcement of promises of indemnity. Chapter two addresses the content of the promise: what is the indemnifier required to do and how may it be done? General principles of construction applicable to indemnities are considered in chapter three. Chapter four then examines the extent of protection provided by an indemnity. The most common type of dispute appearing in the cases is whether a particular loss falls within the scope of the indemnity, so that the indemnified party is entitled to be protected against it. Chapter five considers the enforcement of indemnity promises in relation to loss that has already occurred and (briefly) in relation to prospective loss. Chapter five also develops the second part of the theory of exact protection, by explaining how the indemnified party is exactly protected in the process of enforcing the indemnity.

Part three, comprising chapters six to ten, is concerned with four particular types of contractual indemnity. The chapters examine each type separately: in chapters six and seven, indemnities against claims by or liabilities to third parties; in chapter eight, indemnities against claims by or liabilities to the indemnifier; in chapter nine, indemnities against third party non-performance; and in chapter 10, indemnities against the consequences of the indemnifier's breach of contract. These types are not mutually exclusive, nor are they exhaustive of all possible forms of indemnity. They have been chosen because they arise most often in practice (and in the cases) and because each type exhibits characteristics and presents legal issues peculiar to that type.

Influences of Legal History

[1–18] General. This book does not provide a historical account of contractual indemnities, but the influences of legal history are sufficiently clear in modern cases on enforcement to deserve some mention. It is still relevant, for example, to distinguish between loss that has already occurred and loss that is anticipated, because the point affects both the right to indemnification and the manner in which the indemnifier may be compelled to perform. Part of the controversy surrounding the application of rules of causation, remoteness or mitigation can be traced back to the forms of action.

Before the forms of action were abolished and the administration of law and equity unified, there were two significant distinctions, one of substance, one of form. For protection against a loss that was merely anticipated, the indemnified party had to seek relief in a court

---

[40] See [1–10].

of equity.[41] This was because the promise to indemnify was generally a promise to keep the indemnified party harmless against a loss; the contract would only be broken when the indemnified party suffered loss. The remedies provided by the common law courts were inefficacious to protect the indemnified party beforehand. Intervention in equity rested upon the power of a court of equity to compel specific performance of a contract of indemnity.

Where a loss had already been sustained, the indemnified party could bring an action at law. Here, further distinctions were made in relation to the form of action. Claims might be brought in covenant, special assumpsit, debt or indebitatus assumpsit.

[1–19] Covenant and special assumpsit.[42] Claims were often brought in special assumpsit[43] on simple contracts, or in covenant[44] on agreements under seal. The claimant's declaration usually averred the existence of the agreement, the event or events amounting to damnification, and the failure of the defendant to indemnify the claimant at that time or at any time thereafter. There could be no breach unless a loss had occurred and that loss fell within the terms of the indemnity.[45] The action was for damages. The modern law, as it applies to enforcement of indemnities in relation to actual loss, derives from these cases. The indemnified party's claim for its actual loss is nowadays generally one for unliquidated damages for breach of contract; the breach occurs because the indemnifier has failed to indemnify against loss.[46]

Claims for actual loss under contracts of indemnity insurance were also regarded as claims for unliquidated damages,[47] except where there was a total loss under a valued policy, in which case the claim was for liquidated damages.[48] In England, the nature of the insured's claim and of the insurer's promise have proven controversial in recent times. The effect of the common law approach has been to deny the insured recovery for additional loss suffered where the insurer fails to provide compensation in a timely manner.[49]

---

[41] See further [7–18]–[7–21].

[42] See generally E Bullen and SM Leake, *Precedents of Pleadings in Personal Actions in the Superior Courts of Common Law*, 3rd edn (London, Stevens and Sons, 1868), 175ff.

[43] See, eg, *Hardcastle v Netherwood* (1821) 5 B & Ald 93; 106 ER 1127; *Thomas v Cook* (1828) 8 B & C 728; 108 ER 1213; *Williamson v Henley* (1829) 6 Bing 299; 130 ER 1295; *Huntley v Sanderson* (1833) 1 Cr & M 467; 149 ER 483; *Betts v Gibbins* (1834) 2 Ad & E 57; 111 ER 22; *Collinge v Heywood* (1839) 9 Ad & E 634; 112 ER 1352; *Toplis v Grane* (1839) 5 Bing NC 636; 132 ER 1245; *Reynolds v Doyle* (1840) 1 Man & G 753; 133 ER 536; *Groom v Bluck* (1841) 2 Man & G 567; 133 ER 873.

[44] See, eg, *Carr v Roberts* (1833) 5 B & Ad 78; 110 ER 721; *Smith v Howell* (1851) 6 Ex 730; 155 ER 739.

[45] cf *Draper v Thompson* (1829) 4 Car & P 84; 172 ER 618.

[46] *Johnson v Diamond* (1855) 11 Ex 73; 156 ER 750; *Finn v Gavin* [1905] VLR 93 (SC); *Muhammad Issa El Sheikh Ahmad v Ali* [1947] AC 414 (PC), 426; *Firma C-Trade SA v Newcastle Protection and Indemnity Association (The Fanti) (No 2)* [1991] 2 AC 1 (HL), 35–36 (Lord Goff); *Chief Commissioner of State Revenue v Reliance Financial Services Pty Ltd* [2006] NSWSC 1017, [31]–[34]. See further [5–41]–[5–43].

[47] *Grant v Royal Exchange Assurance Co* (1816) 5 M & S 439; 105 ER 1111; *Castelli v Boddington* (1852) 1 El & Bl 66; 118 ER 361; *Luckie v Bushby* (1853) 13 CB 864; 138 ER 1443; *Lewington v Scottish Union and National Insurance Co* (1901) 18 WN (NSW) 275 (SC). See generally *F & K Jabbour v Custodian of Israeli Absentee Property* [1954] 1 WLR 139 (QB), 143–45; *Alexander v Ajax Insurance Co Ltd* [1956] VLR 436 (SC), 445–49; *Chandris v Argo Insurance Co Ltd* [1963] 2 Lloyd's Rep 65 (QB), 74; *Phoenix General Insurance Co of Greece SA v Halvanon Insurance Co Ltd* [1987] 2 WLR 512 (QB), 528; *Penrith City Council v Government Insurance Office of NSW* (1991) 24 NSWLR 564 (SC), 568; *Odyssey Re (Bermuda) Ltd v Reinsurance Australia Corp Ltd* [2001] NSWSC 266; (2001) 19 ACLC 982; *New Cap Reinsurance Corp Ltd (in liq) v AE Grant* [2008] NSWSC 1015; (2008) 221 FLR 164, [87]–[90].

[48] *Irving v Manning* (1847) 1 HLC 287, 307; 9 ER 766, 775; *Alexander v Ajax Insurance Co Ltd* [1956] VLR 436 (SC), 445–46 (Sholl J). Contrast *Sunderland Marine Insurance Co v Kearney* (1851) 16 QB 925, 937; 117 ER 1136, 1141 (debt).

[49] See [2–31]–[2–32].

[1–20] Debt generally. Debt as a form of action was used relatively rarely for indemnities. One reason was that the promise to indemnify was generally construed as a promise to keep the indemnified party harmless against a loss. Such a promise is not a promise to pay the indemnified party directly and it may be performed by other means. Even if the promise were construed to be a promise to pay the indemnified party directly, indemnity requires payment of an amount which varies depending upon the loss actually sustained by the indemnified party. The amount payable by way of indemnity is not a sum certain as was required in the action of debt.[50]

[1–21] Debt on bond of indemnity. Debt was the appropriate form of action where the indemnity was given in the form of a conditional bond. An indemnity bond usually provided for a fixed sum stated as payable as penalty, subject to a condition of defeasance. The condition was in terms that the putative debtor would indemnify the creditor against losses, liabilities or obligations described expressly in the bond or incorporated by reference to another document.[51]

The provision for a fixed penalty is inconsistent with the principle of indemnity. It was recognised at least as early as 1771 that the creditor under the bond of indemnity could claim only the amount of loss actually sustained.[52] The claim was unliquidated in nature unless and until the amount of loss had been ascertained by some method binding upon the parties. Accordingly, an unascertained loss under a bond of indemnity was not subject to set-off[53] nor was it a 'debt' subject to garnishment;[54] and, for some time,[55] the indemnified party's right of proof in the bankruptcy of the indemnifier seems to have been more limited than it would have been for an ordinary 'debt'.[56]

[1–22] Indebitatus assumpsit. Indebitatus assumpsit was used for some claims in relation to indemnities, though none of the common counts was universally applicable. The only common count of real significance was for money paid,[57] usually described more fully as a claim for money paid by the (indemnified) claimant to the use of, or at the request of, the (indem-

---

[50] See generally JB Ames, *Lectures on Legal History* (Cambridge, MA, Harvard University Press, 1913), 89–90; AWB Simpson, *A History of the Common Law of Contract* (Oxford, Clarendon Press, 1975), 61–66; WM McGovern, 'Contract in Medieval England: the Necessity for Quid Pro Quo and a Sum Certain' (1969) 13 *American Journal of Legal History* 173, 186–90. In relation to insurance see CA Keigwin, 'The Action of Debt: Part I' (1922) 11 *Georgetown Law Journal* 20, 39 and CA Keigwin, 'The Action of Debt: Part II' (1923) 12 *Georgetown Law Journal* 28, 40. The modern law applicable to sums payable under the terms of a contract is not so rigid: *Jervis v Harris* [1996] Ch 195 (CA), 202–03 (Millett LJ).

[51] See, eg, *Hodgson v Bell* (1797) 7 TR 97; 101 ER 874; *The Overseers of St-Martin-in-the-Fields v Warren* (1818) 1 B & Ald 491; 106 ER 181; *Taylor v Young* (1820) 3 B & Ald 521; 106 ER 752; *White v Ansdell* (1836) 1 M & W 348; 150 ER 467; *Smith v Day* (1837) 2 M & W 684; 150 ER 931; *Field v Robins* (1838) 8 Ad & E 90; 112 ER 770; *Hankin v Bennett* (1853) 8 Ex 107; 155 ER 1279.

[52] *Goddard v Vanderheyden* (1771) 3 Wils 262, 269–70; 95 ER 1046, 1050.

[53] *Attwooll v Attwooll* (1853) 2 E & B 23; 118 ER 677. See also *Axel Johnson Petroleum AB v MG Mineral Group AG* [1992] 1 WLR 270 (CA), 273–74 (Leggatt LJ).

[54] *Johnson v Diamond* (1855) 11 Ex 73; 156 ER 750. See generally *Randall v Lithgow* (1884) 12 QBD 525 (QB); *Israelson v Dawson* [1933] 1 KB 301 (CA) (garnishee orders and contracts of insurance).

[55] The range of provable claims was gradually extended beyond 'debts' to include various forms of unliquidated claims: see, eg, Bankruptcy Act 1861, ss 153, 154; Bankruptcy Act 1869, s 31.

[56] *The Overseers of St-Martin-in-the-Fields v Warren* (1818) 1 B & Ald 491; 106 ER 181; *Taylor v Young* (1820) 3 B & Ald 521, 527; 106 ER 752, 754 (Abbott CJ), 529; 755 (Bayley J); *Hankin v Bennett* (1853) 8 Ex 107; 155 ER 1279. cf *Re Willis* (1849) 4 Ex 530, 538–39; 154 ER 1324, 1328.

[57] See generally Bullen and Leake, *Precedents of Pleadings in Personal Actions in the Superior Courts of Common Law* (n 42), 42–44. Occasionally, claims might be fitted within other counts: see, eg, *Re The Progress Assurance Co, ex p Bates* (1870) 39 LJ Ch 496 (Ch) (account stated).

nifying) defendant. As the name suggests, it was relevant where the indemnified party had paid expenses or discharged liabilities to third parties. The existence of an express promise of indemnity did not preclude an action for money paid[58] and so some cases could be brought in special assumpsit or in indebitatus assumpsit. The defendant's request for the claimant's payment might be found in the same circumstances that gave rise to the contractual promise of indemnity against the relevant liabilities.[59] Actual payment by the claimant was essential to the action for money paid; that same payment could constitute the actual loss which founded an action for damages in special assumpsit for failure to indemnify.

These points are illustrated by *Crampton v Walker*.[60] The claimant accepted a bill of exchange for the defendant's accommodation, the defendant promising in return to indemnify the claimant against liability on the bill. The claimant was compelled to pay the amount of the bill and interest, and also incurred costs in defending an action by the holder. The claimant claimed these losses as damages for breach of the indemnity and the defendant raised a set-off to each of the heads of loss. To determine whether the claimant's claim was sufficiently liquidated to be subject to set-off, Hill J adopted the test of whether the claimant could have maintained an action for money paid. The defendant's set-off against the amount of the bill plus interest was sound, because the claimant could have sued for that sum in an action for money paid.[61] A claim by the claimant for money paid in relation to the costs would have failed on the pleadings, which stated only that the costs were incurred, not paid.

[1–23] **Scope of indebitatus assumpsit.** The action was available where the payment by the indemnified party had the effect of relieving the indemnifier from a liability. Examples include the cases on bills of exchange in which the indemnified acceptor was compelled to pay the holder of the bill,[62] and payments by guarantors who had provided guarantees at the express or implied request of the debtor.[63] It has been suggested more recently that an analogous claim would be available where the indemnifier and indemnified party are held liable as concurrent tortfeasors, and the indemnified party discharges the common liability to the claimant.[64]

Whether the action was available to an indemnified party in other circumstances is less clear. In *Victorian WorkCover Authority v Esso Australia Ltd*,[65] which concerned a statutory indemnity, Gleeson CJ, Gummow, Hayne and Callinan JJ referred to the 'requirement of the common money count that the payments made by the claimant have exonerated the defendant from liability'.[66] This corresponds with the usual restitutionary analysis.[67] There are, however, some decisions to the contrary that emphasise the element of request.[68] In

---

[58] But see *Toussaint v Martinnant* (1787) 2 TR 100; 100 ER 55.
[59] See further [1–23].
[60] *Crampton v Walker* (1860) 3 El & El 321; 121 ER 463. cf *Brown v Tibbits* (1862) 11 CBNS 854, 866–67; 142 ER 1031, 1036 (Williams J), 868–69; 1037 (Byles J).
[61] *Garrard v Cottrell* (1847) 10 QB 679; 116 ER 258; *Sleigh v Sleigh* (1850) 5 Ex 514, 517; 155 ER 224, 225.
[62] See nn 60–61.
[63] See [2–24].
[64] *State Government Insurance Office (Qld) v Brisbane Stevedoring Pty Ltd* (1969) 123 CLR 228, 245 (Kitto J).
[65] *Victorian WorkCover Authority v Esso Australia Ltd* [2001] HCA 53; (2001) 207 CLR 520.
[66] *Victorian WorkCover Authority v Esso Australia Ltd* [2001] HCA 53; (2001) 207 CLR 520, [16].
[67] cf *Goff and Jones: The Law of Unjust Enrichment* (n 13), 519, para 20-01; K Mason, JW Carter and GJ Tolhurst, *Mason and Carter's Restitution Law in Australia*, 2nd edn (Sydney, LexisNexis Butterworths, 2008), 249–52, para 636.
[68] *Brittain v Lloyd* (1845) 14 M & W 762; 153 ER 683; *Lewis v Campbell* (1849) 8 CB 541; 137 ER 620; *Hutchinson v Sydney* (1854) 10 Ex 438; 156 ER 508. cf J Gleeson and N Owens, 'Dissolving Fictions: What to Do With the Implied Indemnity?' (2009) 25 *Journal of Contract Law* 135, 155–59.

Lewis v Campbell,[69] the claimant was indebted to a third party. Rather than pay the third party directly, the claimant reached an arrangement under which the amount of the debt was credited towards an alleged liability of the third party to the defendant. The defendant promised to indemnify the claimant against claims by the third party. The third party sued the claimant; the defendant assumed responsibility for the defence of the action and lost; the claimant then paid the amount of the judgment against him. Wilde CJ rejected the argument that the action for money paid could only be brought where the claimant's payment had relieved the defendant of a liability to the third party. In the circumstances, the claimant could even succeed independently of the contract of indemnity. The indemnity aside, the request could be inferred from the claimant's conduct in permitting the defendant to defend the action and from the defendant's conduct in so doing.

The point was raised more recently in relation to contracts of reinsurance in *New Cap Reinsurance Corp Ltd (in liq) v AE Grant*.[70] The reinsurance contracts provided indemnity against losses paid by the reinsured. It was held that the reinsured could have recovered such amounts from the reinsurer by analogy with the common count for money paid.[71] If that conclusion is correct, it appears to extend the reasoning in the authorities above. It is not clear that the reinsurer would be liable at all to the original insured, so as to be exonerated by the reinsured's payment. Nor is it clear that there is a request by the reinsurer that the reinsured make the payments, unless that request is to be inferred from the express statement of the scope of the indemnity.[72]

---

[69] *Lewis v Campbell* (1849) 8 CB 541; 137 ER 620.
[70] *New Cap Reinsurance Corp Ltd (in liq) v AE Grant* [2008] NSWSC 1015; (2008) 221 FLR 164.
[71] *New Cap Reinsurance Corp Ltd (in liq) v AE Grant* [2008] NSWSC 1015; (2008) 221 FLR 164, [107]–[108].
[72] cf *New Cap Reinsurance Corp Ltd (in liq) v AE Grant* [2008] NSWSC 1015; (2008) 221 FLR 164, [99].

Part II

General Principles

2

The Nature of the Promise of Indemnity

Introduction

[2–1] **Purpose of chapter.** This chapter provides a theoretical foundation for understanding promises of indemnity. The analysis draws together characteristics of indemnity promises in various contexts, explaining their operation in terms of the unifying concept of exact protection against loss. The principles and characteristics synthesised in this chapter will recur throughout this work. The chapter focuses principally on the nature of the promise of indemnity, that is, what the promise in essence requires the indemnifier to do to protect the indemnified party.

[2–2] **Structure of chapter.** The chapter is divided into five sections. As the first section explains, an indemnity promise can be construed in different ways. The two most common constructions of the promise are considered in the next two sections. The fourth section notes other constructions. The chapter ends by comparing these constructions with the construction of the insurer's promise of indemnity in a contract of indemnity insurance.

Differences in the Nature of Indemnity Promises

[2–3] **What indemnity requires depends upon construction.** At the highest level of generality, a promise of indemnity will, when performed, secure the indemnified party against loss within the scope of the indemnity. How that is to be done involves two further questions. First, what, in general terms, does the indemnity require the indemnifier to do by way of 'indemnity'? Secondly and more particularly, what modes of performance will be sufficient to discharge the obligation to indemnify? There is no uniform rule applicable to either of these questions; rather, the answer depends upon the construction of the contract.

In relation to the first question, two constructions are commonly recognised in the cases. One construction is that the indemnifier will keep the indemnified party from loss; that is, that the indemnifier will prevent or avoid loss to the indemnified party. The other construction is that the indemnifier will compensate the indemnified party for loss it suffers. Thus, in *McIntosh v Dalwood (No 4)*,[1] Street CJ remarked that '[i]n every case the contractual obligation must first be ascertained'. He went on to identify two types of indemnities: 'an obligation to indemnify a person, in the sense of repaying to him a sum of money after

---

[1] *McIntosh v Dalwood (No 4)* (1930) 30 SR (NSW) 415 (FC), 418.

he has paid it'; and 'an obligation to relieve a debtor by preventing him from having to pay his debt'. The former is equivalent to a compensatory construction. The latter is equivalent to the construction that the indemnifier will keep the indemnified party (the debtor) harmless from loss. This is because the usual rule is that the indemnified party sustains a loss upon paying the third party.[2] By interceding and relieving the indemnified party of the debt, the indemnifier has spared the indemnified party from payment and so avoided the loss.

[2–4] **Significance of different constructions.** The distinction between prevention and compensation has implications for the time and manner of performance of the indemnity. For the former class of indemnities, the indemnifier is expected to act before the indemnified party suffers a loss. In contrast, it is implicit in the notion of compensation that the indemnifier is to perform after the indemnified party has already sustained loss. Furthermore, where the indemnity requires the indemnifier to keep the indemnified party harmless from loss, there is often greater variety in the possible modes of performance. Indemnities that operate by way of compensation are performed simply by payment to the indemnified party of a sum equal to its loss according to the terms of the indemnity.

The distinction may have more subtle consequences for the enforcement of the indemnity.[3] An indemnity that operates by way of prevention of loss may be specifically enforced before the indemnified party has sustained loss. That remedy is not appropriate for indemnities of a compensatory nature. The time at which the indemnified party's cause of action accrues may be the same upon either construction; equally, it is possible to conceive of situations in which the action on a compensatory indemnity might arise at a later time.[4] Where the indemnified party claims for consequential losses beyond the scope of the indemnity, the difference in the nature of the promise may affect the extent of recovery.[5] So, for example, under a preventive indemnity, the indemnified party may be debarred from recovering further loss that is caused by a failure to receive timely payment (as damages) for its original loss. Such a claim may be, in substance, one for damages for the 'late' payment of damages.[6]

[2–5] **Limitations of the distinction.** The significance and utility of the distinction between these two constructions of indemnity promises should not be overstated. Many cases are satisfactorily resolved without reference to it. One reason is that disputes often concern the scope of protection and not the essential nature of the promise. A related reason is that the indemnified party may be content to claim for an actual loss that is within scope. Although the underlying technical analysis differs, either construction leads to the result that the indemnified party recovers the amount of that actual loss on the basis prescribed by the indemnity. To this extent, it should not matter whether the indemnified party's claim is regarded as one for damages for breach or as a claim to enforce a primary contractual obligation to pay a money sum as compensation.

A simple taxonomy based on a division into these two classes is problematic in some respects. It is not always easy to apply or meaningful in context. Some indemnities might

---

[2] See [6–23].
[3] See generally R Zakrzewski, 'The Nature of a Claim on an Indemnity' (2006) 22 *Journal of Contract Law* 54, 65–66.
[4] See [5–44].
[5] See [5–51]–[5–56].
[6] See [5–54].

best be regarded as protean or, perhaps, composite, in nature. An agent's indemnity from the principal may operate in a preventive or compensatory manner, depending upon the nature of the loss in the circumstances.[7] Indemnities against the consequences of the indemnifier's breach of contract might generally be regarded as preventive in character, though this classification can be artificial.[8] Such indemnities are often contractual devices designed to enhance the indemnified party's recovery of compensation for loss from breach. Furthermore, the taxonomy is not exhaustive: a party may be indemnified by means other than the prevention of loss or payment of compensation for loss.[9]

The taxonomy is also quite general. Within each of the two classes are different types of indemnity with different characteristics. The indemnifier may promise to keep the indemnified party harmless from loss, but the permitted or required modes of performance may differ depending upon the circumstances. Other factors, such as the scope of the indemnity, may be more significant or distinctive than the classification of the indemnity promise. So, for example, a promise by A to indemnify B against claims by A may be characterised as an indemnity of a preventive kind, but its most important, practical quality is that it may operate to bar action by A against B.[10]

Indemnity as a Promise of Prevention of Loss

[2–6] Prevention as predominant construction. Of the two usual constructions of indemnity promises, prevention of loss is the most commonly recognised. In *Firma C-Trade SA v Newcastle Protection and Indemnity Association (The Fanti) (No 2)*,[11] Lord Goff remarked that 'a promise of indemnity is simply a promise to hold the indemnified person harmless against a specified loss or expense'. To similar effect is the statement of Buckley LJ in *Re Richardson*,[12] that '[i]ndemnity requires that the party to be indemnified shall never be called upon to pay'. The same construction is recognised implicitly by an order for specific enforcement of the indemnity in relation to a liability to a third party. Such relief is only available where the indemnity promise is preventive in nature.[13]

Although the preventive construction is very common, it is doubtful whether it can be described as the default construction for all forms of indemnity. Many of the decisions endorsing this construction have concerned indemnities against claims by or liabilities to third parties.[14]

---

[7] See [2–23]. The nature of a time charterer's indemnity to the shipowner has not yet been clearly established but it may be similar: cf *Telfair Shipping Corp v Inersea Carriers SA (The Caroline P)* [1985] 1 WLR 553 (QB), 568–69.

[8] See [10–28].

[9] See [2–28], [2–29].

[10] See [8–9], [8–15].

[11] *Firma C-Trade SA v Newcastle Protection and Indemnity Association (The Fanti) (No 2)* [1991] 2 AC 1 (HL), 35.

[12] *Re Richardson, ex p the Governors of St Thomas's Hospital* [1911] 2 KB 705 (CA), 716.

[13] See [7–20].

[14] See [6–7]–[6–9].

[2–7] **Promises to perform particular acts and promises of indemnity.** A promise of indemnity by prevention of loss must be distinguished from a promise to perform an act that will, in effect, prevent the indemnified party from suffering loss. So, for example, a promise by A to pay a sum of money to B, in respect of an anticipated liability of B to C, is not a promise of indemnity.[15] The same applies where A promises B to pay the sum directly to C. Timely performance of that promise may 'indemnify' B against the liability to C, but the promise is not a promise of indemnity.[16]

Illustrations

[2–8] **Particular terms.** Expressions such as 'save harmless', 'keep harmless' or 'hold harmless' may indicate the parties' intention that the indemnity be preventive in nature.[17] In *Collinge v Heywood*,[18] Collinge was encouraged to commence an action against another, in return for Heywood's promise 'to save, defend, and keep harmless and indemnified'[19] Collinge against, inter alia, costs, damages and expenses incurred or sustained in connection with the action. Collinge incurred legal costs in 1826 and paid his attorney's bill in part in 1830 and in part in 1831. It was held that Collinge's right of action on the indemnity only accrued once he had paid his attorney. In *Firma C-Trade SA v Newcastle Protection and Indemnity Association (The Fanti) (No 2)*,[20] Lord Jauncey explained the result as follows:

> Heywood would not have been in breach until he had failed to keep Collinge 'harmless and indemnified,' a failure which would only occur when Collinge had had to make payment. The fact that Heywood would be in breach of contract as soon as Collinge paid imports, of necessity, that he was contractually bound to act before Collinge paid

[2–9] **Indemnities against claims by or liabilities to third parties.** Indemnities against claims by or liabilities to third parties are often construed as being preventive in nature.[21] This construction has been adopted in relation to liabilities on bills of exchange,[22] other contractual liabilities to pay money to third parties,[23] liabilities arising under statute[24] and liabilities in tort or for breach of contract.[25] Where an agent has a contractual right to indemnity from the principal, then in some cases[26] the principal may be expected to intervene and keep the agent from loss arising from liabilities to others.[27]

---

[15] *cf Brough v Oddy* (1829) 1 Russ & M 55; 39 ER 22.

[16] *Wren v Mahony* (1972) 126 CLR 212, 226–28 (Barwick CJ).

[17] *Warwick v Richardson* (1842) 10 M & W 284, 288; 152 ER 477, 479 (Alderson B) ('save harmless'). See also [6–8]. *cf Sunbird Plaza Pty Ltd v Maloney* (1988) 166 CLR 245, 254 (Mason CJ) (expression 'keep harmless' used in relation to several cases not all of which were clearly of this nature); *Farstad Supply AS v Enviroco Ltd (The Far Service)* [2010] UKSC 18; [2010] 2 Lloyd's Rep 387, [24]–[27] (Lord Clarke), [57] (Lord Mance) ('hold harmless' effecting exclusion of liability).

[18] *Collinge v Heywood* (1839) 9 Ad & E 634; 112 ER 1352.

[19] This is the form of the indemnity as recited in the declaration. The promise was also described as one to 'save, defend and keep indemnified'.

[20] *Firma C-Trade SA v Newcastle Protection and Indemnity Association (The Fanti) (No 2)* [1991] 2 AC 1 (HL), 41.

[21] See [6–7], [6–9].

[22] See [6–10].

[23] See [6–14].

[24] See [6–12].

[25] See [6–15], [6–16].

[26] Contrast [2–23].

[27] See [6–13].

[2–10] Indemnities against claims by or liabilities to the indemnifier. The distinctive feature of this type of indemnity is that it may provide the indemnified party with a defence to a claim by the indemnifier. The basis of that defence depends upon the construction of the indemnity. Before the fusion of the administration of law and equity, a defence could arise at common law for the avoidance of circuity of action.[28] If the indemnifier's action succeeded and the indemnified party satisfied the judgment, then the indemnified party would have a reciprocal claim against the indemnifier. The claim could be for damages for breach of contract by failing to keep the indemnified party harmless from loss.[29]

Another, more modern perspective is that such an indemnity promise is tantamount to, or carries with it by implication, a promise by the indemnifier not to sue the indemnified party.[30] That perspective is consistent with a preventive construction. By observing its promise not to sue, the indemnifier avoids loss to the indemnified party that would otherwise arise.

[2–11] Indemnities against non-performance by third party. In contrast to indemnities against claims by or liabilities to third parties, it is difficult to identify a usual or default construction that applies to indemnities against non-performance by third parties. *McGuinness v Norwich and Peterborough Building Society*[31] exemplifies a preventive construction. The indemnifier agreed to 'make good' any losses or expenses which the lending bank suffered if the borrower failed to pay the sums owing, or if the obligations in the principal contract were unenforceable against the borrower. It was held that the nature of the indemnity was to save the bank harmless against loss.[32] The indemnifier's breach of that term would give rise to a liability in unliquidated damages. That liability was, therefore, not a 'debt . . . for a liquidated sum' as required by statute for a creditor's petition for bankruptcy.[33]

Method of Indemnification

[2–12] Discretion as to method of performance. The usual construction of a preventive indemnity is that the method of performance is left to the indemnifier's discretion. The point arises most clearly in the cases concerning claims by or liabilities to third parties.[34]

The indemnifier's discretion as to the method of performance may be circumscribed by several factors. The parties may expressly prescribe the manner in which the indemnity is to be performed, though the promise must retain its character as an indemnity.[35] In the absence of express provision, it may be inferred from the surrounding circumstances that the indemnity is to be performed in one of a limited number of ways. A promise to indemnify against liabilities is sometimes construed as a promise to relieve the indemnified party

---

[28] See [8–15].
[29] The defence could also be explained on the basis of a promise to compensate. See further [8–9].
[30] See [8–10].
[31] *McGuinness v Norwich and Peterborough Building Society* [2011] EWCA Civ 1286; [2012] 2 All ER (Comm) 265.
[32] *McGuinness v Norwich and Peterborough Building Society* [2011] EWCA Civ 1286; [2012] 2 All ER (Comm) 265, [8].
[33] Under the Insolvency Act 1986, s 267(2)(b).
[34] See [7–4]–[7–5].
[35] See [2–7].

by preventing that party from having to pay to satisfy the liability.[36] If that description were applied strictly, it would seem to be insufficient for the indemnifier simply to put the indemnified party in funds before the latter paid. That method of performance is, however, acceptable in other circumstances.[37]

Another constraint is that the indemnifier may lack the power to perform in a particular manner. One method of performing an indemnity against claims by third parties, for example, is for the indemnifier successfully to defend an action against the indemnified party. An indemnifier does not, however, have the power generally to take up and control the defence on the indemnified party's behalf.[38] Finally, in some circumstances the indemnified party may obtain specific relief to enforce the indemnity before it suffers loss. The form of the order may exclude or curtail a discretion that the indemnifier could otherwise have exercised had it performed voluntarily.

[2–13] Examples of satisfactory performance of indemnity. The following acts may, in appropriate circumstances, constitute satisfactory performance of a preventive indemnity:

(1) The indemnifier performs some other contractual or legal duty so as to avoid inflicting a loss on the indemnified party, or exposing the indemnified party to potential loss.[39]
(2) The indemnifier successfully defends a claim by a third party against the indemnified party.[40]
(3) The indemnifier pays directly to a third party the amount of the indemnified party's liability to that party.[41]
(4) The indemnifier by some other means procures the release or discharge of the indemnified party from a claim by or liability to the third party.[42]
(5) The indemnifier provides the indemnified party with funds sufficient to satisfy a claim or liability before the indemnified party is called upon to pay.[43]
(6) The indemnifier withholds or withdraws a claim it could otherwise press.[44] Where A indemnifies B against claims by or liabilities to A, this is an obvious method of performance. It may also be relevant where A indemnifies B against claims by third parties. A may, for example, have a claim against C which, if pursued, would cause C to make a corresponding claim against B. This sometimes occurs in the context of carriage of goods. Another possibility is that A and B are under a common liability to C, such that A would be entitled to claim contribution from B. If, however, A were to recover contribution from B, then B would not be completely protected against the liability to C.

---

[36] *Re Richardson, ex p the Governors of St Thomas's Hospital* [1911] 2 KB 705 (CA), 716 (Buckley LJ); *McIntosh v Dalwood (No 4)* (1930) 30 SR (NSW) 415 (FC), 418 (Street CJ); *Re Dixon* [1994] 1 Qd R 7 (FC), 19–20 (Shepherdson J); *Victorian WorkCover Authority v Esso Australia Ltd* [2001] HCA 53; (2001) 207 CLR 520, [17] (Gleeson CJ, Gummow, Hayne and Callinan JJ).
[37] See [7–16].
[38] See [7–7].
[39] *cf* [9–39], [10–28].
[40] See [7–8].
[41] See [7–10].
[42] See [7–11].
[43] See [7–16].
[44] See [7–12]–[7–15].

Prevention of Loss and Exact Protection

[2–14] Prevention of loss in general. The principle of exact protection easily accommodates the preventive construction at an abstract level. One means of protecting the indemnified party against a loss is to prevent that loss ever occurring. The protection is exact from the indemnified party's perspective because there is no question of under-compensation or over-compensation for loss. It is more challenging to demonstrate that the application of a preventive construction in practice conforms to the principle of exact protection. Of the methods of indemnification described earlier,[45] many concern indemnities against claims or liabilities and these require further explanation.

[2–15] Exoneration from claim or liability. Analysis begins with the proposition that the indemnified party generally suffers loss when it pays money to satisfy the claim or liability against it.[46] The existence of a claim or liability represents only a potential loss. By exonerating the indemnified party from the claim or liability, the indemnifier thereby removes the source of potential loss. It follows then, that if the indemnifier acts to eliminate the claim or liability before the indemnified party pays, the indemnifier has exactly protected the indemnified party. On this basis, performance by successfully defending an action, or procuring the release or discharge of a claim or liability, is consistent with the concept of exact protection.

[2–16] Direct payment to third party. It appears to be accepted that this method of performance exonerates the indemnified party or, at least, confers upon the indemnified party a good defence to a claim by the third party.[47] The indemnified party is, then, protected against loss. As the payment is made to the third party, the indemnified party is not directly enriched, nor made poorer; in this respect, the protection is exact.[48]

[2–17] Payment in advance to indemnified party. If the indemnifier pays the indemnified party before the latter pays the third party, the indemnified party can meet the liability without drawing upon its own resources. In that respect, the indemnified party has been protected against loss. There remains a risk that the amount provided will prove to be more than necessary to protect the indemnified party. The indemnified party may, for example, accept the sum and then defend the third party's action successfully, or compromise for less,[49] or suffer judgment but evade enforcement.

There are at least two theoretical solutions. One is to compel the indemnified party to pay over the funds to the third party.[50] Another solution is to compel the indemnified party to account to the indemnifier for any excess. This might be justified on the basis that the overpayment was a mistake,[51] or, perhaps, on the basis that it is implicit in the principle of

---

[45] See [2–13].
[46] See [6–23].
[47] See [7–10].
[48] *cf Transportation Displays Inc v Winston* 870 F Supp 74 (1994) (USDC SDNY) (consequences of overpayment by indemnifier to third party).
[49] *cf British Dominions General Insurance Co Ltd v Duder* [1915] 2 KB 394 (CA) (compromise by reinsured before payment by reinsurer).
[50] See further [7–56], [7–61]–[7–62].
[51] In the insurance context, *cf Stearns v Village Main Reef Gold Mining Co Ltd* (1905) 10 Com Cas 89 (CA) and the analysis of *Castellain v Preston* (1883) 11 QBD 380 (CA) given in *British Traders' Insurance Co Ltd v Monson* (1964) 111 CLR 86, 94 (Kitto, Taylor and Owen JJ).

exact protection and is analogous to the obligation to account for other benefits received after indemnification.[52] It is not clear, however, that all cases of overpayment must be covered by one of these solutions. Where the indemnifier makes the payment voluntarily in performance of the contract, there is some force in the view that the principle of exact protection should not be applied rigorously. In particular, if the method of performance has been left to the indemnifier's discretion, then its payment to the indemnified party in advance involves a choice of one of alternative modes of performance.[53] The indemnifier could have attempted to deal with the third party directly, so it is difficult to see why it ought to be able to complain afterwards that it has overpaid the indemnified party.[54]

[2–18] Abandoning claim. The analysis is substantially the same as that for exoneration. If the indemnifier's claim is the cause of a third party's claim against the indemnified party, then abandoning the claim has the practical effect of eliminating the potential loss emanating from the third party. The same applies where the only claim is by the indemnifier directly against the indemnified party. Where the indemnifier and indemnified party are both liable to the third party, and the indemnifier could claim against the indemnified party in respect of that liability, then abandoning that claim only eliminates one source of potential loss. The indemnifier must also exonerate the indemnified party from the liability to the third party.

Indemnity as a Promise of Compensation for Loss

[2–19] Indemnity by compensation. In *Official Assignee v Jarvis*[55] Salmond J said:

> [A] contract of indemnity was in general construed at common law as being merely a contract to reimburse the indemnified party against loss actually incurred by him. Until and unless he had actually paid the principal creditor, therefore, he had no right of action under the indemnity

The suggestion that compensation was the usual construction might draw limited support from *Spark v Heslop*.[56] The defendant promised 'to be answerable' to the claimant for, inter alia, costs, damages and expenses which the claimant might sustain by bringing an action against another. The question was whether the claimant could recover from the defendant for his own legal costs incurred in the action though he had not yet paid them. Wightman J said that the agreement was 'not a contract of indemnity *in the ordinary sense*. It is a contract, *not merely to repay*, but also to take care that the plaintiff shall not be called upon to pay'.[57]

---

[52] See [4–37].
[53] *Yates v Hoppe* (1850) 9 CB 542; 137 ER 1003. But note Maule J's suggestion (545; 1004) of a 'failure of basis' exception.
[54] *cf Lacey v Hill; Crowley's Claim* (1874) LR 18 Eq 182, 191–92.
[55] *Official Assignee v Jarvis* [1923] NZLR 1009 (CA), 1016. These remarks were approved in *Ramsay v National Australia Bank Ltd* [1989] VR 59 (FC), 66. *cf Re Law Guarantee Trust and Accident Society Ltd* [1914] 2 Ch 617 (CA), 638 (Kennedy LJ).
[56] *Spark v Heslop* (1859) 1 El & El 563; 120 ER 1020.
[57] *Spark v Heslop* (1859) 1 El & El 563, 571; 120 ER 1020, 1024 (emphasis added).

The better view is that there was no difference between common law and equity in the construction of promises of indemnity.[58] Moreover, the old reported cases, most of which concern indemnities against liabilities to third parties, tend to favour a preventive construction. The error in Salmond J's reasoning is that it conflates the construction of the promise of indemnity with its enforcement in practice. Even for preventive indemnities, an action at common law could not be brought until the indemnified party suffered loss by paying the third party. It is in that sense that the award of damages for breach 'reimbursed' the indemnified party.

Compensation for loss is clearly established as a possible construction of a non-insurance indemnity,[59] though it appears less frequently than the preventive construction. A compensatory construction may be made clear by express terms of the contract, or it may be inferred from the commercial context.

[2–20] Promises to pay promisee and promises to indemnify. A distinction must be made between promises to indemnify by compensation, and promises to pay the promisee a sum which may, in effect, compensate the promisee for some loss or expense. A promise to pay a creditor the sum owing by a debtor, if the debtor defaults, may 'indemnify' the creditor but such a promise is usually regarded as one of guarantee.[60] The issuer of a performance bond may promise the beneficiary to pay upon demand a sum which the beneficiary claims is necessary to meet a loss under the principal contract. Yet a performance bond is not in general a contract of indemnity.[61] A promise to pay remuneration for services is distinguishable from a promise to indemnify against remuneration for services to the extent that the fees have not been recovered from another.[62]

Illustrations

[2–21] Express provision for compensation for loss. The terms of the contract may expressly provide that the indemnifier is to compensate for loss actually sustained by the indemnified party. In *Wardley Australia Ltd v Western Australia*,[63] the Western Australian state government provided an indemnity to the lending bank against the bank's 'net loss' arising if the borrower did not satisfy in full its liabilities under a bills facility. The indemnity contained several terms relating to the calculation of 'net loss' and concluded with an undertaking to pay on demand the sum claimed by the bank. Mason CJ, Dawson, Gaudron and McHugh JJ explained that the indemnity 'created a liability on the part of the [government] to the Bank to make payment if and when the Bank's relevant "net loss" was ascertained and quantified, subject to the making of a demand for payment by the Bank'.[64]

Other examples can be found in the cases on leases of chattels or hire-purchase agreements, where a third party indemnifies the lessor/owner in relation to performance by the

---

[58] See further [6–7].
[59] See, eg, *McIntosh v Dalwood (No 4)* (1930) 30 SR (NSW) 415 (FC), 418 (Street CJ); *Newman v McNicol* (1938) 38 SR (NSW) 609 (SC), 626; *Scott Lithgow Ltd v Secretary of State for Defence* 1989 SC (HL) 9, 20; *Paterson v Pongrass Group Operations Pty Ltd* [2011] NSWSC 1588, [57].
[60] See [9–11].
[61] See [9–25].
[62] *Chief Commissioner of State Revenue v Reliance Financial Services Pty Ltd* [2006] NSWSC 1017, [33].
[63] *Wardley Australia Ltd v Western Australia* (1992) 175 CLR 514.
[64] *Wardley Australia Ltd v Western Australia* (1992) 175 CLR 514, 524.

lessee/hirer. In *Yeoman Credit Ltd v Latter*,[65] the third party promised the finance company 'to indemnify . . . against any loss resulting from or arising out of the [hire-purchase] agreement and to pay . . . the amount of such loss on demand'. Another clause of that agreement defined how the loss was to be calculated. Holroyd Pearce LJ and Harman LJ held that the third party's contract with the finance company was an indemnity and not merely a guarantee. The third party's promise was, essentially, to compensate the finance company for loss on the basis stated in the contract.

[2–22] Where indemnifier unable or not expected to intervene. In some circumstances it may be impossible, or commercially impracticable or undesirable, for the indemnifier to intervene in a transaction so as to avoid loss to the indemnified party. The inference may be drawn that the parties intended the indemnified party to be protected by way of compensation for loss and not prevention of loss.[66] This perspective can be illustrated by contrasting two decisions, *Total Oil Products (Australia) Pty Ltd v Robinson*[67] and *Trewheelar v Trukeel Pty Ltd.*[68]

In *Total Oil*, the claimant contracted to purchase land and an associated business from a company of which the defendants were the sole directors and shareholders. Short-term finance for the company was needed to complete the transaction. The bank took as security a mortgage over the company's land and a charge over its assets. The claimant provided a limited guarantee of the company's overdraft account and there was a counter-indemnity from the defendants against, inter alia, losses which the claimant might incur due to 'any default on the part of [the company] . . . in consequence of which [the claimant] shall be called upon as guarantor to make any payment' to the bank. The company defaulted. The bank exercised its power of sale and sold the land and business to the claimant. The company's indebtedness to the bank exceeded the proceeds from sale so the claimant as guarantor made up the difference. The claimant then claimed that sum under the indemnity.

Asprey JA described the defendants' indemnity variously as a promise to save the claimant harmless, as an agreement to 'make good' the claimant's loss, and as a responsibility for 'payment' of loss. The tenor of Asprey JA's reasoning seems to be that the defendants were to pay the claimant's ultimate loss once the transaction had been finalised; that is, the indemnity was compensatory in nature.[69] But it could also be said that the source of the claimant's potential loss was a liability to another party, and that this often entails a preventive construction of the indemnity.[70] The defendants could have averted loss to the claimant by paying the bank directly on the claimant's behalf when the bank called upon the claimant to pay following the company's default.

The compensatory construction adopted in *Total Oil* is best explained by the unusual surrounding circumstances. The resort to short-term credit from the bank was part of an arrangement made by the company, the defendants and the claimant for carrying the contracts for sale to completion. In the event of the company's default, the claimant's net loss

---

[65] *Yeoman Credit Ltd v Latter* [1961] 1 WLR 828 (CA). See also *Royscot Commercial Leasing Ltd v Ismail* (CA, 29 April 1993).

[66] *cf* MA Clarke, 'Nature of Insurer's Liability' [1992] *Lloyd's Maritime and Commercial Law Quarterly* 287, 288; N Campbell, 'The Nature of an Insurer's Obligation' [2000] *Lloyd's Maritime and Commercial Law Quarterly* 42, 63–64 (criticising English insurance decisions on similar grounds).

[67] *Total Oil Products (Australia) Pty Ltd v Robinson* [1970] 1 NSWR 701 (CA).

[68] *Trewheelar v Trukeel Pty Ltd* (1986) Q Conv R 54-223 (SC).

[69] *Total Oil Products (Australia) Pty Ltd v Robinson* [1970] 1 NSWR 701 (CA), 704.

[70] See [6–7], [6–9].

as guarantor would depend on the sum recovered by the bank through a sale of the property and business. Those sales would, in all likelihood, be to the claimant at a price negotiated between the bank and the claimant. This construction was commercially more appropriate than a preventive construction. On the latter construction, the claimant might have compelled the defendants to intervene and satisfy the claimant's liability to the bank for the company's default. This would have been inconsistent with the commercial object of the parties' arrangement that the claimant, and not the defendants, was the guarantor. The amount of the claimant's liability as guarantor immediately upon the company's default would have been much greater than the claimant's net loss after the company's assets had been liquidated. Thus, if the defendants were compelled to indemnify the claimant before the net loss was determined, they would have paid too much initially and had to recoup the excess.

In *Trewheelar*, a contract for the sale of shares in a company contained an indemnity from the purchasers to the vendors. The indemnity covered, inter alia, the vendors' liability as guarantors of the company's obligations as purchaser under a contract for the sale of real property. The company failed to complete the contract and judgment was entered against the vendors as guarantors. Thomas J held that the indemnity to the vendors was preventive in nature and ordered the purchasers to pay the amount of the judgment to the judgment creditor.[71]

Trewheelar and *Total Oil* both concerned an indemnity from A, as directors and shareholders of a company, C, to B, in respect of B's liability as guarantor of C's obligations owed to D. C's obligations in each case were broadly similar in nature, in that they involved the payment of money to D. The critical factual distinction is that in *Trewheelar* the guarantors and vendors, B, were to be freed from further involvement with C and its contract for the property. B's ultimate loss did not depend on any further dealings by them with D, the seller of the property. In *Total Oil*, the position was reversed. B was the intended purchaser of the land and business of C, and D had an interest in those assets by way of security.

[2–23] **Agent's indemnity from the principal.** An agent's right to indemnity from the principal cannot be characterised as wholly preventive or compensatory in nature. One common formulation of the implied contractual indemnity refers to an agent's right to be *reimbursed* all expenses and indemnified against all losses and liabilities incurred in the course of the agency.[72] Another description is that the indemnity applies generally to the consequences and incidents of the agency relationship.[73] In some circumstances the principal may be required to intervene and prevent loss to the agent, for example, by relieving the agent of a liability to a third party.[74] The commercial context may, however, indicate that some outgoings or expenses associated with the agency are to be sustained by the agent and recouped later.

---

[71] *Trewheelar v Trukeel Pty Ltd* (1986) Q Conv R 54-223 (SC), 57,518.

[72] *Re Famatina Development Corp Ltd* [1914] 2 Ch 271 (CA), 282 (Lord Cozens-Hardy MR); *Lezam Pty Ltd v Seabridge Australia Pty Ltd* (1992) 107 ALR 291 (FC), 311 (Sheppard J). See P Watts and FMB Reynolds, *Bowstead & Reynolds on Agency*, 19th edn (London, Sweet & Maxwell, 2010), 327, para 7-056.

[73] *Adamson v Jarvis* (1827) 4 Bing 66, 72; 130 ER 693, 695; *John D Hope & Co v Glendinning* [1911] AC 419 (HL), 431 (Lord Kinnear); *Williams v Lister & Co* (1913) 109 LT 699 (CA), 700 (Vaughan Williams LJ); *Davis v Hueber* (1923) 31 CLR 583, 594 (Higgins J). See G Dal Pont, *Law of Agency*, 2nd edn (Sydney, LexisNexis Butterworths, 2008), 455, para 18.8.

[74] See [6–13].

In *Perishables Transport Co Ltd v N Spyropoulos (London) Ltd*,[75] for example, a forwarding agent arranged for the carriage of a consignment on behalf of its principal. The prevailing practice was that an agent was personally liable for the freight charges even where the principal was disclosed. The agent paid the freight charges because it could not collect them from the consignees at the destination, as the principal had instructed. Concluding that the agent was still entitled to be indemnified, Salmon LJ said that the arrangement with the consignees 'did not affect [the defendant principal's] primary liability to reimburse the plaintiffs should the plaintiffs be called upon to pay in the event of payment [by the consignees] being withheld'.[76]

[2–24] Guarantor's implied indemnity from debtor. Where a guarantor provides a guarantee at the express or implied request of the debtor, the guarantor can generally reclaim from the debtor the amounts it has paid to the creditor in respect of the debtor's liability. There may be an express contractual right to indemnity; alternatively, recovery can be justified on a restitutionary basis.[77] In *Re a Debtor*,[78] the English Court of Appeal identified another ground of recovery: a contract of indemnity between the debtor and guarantor, inferred from the circumstances surrounding the provision of the guarantee. Slesser LJ and Greene LJ characterised the indemnity as a promise to reimburse the guarantor for amounts paid to the creditor,[79] and it seems that the indemnity was enlivened immediately upon payment by the guarantor.[80] The reason for adopting a compensatory, rather than preventive, construction is not entirely clear. The Court may have been influenced by an analogy with the cases in indebitatus assumpsit. Yet, as Slesser LJ noted, a guarantor may have a right to quia timet relief, to compel the debtor to perform its obligation to the creditor and so exonerate the guarantor from liability.[81] Such relief resembles specific enforcement of a promise of indemnity against liability to a third party, which is only available where the indemnity is preventive in nature.

Re a Debtor has been referred to several times without any objection to the construction of the indemnity.[82] A justification may be that a debtor who requests another party to provide a guarantee is not promising that that party will never be required to pay; rather, the debtor merely promises to compensate the guarantor if the guarantee is called upon.

[75] *Perishables Transport Co Ltd v N Spyropoulos (London) Ltd* [1964] 2 Lloyd's Rep 379 (QB). See also, eg, *Imaje Events Pty Ltd v Taylor* [2007] VSC 390; (2008) Aust Contract R 90-276, [34].

[76] *Perishables Transport Co Ltd v N Spyropoulos (London) Ltd* [1964] 2 Lloyd's Rep 379 (QB), 381.

[77] The action was originally one for money paid: *Morrice v Redwyn* (1731) 2 Barn KB 26; 94 ER 333; *Toussaint v Martinnant* (1787) 2 TR 100, 105; 100 ER 55, 57 (Buller J); *Israel v Foreshore Properties Pty Ltd (in liq)* (1980) 30 ALR 631 (HCA), 636 (Aickin J). cf *Owen v Tate* [1976] QB 402 (CA) (where guarantee not requested).

[78] *Re a Debtor* [1937] Ch 156 (CA). See also *Anson v Anson* [1953] 1 QB 636 (QB), 641–42; *Israel v Foreshore Properties Pty Ltd (in liq)* (1980) 30 ALR 631 (HCA), 634–35 (Aickin J); *Marzo v 555/255 Pitt Street Pty Ltd* (1990) 21 NSWLR 1 (SC), 6–7.

[79] *Re a Debtor* [1937] Ch 156 (CA), 161 (Slesser LJ), 163–64 (Greene LJ).

[80] *Re a Debtor* [1937] Ch 156 (CA), 164 (Greene LJ).

[81] See, eg, *Holden v Black* (1905) 2 CLR 768, 782–83; *Ascherson v Tredegar Dry Dock and Wharf Co Ltd* [1909] 2 Ch 401 (Ch); *Watt v Mortlock* [1964] Ch 84 (Ch); *Thomas v Nottingham Incorporated Football Club Ltd* [1972] Ch 596 (Ch); *Moschi v Lep Air Services Ltd* [1973] AC 331 (HL), 348 (Lord Diplock); *Friend v Brooker* [2009] HCA 21; (2009) 239 CLR 129, [55] (French CJ, Gummow, Hayne and Bell JJ).

[82] *Anson v Anson* [1953] 1 QB 636 (QB), 641–42; *McColl's Wholesale Pty Ltd v State Bank of New South Wales* [1984] 3 NSWLR 365 (SC), 376; *Re Last, ex p Butterell* (1994) 124 ALR 219 (FCA), 222; *Re Bank of Credit and Commerce International SA (No 8)* [1998] AC 214 (HL), 229 (Lord Hoffmann).

Method of Indemnification

[2–25] Performance by payment of amount equal to loss. An indemnity that operates by way of compensation for loss is performed by the indemnifier paying to the indemnified party a sum of money equal to the amount of the indemnified party's loss, ascertained in accordance with the terms of the contract.

Compensation for Loss and Exact Protection

[2–26] Nature of the promise. The nature of the promise means that the indemnifier is not obliged to perform until a loss occurs. This avoids the risk of over-compensation that arises where the indemnified party is paid in advance of loss. The principle of exact protection has a similar effect in practice for preventive indemnities, though there is an important difference in the manner in which that principle is manifested. For a preventive indemnity, the indemnified party generally recovers for loss by enforcing the indemnifier's secondary obligation to pay damages for breach of contract. Unless and until there is a loss, there is no breach and, therefore, no secondary obligation is engaged. For an indemnity of a compensatory nature, the primary obligation to indemnify is not engaged unless and until a loss has occurred.

[2–27] Occurrence of loss and calculation of amount of loss. If the amount paid corresponds exactly to the amount of the loss, ascertained in accordance with the terms of the contract, the indemnified party is exactly protected. This assumes that it is possible to identify the occurrence of a loss within scope and to ascertain the amount of that loss. Both are essentially matters of construction, requiring the indemnity to be applied to the circumstances. The contract may provide a mechanism for ascertaining the amount of a loss, which can be applied at any time the indemnity might fall due for performance. This is not, however, always the case. It is possible for a promise of indemnity by compensation to be engaged even when the amount of the loss is not readily ascertainable.[83] That the indemnifier engages to pay a sum which is indeterminate at the time for performance of the indemnity may seem peculiar and difficult to reconcile with the concept of exact protection. Compensation might be paid or accepted provisionally, on the basis that there will be a final accounting when the amount of the loss has been fixed. From a pragmatic perspective, a delay in payment might be compensated by damages or an award of statutory interest.[84]

Other Constructions

[2–28] Indemnity by reinstatement or substitution. A contract of indemnity may permit or require the indemnifier to make good a loss to the indemnified party by performing some act other than the payment of money: for example, by reinstating, repairing or

---

[83] See, eg, *Scott Lithgow Ltd v Secretary of State for Defence* 1989 SC (HL) 9, 20–22. See further [5–44], [5–45].
[84] See [5–52]–[5–53].

replacing property, or procuring the provision of substitute services.[85] Such arrangements are commonly found in contracts of indemnity insurance.[86]

[2–29] **Indemnity as an exclusion of liability.** A promise by A to indemnify B against claims by or liabilities to A may be construed as an exclusion of B's liability to A. The leading decision is *Farstad Supply AS v Enviroco Ltd (The Far Service)*.[87] Under an indemnity clause in a charterparty, the owner promised to 'defend, indemnify and hold harmless' the charterer against, inter alia, claims and liabilities resulting from damage to the chartered vessel. It was held that the clause provided the charterer with a defence to a claim by the owner for damage to the vessel caused by the charterer's negligence. The scope of the clause included claims by or liabilities to the owner.[88] The preferred construction was that the clause effected an outright exclusion of such liabilities; it did not merely provide a defence for the avoidance of circuity of action.[89]

[2–30] **Indemnity defines secondary obligation to pay damages.** A promise by A to indemnify B against the consequences of A's breach of a contract with B may be given one of the two usual constructions.[90] A third construction recognised in this context is that the indemnity states the basis upon which A will pay damages to B for A's breach of contract.[91] The indemnity thus functions as a form of agreed damages clause. Although there is no primary obligation, the indemnity might still be regarded as broadly compensatory in nature, in the sense that it is the source of, or modifies, A's secondary obligation to pay damages to compensate B for loss from A's breach of contract.

Comparison with Indemnity Insurance

[2–31] **Nature of insurer's promise of indemnity.** A distinction between indemnity by prevention of loss and indemnity by compensation for loss is also recognised in indemnity insurance. It has been the subject of marked controversy[92] in England in the past 20 or so

---

[85] See, eg, *Management Corp Strata Title Plan No 1933 v Liang Huat Aluminium Ltd* [2001] BLR 351 (Sing CA).
[86] See, eg, *Re Sentinel Securities plc* [1996] 1 WLR 316 (Ch), 326–27 (provision of substitute goods/services where original supplier ceased to trade); *Re Digital Satellite Warranty Cover Ltd* [2013] UKSC 7; [2013] 1 WLR 605 (repair or replacement of equipment); *CIC Insurance Ltd v Bankstown Football Club Ltd* (1997) 184 CLR 384, 395–97 (Brennan CJ, Dawson, Toohey and Gummow JJ) (reinstatement).
[87] *Farstad Supply AS v Enviroco Ltd (The Far Service)* [2010] UKSC 18; [2010] 2 Lloyd's Rep 387.
[88] See [8–5].
[89] *Farstad Supply AS v Enviroco Ltd (The Far Service)* [2010] UKSC 18; [2010] 2 Lloyd's Rep 387, [25]–[27] (Lord Clarke), [57] (Lord Mance). See generally W Courtney, 'Indemnities, Exclusions and Contribution' [2011] *Lloyd's Maritime and Commercial Law Quarterly* 339. See [8–11].
[90] See [10–16], [10–18].
[91] See [10–20]–[10–23].
[92] See generally Clarke, 'Nature of Insurer's Liability' (n 66); Campbell, 'The Nature of an Insurer's Obligation' (n 66); J Birds, 'No Damages Remedy When Insurers Unjustifiably Repudiate Liability' [1997] *Journal of Business Law* 368; M Hemsworth, 'Consequential Loss Claims for Delayed Insurance Settlements: Creating a Financial Crisis from an Insurance Drama' [1998] *Lloyd's Maritime and Commercial Law Quarterly* 154; M Hemsworth, 'The Nature of the Insurer's Obligation Reconsidered: Property and Liability Insurance' [2001] *Lloyd's Maritime and Commercial Law Quarterly* 296; J Lowry and P Rawlings, 'Insurers, Claims and the Boundaries of Good Faith' (2005) 60 *Modern Law Review* 82, 85–90; C Ying, 'Damages for Late Payment of Insurance Claims' (2006) 22 *Law Quarterly Review* 205; MA Clarke, 'Compensation for Failure to Pay Money Due: A "Blot on English Common Law Jurisprudence" Partly Removed' [2008] *Journal of Business Law* 291. See also English Law Commission,

years, prompted by the decisions of the House of Lords in *Firma C-Trade SA v Newcastle Protection and Indemnity Association (The Fanti) (No 2)*[93] and of Hirst J in *Ventouris v Mountain (The Italia Express) (No 2)*.[94] The distinction can be significant where the insurer fails to meet a claim promptly and the insured suffers consequential losses because, for example, it is unable from its own funds to repair or replace damaged property, or to resume an affected business, or because it must borrow substitute funds from another source.[95] If the insurer's indemnity is preventive in nature, such consequential losses are usually regarded as irrecoverable because they arise from the insurer's failure to perform its secondary obligation to pay damages for breach of the insurance contract.[96] If, however, the insurer's indemnity promise is compensatory in nature, then consequential losses for late payment or non-payment can be recovered in accordance with ordinary damages principles.[97]

Depending on the view taken of the time for performance of a compensatory indemnity, the distinction may also affect the time at which the insured's cause of action accrues.[98]

[2–32] Examples of preventive construction. A preventive construction has been recognised in decisions on liability insurance,[99] though it seems that such indemnities do not employ the same concept of damnification as do non-insurance indemnities.[100] Most controversially, a preventive construction has been accepted in England as applicable to property insurance. In *Ventouris v Mountain (The Italia Express) (No 2)*[101] the insurer refused, for a considerable time, to accept a claim for a total loss of the vessel insured under a valued policy. In addition to the sum fixed by the policy, the insured claimed consequential losses including loss of income which would have been earned by a replacement vessel and loss of capital appreciation in a replacement vessel.

Hirst J dismissed the claim for consequential losses. The principal basis for decision was that sections 67 and 68 of the Marine Insurance Act 1906 conclusively defined the extent of

---

Insurance Contract Law Issues Paper 6: Damages for Late Payment and the Insurer's Duty of Good Faith (2010); English Law Commission, *Insurance Contract Law: Post Contract Duties and Other Issues: Joint Consultation Paper* (2011), ch 1.

[93] *Firma C-Trade SA v Newcastle Protection and Indemnity Association (The Fanti) (No 2)* [1991] 2 AC 1 (HL).

[94] *Ventouris v Mountain (The Italia Express) (No 2)* [1992] 2 Lloyd's Rep 281 (QB).

[95] In Australia, a statutory right to interest is provided by Insurance Contracts Act 1984 (Cth), s 57.

[96] See [2–32].

[97] See generally, *Sempra Metals Ltd (formerly Metallgesellschaft Ltd) v Inland Revenue Commissioners* [2007] UKHL 34; [2008] 1 AC 561 (HL). For examples from other jurisdictions, see [5–53].

[98] cf *Ventouris v Mountain (The Italia Express) (No 2)* [1992] 2 Lloyd's Rep 281 (QB), 291; *Callaghan v Dominion Insurance Co Ltd* [1997] 1 Lloyd's Rep 541 (QB), 544; *Virk v Gan Life Holdings plc* [2000] 1 Lloyd's Rep IR 159 (CA), [9]–[10], [21] (Potter LJ) (apparently no difference as action accrues upon occurrence of loss); *CIC Insurance Ltd v Bankstown Football Club Ltd* (1997) 184 CLR 384, 401–02 (Brennan CJ, Dawson, Toohey and Gummow JJ); *Tropicus Orchids Flowers and Foliage Pty Ltd v Territory Insurance Office* [1998] NTSC 73; (1998) 148 FLR 441, 488–90 (affd without appeal on this point: *Territory Insurance Office v Tropicus Orchids Flowers and Foliage Pty Ltd* [1999] NTCA 16, [33]) (insurer required to pay compensation within reasonable time from claim).

[99] See, eg, *Israelson v Dawson* [1933] 1 KB 301 (CA), 306 (Greer LJ); *Firma C-Trade SA v Newcastle Protection and Indemnity Association (The Fanti) (No 2)* [1991] 2 AC 1 (HL), 35–36 (Lord Goff), 40–41 (Lord Jauncey). cf *Penrith City Council v Government Insurance Office of NSW* (1991) 24 NSWLR 564 (SC); *Commonwealth of Australia v Vero Insurance Ltd* [2012] FCA 826; (2012) 291 ALR 563, [81]–[90].

[100] In insurance, see *West Wake Price & Co v Ching* [1957] 1 WLR 45 (QB), 49; *Cacciola v Fire & All Risks Insurance Co Ltd* [1971] 1 NSWLR 691 (CA); *Distillers Co Bio-Chemicals (Australia) Pty Ltd v Ajax Insurance Co Ltd* (1973) 130 CLR 1, 26 (Stephen J); *Post Office v Norwich Union Fire Insurance Society Ltd* [1967] 2 QB 363 (CA), 373–74 (Lord Denning MR), 377–78 (Salmon LJ); *Bradley v Eagle Star Insurance Co Ltd* [1989] AC 957 (HL), 966 (Lord Brandon); *Orica Ltd v CGU Insurance Ltd* [2003] NSWCA 331; (2003) 59 NSWLR 14, [15]–[17] (Spigelman CJ); *Commonwealth of Australia v Vero Insurance Ltd* [2012] FCA 826; (2012) 291 ALR 563, [84], [99]. cf the position outside insurance, [6–23].

[101] *Ventouris v Mountain (The Italia Express) (No 2)* [1992] 2 Lloyd's Rep 281 (QB).

the indemnity to be provided by the insurer in the case of a valued policy. The alternative ground was that the insurer's promise of indemnity was to prevent loss to the insured, not to compensate the insured for loss. The insured's primary claim was in the nature of damages for the insurer's breach of contract constituted by the loss of the vessel. The consequential losses were, in essence, losses sustained because the insurer had not paid damages promptly after the casualty.[102] But at common law, there is no fixed time for the payment of damages and no right to further damages for the 'late' payment of damages.[103]

The alternative ground was accepted in later decisions. In *Sprung v Royal Insurance (UK) Ltd*,[104] vandals broke into the insured's business premises and wrecked electrical machinery. For almost four years, the insurer refused to pay for a large part of the damage. The insured was unable to find funds to replace or repair the damaged machinery and his business declined. The insured's claim for his business losses was rejected on the ground that it was essentially a claim for loss arising from the insurer's failure promptly to pay damages for breach of contract.

[2–33] Examples of compensatory construction. Notwithstanding the modern English conception of the insurer's promise of indemnity,[105] support can be found in earlier English cases for the view that an indemnity insurer promises to compensate for loss. In *Prudential Insurance Co v Commissioners of Inland Revenue*,[106] for example, Channel J remarked:

> Where you insure a ship or a house you cannot insure that the ship shall not be lost or the house burnt, but what you do insure is that a sum of money shall be paid upon the happening of a certain event.

In *Sunderland Marine Insurance Co v Kearney*,[107] it was held that an action in debt was maintainable for a total loss under a valued policy of insurance of freight.[108] Lord Campbell CJ described the insurer's promise as 'a positive engagement to pay a certain sum of money upon an event which is averred to have happened'.[109]

Other English decisions have treated the promise as compensatory, while adhering to the orthodox view that the insured's claim is generally for damages. In *F&K Jabbour v Custodian of Israeli Absentee Property*,[110] Pearson J remarked:

> [T]he word 'damages' is puzzling and seems to be used in a rather unusual sense, because the right to indemnity arises, not by reason of any wrongful act or omission on the part of the insurer (who did not promise that the loss would not happen or that he would prevent it) but only under his promise to indemnify the insured in the event of a loss.

---

[102] *cf Muhammad Issa El Sheikh Ahmad v Ali* [1947] AC 414 (PC) (a non-insurance indemnity case where consequential losses were recoverable).

[103] *President of India v Lips Maritime Corp (The Lips)* [1988] AC 395 (HL), 424–25 (Lord Brandon).

[104] *Sprung v Royal Insurance (UK) Ltd* [1999] Lloyd's Rep IR 111 (CA). See also *Pride Valley Foods Ltd v Independent Insurance Co Ltd* [1999] Lloyd's Rep IR 120 (CA); *Mandrake Holdings Ltd v Countrywide Assured Group plc* [2005] EWCA Civ 840, [8] (Mance LJ); *Tonkin v UK Insurance Ltd* [2006] EWHC 1120 (TCC); [2006] 2 All ER (Comm) 550, [38]; *Re The Alexandros T* [2013] UKSC 70, [6] (Lord Clarke).

[105] See [2–32].

[106] *Prudential Insurance Co v Commissioners of Inland Revenue* [1904] 2 KB 658 (KB), 663. See also *Dane v Mortgage Insurance Corp Ltd* [1894] 1 QB 54 (CA), 60–61 (Lord Esher MR).

[107] *Sunderland Marine Insurance Co v Kearney* (1851) 16 QB 925; 117 ER 1136.

[108] Contrast *Irving v Manning* (1847) 1 HLC 287, 307; 9 ER 766, 775 (liquidated damages).

[109] *Sunderland Marine Insurance Co v Kearney* (1851) 16 QB 925, 937; 117 ER 1136, 1141.

[110] *F&K Jabbour v Custodian of Israeli Absentee Property* [1954] 1 WLR 139 (QB), 143. *cf* also *CIC Insurance Ltd v Bankstown Football Club Ltd* (1997) 184 CLR 384, 402 fn 42 (Brennan CJ, Dawson, Toohey and Gummow JJ).

In *Forney v Dominion Insurance Co Ltd*,[111] Donaldson J explained that an insured's claim is technically for unliquidated damages but that '[i]n the majority of cases, the only loss suffered is that the underwriter failed to pay the sum due and the result is the same as if the claim had been in debt'.[112] That this characterisation applies even where the indemnity is compensatory in nature is, at least in part, a historical byproduct of limitations of the form of action of debt.[113]

Instances of the insurer's promise being construed as one to compensate the insured can be found in decisions from other jurisdictions, including Australia,[114] New Zealand[115] and Scotland.[116] In *CIC Insurance Ltd v Bankstown Football Club Ltd*[117] the insured club claimed under an industrial special risks policy for losses arising out several fires which caused damage to the club's premises. Brennan CJ, Dawson, Toohey and Gummow JJ said that the 'fundamental obligations' of the insurer under the policy were, 'within a reasonable time of the receipt of the claim . . . to acknowledge liability and then to pay the liquidated sum, for the computation of which the Policy provided'.[118]

[2–34] Effect of 'pay to be paid' or 'paid losses' provisions. Some contracts of liability insurance, such as those offered by P&I clubs, provide coverage in respect of sums that the insured is liable to pay and has in fact paid to a third party.[119] These stipulations are known as 'pay to be paid' provisions. Similarly, some contracts of reinsurance may refer to 'paid losses' or losses 'actually paid' by the reinsured. Whether such expressions are applied literally, so as to make payment by the reinsured a precondition for indemnification, is a matter of construction.[120]

A 'pay to be paid' provision might be given effect in one of two ways. In *Firma C-Trade SA v Newcastle Protection and Indemnity Association (The Fanti) (No 2)*,[121] where such a provision was applied, the House of Lords accepted that a promise of indemnity against liability was usually preventive in character.[122] On that view, the promise is to prevent loss, with payment by the insured being a condition precedent to enforcement. Even so, it seems paradoxical to say that A will prevent loss to B, provided that B suffers loss – by payment – before B can insist on A's performance. An alternative construction may be that a 'pay to be paid', or similar, provision alters the nature of the indemnity promise itself. The insurer promises to compensate the insured after it has suffered loss by making payment in respect of the liability.[123]

---

[111] *Forney v Dominion Insurance Co Ltd* [1969] 1 WLR 928 (QB).

[112] *Forney v Dominion Insurance Co Ltd* [1969] 1 WLR 928 (QB), 936.

[113] cf *F&K Jabbour v Custodian of Israeli Absentee Property* [1954] 1 WLR 139 (QB), 144. See further [1–20].

[114] *CIC Insurance Ltd v Bankstown Football Club Ltd* (1997) 184 CLR 384, 401–02; *Wallaby Grip Ltd v QBE Insurance (Australia) Ltd* [2010] HCA 9; (2010) 240 CLR 444, [28], [30]. See also [5–44] n 190, [5–53].

[115] *Stuart v Guardian Royal Exchange Assurance of New Zealand Ltd (No 2)* (1985) 5 ANZ Ins Cas 60-844 (NZHC); *New Zealand Insurance Co Ltd v Harris* [1990] 1 NZLR 10 (CA).

[116] *Scott Lithgow Ltd v Secretary of State for Defence* 1989 SC (HL) 9, 20; *Strachan v Scottish Boatowners' Mutual Insurance Association* 2010 SC 367 (OH), 371–72, 379.

[117] *CIC Insurance Ltd v Bankstown Football Club Ltd* (1997) 184 CLR 384.

[118] *CIC Insurance Ltd v Bankstown Football Club Ltd* (1997) 184 CLR 384, 401–02.

[119] See generally *Law Society v Shah* [2007] EWHC 2841 (Ch); [2009] Ch 223, [13]–[15]. For a non-insurance example, see *Aluflet SA v Vinave Empresa de Navegaçao Maritima LDA (The Faial)* [2000] 1 Lloyd's Rep 473 (QB) (cl 18 of Barecon 89 form).

[120] See, eg, *Charter Reinsurance Co Ltd v Fagan* [1997] AC 313 (HL).

[121] *Firma C-Trade SA v Newcastle Protection and Indemnity Association (The Fanti) (No 2)* [1991] 2 AC 1 (HL).

[122] *Firma C-Trade SA v Newcastle Protection and Indemnity Association (The Fanti) (No 2)* [1991] 2 AC 1 (HL), 28 (Lord Brandon), 35 (Lord Goff), 40–41 (Lord Jauncey).

[123] cf *New Cap Reinsurance Corp Ltd (in liq) v AE Grant* [2008] NSWSC 1015; (2008) 221 FLR 164, [105]–[108].

3

Construction

Introduction

[3–1] Purpose of chapter. This chapter and the next are concerned with the construction of indemnity clauses and associated provisions. Prior decisions on construction generally do not determine questions of construction in later cases.[1] The treatment in the two chapters proceeds accordingly at a more general level. This chapter examines general principles, techniques and preferences that are employed in the process of construing contractual indemnities. The next chapter focuses on the ascertainment of the scope of the indemnity and its application in the circumstances that have arisen.

[3–2] Structure of chapter. The chapter begins with a brief overview of the various construction issues that may be raised by contractual indemnities. The material to which a court may have resort in the process of construction is considered next. A substantial part of the chapter is then devoted to examining different standards of construction applied to indemnity provisions. The chapter concludes with a discussion of the *contra proferentem* rule. It is, of the various well-known and specific maxims of construction, the one that is most often invoked in connection with indemnities.

Construction Issues

[3–3] Examples of construction issues. Most issues of construction arise in the context of attempts to enforce the indemnity in respect of a particular loss. The following are some examples:

- Whether the language used by the parties creates a promise of indemnity at all.[2]
- If so, the nature of the promise.[3]
- Whether another term of the contract imposes a condition precedent to performance or enforcement of the promise of indemnity.[4]
- Whether the time for performance of the indemnity has arrived.[5]

---

[1] See [3–8].
[2] See, eg, *The Devonshire and St Winfred* [1913] P 13 (P); *Etudes et Enterprises v Snowy Mountains Hydro-Electric Authority* [1962] NSWR 204 (FC); *Total Transport Corp v Arcadia Petroleum Ltd (The Eurus)* [1996] 2 Lloyd's Rep 408 (QB) (affd *Total Transport Corp v Arcadia Petroleum Ltd (The Eurus)* [1998] 1 Lloyd's Rep 351 (CA)).
[3] See [2–3].
[4] See [5–10].
[5] See [5–44], [5–45].

- Whether a loss has occurred.[6]
- Whether the claimed loss falls within the scope of the indemnity.[7]
- Whether the indemnity may be specifically enforced in relation to a prospective loss.[8]
- Whether the provision for indemnity displaces other rights or remedies that the indemnified party would possess against the indemnifier in relation to the loss, such as a right to common law damages for breach of contract.[9]
- Whether a typical incident of a contract of indemnity, such as a right of subrogation, has been excluded or qualified.[10]
- Whether a legal or equitable principle that would normally justify the discharge of the indemnifier has been excluded or qualified.[11]

The issue that arises most often is whether the claimed loss is within the scope of the indemnity. Particular issues of scope are considered in depth in the next chapter. The principles and techniques discussed in this chapter are applicable more generally.

[3–4] Matters of meaning, legal effect or application. Another perspective is to consider the nature of the legal issue that is to be resolved through the process of construction. Construction can be divided into three aspects: the determination of the meaning of words or expressions used in the contract; the determination of the legal status or effect of terms in the contract; and the application of the contract to the circumstances that have arisen.[12] Although questions of meaning do sometimes arise, the most important construction questions relate to the application or legal effect of the indemnity.

Even where the scope of the indemnity is concerned, most issues are issues of application and not linguistic meaning.[13] That distinction can be illustrated by two examples. Many different events adversely affecting the indemnified party meet the definition of a 'loss'. But this does not necessarily reveal whether the indemnity protects against a particular type of loss: that is a question of application. The word 'claim' may indicate a demand for something due or the assertion of a right. This sheds little light on questions such as whether the claim must be sound in law,[14] whether claims in respect of certain types of liability are covered, or by whom the claim must be made. In *Wiltshire County Council v Crest Estates Ltd*,[15] Crest indemnified the council against 'all actions, claims, demands, expenses and proceedings arising out of or in connection with or incidental to the carrying out of the works'. The question was whether the indemnity covered the council's statutory liability to compensate persons whose interest in land had been injuriously affected by the execution of the works. Neuberger LJ remarked that '[a]s a matter of ordinary language, it seems to me that clause 6 is fairly easily capable of bearing the meaning for which either party contends'.[16] The fundamental issue was not the linguistic meaning of the word 'claim' as used in clause 6. Rather, it was a question of application, namely, whether the indemnity

---

[6] See [4–6]–[4–9], [5–39].
[7] See generally ch 4.
[8] See [5–66], [7–20].
[9] See [10–29].
[10] See [4–43].
[11] See, eg, [5–22], [5–25].
[12] See JW Carter, *The Construction of Commercial Contracts* (Oxford, Hart, 2013), 6–14, paras 1-07–1-19.
[13] See further [3–11], [3–12].
[14] See [6–36].
[15] *Wiltshire County Council v Crest Estates Ltd* [2005] EWCA Civ 1087; [2005] BLR 458.
[16] *Wiltshire County Council v Crest Estates Ltd* [2005] EWCA Civ 1087; [2005] BLR 458, [21].

applied to claims for statutory compensation by affected persons. Relying on other contextual considerations, the majority concluded that it did not.

Raw Material

Use of Context

[3–5] **General law principles applicable.** The principles that govern the use of context in construction of contracts in general apply also to contracts of indemnity or indemnity provisions in broader contracts. Contextual material is of two kinds. Internal context encompasses the rest of the content of the parties' agreement. External context refers to that part of the contractual background, 'surrounding circumstances' or 'factual matrix', to which resort is permitted in the process of construction, in accordance with ordinary legal principles.

[3–6] **Internal context.** Where an indemnity provision is one term in a broader contract, other terms of the contract are taken into account in the process of construction of the indemnity. The overall contractual scheme is relevant,[17] as may be material in the recitals.[18] A common illustration is that the presence and scope of exclusion or insurance clauses, risk allocation clauses and other indemnity clauses may bear upon the construction of the indemnity in issue.[19] In *Farstad Supply AS v Enviroco Ltd (The Far Service)*,[20] the owner of the vessel under charter agreed, in clause 33.5 of the charterparty, to 'defend, indemnify and hold harmless the Charterer' from, inter alia, claims in relation to damage to the vessel. It was held that the clause operated to exclude the charterer's liability to the owner for the damage to the vessel. Lord Clarke explained that[21]

> clause 33.5 must be construed in its context as part of clause 33 as a whole, which must in turn be set in its context as part of the charterparty, which in its own turn must be considered against the relevant surrounding circumstances or factual matrix.

A relevant factor was that clause 33 contained a detailed set of provisions for allocating risk of loss; the expression 'defend, indemnify and hold harmless' was used repeatedly throughout that clause, even in places where it could only indicate exclusion.

---

[17] cf *Furness Shipbuilding Co Ltd v London and North Eastern Railway Co* (1934) 50 TLR 257 (HL), 259 (Lord Atkin); *Etudes et Enterprises v Snowy Mountains Hydro-Electric Authority* [1962] NSWR 204 (FC), 205 (Owen J); *Dorset County Council v Southern Felt Roofing Co Ltd* (1989) 48 BLR 96 (CA), 102 (Slade LJ) ('pattern of the conditions, when read as a whole').

[18] *Tidona Pty Ltd v Thunder Project Consultants Pty Ltd* (NSWSC, 7 May 1992); *Albert Shire Council v Vanderloos* (1992) 77 LGRA 309 (QCA), 312; *Pendal Nominees Pty Ltd v Lednez Industries (Australia) Ltd* (1996) 40 NSWLR 282 (SC), 290. cf *Management Corp Strata Title Plan No 1933 v Liang Huat Aluminium Ltd* [2001] BLR 351 (Sing CA), 354 (LP Thean JA).

[19] See, eg, *Federal Steam Navigation Co Ltd v J Fenwick & Co Pty Ltd* (1943) 68 CLR 553; *Canada Steamship Lines Ltd v R* [1952] AC 192 (PC), 214; *Scottish Special Housing Association v Wimpey Construction UK Ltd* [1986] 1 WLR 995 (HL); *Farstad Supply AS v Enviroco Ltd (The Far Service)* [2010] UKSC 18; [2010] 2 Lloyd's Rep 387; *ENE Kos 1 Ltd v Petroleo Brasileiro SA (The Kos) (No 2)* [2012] UKSC 17; [2012] 2 WLR 976, [11] (Lord Sumption); *Kudos Catering (UK) Ltd v Manchester Central Convention Complex Ltd* [2013] EWCA Civ 38. See further [4–61], [4–64].

[20] *Farstad Supply AS v Enviroco Ltd (The Far Service)* [2010] UKSC 18; [2010] 2 Lloyd's Rep 387. The case is discussed further at [8–5], [8–11].

[21] *Farstad Supply AS v Enviroco Ltd (The Far Service)* [2010] UKSC 18; [2010] 2 Lloyd's Rep 387, [21].

[3–7] External context. The use of external context as an aid to construction is clearly recognised in modern indemnity cases[22] that refer expressly to the principles in *Investors Compensation Scheme Ltd v West Bromwich Building Society*.[23] Instances of resort to external context can also be found in many other decisions.[24] One issue in *Caledonia North Sea Ltd v British Telecommunications plc (The Piper Alpha)*[25] was whether an indemnity from a contractor to the operator of an oil platform covered the operator's settlement of claims for death and personal injury, in circumstances where the contractor was not liable to the claimants at common law or under statute. The indemnity was held to apply. Lord Bingham, Lord Mackay and Lord Hoffmann all referred to the usual market practice in the North Sea oil exploration industry, which was for contracting parties generally to accept responsibility for harm to their own employees, regardless of the fault of the other party. Lord Bingham also referred to the applicable regulatory regime, under which the operator was answerable for 'almost any safety failure' which caused death or personal injury.

A leading example from another jurisdiction is *Andar Transport Pty Ltd v Brambles Ltd*.[26] A driver employed by Andar was injured while conducting a laundry delivery round. He succeeded in an action in negligence against Brambles, which had engaged Andar to perform the laundry deliveries. Brambles in turn claimed on an indemnity from Andar contained in an 'independent trucking contractor' agreement between them. In the High Court of Australia, the question of construction was whether the third party claims covered by the indemnity included claims by the driver by whom laundry deliveries were performed. Gleeson CJ, McHugh, Gummow, Hayne and Heydon JJ noted the commercial purpose of the agreement, namely, that the drivers were to be employed by independent contractors but that, to outside observers, the operations were still to appear as if they were conducted by Brambles. In that context, there was a real possibility of a claim based on an allegation of vicarious liability. The indemnity was directed to claims against Brambles by outsiders and not by drivers themselves. The joint judgment also referred[27] to the principles of strict construction for guarantees as stated in *Coghlan v SH Lock (Australia) Ltd*.[28] That reference is still consistent with this reasoning. In *Coghlan*, Lord Oliver had said that those principles did not displace the principle that in cases of ambiguity 'regard may be had to the circumstances surrounding the execution of the document as an aid to construction'.[29]

---

[22] See, eg, *Rank Enterprises Ltd v Gerard* [2000] EWCA Civ 15; [2000] 1 Lloyd's Rep 403, [8] (Mance LJ); *Cosmos Holidays plc v Dhanjal Investments Ltd* [2009] EWCA Civ 316, [15], [17] (Clarke MR).

[23] *Investors Compensation Scheme Ltd v West Bromwich Building Society* [1998] 1 WLR 896 (HL).

[24] See, eg, *Great Western Railway Co v J Durnford and Son Ltd* (1928) 44 TLR 415 (HL), 416 (Viscount Sumner); *Stevens v Britten* [1954] 1 WLR 1340 (CA), 1344 (Evershed MR); *Consultants Group International v John Warman Ltd* (CA, 19 December 1986); *Wiltshire County Council v Crest Estates Ltd* [2005] EWCA Civ 1087; [2005] BLR 458, [50]–[51] (Ward LJ); *Farstad Supply AS v Enviroco Ltd (The Far Service)* [2010] UKSC 18; [2010] 2 Lloyd's Rep 387, [21] (Lord Clarke).

[25] *Caledonia North Sea Ltd v British Telecommunications plc (The Piper Alpha)* [2002] UKHL 4; [2002] 1 Lloyd's Rep 553.

[26] *Andar Transport Pty Ltd v Brambles Ltd* [2004] HCA 28; (2004) 217 CLR 424. See also *Management Corp Strata Title Plan No 1933 v Liang Huat Aluminium Ltd* [2001] BLR 351 (Sing CA), 354–55 (LP Thean JA); *Central Pacific Holdings Pty Ltd v State of Victoria* [2011] VSCA 322.

[27] *Andar Transport Pty Ltd v Brambles Ltd* [2004] HCA 28; (2004) 217 CLR 424, [19].

[28] *Coghlan v SH Lock (Australia) Ltd* (1987) 8 NSWLR 88 (PC).

[29] *Coghlan v SH Lock (Australia) Ltd* (1987) 8 NSWLR 88 (PC), 92. cf *Western Export Services Inc v Jireh International Pty Ltd* [2011] HCA 45; (2011) 282 ALR 604 (reasserting the need for ambiguity before consideration of the external context under Australian law).

Use of Precedent

[3–8] Value of precedent. Conclusions on construction reached in past decisions do not, as a general rule, determine the construction of indemnity provisions in later cases.[30] The utility of precedent depends on the nature of the contract and the nature of the issue.

[3–9] Type of contract. For individual, negotiated contracts, precedent is generally of little or no use in the construction of express terms. A basic reason is that non-insurance indemnity provisions in commercial contracts are rarely expressed in identical terms. Where the indemnity is in the same terms as another considered in a prior decision, the relevant context (internal or external) may be different. As the indemnity must be construed in its appropriate context, the earlier decision cannot be conclusive. Where a particular word or phrase is the same as that considered in a previous decision, its collocation in the indemnity provision may be different.[31]

Precedent may be influential where the indemnity takes its usual form in a standard form contract, such as a charterparty, a construction contract, a contract for the hire of industrial machinery, a towage contract or a contract for carriage by road. There is, for example, a considerable body of case law on the construction of the standard form indemnity that appears in many time charterparties.[32] That indemnity is usually in terms that the charterer will indemnify the owner against the consequences of the master's compliance with the charterer's orders as to the employment of the vessel, or the master signing bills of lading. It is accepted that the connection between the owner's loss and the charterer's order must satisfy a certain standard of causation.[33] There is also a well-established exception for risks associated with navigation. A distinction is thus drawn between risks arising from directions as to the employment of the vessel, which may be within scope, and those relating to navigation, which are beyond scope.[34]

[3–10] Type of issue. Precedent may be more useful where the issue is general rather than specific in nature. In many cases, the issue of construction is how to apply the indemnity to the circumstances that have arisen. Prior decisions on the application of the indemnity to different facts are unlikely to provide a useful basis for comparison. By way of contrast, precedent may be relevant where a contract of indemnity is inferred from circumstances in which certain recognised elements are present.[35] Similarly, where an indemnity is implied by law into an existing contract, the default scope of that indemnity may be determined by precedent. So, for example, an agent's implied indemnity from the principal is generally

---

[30] *Furness Shipbuilding Co Ltd v London and North Eastern Railway Co* (1934) 50 TLR 257 (HL), 259 (Lord Atkin); *Great Western Railway Co v Port Talbot Dry Dock Co Ltd* [1944] 2 All ER 328 (KB), 332; *John Lee & Son (Grantham) Ltd v Railway Executive* [1949] 2 All ER 230 (KB), 232; *Davis v Commissioner for Main Roads* (1967) 117 CLR 529, 537 (Menzies J); *Erect Safe Scaffolding (Australia) Pty Ltd v Sutton* [2008] NSWCA 114; (2008) 72 NSWLR 1, [5] (Giles JA), [89] (Basten JA), [154] (McClellan CJ at CL).

[31] cf *Leighton Contractors Pty Ltd v Smith* [2000] NSWCA 55, [6]–[7] (Mason P and Fitzgerald JA); *F&D Normoyle Pty Ltd v Transfield Pty Ltd* [2005] NSWCA 193; (2005) 63 NSWLR 502, [59], [65] (Ipp JA), [146]–[147] (Bryson JA).

[32] See W Courtney, 'Indemnities in Time Charterparties and the Effect of the Withdrawal of the Vessel' (2013) 30 *Journal of Contract Law* 243.

[33] See [4–13].

[34] *Weir v Union Steamship Co Ltd* [1900] AC 525 (HL); *Larrinaga Steamship Co Ltd v R* [1945] AC 246 (HL).

[35] See, eg, [4–53]–[4–54] (action at the request of the indemnifier), [10–11]–[10–13] (indemnity against breach of contract).

regarded as excluding losses attributable to unauthorised acts, the agent's negligence or default, and acts or transactions by the agent which are known to be, or are obviously, unlawful.[36]

Standards of Construction

[3–11] Different standards of construction. It is difficult to discern any coherent approach to the construction of indemnities before the middle of the twentieth century. References can be found to strict construction against the indemnified party,[37] to construction against the indemnifier as the covenantor,[38] to literal construction,[39] and to consideration of the business object of the indemnity clause.[40] Since the middle of the twentieth century two perspectives have clearly emerged as predominant: 'strict' construction and 'commercial' construction. Although described loosely in terms of 'construction', the two standards are principally concerned with the final stage in the construction process, that is, the application of the indemnity to the circumstances.[41]

The standards are sometimes regarded as conflicting or irreconcilable,[42] though they are not mutually opposed in all respects. Their purpose is to identify and choose between various competing applications of the indemnity. The same or similar potential applications might be identified on either approach; the result of the selection process might also be the same in some cases. As a matter of technique, some of the rules traditionally associated with strict construction may still be used in commercial construction.[43] The judicial hostility to a broad application of indemnity clauses evident in strict construction may be underpinned by sound commercial concerns: for example, that a party does not lightly accept responsibility for loss where it would otherwise not be liable, or where the loss is occasioned by the fault of others.[44] In some circumstances, it appears that commercial expectations may coincide with a strict or (narrow) literal construction of the indemnity.[45]

[3–12] Why use strict or commercial construction? The effects of strict construction or commercial construction are far-reaching, but they are most evident in relation to issues of scope. The scope of an indemnity could in theory be applied literally, that is, as a mere aggregation of the ordinary meanings of its constituent elements. Yet most indemnity provisions are drafted in such general and broad language that it could not seriously be

---

[36] See P Watts and FMB Reynolds, *Bowstead & Reynolds on Agency*, 19th edn (London, Sweet & Maxwell, 2010), 332–33, paras 7-062, 7-065.

[37] *Lewis v Smith* (1850) 9 CB 610, 619; 137 ER 1030, 1033 (Creswell J).

[38] *Fowle v Welsh* (1822) 1 B & C 29, 35; 107 ER 12, 14 (Bayley J).

[39] *Henson v London & North Eastern Railway Co* [1946] 1 All ER 653 (CA), 663 (Cohen LJ), *cf* 658 (Scott LJ).

[40] *Great Western Railway Co v J Durnford and Son Ltd* (1928) 44 TLR 415 (HL), 416 (Viscount Sumner).

[41] See generally Carter, *The Construction of Commercial Contracts* (n 12), 499–500, paras 15-09–15-11.

[42] See, eg, *Schenker & Co (Aust) Pty Ltd v Maplas Equipment and Services Pty Ltd* [1990] VR 834 (FC), 846 (McGarvie J); *Glebe Island Terminals Pty Ltd v Continental Seagram Pty Ltd (The Antwerpen)* (1993) 40 NSWLR 206; [1994] 1 Lloyd's Rep 213 (CA), 242 (Sheller JA); *Valkonen v Jennings Construction Ltd* (1995) 184 LSJS 87 (SAFC), 97–98 (Cox J). *cf Leighton Contractors Pty Ltd v Smith* [2000] NSWCA 55, [9] (Mason P and Fitzgerald JA); *F&D Normoyle Pty Ltd v Transfield Pty Ltd* [2005] NSWCA 193; (2005) 63 NSWLR 502, [64] (Ipp JA).

[43] See [3–29].

[44] See [4–44].

[45] *Agricultural and Rural Finance Pty Ltd v Gardiner* [2008] HCA 57; (2008) 238 CLR 570, [116] (Kirby J) (punctual payment as condition precedent to indemnity).

expected that the parties intended the indemnity to be applied in that manner.[46] The scope of the indemnity in *application* differs from, and is generally narrower than, the scope literally indicated by its terms. Restrictions on the scope of the indemnity, when compared with its apparent literal extent, are derived through construction. The process involves consideration of context and, perhaps also, the use of specific construction principles that serve to narrow the application of the indemnity.

This perspective reinforces the point, made earlier,[47] that the most significant issues of construction for indemnities are matters of application or legal effect, not linguistic meaning. Dictionaries are usually inadequate to resolve questions of application.[48] In *National Roads and Motorists' Association v Whitlam*,[49] Whitlam claimed under an indemnity for, inter alia, loss of reputation, consequential loss of earning capacity and for injury to his feelings. The indemnity was against 'Liabilities', which was defined to mean 'any loss, liability, cost, charge or expense'. Campbell JA listed 13 different dictionary definitions of the word 'loss' and observed that the indemnity could not have been intended to apply to all of them. In concluding that the word 'loss' did not cover harm to Whitlam's reputation and associated losses, Campbell JA was influenced by the textual context in which the word 'loss' appeared, the likely purpose of the indemnity, and a concern to reach a 'commercially realistic' result.[50]

Strict Construction

[3–13] Justification by use of analogies. The adoption of strict construction for contracts of indemnity, or indemnity provisions in broader contracts, has been supported by analogy with exclusion clauses and contracts of guarantee. That rationale rests on two propositions: first, that a strict standard of construction applies to exclusion clauses or guarantees; secondly, that indemnities are sufficiently analogous to apply the same standard of construction. The strength of that first proposition is, perhaps, somewhat diminished nowadays. It is an open question whether strict construction still applies with full rigour to exclusion clauses[51] or guarantees.[52]

[3–14] Analogy with exclusion clauses. The analogy was developed in several leading decisions in which the two types of clause were said to be construed with equivalent strictness, or

---

[46] See, eg, *Larrinaga Steamship Co Ltd v R* [1945] AC 246 (HL), 261 (Lord Porter); *John Lee & Son (Grantham) Ltd v Railway Executive* [1949] 2 All ER 581 (CA), 582 (Evershed MR).

[47] See [3–4].

[48] See, eg, *F&D Normoyle Pty Ltd v Transfield Pty Ltd* [2005] NSWCA 193; (2005) 63 NSWLR 502, [146] (Bryson JA). See generally Carter (n 12), 496–97, para 15-04.

[49] *National Roads and Motorists' Association Ltd v Whitlam* [2007] NSWCA 81; (2007) 25 ACLC 688.

[50] *National Roads and Motorists' Association Ltd v Whitlam* [2007] NSWCA 81; (2007) 25 ACLC 688, [55]–[65].

[51] See, eg, *Photo Production Ltd v Securicor Transport Ltd* [1980] AC 827 (HL), 850 (Lord Diplock) (construction involves degrees of strictness); *Bank of Credit and Commerce International SA v Ali* [2001] UKHL 8; [2002] 1 AC 251, [62] (Lord Hoffmann) ('disappearance of artificial rules'). See generally Carter (n 12), 575–84, paras 17-09–17.17.

[52] *Egan v Static Control Components (Europe) Ltd* [2004] EWCA Civ 392; [2004] 2 Lloyd's Rep 429, [19] (Holman J), [37] (Arden LJ); *Harvey v Dunbar Assets plc* [2013] EWCA Civ 952, [28]–[32] (Gloster LJ). See generally JC Phillips, *The Modern Contract of Guarantee*, 2nd English edn (London, Sweet & Maxwell, 2010), 281–83, paras 5-01–5-06; G Andrews and R Millett, *Law of Guarantees*, 6th edn (London, Sweet & Maxwell, 2011), 115–25, para 4-002.

even greater strictness in the case of indemnities.[53] The same analogy was accepted for a time in Australia. Thus, when the High Court of Australia set the course for a more commercial construction of exclusion clauses,[54] the same approach was transferred to indemnities.[55]

The form of indemnity that most closely approximates an exclusion clause is an indemnity against claims by or liabilities to the indemnifier. Such a clause may bar a claim by the indemnifier against the indemnified party, in effect excluding the indemnified party's liability to the indemnifier in the relevant respect.[56] It is, however, clear that the analogy was not necessarily limited to such forms of indemnity. In *Smith v South Wales Switchgear Co Ltd*,[57] Viscount Dilhorne and Lord Fraser each described an indemnity (in that case, against liability to third parties) as the 'obverse' of an exemption clause. Under an exclusion clause, the injured party must bear its own loss, the responsibility for which would otherwise fall upon the beneficiary of the clause. Under an indemnity, the indemnifier must assume responsibility for a loss to the indemnified party that, in many cases, would not otherwise fall upon the indemnifier. The indemnified party is, correspondingly, spared from a loss or liability that it would otherwise bear.

[3–15] Analogy with guarantees. The analogy with guarantees was drawn by the High Court of Australia in *Andar Transport Pty Ltd v Brambles Ltd*,[58] a case concerning an indemnity against liabilities to third parties. Gleeson CJ, McHugh, Gummow, Hayne and Heydon JJ explained that the strict construction principles applicable in Australia to guarantees[59] were 'relevant' to the construction of indemnities, because 'notwithstanding the differences in the operation of guarantees and indemnities, both are designed to satisfy a liability owed by someone other than the guarantor or indemnifier to a third person'.[60] So described, the analogy does not hold for all indemnities. It would not apply to indemnities against claims by or liabilities to the indemnifier, nor indemnities against 'personal' losses, such as loss of or damage to the indemnified party's property.

The tenderness shown by the law towards guarantors is attributable in part to the fact that, in times long past, they were usually relatives or associates of the debtor and derived no direct reward for or benefit from their undertaking.[61] That is far from universally true today. In any event, no equivalent generalisation can be made for contractual indemnities

---

[53] *Canada Steamship Lines Ltd v R* [1952] AC 192 (PC), 213–14; *Smith v South Wales Switchgear Co Ltd* [1978] 1 WLR 165 (HL), 168 (Viscount Dilhorne), 178 (Lord Keith); *Ailsa Craig Fishing Co Ltd v Malvern Fishing Co Ltd* [1983] 1 WLR 964 (HL), 970 (Lord Fraser). See also *Gillespie Brothers & Co Ltd v Roy Bowles Transport Ltd* [1973] QB 400 (CA), 420 (Buckley LJ); *Antiparos ENE v SK Shipping Co Ltd (The Antiparos)* [2008] EWHC 1139 (Comm); [2008] 2 Lloyd's Rep 237, [32].

[54] *Darlington Futures Ltd v Delco Australia Pty Ltd* (1986) 161 CLR 500.

[55] See [3–30].

[56] See [8–11].

[57] *Smith v South Wales Switchgear Co Ltd* [1978] 1 WLR 165 (HL), 168 (Viscount Dilhorne), 172 (Lord Fraser). See also *Gillespie Brothers & Co Ltd v Roy Bowles Transport Ltd* [1973] QB 400 (CA), 420 (Buckley LJ) ('one is in essence the correlative of the other').

[58] *Andar Transport Pty Ltd v Brambles Ltd* [2004] HCA 28; (2004) 217 CLR 424. See also *Sandtara Pty Ltd v Abigroup Ltd* (1996) 42 NSWLR 491 (CA), 499 (Cole JA). Contrast *Glebe Island Terminals Pty Ltd v Continental Seagram Pty Ltd (The Antwerpen)* (1993) 40 NSWLR 206; [1994] 1 Lloyd's Rep 213 (CA), 243 (Sheller JA) (rejecting analogy); *Scottish & Newcastle plc v Raguz* [2008] UKHL 65; [2008] 1 WLR 2494, [72] (Lord Walker) ('covenant for indemnity [is] not a form of guarantee or liability insurance. There is no reason to bend or stretch its natural meaning in favour' of either party).

[59] *Ankar Pty Ltd v National Westminster Finance (Australia) Ltd* (1987) 162 CLR 549; *Chan v Cresdon* (1989) 168 CLR 242.

[60] *Andar Transport Pty Ltd v Brambles Ltd* [2004] HCA 28; (2004) 217 CLR 424, [23]. cf [71]–[73] (Kirby J).

[61] See, eg, *Corumo Holdings Pty Ltd v C Itoh Ltd* (1991) 24 NSWLR 370 (CA), 377–78 (Kirby P).

past or present. The circumstances of many of the early non-insurance indemnity decisions point in the opposite direction. The indemnified party often assumed a position of risk at the request, or for the benefit, of the indemnifier; the indemnifier provided an indemnity for that reason.

[3–16] **Rationale for strict construction.** Central to the analogies with exclusion clauses and guarantees is a policy concern that the indemnifier is assuming responsibility for a loss that the indemnifier would not otherwise bear according to ordinary legal principles.[62] The indemnity is a potent term. Another concern is the respective culpability of the parties. There may be a greater reluctance to conclude that an indemnity applies where, for example, there is some element of fault on the part of the indemnified party that contributes to the loss.[63] There may also be a suspicion of unfairness, namely, that the transfer of risk has not been adequately priced in the parties' bargain.

These concerns justify caution in the construction of indemnity provisions and scepticism of literal application. Even so, it should not be necessary to address those concerns by adopting a distinct, strict standard of construction. The same concerns can be substantially accommodated, by reference to commercial considerations, upon a commercial construction.

[3–17] **Comparison with indemnity insurance.** Contracts of indemnity insurance offer another point of comparison, though cross-references to principles of construction in insurance are conspicuously rare. The modern approach seems to be that ordinary principles of commercial construction apply to contracts of insurance,[64] together with rules and principles peculiar to insurance law. There are undoubtedly important contextual differences,[65] but it is difficult to see why these should dictate a difference in the general approach to construction of insurance and non-insurance indemnities.

There is usually no identifiable, discrete consideration for the non-insurance indemnifier's promise of indemnity. It does not necessarily follow that the promise is 'gratuitous'. The cost of the risk may have been factored into the total contract price charged by the indemnifier. Alternatively, a benefit may be inherent in the performance of the transaction, as where the indemnifier requests the indemnified party to undertake a particular course of action to the indemnifier's advantage and provides an indemnity in return. Furthermore, English law has not embraced a general distinction between compensated and uncompensated sureties in the construction of guarantees.[66]

Other distinctions may be that indemnities in insurance contracts are generally drafted by the insurer, and often in more comprehensive and specific terms than those found in non-insurance contracts. These are distinctions of form or context, not kind. In any event, not all non-insurance indemnities are distinguishable on this basis. Authorship might be

---

[62] *cf Andar Transport Pty Ltd v Brambles Ltd* [2004] HCA 28; (2004) 217 CLR 424, [68] (Kirby J).

[63] See [4–44].

[64] *Deutsche Genossenschaftsbank v Burnhope* [1995] 1 WLR 1580 (HL); *Gan Insurance Co Ltd v Tai Ping Insurance Co Ltd* [2001] EWCA Civ 1047; [2001] 2 All ER (Comm) 299, [12]–[13] (Mance LJ); *Pratt v Aigaion Insurance Co SA (The Resolute)* [2008] EWCA Civ 1314; [2009] 1 Lloyd's Rep 225, [9]–[14] (Clarke MR). See also *Australian Casualty Co Ltd v Federico* (1986) 160 CLR 513, 520 (Gibbs CJ); *McCann v Switzerland Insurance Australia Ltd* [2000] HCA 65; (2000) 203 CLR 579, [22] (Gleeson CJ); *Wilkie v Gordian Runoff Ltd* [2005] HCA 17; (2005) 221 CLR 522, [15] (Gleeson CJ, McHugh, Gummow and Kirby JJ); *Selected Seeds Pty Ltd v QBEMM Pty Ltd* [2010] HCA 37; (2010) 242 CLR 336, [29], [34].

[65] See [1–14].

[66] *cf* also *Ankar Pty Ltd v National Westminster Finance (Australia) Ltd* (1987) 162 CLR 549, 560–61 (Mason CJ, Wilson, Brennan and Dawson JJ).

taken into account in the application of the *contra proferentem* rule, irrespective of whether the contract is one of insurance.[67]

[3–18] Nature and incidents of strict construction. The concept of strict construction is not easily defined.[68] In broad terms, it involves the application of various techniques and construction preferences which serve to reduce or confine the circumstances in which the indemnity will protect against loss. Thus, a strict construction generally favours the indemnifier, not the indemnified party. These techniques or preferences may apply in relation to the circumstances that engage the indemnity and also in the determination of its extent. The following are some examples:

(1) An insistence on precise compliance by the indemnified party with any non-promissory conditions precedent to performance of the indemnity.
(2) Where the contract contains a promissory term that is associated with the indemnity, the term may be classified as a condition when considerations are otherwise evenly balanced.
(3) The adoption of a literal application of words or phrases where the literal application is a narrow one, and a reluctance to extend by implication the scope of the indemnity.
(4) A requirement of clarity of expression if the indemnity is to protect the indemnified party against the consequences of certain events.
(5) Reliance on technical legal or grammatical rules, such as the *contra proferentem* rule[69] and the *ejusdem generis* rule,[70] particularly when such rules are used to select one of the narrower or narrowest applications of the indemnity from those reasonably available.

[3–19] Satisfaction of condition precedent. One incident of strict construction may be that the indemnified party must demonstrate exact satisfaction of any non-promissory conditions precedent to performance of the indemnity; substantial compliance is not sufficient.[71] In *Agricultural and Rural Finance Pty Ltd v Gardiner*,[72] investors in a primary production scheme were entitled to be indemnified against obligations to repay loans, provided that certain conditions precedent were satisfied. Two of those conditions precedent required the investor to have 'punctually paid' specified instalments of interest and principal. The New South Wales Court of Appeal by majority held that the indemnity in relation to several of the loans was enforceable, even though the investor had failed to make the payments at the time originally fixed by the contract. Spigelman CJ considered that the requirements were not to be construed strictly, so that it was sufficient that the lender accepted the payment as being made punctually.[73] That reasoning was rejected by

---

[67] See [3–35].
[68] *Bright v Sampson and Duncan Enterprises Pty Ltd* (1985) 1 NSWLR 346 (CA), 366–67 (Mahoney JA) (exclusion clause); *Mannai Investment Co Ltd v Eagle Star Assurance* [1997] AC 749 (HL), 776 (Lord Hoffmann). See generally Carter (n 12), 500, 518–19, paras 15-11–15-12, 15-34; G McMeel, *The Construction of Contracts*, 2nd edn (Oxford, Oxford University Press, 2011), 259–61, paras 6.22–6.26; K Lewison, *The Interpretation of Contracts*, 5th edn (London, Sweet & Maxwell, 2011), 60–61, para 2.10.
[69] See [3–35].
[70] See, eg, *F&D Normoyle Pty Ltd v Transfield Pty Ltd* [2005] NSWCA 193; (2005) 63 NSWLR 502, [67] (Ipp JA).
[71] This proposition could be regarded as an instance of literal application: Carter (n 12), 510–13, paras 15-26–15-28.
[72] *Agricultural and Rural Finance Pty Ltd v Gardiner* [2008] HCA 57; (2008) 238 CLR 570.
[73] *Gardiner v Agricultural and Rural Finance Pty Ltd* [2007] NSWCA 235; (2008) Aust Contract R 90-274, [125]–[126]. Basten JA arrived at the same result on the basis that the payment was not punctual ([243]) but that the terms of the agreement had been varied ([255]–[264]).

the High Court of Australia: payments not made at the appointed time were not made punctually.[74]

[3–20] Classification of related promissory terms. Where considerations are otherwise evenly balanced, strict construction may favour a promissory term associated with the indemnity being classified as a condition, rather than as an intermediate term or a warranty.[75] The indemnified party's failure to perform then confers upon the indemnifier a right to terminate the contract and, accordingly, discharge itself from any further obligation to indemnify.

In *Jiona Investments Pty Ltd v Medihelp General Practice Pty Ltd*,[76] a number of parties, including members of a corporate group, were indemnified against claims brought by certain third parties. A separate clause provided that the indemnifier and another company, which controlled the corporate group, would consult and discuss any settlement negotiations in relation to the claims, and that no settlement would be made by any party without first obtaining the consent of the indemnifier and the controlling company. A settlement was made by one of the indemnified parties without the indemnifier's consent. It was unnecessary to reach a conclusion on the effect of that act, but Muir JA, referring to principles of strict construction, inclined to the view that the term breached was a condition.[77]

[3–21] Literal application to narrow extent of protection. Particular words or phrases in an indemnity provision may be applied literally where this reduces the extent of protection. In *Lowery v Vickers Armstrong (Engineers) Ltd*,[78] Megaw LJ and Russell LJ concluded that personal injuries caused by an explosion from a leaking gas main did not arise 'directly or indirectly out of the supply of gas under the terms of this agreement' as required by the indemnity. This was because the leak occurred externally and before the gas had passed through any of the gas meters used to monitor the supply under the agreement. In *City of Manchester v Fram Gerrard Ltd*,[79] the contractor promised to indemnify the employer against certain losses and liabilities arising out of the execution of the works, provided they were due to the negligence or default 'of the contractor, his servants or agents, or of any sub-contractor'. Adopting a strict construction, Kerr J held that the indemnity did not render the contractor liable for defaults by its *sub-contractor's* sub-contractor.[80] In *Laresu Pty Ltd v Clark*,[81] the owner of a property promised to indemnify the managing agent against all actions, claims, costs and so forth, arising out of the 'performance of any of the powers, duties or authorities' of the agent under the agency agreement. The agent was found liable in negligence to a party who was injured on the premises. The indemnity was held not to protect the agent against the liability because it arose from a failure to perform, rather than 'performance of', the agent's duties.[82]

---

[74] *cf Agricultural and Rural Finance Pty Ltd v Gardiner* [2008] HCA 57; (2008) 238 CLR 570, [38]–[39] (Gummow, Hayne and Kiefel JJ), [116] (Kirby J). The result might also be justified on the basis that a commercial construction would still require strict compliance.

[75] *cf Ankar Pty Ltd v National Westminster Finance (Australia) Ltd* (1987) 162 CLR 549 (application to contract of guarantee).

[76] *Jiona Investments Pty Ltd v Medihelp General Practice Pty Ltd* [2010] QCA 99.

[77] *Jiona Investments Pty Ltd v Medihelp General Practice Pty Ltd* [2010] QCA 99, [16]–[19]. Contrast *Winchester Cigarette Machinery Ltd v Payne* (CA, 4 May 1995).

[78] *Lowery v Vickers Armstrong (Engineers) Ltd* (1969) 8 KIR 603 (CA).

[79] *City of Manchester v Fram Gerrard Ltd* (1974) 6 BLR 70 (QB).

[80] *City of Manchester v Fram Gerrard Ltd* (1974) 6 BLR 70 (QB), 94–95.

[81] *Laresu Pty Ltd v Clark* [2010] NSWCA 180.

[82] *Laresu Pty Ltd v Clark* [2010] NSWCA 180, [88]–[89] (Macfarlan JA).

[3–22] Insistence on clarity of expression. It is sometimes said that parties must use 'clear words' if they intend the indemnity to protect the indemnified party against the consequences of certain events.[83] A common instance is a loss or liability caused by the indemnified party's own negligence.[84] The insistence on clarity to achieve a particular result reveals an important quality of this aspect of strict construction. In many cases the words of the indemnity, literally applied, would cover the losses or liabilities arising from the relevant event. A literal application is not, in the present context,[85] the same as a strict application because it would lead to a broadening, not a narrowing, of the indemnity.

The requirement to be clear is, to a large degree, a requirement to be explicit. *Smith v South Wales Switchgear Co Ltd*[86] contains stringent expressions to this effect. Noting that the *Canada SS* rules were applicable to exclusion clauses and indemnities, Lord Keith said that they applied 'a fortiori in the latter case, since it represents a less usual and more extreme situation'.[87] Viscount Dilhorne suggested that 'a heavier burden lay on the proferens seeking to establish that the other party to an agreement had agreed to indemnify him against liability for his negligence' than where the *proferens* sought only an exemption from liability for negligence.[88]

The insistence on explicitness reflects an inherent hostility[89] to indemnification in certain circumstances. That hostility might be manifested in the form of a presumption against application of the indemnity. Alternatively, it may represent a predisposition to countenance alternative (and narrower) applications of the indemnity clause. The contemplation of alternative applications may be sufficient to raise a doubt which then justifies a narrower construction against the indemnified party.[90]

[3–23] Choosing between alternatives. Many construction disputes require a choice to be made between competing meanings of expressions used in an indemnity provision, or between competing applications of the indemnity. That process involves the identification of possible meanings or applications of the contract, and then the selection of one of them.

The impact of strict construction in the first stage of the process is difficult to assess. In some cases at least, the strict approach seems to have involved an inclination to countenance contrived or strained meanings or applications that lead to a narrow operation of the indemnity. Yet in *Photo Production Ltd v Securicor Transport Ltd*,[91] Lord Diplock regarded a strict construction as being different from a distorted or strained construction. In Australia, following *Andar Transport Pty Ltd v Brambles Ltd*,[92] it has been suggested that the possible meanings or applications must still be realistic or tenable. In *Rava v Logan Wines Pty Ltd*,[93] Campbell JA said:

[83] For examples of the same requirement applied to other aspects of indemnities, see n 121.

[84] See, eg, *Canada Steamship Lines Ltd v R* [1952] AC 192 (PC), 211; *Smith v South Wales Switchgear Co Ltd* [1978] 1 WLR 165 (HL), 168 (Viscount Dilhorne).

[85] Contrast [3–21].

[86] *Smith v South Wales Switchgear Co Ltd* [1978] 1 WLR 165 (HL).

[87] *Smith v South Wales Switchgear Co Ltd* [1978] 1 WLR 165 (HL), 178.

[88] *Smith v South Wales Switchgear Co Ltd* [1978] 1 WLR 165 (HL), 168.

[89] *cf Bank of Credit and Commerce International SA v Ali* [2001] UKHL 8; [2002] 1 AC 251, [61] (Lord Hoffmann) (requirement of clear words suggests judicial perception of unfairness).

[90] See further [3–23].

[91] *Photo Production Ltd v Securicor Transport Ltd* [1980] AC 827 (HL), 850–51.

[92] *Andar Transport Pty Ltd v Brambles Ltd* [2004] HCA 28; (2004) 217 CLR 424. *cf* also *Coghlan v SH Lock (Australia) Ltd* (1987) 8 NSWLR 88 (PC), 95–96.

[93] *Rava v Logan Wines Pty Ltd* [2007] NSWCA 62, [56]. See also *Gardiner v Agricultural and Rural Finance Pty Ltd* [2007] NSWCA 235; (2008) Aust Contract R 90-274, [20] (Spigelman CJ).

[T]he application of the principle for construction of guarantees and indemnities that was adopted by the High Court in *Andar* does not involve preparing a list of all the possible meanings of a clause that the language can bear without breaking, and choosing the meaning that is most favourable to the guarantor or indemnifier. Rather, the choice is limited to choosing amongst meanings that are fairly open by reason of the application of other rules of construction.

At the second stage of the process – the selection of a meaning or application from those available – the *contra proferentem* rule may be invoked. One form of the rule is that an ambiguity or doubt is to be resolved against the indemnified party, as beneficiary of the provision, and in favour of the indemnifier.[94] Applied in this manner, the *contra proferentem* rule is entirely consistent with strict construction because it narrows the operation of the indemnity.

Commercial Construction

[**3–24**] **Incidents of commercial construction.** Commercial construction is, like strict construction, difficult to define in simple terms.[95] Incidents of commercial construction applicable to indemnities may include:

(1) Greater reliance on external context in the construction of the indemnity.
(2) A preference for results that are commercially sensible and give effect to the underlying commercial object of the agreement.
(3) If the scope of the indemnity is to be applied more narrowly than its terms literally suggest, the restriction is justified by reference to commercial considerations, rather than on the basis of technical legal or grammatical rules, or a predisposition to discern ambiguity.

[**3–25**] **Greater use of external context.** The process of commercial construction draws upon the circumstances surrounding entry into the contract. That material aids in the achievement of another aim of commercial construction, which is to arrive at a result that gives effect to the commercial purpose or object of the agreement. Modern decisions on strict construction do, however, also accept that this material may be taken into account.[96] If that is correct, then any meaningful distinction between commercial and strict construction on this point relates to the degree to which such material is relied upon in the construction process.

Morgan Grenfell Development Capital Syndications Ltd v Arrows Autosports Ltd[97] illustrates the contrast between what might be regarded as commercial and strict approaches. MGDCS provided an overdraft facility to Arrows and the principal of Arrows provided an indemnity in relation to Arrows' liability under that facility. The funds advanced by MGDCS were sourced from various entities in the Morgan Grenfell group. One issue was whether those other entities, known as Funds I to V, were entitled to be indemnified against their losses in the transaction. The indemnified persons were defined to be 'the Overdraft Provider and/or any of its affiliates, associates, shareholders, subsidiaries, subsidiary under-

---

[94] See [3–37].
[95] See generally Carter (n 12), ch 16.
[96] See [3–7].
[97] *Morgan Grenfell Development Capital Syndications Ltd v Arrows Autosports Ltd* [2004] EWHC 1015 (Ch).

takings, any holding company and their respective directors, offices [sic], partners, agents, employees and representatives'.

Lindsay J first applied what he termed a 'strict' or 'linguistic' and 'narrow' approach, which focused on the terms of the indemnity and the corporate structure of Morgan Grenfell. On that basis, Funds I to IV satisfied the definition but it was doubtful whether Fund V did so. Lindsay J then went on to consider what he termed a 'broad' approach, which was 'a little freer in "having due regard to the purpose of the contract and the circumstances in which the contract was made"'.[98] In the circumstances, it would have been clear to the indemnifier that the Funds were affiliates or associates of MGDCS. The commercial purpose of the indemnity was to protect the Morgan Grenfell entities against loss that they might suffer as a result of the transaction. On that basis, all of Funds I to V were entitled to be indemnified.

[3–26] **Achieving the commercial purpose and commercially sensible results.** Another aspect of commercial construction is a preference for a construction that produces a commercially sensible or realistic result, and gives effect to the object or purpose of the transaction.[99] In *Rank Enterprises Ltd v Gerard*,[100] contracts for the sale of three vessels contained a warranty by the seller that the vessels were unencumbered. The warranty clause continued: 'Should any claims which have been incurred prior to the time of delivery be made against the vessel, the Seller hereby undertakes to indemnify the Buyers against all consequences of such claims'. There was a separate guarantee in similar terms. At issue was whether the indemnity and the guarantee applied to certain claims made after delivery, which the seller alleged were spurious. Mance LJ considered that the language used in the indemnity tended to favour coverage for claims that were wholly or partly invalid, in addition to valid claims. This was reinforced by various practical considerations. The general commercial purpose of the clause was to protect the buyer after delivery in respect of predelivery events. The seller would usually be in a better position to know the history of the vessel being sold. The buyer of the vessel needed to act with assurance once a claim was made against the vessel, so as to free the vessel for further trading. If the indemnity extended to alleged as well as actual liabilities, it could also cover the buyer's reasonable settlement of claims.

[3–27] **Basis for narrowing application of indemnity.** The process of commercial construction eschews strained or artificial constructions. In applying the indemnity, limitations to scope are derived primarily from commercial or contextual considerations[101]

---

[98] *Morgan Grenfell Development Capital Syndications Ltd v Arrows Autosports Ltd* [2004] EWHC 1015 (Ch), [17].

[99] See, eg, *Richardson v Buckinghamshire City Council* [1971] 1 Lloyd's Rep 533 (CA), 537 (Buckley LJ); *EE Caledonia Ltd v Orbit Valve Co Europe* [1994] 1 WLR 1515 (CA), 1525 (Steyn LJ); *Campbell v Conoco (UK) Ltd* [2002] EWCA Civ 704; [2003] 1 All ER (Comm) 35, [13], [34]–[35] (Rix LJ); *Wiltshire County Council v Crest Estates Ltd* [2005] EWCA Civ 1087; [2005] BLR 458, [50]–[54] (Ward LJ); *National Roads and Motorists' Association Ltd v Whitlam* [2007] NSWCA 81; (2007) 25 ACLC 688, [58]–[62] (Campbell JA); *Cosmos Holidays plc v Dhanjal Investments Ltd* [2009] EWCA Civ 316, [17]–[19] (Clarke MR); *Farstad Supply AS v Enviroco Ltd (The Far Service)* [2010] UKSC 18; [2010] 2 Lloyd's Rep 387, [59] (Lord Mance). cf also *Pervolianakis v GRE Insurance Ltd* (VFC, 4 August 1986) (strict construction avoided where it would have rendered indemnity nugatory).

[100] *Rank Enterprises Ltd v Gerard* [2000] EWCA Civ 15; [2000] 1 Lloyd's Rep 403. cf *Athens Cape Naviera SA v Deutsche Dampfschiffahrtsgesellschaft (The Barenbels)* [1985] 1 Lloyd's Rep 528 (CA).

[101] See, eg, *Great Western Railway Co v J Durnford and Son Ltd* (1928) 44 TLR 415 (HL), 416 (Viscount Sumner) ('Wide as the words look at the outset, their context and purpose evidently subject them to several restrictions').

rather than from use of technical legal[102] or grammatical rules such as the *reddendo singula singulis* rule,[103] the *contra proferentem* rule[104] or the *ejusdem generis* rule.[105] The concern for commercially sensible and reasonable results can be seen across a wide variety of limitations, including those concerning risks assumed by the indemnified party under the contract,[106] those concerning the type of loss or liability[107] or the manner in which it arises,[108] and limitations applied to losses that have been incurred unreasonably.[109]

The potential difference between strict and commercial approaches is illustrated by the contrasting majority and minority judgments in *F&D Normoyle Pty Ltd v Transfield Pty Ltd*.[110] A worker injured on a construction site sued his employer (a sub-contractor) and the main contractor. The main contractor claimed on contractual indemnities from the worker's employer and another sub-contractor. The indemnities covered claims and liabilities 'arising as a result of any act, neglect or default' of the sub-contractor or its employees. The majority of the New South Wales Court of Appeal applied the *ejusdem generis* rule and concluded that 'act', when appearing with 'neglect or default', signified an act involving a breach of legal duty. As the sub-contractors had been found not liable for negligence or breach of contract or statutory duty, the indemnity did not apply. Bryson JA in the minority considered that the appropriate standard of construction was commercial. Strained constructions and rules that promoted the detection of ambiguity were to be avoided. The word 'act' was fault-neutral and there was no other contextual reason for narrowing the application of the indemnity. The injured worker's claim against the main contractor arose from his own act; it was, therefore, an 'act' of an employee within the terms of the indemnity from the worker's employer.

The Present Law

The Rise of Commercial Construction

[3–28] **Movement towards commercial construction.** Strict construction of indemnity clauses reached its apogee in the second half of the twentieth century. In *Smith v South*

---

[102] Some Australian indemnity decisions have deprecated the *Canada SS* rules, particularly the third rule, on the basis that it involves a strained construction which is inconsistent with commercial construction: see [4–48].

[103] *Schenker & Co (Aust) Pty Ltd v Maplas Equipment and Services Pty Ltd* [1990] VR 834 (FC), 840–42 (McGarvie J).

[104] See further [3–35].

[105] cf *John Lee & Son (Grantham) Ltd v Railway Executive* [1949] 2 All ER 230 (KB), 232; *F&D Normoyle Pty Ltd v Transfield Pty Ltd* [2005] NSWCA 193; (2005) 63 NSWLR 502, [67] (Ipp JA) and contrast [146]–[147] (Bryson JA).

[106] See, eg, *Weir v Union Steamship Co Ltd* [1900] AC 525 (HL); *Larrinaga Steamship Co Ltd v R* [1945] AC 246 (HL); *ENE Kos 1 Ltd v Petroleo Brasileiro SA (The Kos) (No 2)* [2012] UKSC 17; [2012] 2 WLR 976, [11]–[12] (Lord Sumption), [60]–[61] (Lord Clarke) (risks borne by owner under charterparty).

[107] See, eg, *Boughen v Frederick Attwood Ltd* [1978] 1 Lloyd's Rep 413 (QB), 415–16 (coverage for claims in relation to goods carried but not personal injury); *EE Caledonia Ltd v Orbit Valve Co Europe* [1994] 1 WLR 1515 (CA), 1525 (Steyn LJ) (no coverage for breach of statutory duty where concurrent negligence); *National Roads and Motorists' Association Ltd v Whitlam* [2007] NSWCA 81; (2007) 25 ACLC 688, [58]–[62] (Campbell JA) (no coverage for loss of reputation).

[108] See, eg, *Clearlite Holdings Ltd v Auckland City Corp* [1976] 2 NZLR 729 (SC), 745–46 (no coverage where indemnifier performed properly); *Glebe Island Terminals Pty Ltd v Continental Seagram Pty Ltd (The Antwerpen)* (1993) 40 NSWLR 206; [1994] 1 Lloyd's Rep 213 (CA), 242–44 (Sheller JA) (no coverage where indemnified party actively facilitated theft of goods).

[109] See [4–29].

[110] *F&D Normoyle Pty Ltd v Transfield Pty Ltd* [2005] NSWCA 193; (2005) 63 NSWLR 502.

Wales Switchgear Co Ltd,[111] where the indemnified party sought protection against a liability for negligence, Lord Fraser regarded an indemnity clause as being sufficiently similar to an exclusion clause that the same principles were to be applied.[112] Viscount Dilhorne and Lord Keith considered that an indemnity clause ought to be construed even more stringently than an exclusion clause in relation to negligence; it was, in Lord Keith's words, a 'less usual and more extreme situation'.[113] In *Ailsa Craig Fishing Co Ltd v Malvern Fishing Co Ltd*,[114] Lord Fraser referred to the 'very strict' principles and 'specially exacting standards' applicable to exclusion clauses and indemnity clauses, which were not to be applied in their full rigour to limitation clauses.

These cases have never been expressly overruled but there is now a clear tendency to approach the construction of indemnities[115] in the same manner as other terms in commercial contracts. There are a number of decisions in the English Court of Appeal that have expressly or impliedly adopted the principles of commercial construction.[116] In *Bank of Scotland v Euclidian (No 1) Ltd*,[117] Field J suggested that the principle of strict construction against the indemnified party had been superseded by later decisions on commercial construction.

[3–29] Relevance of techniques of strict construction. It does not follow that all of the law traditionally associated with strict construction has been discarded. Some of the techniques and rules have been absorbed within the process of commercial construction, though they are to be applied less rigidly and with greater regard to commercial context. Their continuing influence on indemnities is most apparent in two situations: first, where the indemnified party seeks protection for loss caused by its own fault;[118] and secondly, where it is suggested that the terms of the indemnity modify or displace other legal rights. So, for example, the *Canada SS* rules remain viable but with an emphasis that they are guidelines and must not be applied mechanically.[119] Their continued utility in commercial construction rests principally on the proposition, which is not always true,[120] that it is improbable that one party would indemnify another against the consequences of the latter's own

---

[111] *Smith v South Wales Switchgear Co Ltd* [1978] 1 WLR 165 (HL). *cf Canada Steamship Lines Ltd v R* [1952] AC 192 (PC), 211.

[112] *Smith v South Wales Switchgear Co Ltd* [1978] 1 WLR 165 (HL), 172.

[113] *Smith v South Wales Switchgear Co Ltd* [1978] 1 WLR 165 (HL), 168 (Viscount Dilhorne), 178 (Lord Keith).

[114] *Ailsa Craig Fishing Co Ltd v Malvern Fishing Co Ltd* [1983] 1 WLR 964 (HL), 970.

[115] *cf Egan v Static Control Components (Europe) Ltd* [2004] EWCA Civ 392; [2004] 2 Lloyd's Rep 429 (guarantees); Carter (n 12), 575–84, paras 17-09–17-17 (exclusion and limitation clauses).

[116] *EE Caledonia Ltd v Orbit Valve Co Europe* [1994] 1 WLR 1515 (CA), 1525 (Steyn LJ); *Total Transport Corp v Arcadia Petroleum Ltd (The Eurus)* [1998] 1 Lloyd's Rep 351 (CA), 361 (Staughton LJ); *Rank Enterprises Ltd v Gerard* [2000] EWCA Civ 15; [2000] 1 Lloyd's Rep 403, [8] (Mance LJ); *Wiltshire County Council v Crest Estates Ltd* [2005] EWCA Civ 1087; [2005] BLR 458, [50]–[51] (Ward LJ); *Cosmos Holidays plc v Dhanjal Investments Ltd* [2009] EWCA Civ 316, [15], [17]–[19] (Clarke MR); *Kudos Catering (UK) Ltd v Manchester Central Convention Complex Ltd* [2013] EWCA Civ 38, [21], [27]–[28] (Tomlinson LJ). *cf also Campbell v Conoco (UK) Ltd* [2002] EWCA Civ 704; [2003] 1 All ER (Comm) 35, [12]–[13], [34]–[35] (Rix LJ); *Farstad Supply AS v Enviroco Ltd (The Far Service)* [2010] UKSC 18; [2010] 2 Lloyd's Rep 387, [59] (Lord Mance); *ENE Kos 1 Ltd v Petroleo Brasileiro SA (The Kos) (No 2)* [2012] UKSC 17; [2012] 2 WLR 976, [11]–[12] (Lord Sumption).

[117] *Bank of Scotland v Euclidian (No 1) Ltd* [2007] EWHC 1732 (Comm); [2008] Lloyd's Rep IR 182, [32].

[118] See generally [4–44].

[119] *EE Caledonia Ltd v Orbit Valve Co Europe* [1994] 1 WLR 1515 (CA), 1522 (Steyn LJ); *HIH Casualty and General Insurance Ltd v Chase Manhattan Bank* [2003] UKHL 6; [2003] 2 Lloyd's Rep 61, [11] (Lord Bingham), [61]–[63] (Lord Hoffmann), [116] (Lord Scott); *Onego Shipping & Chartering BV v JSC Arcadia Shipping (The Socol 3)* [2010] EWHC 777 (Comm); [2010] 2 Lloyd's Rep 221, [48]–[52]. See further [4–47], [4–49].

[120] *cf Caledonia North Sea Ltd v British Telecommunications plc (The Piper Alpha)* [2002] UKHL 4; [2002] 1 Lloyd's Rep 553; *Shell UK Ltd v Total UK Ltd* [2010] EWCA Civ 180; [2011] QB 86, [13]–[14].

negligence. The insistence on clear words to achieve certain results also persists in relation to some other aspects of indemnities.[121] Where a doubt or ambiguity in construction cannot otherwise be resolved, the *contra proferentem* rule is still relevant.[122]

Comparison with Position in Australia

[3–30] Background. Australian law provides an interesting counterpoint to English developments. The course of construction of contractual indemnities is marked by two decisions of the High Court of Australia: *Darlington Futures Ltd v Delco Australia Pty Ltd*[123] and *Andar Transport Pty Ltd v Brambles Ltd*.[124] The latter represents the present state of the law.

It is difficult to discern any clear pattern in the construction of indemnities prior to *Darlington*. Some cases could be characterised as employing strict construction,[125] some as employing commercial construction or avoiding a strict construction,[126] and others as turning upon textual analysis without an obvious preference for either perspective.[127] *Darlington* itself concerned the construction an exclusion clause and a limitation clause. The Full Court of the Supreme Court of South Australia had construed both clauses 'strictly' but the High Court was concerned to avoid strained or artificial constructions of the clauses. In a well-known passage, Mason, Wilson, Brennan, Deane and Dawson JJ said:[128]

> [T]he interpretation of an exclusion clause is to be determined by construing the clause according to its natural and ordinary meaning, read in the light of the contract as a whole, thereby giving due weight to the context in which the clause appears including the nature and object of the contract, and, where appropriate, construing the clause contra proferentem in case of ambiguity.

That statement is consistent with the concept of commercial construction. Following the lead in *Darlington*, Australian decisions began to apply the same approach to the construction of contractual indemnities.[129] The approach was applied to indemnities in various forms and not limited to indemnities against claims by or liabilities to the indemnifier, which most closely resemble exclusion or limitation clauses.

---

[121] *Liberty Mutual Insurance Co (UK) Ltd v HSBC Bank plc* [2002] EWCA Civ 691, [51], [56] (Rix LJ) (displacement of right of subrogation); *Bank of Scotland v Euclidian (No 1) Ltd* [2007] EWHC 1732 (Comm); [2008] Lloyd's Rep IR 182, [32]. See also [10–30] (whether indemnity against breach displaces common law right to damages).

[122] *Antiparos ENE v SK Shipping Co Ltd (The Antiparos)* [2008] EWHC 1139 (Comm); [2008] 2 Lloyd's Rep 237, [32]; *Cosmos Holidays plc v Dhanjal Investments Ltd* [2009] EWCA Civ 316, [4] (Clarke MR). See further [3–35].

[123] *Darlington Futures Ltd v Delco Australia Pty Ltd* (1986) 161 CLR 500.

[124] *Andar Transport Pty Ltd v Brambles Ltd* [2004] HCA 28; (2004) 217 CLR 424.

[125] *cf Davis v Commissioner for Main Roads* (1967) 117 CLR 529, 534 (Kitto J) (dissenting); *Canberra Formwork Pty Ltd v Civil and Civic Ltd* (1982) 41 ACTR 1 (SC); *Greenwell v Matthew Hall Pty Ltd (No 2)* (1982) 31 SASR 548 (SC).

[126] *Australian Coastal Shipping Commission v PV 'Wyuna'* (1964) 111 CLR 303, 309–10 (Kitto J); *Total Oil Products (Australia) Pty Ltd v Robinson* [1970] 1 NSWR 701 (CA), 704–05 (Asprey JA); *Pervolianakis v GRE Insurance Ltd* (VFC, 4 August 1986).

[127] *Federal Steam Navigation Co Ltd v J Fenwick & Co Pty Ltd* (1943) 68 CLR 553; *Australian Coastal Shipping Commission v PV 'Wyuna'* (1964) 111 CLR 303 (but *cf* n 126 (Kitto J)).

[128] *Darlington Futures Ltd v Delco Australia Pty Ltd* (1986) 161 CLR 500, 510.

[129] *Schenker & Co (Aust) Pty Ltd v Maplas Equipment and Services Pty Ltd* [1990] VR 834 (FC), 845–46 (McGarvie J); *Albert Shire Council v Vanderloos* (1992) 77 LGRA 309 (QCA), 312; *Glebe Island Terminals Pty Ltd v Continental Seagram Pty Ltd (The Antwerpen)* (1993) 40 NSWLR 206; [1994] 1 Lloyd's Rep 213 (CA), 242 (Sheller JA); *Valkonen v Jennings Construction Ltd* (1995) 184 LSJS 87 (SAFC), 98 (Cox J); *Nilsen Electric (SA) Pty Ltd v Mitsubishi Motors Australia Ltd* [1999] SASC 105 (FC), [14] (Bleby J); *Australian Paper Plantations Pty Ltd v Venturoni* [2000] VSCA 71, [17] (Buchanan JA).

[3–31] *Andar Transport v Brambles.* In *Andar Transport Pty Ltd v Brambles Ltd*,[130] Gleeson CJ, McHugh, Gummow, Hayne and Heydon JJ drew an analogy with contracts of guarantee. The principles of construction of guarantees that were relevant to indemnities were those contained in the following passage from *Ankar Pty Ltd v National Westminster Finance (Australia) Ltd*:[131]

> At law, as in equity, the traditional view is that the liability of the surety is *strictissimi juris* and that ambiguous contractual provisions should be construed in favour of the surety. The doctrine of *strictissimi juris* provides a counterpoise to the law's preference for a construction that reads a provision otherwise than as a condition. A doubt as to the status of a provision in a guarantee should therefore be resolved in favour of the surety.

The joint judgment in *Andar* also referred to a statement by Lord Oliver in *Coghlan v SH Lock (Australia) Ltd*[132] concerning 'well-known principles' for the construction of guarantees. These were that '[s]uch a document falls to be construed strictly; it is to be read *contra proferentem*; and, in case of ambiguity, it is to be construed in favour of the surety'.[133]

Referring to the commercial context and considering the relationship between the indemnity clauses and other provisions of the agreement, Gleeson CJ, McHugh, Gummow, Hayne and Heydon JJ favoured a construction that led to the indemnity being inapplicable in the circumstances. To the extent that the clauses remained ambiguous, they were to be construed in favour of the indemnifier and against the indemnified party. This confirmed their preliminary view.

[3–32] Adoption of strict construction? The *ratio decidendi* of *Andar Transport Pty Ltd v Brambles Ltd*[134] has been a matter of some controversy. The most limited reading of the joint judgment is that it only endorses the principle that, in cases of ambiguity or doubt, an indemnity provision is to be construed in favour of the indemnifier.[135] That corresponds to the final part of the passage from *Ankar Pty Ltd v National Westminster Finance (Australia) Ltd*[136] and the last of the three propositions from *Coghlan v SH Lock (Australia) Ltd*.[137] In *Bofinger v Kingsway Group Ltd*,[138] the High Court of Australia described the 'principle' in *Andar* in terms that a doubt as to the construction of an indemnity should be resolved in favour of the indemnifier. In other respects, the approach adopted by Gleeson CJ, McHugh, Gummow, Hayne and Heydon JJ in *Andar* accords with what might be expected of commercial construction.[139] *Andar* and *Darlington Futures Pty Ltd v Delco Australia*

---

[130] *Andar Transport Pty Ltd v Brambles Ltd* [2004] HCA 28; (2004) 217 CLR 424, [23]. See further [3–15].

[131] *Ankar Pty Ltd v National Westminster Finance (Australia) Ltd* (1987) 162 CLR 549, 561 (Mason ACJ, Wilson, Brennan and Dawson JJ).

[132] *Coghlan v SH Lock (Australia) Ltd* (1987) 8 NSWLR 88 (PC).

[133] *Coghlan v SH Lock (Australia) Ltd* (1987) 8 NSWLR 88 (PC), 92

[134] *Andar Transport Pty Ltd v Brambles Ltd* [2004] HCA 28; (2004) 217 CLR 424.

[135] *F&D Normoyle Pty Ltd v Transfield Pty Ltd* [2005] NSWCA 193; (2005) 63 NSWLR 502, [141]–[142] (Bryson JA); *Rava v Logan Wines Pty Ltd* [2007] NSWCA 62, [49]–[57] (Campbell JA); *National Roads and Motorists' Association Ltd v Whitlam* [2007] NSWCA 81; (2007) 25 ACLC 688, [66]–[69] (Campbell JA); *Erect Safe Scaffolding (Australia) Pty Ltd v Sutton* [2008] NSWCA 114; (2008) 72 NSWLR 1, [26]–[30], [82] (Basten JA), *cf* [11] (Giles JA). *cf Westina Corp Pty Ltd v BGC Contracting Pty Ltd* [2009] WASCA 213; (2009) 41 WAR 263, [49]–[50] (Buss JA).

[136] *Ankar Pty Ltd v National Westminster Finance (Australia) Ltd* (1987) 162 CLR 549, 561 (Mason ACJ, Wilson, Brennan and Dawson JJ).

[137] *Coghlan v SH Lock (Australia) Ltd* (1987) 8 NSWLR 88 (PC), 92.

[138] *Bofinger v Kingsway Group Ltd* [2009] HCA 44; (2009) 239 CLR 269, [53].

[139] *cf* also *Pacific Carriers Ltd v BNP Paribas* [2004] HCA 35; (2004) 218 CLR 451, [22], decided less than two months later.

Ltd[140] are, then, consistent.[141] Both accommodate commercial construction, with the clause being construed against the beneficiary in cases of ambiguity or doubt.

The competing view is that *Andar* establishes two principles, namely, that indemnities are to be construed: (1) strictly and (2) in cases of ambiguity, in favour of the indemnifier.[142] This approach is not consistent with *Darlington*. The view is supported by the repeated references in the joint judgment to the 'principles' (plural) of construction of guarantees to be applied to indemnities. Those references identify the doctrine of *strictissimi juris* and, perhaps also, the explicit statement of strict construction from *Coghlan*. Kirby J in *Andar* considered that the joint judgment had adopted a 'strict construction'.[143] Some of the material cited in footnotes might be understood to support the *contra proferentem* rule or strict construction more generally.[144]

As a matter of basic principle, the former view should be preferred to the latter.[145]

[3–33] Limits of *Andar Transport v Brambles*. The fact that the indemnity had been prepared by solicitors acting for the indemnified party was described as a 'significant circumstance' in the joint judgment in *Andar Transport Pty Ltd v Brambles Ltd*.[146] It is not clear whether the principle concerning doubt or ambiguity is to be applied where the indemnifier has drafted the indemnity.[147] The analogy drawn with guarantees in *Andar* was justified on the basis that both types of promise are intended to satisfy a liability owed by someone other than the promisor to a third person. An indemnity against the indemnified party's personal losses does not meet that description, nor does an indemnity against claims by or liabilities to the indemnifier. It is doubtful whether *Andar* was intended to apply to such indemnities.[148] The latter form of indemnity is closer in nature to an exclusion or limitation clause. *Darlington Futures Pty Ltd v Delco Australia Ltd*[149] may therefore be the more appropriate authority.[150]

[3–34] Other implications. Two further points arise if *Andar Transport Pty Ltd v Brambles Ltd*[151] does revert to strict construction of indemnities. First, it might be thought that the third of the *Canada SS* rules, which fell into disfavour after *Darlington*,[152] could be revived. Yet that rule has been rejected even when a strict construction has been applied.[153] Secondly, the ambit of the *strictissimi juris* principle referred to in *Andar* is uncertain. Lord Ellenborough

---

[140] *Darlington Futures Ltd v Delco Australia Pty Ltd* (1986) 161 CLR 500.

[141] *cf Andar Transport Pty Ltd v Brambles Ltd* [2004] HCA 28; (2004) 217 CLR 424, [122]–[123] (Callinan J).

[142] *F&D Normoyle Pty Ltd v Transfield Pty Ltd* [2005] NSWCA 193; (2005) 63 NSWLR 502, [47], [64] (Ipp JA); *BI (Contracting) Pty Ltd v AW Baulderstone Holdings Pty Ltd* [2007] NSWCA 173; (2008) Aust Contract R 90-267, [17]–[25] (Beazley JA); *Laresu Pty Ltd v Clark* [2010] NSWCA 180, [88] (Macfarlan JA). *cf Colliers Jardine Pty Ltd v Castle Mall Properties Pte Ltd* [2005] NSWCA 311, [40]–[41] (Tobias JA); *Gardiner v Agricultural and Rural Finance Pty Ltd* [2007] NSWCA 235; (2008) Aust Contract R 90-274, [15]–[21], [125] (Spigelman CJ).

[143] *Andar Transport Pty Ltd v Brambles Ltd* [2004] HCA 28; (2004) 217 CLR 424, [70].

[144] See *Andar Transport Pty Ltd v Brambles Ltd* [2004] HCA 28; (2004) 217 CLR 424, [23] fn 45.

[145] See [3–16].

[146] *Andar Transport Pty Ltd v Brambles Ltd* [2004] HCA 28; (2004) 217 CLR 424, [10] and *cf* [19].

[147] See [3–38].

[148] *cf Andar Transport Pty Ltd v Brambles Ltd* [2004] HCA 28; (2004) 217 CLR 424, [68]–[71] (Kirby J) (relying on a more general ground).

[149] *Darlington Futures Ltd v Delco Australia Pty Ltd* (1986) 161 CLR 500.

[150] See, eg, *MRT Performance Pty Ltd v Mastro Motors Inc* [2005] NSWSC 316, [37].

[151] *Andar Transport Pty Ltd v Brambles Ltd* [2004] HCA 28; (2004) 217 CLR 424.

[152] See [4–48].

[153] *BI (Contracting) Pty Ltd v AW Baulderstone Holdings Pty Ltd* [2007] NSWCA 173; (2008) Aust Contract R 90-267. See W Courtney, 'Construction of Contractual Indemnities – Out With the Old, In With the New?' (2008) 24 *Journal of Contract Law* 182.

in *Bacon v Chesney*[154] described it as requiring the creditor to show that the terms of a guarantee had been 'strictly complied with'. The principle has been seen to encompass some of the technical rules for the discharge of the guarantor.[155] If that is correct then the adoption of the *strictissimi juris* principle might lead to similar rules being applied to indemnities. *Andar* aside, it has never been clearly established that those rules in general apply to indemnities; the balance of opinion favours some rules but not others.[156]

The *Contra Proferentem* Rule

[3–35] Forms of the rule. A rule that has figured prominently in the construction of indemnities is the *contra proferentem* rule, a shorthand description of the Latin maxim *verba chartarum fortius accipiuntur contra proferentem*. The rule can be expressed as follows: where there is ambiguity or doubt as to the construction of the indemnity clause, it should be resolved in favour of one of the parties and against the other – the *proferens* – because that latter party has a particular status in relation to the indemnity clause. Construction includes issues of the meaning of terms used in, or the legal effect or application of, the indemnity clause.[157]

The characteristic that defines a party as the *proferens* is the subject of differing and potentially conflicting lines of authority.[158] There are at least three different forms of the rule as it has been applied to indemnities:

(1) the *proferens* is the party who drafted or proposed the document or the relevant indemnity clause;[159]

(2) the *proferens* is the party for whose benefit the relevant clause is inserted and who seeks to rely upon it; that is, generally, the indemnified party;[160] and

(3) the *proferens* is the promisor, that is, the indemnifier, irrespective of the proponent of the clause.[161]

---

[154] *Bacon v Chesney* (1816) 1 Stark 192, 193; 171 ER 443, 443. He also referred to *Straton v Rastall* (1788) 2 TR 366, 370; 100 ER 197, 199 (Buller J) ('the contract cannot be carried beyond the strict letter of it').

[155] *Ankar Pty Ltd v National Westminster Finance (Australia) Ltd* (1987) 162 CLR 549, 560 (Mason ACJ, Wilson, Brennan and Dawson JJ); *ST Microelectronics NV v Condor Insurance Ltd* [2006] EWHC 977 (Comm); [2006] 2 Lloyd's Rep 525, [33]–[36].

[156] See [5–20]–[5–29].

[157] See, eg, *Bofinger v Kingsway Group Ltd* [2009] HCA 44; (2009) 239 CLR 269, [53].

[158] *J Fenwick & Co Pty Ltd v Federal Steam Navigation Co Ltd* (1943) 44 SR (NSW) 1 (FC), 5–6 (Jordan CJ). See generally Carter (n 12), 145–47, paras 4-44–4-45; Lewison, *Interpretation of Contracts* (n 68), 362–67, para 7.08.

[159] *John Lee & Son (Grantham) Ltd v Railway Executive* [1949] 2 All ER 581 (CA), 583 (Evershed MR); *Davis v Commissioner for Main Roads* (1967) 117 CLR 529, 534 (Kitto J); *Canberra Formwork Pty Ltd v Civil and Civic Ltd* (1982) 41 ACTR 1 (SC), 23; *Schenker & Co (Aust) Pty Ltd v Maplas Equipment and Services Pty Ltd* [1990] VR 834 (FC), 845 (McGarvie J); *Roads & Traffic Authority of NSW v Palmer* [2003] NSWCA 58, [214] (Spigelman CJ); *Gardiner v Agricultural and Rural Finance Pty Ltd* [2007] NSWCA 235; (2008) Aust Contract R 90-274, [16] (Spigelman CJ); *Re-Source America International Ltd v Platt Site Services Ltd* [2004] EWCA Civ 665; (2004) 95 Con LR 1, [55] (Tuckey LJ); *Cosmos Holidays plc v Dhanjal Investments Ltd* [2009] EWCA Civ 316, [4] (Clarke MR).

[160] *Canada Steamship Lines Ltd v R* [1952] AC 192 (PC), 208, 213–14; *Hair and Skin Trading Co Ltd v Norman Airfreight Carriers Ltd* [1974] 1 Lloyd's Rep 443 (QB), 445; *General Surety & Guarantee Co Ltd v Francis Parker Ltd* (1977) 6 BLR 16 (QB), 21; *Smith v South Wales Switchgear Co Ltd* [1978] 1 WLR 165 (HL), 168 (Viscount Dilhorne), 174 (Lord Fraser), 178 (Lord Keith); *Andar Transport Pty Ltd v Brambles Ltd* [2004] HCA 28; (2004) 217 CLR 424, [19], [29] (Gleeson CJ, McHugh, Gummow, Hayne and Heydon JJ); *Rava v Logan Wines Pty Ltd* [2007] NSWCA 62, [51] (Campbell JA). cf *Nilsen Electric (SA) Pty Ltd v Mitsubishi Motors Australia Ltd* [1999] SASC 105 (FC), [14] (Bleby J).

[161] *Fowle v Welsh* (1822) 1 B & C 29, 35; 107 ER 12, 14 (Bayley J); *Commonwealth v Aurora Energy Pty Ltd* [2006] FCAFC 148; (2006) 235 ALR 644, [41] (North and Emmett JJ).

The rule in its second sense has sometimes been treated as additional to, and distinct from, the rule in its first sense.[162]

[3–36] *Proferens* **is drafter or proponent of indemnity.** One form of the rule is that the *proferens* is the party who put forward or drafted the terms as a whole or, at least, the relevant indemnity provision. The rationale is that the terms put forward by one party are construed as they would be reasonably understood by the other. The former party, being responsible for the ambiguity, should be bound by the more favourable construction adopted by a reasonable person in the position of the recipient.

The rule is generally unhelpful where both parties are involved in drafting the indemnity[163] or where the indemnity is in a form determined by statute.[164] The rule seems to be applied with less consistency in situations where the proponent of the indemnity is not the author. The indemnity may appear in a standard form contract prepared by an independent external body, which then is proffered by one of the parties to the other. In such situations, the influence of the *contra proferentem* rule has varied.[165] Alternatively, one person may mandate that certain terms be used by others in their contracts. Thus, A may provide to B a contract containing an indemnity on terms already determined by C. The *contra proferentem* rule might still be applied against A, as proponent of the terms.[166]

[3–37] *Proferens* **is beneficiary of provision.** Another form of the *contra proferentem* rule treats as the *proferens* the party who receives the benefit of the particular provision. The *Canada SS* rules are framed in this sense.[167] The principle recognised in *Andar Transport Pty Ltd v Brambles Ltd*[168] – that a doubt or ambiguity in the construction of an indemnity provision is resolved against the indemnified party and in favour of the indemnifier – also conforms to this sense of the rule. The policy basis of the rule as it applies to indemnities was explained by Kirby J:[169]

> Indemnity clauses are provisions that purport to exempt one party from civil liability which the law would otherwise impose upon it. They are provisions that shift to another party the civil liability otherwise attached by law to the first party. Self-evidently this is a serious thing to do or to attempt to do. Where such indemnities are said to arise out of contracts which are ambiguous or unclear, it is not unreasonable that their provisions should be construed so that any uncertainty is resolved favourably to the party thereby burdened by legal obligations that would not otherwise attach to it.

[3–38] **Potential for conflict.** The two forms of the rule are consistent where the indemnified party prepares or puts forward the indemnity. The two forms of the rule conflict where the indemnifier prepares or puts forward the indemnity, or where the indemnity is stated in affirmative terms but made subject to qualifications or exclusions that are ambiguous.

---

[162] See, eg, *Coghlan v SH Lock (Australia) Ltd* (1987) 8 NSWLR 88 (PC), 92.

[163] *cf Kleinwort Benson Ltd v Malaysia Mining Corp Berhad* [1988] 1 WLR 799 (QB), 809.

[164] *cf Kodak (Australasia) Pty Ltd v Retail Traders Mutual Indemnity Insurance Association* (1942) 42 SR (NSW) 231 (FC), 233; *Insurance Commission of Western Australia v Container Handlers Pty Ltd* [2004] HCA 24; (2004) 218 CLR 89, [98]–[99] (Kirby J).

[165] *cf J Fenwick & Co Pty Ltd v Federal Steam Navigation Co Ltd* (1943) 44 SR (NSW) 1 (FC), 7 (Jordan CJ); *Borkan General Trading Ltd v Monsoon Shipping Ltd (The Borvigilant and The Romina G)* [2003] EWCA Civ 935; [2003] 2 Lloyd's Rep 520, [103] (Clarke LJ).

[166] *Roads & Traffic Authority of NSW v Palmer* [2003] NSWCA 58, [214] (Spigelman CJ).

[167] *Canada Steamship Lines Ltd v R* [1952] AC 192 (PC), 208, 213–14. See also *Smith v South Wales Switchgear Co Ltd* [1978] 1 WLR 165 (HL), 168 (Viscount Dilhorne), 174 (Lord Fraser), 178 (Lord Keith).

[168] *Andar Transport Pty Ltd v Brambles Ltd* [2004] HCA 28; (2004) 217 CLR 424.

[169] *Andar Transport Pty Ltd v Brambles Ltd* [2004] HCA 28; (2004) 217 CLR 424, [68].

For the first type of conflict there are several different approaches. In insurance, the rule is generally applied against the insurer who prepares the policy.[170] Outside the insurance context, it has been suggested in Australia that *Andar Transport Pty Ltd v Brambles Ltd*[171] prefers one form of the rule – resolution in favour of the indemnifier – over the other form of the rule.[172] The better view is, however, that this point was left open in *Andar* as there was no conflict between the two forms of the rule.[173] Another approach is that the different forms of the rule cancel each other out, so that the indemnifier is not necessarily entitled to have ambiguities or doubts resolved in its favour.[174]

A more complex approach can be found in *J Fenwick & Co Pty Ltd v Federal Steam Navigation Co Ltd*,[175] which presented both types of conflict. The tug owner provided the towage contract, which included the UK Standard Towage Conditions. The tug owner claimed indemnity from the hirer under clause 3 and the hirer sought to rely upon an exception in clause 4. Jordan CJ declined to apply the *contra proferentem* rule against the tug owner as the proponent of the terms.[176] They were in a standard form and there was no suggestion that the hirer had any objection to them or was unable to look after its own interests. In applying the other form of the rule, the perceived ambiguity related to the exception in clause 4 rather than the primary obligation of indemnity in clause 3. The hirer was the party relying upon clause 4, so the ambiguity was construed against it and in favour of the indemnified tug owner.[177] In the circumstances, the outcome seems arbitrary and the rule hardly satisfactory.

[3–39] Use of rule. Where the rule applies against the indemnified party as the beneficiary of the indemnity clause, it narrows the operation of the indemnity. That result is consistent with strict construction. Indeed, if the rule is applied directly and immediately to the indemnity, it achieves a form of strict construction. Thus, there are statements in older cases that merge the two concepts: an indemnity is construed strictly against the indemnified party, or strictly in favour of the indemnifier.[178]

The modern approach is that ambiguity or doubt in the construction of the indemnity is a precondition for use of the rule.[179] The rule is one of last resort, to be used only when

---

[170] *Re Etherington and Lancashire and Yorkshire Accident Insurance Co* [1909] 1 KB 591 (CA), 596 (Vaughan Williams LJ), 600 (Farwell LJ); *Western Australian Bank v Royal Insurance Co* (1908) 5 CLR 533, 554 (Griffith CJ), 559 (Barton J), 567 (O'Connor J), cf 574 (Higgins J); *Halford v Price* (1960) 105 CLR 23, 30 (Dixon CJ), 34 (Fullagar J); *Zeus Tradition Marine Ltd v Bell (The Zeus V)* [2000] EWCA Civ 188; [2000] 2 Lloyd's Rep 587, [30] (Potter LJ); *Blackburn Rovers Football & Athletic Club plc v Avon Insurance plc* [2005] EWCA Civ 423; [2005] Lloyd's Rep IR 447, [9]. cf *Youell v Bland Welch & Co Ltd* [1992] 2 Lloyd's Rep 127 (CA), 134 (Staughton LJ).

[171] *Andar Transport Pty Ltd v Brambles Ltd* [2004] HCA 28; (2004) 217 CLR 424.

[172] *Rava v Logan Wines Pty Ltd* [2007] NSWCA 62, [51] (Campbell JA).

[173] *Andar Transport Pty Ltd v Brambles Ltd* [2004] HCA 28; (2004) 217 CLR 424, [10], [19]; *Gardiner v Agricultural and Rural Finance Pty Ltd* [2007] NSWCA 235; (2008) Aust Contract R 90-274, [16] (Spigelman CJ).

[174] *Gardiner v Agricultural and Rural Finance Pty Ltd* [2007] NSWCA 235; (2008) Aust Contract R 90-274, [21] (Spigelman CJ).

[175] *J Fenwick & Co Pty Ltd v Federal Steam Navigation Co Ltd* (1943) 44 SR (NSW) 1 (FC) (affd without use of the rule: *Federal Steam Navigation Co Ltd v J Fenwick & Co Pty Ltd* (1943) 68 CLR 553).

[176] cf n 165.

[177] *J Fenwick & Co Pty Ltd v Federal Steam Navigation Co Ltd* (1943) 44 SR (NSW) 1 (FC), 7 (Jordan CJ), 12 (Maxwell J).

[178] *Lowery v Vickers Armstrong (Engineers) Ltd* (1969) 8 KIR 603 (CA), 614 (Megaw LJ); *Hair and Skin Trading Co Ltd v Norman Airfreight Carriers Ltd* [1974] 1 Lloyd's Rep 443 (QB), 445; *General Surety & Guarantee Co Ltd v Francis Parker Ltd* (1977) 6 BLR 16 (QB), 21.

[179] *Borkan General Trading Ltd v Monsoon Shipping Ltd (The Borvigilant and The Romina G)* [2003] EWCA Civ 935; [2003] 2 Lloyd's Rep 520, [103] (Clarke LJ); *Andar Transport Pty Ltd v Brambles Ltd* [2004] HCA 28; (2004) 217 CLR 424, [17], [19], [29] (Gleeson CJ, McHugh, Gummow, Hayne and Heydon JJ); *Bofinger v Kingsway Group*

other techniques of construction fail to yield a satisfactory answer.[180] This is a logical concomitant of commercial construction, but there are also decisions accepting the same precondition in the context of a strict construction.[181] That view implies that there are other techniques that may first be applied to narrow the operation of the indemnity.

Ltd [2009] HCA 44; (2009) 239 CLR 269, [53]; *Cosmos Holidays plc v Dhanjal Investments Ltd* [2009] EWCA Civ 316, [4] (Clarke MR). *cf Egan v Static Control Components (Europe) Ltd* [2004] EWCA Civ 392; [2004] 2 Lloyd's Rep 429, [37] (Arden LJ) (guarantee).

[180] *J Fenwick & Co Pty Ltd v Federal Steam Navigation Co Ltd* (1943) 44 SR (NSW) 1 (FC), 6 (Jordan CJ); *McCann v Switzerland Insurance Australia Ltd* [2000] HCA 65; (2000) 203 CLR 579, [74] (Kirby J); *Sinochem International Oil (London) Co Ltd v Mobil Sales and Supply Corp* [2000] EWCA Civ 47; [2000] 1 Lloyd's Rep 339, [27] (Mance LJ); *Direct Travel Insurance v McGeown* [2003] EWCA Civ 1606; [2004] 1 All ER (Comm) 609, [13] (Auld LJ); *Andar Transport Pty Ltd v Brambles Ltd* [2004] HCA 28; (2004) 217 CLR 424, [124] (Callinan J).

[181] *Andar Transport Pty Ltd v Brambles Ltd* [2004] HCA 28; (2004) 217 CLR 424, [19], [29] (Gleeson CJ, McHugh, Gummow, Hayne and Heydon JJ); *BI (Contracting) Pty Ltd v AW Baulderstone Holdings Pty Ltd* [2007] NSWCA 173; (2008) Aust Contract R 90-267, [24]–[25] (Beazley JA).

4

The Scope of the Indemnity

Introduction

[4–1] **Purpose of chapter.** This chapter is concerned with identifying the extent of protection provided by a promise of indemnity. The extent of protection is determined by reference to the 'scope' of the indemnity. Whether the indemnified party is entitled to be protected against a loss can be cast in terms of whether the loss is within or beyond the scope of the indemnity.

Ascertainment of the scope of an indemnity is fundamentally a matter of construction, which in turn depends upon context. Prior decisions are usually of limited value in resolving questions of construction of particular words or terms used in a contract.[1] There is, therefore, little advantage in dissecting indemnity provisions into common words and phrases and then analysing decisions on the meaning or application of each component. The treatment in this chapter adopts a more general perspective, considering construction issues that are relevant to indemnities in all forms.

[4–2] **Structure of chapter.** The chapter is divided into five sections. The first section outlines basic concepts concerning scope. The second section examines three general limitations on the scope of an indemnity that resemble concepts found in the law of damages, namely, causation, remoteness and mitigation of loss. The third section examines limitations on scope that may apply because the indemnified party is in some way at fault in causing the loss claimed. The fourth section considers the relationship between indemnities and other risk allocation clauses, such as insurance clauses. The final section considers the recovery of legal costs under an indemnity.

The Concept of Scope

Definition and Structure

[4–3] **Definition of scope.** The scope of an indemnity may be defined as the set of losses against which the indemnifier promises to protect the indemnified party. The concept applies to all indemnities, including implied indemnities.[2] In theory, and subject to statute and public policy, the scope of an indemnity may be unlimited. In practice, an indemnifier

---

[1] See [3–8]–[3–10].

[2] See, eg, *Ullises Shipping Corp v Fal Shipping Co Ltd (The Greek Fighter)* [2006] EWHC 1729 (Comm); [2006] Lloyd's Rep Plus 99, [296], [302].

generally does not undertake to protect the indemnified party against all loss whatsoever from an event: the scope of the indemnity is qualified. For express indemnities, the qualification usually arises in one or more of the following ways:

(1) where the scope of the indemnity is stated affirmatively, it may be inferred that this statement is exhaustive;

(2) the statement of the scope of the indemnity may contain express exclusions, for example, for 'consequential loss', or may be subject to some other qualification, such as a monetary or temporal limit on claims; and

(3) the scope may be subject to implied limitations which arise through construction.

[4–4] Structure of an express statement of scope. The scope of an indemnity may be defined expressly in any manner the parties choose. Many express indemnity provisions employ the following structure:

(1) A list of types of harm or loss, such as 'actions', 'demands', 'claims', 'liabilities', 'expenses', 'costs' or 'damages'. These may be qualified by words describing the status of the loss or harm, for example, expenses 'incurred' or losses 'sustained'.

(2) A causal or connective factor, which relates the types of loss in (1) with the events described in (3). Common expressions include 'caused by', 'arising out of', 'arising from', or 'in connection with'.

(3) The activating or 'triggering' event or circumstances, the occurrence of which may lead to loss as stated in (1) according to the relation described in (2). The trigger may be a specific event, such as a breach of contract by the indemnifier, or it may be a general context, for example, 'the performance of the services' or 'the agency relationship'.

Not every contractual indemnity expressly addresses all three elements. An indemnity often found in time charterparties refers to the 'consequences' of the master's compliance with the charterer's orders.[3] That formulation merges the causal or connective factor (the second element) with a non-specific type of loss (the first element). Alternatively, only the third element may be present, as in a case where the indemnifier promises to indemnify 'against breach of contract' by the indemnifier.[4] The missing elements are supplied through the process of construction.

[4–5] Use of scope. The question of whether the indemnified party is entitled to protection against a particular loss is generally framed in terms of whether the loss is within the scope of the indemnity. The usual approach involves two stages.[5] The scope of the indemnity is first ascertained. The circumstances are then tested against the scope to determine whether the claimed loss falls within or beyond scope. In practice these two stages may be merged, because the ascertainment of scope is directed by the context of the claim for a particular loss.

Issues commonly arising at the first stage include whether the indemnity covers a particular type or basis of liability, or legal costs of defending claims, or a reasonable settlement of a claim, or losses or liabilities caused wholly or partly by the indemnified party's own negligence. At the second stage, where the indemnity is applied to the facts, the question may

---

[3] See further [4–13].
[4] See [10–4].
[5] See, eg, *ENE Kos 1 Ltd v Petroleo Brasileiro SA (The Kos) (No 2)* [2012] UKSC 17; [2012] 2 WLR 976, [56] (Lord Clarke).

relate to the reasonableness of the legal costs incurred, or settlement concluded, by the indemnified party; or whether the relationship between the activating event and the loss satisfies the specified causal or connective factor.

Relationship with Concepts of Loss and Damnification

[4–6] Scope, loss and damnification. In general terms, the scope of an indemnity represents a subset of all possible losses from an event or state of affairs. The concept of loss is more abstract than that of scope. It requires the characterisation of an event by reference to its effect on the indemnified party. The consequences of the event may possess the quality of a loss because they are adverse or harmful to the indemnified party.

Damnification refers to the process of suffering or sustaining a loss. Like the concept of loss, damnification may operate at a more general level than scope. In some circumstances, default construction rules may determine what events damnify the indemnified party. An important feature of express indemnities is that the indemnified party is not necessarily damnified when one of the events or types of harm stated in the scope of the indemnity materialises. So, for example, under a non-insurance indemnity against 'liability', the indemnified party is generally not damnified merely because it incurs a liability.[6] Likewise, under an indemnity against 'breach', the indemnified party is not always damnified by a breach of contract.[7]

A promise of indemnity may protect against detriment to the person, loss of or damage to property, and purely economic losses.

[4–7] Detriment to the person. Many cases concern injury to persons other than the indemnified party. The injured person is often a worker engaged in performing services on a construction project or at an industrial location. From the indemnified party's perspective, the relevant loss is not a loss due to personal injury. It is a loss arising from an actual or potential liability to the injured person. This is an economic loss and so falls into another category.[8]

The non-insurance indemnity cases are rarely concerned with personal harm to the indemnified party. It appears from old decisions that deprivation of liberty, by arrest and imprisonment, amounted to damnification.[9] It also appears that the expenditure of labour,[10] and injury to the indemnified party's reputation[11] may be the subject of an indemnity promise.

[4–8] Loss of or damage to property. Loss of or damage to the indemnified party's property must be distinguished from loss of or damage to property of another person. In the latter case, the loss to the indemnified party generally arises because it is liable to the other person. The loss is, from the indemnified party's perspective, purely economic. The distinction also features in disputes concerning the scope of the indemnity, namely, whether

---

[6] See [6–23].
[7] See [10–25].
[8] See [4–9].
[9] See [6–24].
[10] *Chief Commissioner of State Revenue v Reliance Financial Services Pty Ltd* [2006] NSWSC 1017, though this decision might be better characterised as involving a failure to obtain a benefit from a third party: see [9–32].
[11] *cf National Roads and Motorists' Association Ltd v Whitlam* [2007] NSWCA 81; (2007) 25 ACLC 688, [55] (Campbell JA) (loss of reputation not within the scope of the indemnity in issue).

the indemnified party is to be protected against harm to its own property or only against liability to third parties.[12] In *Great Western Railway Co v Port Talbot Dry Dock Co Ltd*,[13] the defendant was repairing the claimant's vessel when it capsized and sank. The claimant sued in negligence and also under a contractual indemnity from the defendant against 'all actions claims losses and expenses whatsoever in respect of . . . loss of or damage to property' attributable to the execution of the works. Tucker J concluded that the indemnity was not limited to the claimant's liability for damage to third party property, and extended to include loss of the claimant's own property. Accordingly, the defendant was liable under the indemnity for the loss of the vessel.

[4–9] **Economic losses.** Various kinds of economic loss may be the subject of the promise of indemnity. A common instance is the payment of money by the indemnified party to satisfy a liability to a third party.[14] Other losses include: being deprived of a right that would otherwise exist;[15] the diminution in value of property;[16] loss of use of property;[17] reliance losses sustained where expenditure in a venture has become wasted;[18] and losses constituted by the failure of the indemnified party to obtain a particular return from a transaction. The basis of the expectation is often contractual and may be founded in a contract between the indemnified party and the indemnifier or a third party. Thus, A may indemnify B against the consequences of A's breach of a contract with B; B sustains loss because it fails to receive the performance promised by A.[19] Alternatively, A may indemnify B against C's breach of a contract with B; B's loss may be the failure to receive the promised performance from C.[20] The return protected by the indemnity may even exceed the promised performance.[21]

General Limitations

Causation or Connection

Overview

[4–10] **Standard may be express or inferred.** The nature of the connection that must exist between a loss and an event or state of affairs may be defined expressly. There is considerable variety in definitions. Common expressions include: 'caused by', 'arising as a result

---

[12] See, eg, *Great Western Railway Co v Port Talbot Dry Dock Co Ltd* [1944] 2 All ER 328 (KB); *Mobil Oil Canada Ltd v Beta Well Service Ltd* (1974) 2 AR 186 (CA) (affd *Mobil Oil Canada Ltd v Beta Well Service Ltd* (1974) 50 DLR (3d) 158 (SCC)); *Twentieth Super Pace Nominees Pty Ltd v Australian Rail Track Corp Ltd* [2006] VSC 353, [138]–[140]. See also *Pacific Gas and Electric Co v GW Thomas Drayage & Rigging Co* 69 Cal 2d 33 (1968) (Cal CA).
[13] *Great Western Railway Co v Port Talbot Dry Dock Co Ltd* [1944] 2 All ER 328 (KB).
[14] See [6–23].
[15] *Milburn & Co v Jamaica Fruit Importing and Trading Co of London* [1900] 2 QB 540 (CA) (loss of right to general average contribution).
[16] *Guy-Pell v Foster* [1930] 2 Ch 169 (CA); *Muhammad Issa El Sheikh Ahmad v Ali* [1947] AC 414 (PC).
[17] *ENE Kos 1 Ltd v Petroleo Brasileiro SA (The Kos) (No 2)* [2012] UKSC 17; [2012] 2 WLR 976.
[18] *Man Nutzfahrzeuge AG v Freightliner Ltd* [2005] EWHC 2347 (Comm). See [10–56].
[19] See generally ch 10.
[20] See generally ch 9.
[21] See [9–8], [9–45].

of', 'arising out of' and 'in connection with'; several of these expressions may be combined disjunctively in the statement of scope. Where the standard of causation or connection is not expressly stated, it must be inferred as a matter of construction.[22]

It is also possible to find comparisons of the relative strength of connection required by such expressions; on one view, the list given in the preceding paragraph is ordered from strongest to weakest.[23] Abstract comparisons, even when not in conflict, tend to be of limited utility however. The stringency of the causal or connective factor is sensitive to context, particularly the specified event or state of affairs that activates the indemnity. Furthermore, many disputes about causation or connection relate to the application of the indemnity to the factual circumstances.

[4–11] Guiding considerations. As the standard of causation or connection ultimately depends upon construction, it is difficult to articulate specific principles. The following general propositions can be stated as guidance:

(1) There is no identifiable standard of causation or connection that is generally presumed to apply to non-insurance indemnities.

(2) An event can often satisfy the causal or connective element of scope without being the sole cause of the loss.[24] It may be sufficient that the event is 'a' cause of,[25] or an 'effective' cause of,[26] or materially contributes to[27] the loss.

(3) A requirement that the specified event be the sole cause of the loss is unlikely to be inferred in the absence of an express statement to that effect.[28]

[4–12] No general standard of causation or connection. There is no standard of causation or connection that is presumed generally to apply to non-insurance indemnities.[29] In particular, neither factual (*causa sine qua non*) causation,[30] nor common law causation, nor proximate causation[31] serves as a general standard. This is a significant point of departure

---

[22] See, eg, *County and District Properties Ltd v C Jenner & Sons Ltd* [1976] 2 Lloyd's Rep 728 (QB), 735. cf *Boughen v Frederick Attwood Ltd* [1978] 1 Lloyd's Rep 413 (QB), 416.

[23] cf *Dickinson v Motor Vehicle Insurance Trust* (1987) 163 CLR 500, 505; *Campbell v Conoco (UK) Ltd* [2002] EWCA Civ 704; [2003] 1 All ER (Comm) 35, [19] (Rix LJ); *Erect Safe Scaffolding (Australia) Pty Ltd v Sutton* [2008] NSWCA 114; (2008) 72 NSWLR 1, [11] (Giles JA).

[24] *Warrellow v Chandler* [1956] 1 WLR 1272 (Shrop); *Arthur White (Contractors) Ltd v Tarmac Civil Engineering Ltd* [1967] 1 WLR 1508 (HL), 1516–17 (Lord Morris); *Menzies Property Services Ltd v State of New South Wales* [2003] NSWCA 17, [55] (Ipp JA); *ENE Kos 1 Ltd v Petroleo Brasileiro SA (The Kos) (No 2)* [2012] UKSC 17; [2012] 2 WLR 976, [12] (Lord Sumption), [70]–[71] (Lord Clarke).

[25] *Menzies Property Services Ltd v State of New South Wales* [2003] NSWCA 17, [55] (Ipp JA).

[26] *Arthur White (Contractors) Ltd v Tarmac Civil Engineering Ltd* [1967] 1 WLR 1508 (HL), 1516 (Lord Morris); *Onego Shipping & Chartering BV v JSC Arcadia Shipping (The Socol 3)* [2010] EWHC 777 (Comm); [2010] 2 Lloyd's Rep 221, [88]; *ENE Kos 1 Ltd v Petroleo Brasileiro SA (The Kos) (No 2)* [2012] UKSC 17; [2012] 2 WLR 976, [12] (Lord Sumption), [70], [75] (Lord Clarke).

[27] *Erect Safe Scaffolding (Australia) Pty Ltd v Sutton* [2008] NSWCA 114; (2008) 72 NSWLR 1, [97] (Basten JA).

[28] *Lowery v Vickers Armstrong (Engineers) Ltd* (1969) 8 KIR 603 (CA), 609–10 (Salmon LJ); *Leighton Contractors Pty Ltd v Smith* [2000] NSWCA 55, [8] (Mason P and Fitzgerald JA); *Snelgar v Westralia Airports Corp Pty Ltd* [2006] WASCA 83, [77]–[78] (Steytler P).

[29] But see *Royal Greek Government v Minister of Transport (The Ann Stathatos)* (1950) 83 Ll L Rep 228 (KB), 238; *ENE Kos 1 Ltd v Petroleo Brasileiro SA (The Kos) (No 2)* [2012] UKSC 17; [2012] 2 WLR 976, [70] (Lord Clarke).

[30] See [4–16], [4–17].

[31] cf *Lowery v Vickers Armstrong (Engineers) Ltd* (1969) 8 KIR 603 (CA), 610 (Salmon LJ) (no requirement of dominant cause); *State of New South Wales v Tempo Services Ltd* [2004] NSWCA 4, [8] (Meagher JA); *F&D Normoyle Pty Ltd v Transfield Pty Ltd* [2005] NSWCA 193; (2005) 63 NSWLR 502, [90] (Ipp JA); *Beazley Underwriting Ltd v Travelers Companies Inc* [2011] EWHC 1520 (Comm); [2012] 1 All ER (Comm) 1241, [128]; *ENE Kos 1 Ltd v Petroleo Brasileiro SA (The Kos) (No 2)* [2012] UKSC 17; [2012] 2 WLR 976. See further [4–13] (time charterparties).

from indemnities in contracts of insurance, to which the standard of proximate cause is generally applied.

Concepts and techniques drawn from other standards of causation may, however, still be applied by analogy. Thus, it may be relevant to consider whether the connection between the loss and the activating event is too distant or tenuous, or whether an intervening event makes such a contribution to the loss that it 'breaks' the chain of causation from the original event.[32]

[4–13] Standard may be recognised in limited circumstances. A standard of causation or connection may be recognised in more limited circumstances, such as where an indemnity appears in a standard form contract. An example is the indemnity commonly found expressed or implied in time charterparties. The indemnity, from the charterer to the owner, is usually framed to protect against the 'consequences' of the master signing bills of lading or other documents, or complying with orders given by the charterer.

A substantial line of decisions had appeared to establish that the standard was that of 'direct'[33] or 'proximate'[34] causation. However, in *ENE Kos 1 Ltd v Petroleo Brasileiro SA (The Kos) (No 2)*[35] a majority of the Supreme Court of the United Kingdom held that the standard was that of 'effective' cause. That standard was more stringent than factual causation but less stringent than proximate causation or a standard of sole cause. The owner of the *Kos* withdrew the vessel on the basis of the charterer's non-payment of hire. At that point, the vessel had been partly loaded pursuant to orders of the charterer. The owner then claimed under the indemnity for losses incurred in discharging the cargo already aboard. Two causes of the loss were the charterer's order to load and the owner's decision to withdraw the vessel. The majority concluded that the charterer's order was an effective cause of the loss and this was sufficient to apply the indemnity.

Where Causal or Connective Relation Not Satisfied

[4–14] General. The required causal or connective relation may be lacking even though a loss appears to follow from one of the activating events or circumstances specified in the scope of the indemnity. This may be so because:

(1) the loss is properly attributed to an antecedent event or pre-existing circumstances;
(2) the activating event or circumstances merely provide the 'occasion' for the loss;
(3) the connection has been severed by an intervening event; or

---

[32] See [4–18], [4–19].

[33] *Portsmouth Steamship Co Ltd v Liverpool & Glasgow Salvage Association* (1929) 34 Ll L Rep 459 (KB), 462; *Larrinaga Steamship Co Ltd v R* [1945] AC 246 (HL), 263 (Lord Porter); *Actis Co Ltd v Sanko Steamship Co Ltd (The Aquacharm)* [1980] 2 Lloyd's Rep 237 (QB), 244 (and on appeal: *Actis Co Ltd v Sanko Steamship Co Ltd (The Aquacharm)* [1982] 1 WLR 119 (CA), 126 (Griffiths LJ)); *Triad Shipping Co v Stellar Chartering & Brokerage Inc (The Island Archon)* [1994] 2 Lloyd's Rep 227 (CA), 238 (Nicholls VC); *Whistler International Ltd v Kawasaki Kisen Kaisha Ltd (The Hill Harmony)* [2001] 1 AC 638 (HL), 656 (Lord Hobhouse). cf *Sig Bergesen DY & Co v Mobil Shipping and Transportation Co (The Berge Sund)* [1993] 2 Lloyd's Rep 453 (CA), 462 (Staughton LJ).

[34] *Royal Greek Government v Minister of Transport (The Ann Stathatos)* (1950) 83 Ll L Rep 228 (KB), 238; *Vardinoyannis v The Egyptian General Petroleum Co (The Evaggelos Th)* [1971] 2 Lloyd's Rep 200 (QB); *Newa Line v Erechthion Shipping Co SA (The Erechthion)* [1987] 2 Lloyd's Rep 180 (QB), 185; *Ullises Shipping Corp v Fal Shipping Co Ltd (The Greek Fighter)* [2006] EWHC 1729 (Comm); [2006] Lloyd's Rep Plus 99, [302]–[308].

[35] *ENE Kos 1 Ltd v Petroleo Brasileiro SA (The Kos) (No 2)* [2012] UKSC 17; [2012] 2 WLR 976, [12] (Lord Sumption), [70], [75] (Lord Clarke). See generally W Courtney, 'Indemnities in Time Charterparties and the Effect of the Withdrawal of the Vessel' (2013) 30 *Journal of Contract Law* 243.

(4) the connection between the loss and the activating event or circumstances is too distant or tenuous.

[4–15] Loss attributed to antecedent event or pre-existing circumstances. An example is *The Lindenhall.*[36] A towage contract contained an indemnity from the claimants to the defendants against all claims in respect of damage 'arising in the course of and in connexion with the towage'. While the claimants' vessel was being towed, it was damaged by an explosion from an enemy mine dropped some hours earlier during an air raid. The defendants' reliance on the indemnity failed, one reason[37] being that the claimants' loss was not sustained 'in connexion with' the towage.

[4–16] Event or circumstances merely occasion for loss. The activating event or circumstances specified in the scope of the indemnity may be treated as providing only the context or occasion for the loss. Such a characterisation supposes that the indemnity on its proper construction requires a closer connection.[38] This result is sometimes seen where the specified event or circumstances are generally descriptive of the subject-matter of the contract, or of a significant aspect of performance of the contract. Examples include the enjoyment of a lease or licence,[39] the use of an item supplied under the contract,[40] the performance of the contracted services,[41] or the compliance by the master of a vessel with orders given by the time charterer.[42]

The usual justification is that the indemnity would operate in an unacceptably broad manner if the existence or performance of the contractual arrangement were sufficient of itself.[43] In *Great Western Railway Co v J Durnford & Son Ltd,*[44] the defendant granted to the claimant a licence to use a portable gangway that projected over the defendant's railway. The claimant in return agreed to indemnify the defendant against all claims or liability 'arising out of or in connection with the existence or user of the said gangway'. The claimant's lorry was positioned on the gangway when it collided with rolling stock shunted along the line by the defendant. The presence of the lorry upon the gangway was a *causa sine qua non* of the accident, but the House of Lords held that the defendant could not invoke the indemnity. Viscount Sumner explained that if the indemnity applied so broadly, the claimant could

---

[36] *The Lindenhall* [1945] P 8 (CA). See also *Bradstreets British Ltd v Mitchell* [1933] Ch 190 (Ch) (liability for libel preceding breach of contract: see [10–41]). *cf Total Transport Corp v Arcadia Petroleum Ltd (The Eurus)* [1998] 1 Lloyd's Rep 351 (CA), 362 (Staughton LJ) (longstanding timing rule affecting loading of cargo); *Naviera Mogor SA v Societe Metallurgique de Normandie (The Nogar Marin)* [1988] 1 Lloyd's Rep 412 (CA), 422 (master's negligence in signing receipt which was then used to issue clean bills of lading).

[37] See also [8–4].

[38] Contrast, eg, *Furness Shipbuilding Co Ltd v London and North Eastern Railway Co* (1934) 50 TLR 257 (HL); *Mediterranean Freight Services Ltd v BP Oil International Ltd (The Fiona)* [1994] 2 Lloyd's Rep 506 (CA), 522 (Hoffmann LJ). See further [4–20]–[4–21].

[39] *Great Western Railway Co v J Durnford and Son Ltd* (1928) 44 TLR 415 (HL); *John Lee & Son (Grantham) Ltd v Railway Executive* [1949] 2 All ER 581 (CA). *cf Warrellow v Chandler* [1956] 1 WLR 1272 (Shrop).

[40] *Wright v Tyne Improvement Commissioners* [1967] 2 Lloyd's Rep 411 (QB).

[41] See [4–20]–[4–21].

[42] See, eg, *Stag Line Ltd v Ellerman & Papayanni Lines Ltd* (1949) 82 Ll L Rep 826 (KB) (damage to vessel caused by striking obstruction while leaving berth, not by order to go to berth); *AB Helsingfors Steamship Co Ltd v Rederiaktiebolaget Rex (The White Rose)* [1969] 1 WLR 1098 (QB). See further [4–13].

[43] *Great Western Railway Co v J Durnford and Son Ltd* (1928) 44 TLR 415 (HL); *Larrinaga Steamship Co Ltd v R* [1945] AC 246 (HL), 256 (Lord Wright), 261 (Lord Porter); *John Lee & Son (Grantham) Ltd v Railway Executive* [1949] 2 All ER 581 (CA); *Lipman Pty Ltd v McGregor* [2004] NSWCA 6, [30] (Gzell J); *Onego Shipping & Chartering BV v JSC Arcadia Shipping (The Socol 3)* [2010] EWHC 777 (Comm); [2010] 2 Lloyd's Rep 221, [63]–[64], [68]–[69].

[44] *Great Western Railway Co v J Durnford and Son Ltd* (1928) 44 TLR 415 (HL).

safely use the gangway only when the defendant was not engaged in shunting operations. Such a construction would have prejudiced, if not wholly defeated, the commercial object of the licence agreement.

[4–17] Effect of express reference to 'but for' connection. The distinction between a cause of loss and an occasion for loss may be drawn even where the scope of the indemnity is expressed in terms of a 'but for' connection. In *John Lee & Son (Grantham) Ltd v Railway Executive,*[45] a railway engine ejected a spark which set alight a warehouse in which the claimants' goods were stored. The Railway Executive, the defendant in an action for negligence, relied upon a clause in a tenancy agreement for the warehouse between itself, as the landlord, and one of the claimants, as tenant. The clause provided that the tenant would release and indemnify the landlord against liability for loss of or damage to property 'which but for the tenancy hereby created . . . would not have arisen'. Although the existence of the tenancy and the presence of the goods in the warehouse were necessary factual elements in the loss, it was held that the clause did not apply. The clause was limited to liabilities that arose by reason of the relationship of landlord and tenant.

[4–18] Intervening events. The necessary connection between the loss and the event or circumstances may be severed by a subsequent event that is regarded as sufficiently extrinsic and influential in the occurrence of the loss.[46] The decisions on indemnities in time charterparties establish that there must be an unbroken connection between the charterer's order and the loss claimed by the owner.[47] An intervening act of negligence by the master or some casualty may be enough to sever the connection.[48] Settlements by the indemnified party of claims by third parties have been analysed in similar terms. Colman J in *General Feeds Inc Panama v Slobodna Plovidba Yugoslavia*[49] reasoned that unless the settlement was reasonable, the indemnified party would not establish that its loss under the settlement was caused by the eventuality specified in the indemnity. The loss would be attributable to its own act in concluding an unreasonable settlement.[50]

[4–19] Limits to consequences of event or circumstances. The scope of the indemnity may, as a matter of construction, be limited to losses that have a sufficiently tangible con-

[45] *John Lee & Son (Grantham) Ltd v Railway Executive* [1949] 2 All ER 581 (CA). cf *Warrellow v Chandler* [1956] 1 WLR 1272 (Shrop); *Onego Shipping & Chartering BV v JSC Arcadia Shipping (The Socol 3)* [2010] EWHC 777 (Comm); [2010] 2 Lloyd's Rep 221, [63]–[64].

[46] See, eg, *City of Manchester v Fram Gerrard Ltd* (1974) 6 BLR 70 (QB), 91. For another causation perspective on the case, see [4–19].

[47] *Portsmouth Steamship Co Ltd v Liverpool & Glasgow Salvage Association* (1929) 34 Ll L Rep 459 (KB), 462; *AB Helsingfors Steamship Co Ltd v Rederiaktiebolaget Rex (The White Rose)* [1969] 1 WLR 1098 (QB), 1108; *Triad Shipping Co v Stellar Chartering & Brokerage Inc (The Island Archon)* [1994] 2 Lloyd's Rep 227 (CA), 234–36 (Evans LJ), 238 (Nicholls VC); *ENE Kos 1 Ltd v Petroleo Brasileiro SA (The Kos) (No 2)* [2012] UKSC 17; [2012] 2 WLR 976, [51] (Lord Mance) (dissenting on standard of causation), [75] (Lord Clarke).

[48] cf *Royal Greek Government v Minister of Transport (The Ann Stathatos)* (1950) 83 Ll L Rep 228 (KB) (explosion on vessel caused by spark and explosive atmosphere, not by order to load gassy cargo); *Vardinoyannis v The Egyptian General Petroleum Co (The Evaggelos Th)* [1971] 2 Lloyd's Rep 200 (QB) (whether loss caused by order to Suez or subsequent shelling by armed forces); *The Athanasia Comninos and The Georges C Lemos* [1990] 1 Lloyd's Rep 277 (QB), 294 (casualty caused by master's failure to ensure cargo carried with appropriate care); *Actis Co Ltd v Sanko Steamship Co Ltd (The Aquacharm)* [1982] 1 WLR 119 (CA), 126 (Griffiths LJ) (transhipment costs apparently caused by master overloading the vessel); *A/S Hansen-Tangens Rederi III v Total Transport Corp (The Sagona)* [1984] 1 Lloyd's Rep 194 (QB) (losses caused by order to deliver cargo to receivers not entitled to it notwithstanding master's failure to make further enquiries before delivery).

[49] *General Feeds Inc Panama v Slobodna Plovidba Yugoslavia* [1999] 1 Lloyd's Rep 688 (QB), 691–92.

[50] cf *Waite v Paccar Financial plc* [2012] EWCA Civ 901, [30] (McFarlane LJ). See further [6–52].

nection with the event or circumstances that activated the indemnity.[51] Even broad descriptions of connection, such as 'all consequences', are not necessarily unlimited in extent.

In *City of Manchester v Fram Gerard Ltd*,[52] the contractor was engaged to construct an abattoir and facilities for a meat market. The contract contained an indemnity from the contractor to the employer, relevantly, against losses and liabilities 'in respect of any injury or damage whatsoever to any property . . . in so far as such injury or damage arises out of . . . the execution of the works', provided that the same was 'due to' any negligence or default of the contractor or its sub-contractors. The employer sought indemnity for sums it had paid to settle claims for contamination of meat stored in the facilities. One line of argument was that a sub-contractor's default had led to cracks in some of the concrete floors. Those cracks had been sealed by a third party, and the sealant had released a substance which contaminated the meat. The contamination occurred some three years after the original default by the sub-contractor. Kerr J held that the connection between the default and loss was too tenuous to satisfy the phrase 'due to' used in the indemnity.[53]

Services Contracts and Claims by Third Parties

[4–20] **Identifying the causal and consequential elements.** Services contracts can present particularly challenging questions of causation or connection. A typical situation is as follows. A worker or member of the public is injured while on a construction site or at an industrial location. The employer or contractor is found liable for negligence or breach of statutory duty, and in turn claims on an indemnity from a contractor or sub-contractor, respectively, who provides services at the location. The indemnifier may be concurrently liable to the injured claimant. The event or circumstances activating the indemnity are often described using general terms such as 'performance of the services'; likewise, the causal or connective relation, where expressions such as 'arising out of' or 'in connection with' are common.

A preliminary issue is whether an expression such as 'performance of the services' describes the general circumstances or is limited to performance of the services by the *indemnifier*.[54] The latter construction may narrow the scope of the indemnity by focusing attention upon the indemnifier's conduct. The immediate consequential factor must also be identified. The usual candidates are the injury to the claimant, or the liability of the indemnified party.[55] The latter construction may be narrower in scope because it requires consideration of the origin and nature of the indemnified party's liability. That is, it may be easier to establish: (1) that the indemnified party is liable for injuries to the claimant that

---

[51] *cf Australian Coastal Shipping Commission v PV 'Wyuna'* (1964) 111 CLR 303, 316–17 (Owen J); *F&D Normoyle Pty Ltd v Transfield Pty Ltd* [2005] NSWCA 193; (2005) 63 NSWLR 502, [90] (Ipp JA); *Ullises Shipping Corp v Fal Shipping Co Ltd (The Greek Fighter)* [2006] EWHC 1729 (Comm); [2006] Lloyd's Rep Plus 99, [302]; *Antiparos ENE v SK Shipping Co Ltd (The Antiparos)* [2008] EWHC 1139 (Comm); [2008] 2 Lloyd's Rep 237, [32]–[33]; *Erect Safe Scaffolding (Australia) Pty Ltd v Sutton* [2008] NSWCA 114; (2008) 72 NSWLR 1, [11] (Giles JA).

[52] *City of Manchester v Fram Gerard Ltd* (1974) 6 BLR 70 (QB).

[53] *City of Manchester v Fram Gerard Ltd* (1974) 6 BLR 70 (QB), 90–91.

[54] See, eg, *Smith v South Wales Switchgear Co Ltd* [1978] 1 WLR 165 (HL), 169 (Viscount Dilhorne), 173–74 (Lord Fraser), 178 (Lord Keith); *Australian Paper Plantations Pty Ltd v Venturoni* [2000] VSCA 71, [9]–[11] (Buchanan JA); *Roads & Traffic Authority of NSW v Palmer* [2003] NSWCA 58, [213] (Spigelman CJ), [238]–[245] (Giles JA).

[55] See, eg, *Smith v Vange Scaffolding & Engineering Co Ltd* [1970] 1 WLR 733 (QB); *Leighton Contractors Pty Ltd v Smith* [2000] NSWCA 55, [7] (Mason P and Fitzgerald JA); *F&D Normoyle Pty Ltd v Transfield Pty Ltd* [2005] NSWCA 193; (2005) 63 NSWLR 502, [62] (Ipp JA).

were caused by certain acts or omissions; than (2) that the indemnified party's liability for those injuries was caused by the same acts or omissions.

[4–21] Basis and source of liability. The indemnity may cover a basis of liability that involves some element of fault by the indemnified party, such as negligence, or it may be limited to a strict and derivative liability that arises as a result of acts of others, as for some breaches of statutory duties or breach of a non-delegable tortious duty.[56] This is, strictly, an issue distinct from causation. It deserves mention here, however, because the causal or connective relation can affect the construction of the scope of the indemnity as it relates to bases of liability. If, for example, the expression 'performance of the services' (or similar) contemplates performance by the indemnifier,[57] this may suggest that the indemnity is limited to derivative liabilities incurred by the indemnified party as a result of the indemnifier's acts or omissions.[58]

A further consideration is the role that the performance of the services must play in bringing about the indemnified party's liability. Is it sufficient that it is part of the factual context from which the liability arises,[59] or must there be more than a merely temporal connection?[60] If the latter, must some aspect of the performance of the services form an essential ingredient in the claimant's cause of action against the indemnified party?[61] In *Speno Rail Maintenance Australia Pty Ltd v Hamersley Iron Pty Ltd*,[62] Wheeler J observed that a liability in negligence includes aspects of duty and breach; thus, the involvement of the relevant parties needs to be evaluated by reference to that composite concept. The indemnifier's conduct may indirectly affect the indemnified party's legal responsibility, as where the indemnifier creates a risk of harm that the indemnified party, in the fulfilment of its duty of care, would be expected to eliminate.[63]

Exclusion of Concurrent Causes or Concurrent Liabilities

[4–22] General. A loss may be a product of concurrent causes, one being within the scope of the indemnity and the other not. Most cases concern concurrent causes that are inter-

---

[56] See, eg, *Walters v Whessoe Ltd* (1960) 6 BLR 23 (CA), 33 (Sellers LJ), 35 (Devlin LJ); *Smith v South Wales Switchgear Co Ltd* [1978] 1 WLR 165 (HL), 174 (Lord Fraser), 179 (Lord Keith); *Greenwell v Matthew Hall Pty Ltd (No 2)* (1982) 31 SASR 548 (SC), 555; *Erect Safe Scaffolding (Australia) Pty Ltd v Sutton* [2008] NSWCA 114; (2008) 72 NSWLR 1, [89]–[90] (Basten JA). See further [4–56]–[4–57].

[57] See [4–20].

[58] cf *Smith v South Wales Switchgear Co Ltd* [1978] 1 WLR 165 (HL), 169 (Viscount Dilhorne), 173 (Lord Fraser), 178 (Lord Keith); *Canberra Formwork Pty Ltd v Civil and Civic Ltd* (1982) 41 ACTR 1 (SC), 22; *Erect Safe Scaffolding (Australia) Pty Ltd v Sutton* [2008] NSWCA 114; (2008) 72 NSWLR 1, [12] (Giles JA), [155]–[157] (McClellan CJ at CL), cf [97]–[98] (Basten JA).

[59] See, eg, *Furness Shipbuilding Co Ltd v London and North Eastern Railway Co* (1934) 50 TLR 257 (HL); *EE Caledonia Ltd v Orbit Valve Co Europe* [1994] 1 WLR 1515 (CA), 1527 (Steyn LJ); *Campbell v Conoco (UK) Ltd* [2002] EWCA Civ 704; [2003] 1 All ER (Comm) 35, [26]–[29] (Rix LJ), [37] (Tuckey LJ). cf *State of New South Wales v Tempo Services Ltd* [2004] NSWCA 4, [8] (Meagher JA), [20] (Hodgson JA); *Speno Rail Maintenance Australia Pty Ltd v Hamersley Iron Pty Ltd* [2000] WASCA 408; (2000) 23 WAR 291, [10]–[12] (Malcolm CJ), [63]–[68] (Ipp JA) (in context of insurance contract).

[60] *Smith v South Wales Switchgear Co Ltd* [1978] 1 WLR 165 (HL), 173–74 (Lord Fraser), 179 (Lord Keith); *Australian Paper Plantations Pty Ltd v Venturoni* [2000] VSCA 71, [15] (Buchanan JA); *Roads & Traffic Authority of NSW v Palmer* [2003] NSWCA 58, [238], [248]–[249] (Giles JA); *Erect Safe Scaffolding (Australia) Pty Ltd v Sutton* [2008] NSWCA 114; (2008) 72 NSWLR 1, [12] (Giles JA), [157] (McClellan CJ at CL). cf [4–16].

[61] cf *Smith v Vange Scaffolding & Engineering Co Ltd* [1970] 1 WLR 733 (QB), 740.

[62] *Speno Rail Maintenance Australia Pty Ltd v Hamersley Iron Pty Ltd* [2000] WASCA 408; (2000) 23 WAR 291, [127].

[63] *Speno Rail Maintenance Australia Pty Ltd v Hamersley Iron Pty Ltd* [2000] WASCA 408; (2000) 23 WAR 291, [128]–[130] (Wheeler J); *Erect Safe Scaffolding (Australia) Pty Ltd v Sutton* [2008] NSWCA 114; (2008) 72 NSWLR 1, [35]–[36], [44] (Basten JA).

dependent, in the sense that the loss would not have occurred in the absence of any one of them. Instances of independent causes are difficult to find. The existence of an independent cause beyond the scope of the indemnity may, as a matter of fact, negate the causal or connective relation between the loss and the activating event specified in the scope of the indemnity.[64]

Whether the indemnified party can recover for a loss by concurrent causes, one included within scope, another not, is ultimately a matter of construction. The point may be addressed expressly, as where an indemnity provides for a proportionate reduction in coverage based on relative contributions to the loss,[65] or where the contract defines the order of precedence among potentially conflicting terms. In the absence of an express provision, there does not appear to be any well-established default rule. The approach in indemnity insurance is generally as follows.[66] If the loss is attributable to concurrent proximate (and interdependent) causes and one of those causes is expressly excluded by the policy, then the insured cannot recover even though the other proximate cause falls within the policy. If, however, the former cause is neither expressly included nor excluded, then the loss is recoverable.

That approach cannot be transferred directly to non-insurance indemnities. The standard of causation differs among non-insurance indemnities and is not generally one of proximate cause.[67] The distinction between a cause that is expressly excluded and a cause that is merely beyond scope is sound in some circumstances.[68] It does not, however, account for inferred exclusions from scope, which are not uncommon for non-insurance indemnities. That inference may also be drawn from other terms of the contract containing the indemnity. The rule as applied in insurance might thus be adapted to non-insurance indemnities by modifying the references to proximate causation, and by recognising that exclusions may arise expressly or by implication.

[4–23] Exclusion inferred from other terms of contract.

Where the exclusion is alleged to derive from other terms of the contract, reconciliation of the indemnity and those other terms will determine which has priority. In *Mediterranean Freight Services Ltd v BP Oil International Ltd (The Fiona)*,[69] an explosion occurred in the tank of the claimant's vessel while preparing to discharge a cargo carried for the defendant. The carriage was subject to the Hague-Visby Rules. One of the causes of the explosion was found to be the dangerous nature of the cargo. The claimant relied on the indemnity under article IV rule 6, which applied to shipments of inflammable, dangerous or explosive goods without the carrier's informed consent. Another cause of the explosion was the claimant's failure, before the voyage, to clean the tank of residue from the previous cargo. This was a breach of the seaworthiness obligation in article III rule 1. The latter was held to be the superior and overriding term. As the breach of that rule had been one cause of the loss, the claimant was debarred from claiming on the indemnity in article IV rule 6.

---

[64] *cf Menzies Property Services Ltd v State of New South Wales* [2003] NSWCA 17.

[65] See further [4–45].

[66] *Wayne Tank and Pump Co Ltd v Employers' Liability Assurance Corp* [1974] QB 57 (CA); *JJ Lloyd Instruments Ltd v Northern Star Insurance Co Ltd (The Miss Jay Jay)* [1987] 1 Lloyd's Rep 32 (CA); *Global Process Systems Inc v Syarikat Takaful Malaysia Berhad (The Cendor Mopu)* [2011] UKSC 5; [2011] 1 All ER 869; *HIH Casualty & General Insurance Ltd v Waterwell Shipping Inc* (1998) 43 NSWLR 601 (CA), 612 (Sheller JA). *cf McCarthy v St Paul International Insurance Co Ltd* [2007] FCAFC 28; (2007) 157 FCR 402, [92]–[103], [114] (Allsop J).

[67] See [4–12], [4–13].

[68] See, eg, *ENE Kos 1 Ltd v Petroleo Brasileiro SA (The Kos) (No 2)* [2012] UKSC 17; [2012] 2 WLR 976 (loss caused by charterer's order to load cargo and owner's decision to withdraw vessel).

[69] *Mediterranean Freight Services Ltd v BP Oil International Ltd (The Fiona)* [1994] 2 Lloyd's Rep 506 (CA).

[4–24] **Degree of influence and effect of exclusion.** The degree to which the excluded cause must contribute to the loss, and the extent of exemption from coverage, depend upon the construction of the contract and the nature of the loss. The approach is pragmatic rather than technical.[70] It seems generally to be sufficient that the excluded factor is 'a' cause[71] or an 'effective' cause[72] of the loss. If the exclusion relates to the indemnified party's negligence and such negligence is 'a' or an 'effective' cause of an indivisible loss, the usual outcome is that the indemnified party is debarred completely and not merely pro tanto.[73]

The point was considered in *AMF International Ltd v Magnet Bowling Ltd.*[74] The indemnified party and indemnifier were held liable to AMF, responsibility between them being apportioned 40:60 on the tort claims by AMF. On the basis that negligence was impliedly excluded from the scope of the indemnity, the indemnified party argued that it was nonetheless entitled to protection because its negligence (40 per cent) was merely a *causa sine qua non* whereas the indemnifier's negligence (60 per cent) was the real cause of the loss. Mocatta J rejected a distinction based on relative causation. The indemnified party's negligence was an effective cause of the loss and this was sufficient to preclude enforcement of the indemnity.[75]

[4–25] **Concurrent liabilities.** An indemnified party may be liable on multiple bases to a third party in respect of the same loss. Concurrent liabilities for negligence and for breach of statutory duty are a common example.[76] The bases of liability may derive from the same or different acts. If one basis or cause of liability is excluded (for example, negligence) then it is a question of construction whether concurrent liability on another basis is also excluded. In *EE Caledonia Ltd v Orbit Valve Co Europe*,[77] an oil platform operator settled claims by third parties on the basis of liability for negligence and breach of statutory duty. The operator then claimed on an indemnity from a contractor. The English Court of Appeal concluded that the operator was not entitled to be indemnified against its liability on either basis. Treating breach of statutory duty and negligence each as an effective cause of the operator's loss under settlement, Steyn LJ explained that the point was simply one of construction of the agreement in a commercial manner.[78] Properly construed, the indemnity clause allocated to each party the risk of its own negligence. The operator could not, therefore, recover on that basis. Consistently with that allocation of risk, the parties presumably intended that the exclusion of negligence from scope could not be circumvented by relying upon a concurrent liability for breach of statutory duty. Thus, the operator could not recover on this basis either.

---

[70] *EE Caledonia Ltd v Orbit Valve Co Europe* [1994] 1 WLR 1515 (CA), 1525 (Steyn LJ).

[71] *EE Caledonia Ltd v Orbit Valve Co Europe* [1994] 1 WLR 221 (QB), 231–32.

[72] *AMF International Ltd v Magnet Bowling Ltd* [1968] 1 WLR 1028 (QB), 1059; *EE Caledonia Ltd v Orbit Valve Co Europe* [1994] 1 WLR 1515 (CA), 1525 (Steyn LJ). cf *Lowery v Vickers Armstrong (Engineers) Ltd* (1969) 8 KIR 603 (CA), 615 (Megaw LJ) ('major' cause); *Beazley Underwriting Ltd v Travelers Companies Inc* [2011] EWHC 1520 (Comm); [2012] 1 All ER (Comm) 1241, [117] (need not be sole cause).

[73] *Walters v Whessoe Ltd* (1960) 6 BLR 23 (CA); *AMF International Ltd v Magnet Bowling Ltd* [1968] 1 WLR 1028 (QB); *Lowery v Vickers Armstrong (Engineers) Ltd* (1969) 8 KIR 603 (CA); *Greenwell v Matthew Hall Pty Ltd (No 2)* (1982) 31 SASR 548 (SC). cf also *Mediterranean Freight Services Ltd v BP Oil International Ltd (The Fiona)* [1994] 2 Lloyd's Rep 506 (CA), 521 (Hoffmann LJ); *Beazley Underwriting Ltd v Travelers Companies Inc* [2011] EWHC 1520 (Comm); [2012] 1 All ER (Comm) 1241, [133].

[74] *AMF International Ltd v Magnet Bowling Ltd* [1968] 1 WLR 1028 (QB).

[75] *AMF International Ltd v Magnet Bowling Ltd* [1968] 1 WLR 1028 (QB), 1059–60.

[76] See further [4–57].

[77] *EE Caledonia Ltd v Orbit Valve Co Europe* [1994] 1 WLR 1515 (CA). cf *Roads & Traffic Authority of NSW v Palmer* [2003] NSWCA 58, [246]–[249] (Giles JA) (indemnified party concurrently liable for its own negligence and also for breach of a non-delegable duty of care due to indemnifier's conduct).

[78] *EE Caledonia Ltd v Orbit Valve Co Europe* [1994] 1 WLR 1515 (CA), 1525.

Losses Not Reasonably Foreseen or Contemplated

[4–26] **Definition.** The concept of remoteness, as it applies to claims for damages for breach of contract, is concerned to limit recovery of certain kinds of loss from breach. Its operation generally depends upon a consideration of two factors: the knowledge actually possessed by, or imputed to, the parties (at least, the defaulting party) at the time of contract; and the likelihood, in the known circumstances, of the relevant kind of loss eventuating from the breach of contract. An analogous concept can be applied to the scope of the indemnity. That is, the scope is limited to those types of losses that the parties would reasonably have foreseen or contemplated to arise from the specified events or circumstances that activate the indemnity. Losses that are unforeseen or not contemplated are not recoverable because they are beyond scope.

Defined in this manner, the limitation of remoteness arises as a matter of construction of the contract and not as an incident of a claim for common law damages in the enforcement of the indemnity.[79] As the limitation is applied in the abstract it need not be conceptualised in terms of the rule in *Hadley v Baxendale*,[80] though this is the usual reference point for analysis. It may be applied to a variety of events or circumstances and not only breaches of contract. Insofar as the remoteness limitation depends upon what the parties 'reasonably contemplated', it may resemble other inferred limitations on scope, such as those based on the allocation of risk under the broader contract, or exclusions for the indemnified party's negligence or unreasonable conduct. The distinctive feature of the remoteness limitation is that, based upon the parties' knowledge at the time of contract, the type of loss is an unlikely or unpredictable consequence of the activating event or circumstances.

[4–27] **Express terms.** As the remoteness limitation described above[81] is a matter of construction, it may be adopted or excluded by express provision to that effect. In *Schenker & Co (Aust) Pty Ltd v Maplas Equipment and Services Pty Ltd*,[82] for example, a clause stated that the client would hold harmless and indemnify the contractor against claims for loss of or damage to goods 'whether or not the same occurs . . . in circumstances which are in contemplation of the contractor and/or the client or are foreseeable by them or either of them'. It has also been suggested that the causal or connective element in the scope of the indemnity may affect the applicability of a remoteness limitation. In *Mediterranean Freight Services Ltd v BP Oil International Ltd (The Fiona)*,[83] Hoffmann LJ considered that the expression 'directly or indirectly' as used in article IV, rule 6 of the Hague-Visby Rules, although referring to causation, would have the concomitant effect of displacing any remoteness limitation equivalent to the rule in *Hadley v Baxendale*.[84] Indemnities that are drafted in wide and general terms are not necessarily applied literally so as to exclude considerations of remoteness.[85]

---

[79] See further [5–47], [5–49].

[80] *Hadley v Baxendale* (1854) 9 Ex 341; 156 ER 145.

[81] See [4–26].

[82] *Schenker & Co (Aust) Pty Ltd v Maplas Equipment and Services Pty Ltd* [1990] VR 834 (FC).

[83] *Mediterranean Freight Services Ltd v BP Oil International Ltd (The Fiona)* [1994] 2 Lloyd's Rep 506 (CA), 522. *cf* 519 (Hirst LJ).

[84] *Hadley v Baxendale* (1854) 9 Ex 341; 156 ER 145.

[85] *cf Australian Coastal Shipping Commission v PV 'Wyuna'* (1964) 111 CLR 303, 309–10 (Kitto J); *Total Transport Corp v Arcadia Petroleum Ltd (The Eurus)* [1996] 2 Lloyd's Rep 408 (QB), 432 ('all consequences'). But see n 87.

[4–28] Inferred limitation of remoteness. More controversial is whether a limitation of remoteness should be inferred in the absence of any express provision. It has been suggested, for example, that a limitation ought to be presumed to apply where the indemnity is engaged by a legal wrong that would itself attract the remoteness rule.[86] The issue is ultimately a matter of construction, and the justification for a remoteness limitation is sensitive to context. This tends to count against any general presumption applicable to all types of indemnity. It is clear that a limitation of remoteness is not invariably inferred.

A leading illustration is *Triad Shipping Co v Stellar Chartering & Brokerage Inc (The Island Archon)*.[87] The chartered vessel was ordered to Basrah, where the owner incurred loss from cargo claims asserted by Iraqi receivers. Such claims were, typically, highly dubious in nature; the practice was so widespread that it was known as the 'Iraqi system'. The system was notorious when the vessel was ordered to Basrah, but it was neither actually known nor foreseeable when the charterparty was agreed.

It was held that the owner could recover for the loss from the charterer under an indemnity against the consequences of the master complying with the charterer's orders. The scope of the indemnity was limited by reference to the overall allocation of risk under the charterparty. The foreseeability of the risk was relevant, but its significance was inverted from the conventional understanding in a claim for damages. Nicholls VC said: 'the very fact that the loss flowing from charterer's orders was an ordinary and foreseeable risk may lead to the conclusion that it is not within the indemnity'.[88] The owner of the vessel would be taken to have accepted such a risk. Conversely, as the risk of loss from the Iraqi system was not foreseen at the time of the charterparty, it had not been assumed by the owner and so fell within the indemnity. This inverse relationship between foreseeable risk and scope may seem to give the indemnity a very broad operation, but that breadth reflects the power of the charterer to direct the employment of the vessel. As Devlin J explained in *Royal Greek Government v Minister of Transport (The Ann Stathatos)*,[89] if the owner of the vessel 'is to surrender his freedom of choice and put his master under the orders of the charterer, there is nothing unreasonable in his stipulating for a complete indemnity in return'.

Avoided and Reasonably Avoidable Loss

[4–29] General. It has occasionally been said that principles of mitigation do not apply to claims under non-insurance[90] indemnities, though these statements also assume that the

---

[86] See further [10–46]–[10–47] (indemnifier's breach of contract).

[87] *Triad Shipping Co v Stellar Chartering & Brokerage Inc (The Island Archon)* [1994] 2 Lloyd's Rep 227 (CA). See also *ENE Kos 1 Ltd v Petroleo Brasileiro SA (The Kos) (No 2)* [2012] UKSC 17; [2012] 2 WLR 976, [10], [12] (Lord Sumption).

[88] *Triad Shipping Co v Stellar Chartering & Brokerage Inc (The Island Archon)* [1994] 2 Lloyd's Rep 227 (CA), 238. See also *Action Navigation Inc v Bottiglieri di Navigazione SpA (The Kitsa)* [2005] EWHC 177 (Comm); [2005] 1 Lloyd's Rep 432, [25]; *ENE Kos 1 Ltd v Petroleo Brasileiro SA (The Kos) (No 2)* [2012] UKSC 17; [2012] 2 WLR 976, [12] (Lord Sumption).

[89] *Royal Greek Government v Minister of Transport (The Ann Stathatos)* (1950) 83 Ll L Rep 228 (KB), 234.

[90] For the position in insurance, see, eg, J Birds, B Lynch and S Milnes, *MacGillivray on Insurance Law*, 12th edn (London, Sweet & Maxwell, 2012), 920–23, paras 27-009–27-015; MA Clarke, *The Law of Insurance Contracts*, 5th edn, (London, Informa, 2006), 897–906, §28-8G3; PM Eggers, 'Sue and Labour and Beyond: the Assured's Duty of Mitigation' [1998] *Lloyd's Maritime and Commercial Law Quarterly* 228; MA Clarke, 'Wisdom After the Event: the Duty to Mitigate Insured Loss' [2003] *Lloyd's Maritime and Commercial Law Quarterly* 525.

indemnified party's claim is not for damages.[91] The impact of mitigation principles on the indemnified party's claim to enforce the indemnity is considered elsewhere.[92] The present focus is on concepts analogous to mitigation that may apply, as a matter of construction, to restrict the scope of the indemnity.

Authorities on mitigation of damage are cited relatively infrequently. The most direct references appear where the scope of the indemnity covers loss from a legal wrong that would ordinarily be subject to principles of mitigation of damage. The scope of the indemnity may be informed by, or parallel, the common law basis for assessment of damages.[93] More generally, there are several characteristics of indemnities that approximate the effect of mitigation principles though they are not the same in all respects. The characteristics include:

(1) excluding or limiting coverage for loss that ought reasonably to have been avoided by the indemnified party;
(2) excluding or limiting protection where the indemnified party has impaired the indemnifier's rights in relation to the loss (and so affected the ultimate burden borne by the indemnifier);
(3) in limited circumstances, providing coverage for losses incurred in attempts to avoid further loss; and
(4) requiring the indemnified party to account for benefits that diminish the loss, whether received before or after being indemnified.

The first, third and fourth characteristics are considered below. The second characteristic, which involves other considerations, is examined separately.[94]

Avoidable Loss

[4–30] Source and nature of limitation. A requirement of reasonableness may expressly qualify a type of loss described in the scope of the indemnity, as in the case of 'reasonable costs' or a 'reasonable settlement'. Even in the absence of express provision, a limitation on the scope of the indemnity is presumed to arise as a matter of construction. The limitation applies to the conduct of the indemnified party in incurring losses as well as failing to mitigate losses once they have arisen. The indemnified party is not entitled to protection against loss that it ought to have avoided by conduct of a certain standard. The standard is expressed in various ways, usually by one or more of the following: proper,[95]

---

[91] *Royscot Commercial Leasing Ltd v Ismail* (CA, 29 April 1993); *Total Transport Corp v Arcadia Petroleum Ltd (The Eurus)* [1996] 2 Lloyd's Rep 408 (QB), 422; *Scottish and Southern Energy plc v Lerwick Engineering & Fabrication Ltd* [2008] CSOH 41; 2008 SCLR 317, [28]; *Codemasters Software Co Ltd v Automobile Club de L'Ouest (No 2)* [2009] EWHC 3194 (Ch); [2010] FSR 13, [31]–[32].
[92] See [5–47], [5–50].
[93] See [9–52] (indemnities against default by a third party) and [10–40] (indemnities against default by the indemnifier).
[94] See [5–25]–[5–29].
[95] *cf Webster v Petre* (1879) 4 Ex D 127, 131; *Ringrow Pty Ltd v BP Australia Pty Ltd* [2006] FCA 1446, [86]–[88] (equating propriety with requirement of reasonableness and good faith).

fair,[96] reasonable,[97] or 'good faith'.[98] It appears that reasonableness is a minimum standard.

[4–31] Where act increases loss. One aspect of the reasonableness limitation is that the indemnified party should act reasonably in incurring losses under the indemnity. In *Smith v Howell*,[99] defaults by the defendant, as the ultimate assignee of a sub-lease, prompted a cascade of litigation. The holder of the reversionary interest in the lease successfully sued the sub-lessee for rent and repairs; the sub-lessee successfully sued the now-claimant; the claimant sued the defendant. The claimant claimed, under an indemnity from the defendant, substantial legal costs incurred in defending the action by the sub-lessee. It was held that these were not recoverable. Pollock CB said:[100]

> There is no doubt that, at one time, very wild notions were entertained with respect to the contract of indemnity, but these notions are now exploded . . . [T]he party indemnified may recover all such charges as necessarily and reasonably arose out of the circumstances under which the party charged became responsible.

The original proceedings against the sub-lessee had established breaches of the covenants in the sub-lease and the relevant amount of damage. It was unreasonable in the circumstances for the claimant to persist in defending the action by the sub-lessee.

Hooper v Bromet[101] is another example. Hooper and Bromet were the owners of adjoining lots in a housing estate that was subject to a building scheme. When Bromet purchased the lot, the seller had been unable to produce the original deed of the building scheme. The seller instead furnished a copy and agreed to indemnify Bromet against all costs, damages and expenses suffered 'by reason of the building stipulations . . . being other than those set out in the said copy'. The true deed contained restrictions greater than those shown in the copy. Bromet became aware of the greater restrictions in the true deed, but he nonetheless began construction on the lot in contravention of those terms. Hooper obtained an injunction against Bromet and an order that Bromet demolish his buildings insofar as they contravened the restrictions in the deed. Bromet was denied indemnification for the expenses wasted in constructing and then demolishing the buildings. Vaughan Williams LJ said that Bromet 'ought not to have built' when he knew of the restrictions in the true deed.[102]

[4–32] Where failure to act increases or does not diminish loss. An indemnified party may be expected to act reasonably to reduce an existing loss or to prevent a loss accumulating. Such a requirement may be imposed expressly. A broadly analogous situation is where the right to enforce the indemnity is conditioned upon the indemnified party first exhaust-

---

[96] *Smith v Howell* (1851) 6 Ex 730, 737; 155 ER 739, 742 (Pollock CB); *Scottish & Newcastle plc v Raguz* [2007] EWCA Civ 150; [2007] 2 All ER 871, [53]–[54] (Lloyd LJ) (approved: *Scottish & Newcastle plc v Raguz* [2008] UKHL 65; [2008] 1 WLR 2494, [14] (Lord Hoffmann), [16] (Lord Hope), [72] (Lord Walker), [74] (Lord Brown)).

[97] *Smith v Howell* (1851) 6 Ex 730, 737; 155 ER 739, 742 (Pollock CB); *Hornby v Cardwell* (1881) 8 QBD 329 (CA), 337 (Brett LJ); *White Industries Qld Pty Ltd v Hennessey Glass & Aluminium Systems Pty Ltd* [1999] 1 Qd R 210 (CA), 227 (Derrington J); *Scottish & Newcastle plc v Raguz* [2007] EWCA Civ 150; [2007] 2 All ER 871, [53]–[54] (Lloyd LJ) (approved as noted at n 96).

[98] *Ringrow Pty Ltd v BP Australia Pty Ltd* [2006] FCA 1446, [86]–[88].

[99] *Smith v Howell* (1851) 6 Ex 730; 155 ER 739.

[100] *Smith v Howell* (1851) 6 Ex 730, 737; 155 ER 739, 742. See also *Scottish & Newcastle plc v Raguz* [2007] EWCA Civ 150; [2007] 2 All ER 871, [53]–[54] (Lloyd LJ) (approved as noted at n 96). See also [4–77].

[101] *Hooper v Bromet* (1904) 90 LT 234 (CA).

[102] *Hooper v Bromet* (1904) 90 LT 234 (CA), 237 and see also 240 (Cozens-Hardy LJ).

ing its rights against others in respect of the loss.[103] In the absence of any express provision, the implied general requirement of reasonableness may apply. What is reasonable will depend upon the circumstances but the limitation is, in this regard, probably undemanding. The indemnified party is not generally expected to pursue others to diminish the indemnified loss.[104]

Hawkins v Maltby[105] illustrates the implied limitation. It was one of the nineteenth-century share transfer cases in which the ultimate buyer's failure to procure the registration of the transfer left the seller liable for calls on the shares.[106] Two calls were made, each attracting interest at 11 per cent if not paid when due. The seller delayed for some time and then paid the amount of the calls together with an amount for the accrued interest. Lord Romilly MR rejected the seller's claim under the indemnity to recover for the interest accrued at 11 per cent, on the ground that the seller ought to have paid the calls at once.[107] The seller was allowed interest at only four per cent from the time the calls fell due.

[4–33] Where action taken to reduce loss. Where the indemnified party does act to reduce a loss, its actions must be reasonable. In *Goulston Discount Co Ltd v Sims*,[108] a motor dealer promised to indemnify a finance company against loss suffered under a separate hire-purchase agreement. Loss under the indemnity was defined as the amount the hirer would have to pay under the hire-purchase agreement to acquire the goods, plus the finance company's expenses, less amounts received. After the hirer had paid one instalment an accident rendered the vehicle a total loss. The vehicle was insured for £200 but the finance company accepted £180 from the insurer and used the latter figure to calculate its loss under the indemnity. It was held that those calculations should have accounted for the full insured value. Lord Denning MR explained that finance company should 'give credit for the amount which they ought reasonably to have received on the insurance policy'.

Goulston is difficult to reconcile with *Royscot Commercial Leasing Ltd v Ismail*,[109] where there was an indemnity to a lessor in relation to a separate lease of equipment. The indemnifier objected that the indemnified lessor had failed to mitigate its loss in the process of repossessing and selling the leased goods after the lessee's default. The English Court of Appeal held that the lessor's claim under the indemnity was for a 'debt' and so mitigation did not apply as a matter of law. Hirst LJ distinguished *Goulston* as turning on the construction of the contract. Even if Hirst LJ was correct to conclude that the lessor's claim was for a 'debt',[110] that conclusion was relevant only to mitigation in respect of the claim to enforce the indemnity. It did not preclude an argument that an analogous constraint might apply as a matter of construction.[111] This possibility was not canvassed. It is doubtful whether construction was a satisfactory basis for distinguishing *Goulston*. The promises in *Goulston* and *Royscot* were both 'to indemnify' against loss, with loss being defined by the terms of the indemnity.

---

[103] See [9–34].
[104] *cf* [4–42] (subrogation).
[105] *Hawkins v Maltby* (1868) LR 6 Eq 505.
[106] See generally [6–11].
[107] *Hawkins v Maltby* (1868) LR 6 Eq 505, 509.
[108] *Goulston Discount Co Ltd v Sims* (1967) 111 SJ 682 (CA).
[109] *Royscot Commercial Leasing Ltd v Ismail* (CA, 29 April 1993).
[110] See further [5–42], [5–43].
[111] *cf Codemasters Software Co Ltd v Automobile Club de L'Ouest (No 2)* [2009] EWHC 3194 (Ch); [2010] FSR 13, [35], [38]–[39].

[4–34] **Onus.** At common law the onus lies upon the promisor to establish that the promisee failed to act reasonably to avoid a loss following a breach of contract.[112] It is difficult to state the corresponding position for claims under contractual indemnities. Some decisions appear to place the onus upon the indemnified party,[113] and others upon the indemnifier.[114]

As a matter of general principle, two approaches are possible. One approach ties the requirement of reasonableness to the definition of the scope of the indemnity. The usual rules as to onus can then be applied.[115] Thus, if reasonableness is an integral element in the affirmative statement of scope, the indemnified party has to establish, at least prima facie, that the relevant loss was incurred reasonably. If *un*reasonableness is regarded as an exception from scope, then it would fall upon the indemnifier to establish that the loss was incurred unreasonably. The other approach is to follow the ordinary common law damages rule and impose the onus upon the indemnifier. This recognises that the objection of unreasonableness is essentially defensive in nature.

[4–35] **Particular circumstances.** Whichever approach is correct in general, the placement of onus may be affected by particular circumstances.

(1) *Settlements.* The burden generally lies upon the indemnified party to establish that its settlement of a third party claim is reasonable.[116]
(2) *Parallel scheme of liability.* Where loss from a legal wrong is the subject of the indemnity, the scope may be construed to incorporate by analogy some or all of the principles governing the assessment of damages for that loss, including mitigation.[117] That would generally place the onus upon the indemnifier.
(3) *Costs.* Where a curial discretion as to costs is exercised to reflect the contractual entitlement under an indemnity, the basis of assessment adopted under the costs rules may dictate whether the onus lies upon the paying or receiving party.[118]
(4) *Other legal principles.* Other general law principles may apply, independently of the indemnity, to cast the onus upon the indemnified party to establish that it has acted reasonably in relation to a transaction that is covered by the indemnity.[119]

---

[112] *Roper v Johnson* (1873) LR 8 CP 167; *TC Industrial Plant Pty Ltd v Robert's Queensland Pty Ltd* (1963) 180 CLR 130, 138; *Garnac Grain Co Inc v HMF Faure & Fairclough Ltd* [1968] AC 1130n (HL), 1140 (Lord Pearson).

[113] *cf Hornby v Cardwell* (1881) 8 QBD 329 (CA), 337 (Brett LJ); *Re Davis and National Australia Bank Ltd* [1989] FCA 420, [14]–[16]; *Scottish & Newcastle plc v Raguz* [2007] EWCA Civ 150; [2007] 2 All ER 871, [53]–[56] (Lloyd LJ).

[114] *Webster v Petre* (1879) 4 Ex D 127, 131; *Total Oil Products (Australia) Pty Ltd v Robinson* [1970] 1 NSWR 701 (CA), 705–06 (Asprey JA); *Wenkart v Pitman* (1998) 46 NSWLR 502 (CA), 520, 523 (Powell JA); *Macquarie International Health Clinic Pty Ltd v Sydney South West Area Health Service (No 3)* [2010] NSWSC 1139, [30]. *cf* also *Born v Turner* [1900] 2 Ch 211 (Ch), 217. Some support might also be found in *Smith v Compton* (1832) 3 B & Ad 407, 408; 110 ER 146, 147 (Lord Tenterden CJ) and *Lord Newborough v Schroder* (1849) 7 CB 342, 398–99; 137 ER 136, 158–59 (Coltman J) though those remarks might be confined to the issue of proof of the indemnified party's liability and the effect of notice: see [6–44]–[6–46].

[115] See [5–33].

[116] The assessment of reasonableness also differs from that applicable under the general limitation considered presently: see further [6–50].

[117] See n 93.

[118] See generally [4–79]. As to the possibility of conflicts in onus, see *EMI Records Ltd v Ian Cameron Wallace Ltd* [1983] Ch 59 (Ch), 71–72; *Macquarie International Health Clinic Pty Ltd v Sydney South West Area Health Service (No 3)* [2010] NSWSC 1139, [31]–[37].

[119] See, eg, *Total Oil Products (Australia) Pty Ltd v Robinson* [1970] 1 NSWR 701 (CA), 705–06 (Asprey JA) (indemnified party as purchaser under mortgagee sale).

Increased Loss

[4–36] Loss incurred in attempt to avert other loss. One aspect of common law mitigation principles is that the promisee may recover for loss reasonably incurred in an attempt to reduce or avoid loss flowing from breach.[120] A different perspective is required for non-insurance contractual indemnities. A loss incurred in an attempt to mitigate or avoid another loss may itself be sufficiently closely connected with the activating event to fall within the express scope of the indemnity. *Pyman Steamship Co v Admiralty Commissioners*[121] is explicable on this basis. The chartered vessel became disabled and was towed to safety, partly to avoid drifting into minefields. The owner claimed for some of the salvage costs under an indemnity from the charterer against the consequences of hostilities and war-like operations. The charterer was held liable on the basis that a loss incurred to avert an imminent peril was recoverable as a loss by that peril. Scrutton LJ regarded this as a matter of construction of the express contract, bearing in mind its nature as a mercantile document.[122]

If the additional loss is not within the express scope of the indemnity, it may be impliedly included within scope. It is doubtful, however, that there is any general rule for implied coverage of loss that is beyond the express scope of the indemnity, but which is incurred in an attempt to mitigate a loss that is within the express scope.[123] Coverage might be justified on a more specific basis. In some circumstances, a term may be implied to reimburse the indemnified party for expenses incurred in an attempt to avert or mitigate certain kinds of loss.[124] There is also a limited principle that applies in cases of subrogation. If, after being indemnified, an indemnified party reasonably and properly incurs costs in pursuing recovery from a third party in relation to the indemnified loss, then it may deduct those costs from any amounts recovered before accounting to the indemnifier.[125]

The treatment of legal costs incurred by the indemnified party in the defence of an action by a third party exemplifies both the general and limited propositions. Such costs are usually incurred in an attempt to refute the existence or reduce the extent of the asserted liability, that is, to avoid or diminish a potential loss under the indemnity. Costs are often found to be impliedly included within the scope of an indemnity against claims by or liabilities to third parties, if not mentioned expressly. It is, however, ultimately a matter of construction; legal costs are not always covered.[126] Settlements of claims by third parties may be another example. The settlement of a claim by a third party could be seen as a measure taken to avoid a potentially greater loss. But again, the recovery of sums paid in settlement is treated as a matter of construction of the scope of the indemnity.[127]

---

[120] H McGregor, *McGregor on Damages*, 18th edn (London, Sweet & Maxwell, 2009), 284–85, paras 7-091–7-092.

[121] *Pyman Steamship Co v Admiralty Commissioners* [1919] 1 KB 49 (CA).

[122] *Pyman Steamship Co v Admiralty Commissioners* [1919] 1 KB 49 (CA), 55.

[123] *cf National Roads and Motorists' Association Ltd v Whitlam* [2007] NSWCA 81; (2007) 25 ACLC 688, [52] (point raised but not determined). Contrast *Clipper Logistics Group Ltd v Monsoon Accessorize Ltd* [2011] EWHC 419 (Ch), [63].

[124] This happens rarely in the insurance context: see, eg, *Netherlands Insurance Co Est 1845 Ltd v Karl Ljungberg and Co AB* [1986] 2 Lloyd's Rep 19 (PC). *cf Yorkshire Water Services Ltd v Sun Alliance & London Insurance plc* [1997] 2 Lloyd's Rep 21 (CA); *Re Mining Technologies Australia Pty Ltd* [1999] 1 Qd R 60 (CA), 67–68 (Pincus JA), 72 (Davies JA), 86 (McPherson JA); *Baker v Black Sea & Baltic General Insurance Co Ltd* [1998] 1 WLR 974 (HL); *Vero Insurance Ltd v Australian Prestressing Services Pty Ltd* [2013] NSWCA 181, [53]–[56] (Meagher JA).

[125] *Assicurazioni Generali de Trieste v Empress Assurance Corp Ltd* [1907] 2 KB 814 (KB). See also C Mitchell and S Watterson, *Subrogation Law and Practice* (Oxford, Oxford University Press, 2007), 352, para 10.107.

[126] See further [4–76].

[127] See [6–32], [6–35].

Reduced Loss

[4–37] Accounting for benefits that diminish the loss. Under common law principles of mitigation, benefits diminishing the loss that accrue to the promisee as a consequence of the promisor's breach may be taken into account in assessing the quantum of damages.[128] For contractual indemnities, the essential principle of exact protection produces a broadly similar result. Benefits that diminish the indemnified loss are brought to account; if they were not, the indemnified party would be over-compensated. As Lord Blackburn said in *Burnand v Rodocanachi*:[129]

> [W]here there is a contract of indemnity (it matters not whether it is a marine policy, or a policy against fire on land, or any other contract of indemnity) and a loss happens, anything which reduces or diminishes the loss reduces or diminishes the amount which the indemnifier is bound to pay; and if the indemnifier has already paid it, then, if anything which diminishes the loss comes into the hands of the person to whom he has paid it, it becomes an equity that the person who has already paid the full indemnity is entitled to be recouped by having that amount back.

This passage reveals two distinct aspects of the principle of exact protection, one concerning diminution of the loss before indemnification, the other concerning diminution of the loss afterwards.

[4–38] Benefits obtained prior to indemnification. The requirement to account for prior benefits is clearly seen where the indemnified party, B, seeks protection against or payment for a loss from C and then later claims indemnity from A in respect of the same loss. If B has fully recovered for the loss from C, B often cannot enforce its right to indemnity from A.[130] B's loss has already been eliminated. This is one justification for a more specific proposition described by Barwick CJ in *Sydney Turf Club v Crowley*[131] as

> the well established principle that in a case where there are two promises of indemnity in respect of the same liability, the promisee can only recover once and not twice. Being paid pursuant to one such promise, he cannot recover on the other.

In some cases, C's payment to B in respect of the loss is disregarded for the purposes of the later claim on the indemnity from A.[132] Indeed, if subrogation to B's subsisting rights arises upon payment in full by C to B, then this is necessary for a subrogated claim by C against A to succeed.[133] The distinction has been said to depend upon the relative degree of responsibility of A and C for the loss. If A is regarded as bearing primary responsibility for B's loss, and C only secondary responsibility, then C's payment is ignored. The position is

---

[128] McGregor, *McGregor on Damages* (n 120), 288ff, paras 7-097ff.

[129] *Burnand v Rodocanachi* (1882) 7 App Cas 333 (HL), 339.

[130] *Morgan v Price* (1849) 4 Ex 615; 154 ER 1360; *Bruce v Jones* (1863) 1 H & C 769; 158 ER 1094; *Austin v Zurich General Accident and Liability Insurance Co Ltd* [1945] KB 250 (CA), 258; *British Traders' Insurance Co Ltd v Monson* (1964) 111 CLR 86, 95 (Kitto, Taylor and Owen JJ); *Sydney Turf Club v Crowley* [1971] 1 NSWLR 724 (CA), 730 (Jacobs JA), 734 (Mason JA); *Stratti v Stratti* (2000) 50 NSWLR 324 (CA) (no enforceable right of indemnity against partnership after indemnification by insurer); *Morgan Grenfell Development Capital Syndications Ltd v Arrows Autosports Ltd* [2004] EWHC 1015 (Ch), [60] (indemnified lender paid in full by others).

[131] *Sydney Turf Club v Crowley* (1972) 126 CLR 420, 424. cf *Stratti v Stratti* (2000) 50 NSWLR 324 (CA), 331 (Fitzgerald JA) (enforcement of a second indemnity would be unjust).

[132] See also Mitchell and Watterson, *Subrogation Law and Practice* (n 125), 331–32, paras 10.56–10.60.

[133] *Caledonia North Sea Ltd v London Bridge Engineering Ltd* 2000 SLT 1123 (IH), 1134 (Lord Rodger).

different where C bears primary responsibility, or where the liabilities of A and C are co-ordinate.[134]

[4–39] **Relative degree of responsibility for loss.** The assessment of degrees of responsibility for another's loss depends upon the circumstances, including construction of any relevant contracts.[135] A schema is as follows:

(1) As between:

    (a) a liability under a contract of indemnity insurance; and
    (b) a liability in tort, delict or contract (not being a contract of indemnity insurance),

    the former is generally regarded as secondary and the latter as primary.[136]

(2) A corollary of the first proposition is that a contractual non-insurance indemnity is generally regarded as primary and an insurance indemnity as secondary.[137]

(3) As between:

    (a) a liability under a non-insurance contract of indemnity; and
    (b) a liability in tort, delict or contract (not being a contract of indemnity),

    it is difficult to identify a general rule, though the former is often treated as secondary and the latter as primary.[138]

[4–40] **Non-insurance indemnities and other liabilities.** Some examples can be given of the third proposition in the schema.[139] In *Morris v Ford Motor Co Ltd*,[140] Ford was entitled to an indemnity from the contractor and also to claim against its own negligent employee. The analysis in the English Court of Appeal proceeded on the basis that if subrogation was available, then it was the contractor who was to be subrogated to Ford's claim against the employee. Thus, as between the contractor and the employee, the latter was primarily responsible.

Under a contract of indemnity against a third party's non-performance, benefits obtained by the indemnified party from the third party in relation to the contract between them diminish the indemnified loss. In such cases, the indemnity performs a function broadly similar to a guarantee. As between a guarantor and principal debtor, the latter is

---

[134] *Caledonia North Sea Ltd v British Telecommunications plc (The Piper Alpha)* [2002] UKHL 4; [2002] 1 Lloyd's Rep 553, [53]–[56] (Lord Mackay), [89]–[92] (Lord Hoffmann); *Speno Rail Maintenance Australia Pty Ltd v Metals & Minerals Insurance Pte Ltd* [2009] WASCA 31; (2009) 253 ALR 364, [218]–[219] (Beech AJA).

[135] *Speno Rail Maintenance Australia Pty Ltd v Hamersley Iron Pty Ltd* [2000] WASCA 408; (2000) 23 WAR 291, [167]–[168] (Wheeler J); *Caledonia North Sea Ltd v British Telecommunications plc (The Piper Alpha)* [2002] UKHL 4; [2002] 1 Lloyd's Rep 553, [16] (Lord Bingham), [47], [55]–[56] (Lord Mackay), [97] (Lord Hoffmann).

[136] *Castellain v Preston* (1883) 11 QBD 380 (CA); *Sydney Turf Club v Crowley* [1971] 1 NSWLR 724 (CA), 730 (Jacobs JA); *Caledonia North Sea Ltd v British Telecommunications plc (The Piper Alpha)* [2002] UKHL 4; [2002] 1 Lloyd's Rep 553, [16] (Lord Bingham), [62] (Lord Mackay), [89] (Lord Hoffmann); *HIH Claims Support Ltd v Insurance Australia Ltd* [2011] HCA 31; (2011) 244 CLR 72, [40] (Gummow ACJ, Hayne, Crennan and Kiefel JJ).

[137] This is clearest where the indemnity appears in a contract for services: see [4–74]. See also *Larrinaga Steamship Co Ltd v R* [1945] AC 246 (HL), 256 (Lord Wright), 261 (Lord Porter) (charterparty). Contrast *Greene Wood McLean LLP v Templeton Insurance Ltd* [2009] EWCA Civ 65; [2009] 1 WLR 2013, [14] (Longmore LJ) and [2010] EWHC 2679 (Comm); [2011] Lloyd's Rep IR 557, [61]–[62] (litigation funding arrangement). The same result was reached under the Civil Liability (Contribution) Act 1978, by an order for 100% contribution: [83]–[84]. *cf* also *Stratti v Stratti* (2000) 50 NSWLR 324 (CA) (right to indemnity under partnership statute ineffective because loss already satisfied by indemnity insurance payment).

[138] See [4–40].

[139] See [4–39].

[140] *Morris v Ford Motor Co Ltd* [1973] QB 792 (CA).

intended to be ultimately responsible to the creditor. *Morgan Grenfell Development Capital Syndications Ltd v Arrows Autosports Ltd*[141] goes further. The lender was given an indemnity against loss in relation to an overdraft facility provided to the borrower. It later transferred, for full value, its rights under that facility to various investment funds in its corporate group. The borrower substantially defaulted. It was held that the lender, having been paid in full, suffered no loss; the loss was sustained by the investment funds.[142]

The same result may hold for some liabilities that are equitable in nature. Where B and C are co-debtors and A promises to indemnify B against the common liability, A's liability to indemnify B may be regarded as secondary to C's liability to B to contribute in respect of the common liability.[143]

[4–41] **Limitations of distinction.** The distinction between degrees of responsibility does not provide a convincing explanation of all cases.[144] In *Ibrahim v Barclays Bank plc*,[145] a debtor provided a counter-indemnity to the guarantor in respect of the guarantor's liability to the creditor. That counter-indemnity was supported by a letter of credit issued by a bank in favour of the guarantor. It was held that payment by the issuing bank to the guarantor under the letter of credit discharged the indemnifier's liability to the guarantor under the counter-indemnity. That conclusion did not turn upon a distinction between primary and secondary responsibility. Looking at the substance of the transaction, that distinction should have produced the opposite result: the indemnifier was primarily responsible to the guarantor; the letter of credit, operating as a security, was secondary in nature. Instead, Lewison LJ applied the rule that payment by one party under legal compulsion on account of another's debt may discharge that debt. The issuing bank was under a contractual liability to pay the guarantor, and the bank's payment was entirely referable to the indemnifier's liability to the guarantor.

[4–42] **Benefits obtained or obtainable after indemnification.** Lord Blackburn's second proposition from *Burnand v Rodocanachi*[146] describes an aspect of subrogation as that doctrine may be understood in its broader sense.[147] Subrogation in this general context derives from the nature of a contract of indemnity.[148] It gives effect to the concept of exact protection as one of its functions is to avoid over-compensation of the indemnified party.[149] In its

---

[141] *Morgan Grenfell Development Capital Syndications Ltd v Arrows Autosports Ltd* [2004] EWHC 1015 (Ch).

[142] *Morgan Grenfell Development Capital Syndications Ltd v Arrows Autosports Ltd* [2004] EWHC 1015 (Ch), [47]–[48], [60].

[143] This is implicit in *Hodgson v Hodgson* (1837) 2 Keen 704; 48 ER 800.

[144] See the persuasive analysis in C Mitchell, P Mitchell and S Watterson (eds), *Goff and Jones: The Law of Unjust Enrichment*, 8th edn (London, Sweet & Maxwell, 2011), 132, paras 5-54, 5-55. See further [4–42].

[145] *Ibrahim v Barclays Bank plc* [2012] EWCA Civ 640; [2013] Ch 400.

[146] *Burnand v Rodocanachi* (1882) 7 App Cas 333 (HL), 339. See [4–37].

[147] See, eg, *Castellain v Preston* (1883) 11 QBD 380 (CA); *Lord Napier and Ettrick v Hunter* [1993] AC 713 (HL); SR Derham, *Subrogation in Insurance Law* (Sydney, Law Book Co Ltd, 1985), 1. Contrast *British Traders' Insurance Co Ltd v Monson* (1964) 111 CLR 86, 94 (Kitto, Taylor and Owen JJ); *Kern Corp Ltd v Walter Reid Trading Pty Ltd* (1987) 163 CLR 164, 181 (Wilson and Dawson JJ).

[148] *State Government Insurance Office (Qld) v Brisbane Stevedoring Pty Ltd* (1969) 123 CLR 228, 240–41 (Barwick CJ); *Morris v Ford Motor Co Ltd* [1973] QB 792 (CA), 800 (Lord Denning MR), 805–06 (Stamp LJ), 812 (James LJ); *Transport Accident Commission v CMT Construction of Metropolitan Tunnels* (1988) 165 CLR 436, 442 (Wilson, Dawson, Toohey and Gaudron JJ); *Lord Napier and Ettrick v Hunter* [1993] AC 713 (HL), 736 (Lord Templeman), 743–44 (Lord Goff), 752 (Lord Browne-Wilkinson); *Banque Financière de la Cité v Parc (Battersea) Ltd* [1999] AC 221 (HL), 231 (Lord Hoffmann).

[149] See Mitchell and Watterson (n 125), 309–10, 320–22, paras 10.06, 10.30–10.36.

broader sense, subrogation allows the indemnifier to recoup itself from amounts recovered by the indemnified party that diminish the indemnified loss. In its strict sense, subrogation allows the indemnifier to exercise for its own benefit the indemnified party's rights against third parties in diminution of the indemnified loss.

It might be thought that a different perspective on recoupment and subrogation could be adopted in some situations. The indemnifier's payment to the indemnified party, in performance of the indemnity, might discharge a liability properly resting upon a third party. The right to recoupment and remedy of subrogation would then derive from the law of unjust enrichment, independently of the nature of a contract of indemnity. Indemnities against default or non-performance by a third party are obvious candidates for this analysis. The indemnifier seems to occupy much the same position as a guarantor who pays the creditor and so discharges the debtor. Yet this perspective has not flourished.[150]

A factor specific to this context may be that the creditor relies on an indemnity rather than a guarantee for the very reason that there is no enforceable liability of the debtor. Neither subrogation to subsisting rights nor subrogation to extinguished rights is relevant. More generally, it seems that the contractual indemnifier's payment does not discharge a third party's liability because the indemnifier's responsibility is regarded as 'secondary' in nature.[151] In isolation, that proposition is difficult to reconcile with general principles concerning discharge of another's liabilities.[152] The exceptional treatment is tied inextricably to the different conceptual basis for subrogation under contractual indemnities, which is premised upon subsisting rights against others.

[4–43] Exceptions. The right of subrogation may be qualified or excluded, though the parties' intention – express or implied – must be clear.[153] *Morris v Ford Motor Co Ltd*[154] is a leading example. Cleaners engaged by Ford were liable to indemnify Ford against a liability that arose out of the negligence of one of Ford's employees. The English Court of Appeal by majority held that the cleaners were not entitled to be subrogated to Ford's rights against the negligent employee. Lord Denning MR's preferred ground was that subrogation would have been inequitable; in the alternative, there was no implied term permitting subrogation. James LJ and Stamp LJ both regarded the right of subrogation as inherent in the contract and thus a matter to be excluded. James LJ considered that it was excluded by implication in the circumstances; Stamp LJ disagreed. Lord Denning MR and James LJ noted that it was commonly accepted that insurance would cover this kind of risk and that Ford would never have sued its employee in the circumstances for fear of industrial repercussions.[155]

---

[150] cf *Conister Trust Ltd v John Hardman & Co* [2008] EWCA Civ 841, [65], [68] (Lawrence Collins LJ) (indemnifier unable to invoke Mercantile Law Amendment Act 1856, s 5 as a basis for subrogation).

[151] See [4–39].

[152] See [4–41] and see generally *Goff and Jones: The Law of Unjust Enrichment* (n 144), 129–30, paras 5-47–5-50.

[153] *Liberty Mutual Insurance Co (UK) Ltd v HSBC Bank plc* [2002] EWCA Civ 691, [49]–[51] (Rix LJ).

[154] *Morris v Ford Motor Co Ltd* [1973] QB 792 (CA). See also *Atco Controls Pty Ltd (in liq) v Stewart* [2013] VSCA 132, [111]–[120] (Warren CJ), [255] (Redlich JA).

[155] cf *Liberty Mutual Insurance Co (UK) Ltd v HSBC Bank plc* [2002] EWCA Civ 691, [53] (Rix LJ) (the decision 'does not proceed so much by construing the contract as by reaching a conclusion based on the equity of the situation').

Exclusions Based on Fault or Legal Wrongs

The Indemnified Party's Responsibility for the Loss

[4–44] General. The scope of the indemnity may exclude, expressly or by implication, losses or liabilities attributable to legal wrongs or other culpable conduct by the indemnified party. There has been, in general, a greater willingness to conclude that an indemnity covers fault-free losses or liabilities than those that involve fault on the part of the indemnified party. Many of the decisions have concerned exclusion of losses or liabilities arising from the indemnified party's own negligence. In one such case, *Walters v Whessoe Ltd*,[156] Devlin LJ said:

> The law therefore presumes that a man will not readily be granted an indemnity against a loss caused by his own negligence. Such a loss is due to his own fault. No similar presumption can be made if he is made responsible for the negligence of others over whose acts he has no control . . . Similarly, a man may be responsible without negligence on his part for breach of statutory duty committed either by himself or by his servants or by someone for whom he was vicariously liable. In none of these cases is there any negligence on his part and there is therefore no reason to presume an intention to exclude them from the indemnity.

These remarks exemplify strict construction. Commercial construction has largely dispensed with rigid or mechanical distinctions of this nature; the scope of the indemnity is determined by reference to a broader commercial context. Nonetheless, factors such as the nature of the loss or liability, the indemnified party's role in causing it, and any degree of culpability on its part, still remain relevant to the construction of the indemnity.

The following section focuses primarily on exclusions from scope that are based on a legal wrong by the indemnified party. It is not limited to consideration of fault-based liabilities in the sense described by Devlin LJ above. Nor is the analysis entirely restricted to legal wrongs. It is sometimes appropriate to consider whether a loss or liability is excluded from scope on the basis that some other conduct by the indemnified party contributed to it.[157] The section deals with exclusions derived from construction and not with issues of contractual illegality. An indemnity can protect against civil liability for some intentional acts that constitute wrongs[158] and liability for exemplary damages.[159]

[4–45] No apportionment based on relative responsibility. Assuming that a loss or liability is within scope,[160] the indemnified party is entitled to full indemnification.[161] There is no general rule of construction that the extent of protection is adjusted proportionately to

---

[156] *Walters v Whessoe Ltd* (1960) 6 BLR 23 (CA), 35.

[157] See [4–45] and [4–52].

[158] As for some instances of conversion (see [4–54]) or false imprisonment (*Fletcher v Harcot* (1682) 1 Hut 55; 123 ER 1097) though not deceit (*Brown Jenkinson & Co Ltd v Percy Dalton (London) Ltd* [1957] 2 QB 621 (CA)). *cf* Defamation Act 1952, s 11 (indemnity against civil liability for libel). See generally *Burrows v Rhodes* [1899] 1 QB 816 (DC); *Weld-Blundell v Stephens* [1919] 1 KB 520 (CA).

[159] *Albert Shire Council v Vanderloos* (1992) 77 LGRA 309 (QCA).

[160] *cf* [4–22]–[4–25] (concurrent causes and exclusions from scope).

[161] *Osborne v Eales (No 2)* (1864) 2 Moo PC NS 125, 137–38 (Stephen CJ) ('it seems to me impossible to hold that a man indemnifies another against a loss by merely paying a portion of it. If the latter shares the loss he is to that extent clearly not indemnified').

account for the relative responsibility – whether in terms of cause or culpability – of the indemnifier and indemnified party for the loss or liability.[162]

This is seen where the indemnifier and indemnified party are concurrent tortfeasors and yet, as between them, the indemnifier is liable to cover the full amount of the liability to the claimant.[163] It is recognised indirectly in the tortfeasor contribution statutes in various Commonwealth jurisdictions that are derived from section 6 of the Law Reform (Married Women and Tortfeasors) Act 1935. In New South Wales, for example, section 5(1)(c) of the Law Reform (Miscellaneous Provisions) Act 1946 (NSW) states that 'no person shall be entitled to recover contribution under this section from any person entitled to be indemnified by that person in respect of the liability in respect of which the contribution is sought'.[164] It is also recognised in Commonwealth jurisdictions that have adopted schemes for apportioned or proportionate liability. Where the statute permits, the indemnity between wrongdoers may override the allocation of responsibility that would otherwise apply.[165] Furthermore, an indemnity may cover the indemnified party's liability to a third party even though there is no corresponding liability of the indemnifier to the third party.[166]

The default position can be altered by the terms of the contract. The indemnity may be expressed to apply only to the extent that responsibility for the loss is attributable to the indemnifier or others for whom it is responsible.[167] Such drafting may merely replicate the effect of the contribution statute. An adjustment may also be stated in negative terms, so that the indemnity applies except to the extent that the loss is attributable to the indemnified party.[168]

Negligence

[4–46] General. The consequences of the indemnified party's negligence may be excluded from the scope of the indemnity expressly or by inference. An inferred exclusion is usually justified on the basis that it is improbable that the parties intended to protect the indemnified

---

[162] This may be reinforced by express terms of the contract: see, eg, *Furness Shipbuilding Co Ltd v London and North Eastern Railway Co* (1934) 50 TLR 257 (HL); *Arthur White (Contractors) Ltd v Tarmac Civil Engineering Ltd* [1967] 1 WLR 1508 (HL), 1516–17 (Lord Morris); *Smit International (Deutschland) GmbH v Josef Mobius Baugesellschaft GmbH & Co* [2001] EWHC 531 (Comm) (knock-for-knock indemnity regime under cl 18 of the TOWHIRE form of contract); *Acergy Shipping Ltd v Societe Bretonne De Reparation Navale SAS* [2011] EWHC 2490 (Comm); [2012] 1 All ER (Comm) 369 (another knock-for-knock indemnity regime). See further [4–61].

[163] See, eg, *Swan Hunter and Wigham Richardson Ltd v France Fenwick Tyne & Wear Co Ltd (The Albion)* [1953] 1 WLR 1026 (CA); *State Government Insurance Office (Qld) v Brisbane Stevedoring Pty Ltd* (1969) 123 CLR 228; *BI (Contracting) Pty Ltd v AW Baulderstone Holdings Pty Ltd* [2007] NSWCA 173; (2008) Aust Contract R 90-267 (express indemnities); *Linklaters v HSBC Bank plc* [2003] EWHC 1113 (Comm); [2003] 2 Lloyd's Rep 545 (implied indemnity).

[164] See generally *Davis v Commissioner for Main Roads* (1967) 117 CLR 529; *Port of Melbourne Authority v Anshun Pty Ltd* (1981) 147 CLR 589, 596 (Gibbs CJ, Mason and Aickin JJ).

[165] See, eg, *Aquagenics Pty Ltd v Break O'Day Council* [2010] TASFC 3; (2010) 26 BCL 263; *Perpetual Trustee Co Ltd v CTC Group Pty Ltd (No 2)* [2013] NSWCA 58, [11]–[12] (Macfarlan JA). See generally B McDonald, 'Indemnities and the Civil Liability Legislation' (2011) 27 *Journal of Contract Law* 56.

[166] *Caledonia North Sea Ltd v British Telecommunications plc (The Piper Alpha)* [2002] UKHL 4; [2002] 1 Lloyd's Rep 553.

[167] See, eg, *Steele v Twin City Rigging Pty Ltd* (1992) 114 FLR 99 (ACTSC), 111–12; *Volman v Lobb* [2005] NSWCA 348, [62]–[64] (Hodgson JA).

[168] See, eg, *Leighton Contractors Pty Ltd v Mohamad* [2001] NSWCA 453, [69]–[72] (Priestley JA).

party against losses or liabilities brought about by its own carelessness.[169] Such implausibility remains a consideration nowadays, though it is no longer perceived as readily as it was in the past. In some commercial contexts, perhaps supported by appropriate insurance arrangements, an indemnity against negligence may be the very result intended by the parties.[170]

There are two approaches to excluding the consequences of an indemnified party's negligence from the scope of the indemnity. One approach relies on causation: the negligence may amount to an intervening act or otherwise be sufficiently influential in the loss that it negates the causal or connective relation required by the indemnity.[171] Another approach, which is more easily applied to liabilities than to losses personal to the indemnified party, is to treat the exclusion as operating by reference to a basis of liability. This may be a liability in tort for negligence or, perhaps, a liability for breach of another legal duty, the standard of which requires the exercise of reasonable care. An exclusion of 'negligence' is usually understood to refer to common law negligence or a failure to exercise reasonable care.[172] In general, no distinction is drawn between personal negligence of the indemnified party and the indemnified party's vicarious liability for negligence of employees.[173]

[4–47] The *Canada SS* rules. In *Canada Steamship Lines Ltd v R*[174] Lord Morton, delivering the advice of the Judicial Committee of the Privy Council, set out three 'rules' for determining whether an exclusion clause protects the beneficiary of the clause from the consequences its employees' negligence. Although the rules were stated in terms of exemption from the consequences of negligence, Lord Morton also applied them to an indemnity clause in the same lease. That approach was soon followed.[175] The rules were endorsed by the House of Lords sitting on a Scottish appeal in *Smith v South Wales Switchgear Co Ltd*,[176] where Viscount Dilhorne and Lord Keith suggested that the rules ought to be applied even more stringently to indemnity clauses than exclusion clauses.[177]

The rules remain viable nowadays despite the shift towards commercial construction, but with a greater emphasis that they are guidelines and must not be applied mechanically.[178]

---

[169] *Walters v Whessoe Ltd* (1960) 6 BLR 23 (CA), 34–35 (Devlin LJ); *Arthur White (Contractors) Ltd v Tarmac Civil Engineering Ltd* [1967] 1 WLR 1508 (HL), 1529 (Lord Pearson); *Gillespie Brothers & Co Ltd v Roy Bowles Transport Ltd* [1973] QB 400 (CA), 420 (Buckley LJ); *Smith v South Wales Switchgear Co Ltd* [1978] 1 WLR 165 (HL), 168 (Viscount Dilhorne), 178 (Lord Keith).

[170] See, eg, *Gillespie Brothers & Co Ltd v Roy Bowles Transport Ltd* [1973] QB 400 (CA), 417 (Lord Denning MR); *Hair and Skin Trading Co Ltd v Norman Airfreight Carriers Ltd* [1974] 1 Lloyd's Rep 443 (QB), 446; *Valkonen v Jennings Construction Ltd* (1995) 184 LSJS 87 (SAFC), 98–99 (Cox J); *Caledonia North Sea Ltd v British Telecommunications plc (The Piper Alpha)* [2002] UKHL 4; [2002] 1 Lloyd's Rep 553; *HIH Casualty and General Insurance Ltd v Chase Manhattan Bank* [2003] UKHL 6; [2003] 2 Lloyd's Rep 61, [66]–[67] (Lord Hoffmann); *Shell UK Ltd v Total UK Ltd* [2010] EWCA Civ 180; [2011] QB 86, [13]–[14].

[171] See [4–18].

[172] *Murfin v United Steel Companies Ltd* [1957] 1 WLR 104 (CA). cf *Hosking v De Havilland Aircraft Co Ltd* [1949] 1 All ER 540 (KB) ('neglect').

[173] *EE Caledonia Ltd v Orbit Valve Co Europe* [1994] 1 WLR 221 (QB), 229 (affd without reference to this point: *EE Caledonia Ltd v Orbit Valve Co Europe* [1994] 1 WLR 1515 (CA)). cf *Arthur White (Contractors) Ltd v Tarmac Civil Engineering Ltd* [1967] 1 WLR 1508 (HL), 1529 (Lord Pearson) (stronger presumption against indemnification for personal negligence).

[174] *Canada Steamship Lines Ltd v R* [1952] AC 192 (PC), 208. The rules are considered individually at [4–50]–[4–52].

[175] See, eg, *Walters v Whessoe Ltd* (1960) 6 BLR 23 (CA), 36–37 (Slade J); *Gillespie Brothers & Co Ltd v Roy Bowles Transport Ltd* [1973] QB 400 (CA), 419–21 (Buckley LJ), 421 (Orr LJ).

[176] *Smith v South Wales Switchgear Co Ltd* [1978] 1 WLR 165 (HL).

[177] *Smith v South Wales Switchgear Co Ltd* [1978] 1 WLR 165 (HL), 168 (Viscount Dilhorne), 178 (Lord Keith).

[178] *EE Caledonia Ltd v Orbit Valve Co Europe* [1994] 1 WLR 1515 (CA), 1522 (Steyn LJ); *Stent Foundations Ltd v MJ Gleeson Group plc* [2001] BLR 134 (QB), 139–40; *Campbell v Conoco (UK) Ltd* [2002] EWCA Civ 704; [2003] 1 All ER (Comm) 35, [12]–[13] (Rix LJ); *HIH Casualty and General Insurance Ltd v Chase Manhattan Bank* [2003]

[4–48] Comparison with Australian position. The law in Australia has developed along a different course. The rules (or aspects of them) were referred to in several decisions of the High Court of Australia in the twentieth century. One of those decisions, which concerned an indemnity clause, was *Davis v Commissioner for Main Roads*.[179] The rules were acknowledged, though not applied, in the majority judgment of Menzies J and the dissenting judgment of Kitto J. When the High Court endorsed a more commercial and less strained approach to the construction of exclusion clauses in *Darlington Futures Ltd v Delco Australia Pty Ltd*,[180] it did not refer to the *Canada SS* rules. Nonetheless, the view that became dominant in later decisions was that the commercial construction approach in *Darlington* was inconsistent with the *Canada SS* rules, in particular, the third rule.[181] Most recently, in *Andar Transport Pty Ltd v Brambles Ltd*,[182] the High Court may have signalled a return to strict construction of indemnity clauses.[183] The joint judgment cited *Davis* and *Smith* among other authorities.[184] It might be thought that this would lead to renewed interest in the *Canada SS* rules. It was, however, held in *BI (Contracting) Pty Ltd v AW Baulderstone Holdings Pty Ltd*[185] that the third of the *Canada SS* rules was still inapplicable notwithstanding a reversion to strict construction. The present state of the law as established by intermediate appellate decisions is that the first and second of the rules are viable but that the third is generally not.

[4–49] Use in particular contexts. Although the greatest concern with indemnification against negligence may arise where the indemnity benefits only one party, the *Canada SS* rules have been held applicable to contractual schemes that involve reciprocal indemnities.[186] The rules are not the only means of determining whether the scope of the indemnity includes the consequences of the indemnified party's negligence.[187] The first two rules are concerned with expressed intention and so the rules are usually not applied where an indemnity is implied or a contract of indemnity is inferred from the circumstances.[188] It has also been suggested that the rules, as a particular instance of a construction *contra proferentem*, may not apply when the indemnifier has drafted the indemnity.[189]

UKHL 6; [2003] 2 Lloyd's Rep 61, [11] (Lord Bingham), [61]–[63] (Lord Hoffmann), [116] (Lord Scott); *Onego Shipping & Chartering BV v JSC Arcadia Shipping (The Socol 3)* [2010] EWHC 777 (Comm); [2010] 2 Lloyd's Rep 221, [50]–[52].

[179] *Davis v Commissioner for Main Roads* (1967) 117 CLR 529.
[180] *Darlington Futures Ltd v Delco Australia Pty Ltd* (1986) 161 CLR 500.
[181] *Schenker & Co (Aust) Pty Ltd v Maplas Equipment and Services Pty Ltd* [1990] VR 834 (FC), 845–46 (McGarvie J); *Valkonen v Jennings Construction Ltd* (1995) 184 LSJS 87 (SAFC), 97–98 (Cox J); *Australian Paper Plantations Pty Ltd v Venturoni* [2000] VSCA 71, [17]–[18] (Buchanan JA); *Brambles Ltd v Wail* [2002] VSCA 150; (2002) 5 VR 169, [68]–[70] (revd without reference to this point: *Andar Transport Pty Ltd v Brambles Ltd* [2004] HCA 28; (2004) 217 CLR 424); *State of New South Wales v Tempo Services Ltd* [2004] NSWCA 4, [9] (Meagher JA).
[182] *Andar Transport Pty Ltd v Brambles Ltd* [2004] HCA 28; (2004) 217 CLR 424.
[183] See [3–32]–[3–33].
[184] *Andar Transport Pty Ltd v Brambles Ltd* [2004] HCA 28; (2004) 217 CLR 424, [23] fn 45.
[185] *BI (Contracting) Pty Ltd v AW Baulderstone Holdings Pty Ltd* [2007] NSWCA 173; (2008) Aust Contract R 90-267, [89]–[95] (Beazley JA). See W Courtney, 'Construction of Contractual Indemnities – Out with the Old, In with the New?' (2008) 24 *Journal of Contract Law* 182.
[186] *EE Caledonia Ltd v Orbit Valve Co Europe* [1994] 1 WLR 1515 (CA). *cf Nelson v Atlantic Power and Gas Ltd* 1995 SLT (Notes) 102 (IH).
[187] *cf Gillespie Brothers & Co Ltd v Roy Bowles Transport Ltd* [1973] QB 400 (CA), 414–17 (Lord Denning MR); *British Crane Hire Corp Ltd v Ipswich Plant Hire Ltd* [1975] QB 303 (CA).
[188] But see *Actis Co Ltd v Sanko Steamship Co Ltd (The Aquacharm)* [1982] 1 WLR 119 (CA), 123 (Lord Denning MR).
[189] *Re-Source America International Ltd v Platt Site Services Ltd* [2004] EWCA Civ 665; (2004) 95 Con LR 1, [55] (Tuckey LJ).

The rules have been wholly or partly dispensed with where the contract expressly establishes a scheme of risk allocation[190] or where the manifest purpose of the contract is to cover the risk of the indemnified party's negligence.[191] In *Arthur White (Contractors) Ltd v Tarmac Civil Engineering Ltd*,[192] the owner of an excavator supplied it, together with a driver, to the main contractor on a construction site. Clause 8 of the hire contract stated that drivers would be 'regarded as the servants or agents of the hirer who alone shall be responsible for all claims arising in connection with the operation of the plant by the said drivers'. The owner and contractor were held liable to the injured claimant and the owner sought indemnity from the contractor on the basis that the accident was partly caused by the driver's negligence in operating the excavator, for which the contractor was responsible under clause 8. That claim was upheld by the House of Lords, where several of their Lordships appeared to regard clause 8 as operating as a form of indemnity clause.[193] Lord Upjohn dismissed an argument based on the third of the *Canada SS* rules on the basis that it simply did not fit the scheme of the clause: claims for negligence were obviously intended to be covered.[194] Lord Pearson described the clause as 'emphatic' and said that the clause would be inadequate from a commercial perspective unless it covered negligence.[195] It was left undecided whether the third rule applied to clause 13, which was another, more general, indemnity clause in the contract.[196]

[4–50] Express references to negligence. The first of the *Canada SS* rules[197] states that effect will be given to a clause that 'contains language which expressly exempts' the beneficiary from the consequences of negligence. The rule applies, with appropriate changes, so that an indemnity clause will protect the indemnified party against the consequences of its negligence if this is indicated expressly.[198] An express reference is one that is 'clear and unmistakable'[199] or uses the word 'negligence' or some synonym for it.[200]

The first rule has sometimes been stretched further to cover indemnity clauses that appear to have been candidates for the application of the second rule. In *Westcott v JH Jenner (Plasterers) Ltd*,[201] the expression 'Third Party risks' was accepted as 'insurance slang'

---

[190] See [4–67] in relation to express exceptions from scope in construction contracts. *cf* where there is no express exception: *Dorset County Council v Southern Felt Roofing Co Ltd* (1989) 48 BLR 96 (CA); *National Trust v Haden Young Ltd* (1993) 66 BLR 88 (QB) (later the subject of differing views in *National Trust v Haden Young Ltd* (1994) 72 BLR 1 (CA) and *London Borough of Barking & Dagenham v Stamford Asphalt Co Ltd* (1997) 82 BLR 25 (CA)); *Casson v Ostley PJ Ltd* [2001] EWCA Civ 1013; [2003] BLR 147. See generally *Furness Shipbuilding Co Ltd v London and North Eastern Railway Co* (1934) 50 TLR 257 (HL) (predating the rules and *Alderslade v Hendon Laundry Ltd* [1945] KB 189 (CA)); *Davis v Commissioner for Main Roads* (1967) 117 CLR 529.

[191] *Albert Shire Council v Vanderloos* (1992) 77 LGRA 309 (QCA), 312.

[192] *Arthur White (Contractors) Ltd v Tarmac Civil Engineering Ltd* [1967] 1 WLR 1508 (HL).

[193] See further [4–63].

[194] *Arthur White (Contractors) Ltd v Tarmac Civil Engineering Ltd* [1967] 1 WLR 1508 (HL), 1526.

[195] *Arthur White (Contractors) Ltd v Tarmac Civil Engineering Ltd* [1967] 1 WLR 1508 (HL), 1529.

[196] *cf Arthur White (Contractors) Ltd v Tarmac Civil Engineering Ltd* [1967] 1 WLR 1508 (HL), 1520 (Lord Pearce) (rule 'may well apply'), 1526 (Lord Upjohn) (putting it 'no higher' than possibility that rule applies). See *Jose v MacSalvors Plant Hire Ltd* [2009] EWCA Civ 1329; [2010] TCLR 2 (cl 13 of CPA form of contract was an indemnity, not a risk allocation clause, and so *Canada SS* rules applicable).

[197] *Canada Steamship Lines Ltd v R* [1952] AC 192 (PC), 208.

[198] Examples antedating *Canada SS* include *The Millwall* [1905] P 155 (CA) ('faults or defaults'); *The Riverman* [1928] P 33 (P) ('negligence').

[199] *Smith v South Wales Switchgear Co Ltd* [1978] 1 WLR 165 (HL), 169 (Viscount Dilhorne).

[200] *Smith v South Wales Switchgear Co Ltd* [1978] 1 WLR 165 (HL), 173 (Lord Fraser).

[201] *Westcott v JH Jenner (Plasterers) Ltd* [1962] 1 Lloyd's Rep 309 (CA).

for claims in negligence. In *Gillespie Brothers & Co Ltd v Roy Bowles Transport Ltd*[202] Buckley LJ and Orr LJ held that the word 'whatsoever' in an indemnity against 'all claims or demands whatsoever' was sufficient to satisfy the first rule. The indemnity in *Comyn Ching & Co Ltd v Oriental Tube Co Ltd*,[203] which was contained in a series of letters, was expressed to 'cover any eventuality' and the indemnifier agreed to accept responsibility for 'liabilities in every sense of the word'. Goff LJ held that this was sufficient to satisfy the first rule; otherwise, the application of the third rule would have been fatal.

[4–51] Terms sufficiently wide to cover negligence. In the absence of an express reference to negligence, the second of the *Canada SS* rules[204] requires consideration of whether the words are sufficiently wide in their ordinary meaning to cover negligence. A doubt is to be resolved in favour of the indemnifier and against the indemnified party. In England, phrases such as 'all claims' or 'any liability' have on occasion been accepted as potentially wide enough to cover negligence, even without the addition of terms of art such as 'howsoever caused'.[205] In Australia, similar expressions have been sufficient to cover negligence, even where the *Canada SS* rules have not been directly applied.[206]

A leading decision on the second rule is *Smith v South Wales Switchgear Co Ltd*.[207] Clause 23(b) of the services contract provided an indemnity from the contractor to the customer against '[a]ny liability, loss, claim or proceedings whatsoever under statute or common law ... in respect of personal injury to ... any person ... arising out of or in the course of or caused by the execution of this order'. One of the contractor's employees was injured while on the customer's premises and the customer was found liable in negligence and for breach of statutory duty. It was held that the words, in context, were not wide enough to cover the customer's negligence.[208] A significant consideration was that the indemnity related to performance of the work, and it was the contractor's employees, not those of the customer, who were to be involved in that task. This suggested that the liability was to arise out of the acts or omissions of the contractor or its employees and not those of the customer or its employees.

---

[202] *Gillespie Brothers & Co Ltd v Roy Bowles Transport Ltd* [1973] QB 400 (CA). This reasoning was expressly criticised in *Smith v South Wales Switchgear Co Ltd* [1978] 1 WLR 165 (HL), 169 (Viscount Dilhorne), 173 (Lord Fraser).

[203] *Comyn Ching & Co Ltd v Oriental Tube Co Ltd* (1979) 17 BLR 47 (CA).

[204] *Canada Steamship Lines Ltd v R* [1952] AC 192 (PC), 208.

[205] *Walters v Whessoe Ltd* (1960) 6 BLR 23 (CA), 37 (Slade J), cf 33 (Sellers LJ); *Hair and Skin Trading Co Ltd v Norman Airfreight Carriers Ltd* [1974] 1 Lloyd's Rep 443 (QB), 445–46; *Blake v Richards & Wallington Industries Ltd* (1974) 16 KIR 151 (QB); *EE Caledonia Ltd v Orbit Valve Co Europe* [1994] 1 WLR 1515 (CA), 1522 (Steyn LJ); *Jose v MacSalvors Plant Hire Ltd* [2009] EWCA Civ 1329; [2010] TCLR 2. cf *Wright v Tyne Improvement Commissioners* [1967] 2 Lloyd's Rep 411 (QB), 417 (all liabilities for injury 'howsoever caused' sufficient); *Stent Foundations Ltd v MJ Gleeson Group plc* [2001] BLR 134 (QB), 141 ('lost or damaged by fire or any other cause' insufficient).

[206] *Davis v Commissioner for Main Roads* (1967) 117 CLR 529 ('all claims'); *Valkonen v Jennings Construction Ltd* (1995) 184 LSJS 87 (SAFC) ('any liability ... whatsoever'); *Leighton Contractors Pty Ltd v Smith* [2000] NSWCA 55 ('all loss or damage'); *National Vulcan Engineering Insurance Group Ltd v Pentax Pty Ltd* [2004] NSWCA 218; (2004) 20 BCL 398, [46] (MW Campbell AJA) ('all loss, damages, claims ... whatsoever'); *BI (Contracting) Pty Ltd v AW Baulderstone Holdings Pty Ltd* [2007] NSWCA 173; (2008) Aust Contract R 90-267 ('all liability'). cf *Schleimer v Brisbane Stevedoring Pty Ltd* [1969] Qd R 46 (FC) ('any loss, damage or injury whatsoever or howsoever arising').

[207] *Smith v South Wales Switchgear Co Ltd* [1978] 1 WLR 165 (HL).

[208] *Smith v South Wales Switchgear Co Ltd* [1978] 1 WLR 165 (HL), 169 (Viscount Dilhorne), 173–74 (Lord Fraser), 179 (Lord Keith).

[4–52] **Alternative bases of liability.** Where the indemnified party's negligence is the only, or only realistic, basis for a loss or liability within the scope of the indemnity, then the scope is likely to be construed to include negligence. The indemnity would otherwise lack subject-matter.[209] More controversial is the converse proposition that is embodied in the third of the *Canada SS* rules.[210] In relation to indemnities, the rule essentially holds that an indemnity will not cover the consequences of the indemnified party's negligence if a potential liability might be based on some ground other than negligence. The alternative ground ought not to be fanciful or remote.

Many cases concern liabilities arising in connection with construction projects or other services engagements. The potential bases of liability identified as alternatives typically include breach of statutory duty;[211] liability for other torts such as nuisance, conversion or breach of non-delegable tortious duties;[212] or liability for breach of contract.[213] Another ground is liability for costs incurred in the successful defence of a claim for negligence.[214] As it is often possible to find an alternative ground of liability, a rigid application of the third rule tends to preclude indemnification for negligence unless the contract contains an express reference to it. This is not a commercially sensible outcome in some contexts.[215] Nor, more generally, is it satisfactory to measure the improbability of protection by a single factor, namely, the existence of other bases of liability.

Little attention has been given to the adaptation of the third rule to different subject-matter. As the third rule applies to exclusion clauses, the concern is to identify some other ground of legal responsibility to the other contracting party. That concept can be translated directly to indemnities against liabilities of the indemnified party, whether owed to third parties or the indemnifier. An indemnity may also cover losses personal to the indemnified party, such as damage to property, or losses arising from another's non-performance. It is nonsensical to consider possible bases of the indemnified party's liability for its own loss. The starting point must be that the indemnified party bears the loss unless there is some basis for transferring responsibility to the indemnifier. The more relevant question is whether the indemnifier was expected to assume the risk of losses caused wholly or partly by the indemnified party's own heedless or careless conduct.

[4–53] **Implied indemnities.** Where an indemnity is implied into an existing contract or a contract of indemnity is inferred from the circumstances, much depends upon context. The nature of the relationship between the parties and the basis for the implication or

---

[209] *Walters v Whessoe Ltd* (1960) 6 BLR 23 (CA), 34, 35 (Devlin LJ). cf *Alderslade v Hendon Laundry Ltd* [1945] KB 189 (CA), 192 (Lord Greene MR).

[210] *Canada Steamship Lines Ltd v R* [1952] AC 192 (PC), 208. See [4–48] (status in Australian law).

[211] *Walters v Whessoe Ltd* (1960) 6 BLR 23 (CA), 33 (Sellers LJ), 35 (Devlin LJ); *Smith v South Wales Switchgear Co Ltd* [1978] 1 WLR 165 (HL), 179 (Lord Keith); *Greenwell v Matthew Hall Pty Ltd (No 2)* (1982) 31 SASR 548 (SC), 555; *EE Caledonia Ltd v Orbit Valve Co Europe* [1994] 1 WLR 1515 (CA), 1522–23 (Steyn LJ).

[212] *Lowery v Vickers Armstrong (Engineers) Ltd* (1969) 8 KIR 603 (CA), 606 (Russell LJ), 610–11 (Salmon LJ); *Gillespie Brothers & Co Ltd v Roy Bowles Transport Ltd* [1973] QB 400 (CA), 413–14 (Lord Denning MR); *Smith v South Wales Switchgear Co Ltd* [1978] 1 WLR 165 (HL), 174 (Lord Fraser).

[213] *Smith v South Wales Switchgear Co Ltd* [1978] 1 WLR 165 (HL), 174 (Lord Fraser). cf *BI (Contracting) Pty Ltd v AW Baulderstone Holdings Pty Ltd* [2007] NSWCA 173; (2008) Aust Contract R 90-267, [55].

[214] *Walters v Whessoe Ltd* (1960) 6 BLR 23 (CA), 37 (Slade J); *Gillespie Brothers & Co Ltd v Roy Bowles Transport Ltd* [1973] QB 400 (CA), 414 (Lord Denning MR).

[215] See n 170.

inference is important. An agent's indemnity from the principal, for example, generally does not extend to the consequences of the agent's negligence.[216]

Negligence under an indemnity implied in a time charterparty has sometimes been approached as a matter of causation.[217] In *Actis Co Ltd v Sanko Steamship Co Ltd (The Aquacharm)*[218] Lord Denning MR referred to the *Canada SS* rules in concluding that additional costs caused by the master's carelessness were not covered by the indemnity. In *Krüger & Co Ltd v Moel Tryvan Ship Co Ltd*,[219] the owner's loss arose in a different way and this led to a different result. Cargo was lost due to the master's negligence in navigation. The owner was exempted from liability for such negligence by the terms of the charterparty but was liable under bills of lading which had been presented by the charterer and signed by the master. The owner was allowed to recover from the charterer in respect of its liability on the bills of lading. One ground for that conclusion was that there was an implied indemnity from the charterer to the owner against the more onerous liability under the bills of lading.[220]

Indemnities implied or inferred in connection with agency relationships or charterparties may derive from a broader principle relating to actions upon request. *Sheffield Corp v Barclay*[221] is usually cited as the leading authority. A party may be liable to indemnify another where: the former party requests the latter party to perform an act; the latter party complies with the request; the act turns out to be injurious to the rights of a third party; and the act was not manifestly tortious or illegal to the knowledge of the party acting. The juristic basis of the indemnity is controversial, because it is difficult to accommodate all instances within one of the divisions of the common law of obligations: contract, tort or unjust enrichment.[222] On the whole, it seems to be treated as contractual in nature, based on an inference from the circumstances,[223] but there is also support for the view that it may be imposed by operation of law.[224] Such an indemnity may cover a

---

[216] *Lewis v Samuel* (1846) 8 QB 685; 115 ER 1031; *New Zealand Farmers' Co-operative Distributing Co Ltd v National Mortgage and Agency Co of New Zealand Ltd* [1961] NZLR 969 (SC); *Lezam Pty Ltd v Seabridge Australia Pty Ltd* (1992) 107 ALR 291 (FCAFC), 311 (Sheppard J). cf *James v Commonwealth Bank of Australia* (1992) 37 FCR 445 (FCA), 453 (express exclusion). See generally P Watts and FMB Reynolds, *Bowstead & Reynolds on Agency*, 19th edn (London, Sweet & Maxwell, 2010), 332, para 7-062.

[217] See, eg, *The Athanasia Comninos and The Georges C Lemos* [1990] 1 Lloyd's Rep 277 (QB), 290, 294. See generally [4–18].

[218] *Actis Co Ltd v Sanko Steamship Co Ltd (The Aquacharm)* [1982] 1 WLR 119 (CA), 123.

[219] *Krüger & Co Ltd v Moel Tryvan Ship Co Ltd* [1907] AC 272 (HL).

[220] *Moel Tryvan Ship Co Ltd v Krüger & Co Ltd* [1907] 1 KB 809 (CA), 823–24 (Sir Gorrell Barnes P), 831–32 (Buckley LJ); *Krüger & Co Ltd v Moel Tryvan Ship Co Ltd* [1907] AC 272 (HL), 276 (Lord Loreburn LC). cf *Milburn & Co v Jamaica Fruit Importing and Trading Co of London* [1900] 2 QB 540 (CA) (owner deprived of right to general average contribution where master negligent).

[221] *Sheffield Corp v Barclay* [1905] AC 392 (HL). See also *Birmingham and District Land Co v London and North Western Railway Co* (1886) 34 Ch D 261 (CA), 272 (Cotton LJ), 275 (Bowen LJ), 277 (Fry LJ); *R v Henrickson* (1911) 13 CLR 473; *Secretary of State v Bank of India Ltd* [1938] 2 All ER 797 (PC); *Kai Yung v Hong Kong and Shanghai Banking Corp* [1981] AC 787 (PC); *Naviera Mogor SA v Societe Metallurgique de Normandie (The Nogar Marin)* [1988] 1 Lloyd's Rep 412 (CA).

[222] See generally PS Atiyah, *Essays on Contract* (Oxford, Clarendon Press, 1990), 291–94; N McBride, 'A Fifth Common Law Obligation' (1994) 14 *Legal Studies* 35, 43–45; J Gleeson and N Owens, 'Dissolving Fictions: What to Do with the Implied Indemnity?' (2009) 25 *Journal of Contract Law* 135; B Shaw, 'Indemnities for Acts Done at Another's Request' (2011) 44 *University of British Columbia Law Review* 331.

[223] *Toplis v Grane* (1839) 5 Bing NC 636; 132 ER 1245; *Dugdale v Lovering* (1875) LR 10 CP 196; *Kai Yung v Hong Kong and Shanghai Banking Corp* [1981] AC 787 (PC), 796, 798 (offer of indemnity accepted by acting upon request coupled with intention to create legal relations); *Naviera Mogor SA v Societe Metallurgique de Normandie (The Nogar Marin)* [1988] 1 Lloyd's Rep 412 (CA), 417 (matter of fact except where ministerial duty to act).

[224] *Sheffield Corp v Barclay* [1905] AC 392 (HL), 399, 401 (Lord Davey); *Bank of England v Cutler* [1908] 2 KB 208 (CA), 219–21 (Vaughan Williams LJ); *Naviera Mogor SA v Societe Metallurgique de Normandie (The Nogar*

liability for strict-liability tort that arises necessarily from the performance of the act requested.[225]

Whether the indemnity also covers a loss or liability arising from the carelessness (to use a neutral term) of the indemnified party is less clear. A relevant factor may be whether the want of care occurs in respect of the indemnifier or the third party. If the latter then, in some situations at least,[226] the indemnity may still apply. The point can arise where the indemnified party has the opportunity to make enquiries or verify the accuracy or authenticity of documents before performing the act. If an entity is under a duty of a ministerial nature to register share transfers, for example, then it seems to be entitled to an indemnity from the party requesting the registration unless it has acted dishonestly or otherwise not in good faith.[227] Mere carelessness in failing to check a specimen signature is insufficient to displace the indemnity.[228]

In two decisions involving stolen cheques, a domestic bank, acting as agent for collection upon a request from a foreign bank, had sought indemnity against a liability for conversion.[229] A statutory defence was available to the bank provided it had acted in good faith without negligence. The defence failed in one case; in the other, the claim was settled. To that extent, in each case it might be said that the bank's liability for conversion arose from its 'negligence'. Such negligence was, however, in respect of the true owner of the cheque. In neither case did the domestic bank default in performing its duties as agent for collection vis-à-vis the foreign collecting bank; thus the domestic bank was entitled to indemnity.[230]

Conversion

[4–54] **Protection against liability for conversion.** An indemnity may protect against a liability for conversion. There are two principal lines of authority. One line of cases concerns instructions given to the master of a vessel to deliver cargo to a nominated party without the production of a bill of lading.[231] The master often acts in reliance on a letter of

---

Marin) [1988] 1 Lloyd's Rep 412 (CA), 417 (where ministerial duty to act). *cf Secretary of State v Bank of India Ltd* [1938] 2 All ER 797 (PC), 800 ('fiction of a contract implied by law adds nothing'); *Groves & Sons v Webb & Kenward* (1916) 114 LT 1082 (CA), 1088 (Bankes LJ) (whether matter of fact or mixed law and fact 'does not seem to matter very much').

[225] See [4–54].

[226] Contrast *W Cory & Son Ltd v Lambton and Hetton Collieries Ltd* (1916) 86 LJKB 401 (CA) (no coverage where negligent performance of otherwise lawful task); *Parmley v Parmley* [1945] SCR 635, 648–49 (Estey J) (no coverage where acting upon request without making further enquiries amounted to professional negligence). *Downs v Chappell* [1997] 1 WLR 426 (CA) might be explained on the basis that the indemnified party was negligent towards the third party and the indemnifier: see esp 445 (Hobhouse LJ).

[227] *Kai Yung v Hong Kong and Shanghai Banking Corp* [1981] AC 787 (PC), 798. *cf Bank of England v Cutler* [1908] 2 KB 208 (CA), 233 (Farwell LJ); *Naviera Mogor SA v Societe Metallurgique de Normandie (The Nogar Marin)* [1988] 1 Lloyd's Rep 412 (CA), 417.

[228] But see *Kai Yung v Hong Kong and Shanghai Banking Corp* [1981] AC 787 (PC), 799–800.

[229] *Middle Temple v Lloyds Bank plc* [1999] 1 All ER (Comm) 193 (QB); *Linklaters v HSBC Bank plc* [2003] EWHC 1113 (Comm); [2003] 2 Lloyd's Rep 545. See EP Ellinger, 'Liabilities of Bank When Crossed Cheque Collected Overseas' (2004) 120 *Law Quarterly Review* 226. *cf National Commercial Banking Corp of Australia Ltd v Batty* (1986) 160 CLR 251, 273 (Brennan J).

[230] *Middle Temple v Lloyds Bank plc* [1999] 1 All ER (Comm) 193 (QB), 234–35; *Linklaters v HSBC Bank plc* [2003] EWHC 1113 (Comm); [2003] 2 Lloyd's Rep 545, [35]–[37].

[231] Cases in this category may overlap with those in the next: see, eg, *Strathlorne Steamship Co Ltd v Andrew Weir & Co* (1934) 50 Ll L Rep 185 (CA), 193 (Lord Hanworth MR), 193–94 (Slesser LJ); *A/S Hansen-Tangens Rederi III v Total Transport Corp (The Sagona)* [1984] 1 Lloyd's Rep 194 (QB).

indemnity provided directly by the instructing party, or on a chain of such letters, or on an indemnity contained in the charterparty.[232] The indemnity is intended to meet the risk of exposure to a claim for breach of contract or conversion.[233]

In the other line of cases, a party is requested by another to deal with goods or a negotiable instrument in a particular manner, and that dealing leads to a claim by a third party for infringement of some interest in the goods or instrument. An indemnity against the consequences of complying with the request, which may include a liability for conversion, may be inferred from the circumstances.[234] In *Dugdale v Lovering*,[235] for example, the claimants found themselves in possession of trucks which were claimed by two different parties, one of whom was the defendant. The claimants requested an indemnity from the defendant but the defendant responded only with an immediate demand for possession of the trucks. The claimants complied and were then sued for conversion by the other party. In these circumstances, it was possible to infer a contract by the defendant to indemnify the claimants against that liability.

[4–55] Qualifications. Where the indemnity is inferred from the circumstances, and perhaps also where it is express, the act must be done in good faith and must not be manifestly tortious or illegal to the knowledge of the indemnified party.[236]

The indemnified party will not be protected if its role in the conversion of the goods goes beyond what is authorised or contemplated by the contract.[237] The point is illustrated by *Glebe Island Terminals Pty Ltd v Continental Seagram Pty Ltd (The Antwerpen)*,[238] although the claim there was, strictly, for an indemnity against liability arising in the context of a conversion, rather than a liability for conversion. Employees of the operator of a container terminal connived to facilitate the theft of a substantial consignment of goods from the terminal. The terminal operator was liable for customs duty and sales tax on the goods, and it claimed indemnity from the carrier and consignee in reliance on several clauses in its contract for terminal services. One clause specifically concerned claims for duty or sales tax; other clauses covered loss arising out of the use of the terminal or the provision of services by the terminal operator. The New South Wales Court of Appeal applied the 'four corners' principle of construction[239] to conclude that the indemnity clauses did not protect the terminal operator in the circumstances.

---

[232] See, eg, *Pacific Carriers Ltd v BNP Paribas* [2004] HCA 35; (2004) 218 CLR 451; *Laemthong International Lines Co Ltd v Artis (The Laemthong Glory) (No 2)* [2005] EWCA Civ 519; [2005] 1 Lloyd's Rep 688; *Farenco Shipping Co Ltd v Daebo Shipping Co Ltd (The Bremen Max)* [2008] EWHC 2755 (Comm); [2009] 1 Lloyd's Rep 81; *Far East Chartering Ltd v Great Eastern Shipping Co Ltd (The Jag Ravi)* [2012] EWCA Civ 180; [2012] 1 Lloyd's Rep 637.

[233] cf *Sze Hai Tong Bank Ltd v Rambler Cycle Co Ltd* [1959] AC 576 (PC) (exclusion clause in bill of lading ineffective to avoid liability for misdelivery).

[234] *Adamson v Jarvis* (1827) 4 Bing 66; 130 ER 693; *Betts v Gibbins* (1834) 2 Ad & E 57; 111 ER 22; *Toplis v Grane* (1839) 5 Bing NC 636; 132 ER 1245; *Dugdale v Lovering* (1875) LR 10 CP 196; *Secretary of State v Bank of India Ltd* [1938] 2 All ER 797 (PC). See also [4–53].

[235] *Dugdale v Lovering* (1875) LR 10 CP 196.

[236] For implied indemnities, see, eg, *Dugdale v Lovering* (1875) LR 10 CP 196, 199 (Brett J), 201 (Grove J); *Sheffield Corp v Barclay* [1905] AC 392 (HL), 397 (Earl Halsbury LC) and [4–53]. For express indemnities, see *Far East Chartering Ltd v Great Eastern Shipping Co Ltd (The Jag Ravi)* [2012] EWCA Civ 180; [2012] 1 Lloyd's Rep 637, [50]–[52] (Tomlinson LJ).

[237] cf *Farenco Shipping Co Ltd v Daebo Shipping Co Ltd (The Bremen Max)* [2008] EWHC 2755 (Comm); [2009] 1 Lloyd's Rep 81, [34]–[37] (right to indemnity conditional upon delivery being made to specified party).

[238] *Glebe Island Terminals Pty Ltd v Continental Seagram Pty Ltd (The Antwerpen)* (1993) 40 NSWLR 206; [1994] 1 Lloyd's Rep 213 (CA).

[239] *Gibaud v Great Eastern Railway Co* [1921] 2 KB 426 (CA), 435 (Scrutton LJ); *Thomas National Transport (Melbourne) Pty Ltd v May & Baker (Australia) Pty Ltd* (1966) 115 CLR 353, 377 (Windeyer J).

Breach of Statutory Duty

[4–56] Protection against civil liability for breach of statutory duty. The scope of an indemnity may encompass the indemnified party's civil liability for breach of a duty imposed by statute.[240] Indemnification against this type of liability has not traditionally been approached with the same degree of scepticism as indemnification against negligence;[241] indeed, breach of statutory duty is often identified as an alternative ground of liability in the application of the third of the *Canada SS* rules.[242]

[4–57] Effect of exclusion of negligence. An exclusion of negligence from the scope of the indemnity may affect coverage of liability for breach of statutory duty. Two issues arise: whether the exclusion applies to a freestanding liability for breach of statutory duty; and whether the exclusion applies to a liability for breach of statutory duty that exists concurrently with a liability in negligence in respect of the same loss to the claimant.

The first issue ultimately depends upon construction and requires consideration of the nature of the duty breached.[243] In *Murfin v United Steel Companies Ltd*,[244] a workman was killed by electrocution while at the indemnified party's factory. The indemnified party was held not liable for common law negligence but liable for breach of a regulation which required adequate screening of electrified panels. The indemnity from the contractors covered claims 'under any statute or at common law . . . from any cause other than the negligence' of the indemnified party. The indemnity was held to apply because the liability for breach of statutory duty arose without any 'negligence' in the ordinary – and commercially reasonable – sense of common law negligence.[245] A further consideration was that excluding breach of statutory duty would have deprived the indemnity almost entirely of content.[246] The approach is similar where the exclusion of negligence is inferred rather than express. As Devlin LJ explained in *Walters v Whessoe Ltd*,[247] 'what we have to consider is not what negligence means in strict legal analysis but what sort of conduct the parties intended to exclude from the scope of the indemnity'. On that basis, Devlin LJ considered that the inferred exclusion of negligence applied to 'heedless or careless conduct'.

The second issue, relating to concurrent liabilities, also turns upon construction of the indemnity and consideration of the nature of the statutory duty.[248] The standard of duty imposed by the statute may be one of reasonable care, in which case there is no substantial difference between negligence and breach of the statutory duty. Both bases of liability are excluded.[249] Another reason for denying coverage, irrespective of the standard of statutory duty, is that the indemnified party should not isolate and rely upon a breach of statutory

---

[240] *Hosking v De Havilland Aircraft Co Ltd* [1949] 1 All ER 540 (KB); *Murfin v United Steel Companies Ltd* [1957] 1 WLR 104 (CA); *Caledonia North Sea Ltd v British Telecommunications plc (The Piper Alpha)* [2002] UKHL 4; [2002] 1 Lloyd's Rep 553. *cf* also *Hamilton & Co v Anderson & Co* 1953 SC 129 (IH).

[241] See [4–44].

[242] See [4–52].

[243] *Murfin v United Steel Companies Ltd* [1957] 1 WLR 104 (CA), 110–12 (Singleton LJ), 114–15 (Parker LJ).

[244] *Murfin v United Steel Companies Ltd* [1957] 1 WLR 104 (CA).

[245] *Murfin v United Steel Companies Ltd* [1957] 1 WLR 104 (CA), 112 (Singleton LJ), 115 (Parker LJ).

[246] *cf Hosking v De Havilland Aircraft Co Ltd* [1949] 1 All ER 540 (KB).

[247] *Walters v Whessoe Ltd* (1960) 6 BLR 23 (CA), 36.

[248] *Smith v South Wales Switchgear Co Ltd* [1978] 1 WLR 165 (HL), 175 (Lord Fraser); *EE Caledonia Ltd v Orbit Valve Co Europe* [1994] 1 WLR 221 (QB), 232–33 and on appeal: *EE Caledonia Ltd v Orbit Valve Co Europe* [1994] 1 WLR 1515 (CA), 1524–25 (Steyn LJ).

[249] *Jose v MacSalvors Plant Hire Ltd* [2009] EWCA Civ 1329; [2010] TCLR 2, [19] (Ward LJ).

duty so as to evade the exclusion of negligence.[250] This is one facet of the more general question of the treatment of losses or liabilities that arise concurrently on two bases or from two sources, one being included and the other being excluded from the scope of the indemnity.[251]

Breach of Contract

[4–58] **Types of breach of contract.** There is relatively little authority on the scope of indemnities against the consequences of the indemnified party's breach of contract. The following instances can be distinguished:

(1) an indemnity against the consequences of the indemnified party's breach of its contract with the indemnifier, which applies:

    (a) as between the parties, to bar or limit claims by the indemnifier; or

    (b) in relation to personal losses or claims by third parties; and

(2) an indemnity against the consequences of the indemnified party's breach of a contract with a third party.

[4–59] **Breach of contract with indemnifier.** The indemnity described in situation (1)(a) above[252] is, in effect, a form of exclusion or limitation clause. Two factors may count against this construction. Where the scope of an indemnity is expressed to apply to claims or liabilities in general, without specifying the potential claimants, it is often construed to cover claims by third parties and not the indemnifier.[253] It may also be considered unlikely that the indemnified party was to be excused from the consequences of its breach of contract. If the relevant contractual duty requires the exercise of reasonable care, there is an obvious parallel with the cases on negligence.[254] Such reasoning may also extend to some types of strict contractual duty.[255]

A similar implausibility may be perceived in situation (1)(b), though it can be displaced if the parties' intention is sufficiently clear. In *Swan Hunter and Wigham Richardson Ltd v France Fenwick Tyne & Wear Co Ltd (The Albion)*,[256] a towage contract stated that the towage contractor was not liable for 'any loss or damage whatsoever . . . whether arising from or occasioned by any accident or by any omission, breach of duty, mismanagement, negligence or default'. In the same clause the hiring party, a shipbuilder, promised to indemnify the contractor against 'all liability for the aforegoing matters'. The contractor and shipbuilder were both held liable for loss arising from a collision involving the vessel under tow. The collision was partly caused by the contractor's negligence, which also involved breaches of the towage contract with the shipbuilder. It was held that the contractor was still entitled to be indemnified against the liability. Somervell LJ specifically rejected the

---

[250] *EE Caledonia Ltd v Orbit Valve Co Europe* [1994] 1 WLR 1515 (CA), 1524–25 (Steyn LJ). cf *Smith v South Wales Switchgear Co Ltd* [1978] 1 WLR 165 (HL), 175 (Lord Fraser).

[251] See [4–25].

[252] See [4–58].

[253] See [8–4].

[254] See [4–46].

[255] See, eg, *Taylor Woodrow Property Co of Australia Pty Ltd v Coles Myer Ltd* [1999] NSWCA 204, [46]–[47] (Giles JA) (breach by lessor failing to keep roof weatherproof).

[256] *Swan Hunter and Wigham Richardson Ltd v France Fenwick Tyne & Wear Co Ltd (The Albion)* [1953] 1 WLR 1026 (CA).

argument that a party in breach of contract could not claim an indemnity from the counterparty.[257]

[4–60] **Breach of contract with third party.** An indemnity from A to B against B's liability to C arising from a breach by B of a contract with C can be found in specific commercial contexts. The underlying rationale is usually that A's conduct may bring about B's liability to C.[258] At common law, A may be the assignee of a lease who is to assume responsibility for the performance of the assignor's/lessee's, B's, obligations to the lessor, C.[259] More generally, B's performance of a contract with C may depend upon A's performance of a contract with B. There may be an express or implied indemnity from A to B against B's liabilities to C arising as a result of A's breach of the contract with B.[260]

Other examples can be found in connection with charterparties. The master may sign bills of lading on terms or in circumstances that expose the owner to a more extensive liability in respect of the cargo than it has assumed, vis-à-vis the charterer, under the terms of the charterparty. The owner may be protected by an express or implied indemnity from the charterer against the consequences of the greater liability.[261]

Insurance and Other Risk Allocation Clauses

Types of Risk Allocation Clause

[4–61] **General.** In many sophisticated commercial contracts, promises of indemnity are part of a complex of provisions that are intended to allocate risks of loss associated with the contractual transaction. Subject to statute and public policy, parties are free to alter the allocation of risk that would arise according to ordinary legal principles.[262] Insurance clauses are another element in risk allocation regimes. A party may be required to effect insurance against a specified class of risks for the benefit of a specified class of persons. Another common form of clause may be described as a 'risk' or 'responsibility' clause. The clause usually states that the risk of a particular eventuality, or responsibility for that eventuality, is to be borne (or is not to borne) by one of the parties.

---

[257] *Swan Hunter and Wigham Richardson Ltd v France Fenwick Tyne & Wear Co Ltd (The Albion)* [1953] 1 WLR 1026 (CA), 1032.

[258] See, eg, *Broom v Hall* (1859) 7 CBNS 503; 144 ER 911 (principals, A, wrongfully refusing to accept delivery of goods under a contract arranged by their broker, B, with the seller, C).

[259] See further [10–7]. See now Landlord and Tenant (Covenants) Act 1995, ss 5, 14 (for leases on or after 1 January 1996). *cf Eagon v Dent* [1965] 3 All ER 334 (Ch Lanc) (indemnity to under-lessor/assignor from assignee of reversion).

[260] See, eg, [10–4], [10–11]–[10–13]. *cf* [10–7].

[261] *Moel Tryvan Ship Co Ltd v Krüger & Co Ltd* [1907] 1 KB 809 (CA), 823–24 (Sir Gorrell Barnes P), 831–32 (Buckley LJ); *Krüger & Co Ltd v Moel Tryvan Ship Co Ltd* [1907] AC 272 (HL), 276 (Lord Loreburn LC); *Elder Dempster & Co v CG Dunn & Co Ltd* (1909) 15 Com Cas 49 (HL); *Bosma v Larsen* [1966] 1 Lloyd's Rep 22 (QB); *Telfair Shipping Corp v Inersea Carriers SA (The Caroline P)* [1985] 1 WLR 553 (QB). *cf Ben Shipping Co (Pte) Ltd v An Bord Bainne (The C Joyce)* [1986] 2 All ER 177 (QB); *Ben Line Steamers Ltd v Pacific Steam Navigation Co (The Benlawers)* [1989] 2 Lloyd's Rep 51 (QB).

[262] See, eg, *Furness Shipbuilding Co Ltd v London and North Eastern Railway Co* (1934) 50 TLR 257 (HL); *Davis v Commissioner for Main Roads* (1967) 117 CLR 529; *Caledonia North Sea Ltd v British Telecommunications plc (The Piper Alpha)* [2002] UKHL 4; [2002] 1 Lloyd's Rep 553; *Co-operative Retail Services Ltd v Taylor Young Partnership* [2002] UKHL 17; [2002] 1 WLR 1419, [4] (Lord Bingham), [48] (Lord Hope).

[4–62] **Distinction between promise to indemnify and promise to insure.** A promise to obtain insurance against a particular risk may be used in conjunction with a promise to indemnify against that risk. The two promises can appear in the same clause, as where a contractor promises 'to indemnify and insure' against specified risks.

Although a mere promise to obtain insurance for the benefit of another might loosely be described as a promise to indemnify that person, it is distinct in character.[263] The promisee sues for damages for breach by failing to insure, though a breach will not necessarily cause substantial loss to the promisee. Where the promisor has not insured at all[264] and the relevant risk materialises, the measure of loss is the amount that the promisee ought to have recovered in the circumstances if a policy had been effected.[265] In contrast, a promise of indemnity may in some circumstances be specifically enforced in respect of a potential loss. In relation to actual loss, the indemnified party generally sues for damages for the indemnifier's own failure to protect it against the loss. A breach of the indemnity is predicated upon the existence of a loss to the indemnified party. If, however, the contractual indemnity and the required insurance policy are the same in scope, and the risk materialises, then it is possible that the amount recoverable by the indemnified party will be the same whether it claims under the indemnity or for breach of the promise to insure.

[4–63] **Distinction between promise to indemnify and risk clause.** The characteristics of a risk or responsibility clause depend on context, particularly the source and nature of the risk and the party or parties likely to be affected if it materialises.

A clause by which A agrees with B to accept responsibility for, or the risk of, some eventuality may have one of the following effects:

(1) to exclude B's liability to A for the consequences of the eventuality;
(2) to require A to continue to perform and overcome adverse consequences of the eventuality;[266] or
(3) to require A to indemnify B against the consequences of that eventuality.

A statement that A assumes the risk of or accepts responsibility for an eventuality does not, therefore, necessarily establish an indemnity from A to B against the consequences of that eventuality. Equally, A's disclaimer or renunciation of responsibility does not necessarily create an indemnity from B to A against the consequences of the eventuality.[267]

Two leading authorities can be contrasted. In *Arthur White (Contractors) Ltd v Tarmac Civil Engineering Ltd*,[268] a standard form contract for the hire of an excavator contained a clause (clause 8) stating, in part, that drivers provided with the excavator were to be regarded as servants of the hirer, and that the hirer 'alone shall be responsible for all claims arising in connection with the operation of the plant'. The hirer and owner were both held liable to the claimant, who was injured in an accident involving the excavator. The House of Lords restored the trial judge's order that the hirer indemnify the owner against the

---

[263] See, eg, *Valkonen v Jennings Construction Ltd* (1995) 184 LSJS 87 (SAFC), 95 (Cox J).
[264] cf *Newman v Maxwell* (1899) 80 LT 681 (Ch) (partial insurance).
[265] *Smith v Price* (1862) 2 F & F 748; 175 ER 1268; *Pennant Hills Restaurants Pty Ltd v Barrell Insurances Pty Ltd* (1981) 145 CLR 625, 637–38 (Gibbs J); *Cervellone v Besselink Bros Pty Ltd* (1984) 55 ACTR 1 (SC), 12.
[266] *AE Farr Ltd v Admiralty* [1953] 1 WLR 965 (QB).
[267] *The Richmond* (1902) 19 TLR 29 (P); *The Devonshire and St Winfred* [1913] P 13 (P); *Federal Steam Navigation Co Ltd v J Fenwick & Co Pty Ltd* (1943) 68 CLR 553, 560–61 (Latham CJ). Contrast *Trewheelar v Trukeel Pty Ltd* (1986) Q Conv R 54-223 (SC).
[268] *Arthur White (Contractors) Ltd v Tarmac Civil Engineering Ltd* [1967] 1 WLR 1508 (HL). See further [4–49].

liability. Some of their Lordships appeared to accept that clause 8 was, in the circumstances, effectively a form of indemnity.[269] Lord Pearce, in contrast, insisted that it was neither an exclusion nor an indemnity clause, but rather a clause that allocated vicarious responsibility for the acts of the driver of the excavator.[270]

In *KD Morris & Sons Pty Ltd v GJ Coles & Co Ltd*,[271] the builder was engaged to execute works on premises that were located partly on the employer's own land and partly on adjacent land leased from another. A fire, caused by the builder's negligence, damaged that part of the premises on the leased land. The lessor claimed against the builder and the builder claimed indemnity from the employer. Under clause 14(c) of the building contract, the builder was required to insure against and indemnify the employer against liability or loss in respect of damage to any property due to negligence of the builder. That clause was, in relation to fire, subject to clause 15. Clause 15(b) provided that the existing structures and the works were at the 'sole risk' of the employer as regards loss or damage by fire, and that the employer was to insure against such risks. It was held that clause 15(b) was intended to exclude claims by the employer against the builder in relation to the specified fire risks. It did not provide an indemnity from the employer to the builder against claims by third parties.

Relationship between Clauses

[4–64] Interaction of insurance and indemnity clauses. Questions of the interplay between indemnity, insurance and risk clauses usually arise in the context of a dispute about the assignment of responsibility for a loss on the basis prescribed by the contract. The process involves three stages. First, the scope of the clauses must be ascertained. The existence and extent of insurance or risk clauses may influence the scope of the indemnity and vice versa, even in the absence of express cross-references between them.[272] Secondly, it must be determined whether the claimed loss falls within none, one or more than one of the clauses. Thirdly, if the loss falls within more than one clause, for example, an indemnity clause and an insurance clause, there may be a further question as to who is to bear ultimate responsibility for loss.[273]

Ascertainment of Scope of Clauses

[4–65] Clauses are co-extensive. The scope of an indemnity clause may be co-extensive with that of an insurance clause.[274] One instance is where a single clause commences with

---

[269] *cf Arthur White (Contractors) Ltd v Tarmac Civil Engineering Ltd* [1967] 1 WLR 1508 (HL), 1518 (Lord Morris), 1528 (Lord Pearson). See also *Thompson v T Lohan (Plant Hire) Ltd* [1987] 1 WLR 649 (CA), 657–58 (Dillon LJ), 658 (Woolf LJ). *cf* n 196 (nature of cl 13 in the CPA standard form of contract).

[270] *Arthur White (Contractors) Ltd v Tarmac Civil Engineering Ltd* [1967] 1 WLR 1508 (HL), 1520.

[271] *KD Morris & Sons Pty Ltd v GJ Coles & Co Ltd* (1972) 132 CLR 88. *cf* also *Aberdeen Harbour Board v Heating Enterprises (Aberdeen) Ltd* 1990 SLT 416 (IH).

[272] See, eg, *EE Caledonia Ltd v Orbit Valve Co Europe* [1994] 1 WLR 1515 (CA), 1521 (Steyn LJ); *Ellington v Heinrich Constructions Pty Ltd* [2004] QCA 475; (2005) 13 ANZ Ins Cas 61-646, [21]–[23] (Chesterman J); *Erect Safe Scaffolding (Australia) Pty Ltd v Sutton* [2008] NSWCA 114; (2008) 72 NSWLR 1, [32] (Basten JA), [164]–[167] (McClellan CJ at CL). See generally [3–6] (use of internal context in construction) and [4–67]–[4–72]. *cf Westina Corp Pty Ltd v BGC Contracting Pty Ltd* [2009] WASCA 213; (2009) 41 WAR 263, [75]–[77] (Buss JA).

[273] See [4–74].

[274] See, eg, *Erect Safe Scaffolding (Australia) Pty Ltd v Sutton* [2008] NSWCA 114; (2008) 72 NSWLR 1, [32] (Basten JA), [166]–[167] (McClellan CJ at CL). Contrast, eg, *NSW Arabian Horse Association Inc v Olympic Co-ordination Authority* [2005] NSWCA 210, [34]–[38] (Santow JA).

promises to indemnify and to insure against the same risks, which are then specified in the remainder of the clause. The commercial rationale is usually that the insurance supports the contractual indemnity, either by allowing the indemnifier to call upon it in order to meet its obligation to the indemnified party, or by allowing the indemnified party to call upon it when the indemnifier fails to perform the indemnity.

Where the two clauses coincide to some degree, a question may still arise as to their relative extent. In *Buller Ski Lifts Ltd v Mt Buller Alpine Resort Management Board*,[275] the Board claimed indemnity from a ski lift operator in reliance upon indemnity and insurance clauses in a lease between them. The circumstances were held to be beyond the scope of the indemnity. The insurance clause was stated to apply '[w]ithout in any way limiting the liability' of the operator under the indemnity clause. It required the operator to take out a 'separate and distinct' policy of public liability insurance in the name of the Board. The clause continued: 'whereby the [Board] . . . shall . . . be indemnified against all actions, suits, claims . . . mentioned or referred to' in the indemnity clause. The Victorian Court of Appeal held that those words limited the scope of the insurance clause to that of the indemnity clause. The provision for insurance was intended to address the possibility of the operator's insolvency or some other obstacle that prevented the operator from satisfying a claim by the Board under the indemnity clause.[276]

[4–66] Clauses are not co-extensive. The scope of the indemnity clause and the scope of the insurance or risk clause may coincide to some degree, or they may be disjoint. There are three common reasons for disjunction: loss covered by one clause is expressly excluded from the scope of another;[277] loss covered by one clause is impliedly excluded from the scope of another;[278] or the clauses have different spheres of operation.[279] The last two possibilities are in substance the same; the distinction reflects a difference in the process of construction. In cases of the second kind, the clauses might appear to coincide but, through construction, one is subordinated to the other by way of an exclusion from scope. In cases of the third kind, the clauses are not perceived to coincide.

[4–67] Express exclusion. An indemnity clause may expressly exclude losses covered by an insurance or risk clause. There may remain a question as to the scope of the insurance or risk clause and thus the corresponding extent of the exception to the indemnity. Examples can be found in decisions on standard form construction contracts, where the point has arisen in relation to losses caused by the negligence of the indemnifier, usually the contractor, or those for whom it is responsible. A tension arises from opposing commercial considerations. There is the typical reluctance to absolve a party, in this instance the indemnifier, from the consequences of its own negligence. Yet, as the exclusion is connected to a separate insurance or risk clause, it may seem peculiar to require insurance against specified risks except insofar as they are caused by the indemnifier's negligence. In this context the *Canada SS* rules[280] are not particularly useful.[281]

---

[275] *Buller Ski Lifts Ltd v Mt Buller Alpine Resort Management Board* [2000] VSCA 31. See also, eg, *Steele v Twin City Rigging Pty Ltd* (1992) 114 FLR 99 (ACTSC), 112–14.
[276] *Buller Ski Lifts Ltd v Mt Buller Alpine Resort Management Board* [2000] VSCA 31, [16] (Phillips JA).
[277] See [4–67].
[278] See [4–68].
[279] See [4–73].
[280] *Canada Steamship Lines Ltd v R* [1952] AC 192 (PC), 208. See [4–47].
[281] See, eg, *James Archdale & Co Ltd v Comservices Ltd* [1954] 1 WLR 459 (CA), 461–62 (Somervell LJ); *GD Construction (St Albans) Ltd v Scottish & Newcastle plc* [2003] EWCA Civ 16; [2003] BLR 131, [57] (Longmore LJ).

Where the scope of the indemnity is defined in terms of loss arising from the indemni-fier's negligence, and the risks specified in the risk or insurance clause include those which might arise from such negligence, then loss by negligence is generally within the latter pro-vision and so excluded from the indemnity.[282] In *James Archdale & Co Ltd v Comservices Ltd*,[283] the contractor promised to insure and to indemnify the employer against losses or liabilities in respect of damage to any property due to negligence or default of the contrac-tor or its employees. That clause was expressly made subject to clause 15 insofar as it related to fire risks. Clause 15(b) stated that the existing structures and works were at the 'sole risk' of the employer as regards loss or damage by fire, and that the employer was to insure against the risk. The employer's building and machinery were damaged in a fire caused by the negligence of the contractor's employees. It was held that the loss was within clause 15(b) and so excluded from the scope of the indemnity.

[4–68] Where there is a possible coincidence. The relationship between the indemnity clause and the insurance or risk clause may be left undefined by the express terms of the contract. Whether there is a possibility of coincidence and, if so, the manner in which the clauses are reconciled, are questions of construction. Relevant considerations include the nature of the loss that is the subject of the overlap; whether the other clause is a risk clause, an insurance clause, or a combination of both; and, if it is an insurance clause, the form of the insurance.[284]

Where there is a potential intersection with an indemnity clause, risk clauses and insurance clauses cannot necessarily be treated in the same manner. A clause stating that one party will bear the 'sole risk' of a particular eventuality is prima facie inconsistent with a clause under which that party is to be indemnified by another against that risk. In the absence of any express provision, the clauses might be reconciled on the basis that the risk clause qualifies the scope of the indemnity. The same conflict need not arise between an indemnity clause and an insurance clause. In *Surrey Heath Borough Council v Lovell Construction Ltd*,[285] Dillon LJ explained:

> The effect of the contractual agreement must always be a matter of construction . . . It may be the true construction that a provision for insurance is to be taken as satisfying or curtailing a contrac-tual obligation, or it may be the true construction that a contractual obligation is to be backed by insurance with the result that the contractual obligation stands or is enforceable even if for some reason the insurance fails or proves inadequate.

Where the scope of the insurance coincides with the scope of the indemnity, one may oper-ate as an implied exclusion from the other, or it may be that a loss can fall within both clauses. If both clauses are engaged in the circumstances, it may then become necessary to

---

[282] *James Archdale & Co Ltd v Comservices Ltd* [1954] 1 WLR 459 (CA); *Scottish Special Housing Association v Wimpey Construction UK Ltd* [1986] 1 WLR 995 (HL); *GD Construction (St Albans) Ltd v Scottish & Newcastle plc* [2003] EWCA Civ 16; [2003] BLR 131. See also *KD Morris & Sons Pty Ltd v GJ Coles & Co Ltd* (1972) 132 CLR 88, 94 (Gibbs J). cf *Norwich City Council v Harvey* [1989] 1 WLR 828 (CA) (equivalent drafting qualifying sub-contractor's duty of care to employer).

[283] *James Archdale & Co Ltd v Comservices Ltd* [1954] 1 WLR 459 (CA).

[284] See generally R Merkin and J Steele, *Insurance and the Law of Obligations* (New York, Oxford University Press, 2013), 182–86. See further [4–72] (co-insurance).

[285] *Surrey Heath Borough Council v Lovell Construction Ltd* (1990) 48 BLR 108 (CA), 121. See also *National Trust v Haden Young Ltd* (1994) 72 BLR 1 (CA), 10 (Nourse LJ). cf *Boughen v Frederick Attwood Ltd* [1978] 1 Lloyd's Rep 413 (QB), 416.

determine who, as between the indemnifier and the insurer, is to bear the loss.[286] Thus, the coincidence of the clauses may affect the ultimate extent of the indemnifier's or insurer's responsibility for a loss without affecting their original liability to the indemnified party/ insured for that loss.

As the relationship between the clauses is a matter of construction, no general rule can be identified. Some examples of different approaches are considered below.

[4–69] Construction contracts.[287] The point has proven controversial in a series of decisions on standard form construction contracts, which have lacked internal cross-referencing between the indemnity and the insurance or risk clause. The contractor's indemnity to the employer is usually expressed to protect the employer against the consequences of negligence by the contractor or others for whom it is responsible. The freestanding insurance or risk clause covers a range of risks, some of which might arise from the contractor's negligence, for example, loss or damage by fire.

The view has sometimes been taken that the freestanding insurance or risk clause should complement, rather than overlap with, the indemnity clause. That result might be achieved by construing the insurance or risk clause so as not to cover losses caused by the contractor's negligence.[288] The countervailing view has been that an ordinary policy of insurance against risks such as loss or damage by fire will protect against fire from a variety of causes, including negligent acts or omissions by a person such as the contractor.[289] An obligation to effect insurance should be interpreted accordingly. That construction accepts that the indemnity and insurance clauses may intersect.

[4–70] Leases. A lessee's negligence may cause damage to the premises, for example, by fire. Assuming that there is an insurance policy in favour of the landlord that covers that risk, the question is whether the policy should operate to relieve the lessee from any responsibility to the landlord and, by extension, an insurer exercising a right of subrogation.[290] The cases have generally approached the question in broad terms, and not specifically by reference to the operation of a contractual indemnity.[291] Whether the lessee is relieved of responsibility is probably best regarded as an inference derived through construction of the lease, though it is sometimes approached as an implied term.[292] The following factors may favour exoneration:[293] (1) an obligation upon the landlord or lessee to insure; (2) an obligation

---

[286] See [4–74].

[287] See generally Merkin and Steele, *Insurance and the Law of Obligations* (n 204), 194–200.

[288] See further [4–73]. cf *Casson v Ostley PJ Ltd* [2001] EWCA Civ 1013; [2003] BLR 147 (no indemnity from contractor but risk and insurance clause still construed to exclude contractor's negligence).

[289] *National Trust v Haden Young Ltd* (1994) 72 BLR 1 (CA), 10–11 (Nourse LJ); *GD Construction (St Albans) Ltd v Scottish & Newcastle plc* [2003] EWCA Civ 16; [2003] BLR 131, [39] (Aikens J), [59] (Longmore LJ) though cf [58]. This view is by no means modern: *Shaw v Robberds* (1837) 6 Ad & E 75, 84; 112 ER 29, 33. See generally *Surrey Heath Borough Council v Lovell Construction Ltd* (1990) 48 BLR 108 (CA), 120–21 (Dillon LJ).

[290] cf *Wisma Development Pte Ltd v Sing – The Disc Shop Pte Ltd* [1994] SGCA 43; [1994] 1 SLR(R) 749 where the positions of the parties were reversed.

[291] Though an indemnity obligation was present in the lease in *Bit Badger Pty Ltd v Cunich* [1997] 1 Qd R 136 (SC).

[292] In New Zealand, the matter is now the subject of statute: see Property Law Act 2007 (NZ), ss 268–70, esp s 269(1)(b) (lessee cannot be required to indemnify landlord against reinstatement costs).

[293] *Mark Rowlands Ltd v Berni Inns Ltd* [1986] QB 211 (CA). See also *Agnew-Surpass Shoe Stores Ltd v Cummer-Yonge Investments Ltd* [1976] 2 SCR 221; *Ross Southward Tire Ltd v Pyrotech Products Ltd* [1976] 2 SCR 35; *T Eaton Co Ltd v Smith* [1978] 2 SCR 749; *Marlborough Properties Ltd v Marlborough Fibreglass Ltd* [1981] 1 NZLR 464 (CA). cf *National Oilwell (UK) Ltd v Davy Offshore Ltd* [1993] 2 Lloyd's Rep 582 (QB), 606 (similar criteria applied to contract to supply subsea wellhead system).

upon the lessee to pay or contribute towards the premiums; (3) the damage that occurred is excepted from any general obligation of the lessee to repair the premises; and (4) a provision for the proceeds of insurance to be applied to reinstate the premises. None of these factors is alone decisive,[294] though the first factor is usually regarded as essential.[295]

[4–71] Benefit of P&I insurance to charterer. In *Canadian Transport Co Ltd v Court Line Ltd*,[296] the charterer's failure to stow cargo properly rendered the owner of the vessel liable for the damage to receivers under certain bills of lading. The owner was indemnified by its P&I club and then claimed against the charterer, one ground of claim being an implied indemnity against the liability.[297] There was, however, another term under which the owner purported to give to the charterer 'the benefit of their Protection and Indemnity Club Insurances as far as club rules allow'. On the assumption that the term could confer some benefit upon the charterer (which, in fact, it could not do according to the club rules) Lord Atkin and Lord Wright held that the term did not limit the scope of the charterer's indemnity to the owner.[298] The term could, however, prevent a subrogated action by the P&I insurer. The basis of that view is not entirely clear but it seems to have been that the charterer would have had a defence for the avoidance of circuity of action.

[4–72] Effect of co-insurance. An insurance clause may require one of the parties to procure insurance in the 'joint names' of the contracting parties and perhaps also others involved in the contractual venture. The practical effect may be to bar or restrict claims between those parties in relation to the loss that is the subject of the co-insurance. This result may derive from the contract of insurance itself. The contract may contain an express waiver of rights of subrogation or an implied term to similar effect.[299] Alternatively, an insurer who pays one co-insured may be prevented from enforcing a subrogated claim against another co-insured, for the avoidance of circuity of action.[300]

A requirement to obtain joint names insurance may also directly affect the construction of other terms of the principal contract,[301] particularly indemnity clauses. This is significant because the relevant claim may not be a subrogated one brought by the insurer, or, for various reasons, the potential defendant may not be protected by the policy. In *Co-operative Retail Services Ltd v Taylor Young Partnership*,[302] the indemnity from the contractor to the

---

[294] See, eg, *Marlborough Properties Ltd v Marlborough Fibreglass Ltd* [1981] 1 NZLR 464 (CA) (factors (1), (2) and (4) present, potential difficulty with element (3) overridden); *Leisure Centre Ltd v Babytown Ltd* [1984] 1 NZLR 318 (CA) (elements (1) and (4) present but insufficient); *Bit Badger Pty Ltd v Cunich* [1997] 1 Qd R 136 (SC) (element (2) present but insufficient).

[295] See, eg, *T Eaton Co Ltd v Smith* [1978] 2 SCR 749, 754 (Laskin CJ). Contrast *Tsolon Investments Pty Ltd v Waffle Pod Footing Systems NSW Pty Ltd* [2002] NSWCA 302.

[296] *Canadian Transport Co Ltd v Court Line Ltd* [1940] AC 934 (HL).

[297] As to the nature of that indemnity, see [4–53], [4–60].

[298] *Canadian Transport Co Ltd v Court Line Ltd* [1940] AC 934 (HL), 939 (Lord Atkin), 946 (Lord Wright), *cf* 952–53 (Lord Porter).

[299] *National Oilwell (UK) Ltd v Davy Offshore Ltd* [1993] 2 Lloyd's Rep 582 (QB), 613–14; *Co-operative Retail Services Ltd v Taylor Young Partnership* [2002] UKHL 17; [2002] 1 WLR 1419, [64]–[65] (Lord Hope); *Tyco Fire & Integrated Solutions (UK) Ltd v Rolls-Royce Motor Cars Ltd* [2008] EWCA Civ 286; [2008] BLR 285, [75]–[76] (Rix LJ). *cf Buller Ski Lifts Ltd v Mt Buller Alpine Resort Management Board* [2000] VSCA 31, [23] (Phillips JA).

[300] *Petrofina (UK) Ltd v Magnaload Ltd* [1984] 1 QB 127 (QB), 139–40. See also *Co-operative Bulk Handling Ltd v Jennings Industries Ltd* (1996) 17 WAR 257 (FC), 275–76 (Franklyn J).

[301] *cf British Telecommunications plc v James Thomson & Sons (Engineers) Ltd* [1999] 1 WLR 9 (HL), 15–16 (Lord Mackay) (effect on sub-contractor's duty of care to employer).

[302] *Co-operative Retail Services Ltd v Taylor Young Partnership* [2002] UKHL 17; [2002] 1 WLR 1419. See also *GD Construction (St Albans) Ltd v Scottish & Newcastle plc* [2003] EWCA Civ 16; [2003] BLR 131.

employer in clause 20.2 covered losses due to the contractor's negligence. By clause 20.3, risks to the works and site materials were expressly excluded from the scope of the indemnity in clause 20.2. The contractor was required by clause 22A to obtain joint names insurance in respect of such risks, though there was no express cross-reference between clause 22A and the indemnity in clause 20.2. Clause 22A also set out a detailed scheme for the reinstatement of damaged works, to be paid for using the proceeds of the insurance. The works were damaged by fire, it was assumed, due to the negligence of the contractor and others. The House of Lords held that the contractor was not liable to the employer for the loss.

The position in *Co-operative Retail Services* was made abundantly clear by the combined effect of the express exclusion from the scope of the indemnity, and the detailed provisions relating to the joint names insurance. Where there is no express exclusion from the scope of the indemnity, the existence of a provision for joint names insurance may lend support to an inferred exclusion for the insured risks. The rationale is that the parties, by requiring joint names insurance, have indicated that 'matters are to be settled between them not on the basis of liability and litigation, but on the basis of an insurance funded solution'.[303] There is, however, no overriding legal principle that losses within the scope of joint names insurance arrangements must be excluded from the scope of a contractual indemnity.[304]

[4–73] **Different spheres of operation.** Indemnity and insurance or risk clauses may be construed to be distinct and complementary, in the sense that each is intended to cover a different risk in the contractual venture. This perspective has been adopted in some of the decisions on standard form construction contracts, where there has been no express indication of the relationship between the two types of clause.[305] One basis of demarcation is the contractor's negligence.[306] The indemnity clause is often expressed to cover losses due to the negligence of the contractor or others for whom it is responsible. The insurance or risk clause may then, accordingly, be construed to cover losses not due to such negligence.

Colliers Jardine Pty Ltd v Castle Mall Properties Pte Ltd[307] provides a different illustration. The manager of a shopping mall successfully defended a claim in negligence by a person injured on the premises and then claimed the costs of its defence from the owner of the mall under an indemnity in a contract between them. The indemnity covered claims, actions and losses 'for which the Manager in the course of properly performing its duties hereunder may render itself legally liable'. The indemnity was held not to apply. A significant consideration was that another term of the contract required the owner to maintain, at

---

[303] *Tyco Fire & Integrated Solutions (UK) Ltd v Rolls-Royce Motor Cars Ltd* [2008] EWCA Civ 286; [2008] BLR 285, [78] (Rix LJ). See also *Talbot Underwriting Ltd v Nausch, Hogan & Murray Inc (The Jascon 5)* [2006] EWCA Civ 889; [2006] 2 Lloyd's Rep 195, [55] (Moore-Bick LJ).

[304] *Surrey Heath Borough Council v Lovell Construction Ltd* (1990) 48 BLR 108 (CA), 120–21 (Dillon LJ); *Co-operative Retail Services Ltd v Taylor Young Partnership* [2002] UKHL 17; [2002] 1 WLR 1419, [43]–[45], [65] (Lord Hope); *GD Construction (St Albans) Ltd v Scottish & Newcastle plc* [2003] EWCA Civ 16; [2003] BLR 131, [54] (Aikens J), [60] (Longmore LJ); *Tyco Fire & Integrated Solutions (UK) Ltd v Rolls-Royce Motor Cars Ltd* [2008] EWCA Civ 286; [2008] BLR 285, [77]–[80] (Rix LJ).

[305] cf *Buckinghamshire County Council v James Lovell & Sons Ltd* [1956] JPL 196 (QB); *Dorset County Council v Southern Felt Roofing Co Ltd* (1989) 48 BLR 96 (CA); *London Borough of Barking & Dagenham v Stamford Asphalt Co Ltd* (1997) 82 BLR 25 (CA), 33–36 (Auld LJ); *GD Construction (St Albans) Ltd v Scottish & Newcastle plc* [2003] EWCA Civ 16; [2003] BLR 131, [58] (Longmore LJ); *Tyco Fire & Integrated Solutions (UK) Ltd v Rolls-Royce Motor Cars Ltd* [2008] EWCA Civ 286; [2008] BLR 285, [69] (Rix LJ).

[306] Contrast *Dorset County Council v Southern Felt Roofing Co Ltd* (1989) 48 BLR 96 (CA) (division between claims by third parties and damage to employer's property).

[307] *Colliers Jardine Pty Ltd v Castle Mall Properties Pte Ltd* [2005] NSWCA 311.

its expense, a policy of public liability insurance which included the manager as an insured. The structure of the agreement indicated that the parties intended the manager's legal costs to be covered by the insurance policy, not the indemnity.[308]

Ultimate Responsibility for Loss

[4–74] **Whether indemnifier or insurer ultimately responsible.** If a loss is covered by an insurance policy and a contractual indemnity, there arises the further question of who, as between the insurer and indemnifier, is ultimately to bear the burden of the loss. One of them may pay the insured/indemnified party and then purport to exercise a right of subrogation to recover from the other.

In contracts for services, the contractual indemnifier's responsibility is usually regarded as primary and the insurer's responsibility as secondary; thus the burden of the loss ultimately falls upon the indemnifier.[309] The leading decision is *Caledonia North Sea Ltd v British Telecommunications plc (The Piper Alpha)*.[310] An explosion on an oil platform resulted in many deaths, including that of an employee of the contractor. A claim in respect of that death was settled by the platform operator, who was indemnified by its insurers. The insurers then brought a subrogated claim against the contractor, relying on an indemnity clause in the contract between the contractor and operator. The subrogated claim was upheld on the basis that the contractor's indemnity was the primary liability and the operator's insurance was, from the contractor's perspective, *res inter alios acta*.

This arrangement of relative responsibility is not invariable and it may be altered by contract.[311] In *The Piper Alpha*, Lord Mackay and Lord Hoffmann each pointed out that the operator was under no contractual obligation to obtain its own insurance.[312] The existence of such an obligation might have provided some support for the view that the insurance was not secondary. In this respect, the nature of the insurance to be obtained and provisions for the application of any proceeds are relevant considerations.[313] Lord Hoffmann added that the parties could, theoretically, have drafted the indemnity to apply only to the extent that the operator did not recover from insurance.[314]

---

[308] *Colliers Jardine Pty Ltd v Castle Mall Properties Pte Ltd* [2005] NSWCA 311, [34]–[35] (Tobias JA).

[309] *Speno Rail Maintenance Australia Pty Ltd v Hamersley Iron Pty Ltd* [2000] WASCA 408; (2000) 23 WAR 291; *Caledonia North Sea Ltd v British Telecommunications plc (The Piper Alpha)* [2002] UKHL 4; [2002] 1 Lloyd's Rep 553; *HIH Claims Support Ltd v Insurance Australia Ltd* [2011] HCA 31; (2011) 244 CLR 72, [40] (Gummow ACJ, Hayne, Crennan and Kiefel JJ). *cf Speno Rail Maintenance Australia Pty Ltd v Metals & Minerals Insurance Pte Ltd* [2009] WASCA 31; (2009) 253 ALR 364, [239]–[245] (Beech AJA) (effect of merger in judgment). Examples of other contracts are noted at [4–39].

[310] *Caledonia North Sea Ltd v British Telecommunications plc (The Piper Alpha)* [2002] UKHL 4; [2002] 1 Lloyd's Rep 553.

[311] *Speno Rail Maintenance Australia Pty Ltd v Hamersley Iron Pty Ltd* [2000] WASCA 408; (2000) 23 WAR 291, [168] (Wheeler J).

[312] *Caledonia North Sea Ltd v British Telecommunications plc (The Piper Alpha)* [2002] UKHL 4; [2002] 1 Lloyd's Rep 553, [55] (Lord Hope), [97] (Lord Hoffmann).

[313] *cf* [4–70], [4–72].

[314] *cf National Trust v Haden Young Ltd* (1994) 72 BLR 1 (CA), 10 (Nourse LJ); *Tyco Fire & Integrated Solutions (UK) Ltd v Rolls-Royce Motor Cars Ltd* [2008] EWCA Civ 286; [2008] BLR 285, [79] (Rix LJ). *cf* also the treatment of the insurance proceeds in *Goulston Discount Co Ltd v Sims* (1967) 111 SJ 682 (CA).

Costs

[4–75] Costs determined by scope of indemnity. Whether the indemnified party's legal costs are recoverable under the contract is generally determined by the scope of the indemnity.[315] The matter is, therefore, one of construction. Costs may be incurred by the indemnified party in different contexts. Not all legal costs relate to actual or anticipated legal proceedings. Where they are so incurred, the indemnified party may be pursuing or defending a claim; those proceedings may involve a third party or the indemnifier; the proceedings may be at first instance or on appeal; on any of these permutations, the outcome of the proceedings may be favourable or adverse to the indemnified party. Where costs are an included head of loss, the costs incurred must satisfy all other elements in the definition of the scope of the indemnity. Thus, it is an over-generalisation to say that 'in all cases' the indemnified party can recover for the costs of legal proceedings, properly incurred.[316]

[4–76] Implied inclusion of costs. In the absence of an express reference to 'costs', legal costs may be included by implication within the scope of the indemnity. This is seen most clearly where the indemnity contemplates claims by or liabilities to third parties. The costs of the indemnified party's defence of an action are often recoverable even when not mentioned expressly.[317] The rationale is, presumably, that the indemnified party ought reasonably to test or challenge the third party's claim and not simply capitulate to every demand. A reasonable defence enures to the benefit of the indemnifier also, as it may reduce or invalidate the alleged liability that is the subject of the indemnity. Legal costs incurred in defending actions by third parties are not, however, always included by implication.[318]

[4–77] Limitation to costs reasonably or properly incurred. The scope of the indemnity is generally limited to legal costs that have been reasonably or properly incurred.[319] The content of that requirement is difficult to state in general terms, though relevant considerations may

---

[315] Contrast *The Millwall* [1905] P 155 (CA), 175 (Collins MR) (subsequent contract related to contract of indemnity).

[316] As does *Halsbury's Laws of England*, 5th edn (London, LexisNexis, 2008), vol 49, para 1265.

[317] *Howard v Lovegrove* (1870) LR 6 Exch 43; *The Millwall* [1905] P 155 (CA), 174–75 (Collins MR); *Williams v Lister & Co* (1913) 109 LT 699 (CA); *Re Famatina Development Corp Ltd* [1914] 2 Ch 271 (CA); *Richardson v Buckinghamshire City Council* [1971] 1 Lloyd's Rep 533 (CA), 536 (Buckley LJ); *Wenpac Pty Ltd v Allied Westralian Finance Ltd* (1994) 123 FLR 1 (WASC), 67–68; *Tempo Services Ltd v State of New South Wales* [2004] NSWCA 4, [21] (Hodgson JA); *National Roads and Motorists' Association Ltd v Whitlam* [2007] NSWCA 81; (2007) 25 ACLC 688, [74] (Campbell JA).

[318] *Link Investments Pty Ltd v Zaraba Pty Ltd* [2001] NSWCA 14 (costs of successful defence not included because indemnity limited to actual liabilities); *Colliers Jardine Pty Ltd v Castle Mall Properties Pte Ltd* [2005] NSWCA 311, [34]–[35] (costs of successful defence intended to be covered by liability insurance policy). cf *Tomlinson v Adamson* 1935 SC (HL) 1 (action against indemnified party not sufficiently connected with his role as director of the indemnifying company). Contrast *The Millwall* [1905] P 155 (CA), 176 (Cozens-Hardy LJ).

[319] *Gillett v Rippon* (1829) M & M 406; 173 ER 1204; *Smith v Howell* (1851) 6 Ex 730; 155 ER 739; *Born v Turner* [1900] 2 Ch 211 (Ch), 217; *Hooper v Bromet* (1904) 90 LT 234 (CA), 238 (Vaughan Williams LJ); *The Millwall* [1905] P 155 (CA), 174–75 (Collins MR); *Hornby v Cardwell* (1881) 8 QBD 329 (CA), 337 (Brett LJ); *Wenpac Pty Ltd v Allied Westralian Finance Ltd* (1994) 123 FLR 1 (WASC), 68; *State of New South Wales v Tempo Services Ltd* [2004] NSWCA 4, [21] (Hodgson JA); *Ringrow Pty Ltd v BP Australia Pty Ltd* [2006] FCA 1446, [84], [86]; *National Roads and Motorists' Association Ltd v Whitlam* [2007] NSWCA 81; (2007) 25 ACLC 688, [74]–[77] (Campbell JA). See generally *Wallersteiner v Moir (No 2)* [1975] QB 373 (CA), 403 (Buckley LJ).

include:[320] the principal subject-matter of the indemnity; its relationship with the legal work for which costs are claimed; whether such work was reasonably necessary or contemplated; the rates charged for the work; and, in the event of litigation, the apparent prospects of success of the indemnified party's defence or claim. It has been said, for example, that the indemnified party might be expected to raise any defence that the indemnifier itself would raise if it were controlling the defence.[321] An indemnity will not necessarily extend to the costs of an appeal from a decision at first instance.[322]

[4–78] Basis of assessment. Subject to statute and public policy,[323] a contractual provision as to costs will be given effect. At general law, a simple agreement to pay costs has usually been interpreted to mean costs on the standard or party-party basis.[324] Where, however, the contract expressly uses the terms 'indemnify' or 'indemnity' in connection with 'costs', this is generally understood as full or whole costs, subject to considerations of reasonableness.[325] Thus, the measure has been described in terms of costs as between solicitor and the indemnified party as client (a solicitor-own client basis) or costs on an indemnity basis.[326] The purport of those expressions seems to be substantially the same in this context.[327]

[4–79] Relationship with curial discretion as to costs. Where the indemnifier and indemnified party are parties to the same proceedings, the question of costs can be dealt with as a matter of curial discretion. The curial discretion to award costs stands independently of a contractual right to indemnity against costs, but it is, ordinarily, exercised in conformity with that contractual right.[328] It may be necessary to translate the scope of the indemnity into a basis of assessment recognised by the applicable costs rules.[329] Where there is no basis

---

[320] See, eg, *Black v ASB Bank Ltd* [2012] NZCA 384, [80].
[321] *Hooper v Bromet* (1904) 90 LT 234 (CA), 238 (Vaughan Williams LJ). *cf The Millwall* [1905] P 155 (CA), 174–75 (Collins MR).
[322] *Maxwell v British Thomson Houston Co Ltd* [1904] 2 KB 342 (KB). The decision could be put on the basis that the scope of the indemnity did not extend to the costs of an appeal, or on the basis that it was unreasonable to pursue the (unsuccessful) appeal.
[323] See generally *ANZ Banking Group (NZ) Ltd v Gibson* [1986] 1 NZLR 556 (CA), 566 (Richardson J); *Hawkins v Permarig Pty Ltd* [2004] QCA 76; [2004] 2 Qd R 388, [17]–[18] (McPherson JA); *Laverty v Para Franchising Ltd* [2006] 1 NZLR 650 (CA), [45]–[47].
[324] See, eg, *Re Adelphi Hotel (Brighton) Ltd* [1953] 1 WLR 955 (Ch), 961 (agreement adopting another basis must be 'plainly and unambiguously expressed'); *Chen v Kevin McNamara & Son Pty Ltd (No 2)* [2012] VSCA 229, [8], [20] (Redlich JA). *cf* CPR, r 44.5 (presumed basis for contractual entitlement to costs).
[325] Contrast *Maxwell v British Thomson Houston Co Ltd* [1904] 2 KB 342 (KB), 344; *Kheirs Financial Services Pty Ltd v Aussie Home Loans Pty Ltd* [2010] VSCA 355, [119].
[326] *Howard v Lovegrove* (1870) LR 6 Exch 43, 44–45 (Kelly CB); *Born v Turner* [1900] 2 Ch 211 (Ch), 217; *Great Western Railway Co v Fisher* [1905] 1 Ch 316 (Ch), 324–25; *Williams v Lister & Co* (1913) 109 LT 699 (CA); *Simpson and Miller v British Industries Trust Ltd* (1923) 39 TLR 286 (KB) (defence of action by third party, but only party-party costs for action against indemnifier); *The Riverman* [1928] P 33 (P), 40; *Abigroup Ltd v Sandtara Pty Ltd* [2002] NSWCA 45, [17] (Stein JA); *National Roads and Motorists' Association Ltd v Whitlam* [2007] NSWCA 81; (2007) 25 ACLC 688, [77] (Campbell JA); *Watson & Son Ltd v Active Manuka Honey Association* [2009] NZCA 595, [22]–[25]; *Chen v Kevin McNamara & Son Pty Ltd (No 2)* [2012] VSCA 229, [13] (Redlich JA).
[327] *EMI Records Ltd v Ian Cameron Wallace Ltd* [1983] Ch 59 (Ch), 65, 71; *Macquarie International Health Clinic Pty Ltd v Sydney South West Area Health Service (No 3)* [2010] NSWSC 1139, [11]. Contrast *Taree Pty Ltd v Bob Jane Corp Pty Ltd* [2008] VSC 228, [36]–[37].
[328] See generally *Gomba Holdings (UK) Ltd v Minores Finance Ltd (No 2)* [1993] Ch 171 (CA), 194 (Scott LJ); *Abigroup Ltd v Sandtara Pty Ltd* [2002] NSWCA 45, [8]–[9] (Stein JA); *Venture Finance plc v Mead* [2005] EWCA Civ 325; [2006] 3 Costs LR 389, [22] (Chadwick LJ); *Platinum United II Pty Ltd v Secured Mortgage Management Ltd (in liq)* [2011] QCA 229; *Chen v Kevin McNamara & Son Pty Ltd (No 2)* [2012] VSCA 229, [8] Redlich JA).
[329] See, eg, *AstraZeneca UK Ltd v IBM Corp* [2011] EWHC 3373 (TCC), [40], [45]. See generally CPR, rr 44.3, 44.4.

that corresponds precisely to the indemnity, the most closely analogous basis may be adopted.[330]

An order as to costs does not usually raise any question of *res judicata* or estoppel in respect of the indemnified party's contractual entitlement; one reason is that the accumulation of costs under the indemnity only becomes complete at the conclusion of the proceedings.[331] Thus, the fact that costs have been awarded in the exercise of the curial discretion does not necessarily prevent the indemnifier bringing a later action on the indemnity for outstanding costs on a different, and more favourable, basis.[332]

---

[330] *Macquarie International Health Clinic Pty Ltd v Sydney South West Area Health Service (No 3)* [2010] NSWSC 1139, [28], [32]–[37]. *cf Taree Pty Ltd v Bob Jane Corp Pty Ltd* [2008] VSC 228, [47]–[48] (discretion not exercised where conflicting contractual provisions as to basis of assessment).

[331] *Abigroup Ltd v Sandtara Pty Ltd* [2002] NSWCA 45, [10]–[11] (Stein JA); *John v Price Waterhouse* [2002] 1 WLR 953 (Ch), 959. Contrast *Taree Pty Ltd v Bob Jane Corp Pty Ltd* [2008] VSC 228, [60].

[332] *Barnett v Eccles Corp* [1900] 2 QB 423 (CA), 428 (Vaughan Williams LJ); *Abigroup Ltd v Sandtara Pty Ltd* [2002] NSWCA 45; *John v Price Waterhouse* [2002] 1 WLR 953 (Ch), 961–62; *Boman Irani Pty Ltd v St George Bank Ltd* [2008] VSCA 246; (2008) 22 VR 135, [62]–[63] (Hargrave AJA).

5

Enforcement

Introduction

[5–1] Purpose of chapter. This chapter examines the enforcement of promises of indemnity in respect of an actual or potential loss to the indemnified party. The manner in which an indemnity is enforced depends on several factors including: the nature of the indemnity promise; whether the loss is within the scope of the indemnity; and whether the loss has actually occurred or is merely anticipated. The first two of those factors have already been considered in general terms,[1] but in this chapter they are considered specifically in relation to enforcement of the indemnity. The chapter also considers the third factor.

[5–2] Structure of chapter. The chapter begins by examining restrictions on enforcement. Formal requirements are considered. Other restrictions may arise because the indemnified party has not complied with another term of the contract. The term may be a condition precedent to performance or enforcement of the indemnity, or a promissory term that has been breached by the indemnified party in such a way as to entitle the indemnifier to terminate the contract. Other limitations apply where the indemnified party's conduct adversely affects the extent of the indemnifier's responsibility for loss within the scope of the indemnity. The remainder of the chapter considers the enforcement of indemnities in respect of actual and potential losses, and also the use of declaratory relief to determine the rights of the indemnifier and indemnified party.

[5–3] Summary of chapter. The main propositions advanced in this chapter can be summarised as follows.

(1) The indemnified party generally has a right to recover a sum corresponding to the amount of a loss:

    (a) where the indemnified party has actually sustained that loss;
    (b) the loss is within the scope of the indemnity; and
    (c) there is no bar to enforcement of the indemnity.

(2) The indemnified party may obtain relief in respect of a loss:

    (a) where the loss remains potential only;
    (b) the loss is within the scope of the indemnity;
    (c) the circumstances (in particular, the nature of the indemnity and the nature of the loss) justify the award of relief; and
    (d) there is no bar to enforcement of the indemnity.

---

[1] See ch 2 and ch 4.

(3) Whether an indemnified party can recover for a loss that is beyond the scope of the indemnity depends on the construction of the contract. If recovery is possible at all, the conditions appear to be:

(a) that the loss has actually occurred;

(b) that the indemnity has been activated by some other loss within the scope of the indemnity; and

(c) that the loss that is beyond scope satisfies other legal principles applicable to a claim for damages for breach of the contract of indemnity.

Restrictions on Enforcement

Formal Requirements

The Statute of Frauds

[5–4] Statute of Frauds not applicable.[2] In contemporary language, section 4 of the Statute of Frauds 1677 provides that no action shall be brought on any 'special promise to answer for the debt, default or miscarriages of another person'. Derivative provisions exist in various jurisdictions around the Commonwealth.[3]

Where the indemnified party's loss has no connection with a third party's default then, clearly, the statute is irrelevant. A more difficult question, which has sometimes arisen, is whether section 4 applies to promises of indemnity where the relevant loss or liability of the indemnified party might be triggered by the default of a third party. The modern position can be stated shortly. Section 4 generally does not apply to promises of indemnity, even though the loss or liability may arise from a default by a third party, and even though the loss might be the indemnified party's failure to receive performance from that party.[4] This distinction between guarantees and indemnities is not entirely satisfactory as a matter of logic or policy.

[5–5] Liability associated with another's default. Some forms of indemnity are properly outside the scope of section 4 of the Statute of Frauds 1677. In one line of cases, A promised to protect B against a liability to C, the liability often being assumed by B at A's request and arising upon the default of another, D, in performing some obligation owed to C.[5] These

---

[2] For a thorough review of the position in the United States, see AL Corbin, 'Contracts of Indemnity and the Statute of Frauds' (1928) 41 *Harvard Law Review* 689; AL Corbin, *Corbin on Contracts*, vol 4 (St Paul's, MN, JM Perillo ed, revised edn, Lexis Law Publishing, 1997), 368–85, §§16.16–16.18.

[3] *cf* Property Law Act 1974 (Qld), s 56, which refers to a 'promise to guarantee any liability of another'.

[4] For statements in general terms, see *Re Hoyle; Hoyle v Hoyle* [1893] 1 Ch 84 (CA), 97 (Lindley LJ), 99 (Bowen LJ); *Sutton & Co v Grey* [1894] 1 QB 285 (CA), 287 (Lord Esher MR); *Clipper Maritime Ltd v Shirlstar Container Transport Ltd (The Anemone)* [1987] 1 Lloyd's Rep 546 (QB); *Sunbird Plaza Pty Ltd v Maloney* (1988) 166 CLR 245, 254 (Mason CJ); *Pitts v Jones* [2007] EWCA Civ 1301; [2008] QB 706, [21] (Smith LJ); *Associated British Ports v Ferryways NV* [2009] EWCA Civ 189; [2009] 1 Lloyd's Rep 595, [1] (Kay LJ); *WS Tankship II BV v Kwangju Bank Ltd* [2011] EWHC 3103 (Comm), [151]. For more specific statements in relation to liabilities arising from a third party's default, see n 6.

[5] *Thomas v Cook* (1828) 8 B & C 728; 108 ER 1213; *Wildes v Dudlow* (1874) LR 19 Eq 198; *Re Bolton* (1892) 8 TLR 668 (Ch); *Guild & Co v Conrad* [1894] 2 QB 885 (CA).

were regarded as 'indemnity' cases;[6] more particularly, they were instances of indemnity against liability. In one sense, it can be seen why such promises might have been thought to be within the statute. The indemnifier's obligation could be activated by another's default, and section 4 does not say to whom the promisor is to be answerable. It was, however, established that section 4 applies to promises made to the *creditor* in respect of another's obligations.[7] In these indemnity cases, B was a debtor vis-à-vis C, not a creditor of C; the distinction was critical.[8]

This is not quite a full explanation. Where B is responsible to C for D's obligations, there may be an associated obligation of D to B in respect of B's liability to C. So, for example, D as debtor may be liable to indemnify or reimburse B as guarantor in respect of sums payable or paid to C. From that perspective, A's promise to B could potentially be regarded as a promise to a creditor vis-à-vis D.[9] That view is, however, generally not adopted.[10] The subject-matter of the indemnity is characterised as a liability to C, rather than a loss due to default by D vis-à-vis B. It follows that B's right to enforce the indemnity is independent of D's performance or default. A's promise is to indemnify at all events; it is not a promise to answer for D's default, in terms of the statute.[11] It has also been suggested that the usual policy justification for the Statute of Frauds does not apply in these circumstances. There is relatively little danger of fraud. In many cases, the principal motive for B accepting responsibility for D's obligations is that B has been promised an indemnity by another person, A. Furthermore, it would be unjust to allow A, who induced B to accept that responsibility on the faith of a promise of indemnity, to escape liability on a technicality; indeed, this might encourage fraud.[12]

[5–6] Lost benefit of performance. The subject-matter of the indemnity may be loss suffered by the indemnified party as creditor due to the debtor's failure to perform obligations owed to the indemnified party. The analogy with guarantees is stronger here than in the liability cases. If the activating event is simply 'non-performance' by the debtor, the indemnity can be regarded as outside section 4 of the Statute of Frauds 1677 on the basis that it is, strictly, not dependent upon the debtor's default. Where the activating event is a default by the debtor, it is difficult to justify the distinction between guarantees and indemnities that is drawn for the purposes of the statute. That distinction is not obviously suggested by the language of section 4 itself, which refers only to a promise to 'answer for' a default. That expression might reasonably be understood to mean 'be responsible for the consequences of'.[13]

The fragility of the distinction is apparent when comparing *Sutton & Co v Grey*[14] and *Montagu Stanley & Co v JC Solomon Ltd.*[15] In each case, clients were introduced to brokers

---

[6] See, eg, *Guild & Co v Conrad* [1894] 2 QB 885 (CA), 893–94 (Lindley LJ), 895 (Lopes LJ), 896 (Davey LJ); *Harburg India Rubber Comb Co v Martin* [1902] 1 KB 778 (CA), 784–85 (Vaughan Williams LJ); *Davys v Buswell* [1913] 2 KB 47 (CA), 54–55 (Vaughan Williams LJ).

[7] *Eastwood v Kenyon* (1840) 11 Ad & E 438, 446; 113 ER 482, 485; *Forth v Stanton* (1845) 1 Wms Saund 210; 85 ER 217 (notes); *Reader v Kingham* (1862) 13 CBNS 344, 353; 143 ER 137, 141 (Erle CJ).

[8] See also Restatement (2d) Contracts, §118; Restatement (3d) Suretyship and Guaranty, §11(3)(d).

[9] See Corbin, *Corbin on Contracts* (n 2), vol 4, 377, §16.17.

[10] *Mallet v Bateman* (1865) LR 1 CP 163 (Exch Ch) might be viewed as an exception. D was liable as buyer to pay for goods sold by B. B drew bills on D, which D accepted. A promised B to take the bills as indorsee without recourse to B, and to indemnify B against any liability on the bills arising due to D's default. The promise of indemnity was held to be within the statute.

[11] See [9–16].

[12] cf *Wildes v Dudlow* (1874) LR 19 Eq 198, 200; Corbin (n 2), vol 4, 378, §16.17.

[13] cf *Moschi v Lep Air Services Ltd* [1973] AC 331 (HL), 357 (Lord Simon).

[14] *Sutton & Co v Grey* [1894] 1 QB 285 (CA).

[15] *Montagu Stanley & Co v JC Solomon Ltd* [1932] 2 KB 287 (CA).

on the stock exchange. The terms of the agreements between the introduction agents and brokers were, for present purposes, the same: the agent was to share half of any commission and to indemnify the brokers against half of any losses incurred in connection with such business. In *Sutton & Co*, the latter part of the agreement was held to be outside the statute on the basis of an exception, namely, that the agent had an interest in the transaction, or that it was only an incident of a broader transaction. In *Montagu Stanley & Co*, where the requirement of writing was not in issue, the agreement was clearly regarded as including an indemnity in the strict sense.

There are also older decisions in which it was accepted that promises of indemnity might be within the statute.[16] In *Cripps v Hartnoll*,[17] Pollock CB said:

> [A] mere promise of indemnity is not within the Statute of Frauds . . . On the other hand, an undertaking to answer for the debt or default of another is within the Statute of Frauds, and no doubt some cases might be put where it is both the one and the other, that is to say where the promise to answer for the debt or default of another would involve what might, very properly and legally, be called an indemnity. Where that is the case (which it is not here), in all probability the undertaking would be considered as within the Statute of Frauds if it were to answer for the debt or default of another, notwithstanding it might also be an indemnity.

But this is not the modern law. The adherence to a distinction between guarantees and indemnities may have hardened through an over-generalisation of the cases on indemnities against liabilities.[18] It may also reflect general dissatisfaction with the policy of the statute, and a desire to limit its operation.

Consumer Protection

[5–7] Consumer credit legislation. A requirement of writing may be imposed by consumer credit legislation. Under section 105(1) of the Consumer Credit Act 1974, any 'security' provided in relation to certain consumer agreements must be in writing.[19] The principal agreements are consumer credit agreements and consumer hire agreements. In very general terms, a consumer credit agreement is one in which an individual, the debtor, is provided by another person, the creditor, with credit of any amount.[20] 'Credit' is not defined exhaustively, but includes any kind of financial accommodation.[21] A consumer hire agreement is an agreement for the hire (not hire-purchase[22]) of goods to an individual, the term of which may exceed three months.[23]

'Security' is then defined to include, inter alia, any indemnity or guarantee provided at the debtor's or hirer's request, to secure the performance of the debtor's or hirer's obligations

---

[16] One is *Winckworth v Mills* (1796) 2 Esp 484; 170 ER 428, though it is not a convincing authority. Another, *Green v Cresswell* (1839) 10 Ad & E 453; 113 ER 172 cannot stand after *Batson v King* (1859) 4 H & N 739, 740; 157 ER 1032, 1033 (Pollock CB); *Reader v Kingham* (1862) 13 CBNS 344; 143 ER 137; *Wildes v Dudlow* (1874) LR 19 Eq 198; *Guild & Co v Conrad* [1894] 2 QB 885 (CA), 893–94 (Lindley LJ); *Davys v Buswell* [1913] 2 KB 47 (CA), 54–55 (Vaughan Williams LJ). A third is *Mallet v Bateman* (1865) LR 1 CP 163 (Exch Ch) (see n 10).
[17] *Cripps v Hartnoll* (1863) 4 B & S 414, 419; 122 ER 514, 516.
[18] See [5–5].
[19] Separate provision is made for security provided by the debtor or hirer: ss 105(6), 105(9).
[20] Consumer Credit Act 1974, s 8(1). There is, however, a monetary limit of £25,000 applicable where the credit is obtained wholly or predominantly for business purposes: s 16B(1).
[21] Consumer Credit Act 1974, s 9(1).
[22] Hire-purchase agreements are subsumed within the definition of consumer credit agreement in s 8(1) by the definition of 'credit' in s 9(3).
[23] Consumer Credit Act 1974, s 15(1).

under the principal agreement.[24] A person who provides such a guarantee or indemnity falls within the definition of 'surety'.[25]

Requirements as to the form of certain securities – guarantees and indemnities – have been prescribed by regulations.[26] The security instrument must contain a prominent heading, as the case may be: 'Guarantee subject to the Consumer Credit Act 1974'; 'Indemnity subject to the Consumer Credit Act 1974'; or 'Guarantee and Indemnity subject to the Consumer Credit Act 1974'.[27] The names and postal addresses of the creditor or owner, debtor or hirer, and surety must be given, as must a description of the subject-matter to which the security relates.[28] The instrument must also contain a statement of the surety's rights, and a signature box, in the prescribed form.[29] The instrument must be legible.[30]

If the security is not in writing, or the security instrument is improperly executed, then, insofar as it relates to the principal agreement, it can only be enforced against the surety by court order.[31] Improper execution extends to include cases where: the instrument does not comply with the requirements prescribed by the regulations;[32] the instrument does not embody all terms of the security other than implied terms;[33] the surety is not provided with a copy of the security instrument;[34] or the surety is not provided with an executed copy of the associated principal agreement at the required time.[35]

Non-Compliance with Terms of Contract Containing Indemnity

General

[5–8] Nature of restriction. Non-compliance may take effect in several ways. A condition precedent to performance of the indemnity may not have been satisfied, so that the primary obligation to indemnify is not enlivened.[36] The condition may attach to enforcement instead of performance. In that case, although the indemnifier is technically obliged to perform, the indemnified party cannot enforce the indemnity unless and until the condition is fulfilled. Alternatively, the indemnified party may have committed a breach of a promissory term of the contract that confers upon the indemnifier a right to terminate the contract. Exercise of that right discharges the indemnifier from further performance of the contract, including further performance of the promise to indemnify. The effect of breach

---

[24] Consumer Credit Act 1974, s 189(1).

[25] Consumer Credit Act 1974, s 189(1).

[26] Consumer Credit (Guarantees and Indemnities) Regulations 1983, SI 1983/1556. Such regulations are contemplated by Consumer Credit Act 1974, s 105(2).

[27] Consumer Credit (Guarantees and Indemnities) Regulations 1983, reg 3(1)(a), sch pt I.

[28] Consumer Credit (Guarantees and Indemnities) Regulations 1983, reg 3(1)(b), sch pt II.

[29] Consumer Credit (Guarantees and Indemnities) Regulations 1983, regs 3(1)(c) and (d), sch pts III and IV respectively.

[30] Consumer Credit (Guarantees and Indemnities) Regulations 1983, reg 4.

[31] Consumer Credit Act 1974, s 105(7).

[32] Consumer Credit Act 1974, s 105(4)(a).

[33] Consumer Credit Act 1974, s 105(4)(b).

[34] Consumer Credit Act 1974, s 105(4)(d).

[35] Consumer Credit Act 1974, s 105(5).

[36] See, eg, *Re-Source America International Ltd v Platt Site Services Ltd* [2004] EWCA Civ 665; (2004) 95 Con LR 1, [56] (Tuckey LJ) (condition that fire blankets be used in performance of work); *Agricultural and Rural Finance Pty Ltd v Gardiner* [2008] HCA 57; (2008) 238 CLR 570 (condition that payments be made punctually); *Farenco Shipping Co Ltd v Daebo Shipping Co Ltd (The Bremen Max)* [2008] EWHC 2755 (Comm); [2009] 1 Lloyd's Rep 81, [34] (condition that cargo be delivered to named party).

by the indemnified party is clearest where the indemnity is the only substantial executory obligation of the indemnifier under the contract.

[5–9] Relationship between failure of condition precedent and breach. Discharge for breach and non-fulfilment of a condition precedent are distinct grounds for refusing to perform the indemnity.[37] So, for example, A may promise to indemnify B on the condition that B make punctual payments to C according to the terms of a contract between B and C. In relation to A's promise to indemnify, B's punctual payments are merely a condition precedent: B's promise of performance is made to C, not A.[38] B's failure to perform does not, therefore, confer upon A a right to terminate for breach by B. But A's obligation to perform the indemnity is not engaged if B does not satisfy the condition precedent. There is also, possibly, a difference in onus. The indemnified party may have to establish satisfaction of a condition precedent to performance of the indemnity,[39] whereas the indemnifier must establish the breach of contract upon which it relies as a basis for discharge.

The consequences of non-compliance can be more favourable to the indemnified party in the case of a breach of a promissory term than in the case of a failure to satisfy a condition precedent. The right to discharge the contract for breach is, in the absence of any express right, governed by common law principles. The indemnified party's failure to perform may not be so serious as to confer upon the indemnifier the right to terminate. The contract, and thus the indemnity, remains enforceable by the indemnified party, though that party is liable to pay damages to the indemnifier.

In other cases, both perspectives lead to the same result. In *Guy-Pell v Foster*,[40] the defendant promised to indemnify the claimant against any loss on an investment in certain debentures, in return for an entitlement to one-quarter of any gain upon redemption. The claimant sold the debentures before the maturity date at a great loss and sued the defendant for that loss. The House of Lords held that the loss was to be ascertained at the relevant maturity date and so the action was brought too soon. The claimant then repurchased the debentures and, upon the debtor company entering liquidation (which rendered the principal and interest immediately payable) brought another action against the defendant. That action also failed. The ground preferred by the English Court of Appeal was that the claimant had repudiated the contract or breached an essential term by failing to retain the debentures. The other ground was that retention of the debentures, although not promised by the claimant, was a condition of the defendant's obligation to perform the indemnity.

Condition Precedent

[5–10] Identification of condition precedent. Whether a term is a condition precedent is a matter of construction. A leading illustration is *Scott Lithgow Ltd v Secretary of State for Defence*.[41] In 1974, the head contractor discovered that some materials supplied by a third party were defective and had to be replaced. In October 1977, the contractor notified the Ministry of Defence of its claim under an indemnity in the contract between them. It issued

---

[37] cf *Bank of Nova Scotia v Hellenic Mutual War Risks Association (Bermuda) Ltd (The Good Luck)* [1992] 1 AC 233 (HL), 262–63 (Lord Goff) (nature of warranties in insurance contracts).

[38] *Agricultural and Rural Finance Pty Ltd v Gardiner* [2008] HCA 57; (2008) 238 CLR 570, [65]–[66] (Gummow, Hayne and Kiefel JJ).

[39] See [5–11].

[40] *Guy-Pell v Foster* [1930] 2 Ch 169 (CA).

[41] *Scott Lithgow Ltd v Secretary of State for Defence* 1989 SC (HL) 9.

an arbitration notice against the Ministry in July 1982. At issue was whether the contractor's action on the indemnity from the Ministry was beyond the five-year limitation imposed by statute. The contractor argued that clause 15.5 of the contract established a condition precedent. The clause provided that where an event might result in a claim under the indemnity, the contractor should report the incident immediately and, 'in the interests of prompt settlement, should submit his priced claim as soon as possible thereafter. An estimate . . . is to be included in the initial notification of the incident or submitted within 14 days thereafter'. The contractor's action was out of time by reference to the occurrence of the loss in 1974,[42] but just within time by reference to the claim in October 1977. It was held that clause 15.5 was not a condition precedent to performance of the indemnity. The repeated use of the word 'should' suggested that the term was administrative in character. Furthermore, if clause 15.5 were a condition precedent, it could have operated harshly to deprive the contractor of the right to indemnity where the contractor had not acted 'as soon as possible'.[43]

[5–11] **Onus of proof.** A particular stipulation may be a condition precedent to the indemnity or merely a limited exception or qualification to the scope of the indemnity. If the latter, the burden generally lies upon the indemnifier to establish that the exception or qualification applies.[44] The point is more difficult where the stipulation is a condition precedent in the strict sense. It may be regarded as an element essential to the existence of the right to indemnity, which suggests that the onus lies upon the indemnified party to establish satisfaction. Even so, the approach taken in the insurance context is not uniform.[45] In *Wardle v Agricultural and Rural Finance Pty Ltd*,[46] which concerned a non-insurance indemnity, it was held that the burden rested upon the indemnified party to establish satisfaction of a condition precedent. That conclusion was, however, influenced by the terms of the investment scheme in question. The indemnified party asserted an entitlement to be indemnified in order to invoke an exception to a general liability to make repayments to the lender. In that context, the onus rested upon the indemnified party as the party relying upon the exception.[47]

[5–12] **Demands.** In considering whether a demand is a condition precedent to performance or enforcement of the indemnity, it is necessary to distinguish the following situations. The indemnified party may make a demand upon the indemnifier, seeking indemnification. Alternatively, a demand may be made by another person, such as a creditor, upon the indemnified party. This is most relevant to indemnities against claims by or liabilities to third parties. Finally, a demand may be made by the indemnified party upon another person, for example, a debtor. This is most relevant to indemnities against non-performance by third parties.

---

[42] See further [5–45].
[43] *Scott Lithgow Ltd v Secretary of State for Defence* 1989 SC (HL) 9, 21 (Lord Keith).
[44] See [5–33].
[45] In England, the onus is on the insurer to show non-satisfaction: *Bond Air Services Ltd v Hill* [1955] 2 QB 417 (QB). See also *Bedford v James* [1986] 2 Qd R 300 (SC); *Cee Bee Marine Ltd v Lombard Insurance Co Ltd* [1990] 2 NZLR 1 (CA); *Australian Associated Motor Insurers Ltd v Wright* (1997) 70 SASR 110 (FC). Contrast *Kodak (Australasia) Pty Ltd v Retail Traders Mutual Indemnity Insurance Association* (1942) 42 SR (NSW) 231 (FC); *Verna Trading Pty Ltd v New India Assurance Co Ltd* [1991] 1 VR 129 (CA); *Wallaby Grip Ltd v QBE Insurance (Australia) Ltd* [2010] HCA 9; (2010) 240 CLR 444, [25] (onus on insured to show satisfaction).
[46] *Wardle v Agricultural and Rural Finance Pty Ltd* [2012] NSWCA 107.
[47] *Wardle v Agricultural and Rural Finance Pty Ltd* [2012] NSWCA 107, [242]–[253] (Campbell JA).

[5–13] Demand by indemnified party upon indemnifier. A prior demand by the indemni-fied party upon the indemnifier is generally not a precondition to performance or enforce-ment of the indemnity.[48] An express stipulation for a demand can, however, be given effect.[49] Such a requirement may have one of the following consequences:

(1) the indemnifier's primary obligation to indemnify is not engaged unless and until the indemnified party makes a demand;
(2) the obligation to indemnify is already enlivened but the indemnified party's right to enforce the indemnity does not arise until it has made a demand;[50] or
(3) the indemnified party has a contractual right to obtain payment in advance for poten-tial losses.[51]

The third construction is not presently relevant. The first construction may be more apt for indemnities of a compensatory, rather than preventive, nature. It is not clear that a preven-tive indemnity would be effective where the demand is made in respect of a loss already sustained. The second construction might have practical utility where the indemnified loss relates to non-performance by a third party, or where there is a procedure for investigating and ascertaining the amount of the loss claimed by the indemnified party. Whether the first or second construction applies, the practical result is that a demand is, at least, a pre-condition to enforcement of the indemnity.

[5–14] Demand by third party upon indemnified party. A demand may be required by the terms of the contract between the third party and the indemnified party. Such a require-ment may be indirectly relevant to enforcement of the indemnity, insofar as it affects the existence and nature of the indemnified party's liability to the third party. In some circum-stances, it appears that the indemnity can be enforced in respect of that liability even though the third party has yet not made the requisite demand.[52]

As between the indemnified party and indemnifier, a demand by a third party upon the indemnified party is generally not a condition precedent to enforcement of the indemni-ty.[53] The context or terms of the contract of indemnity may indicate otherwise. In *Bradford v Gammon*,[54] a partnership deed provided for the sale of a deceased partner's share of the partnership property to the remaining partners, and for an indemnity to the deceased part-ner's executors against future claims and liabilities in respect of the partnership property. An executor sought quia timet relief in the form of an order that the partnership procure the release of the deceased partner's estate from, inter alia, liability under the partnership's overdraft account. The bank had closed the account and ascertained the total sum owing, but had made no demand for payment. Eve J held that the indemnity could only be enforced once a demand had been made by a creditor. A significant consideration was that

---

[48] *Chandris v Argo Insurance Co Ltd* [1963] 2 Lloyd's Rep 65 (QB), 74; *Scott Lithgow Ltd v Secretary of State for Defence* 1989 SC (HL) 9. *cf Re Taylor, ex p Century 21 Real Estate Corp* (1995) 130 ALR 723 (FCA), 729–30. *cf* [5–16].
[49] *Harrison v Mitford* (1792) 2 Bulst 229; 80 ER 1082; *Wardley Australia Ltd v Western Australia* (1992) 175 CLR 514, 524 (Mason CJ, Dawson, Gaudron and McHugh JJ); *Australia and New Zealand Banking Group Ltd v Coutts* [2003] FCA 968; (2003) 201 ALR 728, [35]–[36]. *cf* generally *Joachimson v Swiss Bank Corp* [1921] 3 KB 110 (CA), 129 (Atkin LJ). See further [9–49] (effect of principal debtor clause).
[50] *cf Stimpson v Smith* [1999] Ch 340 (CA), 354 (Tuckey LJ) (effect of requirement of demand in guarantee).
[51] But see *K/S Preston Street v Santander (UK) plc* [2012] EWHC 1633 (Ch), [29].
[52] *cf Thomas v Nottingham Incorporated Football Club Ltd* [1972] Ch 596 (Ch) (debtor's exoneration of guarantor).
[53] *cf* [6–29], [7–29].
[54] *Bradford v Gammon* [1925] Ch 132 (Ch).

the business of the partnership could be seriously disrupted if the partnership were required to satisfy creditors who were not pressing for payment.

[5–15] Demand by indemnified party upon third party. There may be several persons against whom an indemnified party can seek to recover for a loss. Unless the contract provides otherwise,[55] there is no general requirement that an indemnified party pursue or exhaust its rights against a third party before enforcing an indemnity.[56] If that were the case, the doctrine of subrogation would have developed differently. A demand made upon a third party that remains unsatisfied may, however, be a factor that goes to establish that the indemnified party has sustained loss by failing to recover from that party.[57]

[5–16] Notice. Notice to the indemnifier that the indemnified party has sustained a loss or been subjected to a claim is not a condition precedent to enforcement of the indemnity, unless the contract expressly so provides.[58]

[5–17] Payment by indemnified party. Generally, the indemnified party has no right to recover in respect of a liability to a third party unless and until the indemnified party pays a sum towards discharge of the liability. This does not mean that payment is to be regarded as a condition precedent to enforcement of the indemnity.[59] Rather, the limitation is a product of two substantive characteristics of indemnities: actual loss is an essential ingredient in an action to enforce the indemnity by way of common law remedy; and such loss generally arises upon payment and not merely because a liability exists.[60] Where the indemnified party claims in respect of a sum already paid, the distinction between payment as a form of loss and payment as a condition precedent is of little import.

The distinction becomes significant when specific enforcement is considered. If the indemnity is construed to be preventive in nature, then the indemnified party may be able to obtain an order for exoneration before it pays the third party. If, however, payment to the third party is made a condition precedent to enforcement, then the condition holds and relief in advance of payment is not possible.[61] The order for specific enforcement would conflict with the terms of the contract.

Discharge for Breach of Contract

[5–18] Discharge for breach by indemnified party. The common law basis for discharge for breach of contract is relatively straightforward. If the indemnified party's breach of contract is sufficiently serious,[62] the indemnifier may terminate the contract and so discharge itself from any further obligation to perform the indemnity.[63] If the breach is not

---

[55] See [9–34].

[56] *cf Dane v Mortgage Insurance Corp Ltd* [1894] 1 QB 54 (CA), 61 (Lord Esher MR).

[57] *cf* [9–32].

[58] *Cutler v Southern* (1667) 1 Wms Saund 116; 85 ER 125; 1 Lev 194; 83 ER 365; *Duffield v Scott* (1789) 3 TR 374; 100 ER 628; *Scott Lithgow Ltd v Secretary of State for Defence* 1989 SC (HL) 9.

[59] *Firma C-Trade SA v Newcastle Protection and Indemnity Association (The Fanti) (No 2)* [1991] 2 AC 1 (HL), 28 (Lord Brandon), 35–36 (Lord Goff), 40 (Lord Jauncey).

[60] See [6–23].

[61] *Firma C-Trade SA v Newcastle Protection and Indemnity Association (The Fanti) (No 2)* [1991] 2 AC 1 (HL); *Paterson v Pongrass Group Operations Pty Ltd* [2011] NSWSC 1588, [79]. See also [2–34], [7–20].

[62] In the sense of a breach of condition or fundamental breach of an intermediate term.

[63] *Guy-Pell v Foster* [1930] 2 Ch 169 (CA). *cf Jiona Investments Pty Ltd v Medihelp General Practice Pty Ltd* [2010] QCA 99, [19]–[20] (Muir JA).

sufficiently serious, and the term breached is not a condition precedent to performance of the indemnity, then the indemnifier will remain liable to indemnify.[64] Where the indemnifier relies on an express contractual right of termination that is enlivened by breach, the central question is whether the conditions for the exercise of the right have been satisfied. Termination pursuant to an express contractual right generally produces the same result, in relation to discharge of the parties, as termination on the common law basis.

[5–19] Discharge for breach by indemnifier. Termination of a contract generally discharges both parties from further performance of all primary obligations under it. It should, therefore, follow that termination by the indemnified party will deprive it of a right to further performance of the indemnity from the indemnifier. This was not the result in *ENE Kos 1 Ltd v Petroleo Brasileiro SA (The Kos) (No 2)*.[65] The owner of the vessel, which was on a time charter, exercised a contractual right to withdraw the vessel for the charterer's non-payment of hire. The owner then sustained losses in discharging cargo already aboard at the time of withdrawal. The Supreme Court of the United Kingdom held, by majority, that the owner was entitled to recover these losses under the standard form indemnity from the charterer against the consequences of the master complying with the charterer's orders. The charterer's order to load the cargo occurred before the charterparty was terminated. Even so, according to the conventional analysis, it would be the subsequent loss, and not that order, that would crystallise the right to enforce the indemnity. The indemnity would not have been engaged until after termination. It appears to have been assumed that the indemnity continued notwithstanding the termination of the charterparty, though it is not clear why the provision was exceptional.

Other Conduct Affecting the Indemnity

[5–20] General. The extent of the indemnifier's ultimate responsibility for loss may be affected by acts of other persons. Those acts may, for example, alter the nature of the risk, or increase the probability of loss occurring or its potential extent, or prejudice the indemnifier's rights against others in relation to the loss if it materialises. The question is whether certain conduct will relieve the indemnifier of its obligation to indemnify.

A parallel might be drawn between the position of an indemnifier and that of a guarantor, whose liability under a contract of guarantee may be affected by subsequent dealings by the debtor or creditor. Consideration of the point in the indemnity cases has often occurred in relation to indemnities against non-performance by third parties, where the analogy with guarantees is strongest. The principles applied to guarantees cannot be determinative because promises of indemnity and guarantee are essentially different. An indemnity promise does not, for example, necessarily share the characteristics of dependency and co-extensiveness.[66] In *Scottish & Newcastle plc v Raguz*,[67] Morritt VC remarked:

---

[64] *Briant v Pilcher* (1855) 16 CB 354; 139 ER 795; *Bowmaker (Commercial) Ltd v Smith* [1965] 1 WLR 855 (CA); *Direct Acceptance Finance Ltd v Cumberland Furnishing Pty Ltd* [1965] NSWR 1504 (FC); *Australia and New Zealand Banking Group Ltd v Beneficial Finance Corp Ltd* [1983] 1 NSWLR 199 (PC), 204; *Winchester Cigarette Machinery Ltd v Payne* (CA, 4 May 1995).

[65] *ENE Kos 1 Ltd v Petroleo Brasileiro SA (The Kos) (No 2)* [2012] UKSC 17; [2012] 2 WLR 976. See also W Courtney, 'Indemnities in Time Charterparties and the Effect of the Withdrawal of the Vessel' (2013) 30 *Journal of Contract Law* 243.

[66] See [9–17].

[67] *Scottish & Newcastle plc v Raguz* [2003] EWCA Civ 1070; [2004] L & TR 11, [8].

In a contract of indemnity the indemnifier undertakes an independent obligation which does not depend on the existence of any other obligation on the part of any other person ... By contrast a contract of guarantee presupposes some principal obligation of a principal obligor to which the guarantee is secondary or ancillary ... [T]he obligation of a guarantor may be discharged by transactions between the creditor and principal debtor, for example by giving time, the release of securities or novation of the obligation because any of those transactions may alter the mutual rights and obligations of the guarantor and the principal debtor. As there is no need for a principal obligation in the case of an indemnity its discharge depends on the usual rules of contract.

But these differences do not necessarily entail the wholesale rejection of all principles applicable to guarantees.[68] The approach for indemnities must be more general because the same issues arise for different forms of indemnity. Where an indemnity protects against the consequences of non-performance by a third party, a variation in the third party's obligations to the indemnified party may correspondingly affect the extent of the indemnifier's liability. This is also true where an indemnity protects against a liability to a third party, and there is a variation of the indemnified party's obligations to that third party.

[5–21] **Types of conduct.** Three types of conduct must be considered. Dealings involving the indemnified party and others may affect the subject-matter of the indemnity.[69] These include variations to liabilities of, or to, the indemnified party; extensions of time granted by, or to, the indemnified party; and releases given by, or to, the indemnified party. Other dealings may affect the indemnifier's ability ultimately to recoup itself in relation to the indemnified loss.[70] Finally, the indemnified party may, by acting unreasonably, incur or increase a loss that would otherwise fall within the scope of the indemnity.[71]

Dealings Affecting the Subject-Matter of the Indemnity

[5–22] **Variation of liabilities of, or to, indemnified party.** In the guarantee context, the general rule is that a guarantor is discharged where the debtor and creditor agree to vary the principal contract, unless it is clear that the variation is unsubstantial or cannot be prejudicial to the guarantor.[72] There is some discord as to whether a similar principle applies to non-insurance[73] indemnities, whether against liabilities of the indemnified party to third parties, or against loss to the indemnified party caused by a third party's non-performance. The point in substance concerns a change in the underlying circumstances which, correspondingly, affects the nature or extent of the promisor's liability. It is doubtful that the variation principle should rest entirely upon the characteristics of dependency or co-extensiveness inherent in a promise of guarantee. From a more general perspective, however, it might be queried whether it is nowadays necessary to apply a legal rule, or

---

[68] See, eg, *Total Oil Products (Australia) Pty Ltd v Robinson* [1970] 1 NSWR 701 (CA), 704 (Asprey JA) but contrast *Tullow Uganda Ltd v Heritage Oil and Gas Ltd* [2013] EWHC 1656 (Comm), [105].

[69] See [5–22].

[70] See [5–25].

[71] See [4–29].

[72] *Holme v Brunskill* (1878) 3 QBD 495 (CA); *Ward v National Bank of New Zealand* (1883) 8 App Cas 755 (PC), 763–64; *Ankar Pty Ltd v National Westminster Finance (Australia) Ltd* (1987) 162 CLR 549, 558–59 (Mason CJ, Wilson, Brennan and Dawson JJ), *cf* 568–69 (Deane J).

[73] For the position in reinsurance where the original policy is varied, see, eg, *Lower Rhine and Würtemberg Insurance Association v Sedgwick* [1899] 1 QB 179 (CA); *Norwich Union Fire Insurance Society v Colonial Mutual Fire Insurance Co* [1922] 2 KB 461 (KB); *HIH Casualty & General Insurance Ltd v New Hampshire Insurance Co* [2001] EWCA Civ 735; [2001] 2 Lloyds Rep 161, [109]–[111] (Rix LJ).

simply to determine the extent of the indemnifier's responsibility as a matter of construction of the contract. That is, the issue is whether the altered loss or liability remains within the scope of the indemnity as originally agreed, not whether the indemnifier has been 'discharged' by certain events.

An old decision concerning an indemnity against liability is *Webster v Petre*.[74] The claimant was liable on a bond to the Crown, conditioned to be void if a certain railway were completed on time. The defendants promised to indemnify the claimant against 'all liability which he . . . might incur in giving the said bond . . . to the extent of £10,000'. The railway was abandoned and, pursuant to a statute enacted after the bond had been given, the claimant arranged for the bond to be cancelled in return for the claimant paying a sum into court. Pollock B accepted that the rule in *Holme v Brunskill*[75] could apply to discharge the defendants if these events amounted to a variation of the claimant's liability without the defendants' consent. The decision essentially turned on the construction of the scope of the indemnity.[76] The payment by the claimant answered the description of a liability which he might incur in giving the bond; it was not a variation of the indemnified liability.

More recent decisions are divided. Dicta in English cases weigh against applying the variation rule to indemnities.[77] In Canada, the variation rule has been applied.[78] The position in New Zealand is not clear.[79] In Australia, the point was touched on in *Schoenhoff v Commonwealth Bank of Australia*.[80] The argument of the guarantors/indemnifiers proceeded on the basis that the principal contract *could* be varied, subject to any express or implied term to the contrary.[81] The assertion of such an implied term failed because it was inconsistent with an express term stating that the guarantors'/indemnifiers' liability was not affected by a variation.[82] Stein AJA left open the question of whether the variation rule applied to indemnities.

[5–23] **Allowance of time.** Where there is an indemnity to a creditor against loss arising from the debtor's default or non-performance, it appears that the allowance of time by the creditor to the debtor will not necessarily discharge the indemnifier.[83] Where there is an

---

[74] *Webster v Petre* (1879) 4 Ex D 127.

[75] *Holme v Brunskill* (1878) 3 QBD 495 (CA).

[76] *Webster v Petre* (1879) 4 Ex D 127, 131.

[77] *Associated British Ports v Ferryways NV* [2009] EWCA Civ 189; [2009] 1 Lloyd's Rep 595, [1] (Kay LJ); *Vossloh AG v Alpha Trains (UK) Ltd* [2010] EWHC 2443 (Ch); [2011] 2 All ER (Comm) 307, [26]–[27]. *cf Scottish & Newcastle plc v Raguz* [2003] EWCA Civ 1070; [2004] L & TR 11, [8] (Morritt VC) (discounting applicability of other rules for discharge but not specifically mentioning the variation rule); *Marubeni Hong Kong and South China Ltd v Ministry of Finance of Mongolia* [2005] EWCA Civ 395; [2005] 1 WLR 2497, [35] (Carnwath LJ); *CIMC Raffles Offshore (Singapore) Ltd v Schahin Holding SA* [2013] EWCA Civ 644; [2013] 2 All ER (Comm) 760, [30], [57] (Sir Bernard Rix).

[78] *Guinness Tower Holdings Ltd v Extranc Technologies Inc* [2004] BCSC 367; *1212763 Ontario Ltd v Bonjour Café* [2012] ONSC 823.

[79] *cf Friedlander v Rusher* [2002] NZCA 195, [25]–[29] (apparently suggesting rule may apply).

[80] *Schoenhoff v Commonwealth Bank of Australia* [2004] NSWCA 161. *cf Total Oil Products (Australia) Pty Ltd v Robinson* [1970] 1 NSWR 701 (CA), 704–05 (Asprey JA).

[81] *cf Friedlander v Rusher* [2002] NZCA 195, [30]–[33].

[82] *Schoenhoff v Commonwealth Bank of Australia* [2004] NSWCA 161, [27]–[29] (Stein AJA).

[83] *Western Credit Ltd v Alberry* [1964] 1 WLR 945 (CA), 950 (Davies LJ); *Peters v NZHB Holdings Ltd* [2004] NZCA 245, [23]; *Walker Crips Stockbrokers Ltd v Savill* [2007] EWHC 2598 (QB), [76]; *Associated British Ports v Ferryways NV* [2009] EWCA Civ 189; [2009] 1 Lloyd's Rep 595, [1] (Kay LJ); *Vossloh AG v Alpha Trains (UK) Ltd* [2010] EWHC 2443 (Ch); [2011] 2 All ER (Comm) 307, [27].

indemnity to a debtor in respect of a liability to the creditor, the indemnifier will not be discharged merely because the creditor allows more time to pay.[84]

This position has been reached in the indemnity cases without close consideration of the basis for the rule as it applies to guarantees. There, the rationale for discharge is said to be that it would otherwise lead to one of two unacceptable consequences where the guarantor makes timely payment to the creditor. Either the guarantor's position would be altered because it would be barred from exercising, by subrogation, the creditor's rights against the debtor until the extended period has elapsed; or the guarantor could sue at the original time but with the effect of undermining the agreement between the creditor and debtor.[85]

The fundamental premise seems to be that, as the guarantor's obligation corresponds to the debtor's, the guarantor is entitled to be discharged from the liability to the creditor at the time originally fixed for performance by the debtor and, if necessary, may proceed immediately against the debtor. That premise does not hold for indemnities generally. Whether the indemnity applies to a liability to a third party, or to non-performance by a third party, the essential concern is loss to the indemnified party, not timely performance of the indemnified obligation. Actual loss may not crystallise until some time after the indemnified obligation has fallen due for performance.[86]

The reluctance to extend this rule of discharge to indemnities may also reflect existing dissatisfaction with the rule as it applies to guarantees.[87]

[5–24] **Release of debtor by creditor.** Indemnities against claims by or liabilities to third parties must be distinguished from indemnities against loss from non-performance by a third party.[88]

Under an indemnity against claims or liabilities, the indemnified party is the debtor. Where the third party creditor releases the indemnified debtor without payment, the indemnifier will not thereafter be obliged to perform the indemnity. This is not because the indemnifier is 'discharged' by the release. Rather, the potential loss against which the indemnity was to protect the debtor, namely, the liability to the third party, has ceased to exist. The indemnified debtor requires no further protection and so the indemnity lacks subject-matter upon which to operate.[89]

An indemnity against non-performance by a third party is primarily concerned with a different kind of loss, namely, the indemnified creditor's failure to receive performance from the debtor. The creditor's release of the debtor before the debtor has fully performed confirms that the creditor will not receive the expected performance; a potential loss may

---

[84] *Way v Hearn* (1862) 11 CBNS 774; 142 ER 1000; *Way v Hearn* (1862) 13 CBNS 292; 143 ER 117. See generally *Scottish & Newcastle plc v Raguz* [2003] EWCA Civ 1070; [2004] L & TR 11, [8] (Morritt VC); *Gardiner v Agricultural and Rural Finance Pty Ltd* [2007] NSWCA 235; (2008) Aust Contract R 90-274, [128] (Spigelman CJ) (point not pressed on appeal: *Agricultural and Rural Finance Pty Ltd v Gardiner* [2008] HCA 57; (2008) 238 CLR 570, [7]).

[85] *Polak v Everett* (1876) 1 QBD 669 (CA), 673–74 (Blackburn J); *Swire v Redman* (1876) 1 QBD 536 (QB), 541–42 (Cockburn CJ and Blackburn J); *Deane v City Bank of Sydney* (1905) 2 CLR 198, 210–11. *cf Moschi v Lep Air Services Ltd* [1973] AC 331 (HL), 348 (Lord Diplock).

[86] See [6–23] (liabilities), [9–32]–[9–34] (non-performance).

[87] *Gardiner v Agricultural and Rural Finance Pty Ltd* [2007] NSWCA 235; (2008) Aust Contract R 90-274, [128] (Spigelman CJ).

[88] Falling somewhere between the two situations discussed in the text is *Total Oil Products (Australia) Pty Ltd v Robinson* [1970] 1 NSWR 701 (CA) (A indemnifying B against liability as guarantor of C's obligations to D; B releasing C from obligations under separate agreement between them).

[89] See further [7–30]. *cf Union Bank of Australia Ltd v Rudder* (1911) 13 CLR 152, 163 (Griffith CJ).

still remain. For this reason it is not appropriate to rely on the principle, drawn from the liability cases, that a 'liability to indemnify against a liability which has no existence, and which can never arise, is a contradiction in terms'.[90] Nor do guarantees provide a direct analogy. The creditor's release of the debtor discharges the guarantor because the guarantor's obligation is dependent upon the debtor's.[91] That is not an inherent characteristic of a promise of indemnity.[92]

Whether the indemnity continues to operate notwithstanding the indemnified creditor's release of the debtor is ultimately a matter of construction.[93] An indemnity can remain effective after a debtor has been released on other grounds, if there is sufficiently clear language in this respect.[94] Conversely, the absence of an enforceable liability of the debtor to the indemnified creditor may lead to the result that there is no relevant loss within the scope of the indemnity.[95]

Other characterisations of events are also possible. It may be that the indemnified creditor has exacerbated the indemnified loss by acting unreasonably in releasing the debtor; alternatively, the indemnified creditor may have impaired or extinguished rights to which the indemnifier would succeed by subrogation.[96] On either basis, the indemnifier's liability could be reduced by an amount corresponding to the extent of the prejudice.

Dealings Affecting the Indemnifier

[5–25] **Rights that diminish the loss.** The indemnified party's dealings with rights against others or securities associated with the indemnified subject-matter may affect the indemnifier in two ways. First, where such rights are exercised by the indemnified party before indemnification, the loss may be diminished and the extent of the indemnifier's liability reduced accordingly. Secondly, upon payment in full, the indemnifier is by subrogation entitled to exercise rights possessed by the indemnified party in diminution of the indemnified loss. By impairing or releasing such rights, the indemnified party may reduce the extent to which the indemnifier can recoup itself and so increase the loss the indemnifier ultimately must bear. This rationale applies to promises of indemnity in all forms.

A requirement to acquire or maintain rights against third parties or to securities may be a promissory term of the contract of indemnity, or a condition precedent to the obligation to indemnify.[97]

---

[90] Contrast *Housing Guarantee Fund Ltd v Johnson* (1995) V Conv R 54-524 (FC), 66,223 (Ormiston J); *McIntosh v Linke Nominees Pty Ltd* [2008] QCA 275, [29] (Muir JA), [46] (Douglas J). The quoted text is from *Re Perkins; Poyser v Beyfus* [1898] 2 Ch 182 (CA), 189 (Lindley MR).

[91] *cf* JC Phillips, *The Modern Contract of Guarantee*, 2nd English edn (London, Sweet & Maxwell, 2010), 382–83, paras 6-54, 6-56.

[92] See [9–12].

[93] *McIntosh v Linke Nominees Pty Ltd* [2008] QCA 275, [29] (Muir JA), [46] (Douglas J). *cf Vossloh AG v Alpha Trains (UK) Ltd* [2010] EWHC 2443 (Ch); [2011] 2 All ER (Comm) 307, [27].

[94] *Clement v Clement* (CA, 20 October 1995); *Sandtara Pty Ltd v Abigroup Ltd* (1996) 42 NSWLR 491 (CA) (disclaimer by liquidator of debtor company); *Citibank Savings Ltd v Nicholson* (1997) 70 SASR 206 (SC), 235–36 (dissolution of debtor company). See generally [9–48].

[95] *cf* [9–41].

[96] See [5–25]–[5–26].

[97] See, eg, *James v Surf Road Nominees Pty Ltd* [2004] NSWCA 475, [65]–[67], [76], [81] (implied term in deed of guarantee and indemnity). *cf Australia and New Zealand Banking Group Ltd v Beneficial Finance Corp Ltd* [1983] 1 NSWLR 199 (PC), 203 (unsuccessful argument that obtaining security by a particular date was a condition precedent to indemnity).

There is also a more general limitation applicable to non-insurance indemnities, though it is relatively undeveloped. An analogy may be drawn with guarantees or indemnity insurance.[98] A guarantor's liability may be reduced pro tanto by certain acts of the creditor that adversely affect securities relating to the guaranteed obligations, and to the benefit of which the guarantor is or would have been entitled upon payment.[99] In indemnity insurance, it has been said that the insured 'may not release, diminish, compromise or divert the benefit of any right to which the insurer is or will be entitled to succeed and enjoy under his right of subrogation'.[100] Another formulation is that the insured must act in good faith and reasonably with regard to the insurer's interests.[101] The duty has been characterised as equitable in nature[102] or based upon an implied term.[103] A breach does not absolutely discharge the insurer, but the insurer has a countervailing claim against the insured for compensation for the resulting loss.

[5–26] **Illustrations.** *Hodgson v Hodgson*[104] is a leading example. The defendant promised to indemnify the claimant against his liability as a co-surety for the due administration of a lunatic's estate. The claimant paid sums due for maladministration, released his co-surety from any claims for contribution, and then claimed the full amount paid from the defendant. The defendant was thus deprived of the benefit of the claimant's right to contribution from the co-surety, to which she would have succeeded upon indemnifying the claimant. It was held accordingly that the defendant was relieved pro tanto from the obligation to indemnify.

Another illustration may be *Goulston Discount Co Ltd v Sims*.[105] A vehicle let on hire-purchase was rendered a total loss in an accident. The vehicle had been insured for £200 but the finance company accepted a lesser sum and used that figure to calculate its loss in its claim for indemnity under a separate recourse agreement with a motor dealer. It was held that the finance company had to account for the full insured value, as that was what it 'ought reasonably to have received'. One explanation[106] is that the finance company, as the indemnified party, had improperly exercised a right to which the indemnifier would have been subrogated. The recourse agreement provided that, upon payment, the motor dealer would become entitled to the finance company's rights 'in respect of the hirer, the goods

---

[98] See, eg, *Barclays Bank plc v Kingston* [2006] EWHC 533 (QB); [2006] 2 Lloyd's Rep 58, [36] (creditor owes indemnifier same duty as guarantor in relation to realisation of securities).

[99] See generally Phillips, *The Modern Contract of Guarantee* (n 91), 499–502, paras 8-49–8-54; G Andrews and R Millett, *Law of Guarantees*, 6th edn (London, Sweet & Maxwell, 2011), 428–40, paras 9-041–9-043.

[100] *State Government Insurance Office (Qld) v Brisbane Stevedoring Pty Ltd* (1969) 123 CLR 228, 241 (Barwick CJ). See also *West of England Fire Insurance Co v Isaacs* [1897] 1 QB 226 (CA); *Phoenix Assurance Co v Spooner* [1905] 2 KB 753 (KB); *Arthur Barnett Ltd v National Insurance Co of New Zealand* [1965] NZLR 874 (CA). See generally C Mitchell and S Watterson, *Subrogation Law and Practice* (Oxford, Oxford University Press, 2007), 370–73, paras 10.157–10.164.

[101] *Horwood v Land of Leather Ltd* [2010] EWHC 546 (Comm); [2010] Lloyd's Rep IR 453, [67]. *cf Globe & Rutgers Fire Insurance Co v Truedell* [1927] 2 DLR 659 (Ont CA).

[102] *Commercial Union Assurance v Lister* (1874) LR 9 Ch App 483, 487 (James LJ).

[103] *Sola Basic Australia Ltd v Morganite Ceramic Fibres Pty Ltd* (NSWCA, 11 May 1989), 32 (Meagher JA); *Horwood v Land of Leather Ltd* [2010] EWHC 546 (Comm); [2010] Lloyd's Rep IR 453, [56]–[67].

[104] *Hodgson v Hodgson* (1837) 2 Keen 704; 48 ER 800 (referred to with approval: *Hancock v Williams* (1942) 42 SR (NSW) 252 (FC), 256 (Jordan CJ)).

[105] *Goulston Discount Co Ltd v Sims* (1967) 111 SJ 682 (CA). *cf Barclays Bank plc v Kingston* [2006] EWHC 533 (QB); [2006] 2 Lloyd's Rep 58, [36].

[106] See [4–33] for another explanation.

and any other indemnifier'.[107] The dealer's liability as indemnifier was, in effect, reduced pro tanto.

It appears that the indemnified party can relinquish a right as part of a reasonable settlement within the scope of the indemnity. In *Comyn Ching & Co Ltd v Oriental Tube Co Ltd*,[108] the indemnified party was one of several parties to an agreement to settle disputes arising out of a construction project. The settlement terms required the indemnified party to pay a sum to the employer and to surrender a claim against another. The indemnifier objected that it had been prejudiced by the abandonment of the claim. Goff LJ held that the reasonableness of the settlement was to be determined as a whole. As the settlement was reasonable overall, the indemnifier's objection was dismissed.[109]

[5–27] Release of co-indemnifier. A threshold question is whether the arrangement between the indemnified party and a co-indemnifier releases the latter. In *Johnson v Davies*,[110] for example, one of three joint indemnifiers entered a voluntary arrangement, in which the indemnified parties participated, under the Insolvency Act 1986. A term of the arrangement stated: 'When all moneys to be made available under these proposals have been realised and distributed to creditors in accordance with the terms herein I will be released from any further liability to them'. It was held that the arrangement did not effect an absolute or immediate release of the indemnified parties' claim against the insolvent indemnifier. The other joint indemnifiers were, therefore, still bound to perform the indemnity.

Where there is a release, in the strict sense, of one co-indemnifier, other co-indemnifiers may be discharged:

(1) absolutely, by the common law rule that a release of one of joint or joint and several debtors releases all;[111]
(2) absolutely, because the indemnity is subject to an express or implied condition that other co-indemnifiers remain liable;[112] or
(3) to the extent that the right to contribution from the released co-indemnifier has been prejudiced.

In applying the common law rule concerning releases, a distinction has traditionally been drawn between a release and a mere covenant not to sue.[113] The latter arrangement does not discharge the liabilities of other co-debtors to the creditor. This distinction has been

---

[107] This provision might explain the departure from the usual rule that insurance recoveries are not counted as diminishing the loss for the purposes of a later claim on a contractual non-insurance indemnity: see [4–38]–[4–39], [4–74].

[108] *Comyn Ching & Co Ltd v Oriental Tube Co Ltd* (1979) 17 BLR 47 (CA).

[109] *Comyn Ching & Co Ltd v Oriental Tube Co Ltd* (1979) 17 BLR 47 (CA), 90–91.

[110] *Johnson v Davies* [1999] Ch 117 (CA). See also *Field v Robins* (1838) 8 Ad & E 90; 112 ER 770.

[111] See generally *Nicholson v Revill* (1836) 4 Ad & E 675; 111 ER 941; *Re EWA (a debtor)* [1901] 2 KB 642 (CA); *Walker v Bowry* (1924) 35 CLR 48; *Deanplan Ltd v Mahmoud* [1993] Ch 151 (Ch). But see, in New Zealand, *Robinson v Tait* [2001] NZCA 217; [2002] 2 NZLR 30, [75]–[77] (Keith, Blanchard and McGrath JJ) (joint and several liability).

[112] As to a condition that a co-indemnifier *become* liable, see: *Fitzgerald v McCowan* [1898] 2 IR 1 (QB); *Richview Investments Inc v Dynasty Social Club* (1997) 87 BCAC 223 (CA); *Capital Bank Cashflow Finance Ltd v Southall* [2004] EWCA Civ 817; [2004] 2 All ER (Comm) 675, [15]–[17] (Mance LJ).

[113] *Solly v Forbes* (1820) 2 Br & B 38; 129 ER 871; *Re EWA (a debtor)* [1901] 2 KB 642 (CA), 648–49 (Collins LJ); *Deanplan Ltd v Mahmoud* [1993] Ch 151 (Ch), 170.

criticised in England,[114] where the appropriate perspective may now be to consider whether the releasing party has given an absolute release or a release with a reservation of its rights against others.[115]

[5–28] Where release affects right to contribution. A creditor's release of one co-guarantor will discharge other co-guarantors to the extent that the release impairs their right to contribution from the released co-guarantor in relation to the guaranteed obligations.[116] The question is whether co-indemnifiers ought to be protected in the same manner as co-guarantors, assuming that the right to contribution exists or would exist among the co-indemnifiers, and that the indemnified party's release of one (or more) of them has adversely affected that right.[117] Two considerations suggest an affirmative answer. First, the rule as it applies to guarantees is concerned with the share of the burden ultimately borne by a co-guarantor in respect of the guaranteed obligations. This same concern applies to co-indemnifiers in relation to the indemnified loss. Secondly, there is a close connection between this rule and the rule that a guarantor is discharged pro tanto where the creditor impairs or releases securities for the guaranteed obligations.[118] An analogous principle has been recognised for promises of indemnity.[119]

[5–29] Other conduct that prejudices the indemnifier. Canadian decisions aside, it is difficult to find support for the discharge of an indemnifier on the general ground of prejudicial conduct by the indemnified party.[120] Such conduct might still be challenged on another basis, for example, as unreasonable conduct that increases loss under the indemnity.[121] In Canada, principles applicable in the law of guarantees[122] have been extended to indemnities against non-performance by a third party. Thus, an indemnifier will be absolutely discharged where the indemnified party commits a breach of the principal contract which materially increases the magnitude, or likelihood of materialisation, of the risk accepted by the indemnifier under the indemnity.[123]

Unfair Contract Terms

[5–30] Unfair Contract Terms Act 1977. Some forms of indemnity are regulated by the Unfair Contract Terms Act 1977. Two important sets of restrictions are set out in

---

[114] In New Zealand, *cf Robinson v Tait* [2001] NZCA 217; [2002] 2 NZLR 30, [69]–[77] (Keith, Blanchard and McGrath JJ). The distinction continues to be observed in Australia: *Dorgal Holdings Pty Ltd v Buckley* (1996) 22 ACSR 164 (NSWSC), 167; *Murray-Oates v Jjadd Pty Ltd* [1999] SASC 537; (1999) 76 SASR 38 (FC), [83]–[87] (Wicks J); *Pollak v National Australia Bank Ltd* [2002] FCAFC 55, [14]–[17].

[115] *Watts v Aldington* (CA, 16 December 1993) (joint and several liability); *Johnson v Davies* [1999] Ch 117 (CA), 127–28 (Chadwick LJ) (joint liability). *cf Morris v Wentworth-Stanley* [1999] QB 1004 (CA), 1011–12 (Potter LJ) (joint liability).

[116] See generally Phillips (n 91), 490–91, paras 8-26–8-28; Andrews and Millett, *Law of Guarantees* (n 99), 426–28, para 9-040.

[117] *cf Gainers Inc v Edmonton Oilers Hockey Corp* (1994) 164 AR 39 (Alta QB), 45–46.

[118] See, eg, *Ward v National Bank of New Zealand* (1883) 8 App Cas 755 (PC), 764–66; *Re Wolmershausen* (1890) 62 LT 541 (Ch), 546; *Hancock v Williams* (1942) 42 SR (NSW) 252 (FC), 256 (Jordan CJ).

[119] See [5–25], [5–26].

[120] *cf Scottish & Newcastle plc v Raguz* [2006] EWHC 821 (Ch); [2006] 4 All ER 524, [101]–[103] (affd without consideration of this point: *Scottish & Newcastle plc v Raguz* [2008] UKHL 65; [2008] 1 WLR 2494); *Dubai Islamic Bank PJSC v PSI Energy Holding Company BSC* [2011] EWHC 2718, [46]–[47].

[121] See [4–30]–[4–33].

[122] See *Bank of Montreal v Wilder* [1986] 2 SCR 551.

[123] *Jens Hans Investments Co Ltd v Bridger* [2004] BCCA 340; (2004) 29 BCLR (4th) 1. See also [9–47].

sections 2 and 4. Certain exceptions aside, these sections apply to contractual indemnities against business liabilities. A business liability is one that arises from conduct in the course of a business, or from the occupation of premises used for business purposes.[124] In the following discussion, assume that A has promised to indemnify B against such liabilities. The nature of the restriction then depends on the circumstances.

If the indemnity applies to B's liability to A, then the indemnity is similar to a clause that excludes or limits B's liability to A.[125] The indemnity is rendered ineffective insofar as it covers B's liability to A for death or personal injury resulting from negligence.[126] Whether the indemnity is effective to protect B against liability in negligence for other loss or damage to A depends on whether the indemnity satisfies the requirement of reasonableness.[127] These restrictions are concerned with an effective exclusion or limitation of liability between B and A, as the victim. They do not apply where B (possibly along with A) is liable to C, and seeks to enforce the indemnity from A in respect that liability.[128] The indemnity operates inter partes and does not affect C's rights against A or B. These restrictions can apply where A and B are commercial parties.[129]

Where A deals as a consumer there is another, broader restriction.[130] It applies where the indemnity covers B's liability to A or to another, C.[131] B's liability may be in negligence or for breach of contract. The indemnity is ineffective except to the extent that it satisfies the test of reasonableness. There is no express distinction between liability for personal harm and liability for other loss or damage.

Enforcement Generally

Scope

[5–31] Requirement for loss within scope. The fact that the indemnified party has suffered or will suffer loss is not a sufficient basis for enforcing the indemnity. There must be an actual or potential loss within the scope of the indemnity.[132] In the case of preventive indemnities, if there is no actual loss within scope, there is no breach of contract by failing to indemnify. If there is no potential loss within scope, there is no reason to order specific enforcement of the indemnity. Similarly, an indemnifier under a compensatory indemnity only promises to protect the indemnified party against losses within scope. If there is no loss within scope, the promise to indemnify is not enlivened. The indemnity cannot be enforced directly against the indemnifier, nor can the indemnifier be liable for a failure to perform the indemnity.

---

[124] Unfair Contract Terms Act 1977, s 1(3).
[125] See generally ch 8. *cf* Unfair Contract Terms Act 1977, s 13(1)(b).
[126] Unfair Contract Terms Act 1977, s 2(1).
[127] Unfair Contract Terms Act 1977, ss 2(2), 11. See *Phillips Products Ltd v Hyland* [1987] 1 WLR 659n (CA).
[128] *Thompson v T Lohan (Plant Hire) Ltd* [1987] 1 WLR 649 (CA); *Hancock Shipping Co Ltd v Deacon & Trysail (Private) Ltd (The Casper Trader)* [1991] 2 Lloyd's Rep 550 (QB).
[129] See generally R Brownsword and J Adams, 'Double Indemnity – Contractual Indemnity Clauses Revisited' [1988] *Journal of Business Law* 146.
[130] Unfair Contract Terms Act 1977, s 4.
[131] Unfair Contract Terms Act 1977, s 4(2)(b).
[132] *AMF International Ltd v Magnet Bowling Ltd* [1968] 1 WLR 1028 (QB), 1060.

[5–32] Protection against loss within scope. The indemnified party is entitled to be protected against any and all loss within the scope of the indemnity.[133] The proposition is widely accepted, but is so basic that it is often assumed rather than articulated. In *Zaccardi v Caunt*,[134] Campbell JA observed that 'the amounts that can be recovered under an indemnity depend simply upon whether a loss that the person indemnified has suffered falls within the scope of the indemnity'.[135] Lord Hoffmann made a similar observation in *Caledonia North Sea Ltd v British Telecommunications plc (The Piper Alpha)*.[136] Considering the recovery of sums paid on behalf of the indemnified party in settlements with claimants, Lord Hoffmann said:[137]

> The liability either falls within the scope of the indemnity or it does not. The kind of loss for which indemnity was claimed fell within the indemnity simply because it was loss arising out of liability for death or injury in respect of the contractor's employees.

[5–33] Onus of proof. Enforcement of an indemnity in respect of a loss generally involves two stages. The scope of the indemnity is first ascertained. The indemnity is then applied to the circumstances, to determine whether there is a loss within scope and, if so, to ascertain the amount of the loss.[138]

The onus of establishing facts that satisfy particular elements of the indemnity may be cast upon one or the other party expressly by the terms of the contract.[139] Where there is no such express provision, it is necessary to distinguish: (1) elements that define the basis of the general promise to indemnify, from (2) those elements that form a limited exception or qualification to the general promise to indemnify. The distinction is not always easy to draw and is ultimately a matter of construction. The legal onus generally rests upon the indemnified party to establish satisfaction of the former elements, and upon the party relying on the limited exception or qualification to establish satisfaction of the latter elements.[140] Thus, the onus generally rests upon the indemnified party to prove the facts that establish a loss that is, prima facie, within the affirmative definition of the scope of the indemnity, and upon an indemnifier to establish facts that bring the loss within an exception to scope.

---

[133] See, eg, *Furness Shipbuilding Co Ltd v London and North Eastern Railway Co* (1934) 50 TLR 257 (HL), 259 (Lord Atkin); *Scottish & Newcastle plc v Raguz* [2008] UKHL 65; [2008] 1 WLR 2494, [16] (Lord Hope), [72] (Lord Walker); *ENE Kos 1 Ltd v Petroleo Brasileiro SA (The Kos) (No 2)* [2012] UKSC 17; [2012] 2 WLR 976, [10]–[13] (Lord Sumption), [34] (Lord Phillips), [58]–[59] (Lord Clarke). See also *Australian Coastal Shipping Commission v PV 'Wyuna'* (1964) 111 CLR 303, 306 (Barwick CJ), 310 (Kitto J), 311 (Menzies J), 316–17 (Owen J); *Davis v Commissioner for Main Roads* (1967) 117 CLR 529, 536 (Menzies J), 537–38 (Kitto J).

[134] *Zaccardi v Caunt* [2008] NSWCA 202.

[135] *Zaccardi v Caunt* [2008] NSWCA 202, [33].

[136] *Caledonia North Sea Ltd v British Telecommunications plc (The Piper Alpha)* [2002] UKHL 4; [2002] 1 Lloyd's Rep 553.

[137] *Caledonia North Sea Ltd v British Telecommunications plc (The Piper Alpha)* [2002] UKHL 4; [2002] 1 Lloyd's Rep 553, [100].

[138] *ENE Kos 1 Ltd v Petroleo Brasileiro SA (The Kos) (No 2)* [2012] UKSC 17; [2012] 2 WLR 976, [58] (Lord Clarke). See also [4–5].

[139] See, eg, *J Fenwick & Co Pty Ltd v Australian Coastal Shipping Commission* [1965] NSWR 97 (SC), 104 (proof of unseaworthiness).

[140] *Federal Steam Navigation Co Ltd v J Fenwick & Co Pty Ltd* (1943) 68 CLR 553, 563 (Latham CJ); *ENE Kos 1 Ltd v Petroleo Brasileiro SA (The Kos) (No 2)* [2012] UKSC 17; [2012] 2 WLR 976, [59] (Lord Clarke); *Tetra Pak Manufacturing Pty Ltd v Challenger Life Nominees Pty Ltd* [2013] NSWSC 349, [47]. In insurance, see *Munro, Brice & Co v War Risks Association* [1918] 2 KB 78 (KB), 88–89; *Kodak (Australasia) Pty Ltd v Retail Traders Mutual Indemnity Insurance Association* (1942) 42 SR (NSW) 231 (FC), 237 (Jordan CJ); *Wallaby Grip Ltd v QBE Insurance (Australia) Ltd* [2010] HCA 9; (2010) 240 CLR 444, [25]–[28]; *Omega Proteins Ltd v Aspen Insurance UK Ltd* [2010] EWHC 2280 (Comm); [2011] 1 All ER (Comm) 313, [88]–[95]. See also [5–11] (onus and conditions precedent).

Indemnified Parties and Others

[5–34] Loss to an indemnified party. The general rule is that the loss must be to a person who, according to the terms of the contract, is to be protected by the promise of indemnity. It makes little sense to indemnify one person against a loss to another. The point has arisen in several cases concerning share sales, where there has been a promise to indemnify the purchaser in respect of a liability of the company whose shares are being sold.[141] In *Waterloo Holdings Pty Ltd v Timso*[142] the deed effecting the share sale included a draft financial statement for the company and an indemnity from the vendor to the purchaser against 'any liabilities of the company which exist at this date and which are not shown in such financial statements'. The purchaser later discovered undisclosed liabilities of the company and claimed under the indemnity. Sheller JA, with whom Powell JA agreed, described the language used in the indemnity clause as 'obscure and intractable'. Sheppard AJA considered that it was not a 'true' indemnity. The vendor, as indemnifier, was not promising to protect the company against its liabilities; nor was an undisclosed liability of the company a direct liability or loss of the purchaser as the indemnified party. The relevant loss to the purchaser was the diminution in the value of the shares purchased, but the indemnity clause was not drafted in those terms. Sheppard AJA was prepared to construe the clause as a simple promise to pay the purchaser the amount of any liabilities that were existing at the time of the sale but undisclosed in the financial statements.

A different approach was taken in *Kostka v Addison*.[143] The vendors of the shares indemnified the purchasers against 'all claims, demands or liabilities against or of the Company . . . whether contingent or actual, or which may accrue or become due at any subsequent date'. A third party obtained judgment against the company and the purchasers sought to set-off amounts payable by the vendors under the indemnity against amounts owing to the vendors under the contract of sale. McPherson J remarked that the promise was not an indemnity 'in the ordinary sense' because it was not directly concerned with a loss to the purchasers, but rather a liability of the company. Assuming that ordinary indemnity principles could still be applied, McPherson J allowed the purchasers credit for the full amount of the judgment against the company, on the basis that the purchasers could have obtained in equity an order for payment to themselves of that sum. Whether that form of relief would properly have been available in the circumstances is unclear.[144] The result is open to the criticism that this sum may not have reflected the purchasers' true loss. McPherson J himself acknowledged that the measure of damages for breach of the indemnity clause would not necessarily be the amount of the judgment against the company.[145]

[5–35] The effect of assignment.[146] Subject to any contrary terms in the contract, the benefit of a non-insurance promise of indemnity is generally regarded as non-personal and

---

[141] In addition to the cases referred to in the text, see *De Santo v Munduna Investments Ltd (in liq)* (1981) 12 ATR 517 (NSWCA). For a different context, see *Morgan Grenfell Development Capital Syndications Ltd v Arrows Autosports Ltd* [2004] EWHC 1015 (Ch), [58]–[59] (financing arrangement).

[142] *Waterloo Holdings Pty Ltd v Timso* (NSWCA, 28 August 1997).

[143] *Kostka v Addison* [1986] 1 Qd R 416 (SC).

[144] McPherson J was influenced by the interest rule, as to which see [7–44], [7–56], [7–62].

[145] *Kostka v Addison* [1986] 1 Qd R 416 (SC), 419.

[146] See generally GJ Tolhurst, *The Assignment of Contractual Rights* (Oxford, Hart Publishing, 2006), 395–96, para 8.13.

assignable.[147] Assignment does not alter the scope of the indemnity unless the terms of the contract indicate otherwise. The relevant loss continues to be the loss to the indemnified party/assignor and not the assignee; this is so even where the assignment is made before actual loss has occurred.[148] In *Pendal Nominees Pty Ltd v Lednez Industries (Australia) Ltd*,[149] the indemnity was given to two parties, Darlings and Allied, in connection with a land reclamation project. The scope of the indemnity included claims, costs and damages 'to which Darlings or Allied shall or may be liable' by reason of the land filling being unsuitable, or the indemnifier failing to perform its obligations under the reclamation agreement. Allied sold part of the reclaimed land and assigned to the purchaser the benefit of the right to indemnity. Some time later, an environmental agency issued a contamination notice in relation to the land. It was held that the purchaser, as assignee of the indemnity, was not entitled to protection against its own losses or liabilities relating to the land. At most, the purchaser as assignee had a right to enforce the indemnity in respect of any losses suffered by Allied.[150]

There is, then, a risk of irrecoverable loss if the original indemnified party disposes of its interest in the subject-matter associated with the indemnity to the assignee for full value. The result may be different where the indemnified party is liable to the assignee and that liability is within the scope of the indemnity. Consider the following situation: A promises to indemnify B against a liability to C; B, being unable to meet a claim by C, assigns to C the benefit of the indemnity from A; C, as assignee, enforces the indemnity against A. C may obtain from A the full amount owed by B to C.[151] This is not, however, a matter of enforcing the indemnity in respect of a loss to C. The indemnity is enforced in respect of B's potential loss, namely, its liability to C. The amount of the potential loss to B corresponds to the amount owed to C. The situation is, therefore, only very loosely analogous to that where A provides to C a guarantee of B's debts.[152]

[5–36] Where indemnified person is not a party to the contract.[153] It is not uncommon for a party to seek protection for itself and others, such as its employees or agents, related companies in the same corporate group, or other contractors engaged in a common venture. Those persons may not be parties to the contract. Accordingly, consider the case where A promises to indemnify B and C, B is a party to the contract but C is not. Enforcement of the indemnity to protect C, as an intended beneficiary of the indemnity,[154] can be approached

---

[147] *Maloney v Campbell* (1897) 28 SCR 228; *Re Perkins; Poyser v Beyfus* [1898] 2 Ch 182 (CA); *British Union and National Insurance Co v Rawson* [1916] 2 Ch 476 (CA), 483–84 (Pickford LJ), 485–86 (Warrington LJ); *Taylor v Sanders* [1937] VLR 62 (FC), 65; *Geo Thompson (Aust) Pty Ltd v Vittadello* [1978] VR 199 (FC), 211 (Gillard J); *Shaw v Lighthouseexpress Ltd* [2010] EWCA Civ 161, [16]–[18] (Jacob LJ). Contrast *Rendall v Morphew* (1914) 84 LJ Ch 517 (Ch). For the position in insurance, see J Birds, B Lynch and S Milnes, *MacGillivray on Insurance Law*, 12th edn (London, Sweet & Maxwell, 2012), 637–42, paras 21-001–21.010.

[148] See, eg, *Maloney v Campbell* (1897) 28 SCR 228, 233–34; *British Union and National Insurance Co v Rawson* [1916] 2 Ch 476 (CA); *Taylor v Sanders* [1937] VLR 62 (FC); *Housing Guarantee Fund Ltd v Yusef* [1991] 2 VR 17 (FC) (guarantee and indemnity); *Pendal Nominees Pty Ltd v Lednez Industries (Australia) Ltd* (1996) 40 NSWLR 282 (SC).

[149] *Pendal Nominees Pty Ltd v Lednez Industries (Australia) Ltd* (1996) 40 NSWLR 282 (SC).

[150] *Pendal Nominees Pty Ltd v Lednez Industries (Australia) Ltd* (1996) 40 NSWLR 282 (SC), 290–92.

[151] See [7–50].

[152] cf *British Union and National Insurance Co v Rawson* [1916] 2 Ch 476 (CA), 484 (Pickford LJ); *Taylor v Sanders* [1937] VLR 62 (FC), 66.

[153] See generally MP Furmston and JW Carter, 'Indemnities for the Benefit of Others' (2011) 27 *Journal of Contract Law* 82.

[154] If C is not an intended beneficiary of A's promise, C may attempt to obtain the benefit of B's indemnity from A, either by a claim against A as assignee (see [5–35]) or B (see [7–63]–[7–64]).

from two perspectives: C enforces the indemnity directly against A, or B enforces the indemnity against A for C's benefit.

[5–37] Direct enforcement by non-party. The obvious obstacle is the common law doctrine of privity. In England, and in some other common law jurisdictions, the indemnified non-party may circumvent that limitation by relying upon statute.[155] There are also Australian decisions accepting that non-insurance indemnities against liabilities to third parties may fall within a limited common law exception to the privity doctrine.[156] Another possibility is that a party to the contract purported to enter as agent for the indemnified principal.[157] The device of agency may require two further doctrinal matters to be resolved: the provision of consideration by or on behalf of the principal; and, where the terms of the indemnity refer to a class of indemnified persons, the principal may have to be known or ascertainable as a member of that class at the time of contract.[158]

[5–38] Enforcement by party for benefit of non-party. It may be possible to discern an intention to create a trust of the benefit of the indemnity, to be held by the contracting party for the indemnified non-party.[159] Although the indemnity is enforced by the contracting party as trustee, the relevant loss is that of the non-party as beneficiary.[160]

The law of trusts aside, the contracting party may seek to enforce the promise of indemnity as a primary obligation for the benefit of the non-party. Two different situations must be considered. Where the subject-matter of the indemnity is a loss to the indemnified non-party, or a liability of the indemnified non-party to another, the indemnity can, in appropriate circumstances, be specifically enforced. In *Trident General Insurance Co Ltd v McNiece Bros Pty Ltd*,[161] Mason CJ and Wilson J remarked that

> [t]here is no reason to doubt that the courts will grant specific performance of a contract of indemnity or insurance, even if it involves payment of a lump sum, at least where the payment is to be made to a third party, damages being an inadequate remedy.

There is a clear analogy with the enforcement of promises to pay a third party.[162]

[155] See Contracts (Rights of Third Parties) Act 1999; *Laemthong International Lines Co Ltd v Artis (The Laemthong Glory) (No 2)* [2005] EWCA Civ 519; [2005] 1 Lloyd's Rep 688; *Far East Chartering Ltd v Great Eastern Shipping Co Ltd (The Jag Ravi)* [2012] EWCA Civ 180; [2012] 1 Lloyd's Rep 637 (shipowner enforcing letter of indemnity issued to charterer). cf *Pendal Nominees Pty Ltd v Lednez Industries (Australia) Ltd* (1996) 40 NSWLR 282 (SC) (unsuccessful attempt to rely upon Conveyancing Act 1919 (NSW), s 70).

[156] *Sandtara Pty Ltd v Abigroup Ltd* (NSWSC, 25 and 29 September 1997); *Gate Gourmet Australia Pty Ltd (in liq) v Gate Gourmet Holding AG* [2004] NSWSC 149, [250]–[255] (extending the exception recognised in *Trident General Insurance Co Ltd v McNiece Bros Pty Ltd* (1988) 165 CLR 107, 123–24 (Mason CJ and Wilson J), 172 (Toohey J)).

[157] See, eg, *Borkan General Trading Ltd v Monsoon Shipping Ltd (The Borvigilant and The Romina G)* [2003] EWCA Civ 935; [2003] 2 Lloyd's Rep 520.

[158] *Trident General Insurance Co Ltd v McNiece Bros Pty Ltd* (1987) 8 NSWLR 270 (CA), 276–77 (McHugh JA); *Trident General Insurance Co Ltd v McNiece Bros Pty Ltd* (1988) 165 CLR 107, 112–13 (Mason CJ and Wilson J). But see P Watts and FMB Reynolds, *Bowstead & Reynolds on Agency*, 19th edn (London, Sweet & Maxwell, 2010), 78–80, para 2-065. cf the requirement under Contracts (Rights of Third Parties) Act 1999, s 1(3).

[159] *Trident General Insurance Co Ltd v McNiece Bros Pty Ltd* (1988) 165 CLR 107; *Sandtara Pty Ltd v Abigroup Ltd* (NSWSC, 25 and 29 September 1997); *Gate Gourmet Australia Pty Ltd (in liq) v Gate Gourmet Holding AG* [2004] NSWSC 149, [256]–[262]. cf *Hepburn v A Tomlinson (Hauliers) Ltd* [1966] AC 451 (HL), 467–68 (Lord Reid) (insurance of goods by bailee).

[160] cf *Lloyd's v Harper* (1880) 16 Ch D 290 (CA), 321 (Lush J); *Coulls v Bagot's Executor and Trustee Co Ltd* (1967) 119 CLR 460, 501 (Windeyer J); *Beswick v Beswick* [1968] AC 58 (HL), 88 (Lord Pearce), 101 (Lord Upjohn).

[161] *Trident General Insurance Co Ltd v McNiece Bros Pty Ltd* (1988) 165 CLR 107, 120. See also *Morgan Grenfell Development Capital Syndications Ltd v Arrows Autosports Ltd* [2004] EWHC 1015 (Ch), [49]; *Affinity Health Pty Ltd v Symbion Health Ltd* [2011] VSC 210, [22].

[162] See, eg, *Beswick v Beswick* [1968] AC 58 (HL).

The other situation is where the indemnity applies to claims by or liabilities to the indemnifier. Indemnities in this form are generally intended to have a prophylactic effect and may be construed as equivalent to, or as importing, a promise not to sue the indemnified persons.[163] If the contracting party can demonstrate a sufficient interest in enforcing the promise to indemnify the non-party, the court may order a stay of the indemnifier's proceedings against the indemnified non-party. The requisite interest may be that the indemnifier's action against the indemnified non-party will lead, or has led, to a corresponding action by the indemnified non-party against the contracting party.[164]

Actual Loss and Potential Loss

[5–39] Distinction between actual and potential loss. The need to distinguish between actual loss and potential loss derives partly from the nature of an indemnity promise and partly from the remedies available to enforce it. As a matter of legal history, contractual rights of indemnity were enforced in courts of common law and in courts of equity.[165] Recovery for actual loss was generally effectuated by remedies of common law origin, in particular, damages for breach of contract. Enforcement of the indemnity in respect of an anticipated loss involved relief that was equitable in nature. That distinction in remedy remains significant nowadays.

Identifying the point of damnification, where a potential loss materialises into an actual loss, involves construction of the contract and characterisation of the circumstances that constitute the loss. Default rules may apply in different contexts to determine when loss occurs. One well-established default rule, for example, is that a mere liability of the indemnified party to a third party is generally regarded as a potential loss only, but a payment to the third party is an actual loss.[166]

[5–40] Accrual of right to enforce indemnity. In broad terms, the time at which the right to enforce the indemnity arises depends upon construction of the contract.[167] A more detailed treatment is given elsewhere[168] but it is appropriate here to outline the major considerations. There are different modes of enforcement, determined by whether the indemnified party seeks protection against an actual loss or a potential loss. The latter mode of enforcement is only available in limited circumstances.[169] If it is available then, clearly, it arises earlier in time than enforcement in relation to actual loss. Where both modes of enforcement are possible – as where a potential loss later crystallises into an actual loss – there has been some suggestion that the earlier mode of enforcement should be used to calculate the running of time for the purposes of limitations statutes.[170]

---

[163] See [8–10].

[164] *Deepak Fertilisers and Petrochemicals Corp v ICI Chemicals & Polymers Ltd* [1999] 1 Lloyd's Rep 387 (CA), 401–02. See further [8–17].

[165] See [1–18]–[1–23], [5–66].

[166] See [6–23].

[167] *Bosma v Larsen* [1966] 1 Lloyd's Rep 22 (QB), 27–28; *Telfair Shipping Corp v Inersea Carriers SA (The Caroline P)* [1985] 1 WLR 553 (QB), 566; *Firma C-Trade SA v Newcastle Protection and Indemnity Association (The Fanti) (No 2)* [1989] 1 Lloyd's Rep 239 (CA), 255 (Bingham LJ); *City of London v Reeve & Co Ltd* [2000] EWHC 138 (TCC); [2000] BLR 211, [30]–[35].

[168] See [5–44]–[5–46].

[169] See [5–66]–[5–68].

[170] *County and District Properties Ltd v C Jenner & Sons Ltd* [1976] 2 Lloyd's Rep 728 (QB), 732, 735–36; *Telfair Shipping Corp v Inersea Carriers SA (The Caroline P)* [1985] 1 WLR 553 (QB), 569–70; *R&H Green & Silley Weir*

Otherwise, the indemnified party is limited to enforcing the indemnity for an actual loss. Whether the cause of action accrues immediately upon the occurrence of the loss, or only at some later point, depends upon the nature of the indemnity promise and any conditions precedent.

Enforcement after Loss

Nature of Enforcement

[5–41] Claim is generally for damages. The conventional view is that the indemnified party recovers for its actual loss under the indemnity by way of a claim for damages for breach of contract.[171] That is, the indemnified party enforces not the primary obligation to indemnify but, instead, the indemnifier's secondary obligation to pay compensation for breach by failing to perform the indemnity. It is then necessary to distinguish the different constructions of the promise of indemnity. For preventive indemnities, Lord Goff's analysis in *Firma C-Trade SA v Newcastle Protection and Indemnity Association (The Fanti) (No 2)*[172] is authoritative. Lord Goff said: 'at common law, a contract of indemnity gives rise to an action for unliquidated damages, arising from the failure of the indemnifier to prevent the indemnified person from suffering damage, for example, by having to pay a third party'.[173] For compensatory indemnities, the relevant breach is the failure to compensate the indemnified party for its loss at the appointed time. An obvious loss suffered by the indemnified party as a result of the breach is the failure to receive the sum that ought to have been paid.[174]

[5–42] Alternative characterisations of the claim. Other characterisations of the indemnified party's claim are possible.[175] A particular case may fall within the circumstances covered by the old form of action for money paid, which are now subsumed within the law of unjust enrichment.[176] Such a claim is not a claim for damages for breach of contract. It has also been suggested that, in the case of a compensatory indemnity, the indemnified party may enforce the indemnifier's primary obligation to pay compensation for actual loss.

In *Royscot Commercial Leasing Ltd v Ismail*,[177] a director of the lessee company entered into a separate contract of indemnity with the lessor, in respect of the lessee's performance under the lease. Hirst LJ accepted the lessor's submission that its claim against the director

---

Ltd v British Railways Board [1985] 1 WLR 570 (QB), 574. *cf City of London v Reeve & Co Ltd* [2000] EWHC 138 (TCC); [2000] BLR 211, [30]–[34].

[171] See [1–19].

[172] *Firma C-Trade SA v Newcastle Protection and Indemnity Association (The Fanti) (No 2)* [1991] 2 AC 1 (HL).

[173] *Firma C-Trade SA v Newcastle Protection and Indemnity Association (The Fanti) (No 2)* [1991] 2 AC 1 (HL), 35.

[174] *cf Forney v Dominion Insurance Co Ltd* [1969] 1 WLR 928 (QB), 936.

[175] See, eg, *Royscot Commercial Leasing Ltd v Ismail* (CA, 29 April 1993); *Codemasters Software Co Ltd v Automobile Club de L'Ouest (No 2)* [2009] EWHC 3194 (Ch); [2010] FSR 13, [31]–[32], [35]; *New Cap Reinsurance Corp Ltd (in liq) v AE Grant* [2008] NSWSC 1015; (2008) 221 FLR 164, [91]–[112]. *cf* also the position in Scotland: *Scott Lithgow Ltd v Secretary of State for Defence* 1989 SC (HL) 9, 20 (Lord Keith); *Scottish and Southern Energy plc v Lerwick Engineering & Fabrication Ltd* [2008] CSOH 41; 2008 SCLR 317, [28].

[176] See [1–22] but *cf* [1–23].

[177] *Royscot Commercial Leasing Ltd v Ismail* (CA, 29 April 1993).

under the indemnity was for a 'debt', so that it was not required to mitigate its loss. If correct,[178] that conclusion must rest on a combination of two factors: first, the indemnity promise was essentially to pay the lessor for loss; secondly, the terms of the indemnity were sufficiently detailed and prescriptive to liquidate the loss. Hirst LJ said that the lessor's argument was advanced as a matter of principle 'without recourse to the actual terms of the indemnity or of the lease agreement', but this cannot be taken literally. The lessor's argument supposed that the indemnity was a promise to pay a readily ascertainable sum upon an event. The measure of loss in the indemnity contract was expressly defined by reference to the lease, which itself contained a detailed formula for calculating the amount due from the lessee company in the event of termination.

[5–43] **Critique of alternative characterisations.** There is no objection in theory to recognising that an indemnified party may, in appropriate cases, enforce a primary right to be indemnified by compensation for an actual loss. To characterise such a claim as one in 'debt' may, however, mislead. The question of whether that label applies has arisen in the cases principally in connection with two issues.[179] The first is whether the claim falls within certain statutory provisions or rules of court which refer, for example, to a 'debt' or 'debt or liquidated demand'.[180] The cases decided before the forms of action were abolished do not *generally* support that characterisation of the claim.[181] More importantly, the meaning of such expressions is not necessarily confined to the old forms of pleading.[182] It may be more to the point to consider whether the claim (even if one in damages) is liquidated in nature. That will depend, in each case, on the terms of the indemnity and the nature of the loss being claimed. It does not necessarily follow that a claim must be liquidated merely because the indemnity is compensatory in nature.[183] Conversely, it is possible (though unusual) for a preventive indemnity to give rise to a claim in damages for a liquidated sum.[184]

The other purpose of characterisation, apparent in cases such as *Royscot Commercial Leasing Ltd v Ismail*,[185] is to justify why ordinary damages principles such as remoteness and mitigation do not apply to the indemnified party's claim. The view advanced in this

---

[178] Contrast *Goulston Discount Co Ltd v Sims* (1967) 111 SJ 682 (CA). See [4–33].

[179] For examples of others, see *F&K Jabbour v Custodian of Israeli Absentee Property* [1954] 1 WLR 139 (QB); *Edmunds v Lloyds Italico* [1986] 1 WLR 492 (CA).

[180] See, eg, *Johnson v Diamond* (1855) 11 Ex 73; 156 ER 750; *Finn v Gavin* [1905] VLR 93 (SC); *Israelson v Dawson* [1933] 1 KB 301 (CA); *Alexander v Ajax Insurance Co Ltd* [1956] VLR 436 (SC); *Odyssey Re (Bermuda) Ltd v Reinsurance Australia Corp Ltd* [2001] NSWSC 266; (2001) 19 ACLC 982; *New Cap Reinsurance Corp Ltd (in liq) v AE Grant* [2008] NSWSC 1015; (2008) 221 FLR 164. cf *Victorian WorkCover Authority v Esso Australia Ltd* [2001] HCA 53; (2001) 207 CLR 520 (nature of statutory right of indemnity). cf also cases on set-off, where the availability of an action for money paid was a factor: *Hardcastle v Netherwood* (1821) 5 B & Ald 93; 106 ER 1127; *Attwooll v Attwooll* (1853) 2 E & B 23; 118 ER 677; *Hutchinson v Sydney* (1854) 10 Ex 438; 156 ER 508; *Crampton v Walker* (1860) 3 El & El 321; 121 ER 463; *Brown v Tibbits* (1862) 11 CBNS 854; 142 ER 1031. See generally W Courtney and JW Carter, 'Debts, Liquidated Sums and the Enforcement of Claims under Guarantees and Indemnities' (2013) 30 *Journal of Contract Law* 70.

[181] See [1–20]–[1–21] (debt), [1–22]–[1–23] (action for money paid).

[182] *Workman, Clark & Co v Lloyd Brazileño* [1908] 1 KB 968 (CA); *Victorian WorkCover Authority v Esso Australia Ltd* [2001] HCA 53; (2001) 207 CLR 520, [29] (Gleeson CJ, Gummow, Hayne and Callinan JJ).

[183] See, eg, *Scott Lithgow Ltd v Secretary of State for Defence* 1989 SC (HL) 9, 22 (Lord Keith) (action accruing on occurrence of loss though loss might not be ascertainable for some time thereafter).

[184] See [1–19].

[185] *Royscot Commercial Leasing Ltd v Ismail* (CA, 29 April 1993). See also *Total Transport Corp v Arcadia Petroleum Ltd (The Eurus)* [1996] 2 Lloyd's Rep 408 (QB), 422; *Codemasters Software Co Ltd v Automobile Club de L'Ouest (No 2)* [2009] EWHC 3194 (Ch); [2010] FSR 13, [31]–[32].

work is that such principles are generally not relevant even where the claim is one for damages for loss within the scope of the indemnity.[186] If that view is accepted, it is unnecessary to characterise the claim as one in debt to arrive at the same result.

Losses within the Scope of the Indemnity

Accrual of Right to Enforce Indemnity

[5–44] **Recovery for actual loss.** The general rule is that the indemnified party's cause of action under a preventive indemnity accrues immediately upon the occurrence of a loss within scope. It is at that point that the indemnifier has failed to keep the indemnified party harmless from loss.[187] It is difficult to identify a general position for compensatory indemnities. The promise to indemnify is not activated unless and until the indemnified party suffers a loss within the scope of the indemnity. The indemnified party's cause of action cannot accrue any earlier. However, there remain various possible constructions. The indemnifier may be required to compensate the indemnified party immediately upon the occurrence of a loss; this has been described as a prima facie construction.[188] Alternatively, the indemnifier may be required to pay compensation only when the amount of the loss is ascertainable and a demand has been made.[189] Another possibility is that the indemnifier is required to pay compensation within a reasonable time after loss.[190]

[5–45] **Ascertainment of actual loss generally not required.** In general, it is not a prerequisite for enforcement that the actual loss be ascertained or readily ascertainable. The terms of the indemnity may provide otherwise.[191] The general position follows directly from the nature of a preventive indemnity, because the cause of action for breach of contract arises upon the occurrence of loss within scope.[192] In relation to compensatory indemnities, the leading decision is *Scott Lithgow Ltd v Secretary of State for Defence*.[193] The House of Lords held, for the purposes of the applicable limitations statute, that the indemnified party's action accrued upon the occurrence of loss, even though the loss could not be precisely quantified at that point. The decision is a striking illustration of the general rule because the contract expressly provided for the indemnified party to submit a priced claim as soon

---

[186] See [5–47]–[5–50].

[187] *Huntley v Sanderson* (1833) 1 Cr & M 467; 149 ER 483; *Collinge v Heywood* (1839) 9 Ad & E 634; 112 ER 1352; *Re Richardson, ex p the Governors of St Thomas's Hospital* [1911] 2 KB 705 (CA), 709 (Cozens-Hardy MR), 712 (Fletcher Moulton LJ); *Rankin v Palmer* (1912) 16 CLR 285, 290 (Griffiths CJ); *Official Assignee v Jarvis* [1923] NZLR 1009 (CA), 1016 (Salmond J); *Wren v Mahony* (1972) 126 CLR 212, 225–26, 230 (Barwick CJ); *Firma C-Trade SA v Newcastle Protection and Indemnity Association (The Fanti) (No 2)* [1991] 2 AC 1 (HL), 35–36 (Lord Goff), 40 (Lord Jauncey).

[188] *Scott Lithgow Ltd v Secretary of State for Defence* 1989 SC (HL) 9, 21–22 (Lord Keith).

[189] See [2–21].

[190] *cf* insurance decisions in Australia and New Zealand: *Stuart v Guardian Royal Exchange Assurance of New Zealand Ltd (No 2)* (1985) 5 ANZ Ins Cas 60-844 (NZHC), 75,279; *Settlement Wine Co Pty Ltd v National & General Insurance Co Ltd* (1994) 62 SASR 40 (SC), 70; *CIC Insurance Ltd v Bankstown Football Club Ltd* (1997) 184 CLR 384, 401–02 (Brennan CJ, Dawson, Toohey and Gaudron JJ); *Tropicus Orchids Flowers and Foliage Pty Ltd v Territory Insurance Office* [1998] NTSC 73; (1998) 148 FLR 441, 487–89 (point not challenged on appeal: *Territory Insurance Office v Tropicus Orchids Flowers and Foliage Pty Ltd* [1999] NTCA 16, [33]); *Brescia Furniture Pty Ltd v QBE Insurance (Australia) Ltd* [2007] NSWSC 598; (2007) 14 ANZ Ins Cas 61-740, [88].

[191] See, eg, [2–21].

[192] See generally *Chandris v Argo Insurance Co Ltd* [1963] 2 Lloyd's Rep 65 (QB), 74; *Castle Insurance Co Ltd v Hong Kong Islands Shipping Co Ltd* [1984] AC 226 (PC), 237–38.

[193] *Scott Lithgow Ltd v Secretary of State for Defence* 1989 SC (HL) 9. See further [5–10].

as possible after an incident giving rise to a loss. Lord Keith, who delivered the leading judgment, was not persuaded by the argument that this construction meant that 'payment might have to be made or accepted on the basis of a rough or inadequate estimate of the loss'.[194]

[5–46] Multiple losses. Assume that there are several consecutive and distinct losses, L1, L2, L3 and so on, all of which are within the scope of the indemnity. An issue that has occasionally arisen is whether there is one breach of the indemnity with several losses, or several breaches of the indemnity, each breach corresponding to the occurrence of a loss. The latter view is correct, at least where each loss is discrete.[195] The point arose in *Crampton v Walker*.[196] The claimant sued for damages for breach of a contract to indemnify the claimant against 'any loss or damage' suffered by reason of accepting a bill of exchange drawn by the defendant. The claimant claimed the amount of the bill with interest as paid, and also costs incurred defending an action brought by the holder. The defendant pleaded a set-off against particular items of loss, and the claimant objected that this was not possible as the losses were all consequences of a single breach of the contract of indemnity. Cockburn CJ dismissed that argument, explaining that 'the cause of action arises only when loss or damage is sustained by the plaintiff, and . . . every fresh loss or damage is a fresh cause of action'.[197]

It follows that it is unnecessary to apply a consequential or compound analysis to distinct losses within the scope of the indemnity. In the example referred to earlier, losses L1, L2 and L3 are considered separately. Whether L2 is recoverable is determined by reference to the breach associated with L2, rather than by considering whether an amount for L2 can be added to L1 as loss flowing from the earlier breach associated with the occurrence of L1.

Impact of Contract Damages Principles

[5–47] Principles appear not to affect recovery for loss within scope. The extent to which, if at all, ordinary contractual damages principles or concepts govern the assessment of loss under an indemnity is somewhat uncertain. A striking feature of the case law is just how rarely reference is made to well-established principles or authorities on contractual damages. It is, consequently, difficult to find clear and authoritative statements accepting or denying that damages principles apply to claims under indemnities. The better view appears to be this: if a loss falls within the scope of the indemnity, then it can be recovered without any further limitation being imposed by the application of contractual damages principles.[198]

---

[194] *Scott Lithgow Ltd v Secretary of State for Defence* 1989 SC (HL) 9, 22.
[195] *Crampton v Walker* (1860) 3 El & El 321; 121 ER 463; *Ex p Wiseman; re Kelson Tritton & Co* (1871) LR 7 Ch App 35, 43 (Mellish LJ) ('contract . . . broken repeatedly at different times upon the happening of various contingencies'); *BNP Paribas v Pacific Carriers Ltd* [2005] NSWCA 72, [5] (Handley JA). *cf* also statutory rights of indemnity: *Attorney-General v Arthur Ryan Automobiles Ltd* [1938] 2 KB 16 (CA); *Howard Rotavator Pty Ltd v Wilson* (1987) 8 NSWLR 498 (CA); *Victorian WorkCover Authority v Esso Australia Ltd* [2001] HCA 53; (2001) 207 CLR 520, [18] (Gleeson CJ, Gummow, Hayne and Callinan JJ); *South Eastern Sydney Area Health Service v Gadiry* [2002] NSWCA 161; (2002) 54 NSWLR 495.
[196] *Crampton v Walker* (1860) 3 El & El 321; 121 ER 463.
[197] *Crampton v Walker* (1860) 3 El & El 321, 328; 121 ER 463, 466.
[198] But see [10–58]–[10–60] (application of law of penalties).

One justification is that such principles do not apply because the indemnified party's claim is not for damages.[199] That may be so in some circumstances, but this is an exception to the general position. The explanation is therefore not sufficient.

More generally, the view is supported by three related perspectives. One perspective is inferential. It draws upon the relative rarity of references to damages principles, and also upon statements to the effect that protection against loss is a matter of scope.[200] The scope of the indemnity defines the extent of the indemnifier's responsibility for the indemnified party's loss.[201] If a loss is within scope, there is no room for the further application of damages principles.

A second perspective is that limitations on the scope of the indemnity may resemble, or be incorporated by reference to, concepts found in the law of damages. The scope may, for example, be limited to losses that have not been incurred unreasonably.[202] Thus, if a loss falls within the scope of the indemnity, it also satisfies the limitations that would be imposed as a matter of law; the application of damages principles to the indemnified party's claim is no more restrictive. Whether a loss is within scope must be determined before damages principles can be applied to a claim for breach by failing to indemnify. Thus, where the loss is beyond scope, it can generally be said that it has been excluded as a matter of construction, not as a matter of law.

A third perspective is that, whatever the limitations on the scope of the indemnity, damages principles may be applied to the breach of the indemnity in such a way that they do not affect the accumulation of loss within scope.

The theoretical analysis that underpins these perspectives is developed elsewhere.[203] For the present, it is sufficient to consider briefly the three significant limiting damages principles, namely, causation, remoteness and mitigation.

[5–48] Causation. Issues of causation arise at two stages. There is, first, the question of whether a particular loss is within scope. That depends on whether the loss follows from the activating event or circumstances according to the causal or connective relation required by the indemnity. A second issue is whether a particular loss to the indemnified party has been caused by breach of the indemnity and is recoverable as damages for that breach. Principles of causation apply as a matter of law only at the second stage; the first stage is a matter of construction. Yet, it is at the first stage, and not the second, that issues of causation are disputed. Provided that the loss is within scope, it seems that legal causation for the breach is easily established for each of the two common constructions of promises of indemnity.[204]

[5–49] Remoteness. The scope of the indemnity may be limited, as a matter of construction, by analogy with the concept of remoteness.[205] Regardless of whether such a limitation applies, once it has been determined that a loss is within scope, then principles of remoteness of

---

[199] See [5–42]–[5–43].
[200] See [5–31]–[5–32].
[201] cf *Transfield Shipping Inc v Mercator Shipping Inc (The Achilleas)* [2008] UKHL 48; [2009] 1 AC 61, [31]–[32] (Lord Hoffmann).
[202] See [4–29]–[4–33].
[203] See [5–57]–[5–65].
[204] See [5–59], [5–61], [5–65].
[205] See [4–26]–[4–28], [10–47].

damage do not further restrict recovery for that loss as a matter of law.[206] Losses beyond the scope of the indemnity are treated differently.[207]

A leading example is *Muhammad Issa El Sheikh Ahmad v Ali*.[208] A contract for the sale of land was not carried to completion, and the vendors entered into a second contract to sell the land to new purchasers. The second contract addressed the possibility that the first purchaser might claim damages or a refund of his part payment under the first contract. In clause 3, the new purchasers undertook 'to guarantee and to pay all these amounts on behalf of the [vendors] on condition that they will not exceed the amount of £P 2017'. Clause 7 dealt with notification of actions and the conduct of a defence. The first purchaser sued the vendors and obtained a judgment against them. The judgment was later enforced by execution against other property of the vendors. That property was sold at a public auction for an amount well below its market value, with some of the proceeds being used to satisfy the balance of the judgment owing to the first purchaser.

At issue was whether the capital loss at auction was too remote to recover as damages for the second purchasers' breach of clause 3. The clause was, in substance, a promise to indemnify the vendors against the first purchaser's claim. The capital loss was held to be recoverable. Lord Uthwatt said:[209]

> Whether the contract be read as a contract to indemnify the vendors at all stages or as a contract to indemnify the vendors against the amounts due to [the first purchaser] with a right in the vendors to fight [him] to such extent as they chose, the result is, in their Lordships' opinion, the same . . . On the first basis the damages claimed fall within the terms of the contract on its true construction, and on the second they are damages which, on the facts found by the trial judge, might reasonably be expected to be in the contemplation of the parties.

The difference between the two constructions of the contract is instructive. On the first interpretation, the scope of the indemnity extended to loss arising through the first purchaser enforcing his claim against the vendors. The capital loss at auction was within scope and so Lord Uthwatt made no reference to principles of remoteness. On the second interpretation, the indemnity only covered the amount due from the vendors to the first purchaser, and legal costs incurred by the vendors in defending the claim. The capital loss at auction was a consequential loss beyond the scope of the indemnity and subject to principles of remoteness.

Although the decision concerned an indemnity that was preventive in nature, remoteness should be equally irrelevant to claims for loss within the scope of compensatory indemnities.[210]

---

[206] *Muhammad Issa El Sheikh Ahmad v Ali* [1947] AC 414 (PC); *Triad Shipping Co v Stellar Chartering & Brokerage Inc (The Island Archon)* [1994] 2 Lloyd's Rep 227 (CA); *Mediterranean Freight Services Ltd v BP Oil International Ltd (The Fiona)* [1994] 2 Lloyd's Rep 506 (CA), 522 (Hoffmann LJ); *Total Transport Corp v Arcadia Petroleum Ltd (The Eurus)* [1996] 2 Lloyd's Rep 408 (QB), 432 (remoteness a matter of construction only) (but *cf Total Transport Corp v Arcadia Petroleum Ltd (The Eurus)* [1998] 1 Lloyd's Rep 351 (CA), 360–61 (Staughton LJ)); *Caledonia North Sea Ltd v London Bridge Engineering Ltd* 2000 SLT 1123 (IH), 1177–78 (Lord Sutherland) and on appeal: *Caledonia North Sea Ltd v British Telecommunications plc (The Piper Alpha)* [2002] UKHL 4; [2002] 1 Lloyd's Rep 553, [100]–[101] (Lord Hoffmann); *Bovis Lend Lease Ltd v RD Fire Protection Ltd* [2003] EWHC 939 (TCC); (2003) 89 Con LR 169, [65]; *Zaccardi v Caunt* [2008] NSWCA 202, [33] (Campbell JA). See also [10–45]–[10–47].

[207] See [5–52]–[5–55].

[208] *Muhammad Issa El Sheikh Ahmad v Ali* [1947] AC 414 (PC).

[209] *Muhammad Issa El Sheikh Ahmad v Ali* [1947] AC 414 (PC), 427.

[210] See [5–59].

[5–50] **Mitigation.** Insofar as principles of mitigation are mentioned at all in indemnity decisions, it is usually in connection with the accumulation or reduction of losses within the scope of the indemnity. So, for example, mitigation of damage may be raised where the indemnity covers loss arising from default by a third party under a contract with the indemnified party.[211] The reference point is generally the third party's failure to perform, which is the subject of the indemnity, rather than the indemnifier's breach of contract by failing to indemnify.

The choice of an internal, rather than external, reference point seems to be explained by two factors. First, there are other characteristics of indemnities that resemble principles of mitigation and which are applied through construction.[212] A restriction on the scope of the indemnity to exclude losses incurred unreasonably is one example. Mitigation principles might then be irrelevant because they have been displaced by the parties' agreement, or, perhaps, because they substantially duplicate those other characteristics and are no more restrictive. Secondly, considering the manner in which the indemnifier breaches the contract by failing to indemnify, principles of mitigation of damage will often be engaged too late to have any meaningful effect on the accumulation of loss within scope.[213]

Losses beyond the Scope of the Indemnity

[5–51] **Nature of consequential loss.** The expression 'consequential loss' is used here to describe a loss that arises from the indemnifier's failure to perform the indemnity, but which is not within the scope of the indemnity.[214] Consequential loss may be beyond the scope of the indemnity for various reasons. The loss may simply not fall within the express statement of scope, or it may be covered by an express or implied exception to scope.

The existence of a consequential loss implies that there is a prior loss that is within scope; otherwise, there would have been no failure to perform the indemnity. If the indemnity has not been engaged, a loss that is beyond scope is clearly not recoverable. There must also be a sufficient connection between the prior loss and the consequential loss. That connection depends upon the nature of the indemnity promise. In the case of a compensatory indemnity, consequential losses arise from the same type of event, namely, late payment or non-payment of the sum due by way of compensation. Preventive indemnities are more difficult to analyse. Consequential losses may follow the occurrence of any type of loss within scope. Recovery for consequential losses may then be restricted through construction of the indemnity, or by applying damages principles. A significant principle in this context is that there is no right to damages for a loss that, in substance, arises from a failure to pay damages promptly.

The discussion that follows is not concerned with the possibility that consequential losses might be recovered on some other basis not associated with the indemnity.

---

[211] See also [4–29], [9–52].

[212] See [4–29].

[213] See [5–59], [5–63].

[214] It is not necessary to enter the debate about the meaning of that expression as used in exclusion clauses, in particular, whether it describes an aspect of remoteness of loss (*Croudace Construction Ltd v Cawoods Concrete Products Ltd* [1978] 2 Lloyd's Rep 55 (CA) but cf *Caledonia North Sea Ltd v British Telecommunications plc (The Piper Alpha)* [2002] UKHL 4; [2002] 1 Lloyd's Rep 553, [100] (Lord Hoffmann)) or an aspect of measure of loss (*Environmental Systems Pty Ltd v Peerless Holdings Ltd* [2008] VSCA 26; (2008) 19 VR 358) or an aspect of causation of loss.

Compensatory Indemnities

[5–52] Damages for late payment or non-payment of compensation. Consider a case involving successive discrete losses, L1 and L2. L1 is within the scope of the indemnity. L2 is not, but arises from the indemnifier's breach of contract. The breach is the indemnifier's failure to pay compensation for L1 at the appointed time. Where this occurs, the indemnified party can suffer two kinds of loss: (1) loss of the compensation that ought to have been paid (that is, the amount due for L1); and (2) other losses in addition to that sum, such as interest costs on money borrowed in its place, or losses sustained through being unable to apply that sum productively to its business (L2).

It will be seen[215] that the indemnified party's right to recover for L2 is determined simply by applying ordinary damages principles to the indemnifier's breach of contract. It is, of course, possible for the contract to limit or exclude the right to damages for L2. One instance may be where L2 would otherwise have been within the scope of the indemnity, but for being caught by an express or implied exclusion from scope. In general, however, the statement of scope of a compensatory indemnity seems to be understood to define the extent of the primary obligation to indemnify, but not also to limit the secondary obligation to pay damages for breach.

[5–53] Illustrations. Decisions involving non-insurance indemnities are rare. One obstacle has been the common law's traditional reluctance to allow damages for the defendant's failure to pay money to the claimant on time.[216] In a number of insurance decisions in Australia and New Zealand,[217] an insured has recovered for consequential losses due to the insurer's breach by failing to make timely payment.[218] A non-insurance example is *Krehic v Clark*.[219] The claimant provided a guarantee to a finance company and the defendant agreed to indemnify the claimant in respect of his liability as guarantor. There was no express provision in the indemnity for interest on sums paid. The claimant was called upon to pay and, in doing so, he was forced to break a lucrative investment and to borrow money at a high rate of interest. The claimant was awarded damages for those losses on the basis that they were within the contemplation of the parties and were caused by the defendant's breach of the indemnity by failing to repay the claimant at the required time.

---

[215] See [5–53].

[216] But now see, eg, *Hungerfords v Walker* (1989) 171 CLR 125; *Sempra Metals Ltd (formerly Metallgesellschaft Ltd) v Inland Revenue Commissioners* [2007] UKHL 34; [2008] 1 AC 561 (HL).

[217] As to the English position, see [2–31]–[2–32].

[218] See, eg, *Stuart v Guardian Royal Exchange Assurance of New Zealand Ltd (No 2)* (1985) 5 ANZ Ins Cas 60-844 (NZHC); *New Zealand Insurance Co Ltd v Harris* [1990] 1 NZLR 10 (CA); *Settlement Wine Co Pty Ltd v National & General Insurance Co Ltd* (1994) 62 SASR 40 (SC), 82; *CIC Insurance Ltd v Bankstown Football Club Ltd* (1995) 8 ANZ Ins Cas 61-232 (NSWCA), 75,565–66 (Kirby P), 75,571 (Priestley JA), 75-597–98 (Powell JA) (revd but this point left open: *CIC Insurance Ltd v Bankstown Football Club Ltd* (1997) 184 CLR 384, 411); *Tropicus Orchids Flowers and Foliage Pty Ltd v Territory Insurance Office* [1998] NTSC 73; (1998) 148 FLR 441, 487–89 (affd without appeal on this point: *Territory Insurance Office v Tropicus Orchids Flowers and Foliage Pty Ltd* [1999] NTCA 16, [33]); *Brescia Furniture Pty Ltd v QBE Insurance (Australia) Ltd* [2007] NSWSC 598; (2007) 14 ANZ Ins Cas 61-740, [497]–[510]. See also N Campbell, 'Monetary Remedies for Wrongful Declinatures of Insurance Claims' (2004) 15 *Insurance Law Journal* 185; S Drummond, 'Damages for Consequential Loss When the Insurer Fails to Pay' (2005) 16 *Insurance Law Journal* 128. *cf* the statutory right to interest under Insurance Contracts Act 1984 (Cth), s 57.

[219] *Krehic v Clark* [1991] 1 NZLR 703 (HC). *cf Petre v Duncombe* (1851) 20 LJQB 242 (see [10–22]); *Ex p Bishop; re Fox, Walker & Co* (1880) 15 Ch D 400 (CA), 421–22; *McColl's Wholesale Pty Ltd v State Bank of New South Wales* [1984] 3 NSWLR 365 (SC), 376–77. The latter two authorities refer to common law damages principles and also to equitable principles concerning suretyship.

Preventive Indemnities

[5–54] Restrictions on recovery. Consider again a case where the indemnified party sustains two discrete losses: L1 and later L2. L1 is within the scope of the indemnity. L2 is not, but arises as a consequence of L1. For the indemnified party to recover an amount for L2 as damages for breach of contract, the following conditions must be met:

(1) L2 satisfies general damages principles as applied to the breach associated with the occurrence of L1;

(2) properly characterised, L2 is not merely a loss arising from the 'late' payment of damages for L1;[220] and

(3) the terms of the contract do not preclude recovery for L2.

[5–55] Illustrations. One of the lines of analysis in *Muhammad Issa El Sheikh Ahmad v Ali*[221] acknowledges the possibility of recovery for loss that is beyond the scope of the indemnity. It will be recalled[222] that the indemnifiers did not protect the indemnified parties against a specified liability to another. This led eventually to an execution sale, at a substantial undervalue, of certain property of the indemnified parties. Lord Uthwatt reasoned that the capital loss in the sale was recoverable even if the scope of the indemnity was limited to the specified liability. The loss was a consequence of the indemnifiers' breach of the contract to indemnify, and was within the parties' reasonable contemplation. Furthermore, although the indemnity clause attached a monetary limit to the specified liability, that limit did not apply to the claim for damages for breach of contract.

[5–56] Exclusion of loss beyond scope. A typical indemnity clause is drafted in the form an affirmative statement of scope, perhaps together with express exclusions for particular kinds of loss, such as lost profits or 'indirect' or 'consequential' loss. A claim for a loss, L2, that follows from another loss within scope, L1, may fail at the threshold because L2 is expressly excluded from the scope of the indemnity. The same reasoning should apply where L2 falls within an implied exclusion from scope that is justified on a specific basis, such as the indemnified party's negligence.

Alternatively, L2 might be excluded on the more general ground that the statement of scope exhaustively defines the extent of the indemnifier's responsibility. Whether it does so is a matter of construction.[223] The parties may expressly provide that the indemnity is exhaustive or non-exhaustive. Where there is no expression of intention then, in many cases if not all, the appropriate inference may be that the indemnity is exhaustive. That inference seems particularly compelling where there is a detailed indemnity clause in a written contract. A similar argument might be made for indemnities specifically against the consequences of the indemnifier's wrong, such as negligence or breach of contract.[224] The indemnified party would already have a legal right to recover for loss from the wrong. The purpose of the indemnity is, presumably, to prescribe a different (and usually more

---

[220] *President of India v Lips Maritime Corp (The Lips)* [1988] AC 395 (HL), 424–25 (Lord Brandon); *Ventouris v Mountain (The Italia Express) (No 2)* [1992] 2 Lloyd's Rep 281 (QB); *Sprung v Royal Insurance (UK) Ltd* [1999] Lloyd's Rep IR 111 (CA). See further [2–32].

[221] *Muhammad Issa El Sheikh Ahmad v Ali* [1947] AC 414 (PC), 427.

[222] See [5–49].

[223] *cf Ventouris v Mountain (The Italia Express) (No 2)* [1992] 2 Lloyd's Rep 281 (QB) (statute fixing extent of liability under a valued policy of marine insurance).

[224] *cf* [10–20].

favourable) basis for protection against loss from the wrong. It seems unlikely that the parties intended to allow recovery of further consequential losses, caused by the indemnifier's failure to prevent other loss from the wrong.

Support for the view that an indemnity is often exhaustive might be drawn from two sources. First, there are judicial statements in terms that the indemnified party's right to be protected against loss is determined simply by reference to the scope of the indemnity.[225] Secondly, cases where L2 is a loss incurred in an attempt to mitigate the loss L1 would be clear candidates for the application of a consequential loss analysis. Yet, it is doubtful that this inclusionary aspect of mitigation is generally applicable to claims under indemnities.[226]

Theoretical Justifications

[5–57] **Concept of exact protection.** These principles governing the recovery of actual loss embody the concept of exact protection in two important respects. There is the requirement that an indemnified party suffer actual loss before it has a right at law to recover for that loss. For compensatory indemnities, the requirement is inherent in the nature of the promise of indemnity. For preventive indemnities, the need for actual loss derives from the manner in which the promise of indemnity is enforced.

There is no difficulty with allowing an indemnified party to obtain payment for a loss once it has actually occurred. But the indemnified party may be over-compensated if it is allowed to recover for a loss that has not yet arisen. The loss may never occur, or it may occur but to a lesser extent than anticipated. As Fletcher Moulton LJ explained in *Re Richardson*,[227] the common law 'would not help a man to make a profit out of what was merely an indemnity'. An indemnified party may, in appropriate cases, obtain relief before suffering loss, but this does not undermine the validity of the explanation as it concerns claims for actual loss. The indemnified party has a right to damages for its actual loss, whereas an order for specific enforcement involves discretionary factors. The relief takes a variety of forms and does not necessarily compel payment by the indemnifier directly to the indemnified party.

The other aspect is that protection against actual loss within the scope of the indemnity is determined by construction. Recovery for such loss is not further limited by common law damages principles, even though the indemnified party's claim is conventionally regarded as one for damages for breach of contract. This characteristic must, however, be reconciled with orthodox contract doctrine.[228]

[5–58] **Uniformity in protection.** The characteristics above produce substantial uniformity in the extent of protection among various modes of enforcement of the indemnity, and also between performance and enforcement of the indemnity. There are, of course, significant differences between a claim for damages for breach of contract and a claim for a sum payable pursuant to a primary contractual obligation. Where, however, the indemnified party merely claims for an actual loss within the scope of the indemnity, the extent of protection ought generally to be the same. Common law damages principles do not further

---

[225] See [5–32].
[226] See [4–36], [5–63].
[227] *Re Richardson, ex p the Governors of St Thomas's Hospital* [1911] 2 KB 705 (CA), 712.
[228] See [5–59]–[5–65].

restrict recovery of loss within scope for either form of claim. Both forms of claim are subject to any limitations that apply as a matter of construction, such as the expectation that the indemnified party act reasonably in accumulating losses within the scope of the indemnity.

The indemnified party's right to recover for actual loss within scope is no less extensive than its right to receive performance of the indemnity in respect of such loss. This is so, whether the indemnity is performed voluntarily or the indemnifier is compelled by law to perform the indemnity in relation to a potential loss before it crystallises into an actual loss. In neither case do common law principles of causation, remoteness or mitigation of damage enter the question.

Compensatory Indemnities

[5–59] **Why recovery not limited by damages principles.** It is relatively straightforward to explain why causation, remoteness and mitigation do not affect the recovery of losses within the scope of the indemnity. Those concepts generally apply to the non-payment of compensation, rather than to the accumulation of loss within scope.[229]

The indemnifier commits a breach of contract by failing to pay compensation at the appointed time. That breach causes the indemnified party to suffer a loss at least equal to the sum not paid. But, by definition, this is the amount of the indemnified party's loss within scope as determined in accordance with the terms of the contract. The remoteness analysis is simple to the point of redundancy. The loss of the sum is a natural consequence of the indemnifier's breach by failing to pay it. Thus, the amount of the indemnified party's loss within the scope of the indemnity is always recoverable as damages because it constitutes a loss under the first limb of *Hadley v Baxendale*.[230]

A promisee is not expected to mitigate loss until breach occurs[231] and principles of mitigation are directed to the consequences of breach. Thus, to the extent that such principles would apply to a breach of the indemnity, they operate at a time and in a manner that generally does not affect the accumulation of loss within scope. Conversely, there are characteristics of indemnities that resemble principles of mitigation of damage but cannot be explained by reference to such principles. An indemnified party may, for example, be expected to act reasonably in incurring loss,[232] even though such conduct occurs before the indemnity is enlivened or breached.

Preventive Indemnities

[5–60] **Why recovery not limited by damages principles.** There are at least two theoretical perspectives. One perspective is that ordinary damages principles do apply to claims for losses within scope but that, in their application, such principles do not limit recovery. This is described as the orthodox analysis. Another perspective is that the scope of the indemnity represents an agreement that the indemnifier will be responsible for loss exclusively on the stated basis.[233] This is described as the 'agreed damages' analysis.

---

[229] See [5–52].
[230] *Hadley v Baxendale* (1854) 9 Ex 341; 156 ER 145.
[231] H McGregor, *McGregor on Damages*, 18th edn (London, Sweet & Maxwell, 2009), 243–45, paras 7-020–7-022.
[232] See [4–29].
[233] *cf* [5–56].

Orthodox Analysis

[5–61] Causation. Assuming that a loss is within the scope of the indemnity, the causation analysis applied to the breach is trivial. The indemnifier promises to keep the indemnified party harmless from losses within scope. The indemnified party sustains a loss within scope *because* the indemnifier has failed to prevent it. Where there are multiple losses within scope, each loss is assessed by reference to the breach corresponding to the occurrence of the loss.[234]

[5–62] Remoteness. The occurrence of a particular loss within the scope of the indemnity is a natural and reasonably expected consequence of the indemnifier's breach by failing to prevent it. The loss is not too remote to recover as damages for that breach because it satisfies the first, or at least the second, limb of *Hadley v Baxendale*.[235] This explanation may derive some support from Lord Hoffmann's judgment in *Caledonia North Sea Ltd v British Telecommunications plc (The Piper Alpha)*.[236] One issue was whether the indemnifier could rely on a separate exclusion clause in the contract to resist a claim under the indemnity for losses sustained by the indemnified party in the settlement of third party claims. The indemnifier's argument went thus. The exclusion clause applied to 'indirect or consequential losses'. These were losses that would be recoverable, if at all, under the second limb of *Hadley v Baxendale*. The settlement figures were above the level that would have been awarded under Scots law. The excess was a loss that did not arise naturally, that is, under the first limb, and could only be recovered under the second limb. The exclusion clause thus prevented recovery of the excess under the indemnity.

Lord Hoffmann considered that the exclusion clause applied to claims for breaches of other terms of the contract and not to claims under the indemnity for liabilities arising outside the contract. The indemnifier's reliance on the distinction between the first and second limbs of *Hadley v Baxendale* was, therefore, irrelevant. However, Lord Hoffmann went on to say:[237]

> In any case, even if the *Hadley v Baxendale* dichotomy had any relevance, I do not think that the increase in the quantum of damages can be regarded as a different kind of loss. . . . It remains compensation for death or injury. If such compensation falls in principle within the scope of the indemnity, I do not think that it matters that, perhaps for reasons of which the indemnifier was unaware, it turns out to be greater than he might have expected.

Lord Hoffmann's point was that the loss was of a kind within the scope of the indemnity; its magnitude alone did not alter its character. But if it is right to interpret his remarks as rebutting the argument based on the second limb of *Hadley v Baxendale*, those remarks seem to imply that a loss of a kind within scope could be assigned to the first limb.

[5–63] Mitigation. The concept of mitigation is the most difficult to reconcile with the orthodox analysis. Principles of mitigation apply to the consequences of breach, which occurs when the indemnified party suffers a loss within scope. This leads to one point of similarity with, and one point of departure from, the analysis for compensatory indemni-

---

[234] See [5–46].
[235] *Hadley v Baxendale* (1854) 9 Ex 341; 156 ER 145.
[236] *Caledonia North Sea Ltd v British Telecommunications plc (The Piper Alpha)* [2002] UKHL 4; [2002] 1 Lloyd's Rep 553.
[237] *Caledonia North Sea Ltd v British Telecommunications plc (The Piper Alpha)* [2002] UKHL 4; [2002] 1 Lloyd's Rep 553, [101].

ties. As with compensatory indemnities, mitigation principles are insufficient to sustain the expectation that the indemnified party act reasonably in incurring losses within the scope of the indemnity. Such conduct precedes the breach of the indemnity associated with the occurrence of the loss. The limitation must, therefore, be applied as a matter of construction.

The point of difference is that mitigation principles could operate in relation to loss within scope once it has arisen. The best explanation – though not wholly satisfactory – may be that principles of mitigation operate concurrently with other characteristics of the promise of indemnity. Insofar as the two might overlap, the relevant characteristics of indemnities have the same effect as, or are no less stringent than, principles of mitigation. Mitigation principles then have no further restrictive effect as a matter of law. The emphasis thus falls naturally on characteristics of the promise of indemnity rather than damages principles applicable upon breach.

The expectation of reasonable conduct that limits the scope of the indemnity appears to be substantially similar to the corresponding principle that would be applied as a matter of mitigation. It is conceptually more coherent to treat reasonableness as a matter of scope in relation to all losses, rather than to rely upon construction for conduct before loss is incurred and damages principles for conduct afterwards. The requirement to account for benefits that diminish the indemnified loss has a limiting effect similar to that aspect of mitigation which requires benefits from breach to be brought to account. This characteristic of an indemnity promise goes further, because it encompasses subrogation.[238]

Another aspect of mitigation permits the promisee to recover for increased loss brought about in an attempt to avoid loss, provided that the promisee's conduct was reasonable. This is an inclusionary rather than exclusionary principle. If the additional loss is itself a loss within the scope of the indemnity, then it is recoverable on that basis. This is sufficient to sustain the argument that mitigation principles do not further *restrict* recovery for loss within scope. It is, however, doubtful whether this aspect of mitigation can generally be invoked to recover losses that are beyond scope.[239] If the orthodox analysis is correct in principle, it is difficult to see why this is so. It may reflect a concern that the inclusionary principle would unduly extend the indemnifier's responsibility for loss beyond the limits set by the scope of the indemnity. This is, in essence, a corollary of the constructional approach that treats the scope of the indemnity as a definitive statement of the indemnifier's responsibility for loss.[240]

Agreed Damages Analysis

[5–64] Indemnity states basis of responsibility for loss. On this view, the promise of indemnity is a statement of the indemnifier's responsibility for the indemnified party's loss, which functions on two levels. There is a primary obligation with an active element: to prevent loss within the scope of the indemnity. On another level, there is an implicit agreement about the damages recoverable by the indemnified party for losses within scope. It is as follows. If a loss within the scope of the indemnity occurs (a breach) then the amount of that loss may be recovered (as damages) on an indemnity measure, subject only to the terms of the contract. As the arrangement concerns the damages payable by the indemnifier upon

---

[238] See [4–37], [4–42].
[239] See [4–36].
[240] See [5–56], [5–64].

breach of a contractual obligation it owes to the indemnified party, it is, in effect, a form of agreed damages clause.

This agreement on damages may determine the kind of loss recoverable and the basis upon which the loss is quantified. An indemnity does not, characteristically, fix any particular sum in advance as the amount of a loss. Each discrete occurrence of a loss within the scope of the indemnity is a distinct breach for which damages can be recovered on the agreed basis. This is consistent with general principle.[241] The agreed damages perspective also tends to support the view that the scope of the indemnity is an exhaustive statement of the indemnifier's responsibility,[242] just as an agreed damages provision generally replaces the promisee's right to damages assessed on a common law basis. If losses beyond scope are to be recoverable, it must be that the indemnity is a definitive statement of responsibility for loss within scope, but not exhaustive in relation to consequential losses. That is an unlikely construction.

[5–65] Causation, remoteness and mitigation. The indemnified party establishes a breach of contract by proving the existence of a loss within scope. The agreed damages aspect of the indemnity promise then governs recovery for that loss. The occurrence of loss within scope is caused by the indemnifier's breach of contract by failing to prevent it. But it is, strictly, not necessary to go even that far: it is sufficient that the agreed damages element of the indemnity is engaged by breach. An agreement on damages for breach of contract can also displace the operation of principles of remoteness[243] and mitigation.[244] The implicit agreed damages aspect of the indemnity has precisely that effect for losses within scope. Although remoteness and mitigation are inapplicable as a matter of law, the agreed damages analysis is entirely compatible with analogous limitations being applied to the scope of the indemnity as a matter of construction.

Enforcement before Loss

Orders for Indemnification

Nature of Relief

[5–66] Specific enforcement of promise of indemnity. Before the administration of law and equity was unified, there were various common law remedies available to enforce contractual promises of indemnity;[245] damages for breach of contract was by far the most significant. The common feature of all of these remedies was that no action could be brought until the indemnified party was damnified by a loss within the scope of the indemnity. Common law remedies were, therefore, inefficacious to avert harm to the indemnified party even where the promise of indemnity was preventive in nature.

---

[241] See [5–46].
[242] cf *Ventouris v Mountain (The Italia Express) (No 2)* [1992] 2 Lloyd's Rep 281 (QB), 291.
[243] *C Czarnikow Ltd v Koufos* [1966] 2 QB 695 (CA), 731 (Diplock LJ); *Robophone Facilities Ltd v Blank* [1966] 1 WLR 1428 (CA), 1448 (Diplock LJ).
[244] *Abrahams v Performing Right Society Ltd* [1995] 1 ICR 1028 (CA).
[245] See [1–18].

A contractual indemnity could be enforced in advance of loss in a court of equity. The basis for enforcement was the jurisdiction of courts of equity to decree specific performance of contracts of indemnity.[246] It is more accurate to describe the relief as a form of specific enforcement which approximates specific performance. Such relief can be described as quia timet in nature because it is sought and provided in respect of an anticipated loss. There are also other forms of quia timet relief that vindicate the indemnified party's rights or protect its position.[247] The following sections give a brief outline of the relevant principles. For reasons that will become clear, a comprehensive treatment is provided later, in relation to indemnities against claims by or liabilities to third parties.[248]

[5–67] Basis of specific enforcement. Specific enforcement is relevant only for promises of indemnity that are preventive in nature. An order for specific enforcement generally requires the indemnifier to act to ensure that an anticipated loss does not crystallise into an actual loss. Confining specific enforcement to preventive indemnities is consistent with the nature of the remedy. Specific enforcement compels performance of the indemnity according to its terms. If the indemnity is compensatory in nature then the indemnifier has not promised to act before the indemnified party sustains a loss. An order compelling performance in advance of loss would depart from the contractual bargain. The limitation is also consistent with the principle that specific enforcement is granted because the remedy at law is inadequate.[249]

Conditions for and Form of Relief

[5–68] Types of potential loss. Specific enforcement is available where the potential loss arises from a liability of the indemnified party to a third party. In the paradigm case, A promises to indemnify B against liabilities to C, C makes a claim upon B in respect of a liability and B obtains an order to compel A to relieve B of that liability. The jurisdiction has not so far been developed in relation to other categories of potential loss. There is no rule specifically against such a development; instead, it may be a product of factual considerations superimposed upon existing principles. Other types of potential loss may lack the characteristics generally regarded as necessary for an order for specific enforcement. Even if those qualities are present, the conduct required to avoid loss to the indemnified party in the circumstances may go beyond the appropriate bounds of an order for specific enforcement.

[5–69] Loss is sufficiently imminent. The prospect of loss must be sufficiently imminent. The position of the indemnified party has been described metaphorically as that of a person with an overhanging cloud, which is to be removed before it begins to rain.[250] The concept can be articulated in more precise terms in relation to liabilities to third parties. The indemnified party must generally establish three matters:[251] that there is a clear and definite liability to a third party; that the liability is presently accrued and enforceable; and that there is some possibility that the liability will be enforced against the indemnified

---

[246] See [7–19].
[247] See [5–74] (preservation orders) and [5–76] (declarations).
[248] See generally ch 7.
[249] See [7–21].
[250] *Earl of Ranelaugh v Hayes* (1683) 1 Vern 189, 190; 23 ER 405, 406; *Hobbs v Wayet* (1887) 36 Ch D 256 (Ch), 259; *Thomas v Nottingham Incorporated Football Club Ltd* [1972] Ch 596 (Ch), 606; *Abigroup Ltd v Abignano* (1992) 39 FCR 74 (FC), 82.
[251] See [7–24].

party. For other types of potential loss, it may be difficult in practice to demonstrate that a loss is sufficiently likely and imminent, and yet still sufficiently distant that the indemnified party has time to bring proceedings before it materialises. A risk of loss of property due to a natural disaster or an industrial accident is an obvious example. A similar difficulty may exist where the potential loss arises from an anticipated failure of a third party to perform.[252]

[5–70] **Form of order.** The form of the order for indemnification is not fixed and is tailored to fit the circumstances of the case. Where the potential loss arises from the indemnified party's liability to a third party, the indemnifier may, for example, be ordered to procure the release or discharge of the indemnified party from that liability.[253] This leaves the method of performance to the discretion of the indemnifier. Alternatively, the order may be more particular, as where the indemnifier is directed to pay the amount of the liability to the third party.[254]

Whatever the form of order, the nature of the potential loss in these cases means that the indemnifier can, at a minimum, perform the indemnity by paying a definite amount to another. If the jurisdiction were extended to other types of potential loss, the prevention of loss to the indemnified party could involve a much broader range of conduct. It is not clear whether specific enforcement would be limited to circumstances in which the required performance involved an act no more onerous than payment. A further consideration would have to be whether the cost to be incurred in avoiding the loss was proportionate to the ultimate loss anticipated.

Theoretical Justification

[5–71] **Concept of exact protection.** A balance must be struck between two competing considerations. One is that the indemnifier should act in a timely manner to keep the indemnified party from loss. The other is that the indemnifier should not be forced to act unnecessarily nor in a manner that will over-compensate the indemnified party. These considerations correspond to the two aspects of the concept of exact protection: the former is concerned with efficacy of protection and the latter with exactness of protection. The considerations are taken into account in the process of moulding an order for specific enforcement to fit the circumstances.

[5–72] **Efficacy of protection.** In the present context this requirement is the less challenging of the two aspects of exact protection. The cases on liabilities to third parties furnish examples. Two of the common forms of order – procurement of a release or discharge, and payment to the third party – will, when performed by the indemnifier, relieve the indemnified party from the liability. If the indemnified party's liability to the third party is extinguished then so too is the potential for loss. Another recognised form of order is that the indemnifier pay to the indemnified party the amount of the liability, so that the indemnified party may then pay the third party. The object of the order is not to avoid expenditure by the indemnified party, but to avoid the diminution in the indemnified party's wealth that occurs if it must first pay from its own resources.[255] If the indemnifier provides the

---

[252] See [9–54].
[253] See [7–41].
[254] See [7–42].
[255] See also [6–20], [7–16].

indemnified party in advance with a sum equal to the amount of the liability, the indemnified party may satisfy the liability using those funds without drawing upon its own. In that sense, the indemnified party is effectively protected against loss.

[5–73] Exactness of protection. A concern for exactness in protection can be perceived in the preconditions attached to relief and also in the terms upon which that relief is granted. Specific enforcement is only available when the indemnified party can establish that the risk of loss is sufficiently imminent. In relation to liabilities to third parties, this generally requires a definite and presently accrued liability, which might be enforced against the indemnified party. Some of the common forms of order for indemnification require the indemnifier to deal directly with the third party. No funds are directed into the hands of the indemnified party, so there is no chance of under- or over-compensation. An order for payment in advance by the indemnifier to the indemnified party does present difficulties, because the indemnified party might compromise for less, or pay less than the full amount owing and evade further enforcement by the third party.[256] The circumstances in which such an order will be made are not clearly defined. A relevant factor seems to be whether the indemnified party can or will pass on in full the amount received from the indemnifier.[257] This consideration is consistent with the concept of exact protection, because it reflects a concern to avoid over-compensation of the indemnified party.

Orders to Preserve Assets

[5–74] Nature of relief. There is an equitable jurisdiction to make orders to separate and preserve assets of the indemnifier against which a right to indemnity might later be exercised. In *Re Richardson*,[258] Cozens-Hardy MR and Fletcher Moulton LJ explained that the Court of Chancery could order the establishment of a fund from which liabilities of the indemnified party could be met as and when they arose.[259] The jurisdiction continues to be recognised, though it appears to be invoked relatively rarely.[260] It is distinct from the jurisdiction associated with freezing orders.[261] The jurisdiction has developed in relation to anticipated liabilities of the indemnified party though there seems to be no reason why it could not be extended, in appropriate cases, to other sources of potential loss.

---

[256] *cf Lacey v Hill; Crowley's Claim* (1874) LR 18 Eq 182, 191–92; *Re Alfred Shaw and Co Ltd, ex p Murphy* (1897) 8 QLJ 70 (SC), 73–74.

[257] See [7–44].

[258] *Re Richardson, ex p the Governors of St Thomas's Hospital* [1911] 2 KB 705 (CA).

[259] *Re Richardson, ex p the Governors of St Thomas's Hospital* [1911] 2 KB 705 (CA), 709 (Cozens-Hardy MR), 713 (Fletcher Moulton LJ). This part of Fletcher Moulton LJ's judgment was cited with approval in *Rankin v Palmer* (1912) 16 CLR 285, 290 (Griffith CJ). See also *Lacey v Hill; Crowley's Claim* (1874) LR 18 Eq 182, 191.

[260] *Bosma v Larsen* [1966] 1 Lloyd's Rep 22 (QB), 29; *Telfair Shipping Corp v Inersea Carriers SA (The Caroline P)* [1985] 1 WLR 553 (QB), 569; *Abigroup Ltd v Abignano* (1992) 39 FCR 74 (FC), 83; *Rowland v Gulfpac Ltd* [1999] 1 Lloyd's Rep Bank 86 (QB); *Papamichael v National Westminster Bank plc* [2002] 1 Lloyd's Rep 332 (QB); *Paterson v Pongrass Group Operations Pty Ltd* [2011] NSWSC 1588, [85]–[86]; *Starlight Shipping Co v Allianz Marine & Aviation Versicherungs AG (The Alexandros T)* [2011] EWHC 3381 (Comm); [2012] 2 Lloyd's Rep 162, [37]–[38].

[261] *Papamichael v National Westminster Bank plc* [2002] 1 Lloyd's Rep 332 (QB), [62]. An order can be made before the indemnified party has a cause of action against the indemnifier.

The order might be regarded as an aspect of specific enforcement of the indemnity,[262] or as an ancillary form of relief based on more general considerations.[263] Whichever basis is correct, such orders are distinct from orders for indemnification. The purpose of the order is to protect the indemnified party's position vis-à-vis the indemnifier, rather than finally to protect the indemnified party against a particular potential loss. The establishment of a fund is, of itself, only an intermediate stage of protection. The fund must later be applied to discharge the indemnified party's liabilities. The conditions for the order are different from those generally applied to orders for indemnification.

[5–75] **Conditions for relief.** As described in *Re Richardson*,[264] orders to preserve assets are part of a remedial procedure that is intended ultimately to save the indemnified party harmless from loss. It may follow that orders are available only where the indemnity promise is preventive in character. If such orders are properly regarded as an aspect of specific enforcement of the indemnity,[265] this is a necessary limitation.

Modern descriptions of the jurisdiction identify three other factors. First, there must be a reasonably clear or arguable case that a liability will fall upon the indemnified party.[266] This is less demanding than the requirements that the indemnified party's liability be clearly established and presently accrued, which generally apply to orders for indemnification.[267] It is also consistent with Cozens-Hardy MR's statement in *Re Richardson*[268] that the established fund was to meet liability 'as and when it arose'. Secondly, it should be clear that when the liability crystallises, the indemnified party will have a right to indemnity from the indemnifier.[269] Thirdly, the exercise of the discretion to grant relief requires a balance to be struck between the severity of the protection and the perceived threat of the dissipation of assets.[270] One factor, for example, may be that there is a clear indication that the indemnifier intends to ignore its obligations.

Declaratory Relief

[5–76] **Utility.** Although declaratory relief is not executory or coercive in nature, it is practically useful as a means of determining parties' rights in relation to a contractual indemnity. A declaration may be used to resolve disputes over matters such as: whether an indemnity

---

[262] *Starlight Shipping Co v Allianz Marine & Aviation Versicherungs AG (The Alexandros T)* [2012] EWCA Civ 1714; [2013] 1 Lloyd's Rep 217, [20] (Longmore LJ).
[263] cf *Rowland v Gulfpac Ltd* [1999] 1 Lloyd's Rep Bank 86 (QB), 98; *Papamichael v National Westminster Bank plc* [2002] 1 Lloyd's Rep 332 (QB), [57], [62]; *Starlight Shipping Co v Allianz Marine & Aviation Versicherungs AG (The Alexandros T)* [2011] EWHC 3381 (Comm); [2012] 2 Lloyd's Rep 162, [38] (preventing court's action from being stultified).
[264] *Re Richardson, ex p the Governors of St Thomas's Hospital* [1911] 2 KB 705 (CA), 709 (Cozens-Hardy MR), 713 (Fletcher Moulton LJ).
[265] See n 262.
[266] *Rowland v Gulfpac Ltd* [1999] 1 Lloyd's Rep Bank 86 (QB), 98; *Papamichael v National Westminster Bank plc* [2002] 1 Lloyd's Rep 332 (QB), [66], [68].
[267] See [7–24].
[268] *Re Richardson, ex p the Governors of St Thomas's Hospital* [1911] 2 KB 705 (CA), 709.
[269] *Papamichael v National Westminster Bank plc* [2002] 1 Lloyd's Rep 332 (QB), [64], [66].
[270] *Rowland v Gulfpac Ltd* [1999] 1 Lloyd's Rep Bank 86 (QB), 98; *Papamichael v National Westminster Bank plc* [2002] 1 Lloyd's Rep 332 (QB), [64], [66].

provision is rendered ineffective by statute;[271] whether a particular loss is within the scope of an indemnity;[272] whether a person is a beneficiary of an indemnity;[273] whether the indemnified party is presently entitled to enforce an indemnity[274] or will be at some future time;[275] and whether the right to enforce the indemnity has been lost by the effluxion of time.[276] An important advantage of declaratory relief is that it can be used to determine rights in relation to an indemnity at a time when the indemnified party cannot enforce the indemnity by other means.

[5–77] Declaratory relief before actual loss. An indemnified party can seek declaratory relief before it sustains actual loss under the indemnity, for example, by paying a third party. In *Re Richardson*,[277] Fletcher Moulton LJ adverted to this limitation of the common law remedies and then continued:[278]

> [T]he rule in Chancery was somewhat different, and yet, to my mind, it emphasizes the fundamental principle that you must have paid before you have a right to indemnity, because the remedy which equity gave was a declaration of a right. You could file a bill against the principal debtor to make him pay the debt so that you would not be called upon to pay it, and then you obtained a declaration that you were entitled to an indemnity.

Re Dixon[279] is a modern illustration. The purchaser of shares in a company agreed to indemnify the vendors against certain tax liabilities. The vendors were issued with adverse notices of assessment and reached a settlement with the taxation authority. The purchaser refused to indemnify the vendors and the vendors sought a declaration of their right to indemnity. The purchaser argued that the 'right' to an indemnity arose only when the vendors sustained a loss by paying the tax due; as they had not yet done so, no declaration could be made. The Full Court of the Supreme Court of Queensland rightly rejected that argument and affirmed, with a slight variation, the declaration made at first instance.

[5–78] Use in conjunction with specific relief. A court may declare a right to indemnity and, at the same time, make orders specifically enforcing the indemnity.[280] Judgments in this form can be found in the decisions on share transfers in the second half of the nineteenth century.[281] The transferor was subjected to calls on the shares after the agreement to transfer but before the transfer was registered. The court might declare that the defendant

---

[271] *Qantas Airways Ltd v Aravco Ltd* (1996) 185 CLR 43.

[272] *Travers v Richardson* (1920) 20 SR (NSW) 367 (SC).

[273] *Re Dixon* [1994] 1 Qd R 7 (FC).

[274] *Ascherson v Tredegar Dry Dock and Wharf Co Ltd* [1909] 2 Ch 401 (Ch); *Re Law Guarantee Trust and Accident Society Ltd* [1914] 2 Ch 617 (CA).

[275] *Re Perkins; Poyser v Beyfus* [1898] 2 Ch 182 (CA); *Thanh v Hoang* (1994) 63 SASR 276 (FC).

[276] *Telfair Shipping Corp v Inersea Carriers SA (The Caroline P)* [1985] 1 WLR 553 (QB); *R&H Green & Silley Weir Ltd v British Railways Board* [1985] 1 WLR 570 (QB). cf *Cathiship SA v Allanasons Ltd (The Catherine Helen)* [1998] 2 Lloyd's Rep 511 (QB).

[277] *Re Richardson, ex p the Governors of St Thomas's Hospital* [1911] 2 KB 705 (CA).

[278] *Re Richardson, ex p the Governors of St Thomas's Hospital* [1911] 2 KB 705 (CA), 712–13. See also *Firma C-Trade SA v Newcastle Protection and Indemnity Association (The Fanti) (No 2)* [1989] 1 Lloyd's Rep 239 (CA), 258 (Stuart-Smith LJ).

[279] *Re Dixon* [1994] 1 Qd R 7 (FC).

[280] Examples beyond the share cases discussed in the text include: *Rankin v Palmer* (1912) 16 CLR 285, 287 (decree at first instance), 292 (as varied); *Abigroup Ltd v Abignano* (1992) 39 FCR 74 (FC), 77 (and see further *Wenkart v Pitman* (1998) 46 NSWLR 502 (CA), 514); *Thanh v Hoang* (1994) 63 SASR 276 (FC); *Paterson v Pongrass Group Operations Pty Ltd* [2011] NSWSC 1588, [97].

[281] See [6–11].

was liable to indemnify the transferor against the calls, and make orders giving effect to the indemnity in accordance with the declaration.[282] These included orders that the defendant repay amounts already paid by the transferor,[283] or relieve the transferor from outstanding calls,[284] or put the transferor in funds to meet them.[285]

[5–79] Future losses or liabilities. Declaratory relief can be given even before the indemnified party could obtain an order specifically enforcing the indemnity. Specific enforcement might be unavailable or inappropriate because the liability against which protection is sought has not yet arisen[286] or because the amount of that liability is not yet fixed and known.[287]

A court may declare the right to indemnity and grant liberty to apply.[288] Liberty to apply may be given in respect of the implementation of orders made at the same time as the declaration,[289] but it may also extend to the enforcement of the indemnity for losses or liabilities in the future.[290] To the contrary is *Lloyd v Dimmack*.[291] Fry J refused to make a general declaration of the assignor-lessee's right to be indemnified against future breaches of the leases by the assignee, with liberty to apply *toties quoties*. One reason[292] given was that there was no sound precedent for such an order. Fry J recanted that view when faced with a similar argument five years later in *Hughes-Hallett v Indian Mammoth Gold Mines Co*.[293] Although he refused relief in that case, Fry J said that there were 'undoubtedly' cases in which 'the Court has declared the right to indemnity generally, and has put matters in such a train that, when the subsequent right to indemnity should arise, the indemnity might be worked out'.[294]

The cases in which a declaration is made and liberty is given to apply in respect of further losses or liabilities generally share two characteristics. First, the indemnified party has already suffered loss or incurred a definite liability within the scope of the indemnity.[295]

---

[282] See generally CC Dale, WT King and WO Goldschmidt (eds), *Seton's Forms of Judgments and Orders*, 6th edn, (London, Stevens and Sons, 1901), 2357–63.

[283] *Evans v Wood* (1867) LR 5 Eq 9; *Shepherd v Gillespie* (1867) LR 5 Eq 293 (affd *Shepherd v Gillespie* (1868) LR 3 Ch App 764); *Hodgkinson v Kelly* (1868) LR 6 Eq 496; *Hawkins v Maltby* (1868) LR 6 Eq 505 (affd *Hawkins v Maltby* (1869) LR 4 Ch App 200).

[284] *Cruse v Paine* (1869) LR 4 Ch App 441. cf *Re National Financial Co, ex p Oriental Commercial Bank* (1868) LR 3 Ch App 791; *Brown v Black* (1873) LR 15 Eq 363 (decree varied: *Brown v Black* (1873) LR 8 Ch App 939) (trust).

[285] *Evans v Wood* (1867) LR 5 Eq 9; *Shepherd v Gillespie* (1867) LR 5 Eq 293 (affd *Shepherd v Gillespie* (1868) LR 3 Ch App 764).

[286] *Hobbs v Wayet* (1887) 36 Ch D 256 (Ch); *Re Perkins; Poyser v Beyfus* [1898] 2 Ch 182 (CA), 190 (Lindley MR); *Thanh v Hoang* (1994) 63 SASR 276 (FC), 284 (Duggan J). See further [7–31].

[287] *Saunders v Peet* [1936] NZLR s73 (SC), 80; *Holmes v Margolese* (1983) 27 RPR 158 (BCSC); *Ozzy Loans Pty Ltd v New Concept Pty Ltd* [2012] NSWSC 814, [32], [84]. cf *Telfair Shipping Corp v Inersea Carriers SA (The Caroline P)* [1985] 1 WLR 553 (QB), 557. See further [7–28].

[288] See, eg, *Shepherd v Gillespie* (1867) LR 5 Eq 293 (affd *Shepherd v Gillespie* (1868) LR 3 Ch App 764); *Hughes-Hallett v Indian Mammoth Gold Mines Co* (1882) 22 Ch D 561 (Ch); *Re Perkins; Poyser v Beyfus* [1898] 2 Ch 182 (CA); *Travers v Richardson* (1920) 20 SR (NSW) 367 (SC).

[289] See generally *Cruse v Paine* (1869) LR 4 Ch App 441; *Abigroup Ltd v Abignano* (1992) 39 FCR 74 (FC), 87–88.

[290] See, eg, *Shepherd v Gillespie* (1867) LR 5 Eq 293, 299–300 (affd *Shepherd v Gillespie* (1868) LR 3 Ch App 764); *Hughes-Hallett v Indian Mammoth Gold Mines Co* (1882) 22 Ch D 561 (Ch), 565; *Re Perkins; Poyser v Beyfus* [1898] 2 Ch 182 (CA), 190 (Lindley MR).

[291] *Lloyd v Dimmack* (1877) 7 Ch D 398 (Ch).

[292] See further [5–80].

[293] *Hughes-Hallett v Indian Mammoth Gold Mines Co* (1882) 22 Ch D 561 (Ch).

[294] *Hughes-Hallett v Indian Mammoth Gold Mines Co* (1882) 22 Ch D 561 (Ch), 565.

[295] cf *Hughes-Hallett v Indian Mammoth Gold Mines Co* (1882) 22 Ch D 561 (Ch), 564–65.

Secondly, the anticipated further loss or liability is the same or similar in nature, so that it is clear that it will also fall within the scope of the indemnity if it materialises.[296]

[5–80] Refusal to make declaration. It is possible to make a declaration of a future entitlement to be indemnified,[297] though a court will be reluctant to do so where the issue is theoretical or hypothetical. This is reflected in the contrast between two trustee indemnity cases, *Hughes-Hallett v Indian Mammoth Gold Mines Co*[298] and *Hobbs v Wayet.*[299] There was, in each case, a concern that the trustee would be subject to calls on shares held for the benefit of another. In *Hughes-Hallett*, Fry J refused to make a declaration of the trustee's right to indemnity from the beneficiary. There was no evidence of a call on the shares, nor that a call would be made in the future. In *Hobbs*, the declaration was granted. No call had been made on the shares but the company liquidator had included the trustee's executor on the list of contributories and indicated that a call for a certain sum would be made.

A similar problem arises where the indemnified party seeks a declaration of its right to indemnity for an alleged liability that may, in fact, exist, though it has not yet been established in law. The issue may be regarded as hypothetical because the liability may never be established against the indemnified party, or it may be impossible to say whether the liability will be within scope until the basis upon which the liability is established is known.[300] Conversely, an indemnifier cannot obtain a declaration that it is *not* liable to indemnify in circumstances where the indemnified party has not made a claim under the indemnity.[301]

A declaration of a general right to indemnity with the grant of liberty to apply may be inappropriate where the future loss or liability extends for some considerable time or indefinitely. In *Lloyd v Dimmack*,[302] the indemnified party, who had assigned several leases, sought an order in this form in relation to future breaches of the leases by the assignee. Fry J refused to make the order, one reason being that it would have been highly inconvenient as the leases still had over 80 years to run.[303]

---

[296] As in *Re Perkins; Poyser v Beyfus* [1898] 2 Ch 182 (CA) (future breaches of covenants in lease).

[297] See [5–79]. *cf Hordern-Richmond Ltd v Duncan* [1947] KB 545 (KB) (right to indemnity or contribution under statute).

[298] *Hughes-Hallett v Indian Mammoth Gold Mines Co* (1882) 22 Ch D 561 (Ch).

[299] *Hobbs v Wayet* (1887) 36 Ch D 256 (Ch).

[300] *Forstaff Adelaide Pty Ltd v Hills Industries Ltd* [2006] SASC 88 (FC), [16]–[18] (Doyle CJ), [26] (Duggan J), [58]–[67] (Anderson J). See also *AMP Fire and General Insurance Co Ltd v Dixon* [1982] VR 833 (FC), 837–38, 840; *Horbury Building Systems Ltd v Hampden Insurance NV* [2004] EWCA Civ 418; [2007] Lloyd's Rep IR 237, [13] (Keene LJ), [29]–[30] (Mance LJ) (liability insurance). *cf Brice v JH Wackerbarth (Australasia) Pty Ltd* [1974] 2 Lloyd's Rep 274 (CA), 275–76 (Lord Denning MR).

[301] *Re Clay; Clay v Booth* [1919] 1 Ch 66 (CA). See also *Hume v Munro (No 2)* (1943) 67 CLR 461, 474 (Latham CJ), 478 (Starke J).

[302] *Lloyd v Dimmack* (1877) 7 Ch D 398 (Ch).

[303] *cf Re Perkins; Poyser v Beyfus* [1898] 2 Ch 182 (CA).

Part III

Particular Indemnities

6

Claims by or Liabilities to Third Parties: Classification and Establishing Loss

Introduction

[6–1] **Purpose of part.** Part two was concerned with general principles applicable to promises of indemnity in various forms. This part examines principles and issues of construction that relate to particular forms of indemnity. Four distinct forms are considered: indemnities against claims by or liabilities to third parties; indemnities against claims by or liabilities to the indemnifier; indemnities against breach or non-performance by third parties; and indemnities against breach of contract by the indemnifier.

That division provides a convenient framework for analysing issues specific to different subject-matter. The categories are not, however, mutually exclusive because the defining characteristics are not mutually exclusive. The third and fourth categories are defined by the event giving rise to the loss. The first and second categories are defined by the type of loss. Accordingly, where A promises to indemnify B against breach by A of a contract with B, the indemnity may be intended to protect B against liabilities to C which arise from A's breach. Alternatively, where A promises to indemnify B against non-performance by C, a possible consequence of C's non-performance is that B incurs a liability to another, D. On one view, *Lloyd v Dimmack*[1] crossed the first, third and fourth categories: A promised B, the assignor of certain leases, that C, the assignee, would pay the rent and perform the covenants in the leases and promised to indemnify B against default. C's default in paying rent and performing the covenants caused B to incur liabilities to the lessors and others.

[6–2] **Purpose of chapter.** This chapter and the next examine the operation of the archetypal non-insurance promise of indemnity: an indemnity against claims by or liabilities to third parties. It is the form of indemnity in respect of which the law is most fully developed. Its distinctive characteristics include the default rules relating to the occurrence of loss and to proof of the indemnified party's liability. Another important feature is the use of specific enforcement to protect the indemnified party before it suffers loss.

[6–3] **Structure of chapter.** The structure adopted in this and the following chapter is repeated in later chapters on other forms of indemnity. The chapter begins with a definition of an indemnity against claims by or liabilities to third parties. Considered next is the nature of the promise of indemnity. It will be seen that indemnities in this form are usually construed to require the indemnifier to avoid or prevent loss to the indemnified party. The following section is then concerned with establishing loss under the indemnity. The distinctive

---

[1] *Lloyd v Dimmack* (1877) 7 Ch D 398 (Ch).

rules concerning the occurrence of loss and proof of liability receive extensive treatment. The analysis continues in the next chapter, which considers performance and enforcement of this form of indemnity.

Classification

[6–4] **Definition.** The expression 'indemnity against claims by or liabilities to third parties' is used to describe a promise of indemnity under which the indemnifier engages to protect the indemnified party against a loss from one or both of the following:

(1) an actual liability of the indemnified party to a third party;
(2) an assertion by a third party of a liability owed to it by the indemnified party, whether or not the alleged liability actually exists.

The reference to loss 'from' a liability or a claim acknowledges a general rule about the occurrence of loss under this form of indemnity. The indemnified party is not damnified merely because it incurs a liability to, or is subject to a claim by, a third party. Loss usually occurs when the indemnified party makes a payment to satisfy the claim or liability. The scope of the indemnity often extends to other losses, such as legal costs, incidental to the liability or claim.

The definition is independent of the event that leads to the actual or alleged liability.[2] Also within the definition are indemnities that are broader in scope, to the extent that they cover claims by or liabilities to third parties. In this respect, specific principles or construction preferences may be applied differentially to distinct aspects of the scope of the indemnity. So, for example, where an indemnity protects against claims against the indemnified party by any person, it may be treated as an indemnity against claims by third parties to that extent and otherwise as an indemnity against claims by the indemnifier.[3]

[6–5] **Express indemnities.** A promise of indemnity against claims by or liabilities to third parties is usually created expressly, by identifying certain heads of loss as the subject of the indemnity. A typical clause will refer to one or more of: 'liabilities', 'claims', 'demands', 'actions', 'proceedings', 'suits', or 'causes of action'. References in more general terms, to 'loss' or to the 'consequences' of an event, may be sufficient to encompass loss from a liability or claim.[4] An express reference to an event only, as in a promise to indemnify 'against breach', may also be sufficient to cover liabilities or claims arising from that event.[5]

[6–6] **Implied indemnities.** A promise to indemnify against claims by or liabilities to third parties may be implied as a term in an existing contract, or form part of a contract that is inferred from the circumstances. Examples include: an agent's implied indemnity from the principal;[6] an indemnity from a debtor to a guarantor who provides a guarantee at the

---

[2] Events may include a breach of contract by the indemnifier (see [10–3]) or a breach of contract by a third party (see [9–3]).
[3] cf *Farstad Supply AS v Enviroco Ltd (The Far Service)* [2010] UKSC 18; [2010] 2 Lloyd's Rep 387, [59] (Lord Mance).
[4] See, eg, *Australian Coastal Shipping Commission v PV 'Wyuna'* (1964) 111 CLR 303.
[5] See, eg, *County and District Properties Ltd v C Jenner & Sons Ltd* [1976] 2 Lloyd's Rep 728 (QB).
[6] See [2–23].

debtor's request;[7] an indemnity implied, in some circumstances, in favour of the owner of the vessel whose master complies with the charterer's orders or signs bills of lading;[8] an indemnity from the drawer to the acceptor of an accommodation bill of exchange;[9] an indemnity in favour of a person who performs certain acts at the request of another;[10] an implied indemnity against breach of contract;[11] and an indemnity in favour of a vendor of shares against liability on the shares pending registration of the transfer.[12]

Nature of Indemnity

Usual Construction is to Prevent Loss

[6–7] **Preventive construction is predominant.** An indemnity against claims by or liabilities to third parties is usually construed to require the indemnifier to intercede and prevent loss to the indemnified party. This construction is adopted for such a wide variety of situations and types of liability that it can be regarded as a default construction in this context.[13] It has occasionally been suggested that this is a 'rule' of equity, which superseded the common law approach. In *Official Assignee v Jarvis*,[14] Salmond J observed that a promise of indemnity was construed at common law as a promise of reimbursement, and then continued:[15]

> In equity, however, a contract of indemnity had a wider operation than this, for it was specifically enforceable. Before any payment had been made or loss incurred by the party entitled to the indemnity he could sue the other party in equity and obtain an order for payment to the principal creditor, or even in a proper case for payment to himself, of the amount of the liability to which the indemnity related.

The transition from reimbursement to the discussion of specific enforcement omits an important step. If the promise were construed as one of reimbursement, there would be no cause for equity to intervene because damages would be an adequate remedy.[16] Furthermore, an order for specific enforcement would effect reimbursement, not payment to another and certainly not payment to the indemnified party before the indemnified party had paid.[17] Salmond J's suggestion of a wider operation implies that courts of equity construed the promise of indemnity differently from the courts of common law. Kennedy LJ considered the nature of the promise more directly in *Re Law Guarantee Trust and Accident Society Ltd*,[18] where he said that

[7] See [2–24].

[8] See generally [4–13], [4–53].

[9] See [6–10].

[10] See [4–53].

[11] See [10–10]–[10–13].

[12] See [6–11].

[13] See [6–9].

[14] *Official Assignee v Jarvis* [1923] NZLR 1009 (CA). See also [2–19].

[15] *Official Assignee v Jarvis* [1923] NZLR 1009 (CA), 1016. See also *Ramsay v National Australia Bank Ltd* [1989] VR 59 (FC), 66.

[16] *McIntosh v Dalwood (No 4)* (1930) 30 SR (NSW) 415 (FC), 418 (Street CJ).

[17] cf *Re Richardson, ex p the Governors of St Thomas's Hospital* [1911] 2 KB 705 (CA), 712–13 (Fletcher Moulton LJ).

[18] *Re Law Guarantee Trust and Accident Society Ltd* [1914] 2 Ch 617 (CA), 638. See also *Re Richardson, ex p the Governors of St Thomas's Hospital* [1911] 2 KB 705 (CA), 715–16 (Buckley LJ).

in the view of a Court of Equity, to indemnify does not merely mean to reimburse in respect of moneys paid, but (in accordance with its derivation) to save from loss in respect of the liability against which the indemnity has been given.

Despite such statements, the effect given to an indemnity against claims by or liabilities to third parties depends upon construction and not upon any rule of law or difference in approach between law and equity. The dichotomy postulated in cases such as *Official Assignee v Jarvis*, of a common law construction of reimbursement for loss and an equitable construction of prevention of loss, must be rejected.[19] In a common law court or a court of equity, it was always a matter of construing the particular contract in the circumstances of the case. Decisions such as *Reynolds v Doyle*[20] show that the common law courts were willing to place a preventive construction on the promise if the circumstances warranted it. *McIntosh v Dalwood (No 4)*,[21] decided before the administration of law and equity was unified in New South Wales, recognised both constructions as possible. Fusion of law and equity did not, therefore, have the result that an 'equitable' construction superseded a 'legal' construction.

Part of the argument addressed to the House of Lords in *Firma C-Trade SA v Newcastle Protection and Indemnity Association (The Fanti) (No 2)*[22] was that a court of equity could have disregarded or overridden certain terms of a contract of indemnity against liability that a common law court would have observed. This was unanimously rejected. Lord Brandon saw the difference between common law and equity as one of remedy only. References made in some of the older cases to the greater protection available for the indemnified party in equity can be understood, accordingly, as references to the expanded remedy and not to differences in construction. Lord Goff observed that '[e]quity does not mend men's bargains; but it may grant specific performance of a contract, consistently with its terms'.[23] Lord Jauncey said: 'Although equity may distinguish between what is a matter of substance and what is a matter of form . . . a contract will be construed alike both in equity and at law'.[24] The result in *The Fanti* reinforces the primacy of construction. The indemnity, which was in the form of insurance against liability, might have been preventive in operation but for an express stipulation for prior payment by the insured. The stipulation was to be applied, so that the indemnity could not be enforced until the insured had paid.

[6–8] Prevention justified by particular language or circumstances. A preventive construction might be justified by reference to particular language in the contract or to the surrounding circumstances at the time of contract.[25] In *Warwick v Richardson*[26] Alderson B

---

[19] cf *Harrington v Browne* (1917) 23 CLR 297, 307 (Isaacs J); *Bank of Credit and Commerce International SA v Ali* [2001] UKHL 8; [2002] 1 AC 251, 263 (Lord Bingham), 282 (Lord Clyde) (rejecting distinction between legal and equitable constructions in general).

[20] *Reynolds v Doyle* (1840) 1 Man & G 753; 133 ER 536. See further [6–10].

[21] *McIntosh v Dalwood (No 4)* (1930) 30 SR (NSW) 415 (FC). cf *McIntosh v Dalwood (No 3)* (1930) 30 SR (NSW) 332 (SC), 334.

[22] *Firma C-Trade SA v Newcastle Protection and Indemnity Association (The Fanti) (No 2)* [1991] 2 AC 1 (HL).

[23] *Firma C-Trade SA v Newcastle Protection and Indemnity Association (The Fanti) (No 2)* [1991] 2 AC 1 (HL), 36.

[24] *Firma C-Trade SA v Newcastle Protection and Indemnity Association (The Fanti) (No 2)* [1991] 2 AC 1 (HL), 42.

[25] cf *Farstad Supply AS v Enviroco Ltd (The Far Service)* [2010] UKSC 18; [2010] 2 Lloyd's Rep 387, [23]–[28] (Lord Clarke); *Paterson v Pongrass Group Operations Pty Ltd* [2011] NSWSC 1588, [57].

[26] *Warwick v Richardson* (1842) 10 M & W 284, 288; 152 ER 477, 479. See also [2–8].

observed, of an undertaking to save harmless, that '[t]o restore a party to his former state, after suffering him to receive harm, is not to save him harmless'. In *Re Dixon*,[27] an agreement 'to indemnify' against certain tax liabilities also received a preventive construction. One relevant factor was that the deed of indemnity conferred upon the indemnifier the right to prosecute objections to the assessments made by the taxation authority. Another factor was that the applicable taxation statute rendered the assessed amount payable as a debt due before the resolution of any objection.

[6–9] Prevention as a default construction. The preventive construction is usually adopted in the absence of a clear indication to the contrary.[28] It can even be regarded as a default construction in this context. Apart from its repetition in leading cases, the preference for a preventive construction may rest on three considerations. The first is one of legal policy: the construction may represent a preference for prevention over cure.[29]

The second consideration is that the indemnifier may be able to anticipate the indemnified party's loss. A claim against or liability of the indemnified party foreshadows loss. The liability may be patent or there may be some process through which the existence and extent of the liability is established.[30]

The third consideration concerns the indemnifier's capacity to prevent loss to the indemnified party. To some extent, that capacity depends on the indemnifier anticipating the loss. Once a liability has become definite, the indemnifier will often have some opportunity to intervene before the indemnified party is compelled to satisfy the liability. The indemnifier's capacity to avoid loss to the indemnified party also depends on the methods available to do so. A potential loss in the form of a liability can be satisfied by the payment of money. An obvious and simple means of saving harmless the indemnified party is for the indemnifier to pay the third party on the indemnified party's behalf.[31] It is not unreasonable to expect this mode of performance at a minimum.

Illustrations

[6–10] Liability as acceptor on bill of exchange. In one line of cases, a party has agreed to accept a bill of exchange for the accommodation of the drawer, the drawer in return expressly or impliedly promising to indemnify the acceptor against the liability incurred by so acting.[32] That promise is generally construed as one to prevent loss to the acceptor. In

---

[27] *Re Dixon* [1994] 1 Qd R 7 (FC). See also *Paterson v Pongrass Group Operations Pty Ltd* [2011] NSWSC 1588, [64]–[68] (tax indemnity to impecunious company director).

[28] *Johnston v Salvage Association* (1887) 19 QBD 458 (CA), 460–61 (Lindley LJ); *Official Assignee v Jarvis* [1923] NZLR 1009 (CA), 1016 (Salmond J); *Re Richardson, ex p the Governors of St Thomas's Hospital* [1911] 2 KB 705 (CA), 715–16 (Buckley LJ); *Re Law Guarantee Trust and Accident Society Ltd* [1914] 2 Ch 617 (CA), 638 (Kennedy LJ); *Rankin v Palmer* (1912) 16 CLR 285, 290–91 (Griffith CJ); *Travers v Richardson* (1920) 20 SR (NSW) 367 (SC), 370–71; *McIntosh v Dalwood (No 3)* (1930) 30 SR (NSW) 332 (SC), 334; *Firma C-Trade SA v Newcastle Protection and Indemnity Association (The Fanti) (No 2)* [1991] 2 AC 1 (HL), 28 (Lord Brandon), 35 (Lord Goff), 40–41 (Lord Jauncey).

[29] cf *Re Anderson-Berry; Harris v Griffith* [1928] Ch 290 (CA), 307 (Sargant LJ); *Friend v Brooker* [2009] HCA 21; (2009) 239 CLR 129, [52] (French CJ, Gummow, Hayne and Bell JJ).

[30] See [6–34].

[31] See [7–10].

[32] See, eg, *Chilton v Whiffin* (1768) 3 Wils 13; 95 ER 906; *Reynolds v Doyle* (1840) 1 Man & G 753; 133 ER 536; *Yates v Hoppe* (1850) 9 CB 542; 137 ER 1003; *Crampton v Walker* (1860) 3 El & El 321; 121 ER 463. cf *Huntley v Sanderson* (1833) 1 Cr & M 467; 149 ER 483 (liability as drawer on bill drawn for benefit of another).

Coles Myer Finance Ltd v Commissioner of Taxation,[33] the taxpayer drew bills of exchange on a bank, procuring the bank's acceptance, and then sold the instruments at a discount to their face value. The timing of the taxpayer's entitlement to claim deductions turned upon the nature of the obligation to indemnify contracted by the taxpayer as drawer when it procured the bank's acceptance of the bills.

One view of the law considered by the High Court of Australia was that the obligation of the drawer was either: (1) to put the bank in funds in advance of maturity; or (2) to pay the bank or holder of the bill at maturity; or (3) to indemnify the bank against the consequences of non-payment, the drawer's obligation to indemnify not arising until the acceptor had actually paid the holder. Mason CJ, Brennan, Deane, Dawson and Toohey JJ rejected the last of those possibilities, explaining: 'There is no cause of action at the suit of the acceptor until he pays. But the decisions are quite consistent with the proposition that the liability arises and can be satisfied at an earlier time'.[34] The 'cause of action' was an action for breach of the contract of indemnity, or for money paid by the acceptor to the drawer's use. The 'liability' referred to in the second sentence was the drawer's obligation to indemnify the acceptor, which came into existence upon the acceptor accepting the bill. The nature of the indemnity was to prevent the acceptor being damnified by acceptance. The indemnity could be performed by the drawer before the acceptor was forced to pay and so sustained a loss.[35]

[6–11] Liability on shares. A series of indemnity cases in the second half of the nineteenth century concerned share transfers.[36] The circumstances were typically as follows. Shares in companies were sold but the transfers not registered,[37] or registered in the name of ineligible nominees,[38] so that the transferor remained liable for calls on the shares. The transferor would then seek indemnity against the calls from the party regarded as the ultimate purchaser and transferee[39] or, sometimes, the real purchaser who stood behind the nominated transferee,[40] or a party who acted as intermediary.[41] The transferor's right to indemnity was often regarded as contractual.[42] Where the transferor was entitled to be indemnified against those calls, the indemnity was generally given preventive effect. Thus, the indemnifier might have been ordered to intervene and meet the calls or otherwise relieve the transferor of the liability.[43]

---

[33] *Coles Myer Finance Ltd v Commissioner of Taxation* (1992) 176 CLR 640.

[34] *Coles Myer Finance Ltd v Commissioner of Taxation* (1992) 176 CLR 640, 659.

[35] *Yates v Hoppe* (1850) 9 CB 542, 545; 137 ER 1003, 1006 (Moule J); *KD Morris & Sons Pty Ltd (in liq) v Bank of Queensland Ltd* (1980) 146 CLR 165, 202 (Aickin J). See further [7–16].

[36] cf *British Union and National Insurance Co v Rawson* [1916] 2 Ch 476 (CA); *Saunders v Peet* [1936] NZLR s73 (SC).

[37] As in *Evans v Wood* (1867) LR 5 Eq 9; *Hawkins v Maltby* (1869) LR 4 Ch App 200; *Cruse v Paine* (1869) LR 4 Ch App 441.

[38] As in *Brown v Black* (1873) LR 8 Ch App 939; *Nickalls v Merry* (1875) LR 7 HL 530.

[39] *Evans v Wood* (1867) LR 5 Eq 9; *Hodgkinson v Kelly* (1868) LR 6 Eq 496; *Shepherd v Gillespie* (1868) LR 3 Ch App 764; *Hawkins v Maltby* (1869) LR 4 Ch App 200; *Crabb v Miller* (1871) 24 LT 892 (Ch App).

[40] *Castellan v Hobson* (1870) LR 10 Eq 47; *Brown v Black* (1873) LR 8 Ch App 939.

[41] *Cruse v Paine* (1869) LR 4 Ch App 441; *Nickalls v Merry* (1875) LR 7 HL 530. cf *Coles v Bristowe* (1868) LR 4 Ch App 3; *Maxted v Paine (No 2)* (1871) LR 6 Exch 132.

[42] *Wynne v Price* (1849) 3 De G & S 310; 64 ER 493; *Walker v Bartlett* (1856) 18 CB 845; 139 ER 1604; *Evans v Wood* (1867) LR 5 Eq 9; *Maxted v Paine (No 2)* (1871) LR 6 Exch 132, 134 (Montague Smith J), 157 (Blackburn J); *Bowring v Shepherd* (1871) LR 6 QB 309; *Kellock v Endthoven* (1873) LR 8 QB 458. The indemnity was also explained on the basis of a trust: *Coles v Bristowe* (1868) LR 4 Ch App 3, 12; *Castellan v Hobson* (1870) LR 10 Eq 47, 51; *Brown v Black* (1873) LR 15 Eq 363 (decree varied: *Brown v Black* (1873) LR 8 Ch App 939).

[43] See [5–78].

[6–12] Liability to taxation. Indemnities against liabilities to taxation have received a preventive construction in several cases, with effect that the taxpayer has been entitled to be indemnified before paying the tax authority.[44] A factor in one case was that the parties knew that the indemnified party was impecunious and so could not meet the tax liability himself.[45] Other contextual factors may include: the indemnifier's contractual right to prosecute objections to any tax assessment; and the effect of the taxation statute in rendering the amount of the assessment conclusive, unless successfully challenged, and due and payable before objections to the assessment would be resolved.

[6–13] Personal liabilities of agent incurred in course of agency. Accepting that an agent's right to indemnity from the principal will often have a contractual basis,[46] the indemnity appears to defy classification as entirely preventive or compensatory.[47] In some circumstances, a principal is expected to intervene and prevent loss to the agent by satisfying a liability of the agent to a third party. A leading example is *Rankin v Palmer*.[48] The agent had collected money from third parties and paid it over to the principal, but was liable to refund that money when the planned venture failed to proceed. The principal was ordered to procure the release or discharge of the agent's estate from such liabilities. At the time of the order the agent was bankrupt and had not paid the third parties. The order, in effect, required the principal to act before the agent himself sustained a loss by payment.

[6–14] Contractual obligations involving payment of money. A may promise to indemnify B in relation to B's primary contractual obligations to C. Such indemnities take a variety of forms; there may also be a separate promise by A to assume responsibility for the performance of B's obligations to C.[49] Where B's obligations to C must, or may, be performed by the payment of money, A's indemnity to B may be construed to require A to make payment before B has paid C.[50] The loss confronted by B is the payment to C; thus, A's intervention prevents that loss.

This construction may apply to a chain of indemnities from A to B to C and so forth. In *Sandtara Pty Ltd v Abigroup Ltd*,[51] W promised to indemnify P against certain liabilities, including liability arising under a contractual indemnity from P to G and A1. G and A1

---

[44] *Re Dixon* [1994] 1 Qd R 7 (FC); *Paterson v Pongrass Group Operations Pty Ltd* [2011] NSWSC 1588. *cf Wren v Mahony* (1972) 126 CLR 212, 225–26 (Barwick CJ); *Munduna Investments Ltd v Stan R Freeman (Holdings) Pty Ltd* (1981) 11 ATR 681 (NSWSC), 684–85 (specific enforcement not in issue). *cf* also *Adams v Morgan and Co Ltd* [1924] 1 KB 751 (CA); *Stevens v Britten* [1954] 1 WLR 1340 (CA); *Re Hollebone's Agreement; Hollebone v WJ Hollebone & Sons Ltd* [1959] 1 WLR 536 (CA) (nature of indemnity not in issue as claims made after payment by taxpayer).

[45] *Paterson v Pongrass Group Operations Pty Ltd* [2011] NSWSC 1588, [67]–[68].

[46] See P Watts and FMB Reynolds, *Bowstead & Reynolds on Agency*, 19th edn (London, Sweet & Maxwell, 2010), 328, para 7-058. See, eg, *Re Famatina Development Corp Ltd* [1914] 2 Ch 271 (CA), 282 (Lord Cozens-Hardy MR); *Re Clune* (1988) 14 ACLR 261 (FCA), 266; *National Roads and Motorists' Association Ltd v Whitlam* [2007] NSWCA 81; (2007) 25 ACLC 688, [89], [95]–[96] (Campbell JA).

[47] See [2–9], [2–23].

[48] *Rankin v Palmer* (1912) 16 CLR 285 (see further [7–41]). See also *Lacey v Hill; Crowley's Claim* (1874) LR 18 Eq 182; *Fraser v Equatorial Shipping Co Ltd (The Ijaola)* [1979] 1 Lloyd's Rep 103 (QB), 112, 120–21 (payment in advance to agent); *Mercantile Credits v Jarden Morgan Australia Ltd* (1989) 1 ACSR 51 (QSC), 66. *cf Shapowloff v Dunn* (1981) 148 CLR 72, 77 (Stephen J).

[49] *cf* [10–7].

[50] See, eg, *Travers v Richardson* (1920) 20 SR (NSW) 367 (SC); *McIntosh v Dalwood (No 4)* (1930) 30 SR (NSW) 415 (FC); *McMahon v Ambrose* [1987] VR 817 (FC), 825 (McGarvie J).

[51] *Sandtara Pty Ltd v Abigroup Ltd* (NSWSC, 25 and 29 September 1997). See also *BNP Paribas v Pacific Carriers Ltd* [2005] NSWCA 72, [2]–[3], [5] (Handley JA), [112] (Giles J).

promised to indemnify A2 in relation to liability under a combined indemnity and guarantee given by A2 to S for performance by C. The orders made by Hunter J required each indemnifier to act before the corresponding indemnified party paid money to the next party in the chain. Thus, W was ordered to indemnify P even though P had not paid G or A1 and thus suffered a loss; P was ordered to indemnify A1 before A1 had suffered a loss by paying A2, and so on.[52]

A preventive construction may also apply to some promises to indemnify a surety against the liability to the creditor.[53] In *Thanh v Hoang*,[54] A was liable under a moneylending scheme to repay amounts to various parties, collectively, C. Two terms in the scheme were a promise by B to C to 'make good' any default by A,[55] and an indemnity from A to B against any contributions that B might have to make on that account. A defaulted, rendering B liable. A was ordered to pay B an amount for B's accrued liabilities to C, even though B had not yet discharged those liabilities by paying C.[56]

[6–15] Liability for damages for breach of contract. The scope of an indemnity from A to B may include B's liability to C for B's breach of a contract with C.[57] Such an indemnity may be construed to require A to prevent loss to B, as *Telfair Shipping Corp v Inersea Carriers SA (The Caroline P)*[58] demonstrates. The owner of the chartered vessel was sued to judgment by cargo receivers on bills of lading that had been signed on behalf of the master. The owner was entitled to the usual indemnity from the charterer for the liability to the receivers and other incidental losses, but the issue was whether the owner's claim was out of time. Neill J acknowledged that the owner might have been entitled to equitable relief, such that time would have begun to run when the owner's liability was ascertained by the judgment of the court at first instance.[59] At that point, of course, the owner would not have sustained actual loss by payment of the judgment sum. This view implies that the indemnity was preventive in nature.

[6–16] Liability for damages in tort. Most non-insurance indemnity decisions on liability in tort relate to negligence, breach of statutory duty or conversion.[60] The nature of the indemnity promise has been explicitly considered less frequently than might be expected. This is partly due to the reluctance to extend the scope of indemnities to the consequences of the indemnified party's own negligence and, perhaps also, partly due to the nature of proceedings in such cases. The right to indemnity is sometimes recognised only incidentally in the orders made upon judgment against the indemnified party. In some cases a declaration of that right is sufficient.[61]

---

[52] See also *Wenkart v Pitman* (1998) 46 NSWLR 502 (CA), 533–34 (Powell JA) (on appeal).

[53] See, eg, *Wooldridge v Norris* (1868) LR 6 Eq 410; *Trewheelar v Trukeel Pty Ltd* (1986) Q Conv R 54-223 (SC); *Thanh v Hoang* (1994) 63 SASR 276 (FC). For contrary examples, see [2–22], [2–24].

[54] *Thanh v Hoang* (1994) 63 SASR 276 (FC).

[55] Suggesting that B's obligation to pay C was a primary obligation (a conditional promise to pay if A did not) and not a secondary obligation in damages for breach by failing to ensure A's performance. *cf* [6–15].

[56] See further [7–31].

[57] See [4–60].

[58] *Telfair Shipping Corp v Inersea Carriers SA (The Caroline P)* [1985] 1 WLR 553 (QB). *cf Bosma v Larsen* [1966] 1 Lloyd's Rep 22 (QB).

[59] *Telfair Shipping Corp v Inersea Carriers SA (The Caroline P)* [1985] 1 WLR 553 (QB), 567, 568–69.

[60] See [4–46], [4–56] and [4–54] respectively.

[61] See, eg, *Albert Shire Council v Vanderloos* (1992) 77 LGRA 309 (QCA); *Qantas Airways Ltd v Aravco Ltd* (1996) 185 CLR 43; *Leighton Contractors Pty Ltd v Smith* [2000] NSWCA 55.

In *Port of Melbourne Authority v Anshun Pty Ltd*,[62] the indemnifier and indemnified party were held liable to the claimant in negligence and liability was apportioned between them for the purposes of contribution under statute. The indemnified party later brought a separate action to enforce the indemnity. In the course of considering whether the claim should have been raised earlier, Gibbs CJ, Mason and Aickin JJ said that 'the right to an indemnity arises on payment of the liability to which it relates and not before'.[63] Properly understood, those remarks recognise that the indemnified party generally cannot enforce the indemnity to obtain a common law remedy until it has sustained an actual loss, for example, by payment. Gibbs CJ, Mason and Aickin JJ were not concerned with specific enforcement in advance of loss, nor were they suggesting that a promise of indemnity operates only by way of compensation.[64]

The point was addressed in an earlier decision of the High Court of Australia, *State Government Insurance Office (Qld) v Brisbane Stevedoring Pty Ltd*.[65] Barwick CJ considered the position of concurrent tortfeasors, A and B, A having promised to indemnify B against the liability to the claimant. He said, of B's indemnity from A:[66]

> That right may be asserted before B has paid the amount of the verdict and an order may be made that A indemnify B. Such an order calls, not of course for a payment by A to B, but for the payment by A of the verdict.

An order for indemnity was made at first instance in that case.[67] But B would only suffer a loss under the indemnity when it paid the amount of the verdict. To order A to pay the verdict and so indemnify B implies that A must intervene before B suffers a loss.

What is meant by Preventing Loss?

[6–17] Particular senses of prevention of loss. It has been said that an indemnity against claims by or liabilities to third parties is usually construed to require the indemnifier to prevent loss to the indemnified party. This is a general description that encompasses several more specific senses of prevention of loss. An indemnity clause can specify the manner in which the indemnified party is to be kept harmless.[68] Sophisticated clauses may include a procedure for the notification, defence and settlement of claims. In the absence of an express provision as to the mode of performance, a more specific sense of prevention of loss may be inferred. There are at least three different formulations, namely:

(1) the indemnified party is not to be troubled by claims, demands or actions, nor encumbered by liabilities;

[62] *Port of Melbourne Authority v Anshun Pty Ltd* (1981) 147 CLR 589.
[63] *Port of Melbourne Authority v Anshun Pty Ltd* (1981) 147 CLR 589, 595.
[64] *Re Dixon* [1994] 1 Qd R 7 (FC), 18 (Shepherdson J), *cf* 32 (de Jersey J); *Thanh v Hoang* (1994) 63 SASR 276 (FC), 284 (Duggan J).
[65] *State Government Insurance Office (Qld) v Brisbane Stevedoring Pty Ltd* (1969) 123 CLR 228.
[66] *State Government Insurance Office (Qld) v Brisbane Stevedoring Pty Ltd* (1969) 123 CLR 228, 240 and *cf* also 253 (Walsh J).
[67] *Schleimer v Brisbane Stevedoring Pty Ltd* [1969] Qd R 46 (SC), 67. For other examples of such orders, see, eg, *Arthur White (Contractors) Ltd v Tarmac Civil Engineering Ltd* [1967] 1 WLR 1508 (HL); *Smith v Vange Scaffolding & Engineering Co Ltd* [1970] 1 WLR 733 (QB); *Steele v Twin City Rigging Pty Ltd* (1992) 114 FLR 99 (ACTSC), 112; *BGC Contracting Pty Ltd v Webber* [2005] WASCA 112, [103] (McLure J). *cf Winford v Permanent Nominees (Aust) Ltd* [2002] ACTSC 21; (2002) Aust Torts Reports 81-654, [73]–[75] (third party proceedings).
[68] See generally [7–4].

(2) the indemnified party is to be relieved from a definite liability to a third party, and so spared from making any payments itself; and

(3) the indemnified party need not draw from its own resources to satisfy a claim by or liability to a third party.

This ordering also reflects the relative stringency of the indemnifier's obligation. The first formulation has little support in modern decisions. The second and third formulations are widely acknowledged. They are also consistent with the default rule concerning damnification, namely, that the indemnified party generally sustains loss upon paying the third party and not beforehand.[69]

[6–18] Freedom from claims or avoidance of liabilities. One approach, broadly, is that the indemnifier will ensure that the indemnified party is not burdened by claims or liabilities. Thus, the indemnifier may be required to prevent the indemnified party from incurring a liability,[70] or to prevent a claim being made or action brought against the indemnified party, or to defend or free the indemnified party from such a claim or action before any liability is established by judgment.[71] Most examples are found in older authorities. In *McIntosh v Dalwood (No 4)*,[72] Street CJ referred to a passage from *Fry on Specific Performance*[73] which stated that an indemnity against claims and demands was breached as soon as a third party made a claim. This is not, however, the conventional view under the modern law. The statement in that text and reference to 'breach' is perhaps best understood in relation to the conditions for specific enforcement.[74]

[6–19] Relief from a definite liability. A second construction is that the indemnifier is to relieve the indemnified party from a definite liability to a third party and so spare the indemnified party from having to pay money itself.[75] Even so, there is generally no breach of contract until the indemnified party pays.[76] This is a more plausible construction where the indemnifier could not reasonably be expected to prevent the indemnified party from incurring a liability or being subjected to a claim by a third party. Indemnities against liability to taxation are obvious examples. This construction is also less burdensome to the indemnifier where the indemnified party's liability is in dispute. The indemnifier is not

---

[69] See [6–23].

[70] *Bosma v Larsen* [1966] 1 Lloyd's Rep 22 (QB). *cf Telfair Shipping Corp v Inersea Carriers SA (The Caroline P)* [1985] 1 WLR 553 (QB), 566, 568. See further [6–28], [6–29].

[71] *Earl of Ranelaugh v Hayes* (1683) 1 Vern 189; 23 ER 405; *Challoner v Walker* (1758) 1 Burr 574; 97 ER 455; 2 Keny 297; 96 ER 1188; *Bullock v Lloyd* (1825) 2 Car & P 119; 172 ER 54; *Ex p Marshall* (1834) 3 Deac & Ch 120, 123–24. This is also one possible interpretation of *Warwick v Richardson* (1842) 10 M & W 284, 296; 152 ER 477, 482, but see [6–27].

[72] *McIntosh v Dalwood (No 4)* (1930) 30 SR (NSW) 415 (FC), 419.

[73] GR Northcote, *Fry on Specific Performance*, 6th edn (London, Stevens and Sons Ltd, 1921), 731. *cf* also WT Barbour, *The History of Contract in Early English Equity*, vol 4 (Oxford, P Vinogradoff ed, Clarendon Press, 1914), 137.

[74] Even then, the statement is too favourable to the indemnified party under the modern law: see [7–24], [7–29].

[75] *Johnston v Salvage Association* (1887) 19 QBD 458 (CA), 460–61 (Lindley LJ); *Re Richardson, ex p the Governors of St Thomas's Hospital* [1911] 2 KB 705 (CA), 716 (Buckley LJ); *McIntosh v Dalwood (No 3)* (1930) 30 SR (NSW) 332 (SC), 334–35; *McIntosh v Dalwood (No 4)* (1930) 30 SR (NSW) 415 (FC), 418 (Street CJ); *Firma C-Trade SA v Newcastle Protection and Indemnity Association (The Fanti) (No 2)* [1991] 2 AC 1 (HL), 35–36 (Lord Goff), 40 (Lord Jauncey). *Victorian WorkCover Authority v Esso Australia Ltd* [2001] HCA 53; (2001) 207 CLR 520, [17] (Gleeson CJ, Gummow, Hayne and Callinan JJ).

[76] *cf Wren v Mahony* (1972) 126 CLR 212, 229–30 (Barwick CJ). See generally [6–23].

obliged to defend or settle the action by the third party against the indemnified party.[77] The indemnified party's costs of defence are, however, often included within the scope of the indemnity. To that extent, the indemnifier may remain financially responsible for the defence of the action.

[6–20] **Avoiding diminution of wealth.** The third construction is the most general. The object is not necessarily to spare the indemnified party from paying the third party to satisfy the liability but, rather, to ensure that the indemnified party need not draw from its existing resources to do so. A direct arrangement by the indemnifier with the third party to release the indemnified party would be sufficient performance on either of those constructions. On the latter construction, the indemnifier may also perform by placing the indemnified party in funds so that it can then pay the third party. This is not, strictly, sufficient performance under the former construction, because the indemnifier's payment to the indemnified party does not relieve the latter of its liability to the third party.

This construction is acknowledged in the cases on bills of exchange.[78] It is also implicit in the proposition that an indemnity may be specifically enforced by an order for payment by the indemnifier to the indemnified party.[79]

Exceptions to Preventive Construction

[6–21] **Where indemnity does not require prevention of loss.** As both the nature of the promise and the nature of loss are determined by construction, the relationship between them is fluid. Where a promise of indemnity deviates from the usual, it can be difficult to discern whether this is because of a difference in the sense of indemnity, or in the concept of loss or damnification, or both.[80] Consider, for example, a promise by A to indemnify B against liabilities to C, the indemnity expressed to be enforceable by payment to B immediately upon B incurring any such liability. Such a promise might adhere to the conventional sense of loss – B drawing upon its own resources to pay C – but with an unusually stringent sense of prevention. Alternatively, it may be construed as a typical promise of compensation based upon an unconventional sense of loss, namely, the incurring of a liability rather than its discharge by payment.

Assuming a conventional sense of indemnity and loss, a compensatory indemnity against claims by or liabilities to third parties will usually require the indemnified party first to pay the third party and then recover the amount paid from the indemnifier. A contract of indemnity that is subject to a 'pay to be paid' stipulation could be regarded as one example.[81] A guarantor's implied indemnity from the debtor is compensatory in nature.[82] The indemnified party's role in other commercial arrangements may be such that the parties expect the indemnified party to meet liabilities as they arise and then seek recoupment later.[83]

---

[77] See [7–7].
[78] See [7–16].
[79] See [7–43]–[7–44].
[80] See [6–25]–[6–29].
[81] cf *Aluflet SA v Vinave Empresa de Navegaçao Maritima LDA (The Faial)* [2000] 1 Lloyd's Rep 473 (QB) (cl 18 of Barecon 89 form). See [2–34].
[82] See [2–24].
[83] See [2–22], [2–23].

Establishing Loss

Existence of Loss

[6–22] General. Identifying the occurrence of loss under the indemnity is ultimately a matter of construction of the contract.[84] The parties may expressly define the events that constitute damnification; otherwise, a default construction rule applies.

Default Construction

[6–23] Indemnified party damnified by payment. Where the parties have not provided otherwise, a default construction rule applies. The indemnified party does not sustain a loss merely because it incurs a liability to a third party, or is subject to a claim, demand or action by a third party. The indemnified party generally suffers loss when it pays an amount from its own resources[85] in full or partial satisfaction of the claim or liability.

The rule was established in a series of early cases, of which *Collinge v Heywood*[86] is probably the best known. It has been affirmed since on many occasions.[87] The leading modern English decision is *Firma C-Trade SA v Newcastle Protection and Indemnity Association (The Fanti) (No 2)*.[88] Lord Goff cited *Collinge* as authority for the proposition that 'at common law, the cause of action does not (unless the contract provides otherwise) arise until the indemnified person can show actual loss'; an example of such loss was 'having to pay a third party'.[89] Lord Brandon and Lord Jauncey expressed similar views.[90]

Wren v Mahony[91] is a leading Australian decision. Wren indemnified Mahony against 'all proceedings actions claims and demands made by the Commissioner of Taxation in connexion with any income tax payable' by Mahony. Mahony was assessed as liable to pay an amount for income tax. Before Mahony had paid any of that sum, he sued Wren by a

---

[84] cf *Firma C-Trade SA v Newcastle Protection and Indemnity Association (The Fanti) (No 2)* [1989] 1 Lloyd's Rep 239 (CA), 255 (Bingham LJ); *Total Liban SA v Vitol Energy SA* [2001] QB 643 (QB), 659–60.

[85] cf *North American Accident Insurance Co v Newton* (1918) 57 SCR 577, 578–79 (Idington J), 581 (Anglin J) (where indemnified party obtains funds from other sources).

[86] *Collinge v Heywood* (1839) 9 Ad & E 634; 112 ER 1352 (see [2–8]). See also *Young v Hockley* (1772) 3 Wils 346; 95 ER 1092; *Taylor v Young* (1820) 3 B & Ald 521; 106 ER 752; *Penny v Foy* (1828) 8 B & C 11, 13–14; 108 ER 947, 948 (Bayley J); *Huntley v Sanderson* (1833) 1 Cr & M 467; 149 ER 483; *Reynolds v Doyle* (1840) 1 Man & G 753; 133 ER 536. Contrast [6–18].

[87] *Johnston v Salvage Association* (1887) 19 QBD 458 (CA), 460–61 (Lindley LJ); *Blyth v Fladgate* [1891] 1 Ch 337 (Ch), 362; *Re Richardson, ex p the Governors of St Thomas's Hospital* [1911] 2 KB 705 (CA); *British Union and National Insurance Co v Rawson* [1916] 2 Ch 476 (CA), 481–82 (Pickford LJ); *M'Gillivray v Hope* [1935] AC 1 (HL), 10 (Lord Tomlin); *Firma C-Trade SA v Newcastle Protection and Indemnity Association (The Fanti) (No 2)* [1991] 2 AC 1 (HL). In Australia, see, eg, *Rankin v Palmer* (1912) 16 CLR 285, 290 (Griffith CJ); *McIntosh v Dalwood (No 3)* (1930) 30 SR (NSW) 332 (SC), 334–35; *McIntosh v Dalwood (No 4)* (1930) 30 SR (NSW) 415 (FC), 418 (Street CJ); *Wren v Mahony* (1972) 126 CLR 212; *Port of Melbourne Authority v Anshun Pty Ltd* (1981) 147 CLR 589, 595 (Gibbs CJ, Mason and Aickin JJ); *Re Dixon* [1994] 1 Qd R 7 (FC), 18–19 (Shepherdson J); *Thanh v Hoang* (1994) 63 SASR 276 (FC), 284 (Duggan J). In Canada, see *Conohan v The Co-Operators* [2002] 3 FC 421 (CA), [18] (Stone JA). In New Zealand, see *Official Assignee v Jarvis* [1923] NZLR 1009 (CA), 1016 (Salmond J).

[88] *Firma C-Trade SA v Newcastle Protection and Indemnity Association (The Fanti) (No 2)* [1991] 2 AC 1 (HL).

[89] *Firma C-Trade SA v Newcastle Protection and Indemnity Association (The Fanti) (No 2)* [1991] 2 AC 1 (HL), 35.

[90] *Firma C-Trade SA v Newcastle Protection and Indemnity Association (The Fanti) (No 2)* [1991] 2 AC 1 (HL), 28 (Lord Brandon), 40 (Lord Jauncey).

[91] *Wren v Mahony* (1972) 126 CLR 212.

specially endorsed writ, claiming the amount as for a debt due, and obtained a judgment for the amount plus interest. The judgment went unsatisfied and Mahony presented a petition for bankruptcy against Wren. The High Court of Australia, by majority, held that the underlying judgment was in error. Barwick CJ explained that Mahony would have acquired a cause of action against Wren under the indemnity only after Mahony had paid the tax to the Commissioner and so sustained actual loss.

As the default construction emphasises actual loss by payment, no finer distinctions are made among antecedent events that fall short of that threshold. Actual liabilities are generally not differentiated from claims or actions asserting liability.[92] Nor is there a distinction in principle between situations where the indemnified party is liable in fact, in the sense that the third party's cause of action has accrued, and situations where the indemnified party has been adjudged liable. An adverse judgment, of itself, is not a loss.[93] Similarly, no distinction is drawn between liabilities to compensate for wrongs and other types of liability.

[6–24] Other forms of damnification. The default rule is principally concerned with distinguishing liability from voluntary payment, but damnification can occur in other ways. If the indemnified party neglects or refuses to pay, it may suffer loss when it is compelled by legal process to pay or provide some other form of satisfaction for the liability: for example, under a garnishee order; by execution levied on the indemnified party's property;[94] or in the course of the administration of the indemnified party's affairs in insolvency. In the old cases, an indemnified debtor was considered to be damnified by being arrested and imprisoned for non-payment of the debt.[95]

Where the scope of the indemnity includes losses related to the principal claim or liability, such as legal costs, the indemnified party may be damnified by such losses before it pays to satisfy the principal claim or liability.[96] An indemnified party may also suffer loss without payment to the third party because it has taken action to avoid or reduce a liability that would otherwise arise, for example, due to infringement of the third party's intellectual property rights.[97]

Other Constructions

[6–25] Difference in promise or in concept of loss? Cases in which the default construction is not applied must be explained on the basis that the parties, expressly or by implication, made some other arrangement for the protection of the indemnified party. The point of departure may be that the promise is not an indemnity in the strict sense, or it may be that

---

[92] *cf Taylor v Young* (1820) 3 B & Ald 521; 106 ER 752; *Carr v Roberts* (1833) 5 B & Ad 78; 110 ER 721; *Wren v Mahony* (1972) 126 CLR 212, 227–29 (Barwick CJ). See also [6–29].

[93] *Carr v Roberts* (1833) 5 B & Ad 78; 110 ER 721 (turning upon promise to pay rather than promise to indemnify); *Eddowes v Argentine Loan and Mercantile Agency Co Ltd* (1890) 63 LT 364 (CA); *British Union and National Insurance Co v Rawson* [1916] 2 Ch 476 (CA) (reliance upon equitable relief).

[94] See, eg, *Muhammad Issa El Sheikh Ahmad v Ali* [1947] AC 414 (PC) (indemnified party sustaining capital loss in execution sale).

[95] *Chilton v Whiffin* (1768) 3 Wils 13; 95 ER 906; *Lewis v Smith* (1850) 9 CB 610, 616–17; 137 ER 1030, 1032; *Spark v Heslop* (1859) 1 El & El 563, 569; 120 ER 1020, 1023. Even the threat of arrest may have been sufficient: *cf Cutler v Southern* (1667) 1 Wms Saund 116; 85 ER 125; 1 Lev 194; 83 ER 365.

[96] See, eg, *Ex p Wiseman; re Kelson Tritton & Co* (1871) LR 7 Ch App 35, 42–43. *Challoner v Walker* (1758) 1 Burr 574; 97 ER 455; 2 Keny 297; 96 ER 1188 might also be explicable on this basis: *cf* [6–18].

[97] See, eg, *Codemasters Software Co Ltd v Automobile Club de L'Ouest (No 2)* [2009] EWHC 3194 (Ch); [2010] FSR 13 (loss due to withdrawing allegedly infringing material from computer game).

the promise is an indemnity but that the concept of damnification differs from that according to the default construction.

[6–26] Promises to pay a third party. In one group of cases[98] there has been a promise to pay a third party to whom the promisee is liable, instead of, or in addition to, a promise to indemnify. The promisee can recover damages for breach of that term even though it has not paid the third party and so sustained a loss as would be necessary for a claim under an indemnity.

Carr v Roberts[99] is a significant decision that has been the subject of different interpretations.[100] The claimant was the administratrix of the deceased estate of Walker. The defendants covenanted to 'save, protect, defend, keep harmless and indemnified' Walker and his administrators against certain liabilities and against 'all actions, suits, claims or demands' in respect of those liabilities. There was also a separate covenant by the defendants to pay those liabilities. One of the liabilities was an annuity that was £500 in arrears at the time Walker died. The annuitant obtained judgment for a sum that greatly exceeded the assets in Walker's estate. The administratrix paid a small amount from the estate and then sued the defendants, who were held liable for the full £500 even though the administratrix had not paid and could not pay that sum to the annuitant.

Littledale J doubted whether the covenant of indemnity alone would have entitled the administratrix to recover, but thought that the defendants' breach of the separate covenant to pay the liabilities was sufficient.[101] Parke J also relied on the breach of the covenant to pay, although he tentatively suggested that the action might have been brought on the indemnity.[102] Patteson J appeared to consider that a covenant 'to indemnify' was insufficient, but that the additional undertaking 'to protect' covered the claim. He was also firmly of the view that the defendants had breached the covenant to pay.[103] Thus, on balance, the decision was against recovery of the £500 for breach of the covenant to indemnify, but all three judges agreed that the claim succeeded under the covenant to pay.

[6–27] Promise to repay money upon demand. *Warwick v Richardson*[104] concerned an indemnity between co-trustees of a legacy. Rather than invest the money as stipulated by the terms of the trust, one of the trustees (Richardson) desired to use it in his private trade. In return for the other co-trustee's (Day's) consent, Richardson undertook to 'save, defend, keep harmless and indemnified' Day against 'all manner of actions, suits, causes of action and suit, proceedings, claims, demands, loss' etc on account of the legacy. The legatees sued the estates of the trustees, both of whom had died, and obtained a decree for payment of the legacy sum plus interest. Day's executor then claimed on the indemnity from Richardson. It was held that Day's estate was entitled to prove for the whole amount of the

[98] *Hodgson v Bell* (1797) 7 TR 97; 101 ER 874; *Penny v Foy* (1828) 8 B & C 11; 108 ER 947; *Loosemore v Radford* (1842) 9 M & W 657; 152 ER 277; *Spark v Heslop* (1859) 1 El & El 563; 120 ER 1020; *Hodgson v Wood* (1863) 2 H & C 649; 159 ER 269; *Ashdown v Ingamells* (1880) 5 Ex D 280; *Re Allen; Adcock v Evans* [1896] 2 Ch 345 (Ch). See also *Official Assignee v Jarvis* [1923] NZLR 1009 (CA), 1014–17 (Salmond J); *Wren v Mahony* (1972) 126 CLR 212, 227–29 (Barwick CJ).

[99] *Carr v Roberts* (1833) 5 B & Ad 78; 110 ER 721.

[100] cf *Ashdown v Ingamells* (1880) 5 Ex D 280, 284 (Bramwell LJ); *Re Perkins; Poyser v Beyfus* [1898] 2 Ch 182 (CA), 187 (North J), 189–90 (Lindley MR); *Re Law Guarantee Trust and Accident Society Ltd* [1914] 2 Ch 617 (CA), 632 (Buckley LJ), 651–52 (Scrutton J).

[101] *Carr v Roberts* (1833) 5 B & Ad 78, 84; 110 ER 721, 723.

[102] *Carr v Roberts* (1833) 5 B & Ad 78, 84-85; 110 ER 721, 723.

[103] *Carr v Roberts* (1833) 5 B & Ad 78, 85; 110 ER 721, 723.

[104] *Warwick v Richardson* (1842) 10 M & W 284; 152 ER 477.

legacy with interest, even though at that point the only amounts actually paid by Day's executor were some costs in the action by the legatees.

Warwick is not easy to reconcile with the default construction, which was already established by the time of the decision. One point of distinction may be that the indemnity contemplated a different kind of loss, namely, loss occurring upon a demand by the legatees, and not merely upon payment.[105] The language used in *Warwick* was, however, not dissimilar to that used in *Collinge v Heywood*.[106] Another explanation may be that the parties intended the 'indemnity' to operate in a specific and unusual way.[107] Richardson's use of the legacy sum was a clear breach of trust, which exposed both co-trustees to liability. The co-trustees' intention was that, upon the legatees making a demand upon Day, Richardson would repay the sum to Day so that the trust could be performed and any further action by the legatees avoided. During argument, counsel for Day's executor said that 'the parties clearly intended present payment, on demand, of the whole £10,000, in order to its being invested pursuant to the will'.[108]

[6–28] Difference in nature of loss. Even where the promise is, strictly, to indemnify, the event that marks the occurrence of loss may be different from that applicable under the default construction. In the field of liability insurance, for example, the indemnity may be activated when liability is established against the insured and before it pays.[109] One explanation is that, for the purposes of the policy, the insured sustains a loss upon that event.[110]

Bosma v Larsen[111] is a non-insurance indemnity decision that departs from the default rule. The owner of the vessel under charter compromised an action brought by receivers of cargo and then claimed on an indemnity from the charterer. The question was whether the owner's claim was out of time; this depended on whether the owner suffered loss: (1) at the latest, when the damaged cargo was discharged, by which point the owner had in fact incurred a liability to the receivers; or (2) only when the owner paid the amount of the compromise or suffered judgment. McNair J concluded that the former characterisation was correct.

Bosma has never been formally overruled but later decisions are, at best, ambivalent about the essential reasoning.[112] An influential factor was that the indemnity clause referred

---

[105] *Warwick v Richardson* (1842) 10 M & W 284, 288, 295–96; 152 ER 477, 479, 482.

[106] *Collinge v Heywood* (1839) 9 Ad & E 634; 112 ER 1352. See [2–8], [6–23].

[107] cf *Wren v Mahony* (1972) 126 CLR 212, 229 (Barwick CJ); *Penrith City Council v Government Insurance Office of NSW* (1991) 24 NSWLR 564 (SC), 568, 569.

[108] *Warwick v Richardson* (1842) 10 M & W 284, 288; 152 ER 477, 479. cf *Smith v Howell* (1851) 6 Ex 730, 738; 155 ER 739, 742 (Alderson B).

[109] *Post Office v Norwich Union Fire Insurance Society Ltd* [1967] 2 QB 363 (CA); *Cacciola v Fire & All Risks Insurance Co Ltd* [1971] 1 NSWLR 691 (CA); *Distillers Co Bio-Chemicals (Australia) Pty Ltd v Ajax Insurance Co Ltd* (1973) 130 CLR 1, 26 (Stephen J); *Bradley v Eagle Star Insurance Co Ltd* [1989] AC 957 (HL), 966 (Lord Brandon). See generally J Birds, B Lynch and S Milnes, *MacGillivray on Insurance Law*, 12th edn (London, Sweet & Maxwell, 2012), 969–70, paras 29-002–29-003; MA Clarke, *The Law of Insurance Contracts*, 5th edn (London, Informa, 2006), 476–77, para 17-4A2. In some contexts, the indemnity may be activated even earlier: see, eg, *Australian Iron and Steel Pty Ltd v Government Insurance Office of NSW* [1978] 2 NSWLR 59 (CA); *Orica Ltd v CGU Insurance Ltd* [2003] NSWCA 331; (2003) 59 NSWLR 14, [15]–[17] (Spigelman CJ), [88] (Santow JA).

[110] *West Wake Price & Co v Ching* [1957] 1 WLR 45 (QB), 49; *Omega Proteins Ltd v Aspen Insurance UK Ltd* [2010] EWHC 2280 (Comm); [2011] 1 All ER (Comm) 313, [49].

[111] *Bosma v Larsen* [1966] 1 Lloyd's Rep 22 (QB).

[112] cf *County and District Properties Ltd v C Jenner & Sons Ltd* [1976] 2 Lloyd's Rep 728 (QB), 735–36; *Telfair Shipping Corp v Inersea Carriers SA (The Caroline P)* [1985] 1 WLR 553 (QB), 566, 568; *R&H Green & Silley Weir Ltd v British Railways Board* [1985] 1 WLR 570 (QB), 574–75; *Penrith City Council v Government Insurance Office of NSW* (1991) 24 NSWLR 564 (SC), 569–70; *City of London v Reeve & Co Ltd* [2000] EWHC 138 (TCC); [2000] BLR 211, [31]–[34]; *Aluflet SA v Vinave Empresa de Navegaçao Maritima LDA (The Faial)* [2000] 1 Lloyd's Rep 473 (QB), 476–78; *Carillion JM Ltd v Phi Group Ltd* [2011] EWHC 1379 (TCC), [157]–[159].

to 'all consequences or liabilities' arising from the master signing bills of lading. McNair J considered that the clause therefore contemplated damnification upon incurring a liability and not upon payment. As a matter of construction, it is unlikely that the mere inclusion of the word 'liability' in the indemnity clause was sufficient to produce this result and displace the default rule.[113] Another concern McNair J raised was that if the indemnified party could not bring an action until it had actually suffered a loss by payment, it might be left in the awkward position of having insufficient funds to meet the liability and yet be unable to claim on the indemnity. But this concern is a general one and it is answered by resort to specific enforcement.

[6–29] Effect of express reference to actions, claims, liabilities etc. The scope of an indemnity usually refers to various types of actual or potential harm: 'actions', 'claims', 'demands', 'liabilities', 'losses' and so forth. It has sometimes been suggested that the application of the default rule may depend on the types of harm listed in the description of scope. The rule is said to apply where there are general references to 'loss' or 'damage' but not where the indemnity clause refers to 'actions', 'claims', 'demands' or 'liabilities'. In the latter case, the reference to the type of harm also defines the occurrence of harm. Thus, the indemnified party is damnified as soon as the action is brought, the claim is made, or the liability is incurred or established. In modern decisions[114] the point has arisen most often in relation to liabilities, where a distinction between indemnities against 'liability', and indemnities against 'payment' or 'general' indemnities, has been contemplated.[115]

The better position seems to be that such language, of itself, does not establish a general exception to the default rule.[116] Attempts to distinguish indemnities against 'liability' from indemnities against 'payment' or 'general' indemnities have not gained widespread acceptance in England.[117] A similar distinction has been rejected in Australia.[118] The distinction would be difficult to reconcile with some leading statements of the common law position, which have been made in general terms.[119] It is also difficult to sustain in light of the development of the equitable jurisdiction specifically to enforce promises of indemnity. That jurisdiction overcame the limitations of the common law remedies where the indemnified party had not yet suffered loss by payment. If incurring or establishing a liability constitutes a loss to the indemnified party, there is no need for equity to intervene. The utility of the jurisdiction would be much diminished.

---

[113] See further [6–29].

[114] See also *Ex p Marshall* (1834) 3 Deac & Ch 120, 123–24; *Warwick v Richardson* (1842) 10 M & W 284, 296; 152 ER 477, 482.

[115] *Bosma v Larsen* [1966] 1 Lloyd's Rep 22 (QB); *Telfair Shipping Corp v Inersea Carriers SA (The Caroline P)* [1985] 1 WLR 553 (QB), 566; *R&H Green & Silley Weir Ltd v British Railways Board* [1985] 1 WLR 570 (QB), 575 and *cf Carillion JM Ltd v Phi Group Ltd* [2011] EWHC 1379 (TCC), [157]–[159]. *cf* also the distinction adopted in the United States: 41 *American Jurisprudence 2d*, Indemnity, §§23–25.

[116] See, eg, *Taylor v Young* (1820) 3 B & Ald 521; 106 ER 752; *Carr v Roberts* (1833) 5 B & Ad 78; 110 ER 721; *Ex p Wiseman; re Kelson Tritton & Co* (1871) LR 7 Ch App 35; *Eddowes v Argentine Loan and Mercantile Agency Co Ltd* (1890) 63 LT 364 (CA); *Wren v Mahony* (1972) 126 CLR 212, 227–29 (Barwick CJ) (all containing references to actions or claims or demands); *County and District Properties Ltd v C Jenner & Sons Ltd* [1976] 2 Lloyd's Rep 728 (QB), 735; *R&H Green & Silley Weir Ltd v British Railways Board* [1985] 1 WLR 570 (QB), 575; *City of London v Reeve & Co Ltd* [2000] EWHC 138 (TCC); [2000] BLR 211, [32]–[34] (references to liability).

[117] *County and District Properties Ltd v C Jenner & Sons Ltd* [1976] 2 Lloyd's Rep 728 (QB), 735; *City of London v Reeve & Co Ltd* [2000] EWHC 138 (TCC); [2000] BLR 211, [31]–[34].

[118] *Wren v Mahony* (1972) 126 CLR 212, 227 (Barwick CJ); *Penrith City Council v Government Insurance Office of NSW* (1991) 24 NSWLR 564 (SC), 570.

[119] See [6–23].

Although the concept of damnification may remain the same, distinctions between types of harm may still be relevant in clarifying or expanding the scope of the indemnity. So, for example, a reference to 'liabilities' in addition to 'losses' may make clear that the indemnity applies to liabilities to third parties and not only personal losses of the indemnified party. Similarly, a reference to 'claims' in addition to 'liabilities' may indicate coverage for losses or expenses associated with the defence or settlement of a claim even where there is no actual underlying liability.[120]

Proof of Liability of Indemnified Party

[6–30] Introduction. The starting point for analysis is that the indemnified party is generally only protected against losses or liabilities within the scope of the indemnity. The indemnified party bears the onus of proving facts that establish, at least prima facie, a loss or liability within scope. The issue can then be approached in three stages.

The first stage is to determine the standard of validity required. That is, must the indemnified party prove an actual liability to the third party, or is some lesser degree of validity – for example, a liability accepted in settlement of a claim – sufficient? Once the standard of validity has been determined, the next stage is to consider the manner in which the indemnified party must establish, to the requisite standard, the existence and extent of the liability. Establishing an actual liability may involve considerations quite different from those involved in determining whether a settlement should be recoverable. Not surprisingly, different construction preferences and legal principles may apply to different standards. Finally, it must be determined whether the liability satisfies the other elements of the scope of the indemnity.

[6–31] Outline of general rules. Proof of liability is complex and, in some respects, controversial.[121] The general rules appear to be as follows.

Standard of validity

(1) Whether an indemnity protects against only actual liabilities, or liabilities established by some process, or liabilities reasonably acknowledged or accepted, is a matter of construction.[122]

Manner of proof

(2) Where the indemnity protects against an actual liability:

    (a) The indemnified party must, if required, establish as against the indemnifier that it is actually liable to the third party.

---

[120] See further [6–36].

[121] In the insurance context, see N Rein, 'Liability Policies: the Relationship of the Claim Against the Insured and the Insured's Claim on the Insurer' (1994) 6 *Insurance Law Journal* 193; K Sutherland, 'An Uneasy Compromise: an Analysis of the Effect of a Settlement Reached by an Insured with a Third Party Claimant vis-a-vis His or Her Insurer' (1998) 9 *Insurance Law Journal* 257; J Marshall and J Potts, 'Indemnity for Settlements: Proof of Underlying Liability?' (2008) 19 *Insurance Law Journal* 97. See generally *VACC Insurance Co Ltd v BP Australia Ltd* [1999] NSWCA 427; (1999) 47 NSWLR 716, [26] (Fitzgerald JA); *Hurlock v Council of the Shire of Johnstone* [2002] QCA 256, [28]–[31] (Williams JA); *Sun Life Assurance Co of Canada v Lincoln National Life Insurance Co* [2004] EWCA Civ 1660; [2005] 1 Lloyd's Rep 606, [55], [59] (Mance LJ); *Lumbermens Mutual Casualty Co v Bovis Lend Lease Ltd* [2004] EWHC 2197 (Comm); [2005] 1 Lloyd's Rep 494; *Omega Proteins Ltd v Aspen Insurance UK Ltd* [2010] EWHC 2280 (Comm); [2011] 1 All ER (Comm) 313.

[122] See [6–32].

   (b) A judgment or arbitral award against, or settlement by, the indemnified party is not of itself conclusive in this respect.

   (c) However, such events may be relevant because:

      (i)   there is an express term as to proof of liability, or an equivalent inference can be drawn from the other terms of the contract;

      (ii) there is an implied term associated with, or an inherent characteristic of, the promise of indemnity;[123]

      (iii) there is an estoppel which operates in favour of the indemnified party against the indemnifier;[124] or

      (iv) the indemnified party entered into a settlement with the third party claimant as a consequence of the indemnifier's repudiation or breach of the contract of indemnity.[125]

(3) Where the indemnity protects against a liability established by an external process, the indemnified party must prove that the liability was determined in the specified manner.[126]

(4) Where the scope of the indemnity includes settlements of alleged liabilities (whether or not well founded) the indemnified party must generally establish that it made a reasonable settlement of the third party's claim.[127]

Liability is otherwise within the scope of the indemnity

(5) The liability, as established by the indemnified party, must satisfy all other elements in the scope of the indemnity.[128]

Standard of Validity

[6–32] Identification of standard. The standard of validity required is a matter of construction.[129] Three standards are common: (1) actual liability; (2) liability established by an external process; and (3) liability that is reasonably acknowledged or accepted by the indemnified party in response to the third party's claim, regardless of whether the claim is sound.

[6–33] Actual liability. The expression 'actual liability' is used to describe a liability of the indemnified party that exists according to a proper legal analysis of the relevant circumstances. Whether the liability has been adjudicated upon is not presently relevant; that is, the liability can be one arising in fact and it need not arise from a judgment or arbitral award.[130]

Actual liability was required in *Travers v Richardson*.[131] The claimant was the purchaser under a contract for the sale of goods by instalments. He later transferred his rights to the

---

[123] See [6–39]–[6–42].
[124] See [6–43]–[6–46].
[125] See [6–47]–[6–48].
[126] See [6–34].
[127] See [6–49]–[6–52].
[128] See [6–54].
[129] *Rust Consulting Ltd v PB Ltd* [2010] EWHC 3243 (TCC); [2011] 1 All ER (Comm) 951, [40]–[42], [45]; *Rust Consulting Ltd v PB Ltd* [2012] EWCA Civ 1070; [2012] BLR 427, [15] (Toulson LJ).
[130] *cf Gracechurch Holdings Pty Ltd v Breeze* (1992) 7 WAR 518 (FC), 525 (Ipp J).
[131] *Travers v Richardson* (1920) 20 SR (NSW) 367 (SC).

defendant, the defendant also accepting responsibility for his obligations and impliedly promising to indemnify him against liability under the sale contract. One instalment was not delivered on time and the defendant thereafter refused to accept deliveries under the contract. The claimant continued to accept and pay for them and then claimed on the indemnity. Street CJ said that the claimant was 'only entitled to be indemnified in respect of compulsory liabilities thrown upon him by the defendant's default. He cannot claim indemnification in respect of payments made voluntarily or unnecessarily'.[132] The claimant had not been obliged to accept and pay for the late delivery and so could not recover the amount paid for that instalment.

[6–34] Liability established by external process. Falling somewhere in the middle are instances where the scope of the indemnity includes liabilities that have been established by an external process. These may be liabilities determined by some form of adjudication,[133] or liabilities imposed by government authorities.[134] Such cases are distinct from those where the result of the external process – for example, a judgment – is relied upon indirectly to prove liability to a different standard, in particular, an actual liability.

[6–35] Liability reasonably acknowledged or accepted. The scope of the indemnity may cover liabilities that have been reasonably acknowledged or accepted by the indemnified party in response to some claim by a third party, regardless of whether the claim was sound in law. A liability accepted by the indemnified party in a compromise with the third party is a common instance.[135]

A guarantor has sometimes recovered under an indemnity from the debtor for amounts paid to the creditor, even though the guarantee was ineffective.[136] In *Argo Caribbean Group Ltd v Lewis*,[137] for example, the guarantor paid the creditor upon demand but the underlying transaction was unenforceable against the debtor due to non-compliance with statute. It appears that this would also have rendered the guarantee unenforceable.[138] It was held that the nature of the guarantor's mandate from the debtor was: 'Pay if I do not' rather than: 'Pay if I do not and I am legally compellable to pay'.[139] The scope of the indemnity from the debtor to the guarantor included the sums paid voluntarily by the guarantor.

Scottish & Newcastle plc v Raguz[140] is a more recent example. The original tenant under two leases was subjected to demands for outstanding rent by the owner of the reversion. The leases had been assigned, so the original tenant had the benefit of an implied statutory

---

[132] *Travers v Richardson* (1920) 20 SR (NSW) 367 (SC), 374–75.

[133] See, eg, cl 23(a) of the TOWHIRE 2008 standard form of contract ('liability adjudged due').

[134] See, eg, *Kelly v Hill* (1993) 26 ATR 138 (VFC), 147–49 (Fullagar and JD Phillips JJ); *Re Dixon* [1994] 1 Qd R 7 (FC), 21 (Shepherdson J), 32 (de Jersey J) and cf *Tullow Uganda Ltd v Heritage Oil and Gas Ltd* [2013] EWHC 1656 (Comm), [66]–[69] (liabilities to taxation).

[135] See further [6–36].

[136] *Alexander v Vane* (1836) 1 M & W 511; 150 ER 537 (oral guarantee); *Re Chetwynd's Estate* [1938] Ch 13 (CA); *Argo Caribbean Group Ltd v Lewis* [1976] 2 Lloyd's Rep 289 (CA) (non-compliance with moneylending statute). cf *Gulf Bank KSC v Mitsubishi Heavy Industries Ltd (No 2)* [1994] 2 Lloyd's Rep 145 (CA) (counter-indemnity to issuer of bond where bond ineffective). Contrast *Sleigh v Sleigh* (1850) 5 Ex 514; 155 ER 224; *Re Morris*; *Coneys v Morris* [1922] IR 81 (CA). See generally JC Phillips, *The Modern Contract of Guarantee*, 2nd English edn (London, Sweet & Maxwell, 2010), 746–47, paras 12-39–12-41.

[137] *Argo Caribbean Group Ltd v Lewis* [1976] 2 Lloyd's Rep 289 (CA).

[138] *Re Chetwynd's Estate* [1938] Ch 13 (CA), 16 (Greene MR); *Eldridge and Morris v Taylor* [1931] 2 KB 416 (CA); *Temperance Loan Fund Ltd v Rose* [1932] 2 KB 522 (CA).

[139] *Argo Caribbean Group Ltd v Lewis* [1976] 2 Lloyd's Rep 289 (CA), 295 (Orr LJ).

[140] *Scottish & Newcastle plc v Raguz* [2007] EWCA Civ 150; [2007] 2 All ER 871; *Scottish & Newcastle plc v Raguz* [2008] UKHL 65; [2008] 1 WLR 2494.

indemnity from the immediate assignee against 'all actions, expenses, and claims on account of the non-payment of the said rent or any part thereof'. The English Court of Appeal held that the original tenant was not liable for a substantial part of the rent claimed, due to non-compliance with statutory requirements. The tenant was, however, entitled to recover for its payment of the rent claimed even if not legally liable for the whole sum, on the basis that the indemnity extended to losses that were fairly and reasonably incurred in the circumstances. The House of Lords by majority held that the original tenant was liable for all the rent paid; this made it unnecessary to address the issue of the scope of the indemnity. A differently constituted majority would have upheld the Court of Appeal's conclusion that the indemnity covered payments fairly and reasonably made by the tenant even where the tenant was not legally liable to pay.[141]

[6–36] Significance of particular expressions. Decisions on contracts of liability insurance are of limited assistance on this point because the terms of such contracts and the context are different.[142] Liability policies commonly refer to amounts for which the insured 'shall become legally liable',[143] whereas a commercial, non-insurance indemnity clause often uses simple terms such as 'action', 'claim', 'loss', 'liable' or 'liability'. Liability policies often contain detailed provisions concerning the notification, defence and settlement of claims, whereas such provisions tend to be found only in more sophisticated non-insurance indemnity clauses.

Terms such as 'loss', 'liable' or 'liability' are protean and sensitive to context. It is not possible to identify typical or default constructions of such terms as used in non-insurance indemnities. The word 'loss' may be wide enough to cover an actual liability, or liability under a reasonable settlement of a claim.[144] The term 'liability' may go beyond actual liabilities, to include a liability accepted under a reasonable settlement.[145]

Terms such as 'actions', 'claims' or 'demands' may refer to proceedings or the assertion of a right against the indemnified party, irrespective of whether there is an underlying actual liability to the third party;[146] the inference may be stronger where the scope of the indemnity includes both 'claims' and 'liabilities'. On that basis, the indemnity may cover a reasonable settlement by the indemnified party without proof of actual liability. This construction was adopted in *Comyn Ching & Co Ltd v Oriental Tube Co Ltd*.[147] A manufacturer promised to indemnify a sub-contractor who used its products in a construction project. The indemnity,

---

[141] *Scottish & Newcastle plc v Raguz* [2008] UKHL 65; [2008] 1 WLR 2494, [14] (Lord Hoffmann), [16] (Lord Hope), [72] (Lord Walker), [74] (Lord Brown); contrast [47] (Lord Scott).

[142] *White Industries Qld Pty Ltd v Hennessey Glass & Aluminium Systems Pty Ltd* [1999] 1 Qd R 210 (CA), 217 (Pincus JA).

[143] See generally nn 109, 110.

[144] *AB Helsingfors Steamship Co Ltd v Rederiaktiebolaget Rex (The White Rose)* [1969] 1 WLR 1098 (QB), 1108–09; *Hancock Shipping Co Ltd v Deacon & Trysail (Private) Ltd (The Casper Trader)* [1991] 2 Lloyd's Rep 550 (QB), 552–53; *BNP Paribas v Pacific Carriers Ltd* [2005] NSWCA 72, [189]–[190] (Giles JA).

[145] *White Industries Qld Pty Ltd v Hennessey Glass & Aluminium Systems Pty Ltd* [1999] 1 Qd R 210 (CA), 225–27 (Derrington J); *Siemens Building Technologies FE Ltd v Supershield Ltd* [2009] EWHC 927 (TCC); [2009] 2 All ER (Comm) 900, [81] ('loss, damage, expense, or liability') (affd without reference to this point: *Supershield Ltd v Siemens Building Technologies FE Ltd* [2010] EWCA Civ 7; [2010] 1 Lloyd's Rep 349).

[146] See, eg, *Nash v Palmer* (1816) 5 M & S 374; 105 ER 1088; *Fowle v Welsh* (1822) 1 B & C 29; 107 ER 12; *Ibbett v De La Salle* (1860) 6 H & N 233; 158 ER 96; *Rank Enterprises Ltd v Gerard* [2000] EWCA Civ 15; [2000] 1 Lloyd's Rep 403, 409 (Mance LJ); *State of New South Wales v Tempo Services Ltd* [2004] NSWCA 4, [21] (Hodgson JA); *Codemasters Software Co Ltd v Automobile Club de L'Ouest* [2009] EWHC 2361 (Ch); [2010] FSR 12, [20], [37]–[38]; *Rust Consulting Ltd v PB Ltd* [2012] EWCA Civ 1070; [2012] BLR 427, [15]–[22] (Toulson LJ).

[147] *Comyn Ching & Co Ltd v Oriental Tube Co Ltd* (1979) 17 BLR 47 (CA).

contained in a series of letters, referred to 'any eventuality', 'any claims' and 'future liabilities in every sense of the word'. The products were defective and the sub-contractor entered into a settlement under which it paid a sum to the employer. Goff LJ explained that the sub-contractor did not have to prove that it was actually liable, but only that it faced a serious claim and that the employer might reasonably have established a case against it.[148] Brandon LJ said that an indemnity against claims would cover a loss arising from a reasonable settlement of a claim that had some prospect or a significant chance of success.[149]

A reference to 'claims' does not always have this effect. The 'claim' may have to be sound, in the sense that it corresponds to an actual liability of the indemnified party. In *Link Investments Pty Ltd v Zaraba Pty Ltd*,[150] the purchaser of real property warranted that it had not been introduced to the property by an agent other than its own 'in circumstances which could give rise to a claim against the vendor for commission'. The purchaser also indemnified the vendor against 'any claim' as described in the warranty. It was held that 'claim' in the indemnity clause meant a good claim. Thus, the vendor was not entitled to its costs incurred in successfully defending an action by an agent for commission.

Proof of Actual Liability

[6–37] Indemnified party must prove liability against indemnifier. Where the scope of the indemnity covers only actual liabilities, the indemnified party must prove, as against the indemnifier, its liability to the third party. There is, in general, no further requirement that the liability be established in a judgment or arbitral award against the indemnified party.[151]

[6–38] General effect of judgment, award or settlement. The indemnified party's liability to the third party may be determined by a judgment or arbitral award after contested proceedings, or by a settlement by the indemnified party with the third party. The question is whether the liability established by these methods is, as against the indemnifier, conclusive of the indemnified party's actual liability to the third party.[152]

The general rule is that a judgment, award or settlement inter partes cannot bind a person who is neither a party nor privy to it. Nor can it be conclusive evidence, against such a person, of the liability of the party who is the subject of the judgment, award or settlement. An indemnifier is not a privy of the indemnified party merely because they are related by a promise of indemnity. The effect of the general rule is that an indemnified party cannot rely solely upon a judgment or award against it, or settlement by it, to establish actual liability and a corresponding right to be indemnified.[153] There appear to be two qualifications to the general rule, though the operation of each is a matter of some uncertainty. One qualification is a limited principle of construction that may apply to judgments against the indemnified party,[154] the other is based on estoppel.[155]

---

[148] *Comyn Ching & Co Ltd v Oriental Tube Co Ltd* (1979) 17 BLR 47 (CA), 83, 89.
[149] *Comyn Ching & Co Ltd v Oriental Tube Co Ltd* (1979) 17 BLR 47 (CA), 92.
[150] *Link Investments Pty Ltd v Zaraba Pty Ltd* [2001] NSWCA 14. cf *Lewis v Smith* (1850) 9 CB 610; 137 ER 1030.
[151] See, eg, *Carillion JM Ltd v Phi Group Ltd* [2011] EWHC 1379 (TCC), [159]. See also [7–27].
[152] See [9–35]–[9–38] for the corresponding position for indemnities against non-performance by third parties.
[153] *King v Norman* (1847) 4 CB 884; 136 ER 757; *Gracechurch Holdings Pty Ltd v Breeze* (1992) 7 WAR 518 (FC); *Rust Consulting Ltd v PB Ltd* [2010] EWHC 3243 (TCC); [2011] 1 All ER (Comm) 951, [42]. cf *The Millwall* [1905] P 155 (CA), 172 (Collins MR).
[154] See [6–39].
[155] See [6–43].

A practical consequence of the general rule is that it may be to the indemnified party's advantage as defendant to join the indemnifier to the proceedings if it is not already a party. Whether the indemnifier is then bound by the judgment against the indemnified party will depend on the form of the proceedings, the applicable rules and any directions given under them.[156] Under the Civil Procedure Rules, the claim on the indemnity may be pursued as an additional claim in proceedings to which the indemnified party and indemnifier are both already parties.[157] Alternatively, if only the indemnified party is involved in the proceedings, then it may make an additional claim against the indemnifier, who becomes a party to the proceedings.[158]

Whether Special Principle Applicable to Judgments

[6–39] Special principle as to conclusiveness of judgments. Mellish LJ in *Parker v Lewis*[159] considered the position of an indemnified party confronted with an action by a third party. After discussing the possibility of compromising the action, Mellish LJ continued:[160]

> On the other hand . . . he may, if he pleases, go on and defend it, and then, if the verdict is obtained against him, and judgment signed upon it, I agree that at law that judgment, in the case of express contract of indemnity is conclusive. But I apprehend it is conclusive on account of what the law considers the true meaning of such a contract of indemnity to be. . . . [I]t would be very hard, indeed, if, when he came to claim the indemnity, the person against whom he claimed it could fight the question over again, and run the chance of whether a second jury would take a different view and give an opposite verdict to the first.

This was, then, a contractual exception to the general rule, which derived from the nature of a promise of indemnity. It could be regarded as a rule of construction or as the basis for an implied term. The remarks were made by reference to express contracts of indemnity, but there appears to be no reason why the same rationale ought not to apply to contracts of indemnity inferred from the circumstances, or indemnities implied into existing agreements. It does not apply to a statutory indemnity.[161]

It is unclear whether Mellish LJ's principle is good law. The remarks were obiter. There are divergent approaches in the insurance context. The balance of English authority seems to weigh against it,[162] whereas Australian decisions tend to support it.[163] Beyond the field

---

[156] See, eg, *The Millwall* [1905] P 155 (CA), 164 (Collins MR), 165 (Cozens-Hardy LJ); *Barclays Bank v Tom* [1923] 1 KB 221 (CA), 224 (Scrutton LJ); *Asphalt and Public Works Ltd v Indemnity Guarantee Trust Ltd* [1969] 1 QB 465 (CA), 473 (Edmund-Davies LJ); *Insurance Exchange v Dooley* [2000] NSWCA 159; (2000) 50 NSWLR 222, [34]–[42] (Handley JA).

[157] CPR, r 20.6.

[158] CPR, rr 20.7 and 20.10(1).

[159] *Parker v Lewis* (1873) LR 8 Ch App 1035.

[160] *Parker v Lewis* (1873) LR 8 Ch App 1035, 1059.

[161] *Cockatoo Docks & Engineering Co Pty Ltd v Dalgety & Co Ltd* (1939) 39 SR (NSW) 295 (FC), 301 (Halse Rogers J).

[162] See, eg, *Enterprise Oil Ltd v Strand Insurance Co Ltd* [2006] EWHC 58 (Comm); [2006] 1 Lloyd's Rep 500, [167]; *Omega Proteins Ltd v Aspen Insurance UK Ltd* [2010] EWHC 2280 (Comm); [2011] 1 All ER (Comm) 313; *Astrazeneca Insurance Co Ltd v XL Insurance (Bermuda) Ltd* [2013] EWHC 349 (Comm); [2013] 2 All ER (Comm) 97, [96]. But *cf Commercial Union Assurance Co plc v NRG Victory Reinsurance Co Ltd* [1998] 2 Lloyd's Rep 600 (CA) (implied term in reinsurance contract); *Sun Life Assurance Co of Canada v Lincoln National Life Insurance Co* [2004] EWCA Civ 1660; [2005] 1 Lloyd's Rep 606, [59] (Mance LJ); *Lumbermens Mutual Casualty Co v Bovis Lend Lease Ltd* [2004] EWHC 2197 (Comm); [2005] 1 Lloyd's Rep 494, [43] (judgment 'normally conclusive').

[163] See, eg, *JN Taylor Holdings Ltd (in liq) v Bond* (1993) 59 SASR 432 (FC), 440 (King CJ); *CE Heath Casualty & General Insurance Ltd v Pyramid Building Society (in liq)* [1997] 2 VR 256 (CA), 291 (Phillips JA); *VACC Insurance Co Ltd v BP Australia Ltd* [1999] NSWCA 427; (1999) 47 NSWLR 716, [26] (Fitzgerald JA); *Insurance*

of insurance, two notable decisions concerning indemnities to guarantors are difficult to reconcile with it.[164] In *King v Norman*,[165] the claimant agreed to become surety for a tax collector and obtained a joint and several bond of indemnity against that liability from the tax collector and the defendant. The claimant was sued as surety and submitted to judgment for £500. It was held that the judgment was not conclusive evidence of liability for the purposes of the claimant's claim on the indemnity from the defendant. In *Gracechurch Holdings Pty Ltd v Breeze*,[166] a husband and wife were co-guarantors, with the husband indemnifying the wife against that liability. In proceedings by the creditor against the husband and wife, the wife conceded liability for the creditor's claim, subject to a defence on one point which was ultimately unsuccessful. The husband did not participate in the proceedings and so judgment by default was entered against him: in favour of the creditor in the principal proceedings, and in favour of the wife in third party proceedings. Those judgments were later set aside, but there arose the question of whether the wife could rely upon the creditor's judgment against her in the claim for indemnity from her husband. It was held that she could not. Ipp J noted *Parker* but did not adopt the general principle as stated above.

[6–40] Different types of judgment. Assuming Mellish LJ's principle in *Parker v Lewis*[167] to be correct, not all judgments can be treated alike. The principle applies to a judgment after contested proceedings. It appears that an award after a contested arbitration may be treated similarly.[168] Judgments by consent and judgments by default are outside this principle, though they might be relevant according to other principles, such as those relating to settlements by the indemnified party.[169] The obvious point is that such judgments are not strongly probative of actual liability. *Parker* might be reconciled with *King v Norman*[170] and *Gracechurch Holdings Pty Ltd v Breeze*[171] on this basis. In each of those cases the indemnified guarantor had, in essence, conceded the liability in respect of which judgment was given. Neither case, however, relied upon this distinction.

[6–41] Distinction between judgments and settlements. Mellish LJ's analysis of the effect of judgments in *Parker v Lewis*[172] is immediately preceded by a discussion of the effect of settlements by the indemnified party. Mellish LJ seems to have considered that different principles applied. Two elements relevant for settlements – notice to the indemnifier and a refusal by the indemnifier to assume the defence of the claim – are absent from the analysis of judgments. The conclusiveness of judgments derived from the nature of a contract of indemnity,

---

Exchange v Dooley [2000] NSWCA 159; (2000) 50 NSWLR 222, [83] (Fitzgerald JA); *Hurlock v Council of the Shire of Johnstone* [2002] QCA 256, [28] (Williams JA).

[164] See also *Rust Consulting Ltd v PB Ltd* [2010] EWHC 3243 (TCC); [2011] 1 All ER (Comm) 951, [45]–[46] (revd on other grounds *Rust Consulting Ltd v PB Ltd* [2012] EWCA Civ 1070; [2012] BLR 427).

[165] *King v Norman* (1847) 4 CB 884; 136 ER 757.

[166] *Gracechurch Holdings Pty Ltd v Breeze* (1992) 7 WAR 518 (FC).

[167] *Parker v Lewis* (1873) LR 8 Ch App 1035, 1059.

[168] *BNP Paribas v Pacific Carriers Ltd* [2005] NSWCA 72, [7] (Handley JA).

[169] *Hurlock v Council of the Shire of Johnstone* [2002] QCA 256, [28]–[29] (Williams JA). *cf Lumbermens Mutual Casualty Co v Bovis Lend Lease Ltd* [2004] EWHC 2197 (Comm); [2005] 1 Lloyd's Rep 494, [43]; *Rust Consulting Ltd v PB Ltd* [2010] EWHC 3243 (TCC); [2011] 1 All ER (Comm) 951, [45]–[46] (revd on other grounds: *Rust Consulting Ltd v PB Ltd* [2012] EWCA Civ 1070; [2012] BLR 427).

[170] *King v Norman* (1847) 4 CB 884; 136 ER 757.

[171] *Gracechurch Holdings Pty Ltd v Breeze* (1992) 7 WAR 518 (FC).

[172] *Parker v Lewis* (1873) LR 8 Ch App 1035.

but Mellish LJ did not identify this same reason for the conclusive effect of settlements. The latter seems to rest on estoppel.[173]

This distinction has sometimes been blurred in later decisions.[174] In *Mercantile Investment and General Trust Co v River Plate Trust, Loan and Agency Co*,[175] Romer J remarked: 'inasmuch as the [indemnified party] defended with the knowledge and approval of the [indemnifier], the latter would be estopped under their covenant of indemnity from disputing the judgment' against the indemnified party. Romer J referred to *Parker*, explaining that the estoppel arose 'by virtue of a term implied in an express covenant of indemnity'. Ipp J in *Gracechurch Holdings Pty Ltd v Breeze*[176] noted that formulation but considered that the estoppel could be independent of the contract. In *Rust Consulting Ltd v PB Ltd*,[177] Edwards-Stuart J adverted to a passage in Mellish LJ's judgment in which he had referred to the indemnified party 'alter[ing] his position in any way on the faith of a contract of indemnity'. These interpretations may suggest that there is no independent principle applicable to judgments under non-insurance indemnities; instead, judgments, arbitral awards and settlements may all be subsumed within the broader ground of estoppel.[178]

[6–42] Limitation of reasonableness. In *Parker v Lewis*,[179] Mellish LJ referred to the indemnified party settling 'on the best terms he can', without mentioning a similar qualification in his discussion of judgments. It is difficult to conceive that a judgment against the indemnified party should be conclusive against the indemnifier even where the indemnified party has conducted the defence unreasonably or incompetently. It should remain open to the indemnifier to contend that the indemnified party acted unreasonably, for example, by failing to raise an effective defence.[180]

Estoppel

[6–43] Estoppel. A more general ground, applicable to judgments, arbitral awards or settlements, is that the indemnifier is estopped from denying that the indemnified party is actually liable to the third party. The estoppel may arise by convention or by representation, the indemnifier having represented that it is content to accept the outcome as binding on itself.[181] It is not possible to provide a comprehensive set of requirements for such an estoppel. Two factors do, however, stand out.

One factor is the indemnifier's knowledge of the third party's claim against the indemnified party. But this is not, of itself, sufficient. It has been held that no estoppel will arise where: (1) the indemnifier is unaware that it is obliged to indemnify against the claim, or positively believes that it is not; and (2) the indemnified party has not actually asserted a

---

[173] See [6–43].

[174] See also an earlier decision, *Lord Newborough v Schroder* (1849) 7 CB 342, 398–99; 137 ER 136, 158–59.

[175] *Mercantile Investment and General Trust Co v River Plate Trust, Loan and Agency Co* [1894] 1 Ch 578 (Ch), 595. cf *McKnight v General Casualty Insurance Co of Paris* [1931] 3 DLR 476 (BCCA), 483 (MA Macdonald JA).

[176] *Gracechurch Holdings Pty Ltd v Breeze* (1992) 7 WAR 518 (FC), 523–24.

[177] *Rust Consulting Ltd v PB Ltd* [2011] EWHC 1622 (TCC); [2011] PNLR 33, [75]–[76].

[178] See [6–43].

[179] *Parker v Lewis* (1873) LR 8 Ch App 1035, 1059.

[180] cf *Lord Newborough v Schroder* (1849) 7 CB 342, 398–99; 137 ER 136, 158–59; *Hooper v Bromet* (1904) 90 LT 234 (CA), 238 (Vaughan Williams LJ).

[181] cf *CGU Insurance Ltd v AMP Financial Planning Pty Ltd* [2007] HCA 36; (2007) 235 CLR 1, [8]–[10] (Gleeson CJ and Crennan J) (circumstances not establishing estoppel in relation to proof of liability), contrast [120]–[122] (Kirby J). See also G Spencer Bower, A Turner and K Handley, *The Doctrine of Res Judicata*, 3rd edn (London, Butterworths, 1996), 117, para 224.

right to indemnity.[182] The point is illustrated by the unusual case of *Rust Consulting Ltd v PB Ltd*.[183] The indemnifier and indemnified party were part of the same corporate group. The indemnified party faced a large claim by third parties and, in the interests of the corporate group, a decision was made that the indemnified party would consent to judgment. The figure was significantly higher than the likely result if the proceedings were contested. Two considerations underlying that decision were that the indemnified party, in any event, had no substantial assets to meet the claim, and that the group had received legal advice that the indemnifier would not be liable under the indemnity. The liquidators of the indemnified party later brought proceedings to enforce the indemnity. On the basis that the indemnity covered only actual liabilities,[184] the argument was that the indemnifier was estopped from denying that the consent judgment was conclusive of actual liability. Edwards-Stuart J held that there was no estoppel even though the indemnifier knew of the claim and gave approval to the consent judgment. The actions of the indemnifier and indemnified party, at the relevant time, were not referable to the enforcement of the indemnity.

Another factor relates to the indemnifier's involvement, or refusal to be involved, in the management of the claim. As Akenhead J said in *Rust Consulting*:[185]

> The active participation of the guarantor or indemnifier in the proceedings, may, depending on the circumstances, level and scope of the participation, go much further to establish an estoppel against it. The positive concurrence by the guarantor or indemnifier with a consent judgment against the beneficiary will go further still.

Akenhead J declined to state the necessary or sufficient factors in more specific terms. Conversely, it has been suggested that an estoppel may arise where the indemnifier has notice of the third party's claim or action and refuses to defend it, although given the opportunity to do so. This proposition is distinct from the point that, in some cases, a failure to acknowledge or defend the claim may constitute a repudiation or breach of contract by the indemnifier.[186]

[6–44] Notice and refusal to defend. The proposition can be traced back to Buller J's judgment in *Duffield v Scott*.[187] The claimant sued for three losses under a bond of indemnity: the amount of a judgment against him; the amount of costs paid to the successful party in that action; and the amount of the claimant's own expenses in the action. The defendant indemnifier did not dispute the liability under judgment but objected to the claim for costs and expenses on the ground that the claimant had not given notice of the action against him. Buller J said:[188]

---

[182] *Rust Consulting Ltd v PB Ltd* [2011] EWHC 1622 (TCC); [2011] PNLR 33, [75]–[77].

[183] *Rust Consulting Ltd v PB Ltd* [2010] EWHC 3243 (TCC); [2011] 1 All ER (Comm) 951; *Rust Consulting Ltd v PB Ltd* [2011] EWHC 1622 (TCC); [2011] PNLR 33; *Rust Consulting Ltd v PB Ltd* [2012] EWCA Civ 1070; [2012] BLR 427.

[184] This point was reversed on appeal: *Rust Consulting Ltd v PB Ltd* [2012] EWCA Civ 1070; [2012] BLR 427, [22] (Toulson LJ).

[185] *Rust Consulting Ltd v PB Ltd* [2010] EWHC 3243 (TCC); [2011] 1 All ER (Comm) 951, [45]. *cf Frixione v Tagliaferro* (1856) 10 Moo PC 175; 14 ER 459 (principals bound by foreign judgment against agent when they were aware of the action and had undertaken to provide evidence to support agent's defence); *Pettman v Keble* (1850) 9 CB 701; 137 ER 1067 (principal not involved in defence but apparently authorising agent's compromise of claim by third party); *Nana Ofori Atta II v Nana Abu Bonsra II* [1958] AC 95 (PC), 101–02.

[186] Contrast *AMP Financial Planning Pty Ltd v CGU Insurance Ltd* [2004] FCA 1330; (2004) 139 FCR 223, [47]. See further [6–47].

[187] *Duffield v Scott* (1789) 3 TR 374; 100 ER 628.

[188] *Duffield v Scott* (1789) 3 TR 374, 377; 100 ER 628, 630.

[T]here are cases which say that, to entitle a person to recover on a bond of indemnity, he must shew that he was compelled by law to pay the debt . . . The purpose of giving notice is not in order to give a ground of action; but if a demand be made which the person indemnifying is bound to pay, and notice be given to him, and he refuse to defend the action, in consequence of which the person to be indemnified is obliged to pay the demand, that is equivalent to a judgment, and estops the other party from saying that the defendant in the first action was not bound to pay the money.

There is some ambiguity in the expressions 'obliged to pay' and 'equivalent to a judgment'. One interpretation is that Buller J was equating a liability determined as between the third party and indemnified party, with a liability established by judgment in favour of the indemnified party against the indemnifier. That is, in the event of notice and the indemnifier's refusal to defend, the indemnifier would be bound by any judgment, and liable for any costs and expenses, in the proceedings brought by the third party against the indemnified party. Mellish LJ in *Parker v Lewis*[189] seems to have adopted a different interpretation, reading the reference to 'judgment' as a judgment in favour of the *third party* against the *indemnified party*. The indemnified party could then, against the indemnifier, rely on the judgment as conclusive evidence of actual liability by invoking a separate principle relating to judgments.[190] If this interpretation is correct, the words 'obliged to pay' suggest some obligation other than one established by judgment; otherwise, the asserted equivalence would be redundant. The obligation might arise from a reasonable settlement of the third party's claim.

Buller J's remarks in *Duffield* must also be understood in the context of the loss claimed by the indemnified party, namely, the costs and expenses incurred in the action. There was also a countervailing view that where a defence was unsuccessful, the associated costs or expenses were wasted or unnecessary and so not recoverable. That view can be found in cases concerning ordinary claims for damages for breach and also in some old indemnity cases.[191] An exception could be justified where the defence was sanctioned or, at least, where notice of the action was given and the promisor failed or refused to defend it.[192]

[6–45] Notice and refusal to defend: developments. As it related to claims for legal costs and expenses under an indemnity, Buller J's proposition from *Duffield v Scott*[193] was superseded by two developments. There was increasing acceptance that such costs and expenses could be recovered under an indemnity (though not necessarily as damages at law) provided they were incurred reasonably.[194] Whether the defence was successful or not was a factor that went to reasonableness. At the same time, there was an evolution in perspective, so that the point simply became a matter of construction of the scope of the indemnity.[195]

---

[189] *Parker v Lewis* (1873) LR 8 Ch App 1035, 1058–59.
[190] See [6–39].
[191] In relation to ordinary claims for damages for breach, see: *Short v Kalloway* (1839) 11 Ad & E 28; 113 ER 322; *Penley v Watts* (1841) 7 M & W 601; 151 ER 907; *Walker v Hatton* (1842) 10 M & W 249; 152 ER 462; *Baxendale v London, Chatham and Dover Railway Co* (1873) LR 10 Ex 35. In that context, remoteness was a factor: see [10–44]. In relation to indemnities or similar obligations, see: *Knight v Hughes* (1828) M & M 247; 173 ER 1147 (contribution); *Gillett v Rippon* (1829) M & M 406; 173 ER 1204; *Beech v Jones* (1848) 5 CB 696; 136 ER 1052.
[192] See also *Lewis v Peake* (1816) 7 Taunt 153; 129 ER 61; *Blyth v Smith* (1843) 5 Man & G 406; 134 ER 622 (claims for breach of contract).
[193] *Duffield v Scott* (1789) 3 TR 374, 377; 100 ER 628, 630.
[194] See, eg, *Broom v Hall* (1859) 7 CBNS 503; 144 ER 911; *The Millwall* [1905] P 155 (CA), 173–74 (Collins MR).
[195] See [4–75], [4–77].

Buller J's analysis was, however, generalised to other types of loss. In *Smith v Compton*,[196] the claimant compromised an action by a third party and then sued the defendant for the amount of the compromise together with the claimant's costs. The defendant resisted both elements of the claim on the ground that no notice had been given. That defence failed. Parke J's judgment as reported merely quotes from Buller J's judgment in *Duffield*. Lord Tenterden CJ said that the only effect of lack of notice was to allow the defendant to prove that the (now) claimant had 'no claim in respect of the alleged loss, or not to the amount alleged' or that the defendant might have obtained a settlement on better terms. By implication, it seems that prior notice would have precluded the defendant from raising such points.[197] *Smith* thus extends the reasoning in *Duffield* to compromises. The claimant's action in *Smith* was for damages for breach of a covenant of good title but nothing was made of that distinction.

The next decision is *Jones v Williams*,[198] where the indemnified party was sued on a bond given to a third party. The action was ultimately stayed by court order, with the indemnified party paying the amount of the debt and costs. The indemnifier refused indemnity on the ground that the indemnified party should have successfully defended the action. The proposed defence was that the third party had not complied with a notice provision in the bond. That objection might be dismissed as a rather technical one which only delayed the inevitable, but, in any event, the point was decided according to the more general principle from *Duffield*. The indemnifier had been given notice of the action and had declined to intervene and defend it; he could not now dispute the indemnified party's liability.

The last of the old decisions is *Parker v Lewis*,[199] where Mellish LJ said:

> [I]f a person has agreed to indemnify another against a particular claim or a particular demand, and an action is brought on that demand, he may then give notice to the person who has agreed to indemnify him to come in and defend the action, and if he does not come in, and refuses to come in, he may then compromise at once *on the best terms he can*, and then bring an action on the contract of indemnity.

The passage represents a refinement of the previous law in its recognition that the settlement by the indemnified party must be reasonable. Such a requirement was not expressed in *Duffield* and Lord Tenterden CJ may even have rejected it by implication in *Smith*. Nonetheless, the qualification should be accepted as correct in principle. It is more consistent with modern authorities.[200] It would be surprising for an estoppel to extend to an unreasonable settlement by the indemnified party, especially where the estoppel is based upon the indemnifier's failure to participate in the defence or settlement of the claim.

[6–46] Notice and refusal to defend: modern perspective. The principle has not flourished.[201] In *Ben Shipping Co (Pte) Ltd v An Bord Bainne (The C Joyce)*,[202] the owners of the

---

[196] *Smith v Compton* (1832) 3 B & Ad 407; 110 ER 146.

[197] Contrast *Rust Consulting Ltd v PB Ltd* [2011] EWHC 1622 (TCC); [2011] PNLR 33, [63].

[198] *Jones v Williams* (1841) 7 M & W 493; 151 ER 860.

[199] *Parker v Lewis* (1873) LR 8 Ch App 1035, 1059 (emphasis added). *cf Smith v Howell* (1851) 6 Ex 730, 737; 155 ER 739, 742 (Pollock CB).

[200] See [6–46].

[201] In addition to the decisions mentioned in the text *cf Edwards v Insurance Office of Australia Ltd* (1933) 34 SR (NSW) 88 (FC), 94 (Davidson J); *Gracechurch Holdings Pty Ltd v Breeze* (1992) 7 WAR 518 (FC), 523–24 (Ipp J); *Jeans v Bruce* [2004] NSWSC 539, [322]–[323], [368] (revd on other grounds: *Harpley Nominees Pty Ltd v Jeans* [2006] NSWCA 176).

[202] *Ben Shipping Co (Pte) Ltd v An Bord Bainne (The C Joyce)* [1986] 2 All ER 177 (QB).

vessel claimed indemnity from the charterers against sums paid in settlement of cargo claims. The owners had informed the charterers of the claims and invited the charterers to assume responsibility for their defence. The charterers declined to do so and did not admit any liability for the claims. The owners failed to establish an implied indemnity in their favour, but Bingham J went on to consider an argument based on the *Duffield* line of cases, namely, that it was sufficient for the owners to show that they had notified the charterers of the claims and that the charterers had declined to take up the defence. Bingham J rejected any such general rule:[203]

> [T]he rule contended for would present the charterers with a choice between taking over the defence of a claim which they believed to be nothing to do with them and thereafter (if that belief was falsified) finding themselves bound to indemnify the owners against settlement of a claim even though the claim could be shown to be ill-founded or the settlement unreasonable. The authorities may well support, and I can see virtue in a much more limited principle, but that would not avail the owners here.

The point was considered more recently in two judgments at first instance in *Rust Consulting Ltd v PB Ltd*.[204] The facts were different from the *Duffield* line of cases because the indemnifier had approved of the indemnified party's submission to a judgment by consent. Neither Akenhead J nor Edwards-Stuart J expressed a clear preference for *The C Joyce* or the *Duffield* line of decisions.

It may be, as Bingham J suggested, that a more limited form of the rule can be sustained.[205] The indemnified party's conduct must be reasonable; this was already recognised by Mellish LJ in *Parker v Lewis*.[206] It is doubtful whether the indemnifier's refusal to defend an action can always be sufficient. There may be legitimate doubt or dispute as to whether the third party's claim falls within the scope of the indemnity. A mere promise to indemnify in a non-insurance contract does not generally import a right or obligation to defend an action against the indemnified party.[207] A broad application of the rule may thus have the effect of compelling the indemnifier to go beyond its contractual obligations to avoid being precluded, at some later stage, from disputing whether the indemnified party was actually liable. The rule might also be limited by reference to the manner in which the liability is established. There is a stronger justification for applying such a rule to a liability established by judgment after contested proceedings than to one accepted, for example, under a consent judgment or settlement.

Where Indemnifier Breaches or Repudiates Contract

[6–47] Reasonable settlement after breach or repudiation. Consider a situation in which the indemnifier breaches or repudiates the contract in respect of its promise to indemnify against liability to a certain third party. (Assume also, in the latter event, that the indemnified party accepts the repudiation.) If the indemnified party consequently enters into a reasonable settlement with that third party, then the indemnified party may recover the

---

[203] *Ben Shipping Co (Pte) Ltd v An Bord Bainne (The C Joyce)* [1986] 2 All ER 177 (QB), 187.

[204] *Rust Consulting Ltd v PB Ltd* [2010] EWHC 3243 (TCC); [2011] 1 All ER (Comm) 951; *Rust Consulting Ltd v PB Ltd* [2011] EWHC 1622 (TCC); [2011] PNLR 33 (revd on other grounds: *Rust Consulting Ltd v PB Ltd* [2012] EWCA Civ 1070; [2012] BLR 427).

[205] *cf* [6–53] and also art 39(1) of the Convention on the Contract for the International Carriage of Goods by Road 1956, as implemented by the Carriage of Goods by Road Act 1965.

[206] *Parker v Lewis* (1873) LR 8 Ch App 1035. See [6–45].

[207] See [7–7].

amount of that settlement as damages in accordance with ordinary contractual principles. This perspective has received most attention in liability insurance cases in jurisdictions outside England.[208] The repudiation or breach may arise, for example, from the insurer's outright denial of liability, or its failure or refusal to perform its obligation to defend the claim.

A leading example is *Edwards v Insurance Office of Australia Ltd.*[209] The insured notified the insurer of the action against him but the insurer refused to defend the action and repudiated liability. The insured then settled upon legal advice. The policy provided indemnity against all sums for which the insured 'shall become legally liable', so the insurer resisted the insured's claim on the basis that there was no evidence of legal liability. Halse Rogers J said that the insurer had committed 'practically an anticipatory breach', so that the insured was entitled to the amount of a reasonable settlement as damages.[210]

The same principles extend to other contracts of indemnity against liability.[211] It may, however, be difficult to establish a breach or repudiation of a non-insurance contract of indemnity. In general, the indemnifier is not obliged to defend claims against the indemnified party, nor is there a particular time fixed for performance of the indemnity. The indemnifier's failure to intervene and pay the third party or defend the claim against the indemnified party does not, therefore, necessarily constitute a breach or repudiation of the contract.

[6–48] Proof of actual liability unnecessary. Subject to the qualification mentioned below, the better view seems to be that an indemnified party who claims on this basis does not have to establish that it was actually liable to the third party, even if the indemnity protects only against actual liabilities.[212] As a matter of general principle, it is clear nowadays that a promisee need not prove, as against the promisor, an actual liability to a third party in order to recover the amount of a reasonable settlement as damages for breach of contract.[213]

The qualification relates to the basis of the indemnifier's conduct. If the indemnifier has refused indemnity on the ground that the indemnified party is not actually liable, there is a problem of circularity. Whether that refusal can be characterised as a breach or repudiation may depend on whether there was an actual liability within scope, so that the indemnifier would have been obliged to perform. That is, proof of an actual liability is necessary to establish that the indemnifier has committed a breach or repudiation of the contract. This problem does not arise where the indemnifier's conduct is independent of the validity

---

[208] *Chamberlain v North American Accident Insurance Co* (1916) 28 DLR 298 (Alta CA); *Edwards v Insurance Office of Australia Ltd* (1933) 34 SR (NSW) 88 (FC); *General Omnibus Co v London General Insurance Co* [1936] IR 596 (CA); *Distillers Co Bio-Chemicals (Australia) Pty Ltd v Ajax Insurance Co Ltd* (1973) 130 CLR 1, 9–10 (Menzies J), 24–25 (Stephen J); *Royal Insurance Fire & General (NZ) Ltd v Mainfreight Transport Ltd* (1993) 7 ANZ Ins Cas 61-172 (NZCA), 77,975–76; *Unity Insurance Brokers Pty Ltd v Rocco Pezzano Pty Ltd* [1998] HCA 38; (1998) 192 CLR 603, [28] (McHugh J), [59]–[64] (Gummow J); *Vero Insurance Ltd v Baycorp Advantage Ltd* [2004] NSWCA 390; (2005) 13 ANZ Ins Cas 61-630, [48]–[49] (Tobias JA); *DA Constable Syndicate 386 v Auckland District Law Society Inc* [2010] NZCA 237; [2010] 3 NZLR 23, [78]–[82].
[209] *Edwards v Insurance Office of Australia Ltd* (1933) 34 SR (NSW) 88 (FC).
[210] *Edwards v Insurance Office of Australia Ltd* (1933) 34 SR (NSW) 88 (FC), 98 and *cf* 97 (Davidson J).
[211] *Unity Insurance Brokers Pty Ltd v Rocco Pezzano Pty Ltd* [1998] HCA 38; (1998) 192 CLR 603, [59]–[64] (Gummow J), *cf* [33]–[34] (McHugh J); *BNP Paribas v Pacific Carriers Ltd* [2005] NSWCA 72, [13] (Handley JA), [187]–[188] (Giles JA). *cf White Industries Qld Pty Ltd v Hennessey Glass & Aluminium Systems Pty Ltd* [1999] 1 Qd R 210 (CA), 217–18 (Pincus JA), 226 (Derrington J).
[212] See generally n 208. *cf* D Derrington and RS Ashton, *The Law of Liability Insurance*, 2nd edn (Sydney, LexisNexis, 2005), 532–35, paras 8-298–8-305.
[213] See [6–50].

of the third party's claim. It suffices to give two examples. The indemnifier may be under a separate obligation to defend all claims (sound or not) against the indemnified party, though the scope of the promise to indemnify is confined to actual liabilities. Alternatively, the indemnifier may indicate that it will not perform the indemnity because any actual liability would fall within an express exception to scope. The alleged repudiation then arises from the indemnifier's erroneous construction of the contract or, perhaps, misapprehension of the facts considered to attract the exception.

Proof of a Reasonable Settlement[214]

[6–49] **Reliance on a reasonable settlement.** The indemnified party may seek indemnity for an amount fixed by a reasonable settlement of a third party's claim, without proving its actual liability to that third party. The claim for indemnity may be propounded on one of these bases:

(1) the applicable standard of validity is that of liability reasonably acknowledged or accepted; that is, loss from a reasonable settlement of a claim is within the scope of the indemnity;

(2) the applicable standard of validity is that of actual liability, but the indemnifier is precluded from denying that the indemnified party is actually liable to the extent of a reasonable settlement; or

(3) the loss from a reasonable settlement is claimed as damages for the indemnifier's breach or repudiation of the contract of indemnity. The standard of validity is generally not relevant here; however, as a practical matter, this form of claim is most advantageous to the indemnified party where the standard of validity is that of actual liability.

[6–50] **Assessment of reasonableness.** The reasonableness of the settlement appears to be assessed in substantially the same manner for all bases. Where the claim is for damages for the indemnifier's breach or repudiation of contract, reasonableness is determined by reference to ordinary damages principles. The same principles are, in general, applied by analogy where the scope of the indemnity extends to reasonable settlements of claims.[215] The same or similar considerations again seem to apply where the indemnified party relies upon a reasonable settlement in conjunction with an estoppel, to establish an actual liability within the scope of the indemnity.[216]

Some of these principles are as follows. The onus rests upon the indemnified party to establish that the settlement was reasonable.[217] Whether the settlement was reasonable

---

[214] See generally W Courtney, 'Settlements Following Breach of Contract' [2013] *Lloyd's Maritime and Commercial Law Quarterly* 157.

[215] *Comyn Ching & Co Ltd v Oriental Tube Co Ltd* (1979) 17 BLR 47 (CA), 89 (Goff LJ); *General Feeds Inc Panama v Slobodna Plovidba Yugoslavia* [1999] 1 Lloyd's Rep 688 (QB), 691–92; *BNP Paribas v Pacific Carriers Ltd* [2005] NSWCA 72, [243]–[250] (Giles JA); *Siemens Building Technologies FE Ltd v Supershield Ltd* [2009] EWHC 927 (TCC); [2009] 2 All ER (Comm) 900, [62], [80] (affd *Supershield Ltd v Siemens Building Technologies FE Ltd* [2010] EWCA Civ 7; [2010] 1 Lloyd's Rep 349).

[216] *CGU Insurance Ltd v AMP Financial Planning Pty Ltd* [2007] HCA 36; (2007) 235 CLR 1, [8] (Gleeson CJ and Crennan J), [112]–[113], [120] (Kirby J). cf *Edwards v Insurance Office of Australia Ltd* (1933) 34 SR (NSW) 88 (FC), 94–95, 97 (Davidson J).

[217] *Edwards v Insurance Office of Australia Ltd* (1933) 34 SR (NSW) 88 (FC), 98 (Halse Rogers J); *Comyn Ching & Co Ltd v Oriental Tube Co Ltd* (1979) 17 BLR 47 (CA), 83, 89 (Goff LJ); *BNP Paribas v Pacific Carriers Ltd* [2005] NSWCA 72, [13]–[14] (Handley JA), [249] (Giles JA); *Codemasters Software Co Ltd v Automobile Club de L'Ouest*

involves two further questions: first, whether in the circumstances it was reasonable to settle at all; and secondly, whether the sum fixed by the settlement was reasonable. In practice, however, the two questions often merge into the single question: was it reasonable to settle at the amount fixed by the settlement?[218]

The reasonableness of the settlement is assessed 'objectively'. It is not enough for the indemnified party simply to show that it acted reasonably, for example, by relying upon legal advice.[219] The basic point of reference is the legal position of the indemnified party in relation to the claim advanced by the third party. An objective assessment requires a pragmatic evaluation of the claim, including consideration of: its prospects of success; the degree of uncertainty involved in the whole or part of the litigation; the likely magnitude of the claim if successful; and the expected cost of the litigation. Purely commercial considerations affecting the indemnified party seem to be extraneous.[220] The assessment is based on material that is, or ought reasonably to have been, available at the time of the settlement.[221]

An appropriate settlement figure will fall within the range of what might reasonably be expected to have been negotiated in the circumstances.[222] Indeed, one aspect of reasonableness may require consideration of the manner in which the indemnified party managed and settled the claim.[223] The indemnified party need not prove that it was actually liable to the third party;[224] and a settlement may still be reasonable even though the settlement figure is around or exceeds the amount of the actual liability.[225]

[6–51] Use of legal advice to establish reasonableness. The requirement that the settlement be objectively reasonable means that it is not sufficient for the indemnified party to show that it or its legal advisers subjectively considered the settlement to be reasonable.[226] The existence of legal advice may be relevant to the extent that the decision to settle was made upon (or contrary to) such advice, but otherwise the contents of the advice and direct evidence of advisers is irrelevant.[227]

[2009] EWHC 2361 (Ch); [2010] FSR 12, [20]. See generally *Biggin & Co Ltd v Permanite Ltd* [1951] 2 KB 314 (CA); *Unity Insurance Brokers Pty Ltd v Rocco Pezzano Pty Ltd* [1998] HCA 38; (1998) 192 CLR 603.

[218] *Comyn Ching & Co Ltd v Oriental Tube Co Ltd* (1979) 17 BLR 47 (CA), 89 (Goff LJ).

[219] *Biggin & Co Ltd v Permanite Ltd* [1951] 2 KB 314 (CA); *Unity Insurance Brokers Pty Ltd v Rocco Pezzano Pty Ltd* [1998] HCA 38; (1998) 192 CLR 603, [6] (Brennan CJ), [69] (Gummow J), [129] (Hayne J); *CA & MEC McInally Nominees Pty Ltd v HTW Valuers (Brisbane) Pty Ltd* [2001] QSC 388; (2001) 188 ALR 439, [53].

[220] *CA & MEC McInally Nominees Pty Ltd v HTW Valuers (Brisbane) Pty Ltd* [2001] QSC 388; (2001) 188 ALR 439, [62]–[64]; *AMP Financial Planning Pty Ltd v CGU Insurance Ltd* [2005] FCAFC 185; (2005) 146 FCR 447, [165] (Gyles J).

[221] *Unity Insurance Brokers Pty Ltd v Rocco Pezzano Pty Ltd* [1998] HCA 38; (1998) 192 CLR 603, [7] (Brennan CJ), [130] (Hayne J); *BNP Paribas v Pacific Carriers Ltd* [2005] NSWCA 72, [249] (Giles JA); *John F Hunt Demolition Ltd v ASME Engineering Ltd* [2007] EWHC 1507 (TCC); [2008] 1 All ER 180, [62]; *Rail Corp NSW v Fluor Australia Pty Ltd* [2009] NSWCA 344, [89] (Macfarlan JA); *Siemens Building Technologies FE Ltd v Supershield Ltd* [2009] EWHC 927 (TCC); [2009] 2 All ER (Comm) 900, [80]. But *cf Biggin & Co Ltd v Permanite Ltd* [1951] 2 KB 314 (CA), 325 (Singleton LJ).

[222] *Unity Insurance Brokers Pty Ltd v Rocco Pezzano Pty Ltd* [1998] HCA 38; (1998) 192 CLR 603, [132] (Hayne J); *Supershield Ltd v Siemens Building Technologies FE Ltd* [2010] EWCA Civ 7; [2010] 1 Lloyd's Rep 349, [28] (Toulson LJ).

[223] See, eg, *BNP Paribas v Pacific Carriers Ltd* [2005] NSWCA 72.

[224] *General Feeds Inc Panama v Slobodna Plovidba Yugoslavia* [1999] 1 Lloyd's Rep 688 (QB), 696; *Siemens Building Technologies FE Ltd v Supershield Ltd* [2009] EWHC 927 (TCC); [2009] 2 All ER (Comm) 900, [80]; *Railcorp NSW v Fluor Australia Pty Ltd* [2009] NSWCA 344, [98]–[102] (Macfarlan JA).

[225] *White Industries Qld Pty Ltd v Hennessey Glass & Aluminium Systems Pty Ltd* [1999] 1 Qd R 210 (CA); *Rail Corp NSW v Fluor Australia Pty Ltd* [2009] NSWCA 344, [109] (Macfarlan JA).

[226] See n 219.

[227] *Biggin & Co Ltd v Permanite Ltd* [1951] 2 KB 314 (CA). *cf DSL Group Ltd v Unisys International Services Ltd* (1994) 67 BLR 127 (QB).

By way of contrast, Australian decisions have taken a broader view. Evidence of legal advice and from legal advisers involved in the management of the claim may be relevant.[228] The extent to which such material may be used is not entirely clear. It seems to be regarded as useful as far as it reveals the investigation made of the claim, and the considerations that informed the evaluation of the claim and the decision to settle it.

[6–52] **Unreasonable settlements.** An indemnified party who makes an unreasonable settlement cannot, on that basis, recover the full amount of the settlement. This result has been analysed in terms of causation, namely, that an unreasonable settlement is not caused by the activating event specified in the scope of the indemnity.[229] More generally, it could be said that a liability fixed by an unreasonable settlement is not a head of loss within the scope of the indemnity, or is an inappropriate measure of such loss.[230]

Several alternatives are open to the indemnified party. The indemnified party could still establish an actual liability to the third party and recover on that basis, with the amount of the settlement imposing an upper limit. It may be possible in some circumstances to sever discrete elements of an unreasonable settlement, so as to permit recovery of reasonable elements.[231] More controversial is the proposition that the indemnified party can instead recover the amount of a hypothetically reasonable settlement.[232] In *BNP Paribas v Pacific Carriers Ltd*,[233] the indemnified party settled a claim of around USD 2.8 million plus interest for USD 2.9 million plus interest. A majority of the New South Wales Court of Appeal considered that the claim was likely to succeed but concluded that the settlement was unreasonable. The indemnified party had squandered the opportunity to negotiate a lower figure through poor strategy. The majority instead allowed a sum of USD 2 million as the amount of a notionally reasonable settlement in the circumstances.

That process of reasoning is, with respect, not entirely convincing.[234] The unreasonable settlement was either beyond the scope of the indemnity or not the appropriate measure of the liability. The substitution of a hypothetical settlement seems inapt, particularly given the emphasis on actual loss in indemnity claims. The indemnified party could have been completely denied recovery on this ground; or, the same result could have been reached by the following route. According to the majority, the indemnified party was likely to be under an actual liability of about USD 2.8 million. This was the prima facie measure of loss. In the circumstances, the indemnified party had failed to reduce its loss by negotiating a reasonable compromise of that liability. The indemnifier might then establish the extent of avoidable loss. A reasonable compromise in the circumstances would have been USD 2 million, hence the prejudice to the indemnifier was USD 800,000. The appropriate sum

---

[228] *Unity Insurance Brokers Pty Ltd v Rocco Pezzano Pty Ltd* [1998] HCA 38; (1998) 192 CLR 603, [6] (Brennan CJ), [35] (McHugh J), [135] (Hayne J); *Rhyse Holdings Pty Ltd v McLaughlins (a firm)* [2002] QCA 122, [19]–[20] (Williams JA); *BNP Paribas v Pacific Carriers Ltd* [2005] NSWCA 72, [249] (Giles JA).

[229] *General Feeds Inc Panama v Slobodna Plovidba Yugoslavia* [1999] 1 Lloyd's Rep 688 (QB), 691–92; *Siemens Building Technologies FE Ltd v Supershield Ltd* [2009] EWHC 927 (TCC); [2009] 2 All ER (Comm) 900, [80].

[230] cf *BNP Paribas v Pacific Carriers Ltd* [2005] NSWCA 72, [64] (Handley JA); *John F Hunt Demolition Ltd v ASME Engineering Ltd* [2007] EWHC 1507 (TCC); [2008] 1 All ER 180, [67], [69]; *Codemasters Software Co Ltd v Automobile Club de L'Ouest* [2009] EWHC 2361 (Ch); [2010] FSR 12, [21].

[231] *John F Hunt Demolition Ltd v ASME Engineering Ltd* [2007] EWHC 1507 (TCC); [2008] 1 All ER 180, [68]. cf *Comyn Ching & Co Ltd v Oriental Tube Co Ltd* (1979) 17 BLR 47 (CA), 90–91 (Goff LJ).

[232] Contrast *BNP Paribas v Pacific Carriers Ltd* [2005] NSWCA 72, [64]–[65] (Handley JA) (dissenting); *John F Hunt Demolition Ltd v ASME Engineering Ltd* [2007] EWHC 1507 (TCC); [2008] 1 All ER 180, [69].

[233] *BNP Paribas v Pacific Carriers Ltd* [2005] NSWCA 72.

[234] See Courtney, 'Settlements Following Breach of Contract' (n 214), 174–75, 178.

was, then, the amount of the actual liability less the loss that ought reasonably to have been avoided: net, USD 2 million.

The Position in the United States

[6–53] **The position in the United States.** In view of the complexity and uncertainty of some of the principles discussed above, the Restatement (2d) Judgments provides an interesting point of comparison.[235] According to §57(1):

> [W]hen . . . an action is brought by the injured person against the indemnitee and the indemnitor is given reasonable notice of the action and an opportunity to assume or participate in its defense, a judgment for the injured person has the following effects on the indemnitor in a subsequent action by the indemnitee for indemnification:
>
> (a) The indemnitor is estopped from disputing the existence and extent of the indemnitee's liability to the injured person; and
> (b) The indemnitor is precluded from relitigating issues determined in the action against the indemnitee if:
>
>   (i)   the indemnitor defended the action against the indemnitee; or
>   (ii) the indemnitee defended the action with due diligence and reasonable prudence.

The basic rule is qualified in two ways. There is §57(2), which applies where there is a conflict of interest between the indemnitor and indemnitee such that the indemnitor could not properly have assumed the defence of the action. A conflict of interest arises where the claim against the indemnitee could be sustained on different grounds, one of which is within scope and another of which is beyond scope. In that event, assuming the indemnitee defended with due diligence and reasonable prudence, the indemnitor is only precluded from relitigating issues in respect of which there was no conflict of interest.

The other qualification is §58, which applies where the indemnitor (such as an insurer) is under an independent obligation to defend claims that might be within the scope of the indemnity. If the indemnitor is given reasonable notice and an opportunity to defend the action, then the indemnitor is estopped as in §57(1)(a). The indemnitor is precluded from relitigating issues in respect of which there was no conflict of interest, but there is no further express requirement corresponding to that in §57(1)(b)(ii) or §57(2)(b).

It also appears that a principle broadly analogous to §57(1)(a) applies to settlements.[236] A party indemnified against liability would usually have to establish an actual liability to the third party. But if the indemnifier is notified of the claim and refuses the opportunity to defend it, then it is sufficient for the indemnified party to show a reasonable settlement of a potential liability.

Liability Must Otherwise be within Scope of Indemnity

[6–54] **Liability must be within scope.** Establishing liability to the requisite standard of validity does not conclude the question of enforcement. The liability must satisfy the other

---

[235] *cf* also Uniform Commercial Code, §2-607(5) (claim against buyer of goods with remedy over against seller or another) and §2-607(6) (where buyer indemnifies seller against infringement).

[236] See, eg, *Chicago RI & PR Co v Dobry Flour Mills Inc* 211 F 2d 785 (1954) (CA 10th circ); *Fashion House Inc v K Mart Corp* 892 F 2d 1076 (1989) (CA 1st circ); *Grand Trunk Western Railroad Inc v Auto Warehousing Co* 686 NW 2d 756 (2004) (Mich CA). *cf* also *West Coast Terminals Co of California v Luckenbach Steamship Co Inc* 349 F 2d 568 (1965) (CA 9th circ). See generally 41 *American Jurisprudence 2d*, Indemnity, §27.

elements of the scope of the indemnity.[237] The indemnifier may contend, for example, that the liability was not caused by the specified event, or that it falls within an exception for negligence or fraud. The indemnifier is generally not restricted to the factual basis of the judgment or award against, or settlement by, the indemnified party.[238]

---

[237] See, eg, *White Industries Qld Pty Ltd v Hennessey Glass & Aluminium Systems Pty Ltd* [1999] 1 Qd R 210 (CA), 218–19 (Pincus JA) (dissenting on point that whole liability under settlement was within scope), 226 (Derrington J). cf *Captain Boyton's World's Water Show Syndicate Ltd v Employers' Liability Insurance Corp Ltd* (1895) 11 TLR 384 (CA) (liability insurance).

[238] Insurance authorities include: *JN Taylor Holdings Ltd (in liq) v Bond* (1993) 59 SASR 432 (FC), 440 (King CJ); *VACC Insurance Co Ltd v BP Australia Ltd* [1999] NSWCA 427; (1999) 47 NSWLR 716, [28] (Fitzgerald JA); *MDIS Ltd v Swinbank London & Edinburgh Insurance Co Ltd* [1999] EWCA Civ 1884; [1999] Lloyd's Rep IR 516; *Enterprise Oil Ltd v Strand Insurance Co Ltd* [2006] EWHC 58 (Comm); [2006] 1 Lloyd's Rep 500, [167], [170]–[171]; *Omega Proteins Ltd v Aspen Insurance UK Ltd* [2010] EWHC 2280 (Comm); [2011] 1 All ER (Comm) 313, [49], [68]–[69].

7

Claims by or Liabilities to Third Parties: Performance and Enforcement

Introduction

[7–1] **Purpose of chapter.** This chapter continues the treatment of indemnities against claims by or liabilities to third parties. The material should be read in conjunction with that presented in the previous chapter.

[7–2] **Structure of chapter.** The chapter is divided into two sections. The first section examines the method of indemnification, that is, the manner in which the indemnifier can perform the promise of indemnity. The usual construction of the promise of indemnity allows the indemnifier considerable latitude in this respect.

The second section of the chapter addresses enforcement. Enforcing this form of indemnity in respect of actual loss is essentially a matter of applying general principles. The section focuses on enforcement in relation to anticipated loss. Generally, the potential loss takes the form of a definite, accrued liability of the indemnified party to another. The object of enforcement is to compel the indemnifier to intervene so that the indemnified party does not have to meet that liability from its own resources. The preconditions for enforcement and forms of order for indemnification are considered in detail. The section closes by considering the indemnified party's use of funds provided by the indemnifier pursuant to the indemnity: does the indemnified party have an obligation to the indemnifier, or third party, to pay over the funds to the third party?

Method of Indemnification

[7–3] **General.** The following section considers the manner in which the indemnifier may perform the promise of indemnity. Each of the modes of performance involves a positive act by the indemnifier or a decision to refrain from action. The indemnifier's performance should possess the quality of finality if it is to discharge the obligation to indemnify: there should be no prospect of the indemnified party being damnified in the future by the relevant claim or liability. But a failure to perform the indemnity in this manner is not necessarily a breach of contract. An uninformed or indifferent indemnifier may do nothing and still not breach the contract because the third party does not pursue its claim against the indemnified party.

The focus is on voluntary performance, in the sense that it is rendered freely by the indemnifier pursuant to the contract. There is considerable similarity between this situation and one where the indemnity is performed under compulsion of an order for specific enforcement. The latter situation raises further issues, such as whether the circumstances justify relief and, if so, the appropriate form of order to give effect to the indemnity.[1]

[7–4] Available modes of performance. The construction of the contract in context is important. The indemnity clause may specify the available modes of performance. Sophisticated clauses may include a procedure for the notification, defence and settlement of claims. Where the indemnity is subject to a 'pay to be paid' condition or is otherwise compensatory in nature, then the contract clearly calls for performance by payment to the indemnified party. There is greater latitude in performance where the indemnity is preventive and unqualified.[2]

Another consideration is that the indemnifier may lack the power to perform in a particular manner. An indemnity can be performed by the indemnifier successfully defending an action against the indemnified party. An indemnifier does not, however, have a general power to take over the defence on behalf of the indemnified party.[3] Finally, where the indemnifier is compelled to perform by an order for specific enforcement of the indemnity, the terms of that order may dictate the available modes of performance.

[7–5] Mode of performance generally at indemnifier's discretion. Within the available modes of performance, the method of indemnification is generally left to the indemnifier's discretion.[4] In *Muhammad Issa El Sheikh Ahmad v Ali*,[5] Lord Uthwatt explained that the indemnity 'might well be performed by satisfaction of [the third party] otherwise than by payment of money, despite the dissent of the [indemnified parties] from that method of performance'. Other illustrations are provided by the cases on accommodation bills of exchange. The drawer accommodated on the bill expressly or impliedly promises to indemnify the acceptor against liability on the bill. The drawer may perform the indemnity in various ways, including by providing funds in advance to meet the bill, by taking up the bill itself, or, upon maturity, by paying the amount of the bill to the acceptor or holder.[6]

[7–6] Common modes of performance. As the promise of indemnity is usually construed to be preventive in nature, commonly accepted modes of performance include:[7] exoneration from the actual or alleged liability to the third party; payment by the indemnifier to the indemnified party before the latter pays the third party; and the indemnifier withdrawing or withholding a claim that it could otherwise press.

---

[1] See [7–24], [7–37].

[2] *cf* [6–17].

[3] See [7–7].

[4] *Ex p Wiseman; re Kelson Tritton & Co* (1871) LR 7 Ch App 35, 43; *Rankin v Palmer* (1912) 16 CLR 285, 291–92 (Griffith CJ); *Muhammad Issa El Sheikh Ahmad v Ali* [1947] AC 414 (PC), 426; *Wren v Mahony* (1972) 126 CLR 212, 227 (Barwick CJ).

[5] *Muhammad Issa El Sheikh Ahmad v Ali* [1947] AC 414 (PC), 426.

[6] See, eg, *Reynolds v Doyle* (1840) 1 Man & G 753; 133 ER 536; *Coles Myer Finance Ltd v Commissioner of Taxation* (1992) 176 CLR 640, 657–59 (Mason CJ, Brennan, Dawson, Toohey and Gaudron JJ), 687–88 (McHugh J). See further [7–16].

[7] *cf Re Richardson, ex p the Governors of St Thomas's Hospital* [1911] 2 KB 705 (CA), 716–17 (Buckley LJ).

Exoneration from Claim by or Liability to Third Party

Defence of Action

[7–7] **Conduct of defence of action.** There is surprisingly little non-insurance authority on this point but the general position appears to be as follows. A mere promise of indemnity does not, subject to statute[8] or other terms of the contract, cast upon the indemnifier an obligation to defend an action against the indemnified party.[9] Nor, subject to statute or other terms of the contract,[10] does the indemnifier have the power to assume responsibility for the defence of the action: the indemnified party remains *dominus litis* and can conduct its own defence.[11]

The contract may specify a procedure for defending or settling claims by third parties. Alternatively, the opening words of the indemnity clause may state that the indemnifier will 'defend' as well as 'indemnify', or 'hold harmless' the indemnified party. In *Codemasters Software Co Ltd v Automobile Club de L'Ouest*,[12] Arnold J suggested that the term 'defend' could mean 'protect from'; in that general sense it may be surplusage. The clause in question did not compel the indemnified party to entrust the defence of an action to the indemnifier, but Arnold J ventured that the indemnified party might have had a right, exercisable at its election, to require the indemnifier to take over the defence.[13]

[7–8] **Successful defence of action.** In general, the indemnified party suffers no loss so long as the action against it is resisted and it makes no payment towards the alleged liability or the costs of the defence. Accordingly, one mode of performance is for the indemnifier to assume responsibility for defence of the action against the indemnified party and to succeed in that defence.

In *Ex p Wiseman; re Kelson, Tritton & Co*,[14] an action was brought against the indemnified party, Wiseman & Co. The indemnifier, Kelson, Tritton & Co, defended the action for some time but then executed a deed of inspectorship and gave up the defence. Wiseman & Co resumed the defence, eventually lost and paid the amount of the judgment and costs. It was held that Wiseman & Co could not have proved as a creditor under the deed of inspectorship for the sums so paid. At the time of the deed there was no apparent breach of the indemnity by Kelson, Tritton & Co. Their defence of the action until their bankruptcy had spared Wiseman & Co from making payments in relation to the claim and so kept Wiseman & Co harmless from loss. The only possible breach – and this was not evident on the facts

---

[8] As an example of a general statutory exception, see the California Civil Code, §2778(4).

[9] This is recognised implicitly in the rules concerning the time at which the indemnified party's right to enforce the indemnity arises: see [5–40], [5–44] and further [7–29], [7–40]. In the insurance context, see, eg, *Distillers Co Bio-Chemicals (Australia) Pty Ltd v Ajax Insurance Co Ltd* (1973) 130 CLR 1, 24 (Stephen J); *Brice v JH Wackerbarth (Australasia) Pty Ltd* [1974] 2 Lloyd's Rep 274 (CA), 277 (Roskill LJ).

[10] See, eg, *Montforts v Marsden* [1895] 1 Ch 11 (CA).

[11] cf *Parker v Lewis* (1873) LR 8 Ch App 1035, 1059 (Mellish LJ); *Born v Turner* [1900] 2 Ch 211 (Ch) (indemnified party justified in severing defence from co-defendant indemnifier); *Forstaff Adelaide Pty Ltd v Hills Industries Ltd* [2006] SASC 88 (FC), [43]–[47] (Anderson J). In the insurance context, see D Derrington and RS Ashton, *The Law of Liability Insurance*, 2nd edn (Sydney, LexisNexis, 2005), 708, para 9-156.

[12] *Codemasters Software Co Ltd v Automobile Club de L'Ouest* [2009] EWHC 2361 (Ch); [2010] FSR 12.

[13] *Codemasters Software Co Ltd v Automobile Club de L'Ouest* [2009] EWHC 2361 (Ch); [2010] FSR 12, [41]. cf *Menzies Property Services Ltd v State of New South Wales* [2003] NSWCA 17, [41] (Santow JA).

[14] *Ex p Wiseman; re Kelson Tritton & Co* (1871) LR 7 Ch App 35.

stated in the special case – was if Wiseman & Co had incurred costs to their own attorney prior to that date.[15]

In *Ex p Wiseman*, the indemnified party was kept harmless up to the point of the indemnifier's bankruptcy but later sustained loss by paying the amount of the judgment and costs. If, however, the indemnifier successfully defends the action against the indemnified party, there is no cause for the indemnified party to pay and so loss is avoided.

[7–9] Unsuccessful defence of action. If the defence mounted by the indemnifier is unsuccessful, the indemnified party will become liable for the judgment sum and, usually, costs. In *Ex p Wiseman; re Kelson, Tritton & Co*,[16] Mellish LJ explained how the indemnifier could have performed the indemnity in that situation:

> [I]f Kelson, Tritton, & Co had continued to defend the action through their own attorney, and then had paid the full sum recovered and the costs to [the claimant in the action] as soon as judgment was signed and before execution could be issued against Wiseman, the contract would never have been broken at all.

This is a specific instance of the more general point that the indemnifier can perform the indemnity by relieving the indemnified party from its liability to the third party.[17]

Extinction of Claim or Liability

[7–10] Payment to third party. The indemnifier can perform the indemnity by paying the third party to whom the indemnified party is, or is alleged to be, liable. The amount paid may be the amount of an undisputed liability of the indemnified party, or it may be an amount agreed in a settlement between the third party and indemnified party or indemnifier in satisfaction of the third party's claim. The purpose of the payment is to extinguish the claim or liability. If it is right to say that an unauthorised payment by a stranger to a creditor generally does not discharge the debtor's debt,[18] then some reason must be found to explain why payment by the indemnifier to the third party is accepted to be satisfactory performance of the indemnity.[19]

The most general explanation is that a promise of indemnity may carry with it, in the absence of contrary terms, an implied authority from the indemnified party to the indemnifier to discharge on its behalf liabilities that are the subject of the indemnity. In *Firma C-Trade SA v Newcastle Protection and Indemnity Association (The Fanti) (No 2)*,[20] Lord Goff was prepared to accept that a P&I club's payment to a third party claimant on the insured's behalf would have been 'expressly or impliedly authorised or ratified' by the insured, and thus effective to discharge the insured's liability.

Of the more specific explanations, the first is that the indemnified party may be involved in the arrangements for the discharge of its liability such that its conduct confers the requi-

---

[15] *Ex p Wiseman; re Kelson Tritton & Co* (1871) LR 7 Ch App 35, 42. Mellish LJ presumably meant that Wiseman had paid the costs and not merely incurred a liability for them: see [2–8], [6–23].

[16] *Ex p Wiseman; re Kelson Tritton & Co* (1871) LR 7 Ch App 35, 42.

[17] See [7–10].

[18] See generally C Mitchell, P Mitchell and S Watterson (eds), *Goff and Jones: The Law of Unjust Enrichment*, 8th edn (London, Sweet & Maxwell, 2011), 128–33, paras 5-44–5-57. cf *Sheahan v Carrier Air Conditioning Pty Ltd* (1996) 189 CLR 407, 430–31 and fn 66 (Dawson, Gaudron and Gummow JJ).

[19] See, eg, *Firma C-Trade SA v Newcastle Protection and Indemnity Association (The Fanti) (No 2)* [1991] 2 AC 1 (HL), 40 (Lord Jauncey).

[20] *Firma C-Trade SA v Newcastle Protection and Indemnity Association (The Fanti) (No 2)* [1991] 2 AC 1 (HL), 35.

site authority on the indemnifier, or so that the arrangements amount to an agreement between the third party, the indemnified party and the indemnifier for the discharge of the liability.[21] A similar instance may be where the third party enforces the right to indemnity as an assignee from the indemnified party.[22]

Secondly, the indemnifier and indemnified party may both be liable to the third party in such a way that the indemnifier's payment discharges the indemnified party's obligation to the same extent. This may occur where they are joint debtors; or where the indemnifying debtor discharges the debt guaranteed by the indemnified party; or where the indemnifying party accommodated on a bill of exchange pays the bill in due course, thus discharging the bill and the indemnified party as accommodation acceptor;[23] or where the indemnifier and indemnified party are concurrent tortfeasors and the indemnifier compensates the victim for the whole of the loss.[24]

Thirdly, the exception for payments made under legal compulsion[25] might be extended to cases where the indemnifier acts pursuant to a court order to discharge the liability.[26]

Finally, even if the indemnifier's payment is unauthorised and does not, strictly, discharge the liability, it may produce a similar result. If the third party accepts the payment in satisfaction of the liability, a subsequent action against the indemnified party may be barred on the ground that it would be an abuse of process.[27]

[7–11] Other means of obtaining release or discharge. Other conduct by the indemnifier is sufficient if it discharges the indemnified party.[28] In *Betts v Gibbins*,[29] the indemnifier attempted to resolve a dispute by supplying replacement goods to the indemnified parties, to be offered to the third party. That offer was rejected by the third party and the indemnified parties then settled the action by payment. The indemnifier failed in his argument that the tender of replacement goods was sufficient performance of the indemnity.

Abandonment of Claim by Indemnifier

[7–12] Situations in which claim may arise. Assuming that A promises to indemnify B against B's liability to C, in some circumstances, A may make a claim that is connected with B's liability to C. There are two common situations:

---

[21] See, eg, *Ramsay v National Australia Bank Ltd* [1989] VR 59 (FC) (common director of indemnifier and indemnified companies arranging for bill to be drawn by indemnifier, discounted by creditor bank, and credited to account of indemnified party).

[22] See [7–50].

[23] Bills of Exchange Act 1882, s 59(3).

[24] *Jameson v Central Electricity Generating Board* [2000] AC 455 (HL), 466 (Lord Lloyd), 471–72 (Lord Hope); *Allison v KPMG Peat Marwick* [1999] NZCA 324; [2000] 1 NZLR 560; *Baxter v Obacelo Pty Ltd* [2001] HCA 66; (2001) 205 CLR 635, [47], [52]–[53] (Gleeson CJ and Callinan J), [62]–[67] (Gummow and Hayne JJ); *Heaton v AXA Equity and Law Life Assurance Society plc* [2002] UKHL 15; [2002] 2 AC 329, [3]–[4] (Lord Bingham).

[25] *Electricity Supply Nominees Ltd v Thorn EMI Retail Ltd* (1992) 63 P & CR 143 (CA), 148 (Fox LJ); *Ibrahim v Barclays Bank plc* [2012] EWCA Civ 640; [2013] Ch 400, [46]–[49] (Lewison LJ).

[26] Strictly, the order compels performance of an obligation owed by the indemnifier to the indemnified party, not the third party as payee. Alternatively, such cases could be rationalised as instances of authorised payments.

[27] *Hirachand Punamchand v Temple* [1911] 2 KB 330 (CA), 339–40 (Fletcher Moulton LJ), 341–42 (Farwell J); *Sheahan v Carrier Air Conditioning Pty Ltd* (1996) 189 CLR 407, 430–31 (Dawson, Gaudron and Gummow JJ).

[28] *Wilson v Lloyd* (1873) LR 16 Eq 60 (indemnified co-debtor in position of surety discharged by variation or allowance of time in compromise between indemnifying co-debtor and creditor); *Muhammad Issa El Sheikh Ahmad v Ali* [1947] AC 414 (PC), 426. See also [7–41].

[29] *Betts v Gibbins* (1834) 2 Ad & E 57; 111 ER 22.

(1) A and B are under a common liability to C, such that A would be entitled to claim contribution from B in respect of that liability.

(2) A has a claim against C and that claim in turn forms the basis of C's claim against B.

In either situation, A may perform the indemnity by withholding or withdrawing a claim that A could otherwise advance.

Claims for Contribution

[7–13] Abandoning claim for contribution. It is necessary to make two assumptions. The first is that the scope of the indemnity covers the common liability to the third party. This may be controversial where, for example, the basis of the indemnified party's liability is negligence. The second assumption is that, but for the effect of the indemnity, the indemnifier would be entitled to obtain contribution from the indemnified party in respect of the common liability. Subject to contrary terms, an indemnity is generally construed to protect the indemnified party against the entire amount of a liability. There is no proportionate adjustment to reflect the indemnifier's and indemnified party's relative responsibility in bringing about the claimant's loss.[30] Accordingly, if the indemnifier were to obtain contribution from the indemnified party, then the latter would not be fully indemnified against the liability.

Abandoning a claim for contribution against the indemnified party may be a necessary, though not sufficient, act of performance. The indemnifier may also have to relieve the indemnified party of the liability to the third party.

Circular Indemnities and Similar Arrangements[31]

[7–14] Carriage of goods. The following situation can arise in transactions involving the carriage of goods.[32] The consignor (A) arranges transport with a carrier or freight forwarder (B) and all or part of the carriage of the goods is entrusted to some other party (C). B offers protection to C against claims for loss of or damage to the goods. The protection may take the form of an express or implied indemnity from B to C against claims generally or, perhaps, only to the extent they exceed C's liability to B under contract. A also indemnifies B against claims by other parties in relation to loss of or damage to the goods. That indemnity may be combined with: (1) a promise by A not to sue third parties, or a promise that no claims will be made against B by others; and/or (2) a *Himalaya* clause. The goods are lost or damaged owing to C's default. A sues C and perhaps also B. C seeks indemnity from B.[33] B claims against A relying, inter alia, on the indemnity from A against B's liability to C.

---

[30] See [4–45].

[31] See R Newell, 'Privity Fundamentalism and the Circular Indemnity Clause' [1992] *Lloyd's Maritime and Commercial Law Quarterly* 97; DA Glass, 'Bailment on Terms and Circular Indemnity' [1997] *Lloyd's Maritime and Commercial Law Quarterly* 478. See further [7–55].

[32] *cf Hair and Skin Trading Co Ltd v Norman Airfreight Carriers Ltd* [1974] 1 Lloyd's Rep 443 (QB); *Nippon Yusen Kaisha v International Import and Export Co Ltd (The Elbe Maru)* [1978] 1 Lloyd's Rep 206 (QB); *Broken Hill Pty Co Ltd v Hapag-Lloyd AG* [1980] 2 NSWLR 572 (SC); *Sidney Cooke Ltd v Hapag-Lloyd AG* [1980] 2 NSWLR 587 (SC); *China Ocean Shipping Co Ltd v PS Chellaram & Co Ltd* (1990) 28 NSWLR 354 (CA); *Schenker & Co (Aust) Pty Ltd v Maplas Equipment and Services Pty Ltd* [1990] VR 834 (FC); *Spectra International plc v Hayesoak Ltd* [1998] 1 Lloyd's Rep 162 (CA); *Chapman Marine Pty Ltd v Wilhelmsen Lines A/S* [1999] FCA 178.

[33] Contrast *PS Chellaram & Co Ltd v China Ocean Shipping Co Ltd* [1989] 1 Lloyd's Rep 413 (NSWSC), 429–30 (revd on other grounds: *China Ocean Shipping Co Ltd v PS Chellaram & Co Ltd* (1990) 28 NSWLR 354 (CA)).

If C's liability to A is within the scope of B's indemnity to C, and B's liability to indemnify C is within the scope of A's indemnity to B,[34] then A might, in effect, save B harmless by eliminating the motivation for C's claim against B. A withdraws its claim against C. Where B's indemnity to C applies only to C's excess liability, then A might save B harmless by confining its claim against C to the specified limit.

[7–15] **Other arrangements.** The same analysis can be extended by analogy to other situations. *Deepak Fertilisers and Petrochemicals Corp v ICI Chemicals & Polymers Ltd*[35] arose out of a project for the construction of a methanol plant. The plant did not perform as intended and was severely damaged in an explosion. A, the employer, sued B, a contractor who supplied supervisory services, technology and know-how for the project, and also C, who had licensed the technology and know-how to B. C, in turn, claimed indemnity from B. Part of the dispute related to two indemnity provisions contained in a contract to which A and B, but not C, were parties. A promised to indemnify B against liability for loss of or damage to A's property. A separate provision stated, in effect, that references to B in the first provision would extend to include C.

The argument in relation to the first provision concerned its application to claims inter partes, rather than to claims by C against B. The indemnity as extended according to the second provision could not be enforced by C, but it was held that B could enforce the indemnity for C's benefit. The court ordered a stay of the proceedings by A against C.[36] This, in effect, eliminated B's potential liability to C.

Payment to Indemnified Party

[7–16] **Payment to indemnified party.** The indemnifier may perform the indemnity by paying the indemnified party an amount equal to its liability to the third party. This mode of performance is appropriate whether the indemnity is (unusually) compensatory or (more commonly) preventive in nature, but the time for performance differs. In the former case, the indemnifier need only pay so much as the indemnified party has already paid to the third party. In the latter case, the indemnifier performs by paying the amount of the liability before the indemnified party pays the third party. This allows the indemnified party to meet the liability without having to draw from its own resources. The loss avoided is the diminution of the indemnified party's wealth.[37] The latter point is illustrated in the cases on accommodation bills of exchange. The drawer expressly or impliedly promises to indemnify the accommodation acceptor against liability on the bill. It is generally understood that such an indemnity is preventive in nature.[38] One of the recognised modes of performance is for the drawer to pay the amount of the bill to the acceptor in advance of maturity.[39]

---

[34] Such points may be disputed: see, eg, *Chas Davis (Metal Brokers) Ltd v Gilyott & Scott Ltd* [1975] 2 Lloyd's Rep 422 (QB); *Schenker & Co (Aust) Pty Ltd v Maplas Equipment and Services Pty Ltd* [1990] VR 834 (FC); *Spectra International plc v Hayesoak Ltd* [1997] 1 Lloyd's Rep 153 (CLCC), 158–59 (revd in part on other grounds: *Spectra International plc v Hayesoak Ltd* [1998] 1 Lloyd's Rep 162 (CA)).
[35] *Deepak Fertilisers and Petrochemicals Corp v ICI Chemicals & Polymers Ltd* [1999] 1 Lloyd's Rep 387 (CA).
[36] See [8–17].
[37] See [6–20].
[38] See [6–10].
[39] *Chilton v Whiffin* (1768) 3 Wils 13, 17; 95 ER 906, 908–09; *Yates v Hoppe* (1850) 9 CB 542, 549–50; 137 ER 1003, 1006 (Maule J); *KD Morris & Sons Pty Ltd (in liq) v Bank of Queensland Ltd* (1980) 146 CLR 165, 202 (Aickin J); *Coles Myer Finance Ltd v Commissioner of Taxation* (1992) 176 CLR 640, 658–59 (Mason CJ, Brennan, Toohey, Dawson and Gaudron JJ).

An order for specific enforcement of an indemnity may, in appropriate cases, require the indemnifier to pay the indemnified party before the latter has paid the third party.[40]

Enforcement

[7–17] **Modes of enforcement.** An indemnity against claims by or liabilities to third parties is usually enforced in one of three ways. The indemnified party may sue for loss actually sustained in connection with the claim or liability. The most common type of loss is expenditure by the indemnified party to satisfy the claim or liability.[41] Claims for actual loss can generally be characterised as claims for damages for breach of contract.[42] Indemnities against claims by or liabilities to third parties possess no special features in this regard and it is sufficient to refer to the general treatment elsewhere.[43] Where a loss has not yet arisen but is anticipated, the indemnified party may seek specific enforcement. The object is to compel the indemnifier to act to prevent a potential loss from materialising, for example, by relieving the indemnified party of the liability before it pays.[44] The final method of enforcement is less common. The indemnified party may rely on the indemnity as having some exculpatory effect in relation to a claim made by the indemnifier.[45] That claim may be made directly against the indemnified party, or it may be made against another party such that it indirectly affects the indemnified party.

Enforcement before Loss

Nature of Enforcement

[7–18] **General.** In appropriate cases, an indemnity against claims by or liabilities to third parties may be enforced before the indemnified party sustains a loss. The general rule is that a claim or liability is not of itself a loss;[46] the loss usually occurs when the indemnified party draws upon its own resources to make payment towards it. Enforcement of the indemnity in advance of loss thus compels the indemnifier to intervene before this happens.

The focus is on orders for indemnification that will, if complied with, fully and finally protect the indemnified party against the relevant liability. Such orders can be described as a form of quia timet relief because they are sought and made in respect of an anticipated loss. An indemnified party's rights can be vindicated or protected in other ways before loss: for example, by declaratory relief,[47] or by an order to preserve assets against which the right to indemnity might later be exercised.[48]

---

[40] See further [7–43]–[7–44].
[41] See [6–23], [6–24].
[42] See [1–22], [1–23] for other possibilities.
[43] See generally ch 5.
[44] See [7–18].
[45] See [7–51].
[46] See [6–23].
[47] See [5–76].
[48] See [5–74].

[7–19] **Juristic basis.** Enforcement in advance of loss derives from the jurisdiction of courts of equity to decree specific performance of contracts of indemnity.[49] As Lord Brandon explained in *Firma C-Trade SA v Newcastle Protection and Indemnity Association (The Fanti) (No 2)*:[50]

> There is no doubt that before the passing of the Supreme Court of Judicature Acts 1873 and 1875, there was a difference between the remedies available to enforce an ordinary contract of indemnity . . . at law on the one hand and in equity on the other. At law the party to be indemnified had to discharge the liability himself first and then sue the indemnifier for damages for breach of contract. In equity an ordinary contract of indemnity could be directed to be specifically performed by ordering that the indemnifier should pay the amount concerned directly to the third party to whom the liability was owed or in some cases to the party to be indemnified. . . . There is further no doubt that since the passing of the Supreme Court of Judicature Acts 1873 and 1875 the equitable remedy has prevailed over the remedy at law.

Such orders for indemnification are more accurately characterised as relief approximate to specific performance rather than specific performance in its strict sense.[51] The relief generally does not require the execution of some instrument or performance of some act that will thereby define the relative legal positions of the parties. Although some decisions refer to a 'contract' of indemnity, relief is available where the indemnity is a term in a larger contract,[52] and it appears that an indemnity can be enforced without an order for specific performance of the entire contract.[53] The time for specific enforcement involves considerations peculiar to the nature of an indemnity promise. For these reasons, the terms 'specific relief' or 'specific enforcement' are used in preference to 'specific performance'.

It does, however, appear that some of the usual requirements for, and defences to, an action for specific performance apply also to an action for specific enforcement of an indemnity.[54]

[7–20] **Relevance of construction.** An order for specific enforcement compels performance of the promise of indemnity according to its terms. Whether specific enforcement is available, and the form it may take, thus depends upon construction of the contract. Specific enforcement is only available where the indemnity is preventive in nature. In *McIntosh v Dalwood (No 4)*[55] Street CJ said:

> In every case the contractual obligation must first be ascertained . . . If the obligation is merely an obligation to indemnify a person, in the sense of repaying to him a sum of money after he has paid

---

[49] *Johnston v Salvage Association* (1887) 19 QBD 458 (CA), 460–61 (Lindley LJ); *Travers v Richardson* (1920) 20 SR (NSW) 367 (SC), 370–71; *McIntosh v Dalwood (No 4)* (1930) 30 SR (NSW) 415 (FC), 418–19 (Street CJ); *Firma C-Trade SA v Newcastle Protection and Indemnity Association (The Fanti) (No 2)* [1991] 2 AC 1 (HL), 28 (Lord Brandon), 36 (Lord Goff), 40–41 (Lord Jauncey); *Management Corp Strata Title Plan No 1933 v Liang Huat Aluminium Ltd* [2001] BLR 351 (Sing CA), 356–57 (LP Thean JA). For early examples, see *Earl of Ranelaugh v Hayes* (1683) 1 Vern 189; 23 ER 405; WT Barbour, *The History of Contract in Early English Equity*, vol 4 (Oxford, P Vinogradoff ed, Clarendon Press, 1914), 135–37.

[50] *Firma C-Trade SA v Newcastle Protection and Indemnity Association (The Fanti) (No 2)* [1991] 2 AC 1 (HL), 28.

[51] R Meagher, D Heydon and M Leeming, *Meagher, Gummow and Lehane's Equity: Doctrines and Remedies*, 4th edn (Sydney, Butterworths LexisNexis, 2002), 661, para 20-050.

[52] *Newman v McNicol* (1938) 38 SR (NSW) 609 (SC), 626; *County and District Properties Ltd v C Jenner & Sons Ltd* [1976] 2 Lloyd's Rep 728 (QB), 734–36; *McMahon v Ambrose* [1987] VR 817 (FC), 825 (McGarvie J).

[53] *Cruse v Paine* (1868) LR 6 Eq 641, 653.

[54] *Anglo-Australian Life Assurance Co v British Provident Life and Fire Society* (1862) 3 Giff 521; 66 ER 515 (misrepresentation); *Paterson v Pongrass Group Operations Pty Ltd* [2011] NSWSC 1588, [80]–[84] (consideration).

[55] *McIntosh v Dalwood (No 4)* (1930) 30 SR (NSW) 415 (FC), 418.

it, no equitable relief is needed. Damages will provide an adequate remedy. If, however, the obligation on its true construction is an obligation to relieve a debtor by preventing him from having to pay his debt, equity will in such a case give relief in the nature of *quia timet* relief, and, instead of compelling the party indemnified first to pay the debt, and perhaps to ruin himself in doing so, will specifically enforce the obligation by ordering the indemnifying party to pay the debt.

The parties may modify or limit the modes of specific enforcement, or exclude that possibility. The leading authority is an insurance case, *Firma C-Trade SA v Newcastle Protection and Indemnity Association (The Fanti) (No 2)*,[56] but the reasoning applies equally to non-insurance indemnities. Insurance provided by P&I clubs afforded cover in respect of claims that the insured 'shall have become liable to pay and shall in fact have paid'. The House of Lords accepted that the usual construction of a promise of indemnity against liability was to keep the indemnified party (here, the insured) harmless from loss.[57] However, the 'pay to be paid' stipulation imposed a condition precedent to enforcement that could not be overridden by resort to equitable principles. An order specifically to enforce the indemnity could only compel performance consistently with the terms of the contract. Those terms required payment first and reimbursement later.

Street CJ's analysis in *McIntosh* reflects the general distinction between preventive and compensatory promises of indemnity in the strict sense. Specific enforcement may also be relevant for promises which, although not indemnities, are similar in effect. A's promise to B to pay a sum of money to C is not an indemnity but it may be specifically enforced.[58] In contrast, specific performance was refused in *Brough v Oddy*.[59] B relinquished possession of certain title deeds to leasehold property, which were then used as security in another transaction under which C was obliged to pay an annuity of £40. In return for B giving up the deeds, A promised B that if C were to default – so that the annuitant might resort to the property as security – then A would pay B about £30 per year. C defaulted. B brought an action for specific performance against A, seeking indemnity against any payments that B might have to make towards the annuity, in order to save the property. Leach MR held that the agreement was not an indemnity, but only a promise by A to pay B upon a certain event.

[7–21] Inadequacy of damages. Street CJ's judgment in *McIntosh v Dalwood (No 4)*[60] identifies another aspect of the jurisdiction to order specific enforcement, namely, the inadequacy of damages. No action could be brought at common law until the indemnified party had suffered actual loss.[61] Damages, and other common law remedies, were therefore inadequate to keep the indemnified party harmless against loss. Where the indemnity is preventive in nature, specific enforcement is necessary to ensure that the indemnified party obtains the

---

[56] *Firma C-Trade SA v Newcastle Protection and Indemnity Association (The Fanti) (No 2)* [1991] 2 AC 1 (HL). See also *Paterson v Pongrass Group Operations Pty Ltd* [2011] NSWSC 1588, [79].

[57] *Firma C-Trade SA v Newcastle Protection and Indemnity Association (The Fanti) (No 2)* [1991] 2 AC 1 (HL), 28 (Lord Brandon), 35 (Lord Goff), 40–41 (Lord Jauncey).

[58] *Coulls v Bagot's Executor and Trustee Co Ltd* (1967) 119 CLR 460; *Beswick v Beswick* [1968] AC 58 (HL).

[59] *Brough v Oddy* (1829) 1 Russ & M 55; 39 ER 22.

[60] *McIntosh v Dalwood (No 4)* (1930) 30 SR (NSW) 415 (FC), 418 (Street CJ). See also *Johnston v Salvage Association* (1887) 19 QBD 458 (CA), 460–61 (Lindley LJ); *McIntosh v Dalwood (No 3)* (1930) 30 SR (NSW) 332 (SC), 334–35; *Firma C-Trade SA v Newcastle Protection and Indemnity Association (The Fanti) (No 2)* [1991] 2 AC 1 (HL), 36 (Lord Goff), 40–41 (Lord Jauncey).

[61] See generally *Re Richardson, ex p the Governors of St Thomas's Hospital* [1911] 2 KB 705 (CA), 709 (Cozens-Hardy MR), 712 (Fletcher Moulton LJ); *Wren v Mahony* (1972) 126 CLR 212, 229–30 (Barwick CJ); *Firma C-Trade SA v Newcastle Protection and Indemnity Association (The Fanti) (No 2)* [1991] 2 AC 1 (HL), 35–36 (Lord Goff). See further [1–18].

essential benefit of the bargain. In contrast, if the indemnity is compensatory then common law remedies – whether for damages for breach of contract or for a sum payable by the terms of the contract – are sufficient to enable the indemnified party to be compensated for its loss.

[7–22] **Time of enforcement.** An order for specific performance may be made before the time for performance of one or more contractual obligations has arrived.[62] The form of the decree is moulded to fit the circumstances, so that a party is not compelled to perform before performance is due. This perspective is not directly applicable to promises of indemnity that are preventive in nature. A striking feature of such promises is that, in general, there is no particular time fixed for performance. So long as the indemnified party suffers no loss within scope, the indemnity is not breached. The object of specific enforcement is to compel the indemnifier to act so that loss – a breach – does not occur. This does not mean that a contractual promise of indemnity is specifically enforceable at will. There are other limiting principles that account for the absence of a temporal reference point. In general terms, those principles confine relief to situations where loss to the indemnified party is sufficiently imminent.[63]

[7–23] **Analogous contexts.** Principles applicable to quia timet claims for indemnity or contribution in other contexts, particularly suretyship and trust, have been influential in the development of the principles governing specific enforcement of contractual indemnities, and vice versa.[64] The principles are the same or similar in many respects, but there remain several important differences.

    The basis of a quia timet right to indemnity in other contexts is not, or at least not relevantly, contractual. Where a guarantor provides a guarantee upon the debtor's request, the implied contract of indemnity appears to operate by way of reimbursement.[65] Such an indemnity would not be susceptible to specific enforcement, yet the guarantor is entitled to quia timet relief according to equitable principles. An order for specific enforcement operates in personam and is concerned with the indemnifier's performance of its contractual obligation to the indemnified party. Not all rights of indemnity are of this nature. A trustee's right of indemnity, for example, comprises both a right to resort to trust assets for recoupment or exoneration and, in appropriate cases, a right to proceed directly against beneficiaries.[66] The relationship between the parties to a contractual indemnity can vary greatly, whereas the other contexts involve a particular type of relationship, such as guarantor and debtor, co-guarantors, or trustee and beneficiary. There may be specific considerations affecting quia timet relief in those contexts that are not relevant to all contracts of indemnity.[67]

Preconditions

[7–24] **Loss must be sufficiently imminent.** Specific enforcement is available where the indemnified party can establish a sufficiently imminent risk of loss. In relation to liabilities to third parties, this requirement can be articulated in more specific terms:

---

[62] *Turner v Bladin* (1951) 82 CLR 463, 472–73; *Hasham v Zenab* [1960] AC 316 (PC), 329–30.
[63] See [7–24].
[64] See, eg, *Wolmershausen v Gullick* [1893] 2 Ch 514 (Ch); *Ascherson v Tredegar Dry Dock and Wharf Co Ltd* [1909] 2 Ch 401 (Ch); *Re Richardson, ex p the Governors of St Thomas's Hospital* [1911] 2 KB 705 (CA).
[65] See [2–24]. Express indemnities to guarantors can be different: see [6–14].
[66] See [1–6].
[67] See, eg, [7–45], [7–56]–[7–57].

(1) there is a clear and definite liability of the indemnified party;
(2) the liability is presently accrued and enforceable; and
(3) there is some prospect that the liability might be enforced against the indemnified party.

These conditions reflect the general proposition that a promise of indemnity is concerned with the avoidance of loss from claims or liabilities, and not directly with the avoidance of claims or liabilities themselves. The first two conditions are substantially similar to those that apply to quia timet orders for exoneration in favour of guarantors.[68] The third condition is sound in principle but its status as a legal rule is uncertain.[69]

[7–25] Existence of liability. The indemnified party is, in general, only entitled to obtain specific enforcement in respect of a definite liability to a third party. It is not sufficient, for example, that the indemnified party might be found to be liable to the third party for some amount once all relevant accounts are settled.[70] The indemnified party's liability to the third party can arise from any source: it may be a primary liability under general law or statute, or in the nature of a secondary liability to pay damages for a wrong. The requirement is expressed in terms of a 'liability' rather than an 'obligation', to indicate that the subject-matter is the payment of money by the indemnified party to the third party. Specific enforcement of indemnities in relation to non-monetary obligations has not so far been recognised.[71]

[7–26] Ascertainment of the liability. It is sometimes said that the indemnified party is only entitled to relief when its liability to the third party has been 'established' or 'ascertained' or 'realised'.[72] Those references contemplate some process involving the indemnified party and third party by which a liability is recognised and perhaps also quantified. That process may be, for example, an action culminating in a judgment in favour of the third party, or a compromise of the third party's claim, or a determination of liability made by a government authority.

The concept of 'ascertainment' performs several functions in relation to the enforcement of the indemnity.[73] One of these functions is to facilitate proof of actual or potential loss within scope. Ascertainment may be relevant because the indemnity protects against liabilities that have been established by certain processes.[74] Alternatively, even if the indem-

---

[68] See *Nisbet v Smith* (1789) 2 Bro CC 579, 582; 29 ER 317, 319 (note 2); *Holden v Black* (1905) 2 CLR 768, 782–83; *Ascherson v Tredegar Dry Dock and Wharf Co Ltd* [1909] 2 Ch 401 (Ch); *Watt v Mortlock* [1964] Ch 84 (Ch); *Thomas v Nottingham Incorporated Football Club Ltd* [1972] Ch 596 (Ch); *National Commercial Bank v Wimborne* (1978) 5 BPR 11,958 (NSWSC); *Woolmington v Bronze Lamp Restaurant Pty Ltd* [1984] 2 NSWLR 242 (SC), 243–44; *Abigroup Ltd v Abignano* (1992) 39 FCR 74 (FC), 81–82; *Friend v Brooker* [2009] HCA 21; (2009) 239 CLR 129, [55] (French CJ, Gummow, Hayne and Bell JJ).
[69] See [7–32].
[70] *Antrobus v Davidson* (1817) 3 Mer 569; 36 ER 219. cf *Hughes-Hallett v Indian Mammoth Gold Mines Co* (1882) 22 Ch D 561 (Ch).
[71] See [5–70].
[72] *County and District Properties Ltd v C Jenner & Sons Ltd* [1976] 2 Lloyd's Rep 728 (QB), 734, 735–36; *Telfair Shipping Corp v Inersea Carriers SA (The Caroline P)* [1985] 1 WLR 553 (QB), 567–68; *R&H Green & Silley Weir Ltd v British Railways Board* [1985] 1 WLR 570 (QB), 574; *City of London v Reeve & Co Ltd* [2000] EWHC 138 (TCC); [2000] BLR 211, [27], [34]. cf *Bradley v Eagle Star Insurance Co Ltd* [1989] AC 957 (HL), 966 (Lord Brandon) (liability insurance).
[73] cf *Lumbermens Mutual Casualty Co v Bovis Lend Lease Ltd* [2004] EWHC 2197 (Comm); [2005] 1 Lloyd's Rep 494, [38]–[42]; *Law Society v Shah* [2007] EWHC 2841 (Ch); [2009] Ch 223, [22]–[24], [44] (function of ascertainment in liability insurance).
[74] See [6–34].

nity protects only against actual liabilities, the indemnified party may rely indirectly upon the process of ascertainment to demonstrate an actual liability.[75]

Ascertainment performs two additional functions that are directly relevant to specific enforcement. First, the process of ascertainment may produce a definite liability where none previously existed (as for a reasonable settlement of an unsound claim), or where there was, in fact, a liability, but there was dispute or uncertainty as to its existence or quantum. This is not to say that the liability produced by the ascertainment process is necessarily well founded, or within the scope of the indemnity, or even that the indemnifier is bound by the outcome of that process. Rather, the basic point is that specific enforcement is generally available for a liability that is identifiable and definite, not one that remains uncertain.

Secondly, the process of ascertainment may convert a clear but inchoate liability into one that is presently accrued and legally enforceable. So, for example, a liability in damages for a wrong may be transformed into a judgment debt; or the terms of a contract between the indemnified party and third party may require some process to be followed to determine the transaction between them and to crystallise a final sum due. A presently accrued and enforceable liability is a distinct precondition for specific enforcement and is considered later.[76]

[7–27] **No particular method of ascertainment required.** For non-insurance indemnities, the indemnified party's liability need not be ascertained by any particular method, such as a judgment, arbitral award or settlement binding on the indemnified party.[77] It is sufficient that the liability be clearly identifiable. In *Re Dixon*,[78] for example, the notices of assessment issued by the taxation authority would have been sufficient. In *McIntosh v Dalwood (No 4)*,[79] the liability arose plainly from the contract. In other cases, the indemnified party has undoubtedly been liable for calls on shares.[80] It is, therefore, not surprising that references to ascertainment by judgment, award or settlement have figured most prominently in cases where the indemnified party has been contesting its liability to pay compensation for an alleged wrong to the third party.

[7–28] **Whether amount of liability must also be ascertained.** A liability may be definite in existence though not in quantum. For some forms of order, clearly, the amount of the liability must be ascertained: an order that the indemnifier pay the third party a sum equal to the amount of the indemnified party's liability is one example. This would not necessarily present an obstacle for other forms of order, such as an order that the indemnifier procure the release or discharge of the indemnified party from an existing liability.

It is probably a general condition for specific enforcement that the amount of the liability be fixed and ascertained or readily ascertainable. Without that condition, the indemnifier might be drawn into a dispute with the third party over quantum, or have to conduct its own investigations into the circumstances from which the liability arose.

---

[75] See [6–31].

[76] See [7–31].

[77] *C Inc plc v L* [2001] EWHC 550 (Comm); [2001] 2 Lloyd's Rep 459, [28] fn 33; *Carillion JM Ltd v Phi Group Ltd* [2011] EWHC 1379 (TCC), [158]–[159].

[78] *Re Dixon* [1994] 1 Qd R 7 (FC). See also [6–34].

[79] *McIntosh v Dalwood (No 4)* (1930) 30 SR (NSW) 415 (FC) (the indemnified party had been sued but there is no mention of judgment against him). See also *Lloyd v Dimmack* (1877) 7 Ch D 398 (Ch), 402; *Rankin v Palmer* (1912) 16 CLR 285; *Thanh v Hoang* (1994) 63 SASR 276 (FC).

[80] See, eg, *Evans v Wood* (1867) LR 5 Eq 9; *Cruse v Paine* (1869) LR 4 Ch App 441. *cf British Union and National Insurance Co v Rawson* [1916] 2 Ch 476 (CA).

Several decisions on the point concern actions against debtors by guarantors seeking to be exonerated from liability to the creditor. In *Morrison v Barking Chemicals Co Ltd*,[81] the terms of the guarantee allowed for the guarantee to be determined by the guarantor or the bank, but the procedure had not been engaged at the time the guarantor sought an order for exoneration. Sargant J declined to make the order because the amount of the guarantor's liability was fluctuating; it would only become fixed when the guarantee was determined by that process. In contrast, in *Re Anderson-Berry*,[82] Lord Hanworth MR suggested that a clear liability of the guarantor was sufficient, even though the amount might be ascertained in subsequent proceedings at a later date. That view is, perhaps, explained by the unusual circumstances of the case. The sureties were liable on an administration bond and sought to restrain the maladministration of the deceased's estate, which would immediately have exposed them to liability.[83]

The intermediate position is that it is sufficient that the amount of the liability is fixed and can readily be ascertained. The principal relief may include incidental orders for inquiries or the taking of accounts. In *Thomas v Nottingham Incorporated Football Club Ltd*,[84] the guarantee had been determined but there was some doubt as to the precise amount of the liability at the time the guarantor sought relief. Goff J made an order for exoneration on the basis that the liability was fixed and the amount was ascertainable. This also appears to be the position for contractual indemnities.[85] Where the amount is ascertainable but not immediately known, there is some variation in the forms of order.[86] The court may be content to declare the right to indemnity and direct an inquiry into the amount due; or it may go further and also order payment of the sum once it has been determined.

[7–29] Effect of actions, claims or demands by third parties. The conditions for specific relief have been stated in terms of a definite and presently accrued liability to a third party. There appears to be no further requirement that the third party have brought an action or made a claim or demand in respect of that liability.[87] The contract may, however, provide otherwise.[88]

It is implicit in the general proposition that a claim, demand or action by a third party is not itself a sufficient basis for specific enforcement. The position might be thought to be different where the scope of the indemnity refers to 'actions', 'claims' or 'demands'. In

---

[81] *Morrison v Barking Chemicals Co Ltd* [1919] 2 Ch 325 (Ch).

[82] *Re Anderson-Berry; Harris v Griffith* [1928] Ch 290 (CA), 304.

[83] *Re Anderson-Berry; Harris v Griffith* [1928] Ch 290 (CA), 309 (Lawrence LJ).

[84] *Thomas v Nottingham Incorporated Football Club Ltd* [1972] Ch 596 (Ch). See also *Holden v Black* (1905) 2 CLR 768, 782–83; *Friend v Brooker* [2009] HCA 21; (2009) 239 CLR 129, [55] (French CJ, Gummow, Hayne and Bell JJ).

[85] Accordingly, no order for specific relief was made in *Holmes v Margolese* (1983) 27 RPR 158 (BCSC) (amount of liability dependent upon third party's choice of remedy); *Ozzy Loans Pty Ltd v New Concept Pty Ltd* [2012] NSWSC 814, [32], [84] (amount of liability not fixed). See also [5–79].

[86] See, eg, *Evans v Wood* (1867) LR 5 Eq 9; *Shepherd v Gillespie* (1867) LR 5 Eq 293 (affd *Shepherd v Gillespie* (1868) LR 3 Ch App 764); *Heritage v Paine* (1876) 2 Ch D 594 (Ch); *Travers v Richardson* (1920) 20 SR (NSW) 367 (SC), 375; *Saunders v Peet* [1936] NZLR s73 (SC), 80–81.

[87] *Earl of Ranelaugh v Hayes* (1683) 1 Vern 189, 190; 23 ER 405, 406; *Wooldridge v Norris* (1868) LR 6 Eq 410, 413–14. The position is the same for guarantors relying on an equitable right to be exonerated by the debtor: *Holden v Black* (1905) 2 CLR 768, 782–83; *Ascherson v Tredegar Dry Dock and Wharf Co Ltd* [1909] 2 Ch 401 (Ch); *Tate v Crewdson* [1938] Ch 869 (Ch); *Thomas v Nottingham Incorporated Football Club Ltd* [1972] Ch 596 (Ch); *Friend v Brooker* [2009] HCA 21; (2009) 239 CLR 129, [55] (French CJ, Gummow, Hayne and Bell JJ).

[88] *Bradford v Gammon* [1925] Ch 132 (Ch). See [5–14].

McIntosh v Dalwood (No 4),[89] Street CJ referred to the following passage from *Fry on Specific Performance:*[90]

> [W]here the contract by A is to indemnify B against all claims and demands of C, there is a breach as soon as C makes the claim, and B may here usefully invoke the aid of a Court of Equity to compel A to satisfy his demand to the relief of B, and thus specifically to perform the contract: and accordingly, in such cases, the Court of Chancery entertained jurisdiction.

This may well be an accurate description of the position in equity in ancient times.[91] In *Earl of Ranelaugh v Hayes,*[92] for example, the Earl assigned to Hayes a share in the excise of Ireland. Hayes agreed in return to stand in his place concerning payments to the King and to indemnify him against all 'debts, accounts, covenants, breaches of covenants, rents and demands, whatsoever'. Upon the King bringing an action against the Earl, the Earl sought specific performance of the indemnity. Lord Keeper North made extensive orders giving effect to the indemnity. Hayes was ordered to clear the Earl from the actions against him within a year. A further order was that, upon being subject to certain suits or demands in the future, the Earl could give notice to Hayes so that Hayes could assume the defence of them. These orders suggest that the object of the indemnity was to spare the Earl from molestation, rather than to discharge definite liabilities.

Whatever may have been the position in ancient times, a distinction between 'liabilities', and 'claims', 'demands' or 'actions', is not significant for specific enforcement under the modern law. The usual construction is that references to 'claims', 'demands' or 'actions' may expand the scope of protection, but that they do not alter or accelerate the method of protection.[93] A simple promise of indemnity is not, generally, a promise that the indemnified party will not be bothered by a claim or action.[94] Nor does it incorporate a promise to defend the indemnified party against claims or actions.[95]

[7–30] Where liability ceases to exist. If the indemnified party is liable to a third party but that liability then ceases to exist, the source of potential loss has disappeared. There is, therefore, no foundation for specific enforcement.[96] The point has arisen where an indemnified company is dissolved, with the effect that its liabilities cease to exist.[97] The point also arises where the indemnified party enters a settlement with the third party on terms that the indemnified party is to be released in return for assigning (or otherwise providing) to the third party the benefit of the indemnity.[98] In *Re Perkins,*[99] the lessee, L, assigned the lease to A1. A1 promised to pay the rent, observe the covenants in the lease and indemnify

---

[89] *McIntosh v Dalwood (No 4)* (1930) 30 SR (NSW) 415 (FC), 419.
[90] GR Northcote, *Fry on Specific Performance,* 6th edn (London, Stevens and Sons, Ltd 1921), 731.
[91] See also Barbour, *The History of Contract in Early English Equity* (n 49), 137.
[92] *Earl of Ranelaugh v Hayes* (1683) 1 Vern 189; 23 ER 405.
[93] See [6–29], [6–36].
[94] See [6–17]–[6–18].
[95] See [7–7].
[96] See also [5–24]. *cf Wenkart v Pitman* (1998) 46 NSWLR 502 (CA), 533–34 (Powell JA) (continued existence of liability not relevant where specific enforcement has resulted in judgment debt).
[97] *Taylor v Sanders* [1937] VLR 62 (FC), 65–66. See also *Holli Managed Investments Pty Ltd v Australian Securities Commission* [1998] FCA 1657; (1998) 90 FCR 341, 348, 352. *cf Butler Estates Co Ltd v Bean* [1942] 1 KB 1 (CA), 11 (Goddard LJ) (covenant to pay and not to indemnify).
[98] *cf Heritage v Paine* (1876) 2 Ch D 594 (Ch); *Re Perkins; Poyser v Beyfus* [1898] 2 Ch 182 (CA); *Josselson v Borst* [1938] 1 KB 723 (CA); *Hydrocarbons Great Britain Ltd v Cammell Laird Shipbuilders Ltd* (1991) 53 BLR 84 (CA). *cf* also *Rendall v Morphew* (1914) 84 LJ Ch 517 (Ch) (discussed at [7–34]).
[99] *Re Perkins; Poyser v Beyfus* [1898] 2 Ch 182 (CA).

L against claims or demands in respect thereof. A1 subsequently assigned the lease to A2, A2 similarly covenanting to pay the rent, perform the covenants in the lease and indemnify A1 against a failure to do so. A2 died. A1 was declared bankrupt. L was compelled to pay outstanding rent and insurance premiums to the lessor and then proved in A1's bankruptcy for those amounts. L and A1's trustee in bankruptcy reached a compromise, under which L released A1's estate in return for an assignment to L of A1's right to indemnity from A2.

L then brought an action as assignee against A2. A2's defence was simple: in compromising L's claim, A1 had been exonerated from liability to L. There was, therefore, nothing upon which the indemnity could operate and so L's action as assignee must fail. The ingenuity of this line of argument has been acknowledged on several occasions.[100] Delivering the judgment of the English Court of Appeal, Lindley MR accepted the argument as correct in principle and remarked: 'A liability to indemnify against a liability which has no existence, and which can never arise, is a contradiction in terms'.[101] The settlement deed was, however, to be construed to avoid defeating its purpose. The extent of the release was limited so as to preserve the assignment to L of A1's right to indemnity and L's claim under it.[102]

[7–31] Liability is presently accrued, not future or contingent. The liability in respect of which specific enforcement is sought must be presently accrued and enforceable.[103] This condition excludes contingent liabilities and other liabilities that are to arise in the future.

Thanh v Hoang[104] illustrates the basic principle. The indemnified parties were liable as sureties for defaults by the indemnifiers in repaying amounts owed to lending syndicates. The trial judge awarded the indemnified parties sums comprising: (1) amounts already paid by them to the creditors; (2) the amount of their liabilities to the creditors accrued up to the date of trial but not yet discharged; and (3) for one of the indemnified parties – an amount for liabilities that had not accrued by the time of trial, but which were anticipated to arise from continuing defaults. The award was upheld on appeal in relation to the first two components, but varied so as to exclude the third component.

A further reason for refusing specific enforcement is that it may not be possible to determine in advance whether a liability will fall within the scope of the indemnity. In *Newman v McNicol*,[105] the claimant was liable to pay an electricity service charge for her property for a fixed term. Before that term expired the claimant sold the property to the defendant, with title being transferred to a nominee company. The claimant claimed that she was thereafter entitled to be indemnified against the service charges, by reference to a clause in the sale contract requiring the defendant to bear all 'working expenses' of the property. Long Innes

---

[100] *Heritage v Paine* (1876) 2 Ch D 594 (Ch), 601 ('parties must have wonderfully miscarried in carrying into effect what they desired to accomplish'); *Total Liban SA v Vitol Energy SA* [2001] QB 643 (QB), 655 ('a spectacular "own goal"').

[101] *Re Perkins; Poyser v Beyfus* [1898] 2 Ch 182 (CA), 189.

[102] *Re Perkins; Poyser v Beyfus* [1898] 2 Ch 182 (CA), 190. See also *Hydrocarbons Great Britain Ltd v Cammell Laird Shipbuilders Ltd* (1991) 53 BLR 84 (CA); *London and Regional (St George's Court) Ltd v Ministry of Defence* [2008] EWCA Civ 1212; [2009] BLR 20, [20] (Hughes LJ).

[103] *McIntosh v Dalwood (No 3)* (1930) 30 SR (NSW) 332 (SC), 334 ('liability must have crystallized into an actual present and enforcible demand'); *Ashby v Commissioner of Succession Duties (SA)* (1942) 67 CLR 284, 294 (Williams J) ('presently enforceable liability'); *Abigroup Ltd v Abignano* (1992) 39 FCR 74 (FC), 83 ('as soon as the [indemnified] person's liability to the third person arises'). See also *C Inc plc v L* [2001] EWHC 550 (Comm); [2001] 2 Lloyd's Rep 459, [28] fn 33.

[104] *Thanh v Hoang* (1994) 63 SASR 276 (FC).

[105] *Newman v McNicol* (1938) 38 SR (NSW) 609 (SC).

J held that the clause did not cover the service charges and, in the alternative, indicated that he would not have ordered indemnity for the charges into the future. The charges could only be a 'working expense' of the property if the owner continued to use the supplied electricity. The claimant's right to indemnity would have depended upon future acts of the nominee company.

Where the liability remains future or contingent in nature, a court may declare the right to indemnity instead of making an order for specific enforcement.[106] Thus, in *Thanh v Hoang*, where the award at first instance was varied on appeal to exclude the indemnified party's future liabilities, the court substituted a declaration of the right to be indemnified against those liabilities.

It is unclear whether references to the liability being 'enforceable' add anything to the requirement that the liability be presently accrued. A distinction could be drawn in some cases between the accrual of the indemnified party's liability and the accrual of the third party's right to enforce it. Even so, it appears that the latter is not always essential to a claim for quia timet relief. In *Thomas v Nottingham Incorporated Football Club Ltd*,[107] the debtor was ordered to exonerate the guarantor from an accrued liability even though the creditor had not made a demand as required by the terms of the guarantee. Goff J reasoned that the provision for a demand operated for the guarantor's benefit. It would have been peculiar for that provision to place the guarantor in a worse position vis-à-vis the indemnifying debtor than he would have occupied in the absence that provision.

[7–32] **Whether indemnified party will sustain loss from the liability.** The object of specific enforcement is to ensure that the indemnified party comes to no (further) loss. The necessary conditions for enforcement considered so far relate to the source of potential loss, namely, a liability to a third party. Assuming that such a liability exists, the further question is whether the indemnified party can or will be damnified by that liability. There are three dimensions to the question.

(1) *Capacity to pay.* The indemnified party may have insufficient means to satisfy the liability in full. This, in turn, limits the possible extent of damnification. Impecuniosity is not, however, an obstacle to specific enforcement.
(2) *Enforceability against assets.* Irrespective of the indemnified party's capacity to pay, there may be no, or insufficient, assets that can be reached by legal process. This is a relevant factor, though it is rarely an issue in practice.
(3) *Prospect of enforcement.* It seems to be relevant to consider whether enforcement by the third party is, in fact, sufficiently likely or imminent. This point is not free from doubt and it is difficult to identify the degree of probability or immediacy required. It may be quite low.

[7–33] **Where indemnified party is impecunious.** The indemnified party is entitled to protection even though it presently lacks the means to meet the liability in full.[108] A theoretical justification may be that some loss is possible, eventually, even if by way of the third party proving as a creditor in some form of administration in insolvency. That rationale

---

[106] See [5–79], [5–80].
[107] *Thomas v Nottingham Incorporated Football Club Ltd* [1972] Ch 596 (Ch). cf *Stimpson v Smith* [1999] Ch 340 (CA); *Friend v Brooker* [2009] HCA 21; (2009) 239 CLR 129, [55]–[59] (French CJ, Gummow, Hayne and Bell JJ) (claims for contribution).
[108] See [7–39].

may not explain all circumstances, such as where the indemnified party has no assets at all.[109] A more general justification is that to refuse protection to an impecunious indemnified party would deprive it of the benefit of the bargain. One of the purposes of a promise of indemnity is to save the indemnified party from ruin by having to pay first and recoup the loss later.[110] To provide less than complete relief could also, perversely, reward the indemnifier for failing to intervene: the less the indemnified party can pay, the lesser the extent of the indemnifier's obligation to indemnify.

[7–34] Where liability cannot be enforced against indemnified party's assets. Specific enforcement may be refused on the ground that the liability cannot be enforced against the indemnified party's assets. In *Eddowes v Argentine Loan and Mercantile Agency Co Ltd*,[111] a husband and wife in partnership were promised indemnity against certain claims or actions by third parties. A third party brought an action against the partnership in England and obtained judgment. The wife, by this time a widow, sued for indemnity against the liability arising from the judgment. The indemnifier objected that the wife had no separate estate and so could not be damnified. That objection failed but the wife was denied relief on a different ground. She resided in Argentina and there was no evidence that there were any assets in England that could be taken to satisfy the judgment.

Another decision that could be explained on a similar basis is *Rendall v Morphew*.[112] The deceased, C, had mortgaged freehold and leasehold property to R to secure the repayment of sums advanced by R to C. After C's death, his executors transferred C's interest in the property, subject to the mortgages, to M. M promised to pay the principal and interest under the mortgages and to indemnify C's estate and each of the executors. M duly paid the relevant sums for about nine years and then ceased payment. The executors assigned to R the 'full benefit' of M's indemnity. R, as assignee of the indemnity, then proceeded directly against M seeking a declaration that M was liable to pay R amounts due for principal and interest.

Eve J concluded that the indemnity was inoperative. R as assignee could only exercise the right to indemnity to protect C's estate and the executors.[113] The relevant claim against which C's estate and the executors might have required protection was the claim by R himself, as creditor. The case has been explained on the basis that there was no longer any liability to R.[114] Alternatively, it could be said that there was a potential liability but that neither C's estate nor the executors could have been damnified by R's claim. The estate had been fully administered, there were no assets remaining against which the liability could be enforced, and so the executors could properly have raised a plea of *plene administravit*.[115]

---

[109] *cf Re Alfred Shaw and Co Ltd, ex p Murphy* (1897) 8 QLJ 70 (SC), 74; *Silver Developments Ltd v Investors Group Trust Co Ltd* (1999) 182 Sask R 64 (QB), [38] (right of indemnity is itself an asset).

[110] *Johnston v Salvage Association* (1887) 19 QBD 458 (CA), 460–61 (Lindley LJ); *Re Richardson, ex p the Governors of St Thomas's Hospital* [1911] 2 KB 705 (CA), 709 (Cozens-Hardy MR); *McIntosh v Dalwood (No 4)* (1930) 30 SR (NSW) 415 (FC), 418 (Street CJ).

[111] *Eddowes v Argentine Loan and Mercantile Agency Co Ltd* (1890) 63 LT 364 (CA).

[112] *Rendall v Morphew* (1914) 84 LJ Ch 517 (Ch).

[113] See generally [5–35] (effect of assignment).

[114] *British Union and National Insurance Co v Rawson* [1916] 2 Ch 152, 159–60 ('attempt to revive a non-existing liability'); *Pendal Nominees Pty Ltd v Lednez Industries (Australia) Ltd* (1996) 40 NSWLR 282 (SC), 291. See [7–30].

[115] See generally *Levy v Kum Chah* (1936) 56 CLR 159, 168–70 (Dixon and Evatt JJ).

[7–35] Where indemnified party has no separate estate. The issue of enforcement against assets arose in a different way in *British Union and National Insurance Co v Rawson*.[116] The indemnified party had been sued to judgment for calls on shares, and then assigned her right to indemnity to the company liquidator. The indemnifier pointed to the indemnified party's status as a married woman. Without separate property, she could not be damnified by the judgment against her, and so there was no reason to enforce the indemnity to compel payment to the liquidator.

It was held that the indemnity was enforceable. Pickford LJ accepted that there was sufficient possibility of damnification because the judgment against the indemnified party operated *quando acciderint*. It could be enforced against any separate property she might acquire in the future, for example, if she were to become widowed. Warrington LJ agreed with that analysis but preferred the explanation that the measure of indemnity was determined by the amount of the liability and not the indemnified party's capacity to pay.[117] That explanation is not entirely convincing. The measure of indemnity is, strictly, distinct from the question of whether the indemnity ought to be enforced at all. Similarly, the indemnified party's capacity to pay is distinct from its susceptibility to enforcement against its assets. Those two factors are often, but are not necessarily, co-extensive. The emphasis on the former does not account for the basis for decision in *Eddowes v Argentine Loan and Mercantile Agency Co Ltd*.[118] It also seems that *Rendall v Morphew*[119] would have to be explained on the ground that there was no liability at all.

[7–36] Prospect of enforcement by third party. Assuming that the liability can be enforced by the third party against the indemnified party's assets, there remains the question of whether the indemnified party must also establish that such enforcement is sufficiently probable or imminent.

A claim, demand or action by the third party is generally not a precondition for specific enforcement.[120] Beyond this, the required degree of likelihood or immediacy is unclear. Pickford LJ's analysis in *British Union and National Insurance Co v Rawson*[121] suggests that enforcement may occur at some indefinite point in the future and that the likelihood of enforcement may be quite low. Even on this analysis, *Rendall v Morphew*[122] falls below the threshold. A plea of *plene administravit* by the executors would still have allowed the creditor to take judgment against assets *quando acciderint*.[123] Eve J did not advert to this possibility presumably because at that stage – some 10 years after the death of the testator – there was no prospect of further assets falling into the estate.[124]

---

[116] *British Union and National Insurance Co v Rawson* [1916] 2 Ch 476 (CA).
[117] See further [7–39].
[118] *Eddowes v Argentine Loan and Mercantile Agency Co Ltd* (1890) 63 LT 364 (CA).
[119] *Rendall v Morphew* (1914) 84 LJ Ch 517 (Ch).
[120] See [7–29].
[121] *British Union and National Insurance Co v Rawson* [1916] 2 Ch 476 (CA), 482–83. cf *Re Anderson-Berry; Harris v Griffith* [1928] Ch 290 (CA), 308 (Sargant LJ) (commenting on the guarantee case *Ascherson v Tredegar Dry Dock and Wharf Co Ltd* [1909] 2 Ch 401 (Ch)).
[122] *Rendall v Morphew* (1914) 84 LJ Ch 517 (Ch).
[123] EV Williams, *A Treatise on the Law of Executors and Administrators*, 1st edn (London, Saunders and Benning, 1832), 1221–22; E Bullen and SM Leake, *Precedents of Pleadings in Personal Actions in the Superior Courts of Common Law*, 3rd edn (London, Stevens and Sons, 1868), 578.
[124] *British Union and National Insurance Co v Rawson* [1916] 2 Ch 476 (CA), 483 (Pickford LJ) ('such a possibility was probably of no importance').

Rawson is more difficult to reconcile with *Eddowes v Argentine Loan and Mercantile Agency Co Ltd*.[125] A difference between the two cases is that the indemnified party in *Eddowes*, being a widow, had separate property. It seems to have been assumed that she would not voluntarily satisfy the English judgment against her. In each case, therefore, there was no immediate prospect of enforcement by the third party against the indemnified party's assets. Bowen LJ in *Eddowes* applied a more stringent standard than that used by Pickford LJ in *Rawson*: the indemnified party had to show that the danger was imminent and not merely a future possibility.[126] Cotton LJ's view in *Eddowes*, and perhaps also Fry LJ's, seems to have been that the facts simply did not establish any prospect of loss by the judgment being enforced.[127] On that basis, the circumstances might have fallen below the threshold suggested by Pickford LJ in *Rawson*.

Orders for Indemnification

[7–37] Form of order dependent upon circumstances. Relief is moulded to fit the circumstances.[128] Relevant considerations include: the commercial context and the terms of the contract;[129] whether the indemnified party's liability to the third party is singular in nature or may recur in the future;[130] (possibly) the solvency of the indemnified party;[131] the relationship between the indemnifier and the third party;[132] and whether another person's rights or interests may be affected by performance of the indemnity.[133]

Under the modern law, orders for specific enforcement generally call for one of the following modes of performance: the indemnifier is to exonerate the indemnified party from the liability, the method being left open to the indemnifier;[134] the indemnifier is to pay the third party directly and so relieve the indemnified party of the liability;[135] or, the indemnifier is to pay the indemnified party in advance, so that the latter can pay the third party.[136] Such orders may be made in conjunction with declarations and other orders of an administrative nature to give effect to the indemnity.

[7–38] Entitlement to specific enforcement not a debt. The indemnified party's equitable right to specific enforcement of the indemnity does not, of itself, establish a 'debt' owed to it by the indemnifier.[137] Similarly, an order that the indemnifier pay the third party directly does not create a debt due by the indemnifier to the indemnified party.[138] However, an

---

[125] *Eddowes v Argentine Loan and Mercantile Agency Co Ltd* (1890) 63 LT 364 (CA).

[126] *Eddowes v Argentine Loan and Mercantile Agency Co Ltd* (1890) 63 LT 364 (CA), 365.

[127] *cf Eddowes v Argentine Loan and Mercantile Agency Co Ltd* (1890) 63 LT 364 (CA), 365 (Cotton LJ), 366 (Fry LJ). Fry LJ referred to a threat to take proceedings in Argentina.

[128] *Taylor v Sanders* [1937] VLR 62 (FC), 66.

[129] See [7–20].

[130] See [7–31], [5–79].

[131] See [7–46].

[132] See [7–56] (the interest rule).

[133] See [7–60].

[134] See [7–41].

[135] See [7–42].

[136] See [7–43].

[137] This proposition originates from the guarantee cases. See *Re Mitchell; Freelove v Mitchell* [1913] 1 Ch 201 (Ch); *Re Fenton, ex p Fenton Textile Association Ltd* [1931] 1 Ch 85 (CA), 113–14 (Lawrence LJ); *Coles Myer Finance Ltd v Commissioner of Taxation* (1991) 28 FCR 7 (FC), 15 (revd on other grounds: *Coles Myer Finance Ltd v Commissioner of Taxation* (1992) 176 CLR 640); *Abigroup Ltd v Abignano* (1992) 39 FCR 74 (FC), 83.

[138] *Abigroup Ltd v Abignano* (1992) 39 FCR 74 (FC), 83.

order for advance payment by the indemnifier to the indemnified party may create an enforceable judgment debt.[139]

[7–39] Extent of protection. The indemnified party is entitled to be protected against the whole amount of the liability, even though it may be unable to pay in full.[140] This applies even where the indemnified party is dead,[141] has been declared bankrupt[142] or is in liquidation.[143] That an impecunious indemnified party may obtain protection against the full amount of its liability does not necessarily controvert the fundamental principle of exact protection against loss.[144]

Another, mathematical, perspective begins with the point that the indemnified party's exposure is determined by the amount of the liability, not its capacity to pay. Assume that the indemnified party is liable for $£x$ and is presently able to pay only a lesser sum $£y$ from its own resources. For simplicity, assume also that the indemnified party is not subject to any insolvency procedures.

If the indemnifier intervenes on the indemnified party's behalf and pays $£y$ to the third party, the indemnified party remains liable for $£x − y$. It has not been fully indemnified against the liability, and so the indemnifier's initial payment is not sufficient performance of the indemnity. Whether the indemnified party could satisfy the balance would depend upon whether $£y$ is greater than half of $£x$. In any event, any further amount the indemnified party itself paid, up to $£x − y$, could be recovered afterwards from the indemnifier.

Alternatively, the indemnifier could intercede and pay $£y$ to the indemnified party before the latter pays the third party. The indemnified party now has a total of $£2y$. Whether this is adequate to discharge the liability of $£x$ will depend upon the circumstances. But, again, the indemnifier's payment is not sufficient performance of the indemnity, because the indemnified party must draw from its own funds to make up the shortfall of $£x − y$. If the indemnified party pays more than a total of $£y$ to the third party, it can recoup the extra amount as its own contribution, up to $£x − y$, from the indemnifier.

Now assume, in both cases, that $£x$ is much greater than $£2y$. The indemnified party decides to pay as much as possible. The indemnifier's initial payment of $£y$ is matched by a contribution of $£y$ from the indemnified party's own resources. The indemnified party can then recover $£y$ from the indemnifier as an actual loss due to its own payment. With the recovery of $£y$, the indemnified party now has the funds to make a second payment of $£y$ to the third party. This, again, is an actual loss for which it can recover, and the process repeats. The 'drip feed' sequence leads eventually to payment of $£x$ by the indemnifier. It is, therefore, correct as a general principle to order indemnification for the whole liability of $£x$ even where the indemnified party cannot presently pay $£x$.

The case of insolvency is more difficult. The indemnified party may be required to divide receipts equally among the general creditors rather than pay them directly to the third party. Repetition of the cycle leads to ever-diminishing payments to the third party and

---

[139] *Wenkart v Pitman* (1998) 46 NSWLR 502 (CA), 530–31 (Powell JA).

[140] *Lacey v Hill; Crowley's Claim* (1874) LR 18 Eq 182, 192; *Wolmershausen v Gullick* [1893] 2 Ch 514 (Ch), 528; *British Union and National Insurance Co v Rawson* [1916] 2 Ch 476 (CA), 482 (Pickford LJ), 487 (Warrington LJ). cf *North American Accident Insurance Co v Newton* (1918) 57 SCR 577 (full reimbursement after payment using funds advanced by another).

[141] *Cruse v Paine* (1869) LR 4 Ch App 441.

[142] *Re Perkins; Poyser v Beyfus* [1898] 2 Ch 182 (CA); *Rankin v Palmer* (1912) 16 CLR 285.

[143] *Re Law Guarantee Trust and Accident Society Ltd* [1914] 2 Ch 617 (CA).

[144] See [7–41]. See further [7–46]–[7–48].

recoveries from the indemnifier. Depending on the circumstances, including the values of £*x*, £*y* and the insolvency dividend ratio, the indemnifier might eventually contribute the full amount of £*x*. But it is quite possible that, even if repeated *ad infinitum*, the series of payments and recoveries will converge to a limiting sum somewhere between £*y* and £*x*. Attempts to apply this mathematical model to an insolvent indemnified party have, however, been rejected.[145] The result is dictated by the policy of the law relating to insolvency and should not be attributed to the indemnified party. The extent of indemnity remains £*x*.

[7–40] Relief from claims, or defence of proceedings. In *Earl of Ranelaugh v Hayes*,[146] Lord Keeper North ordered the indemnifier to clear the indemnified party from the suits presently against him, and further ordered that the indemnified party might give notice of certain future suits or demands, so that the indemnifier might 'take all necessary care in the defence thereof'. Such performance of the indemnity would have kept the indemnified party harmless against loss. It seems that the Lord Keeper considered that the indemnified party was not to be molested by suits or demands, sound or otherwise.[147] The modern view is that a mere promise of indemnity does not require the indemnifier to avoid, or defend the indemnified party against, claims or actions by third parties.[148] Thus, this form of order is generally not appropriate.

[7–41] Exoneration from a definite liability. The indemnifier may be ordered to procure the release or discharge of the indemnified party from a liability to the third party.[149] In *Rankin v Palmer*,[150] an agent was liable to refund money he had collected from third parties on behalf of his principal. The agent sought a declaration that he was entitled to be indemnified by the principal and an order that the principal pay the relevant amounts to him or to the third parties. Rich J ordered the principal to pay the sum over to the agent but that order was varied on appeal to the High Court of Australia. Griffith CJ, with whose judgment Barton and Isaacs JJ concurred, ordered the principal to procure the release or discharge of the agent's estate from each claim 'either by payment or otherwise', within 14 days of being given written notice of a claim. The order left the principal free to make whatever arrangements he thought fit to obtain the release or discharge.[151]

This form of order may be preferred where the indemnifier has a legal or commercial relationship with the third party. The indemnifier may be interested in the discharge of the indemnified party's liability because it relieves the indemnifier of a common or related liability to the third party.[152] More generally, as between the indemnifier and indemnified party, the former may have ultimate responsibility for, or control of, the transaction in which the third party is involved. An order in this form allows the indemnifier flexibility in dealing with the third party. The facts in *Rankin* exemplify both aspects. Griffith CJ remarked that the indemnified agent had 'no right voluntarily to undertake the duty of see-

---

[145] *Re Law Guarantee Trust and Accident Society Ltd* [1914] 2 Ch 617 (CA), 635 (Buckley LJ), 639 (Kennedy LJ), 652 (Scrutton J).

[146] *Earl of Ranelaugh v Hayes* (1683) 1 Vern 189; 23 ER 405.

[147] See also [7–29].

[148] See [7–7], [6–17]–[6–19].

[149] *Cruse v Paine* (1869) LR 4 Ch App 441; *Brown v Black* (1873) LR 15 Eq 363 (order varied on appeal in a manner not presently relevant: *Brown v Black* (1873) LR 8 Ch App 939); *Rankin v Palmer* (1912) 16 CLR 285.

[150] *Rankin v Palmer* (1912) 16 CLR 285.

[151] See also *Re Alfred Shaw and Co Ltd, ex p Murphy* (1897) 8 QLJ 70 (SC), 73.

[152] See [7–45].

ing that the [principal] shall pay his own debts, even to creditors with whom he may effect a settlement on other terms, or who do not wish to be paid'.[153]

This form of order achieves full indemnification. The indemnifier never directs funds into the hands of the indemnified party, so there is no risk of under-compensation or over-compensation. This was a potential issue in *Rankin*, because the agent had been declared bankrupt and may not have been able to pass on the funds in full to the third parties.[154]

[7–42] **Payment by indemnifier to third party.** The indemnifier may be ordered to relieve the indemnified party by paying the amount of the liability directly to the third party.[155] An order in this form has been described as a 'leap frog' order.[156] It seems to be accepted that payment made pursuant to the order is effective to discharge the indemnified party's liability.[157] The order may be made even if the third party is not a party to the proceedings.[158]

A leading example is *McIntosh v Dalwood (No 4)*.[159] McIntosh was liable by contract to pay money by instalments to certain third parties. McIntosh and Dalwood later entered into an agreement under which Dalwood was to assume responsibility for McIntosh's contractual liability and to indemnify him against it. Dalwood defaulted and the third parties brought proceedings against McIntosh. McIntosh sought a declaration of his right to indemnity and an order that Dalwood pay the third parties the amount owing. Dalwood's objection that there was no such right to equitable relief was dismissed.

A similar form of order can be found in cases where a guarantor seeks quia timet relief in respect of an accrued liability to the creditor. A solvent principal debtor may be ordered to exonerate the guarantor by paying the creditor the amount of the liability.[160] Such an order coincides with the debtor's existing legal obligation to the creditor. This is not generally true for claims under indemnities. In *McIntosh*, for example, there was no privity between the indemnifier and the third parties.

The choice of this form of order may depend on several factors. It is an obvious means of giving effect to the construction that the indemnifier is to relieve the indemnified party of its liability and so spare it from having to pay.[161] Another factor is that the indemnifier may be under a common or related liability to the third party, such that it has an interest in

---

[153] *Rankin v Palmer* (1912) 16 CLR 285, 291–92.

[154] cf *Cruse v Paine* (1869) LR 4 Ch App 441. See further [7–45], [7–46].

[155] *Heritage v Paine* (1876) 2 Ch D 594 (Ch); *Lloyd v Dimmack* (1877) 7 Ch D 398 (Ch); *British Union and National Insurance Co v Rawson* [1916] 2 Ch 476 (CA), 482 (Pickford LJ), 486 (Warrington LJ); *McIntosh v Dalwood (No 4)* (1930) 30 SR (NSW) 415 (FC); *Firma C-Trade SA v Newcastle Protection and Indemnity Association (The Fanti) (No 2)* [1991] 2 AC 1 (HL), 28 (Lord Brandon), 40 (Lord Jauncey); *Abigroup Ltd v Abignano* (1992) 39 FCR 74 (FC), 83; *Re Dixon* [1994] 1 Qd R 7 (FC), 20 (Shepherdson J); *Victorian WorkCover Authority v Esso Australia Ltd* [2001] HCA 53; (2001) 207 CLR 520, [17] (Gleeson CJ, Gummow, Hayne and Callinan JJ). cf *Re National Financial Co, ex p Oriental Commercial Bank* (1868) LR 3 Ch App 791; *Shaver v Sproule* (1913) 9 DLR 641 (Ont SC) (order for payment into court, the sum to be applied to discharge third party's liability to fourth party, or indemnified party's corresponding liability to third party).

[156] *Wenkart v Pitman* (1998) 46 NSWLR 502 (CA), 529–30 (Powell JA).

[157] cf *Firma C-Trade SA v Newcastle Protection and Indemnity Association (The Fanti) (No 2)* [1991] 2 AC 1 (HL), 40 (Lord Jauncey); *Sheahan v Carrier Air Conditioning Pty Ltd* (1996) 189 CLR 407, 430–31 fn 66 (Dawson, Gaudron and Gummow JJ). See [7–10].

[158] See also *Abigroup Ltd v Abignano* (1992) 39 FCR 74 (FC), 81 (order made where third party not party to relevant cross-claim between indemnifier and indemnified party). cf *Lacey v Hill; Crowley's Claim* (1874) LR 18 Eq 182, 191; *Wolmershausen v Gullick* [1893] 2 Ch 514 (Ch), 529.

[159] *McIntosh v Dalwood (No 4)* (1930) 30 SR (NSW) 415 (FC).

[160] *Ascherson v Tredegar Dry Dock and Wharf Co Ltd* [1909] 2 Ch 401 (Ch); *Watt v Mortlock* [1964] Ch 84 (Ch); *Thomas v Nottingham Incorporated Football Club Ltd* [1972] Ch 596 (Ch).

[161] *Victorian WorkCover Authority v Esso Australia Ltd* [2001] HCA 53; (2001) 207 CLR 520, [17] (Gleeson CJ, Gummow, Hayne and Callinan JJ).

ensuring that the third party is paid.[162] This form of order also avoids any concerns about over-compensation, because no funds come into the hands of the indemnified party.

[7–43] Advance payment by indemnifier to indemnified party. Fletcher Moulton LJ said in *Re Richardson*:[163]

> I do not think that equity ever compelled a surety to pay money to the person to whom he was surety before the latter had actually paid. He might be ordered to set a fund aside, but I do not think that he could be ordered to pay.

Despite the use of the word 'surety', the context preceding the passage indicates that Fletcher Moulton LJ meant the following: assuming that B is liable to pay C and A is obliged to indemnify B, then, even in equity, B could never obtain payment from A before B had actually paid C.

There were, before *Re Richardson*, instances of orders for payment in advance to the indemnified party.[164] Fletcher Moulton LJ was plainly unaware of them because he criticised Jessel MR for suggesting in *Lacey v Hill*[165] that such cases existed.[166] Later decisions have accepted the same possibility.[167] The position in English law is that, in some circumstances, the indemnifier may be ordered to pay the indemnified party the amount of the liability before the latter pays the third party.

Some doubt concerning the acceptance of this proposition in Australian law can be traced back to the same passage from *Re Richardson*. In *Rankin v Palmer*,[168] Griffith CJ quoted with approval an extensive extract from Fletcher Moulton LJ's judgment that included this passage. That part of Griffith CJ's judgment was quoted and approved in dicta by Barwick CJ in *Wren v Mahony*.[169] The High Court of Australia has, by way of contrast, acknowledged orders for exoneration[170] and for payment to the third party.[171] The most recent appellate consideration of the point, which occurred in the *Wenkart v Pitman* line of cases, is inconclusive. The final orders at first instance required payment in advance to the indemnified parties.[172] An appeal was dismissed by the New South Wales Court of Appeal, though this point was not directly in issue.[173] An objection to the form of order was later raised before the Full Court of the Federal Court of Australia. The Court, which was exercising its jurisdiction in bankruptcy, did not decide the point but described the argu-

---

[162] See [7–45], [7–56].

[163] *Re Richardson, ex p the Governors of St Thomas's Hospital* [1911] 2 KB 705 (CA), 713.

[164] *Evans v Wood* (1867) LR 5 Eq 9; *Shepherd v Gillespie* (1867) LR 5 Eq 293 (affd *Shepherd v Gillespie* (1868) LR 3 Ch App 764).

[165] *Lacey v Hill; Crowley's Claim* (1874) LR 18 Eq 182, 191.

[166] *Re Richardson, ex p the Governors of St Thomas's Hospital* [1911] 2 KB 705 (CA), 713. See *British Union and National Insurance Co v Rawson* [1916] 2 Ch 476 (CA), 487 (Warrington LJ).

[167] *Re Law Guarantee Trust and Accident Society Ltd* [1914] 2 Ch 617 (CA), 633 (Buckley LJ); *British Union and National Insurance Co v Rawson* [1916] 2 Ch 476 (CA), 482 (Pickford LJ), 486–87 (Warrington LJ); *Fraser v Equatorial Shipping Co Ltd (The Ijaola)* [1979] 1 Lloyd's Rep 103 (QB), 120–21; *Firma C-Trade SA v Newcastle Protection and Indemnity Association (The Fanti) (No 2)* [1991] 2 AC 1 (HL), 28 (Lord Brandon), 41 (Lord Jauncey).

[168] *Rankin v Palmer* (1912) 16 CLR 285, 290.

[169] *Wren v Mahony* (1972) 126 CLR 212, 225–26.

[170] *Rankin v Palmer* (1912) 16 CLR 285.

[171] *State Government Insurance Office (Qld) v Brisbane Stevedoring Pty Ltd* (1969) 123 CLR 228, 240 (Barwick CJ), 253 (Walsh J); *Sheahan v Carrier Air Conditioning Pty Ltd* (1996) 189 CLR 407, 430–31 fn 66 (Dawson, Gaudron and Gummow JJ); *Victorian WorkCover Authority v Esso Australia Ltd* [2001] HCA 53; (2001) 207 CLR 520, [17] (Gleeson CJ, Gummow, Hayne and Callinan JJ).

[172] *Sub nom Sandtara Pty Ltd v Abigroup Ltd* (NSWSC, 25 and 29 September 1997).

[173] *Wenkart v Pitman* (1998) 46 NSWLR 502 (CA), 529 (Powell JA).

ment as one that could not 'be dismissed as simply ill-founded or as unworthy of serious consideration'.[174]

The better view in Australia is that an order for advance payment to the indemnified party is possible in appropriate circumstances. This form of order has been used or acknowledged on a number of occasions.[175]

[7–44] Circumstances where order may be appropriate. The circumstances in which this form of order may be used are not well defined. There are some descriptions in very broad terms of the indemnified party's entitlement to obtain payment in advance,[176] but these overstate the position. That there is no general entitlement to this form of order is consistent with the point that an equitable right to enforce the indemnity does not constitute a 'debt' owed by the indemnifier to the indemnified party.[177] In *Firma C-Trade SA v Newcastle Protection and Indemnity Association (The Fanti) (No 2)*,[178] Lord Brandon said that an indemnity could be specifically enforced 'in some cases' by an order that the indemnifier pay the indemnified party. In *Abigroup Ltd v Abignano*,[179] the order was said to be available 'in some circumstances' where the indemnifier was 'under no liability to the third person'. The court later referred to 'special circumstances'.[180]

An order in this form may not be made where it would infringe the interest rule.[181] There are conflicting views as to whether the order is appropriate where the indemnified party is insolvent.[182] Subject to those qualifications, it appears that an order may be made:

(1) in conjunction with an undertaking by the indemnified party to pass on the funds to the third party;[183]
(2) where the third party enforces the indemnity as assignee;[184] or
(3) possibly, in other situations in which there is no real doubt that the indemnified party will pass on the funds in full to the third party.[185]

Leaving to one side the interest rule, the other factors appear to reflect a concern that the indemnified party should not be over-compensated by the order for advance payment.

[7–45] Advance payment and the interest rule. The interest rule may apply in this context.[186] In simple terms, where the indemnifier (or, perhaps, a person claiming under the

---

[174] *Wenkart v Abignano* [1999] FCA 354 (FC), [31]. Special leave to appeal to the High Court was refused: *Wenkart v Pitman* (1999) 16 Leg Rep SL 4b.

[175] *Taylor v Sanders* [1937] VLR 62 (FC), 65–66; *Ramsay v National Australia Bank Ltd* [1989] VR 59 (FC), 66–67; *Abigroup Ltd v Abignano* (1992) 39 FCR 74 (FC), 83; *Thanh v Hoang* (1994) 63 SASR 276 (FC) (but see n 189); *Paterson v Pongrass Group Operations Pty Ltd* [2011] NSWSC 1588.

[176] See, eg, *Lacey v Hill; Crowley's Claim* (1874) LR 18 Eq 182, 191 (if creditor not a party to proceedings); *British Union and National Insurance Co v Rawson* [1916] 2 Ch 476 (CA), 482 (Pickford LJ).

[177] See [7–38].

[178] *Firma C-Trade SA v Newcastle Protection and Indemnity Association (The Fanti) (No 2)* [1991] 2 AC 1 (HL), 28. See also *Thanh v Hoang* (1994) 63 SASR 276 (FC), 284 (Duggan J).

[179] *Abigroup Ltd v Abignano* (1992) 39 FCR 74 (FC), 83.

[180] *Abigroup Ltd v Abignano* (1992) 39 FCR 74 (FC), 84.

[181] See [7–45].

[182] See [7–46]–[7–48].

[183] See [7–49].

[184] See [7–50].

[185] cf *Kostka v Addison* [1986] 1 Qd R 416 (SC), 420. The common law position for ordinary damages claims for breach provides an interesting point for comparison. Although it is, in some respects, more generous to the claimant (see [10–25]), the claimant will still be denied recovery when it is clear that the liability will not be discharged: *Biffa Waste Services Ltd v Maschinenfabrik Ernst Hese GmbH* [2008] EWHC 2210 (TCC); [2009] PNLR 5, [80]–[81].

[186] See further [7–56].

indemnifier) has an interest in ensuring that the funds are received by the third party, then an order for payment to the indemnified party is not appropriate. In the paradigm situation, the indemnifier is also liable to the third party, the nature of that liability being such that it will be correspondingly reduced or extinguished by a discharge of the indemnified party's liability.

Rankin v Palmer[187] is a leading example. An order for advance payment to the indemnified agent was varied on appeal to require the indemnifying principal to exonerate the agent. Griffith CJ's concern was that the principal was also liable to account to the third parties for the sums collected by the agent. If the principal were compelled to pay the agent and the agent did not pass on the funds, the principal might have to pay the money again. This, Griffith CJ said, would be manifestly unfair; the provision of an undertaking to pass on the funds did not obviate that difficulty.[188]

The reasoning in *Rankin* parallels that which applies to guarantees. A guarantor cannot obtain quia timet relief against the debtor in the form of an order directing payment to itself, because this alone will not discharge the debtor from its liability to the creditor.[189]

[7–46] Where indemnified party is insolvent. There is a conflict of opinion, which originates from two different perspectives on the purpose of indemnification. The theoretical concern is that advance payment to an insolvent indemnified party may controvert the fundamental principle of indemnity. The indemnified party receives more from the indemnifier than it ultimately pays to the third party, because receipts are divided among its creditors at large. As Buckley LJ remarked in *Re Richardson*:[190] 'if B [the indemnified party] has not paid the money to A but calls upon C [the indemnifier] to pay the money to him, B, in order that he may pay it to A, then B is not indemnified if the money is paid, not to A alone, but to A and others'.

Even if this perspective is generally correct, it has been suggested that insolvency may be an exceptional situation. The distribution of receipts among the creditors is a consequence of the policy of insolvency law rather than a deficiency with this mode of enforcement of the indemnity.[191] In limited circumstances, and subject to statute, the indemnified party may be placed under an obligation to pass on the funds to the particular third party. One such situation may be where the indemnified party is impecunious but not yet subject to some form of administration in insolvency.[192]

The other perspective is one of equivalence. The measure of indemnity is the amount of the liability and not the indemnified party's capacity to pay.[193] If the indemnifier has to pay a definite sum then, unless it has a particular interest in the application of that sum, the

---

[187] *Rankin v Palmer* (1912) 16 CLR 285. See also *Cruse v Paine* (1869) LR 4 Ch App 441; *Abigroup Ltd v Abignano* (1992) 39 FCR 74 (FC), 83; *Paterson v Pongrass Group Operations Pty Ltd* [2011] NSWSC 1588, [91]–[93], [96].

[188] It is not clear whether Griffith CJ was also concerned that the agent's assignee in bankruptcy could not act in the interests of one creditor to the exclusion of others: *cf Re Alfred Shaw and Co Ltd, ex p Murphy* (1897) 8 QLJ 70 (SC), 74.

[189] *Re Fenton, ex p Fenton Textile Association Ltd* [1931] 1 Ch 85 (CA), 105 (Lord Hanworth MR), 114 (Lawrence LJ), 116 (Romer LJ). *cf Agnes & Jennie Mining Co Ltd v Zen* (1982) 38 BCLR 385 (CA) (express contract of indemnity). *cf Thanh v Hoang* (1994) 63 SASR 276 (FC), 284 (Duggan J) where this point was not considered.

[190] *Re Richardson, ex p the Governors of St Thomas's Hospital* [1911] 2 KB 705 (CA), 717. See also *Re Alfred Shaw and Co Ltd, ex p Murphy* (1897) 8 QLJ 70 (SC).

[191] *Re Law Guarantee Trust and Accident Society Ltd* [1914] 2 Ch 617 (CA), 634–35 (Buckley LJ), 639–40 (Kennedy LJ), 646–47 (Scrutton J).

[192] *cf Sandtara Pty Ltd v Abigroup Ltd* (NSWSC, 25 and 29 September 1997); *Paterson v Pongrass Group Operations Pty Ltd* [2011] NSWSC 1588. See further [7–49].

[193] See [7–39].

choice of payee is irrelevant. If the payment goes to the indemnified party, then what it does with the money afterwards is also immaterial. Furthermore, as a practical matter, if the indemnifier was genuinely concerned that the third party be paid in full, it could have paid the third party directly. This is a valid mode of performance of the indemnity.

Beyond the insurance context, support can be found for each of these perspectives. The balance of authority tends to favour the latter perspective, or treats insolvency as an exception to the former perspective.

[7–47] Authorities favouring payment to insolvent indemnified party. *Re Law Guarantee Trust and Accident Society Ltd*[194] and *Lacey v Hill*[195] are commonly cited as original authorities on this point, though neither is especially strong on close analysis.[196]

In *Re Law Guarantee Trust*, the society promised to debenture holders the due payment of principal and interest by the debtor company. The society then paid a premium to an insurance company in return for a 'guarantee' of part of the risk assumed by the society. The debtor company defaulted and the society soon afterwards entered a voluntary winding-up without having discharged its liabilities to the debenture holders. Those liabilities were ascertained and admitted in the society's liquidation.

It was held that the society was entitled to receive the full amount due from the insurance company without prior payment to the debenture holders. The preferred ground was that the arrangement was a contract of reinsurance and so the matter could be resolved by applying certain principles from insurance law.[197] In contracts of reinsurance and liability insurance, the basic obligation to indemnify is usually[198] not conditional upon prior payment by the reinsured or insured. The insolvency of the reinsured or insured does not affect the measure of indemnity. In the absence of any specific statutory provisions,[199] the insurance moneys are treated like ordinary receipts and are divided among the general creditors. The original insured or claimant is not paid in full.

Buckley LJ and Kennedy LJ held that the same result would have followed if the arrangement were regarded as a contract of indemnity generally and not specifically as a contract of reinsurance. The reasoning went thus. An insolvent indemnified party is entitled to protection against the full amount of the liability. The promise of indemnity was to save harmless, and not merely reimburse, the society. The society would, therefore, have been entitled to specific enforcement of the indemnity. The interest rule[200] then determined whether the insurance company was to pay the society or the debenture holders. As the insurance

---

[194] *Re Law Guarantee Trust and Accident Society Ltd* [1914] 2 Ch 617 (CA).

[195] *Lacey v Hill; Crowley's Claim* (1874) LR 18 Eq 182.

[196] Other decisions that generally support this view, as qualified by the interest rule, include: *British Union and National Insurance Co v Rawson* [1916] 2 Ch 476 (CA), 482 (Pickford LJ), 487 (Warrington LJ); *Official Assignee v Jarvis* [1923] NZLR 1009 (CA); *Taylor v Sanders* [1937] VLR 62 (FC), 65–66; *Re Enhill Pty Ltd* [1983] 1 VR 561 (FC), 564 (Young CJ), 571 (Lush J); *Ramsay v National Australia Bank Ltd* [1989] VR 59 (FC), 66–67; *Firma C-Trade SA v Newcastle Protection and Indemnity Association (The Fanti) (No 2)* [1991] 2 AC 1 (HL), 41 (Lord Jauncey).

[197] See *Re Eddystone Marine Insurance Co, ex p Western Insurance Co* [1892] 2 Ch 423 (Ch); *Charter Reinsurance Co Ltd v Fagan* [1997] AC 313 (HL), 387 (Lord Mustill) (reinsurance); *Re Harrington Motor Co Ltd, ex p Chaplin* [1928] Ch 105 (CA); *Hood's Trustees v Southern Union General Insurance Co of Australasia Ltd* [1928] Ch 793 (CA); *Re Southern Cross Coaches Ltd* (1932) 49 WN (NSW) 230 (SC); *Interchase Corp Ltd v FAI General Insurance Co Ltd* [2000] 2 Qd R 301 (CA), 313–14 (McPherson JA) (liability insurance). See generally J Birds, B Lynch and S Milnes, *MacGillivray on Insurance Law*, 12th edn (London, Sweet & Maxwell, 2012), 975–77, para 29-013.

[198] Contrast [2–34].

[199] The outcome described in the text has been altered by statute: see [7–64].

[200] See further [7–56].

company had no interest in, and was not concerned with, the application of the money to be paid, the society was entitled to receive the payment itself.

This alternative ground is plausible but not beyond criticism. Buckley LJ's and Kennedy LJ's indemnity analysis seems to be at odds with the construction of the agreement advanced elsewhere in their judgments: it was, essentially, a bargain in which the society paid the premium in return for the insurer's promise to pay an amount upon an event.[201] From that perspective, it was commercially sensible that the insolvency of the society was irrelevant, but the commercial context is not necessarily the same for non-insurance indemnities against liability. Furthermore, if the promise really was to pay a sum upon an event that had occurred, it is difficult to see why equitable relief would have been necessary. The status of the interest rule as formulated and applied in the decision is also open to question.[202]

In *Lacey*, stockbrokers incurred substantial liabilities by trading shares on behalf of their principal, who died insolvent. At issue was whether the brokers could prove in the administration of his estate for the total of the liabilities, or only the amount they had so far actually paid in order to be readmitted to the stock exchange. From a modern perspective, this may appear to be merely a matter of valuation of a contingent claim by the brokers. That approach was not open in *Lacey*.[203] Jessel MR allowed proof for the full amount. It was not necessary to decide to whom the amount ought to be paid, but Jessel MR considered that an indemnified party could call for payment to itself if the creditor was not a party to the action.

For two reasons, *Lacey* does not provide unqualified support for the proposition that an insolvent indemnified party is entitled to advance payment in full. The only relevant authority mentioned by Jessel MR in the report of the case is *Cruse v Paine*.[204] Giffard VC there made an order for payment in advance, but there was also an undertaking by the indemnified party's executor to pass on the funds to the third party. In any event, the decree was varied on appeal, with the original order being replaced by an order for exoneration generally.[205] Most importantly of all, the brokers in *Lacey* were not in the position of bankrupts. According to the rules of the stock exchange, their debts had not been discharged on readmission and the brokers would be called upon every year to pay until the liabilities had been met completely. As Jessel MR explained, the brokers would actually have to distribute whatever they recovered to their creditors.[206]

[7–48] Authorities against payment to insolvent indemnified party. Against these decisions stands *Re Alfred Shaw and Co Ltd; ex p Murphy*.[207] The third party proved in the indemnified party's bankruptcy but there were insufficient assets to pay a dividend. The

---

[201] *Re Law Guarantee Trust and Accident Society Ltd* [1914] 2 Ch 617 (CA), 634 (Buckley LJ), 640–41 (Kennedy LJ). See also *Re Law Guarantee Trust and Accident Society Ltd; Godson's Claim* [1915] 1 Ch 340 (Ch), 345–46.

[202] See [7–58].

[203] The Bankruptcy Act 1869, s 31 allowed proof of contingent liabilities, including liabilities under indemnities (*Hardy v Fothergill* (1888) 8 App Cas 351 (HL)) in ordinary cases of bankruptcy, but it was only later that such provisions were extended to the administration in equity of an insolvent estate, by the Judicature Act 1875, s 10. See also WG Walker and EJ Elgood, *The Law and Practice Relating to the Administration of the Estates of Deceased Persons by the Chancery Division of the High Court of Justice* (London, Stevens and Haynes, 1883), 107.

[204] *Cruse v Paine* (1868) LR 6 Eq 641. See further [7–48].

[205] *Cruse v Paine* (1869) LR 4 Ch App 441.

[206] *Lacey v Hill; Crowley's Claim* (1874) LR 18 Eq 182, 191.

[207] *Re Alfred Shaw and Co Ltd, ex p Murphy* (1897) 8 QLJ 70 (SC). cf *Re Richardson, ex p the Governors of St Thomas's Hospital* [1911] 2 KB 705 (CA), a trust case.

indemnifier, a company, subsequently entered liquidation and the indemnified party's trustee in bankruptcy sought to prove in the winding up for the full amount of the liability to the third party. The proof rested on two propositions: first, that the indemnified party was presently entitled to compel performance of the indemnity before sustaining loss by payment; and secondly, that the appropriate order would have been for payment directly to the indemnified party.

The second proposition was rejected as being inconsistent with the fundamental principle of indemnity.[208] The indemnifier's payment of the whole amount of the liability would, in the circumstances, exceed the loss actually sustained by the indemnified party. The funds received would be distributed among the general creditors, so that the third party would be paid a dividend and not in full. Thus, the indemnified party's trustee in bankruptcy could only prove in respect of a contingent liability, as permitted by statute.[209]

In reaching that conclusion, Griffith CJ did not refer to *Lacey v Hill*[210] but did consider *Cruse v Paine*,[211] where the indemnified party had died leaving an estate insufficient to meet liabilities for calls on shares. In Griffith CJ's view it was significant that the order made by Giffard VC – for advance payment by the indemnifiers to the indemnified party's estate – was varied on appeal to require the indemnifiers to exonerate the estate from liability. As to the original order, Griffith CJ said:[212]

> It is, however, plain that the learned Vice-Chancellor would not have directed the defendant to pay the amount of the calls to the plaintiff unconditionally, and without his undertaking to pay it over to the company. The proceeding was in a Court of Equity, and the Court was able to make such an order as to do complete justice. If in the present case, [the indemnified party] were not insolvent and the [indemnifier] not in liquidation, the case would be, to a certain extent, analogous. But I do not know of any principle by which a trustee of an insolvent estate, seeking to recover a debt . . . can do so as trustee for anyone but the body of creditors for whom he is trustee, or can be put under an undertaking to act as trustee for one of those creditors, to the exclusion of the others.

An order for payment to the indemnified party in *Re Alfred Shaw and Co Ltd* would have been inappropriate even if the indemnifier had not been in liquidation. The indemnified party's trustee in bankruptcy might instead have sought an order for payment by the indemnifier to the third party. Although Griffith CJ did not advert to the interest rule, the application of that rule to the facts may have produced the same result.[213]

[7–49] Payment to indemnified party with obligation to pass on funds. Orders in this form can be found in some of the nineteenth-century cases on share transfers.[214] The indemnifier was directed to pay the indemnified party the amount of outstanding calls on shares, with an undertaking by, or on behalf of, the indemnified party to pass on the sum to the liquidator. Although the form of order is sound in principle, its application in those

---

[208] *Re Alfred Shaw and Co Ltd, ex p Murphy* (1897) 8 QLJ 70 (SC), 72.
[209] Contrast n 203.
[210] *Lacey v Hill; Crowley's Claim* (1874) LR 18 Eq 182.
[211] *Cruse v Paine* (1868) LR 6 Eq 641; *Cruse v Paine* (1869) LR 4 Ch App 441.
[212] *Re Alfred Shaw and Co Ltd, ex p Murphy* (1897) 8 QLJ 70 (SC), 74.
[213] The indemnified party's liability to the third party was secured by a mortgage over land which had been transferred from the indemnified party to the indemnifier: see [7–57], [7–59].
[214] See, eg, *Evans v Wood* (1867) LR 5 Eq 9; *Shepherd v Gillespie* (1867) LR 5 Eq 293 (affd *Shepherd v Gillespie* (1868) LR 3 Ch App 764); *Cruse v Paine* (1868) LR 6 Eq 641 (but order varied: *Cruse v Paine* (1869) LR 4 Ch App 441).

particular circumstances must be reconsidered in light of later decisions. It may be that the proper form of order in some of those cases should have been for exoneration.[215]

Sandtara Pty Ltd v Abigroup Ltd[216] is a more recent example without this complication. There was a series of indemnities: from W to P, from P to G and A1, from G and A1 to A2, and from A2 to S. Each indemnity bar the last covered the indemnified party's liability as indemnifier under the next indemnity. S sustained a loss, thus engaging the indemnities in sequence. The final set of orders required each indemnifier to pay the amount of the judgment for S to the corresponding indemnified party, the latter undertaking to pass on the sum to the next party in the series. That is, W was ordered to pay P upon P's undertaking to pass the sum on to A1; P was ordered to pay A1 upon A1's undertaking to pass the sum on to A2, and so on.

The advantage of these orders is that they preserved the liabilities of the parties inter se and yet provided an efficient and final means of passing responsibility for loss down the chain to W. A simple series of 'leap frog' orders would not have accomplished the desired result.[217] Assume, for example, that the orders were for W to pay A1 on behalf of P; for P to pay A2 on behalf of A1; and for A1 to pay S on behalf of A2. This would produce a net gain to A2 and a net loss to P, which should not occur if all parties are solvent. Omitting the middle order resolves that difficulty but the correct outcome would still depend on performance by W and A1. If either of the payments was not made, further orders would be required to adjust the rights of the parties.

Another feature of the decision was that P was impecunious and had been issued with a bankruptcy notice by A1, though no further action had been taken on that notice. P's undertaking to pass on to A1 the payment received from W was supplemented by a condition that P would, in the interim, hold any such payment on trust for A1.

[7–50] Payment to third party as assignee of indemnified party. The following situation occasionally arises. A promises to indemnify B against liability to C; B does not pay C, but assigns to C its right to indemnity from A; C, as the assignee of the indemnity, enforces it against A. Assuming that B's liability to C continues to exist,[218] C can recover from A the full amount of that liability, even though C might not presently recover that amount from B.[219] One explanation is that C exercises the right to indemnity to compel A to pay B's creditor, C, so C obtains payment to itself. A second explanation is that C exercises the right to compel payment in advance to the indemnified party, B, but that C, as the assignee, receives that payment.[220] It is unlikely that the latter form of order would be appropriate where the indemnity is assigned to a stranger, D, because payment to D would not protect B against its liability to C.[221]

---

[215] See [7–61].

[216] *Sandtara Pty Ltd v Abigroup Ltd* (NSWSC, 25 and 29 September 1997). See also *Fraser v Equatorial Shipping Co Ltd (The Ijaola)* [1979] 1 Lloyd's Rep 103 (QB), 121; *Paterson v Pongrass Group Operations Pty Ltd* [2011] NSWSC 1588, [93]–[97].

[217] cf *Abigroup Ltd v Abignano* (1992) 39 FCR 74 (FC), 84–85.

[218] See [7–30].

[219] *Re Perkins; Poyser v Beyfus* [1898] 2 Ch 182 (CA); *British Union and National Insurance Co v Rawson* [1916] 2 Ch 476 (CA); *Bank of Montreal v Barton* (2004) 268 Sask R 193 (QB).

[220] *British Union and National Insurance Co v Rawson* [1916] 2 Ch 476 (CA), 487 (Warrington LJ).

[221] cf *Maloney v Campbell* (1897) 28 SCR 228, 233–34; *Rendall v Morphew* (1914) 84 LJ Ch 517 (Ch), 520. Alternatively, it may depend on the application of the interest rule: cf *British Union and National Insurance Co v Rawson* [1916] 2 Ch 152, 160; *Taylor v Sanders* [1937] VLR 62 (FC), 65–66.

Exculpation

[7–51] Typical situations. A contractual indemnity from A to B against claims by or liabilities to C may be enforced to exculpate B from a liability to A or to C. Exculpation is here used in a general sense to include cases where the indemnity provides a defence to an otherwise extant liability, or prevents a liability ever arising, or has the practical effect of preventing the liability from being enforced. Two common situations are:

(1) A claims contribution from B in respect of a common liability to C.
(2) C makes a claim against B, as a consequence of A's claim against C.

[7–52] Statute expressly bars contribution. In various Commonwealth jurisdictions there remains in force a tortfeasor contribution statute derived from section 6 of the Law Reform (Married Women and Tortfeasors) Act 1935. The text of the original statute, and of many derivatives, expressly recognises that an indemnity from A to B against a liability to C bars a claim by A for contribution from B in respect of that liability.[222] It follows that once the indemnity is found to apply, it is usually unnecessary to apportion responsibility between the indemnified party and indemnifier.[223]

[7–53] Statute does not expressly bar contribution. In other jurisdictions, contribution legislation does not expressly bar claims but recognises that parties may contract for indemnity in relation to their liabilities.[224] Section 7(3)(a) of the Civil Liability (Contribution) Act 1978 states that the Act shall not affect 'any express or implied contractual or other right to indemnity'.

An indemnity from A to B against liabilities to C can, as a matter of general law, provide B with a defence to A's claim for contribution in respect of a common liability to C. Thus, in *Port of Melbourne Authority v Anshun Pty Ltd*,[225] Gibbs CJ, Mason and Aickin JJ remarked that '[a]t common law, the existence of an indemnity is a defence to an action in respect of the liability to which the indemnity relates'. The underlying assumption is that the indemnity protects against the full extent of B's liability to C, irrespective of the relative responsibility of A and B for C's loss.[226] B's defence to A's claim for contribution might then be explained on the basis of avoidance of circuity of action. B would be able to recoup from A, under the indemnity, whatever amount A obtained from B by way of contribution. Another perspective is that the promise of indemnity includes, by implication, a promise by A not to sue B for contribution in respect of the liability to C.[227]

[7–54] Indemnity may exclude equitable contribution. Persons who would be entitled to equitable contribution may displace or modify the operation of those principles by

---

[222] See, eg, Law Reform (Miscellaneous Provisions) Act 1946 (NSW), s 5(1)(c). See further [4–45].
[223] *Swan Hunter and Wigham Richardson Ltd v France Fenwick Tyne & Wear Co Ltd (The Albion)* [1953] 1 WLR 1026 (CA), 1029 ('waste of time'); *State Government Insurance Office (Qld) v Brisbane Stevedoring Pty Ltd* (1969) 123 CLR 228, 235 (Barwick CJ). Apportionment may still be relevant where there are additional wrongdoers, or where the indemnity is expressed to apply only proportionately: see, eg, *Steele v Twin City Rigging Pty Ltd* (1992) 114 FLR 99 (ACTSC), 112, 116.
[224] See, eg, Law Reform (Miscellaneous Provisions) (Scotland) Act 1940, s 3(3)(b); Wrongs Act 1958 (Vic), s 24AD(4)(a).
[225] *Port of Melbourne Authority v Anshun Pty Ltd* (1981) 147 CLR 589, 596. See also *Royal Bank of Scotland plc v Sandstone Properties Ltd* [1998] 2 BCLC 429 (QB), 434–35.
[226] See [4–45].
[227] *cf* [8–10], [8–15].

agreement or otherwise manifesting an intention to do so.[228] *MMI General Insurance Ltd v Copeland*[229] demonstrates that a contractual indemnity against liability may have this effect on rights of contribution between the indemnifier and indemnified party.

Copeland, Sir Laurence Street and others were jointly and severally liable on an indemnity given to MMI. MMI suffered substantial loss and claimed from Copeland, who in turn cross-claimed for contribution from Sir Laurence. Sir Laurence's defence to the cross-claim was that, in return for Sir Laurence joining the indemnity to MMI, Copeland and several others had agreed to indemnify him against claims arising out of that indemnity. Rolfe J noted without disapproval an argument based on the avoidance of circuity of action,[230] but upheld the defence on the narrower ground that the provision of the counter-indemnity indicated the parties' common intention to exclude equitable contribution.

[7–55] Circular indemnities. The paradigm case concerns the carriage of goods.[231] Assume that A, the consignor, promises to indemnify B, the carrier, against claims by other parties in relation to the goods. There may also be a promise by A not to sue third parties or a promise that B will not be sued by others, and a *Himalaya* clause. B promises to indemnify C – to whom all or part of the carriage has been entrusted – against claims by others, either completely or to the extent that they exceed C's liability to B under the contract between them. The goods are lost or damaged. A sues C, which causes C to sue B.

B may seek a stay of A's proceedings against C. Where A's indemnity to B is combined with a promise by A not to sue others, including C, the latter appears to be the preferred ground for ordering a stay of A's action against C.[232] There are, perhaps, two reasons. First, there may be a dispute over the extent to which, if at all, each of the indemnities in the chain responds to the relevant claims. This may not be resolved until after a full hearing.[233] Secondly, the indemnities from A to B and from B to C respectively may not provide complete coverage for the relevant claims. The full amount of A's claim will not necessarily be passed along the chain back to A.

If it has been determined that the indemnities from A to B and from B to C do cover the relevant claims in their entirety, there arises the possibility of 'circuity' among the three parties. The conventional view is that avoidance of circuity as a defence is only available for claims directly between two parties.[234] Judgment should therefore be entered for A against C, for C against B, and for B against A.[235] Another approach, which was adopted by the majority of the Appeal Division of the Supreme Court of Victoria in *Schenker & Co (Aust) Pty Ltd v Maplas Equipment and Services Pty Ltd*,[236] is to enter judgment in favour of

---

[228] *Coulls v Bagot's Executor and Trustee Co Ltd* (1967) 119 CLR 460, 480 (Barwick CJ), 488 (Taylor and Owen JJ); *Muschinski v Dodds* (1985) 160 CLR 583, 597 (Gibbs CJ), 617 (Deane J); *Scholefield Goodman and Sons Ltd v Zyngier* [1986] AC 562 (PC), 572, 574–75.

[229] *MMI General Insurance Ltd v Copeland* [2000] NSWSC 317.

[230] *MMI General Insurance Ltd v Copeland* [2000] NSWSC 317, [50].

[231] See [7–14].

[232] *Nippon Yusen Kaisha v International Import and Export Co Ltd (The Elbe Maru)* [1978] 1 Lloyd's Rep 206 (QB); *Broken Hill Pty Co Ltd v Hapag-Lloyd AG* [1980] 2 NSWLR 572 (SC); *Sidney Cooke Ltd v Hapag-Lloyd AG* [1980] 2 NSWLR 587 (SC); *Chapman Marine Pty Ltd v Wilhelmsen Lines A/S* [1999] FCA 178. See also [8–17].

[233] See, eg, *Broken Hill Pty Co Ltd v Hapag-Lloyd AG* [1980] 2 NSWLR 572 (SC), 584; *PS Chellaram & Co Ltd v China Ocean Shipping Co Ltd* [1989] 1 Lloyd's Rep 413 (NSWSC), 429–30 (revd on other grounds: *China Ocean Shipping Co Ltd v PS Chellaram & Co Ltd* (1990) 28 NSWLR 354 (CA)).

[234] *Aktieselskabet Ocean v B Harding and Sons Ltd* [1928] 2 KB 371 (CA), 384–85 (Scrutton LJ).

[235] *Schenker & Co (Aust) Pty Ltd v Maplas Equipment and Services Pty Ltd* [1990] VR 834 (FC), 851 (Ormiston J) (dissenting on this point). cf *Hair and Skin Trading Co Ltd v Norman Airfreight Carriers Ltd* [1974] 1 Lloyd's Rep 443 (QB), 447.

[236] *Schenker & Co (Aust) Pty Ltd v Maplas Equipment and Services Pty Ltd* [1990] VR 834 (FC).

C against A and to dismiss the indemnity claims between the parties. McGarvie J explained that the orders were not intended to advantage C but, rather, were to achieve an efficient and economical disposition of the dispute.[237]

Other Issues

The Interest Rule

[7–56] **Definition.** The label 'interest rule' is used to describe several related propositions which purport to define the rights and obligations of a party, B, who has received or may receive payment from an indemnifier, A, in respect of B's liability to a third party, C. The interest rule is particularly concerned with B's right to obtain payment from A, and B's obligation to pass on to C any payment received from A.

The rule was first developed in *Re Law Guarantee Trust and Accident Society Ltd*,[238] where Buckley LJ propounded it as a rationalisation of earlier decisions. The extended form of the rule is set out below. It may be assumed that A is to indemnify B against a liability to C; that B is liable to C; and that B has not yet paid C to discharge that liability.

(1) Where A pays B a sum of money in respect of B's liability to C:

    (a) generally – B is under no obligation to A to pass the funds on to C, and may deal with the sum as it pleases; but

    (b) where A has an interest in, or is concerned with, the extinction or reduction of the liability to C – B may be under an obligation to pass the funds on to C.

(2) Where B seeks to compel A's performance of the indemnity against the liability to C, then:

    (a) where A has no interest in, and is not concerned with, the extinction or reduction of B's liability to C – B is entitled to an order for payment to itself; and

    (b) where A has an interest in, or is concerned with, the extinction or reduction of B's liability to C – it is not appropriate to enforce the indemnity by ordering payment of the relevant sum to B.

The first limb of the rule is concerned with B's obligation to A after A has paid B for the liability to C. The second limb of the rule, as it relates to contractual indemnities, is concerned with the appropriate form of an order for specific enforcement. The common basis of the two limbs is that A generally has no right to control B's dealings with C unless A has an interest in or is concerned with the discharge of B's liability to C.

Different aspects of the rule as stated above have been endorsed or applied in various decisions.[239] Rule (1)(a) coincides with the common law position in insurance.[240] The content and

---

[237] *Schenker & Co (Aust) Pty Ltd v Maplas Equipment and Services Pty Ltd* [1990] VR 834 (FC), 849. This outcome avoids the risk of non-recovery from B, for example, due to B's insolvency.

[238] *Re Law Guarantee Trust and Accident Society Ltd* [1914] 2 Ch 617 (CA).

[239] See, eg, *Carr v Roberts* (1833) 5 B & Ad 78; 110 ER 721; *Rankin v Palmer* (1912) 16 CLR 285; *Re Law Guarantee Trust and Accident Society Ltd* [1914] 2 Ch 617 (CA); *British Union and National Insurance Co v Rawson* [1916] 2 Ch 476 (CA); *Official Assignee v Jarvis* [1923] NZLR 1009 (CA); *Taylor v Sanders* [1937] VLR 62 (FC), 65–66; *Re Enhill Pty Ltd* [1983] 1 VR 561 (FC), 564 (Young CJ), 571 (Lush J); *Ramsay v National Australia Bank Ltd* [1989] VR 59 (FC), 66–67; *Firma C-Trade SA v Newcastle Protection and Indemnity Association (The Fanti) (No 2)* [1991] 2 AC 1 (HL), 41 (Lord Jauncey), cf 28 (Lord Brandon); *Abigroup Ltd v Abignano* (1992) 39 FCR 74 (FC), 83; *Paterson v Pongrass Group Operations Pty Ltd* [2011] NSWSC 1588, [85]–[96].

[240] See n 197.

foundation of the interest rule are not, however, free from doubt. Rule (2)(a) is probably too broad[241] and there are different interpretations of rule (2)(b).

[7–57] Scope of application of rule. Aspects of the interest rule have been discussed in connection with contractual indemnities, non-contractual indemnities and promises to pay third parties. Assuming that B is liable to C, but has not paid C, the rule may be relevant where:

(1) A pays money to B in voluntary performance of a contractual promise to indemnify B against the liability to C;[242]
(2) B seeks specific enforcement of a contractual indemnity from A against the liability to C;[243]
(3) B, a guarantor, seeks to be exonerated by A, the debtor, from the liability to C, the creditor;[244]
(4) B, a trustee, seeks to enforce a right to be indemnified by a beneficiary, A, in respect of the liability to C, a trust creditor;[245] or
(5) A pays damages to B for A's breach of contract by failing to pay C, to whom B is liable.[246]

The last situation has been regarded as sufficiently analogous to an indemnity to attract the rule. *Official Assignee v Jarvis*[247] concerned the sale of the equity of redemption in a property that was subject to several mortgages, including a third-ranking mortgage to a particular creditor. There were covenants by the purchasers to pay the money and perform the obligations secured by the mortgages and to indemnify the vendor. The purchasers later sold their interest in the property to another, who made default under the mortgages. The second mortgagee exercised the power of sale but did not recoup the full amount owing, and so there was nothing left recoverable from the property by the creditor as third mortgagee. The vendor, in the meantime, entered bankruptcy and the creditor proved for the outstanding sum that had been secured by the mortgage. The vendor's assignee in bankruptcy then sued the purchasers on the covenants to pay and to indemnify.

It was held that the vendor's assignee in bankruptcy could recover for the sum owing by the vendor to the creditor. It was not necessary to rely upon specific enforcement of the indemnity because there was a separate covenant to pay. An action could be maintained for damages for breach of that covenant even though the vendor had not paid the outstanding sum to the creditor.[248] The next question was whether those damages, as recovered by the vendor's assignee in bankruptcy, were to go directly to the particular creditor or were to be distributed among the creditors generally. Here, the interest rule was applied. The continued existence of an equity of redemption would have given the first

---

[241] See [7–62].
[242] *Re Law Guarantee Trust and Accident Society Ltd* [1914] 2 Ch 617 (CA), 639 (Kennedy LJ).
[243] *Cruse v Paine* (1869) LR 4 Ch App 441; *Re Law Guarantee Trust and Accident Society Ltd* [1914] 2 Ch 617 (CA), 633 (Buckley LJ); *Rankin v Palmer* (1912) 16 CLR 285; *Abigroup Ltd v Abignano* (1992) 39 FCR 74 (FC), 83; *Paterson v Pongrass Group Operations Pty Ltd* [2011] NSWSC 1588.
[244] See [7–42], [7–45].
[245] *Re Richardson, ex p the Governors of St Thomas's Hospital* [1911] 2 KB 705 (CA). *cf Re Byrne Australia Pty Ltd and the Companies Act* [1981] 1 NSWLR 394 (SC), 398 (exercise of right to indemnity against trust assets).
[246] *Carr v Roberts* (1833) 5 B & Ad 78; 110 ER 721; *Loosemore v Radford* (1842) 9 M & W 657, 658; 152 ER 277, 278 (Parke B); *Official Assignee v Jarvis* [1923] NZLR 1009 (CA).
[247] *Official Assignee v Jarvis* [1923] NZLR 1009 (CA).
[248] See [6–26].

purchasers and subsequent purchaser a sufficient interest to direct the funds to the particular creditor. Payment to the creditor would have reduced or discharged the vendor's debt secured by the third mortgage over the property. However, the second mortgagee's sale had destroyed the equity of redemption and with it, the first purchasers' and subsequent purchaser's interest. There being no relevant interest, the funds were to be distributed among the general creditors.

[7–58] Foundation of the rule. The interest rule developed by Buckley LJ and supported by Kennedy LJ in *Re Law Guarantee Trust and Accident Society Ltd*[249] was a synthesis of five decisions: *Carr v Roberts*,[250] *Re Perkins*,[251] *Re Richardson*[252] and two decisions in *Cruse v Paine*.[253] Of these, *Cruse v Paine*, *Re Richardson* and *Re Perkins* were said to be instances where an interest existed; in *Carr v Roberts* the interest was absent. It is, however, doubtful whether *Re Perkins* and *Re Richardson* were valid examples.

In *Re Perkins*, it will be recalled,[254] the first assignee of the lease, A1, assigned to the lessee, L, his right to indemnity from the second assignee of the lease, A2. There was a declaration that A2's estate was liable to L for sums L had paid to the lessor following defaults in the payment of rent and insurance premiums under the lease. In *Re Law Guarantee Trust*, Buckley LJ said that A2's estate had an interest in 'discharging the obligations under the lease'.[255] Another suggestion has been that A2's estate was concerned to avoid forfeiture of the lease.[256] But it is doubtful whether either of these was a real concern. L had already paid the arrears to the lessor and A2's executors had assigned the lease to another person, A3, well before L brought the action. Nor is it entirely clear whether the relevant defaults had all occurred prior to that last assignment, or all afterwards, or some before and some afterwards.[257] A2's estate would only have been liable directly to L or the lessor for defaults occurring before that assignment.[258] The case may illustrate the proposition that the relevant 'interest' can be that of a person claiming under the indemnifier, namely, A3.[259] The obvious and much simpler explanation, however, is that L was exercising A1's right to indemnity as assignee.

In *Re Richardson*, a husband was trustee of two assigned leases for his wife. The landlord sued the husband for arrears in rent and breaches of covenants in the leases. The husband in the meantime was adjudicated a bankrupt. The landlord lodged a proof of debt and obtained an order to use the name of the husband's trustee in bankruptcy to bring an action for indemnity against the beneficiary wife. The wife compromised the claim and paid the money to the landlord. The landlord, pursuant to the prior order, then applied to the court for a determination of whether the whole amount could be retained or was to be

---

[249] *Re Law Guarantee Trust and Accident Society Ltd* [1914] 2 Ch 617 (CA).

[250] *Carr v Roberts* (1833) 5 B & Ad 78; 110 ER 721.

[251] *Re Perkins; Poyser v Beyfus* [1898] 2 Ch 182 (CA).

[252] *Re Richardson, ex p the Governors of St Thomas's Hospital* [1911] 2 KB 705 (CA).

[253] *Cruse v Paine* (1868) LR 6 Eq 641; *Cruse v Paine* (1869) LR 4 Ch App 441.

[254] See [7–30].

[255] *Re Law Guarantee Trust and Accident Society Ltd* [1914] 2 Ch 617 (CA), 633.

[256] JC Phillips, *The Modern Contract of Guarantee*, 2nd English edn (London, Sweet & Maxwell, 2010), 699, para 11-114 fn 257.

[257] The facts as stated in the report of the case (*Re Perkins; Poyser v Beyfus* [1898] 2 Ch 182 (CA), 183) may suggest that the defaults were all attributable to A3, who was a 'man of straw'.

[258] See generally C Harpum, S Bridge and M Dixon, *Megarry and Wade, The Law of Real Property*, 8th edn (London, Sweet & Maxwell, 2012), 959–62, paras 20-053–20-058.

[259] See [7–60].

distributed among the husband's creditors generally. It was held that the landlord was to retain the whole amount.

The case has been regarded as peculiar or exceptional.[260] The substantial difficulty with the interest rule analysis lies in identifying the nature of the wife's interest as beneficiary. It has been said that the beneficiary under a trust has an interest in freeing trust property from any debts or charges to which it is subject.[261] That may generally be so, but it does not fit well with the reasoning in *Re Richardson*. None of the judgments discussed the possibility of claims against trust property. There was no reference to any trust property other than the leases and those leases had expired before the proceedings. It is, therefore, doubtful that the wife had an interest in freeing any trust property from debts or charges thereon or avoiding forfeiture of the leases.[262] More influential in the judgments of Cozens-Hardy MR and Fletcher Moulton LJ was the basic principle that the indemnity arose from the trust relationship and that the trustee was not to profit from it.[263] If the funds had gone into the pool for general creditors, the husband as trustee would have been over-compensated because he would have received more from the beneficiary than he would have paid to the landlord. The right to indemnity by exoneration was to be used to satisfy liabilities to trust creditors only.[264]

The two decisions in *Cruse v Paine* support the interest rule insofar as it concerns specific enforcement of the indemnity. The decisions indicate that an unqualified order for advance payment to the indemnified party is not appropriate where the indemnifier has an interest in the application of the funds.

In summary, and recalling the interest rule as stated earlier,[265] the authorities relied on by Buckley LJ might at best establish rule (1)(a) and rule (2)(b).[266] The reasoning in *Re Law Guarantee Trust* itself purports to apply rule (2)(a).

[7–59] What constitutes an interest? The interest may be financial or proprietary in nature.[267] The indemnifier and indemnified party may each be personally liable to the third party in such a way that discharge of the indemnified party's liability will relieve the indemnifier to a corresponding extent. Several examples can be given. The indemnifier and indemnified party may be co-debtors, with the indemnity covering the common liability.[268]

---

[260] *Re Law Guarantee Trust and Accident Society Ltd* [1914] 2 Ch 617 (CA), 641 (Kennedy LJ), 651 (Scrutton J); *Re Harrington Motor Co Ltd, ex p Chaplin* [1928] Ch 105 (CA), 123 (Atkin LJ).

[261] *Re Law Guarantee Trust and Accident Society Ltd* [1914] 2 Ch 617 (CA), 633 (Buckley LJ); *Official Assignee v Jarvis* [1923] NZLR 1009 (CA), 1018, 1021 (Salmond J); *Re Byrne Australia Pty Ltd and the Companies Act* [1981] 1 NSWLR 394 (SC), 398.

[262] *Re Suco Gold Pty Ltd (in liq)* (1983) 33 SASR 99 (FC), 107 (King CJ). Contrast *Re Enhill Pty Ltd* [1983] 1 VR 561 (FC), 571 (Lush J).

[263] See also *Re Harrington Motor Co Ltd, ex p Chaplin* [1928] Ch 105 (CA), 109 (Eve J), 123 (Atkin LJ).

[264] The correctness of this principle has been controversial in Australia but the weight of opinion supports the result reached in *Re Richardson*: see *Re Byrne Australia Pty Ltd and the Companies Act* [1981] 1 NSWLR 394 (SC); *Re Suco Gold Pty Ltd (in liq)* (1983) 33 SASR 99 (FC); *Re ADM Franchise Pty Ltd* (1983) 7 ACLR 987 (NSWSC); *Re Matheson* (1994) 49 FCR 454 (FCA). See generally, *Federal Commissioner of Taxation v Bruton Holdings Pty Ltd (in liq)* [2008] FCAFC 184; (2008) 173 FCR 472, [47]–[58]; JD Heydon and MJ Leeming, *Jacobs' Law of Trusts*, 7th edn (Sydney, LexisNexis Butterworths, 2006), 575–76, para 2114.

[265] See [7–56].

[266] *cf Federal Commissioner of Taxation v Bruton Holdings Pty Ltd (in liq)* [2008] FCAFC 184; (2008) 173 FCR 472, [50].

[267] Query whether there would have been an interest in *Wooldridge v Norris* (1868) LR 6 Eq 410 (indemnity to surety from debtor's father).

[268] *Official Assignee v Jarvis* [1923] NZLR 1009 (CA), 1018 (Salmond J). *cf Loosemore v Radford* (1842) 9 M & W 657, 658; 152 ER 277, 278 (Parke B).

A debtor may expressly promise to indemnify a guarantor against its liability to the creditor.[269] A principal and an agent may both be liable to a third party in a transaction arising in the course of the agency.[270]

Even where the indemnifier is not personally liable to the third party, the indemnifier may have an interest in property which is affected by the indemnified party's liability. Examples include the following. A purchaser of shares may indemnify the vendor against liability for calls on the shares pending registration of the transfer. The purchaser is said to have an interest in freeing the shares from the calls upon them.[271] The purchaser of the equity of redemption in a property may indemnify the vendor against liabilities secured by a mortgage over the property. For so long as the equity of redemption exists, the purchaser has an interest in freeing the property from encumbrances and is concerned that any money paid by way of indemnity should be directed to the mortgagee for that purpose.[272] A person who enjoys the benefit of a lease may have an interest in preserving the lease and thus be concerned that any money paid by way of indemnity be applied to satisfy liabilities to the lessor. In the trust context, it has been suggested that a beneficiary who is personally liable to indemnify the trustee is concerned with the discharge of trust liabilities, so as to free trust property from any debts or charges.[273]

[7–60] **Whose interest?** The interest of the indemnifier is relevant. It may also be relevant in some circumstances to consider another person who has an interest in affected property that is derived through the indemnifier. In *Official Assignee v Jarvis*,[274] there were successive sales of the equity of redemption in certain land, with each purchaser covenanting to pay the moneys secured by the mortgages and to indemnify the vendor against such liabilities. In one sense, the first purchasers' interest in the property disappeared when they sold the equity of redemption to the second purchaser. It might be thought, similarly, that they would no longer be interested in whether the mortgagee received any payments they were required to make under their covenants with the vendor. However, the first purchasers were entitled to be indemnified by the second purchaser against such payments. Thus, if the first purchasers' payments were not passed on to the mortgagee, the second purchaser could be placed in the invidious position of being liable to pay while still being left with land encumbered as before. In such circumstances, this interest of the second purchaser would have been sufficient.[275]

[7–61] **Where interest exists.** There are two aspects of the interest rule. The first aspect is relevant where the indemnified party has already received funds from the indemnifier. The indemnified party is said to be under an obligation to pay over the funds to the third party.

---

[269] See, eg, *Agnes & Jennie Mining Co Ltd v Zen* (1982) 38 BCLR 385 (CA).

[270] *Rankin v Palmer* (1912) 16 CLR 285.

[271] *Official Assignee v Jarvis* [1923] NZLR 1009 (CA), 1018 (Salmond J); *Re Law Guarantee Trust and Accident Society Ltd* [1914] 2 Ch 617 (CA), 633 (Buckley LJ). See generally [6–11], [5–78].

[272] *Shaver v Sproule* (1913) 9 DLR 641 (Ont SC); *Official Assignee v Jarvis* [1923] NZLR 1009 (CA).

[273] *Re Law Guarantee Trust and Accident Society Ltd* [1914] 2 Ch 617 (CA), 633 (Buckley LJ); *Official Assignee v Jarvis* [1923] NZLR 1009 (CA), 1018 (Salmond J); *Re Enhill Pty Ltd* [1983] 1 VR 561 (FC), 564 (Young CJ), 571 (Lush J). cf *Re Byrne Australia Pty Ltd and the Companies Act* [1981] 1 NSWLR 394 (SC), 398. But see further [7–58].

[274] *Official Assignee v Jarvis* [1923] NZLR 1009 (CA).

[275] *Official Assignee v Jarvis* [1923] NZLR 1009 (CA), 1022. On the facts, the purchasers' interest was extinguished when the second mortgagee exercised the power of sale.

The nature of that obligation has received little attention. In *Official Assignee v Jarvis*,[276] Salmond J in a dictum suggested that it was an equitable obligation, in the nature of a trust. The obligation is owed to the indemnifier, not the third party.

The second aspect of the interest rule concerns specific enforcement of the indemnity. An unconditional order for advance payment to the indemnified party is not appropriate. It might be thought that such an order would be satisfactory if there was a concomitant obligation to pass on the funds to the third party. This aspect of the rule would then be aligned with the other aspect of the rule described above. Although there is some support for that position,[277] the better view is against it: the order should be for exoneration or for payment direct to the third party.[278] Such an order entirely avoids the risk that the indemnified party might not pass on the funds. In this respect, there does not appear to be any relevant distinction between cases where the indemnifier is personally liable to the third party, and cases where the indemnifier's proprietary interests are affected by the indemnified party's liability.

[7–62] Where interest is absent. Where the indemnified party has been paid voluntarily by the indemnifier, there is no obligation to apply that sum to satisfy the claim or liability in respect of which it was given. In *Lacey v Hill*,[279] Jessel MR's response to the objection that the indemnified party might compromise for less, was that 'the person liable to indemnify can go to the creditor and set him right. It is his own fault that the liability remains'. In *Re Law Guarantee Trust and Accident Society Ltd*,[280] Kennedy LJ said that the indemnified party's use of money received under the contract of indemnity is 'in general and apart from special considerations, no concern of the party who, in fulfilment of his contract, has made the payment to him'. The indemnified party need not, of course, pass on the particular funds received from the indemnifier; it could pay an equivalent amount from other sources.[281] But the principle is broader: the indemnified party owes no obligation to the indemnifier to pay the third party, whether from the funds so provided or an equivalent sum from another source.

The interest rule also bears upon orders for specific enforcement of the indemnity. In *Re Law Guarantee Trust*, Buckley LJ said:[282]

> The equitable doctrine is that the party to be indemnified can call upon the party bound to indemnify him specifically to perform his obligation, and to pay him the full amount which the creditor is entitled to receive, and that whether having received it he applies it in payment of that creditor or not is a matter with which the party giving the indemnity is not concerned.

---

[276] *Official Assignee v Jarvis* [1923] NZLR 1009 (CA), 1019, 1022. See also *Ramsay v National Australia Bank Ltd* [1989] VR 59 (FC), 66–67. cf *Loosemore v Radford* (1842) 9 M & W 657, 658; 152 ER 277, 278 (Parke B) ('an equity').

[277] See, eg, *Evans v Wood* (1867) LR 5 Eq 9; *Shepherd v Gillespie* (1867) LR 5 Eq 293 (affd *Shepherd v Gillespie* (1868) LR 3 Ch App 764); *Cruse v Paine* (1868) LR 6 Eq 641. See generally *Re Law Guarantee Trust and Accident Society Ltd* [1914] 2 Ch 617 (CA), 633 (Buckley LJ).

[278] See [7–45].

[279] *Lacey v Hill; Crowley's Claim* (1874) LR 18 Eq 182, 191–92.

[280] *Re Law Guarantee Trust and Accident Society Ltd* [1914] 2 Ch 617 (CA), 639. See also *Carr v Roberts* (1833) 5 B & Ad 78, 84; 110 ER 721, 723 (Littledale J), 85; 723 (Patteson J).

[281] cf *Re Harrington Motor Co Ltd, ex p Chaplin* [1928] Ch 105 (CA), 113 (Lord Hanworth MR).

[282] *Re Law Guarantee Trust and Accident Society Ltd* [1914] 2 Ch 617 (CA), 633. See also *British Union and National Insurance Co v Rawson* [1916] 2 Ch 476 (CA), 482 (Pickford LJ); *Firma C-Trade SA v Newcastle Protection and Indemnity Association (The Fanti) (No 2)* [1991] 2 AC 1 (HL), 41 (Lord Jauncey).

This, arguably, overstates the position.[283] The absence of any interest of the indemnifier is a factor that favours an order for advance payment to the indemnified party. It should not be the only or decisive criterion. For non-insurance indemnities, a further consideration may be whether the indemnified party is, in fact, likely to pass on the funds in full. Conversely, an undertaking to pass on the funds may be attached to the order even where the indemnifier has no apparent interest.[284] Both limitations suggest a concern to avoid over-compensating the indemnified party. The terms of the contract of indemnity are also material.

This aspect of the interest rule is inclusionary rather than exclusionary in effect. The indemnified party may still obtain an order for exoneration or for payment directly to the third party.[285]

Right of Third Party to Benefit of Indemnity

[7–63] **No general right to benefit of indemnity.** Assume that A promises to indemnify B against liability to C, and that there is no other promise by A to indemnify C directly.[286] Whether C receives the benefit of that indemnity has already been considered from two perspectives: B's right to compel A to pay C; and A's right to compel B to pay over to C funds provided by A.[287] It remains to examine the same point from C's perspective, that is, whether C can compel B to pass on the benefit of A's indemnity.

The general rule is that C has no right against B to obtain the benefit of the indemnity from A.[288] This point was established in a series of liability insurance decisions in the first half of the twentieth century,[289] but the reasoning extends also to non-insurance indemnities. The promise of indemnity between A and B is *res inter alios acta* as far as C is concerned.

[7–64] **Exceptions.** The common law position, as it applied to liability insurance, operated unjustly where the insured was insolvent. The insured (B) could recover the whole sum due from the insurer (A) but the money would be distributed among the general creditors, with the result that the injured claimant (C) did not receive full compensation. This injustice led to remedial legislation in the United Kingdom[290] and in other jurisdictions around the Commonwealth.[291] The manner in which such legislation operates varies

---

[283] See [7–44].

[284] *Paterson v Pongrass Group Operations Pty Ltd* [2011] NSWSC 1588, [96]. *cf Sandtara Pty Ltd v Abigroup Ltd* (NSWSC, 25 and 29 September 1997).

[285] See, eg, *McIntosh v Dalwood (No 4)* (1930) 30 SR (NSW) 415 (FC).

[286] The latter situation is considered at [5–36]–[5–38].

[287] See [7–42], [7–56].

[288] *cf Coulls v Bagot's Executor and Trustee Co Ltd* (1967) 119 CLR 460, 502 (Windeyer J); *Beswick v Beswick* [1968] AC 58 (HL), 71 (Lord Reid) (A's promise to B to pay C conferring no general right upon C against B). As to the right of a trust creditor to be subrogated to the trustee's right of indemnity, see D Hayton, P Matthews and C Mitchell, *Underhill and Hayton: Law of Trusts and Trustees*, 18th edn (London, LexisNexis, 2010), 1079–81, paras 81.47–81.53.

[289] *Re Harrington Motor Co Ltd, ex p Chaplin* [1928] Ch 105 (CA); *Hood's Trustees v Southern Union General Insurance Co of Australasia Ltd* [1928] Ch 793 (CA); *Smith v Horlor* [1930] NZLR 537 (SC); *Re Southern Cross Coaches Ltd* (1932) 49 WN (NSW) 230 (SC).

[290] Originally by the Third Parties (Rights Against Insurers) Act 1930. See also Third Parties (Rights Against Insurers) Act 2010, which had not yet commenced at the time of writing.

[291] In Australia, see, eg, Bankruptcy Act 1966 (Cth), s 117; Corporations Act 2001 (Cth), ss 562, 562A; Law Reform (Miscellaneous Provisions) Act 1946 (NSW), s 6; *AssetInsure Pty Ltd v New Cap Reinsurance Corp Ltd (in liq)* [2006] HCA 13; (2006) 225 CLR 331, [75]–[87] (Kirby and Hayne JJ). In New Zealand, see Law Reform Act 1936 (NZ), s 9.

among jurisdictions, but the scope is typically limited to contracts of liability insurance[292] or, in some instances, reinsurance.[293] It is, therefore, not relevant for non-insurance indemnities.

There are two non-statutory solutions. B may hold the benefit of A's promise of indemnity on trust for C. An agreement between B and C that B may or will obtain an indemnity against a certain risk, without any further provision as to the application of the proceeds of the indemnity, is usually not sufficient to give C a beneficial interest in those proceeds.[294] Alternatively, B and C may negotiate a settlement in which B assigns to C the right to indemnity from A, in return for C releasing B or agreeing only to pursue recovery against A.[295]

---

[292] Third Parties (Rights Against Insurers) Act 1930, s 1(5); Third Parties (Rights Against Insurers) Act 2010, s 15.

[293] In Australia, see Corporations Act 2001 (Cth), s 562A; DE Charrett, 'Insured's Access to Insolvent Reinsurer's Reinsurance' (2003) 14 *Insurance Law Journal* 221.

[294] *Lees v Whiteley* (1866) LR 2 Eq 143; *Sinnott v Bowden* [1912] 2 Ch 414 (Ch), 419; *Halifax Building Society v Keighley* [1931] 2 KB 248 (KB) (insurances on mortgaged property); *Henderson v Gray and Winter* (VSC, 20 October 1995), 45; *Re Silverstein, ex p Evenage Pty Ltd* (FCA, 13 March 1998), 39–41 (statutory requirements to obtain professional indemnity insurance). *cf Normid Housing Association Ltd v Ralphs* [1989] 1 Lloyd's Rep 265 (CA), 272–73 (Slade LJ).

[295] See [7–30], [7–50].

8

Claims by or Liabilities to the Indemnifier

Introduction

[8–1] Purpose of chapter. This chapter considers indemnities against claims by or liabilities to the indemnifier. Indemnities in this form are peculiar; they tend to be used in specific contexts, such as settlement agreements or sophisticated liability or risk allocation schemes in commercial contracts. The function of the indemnity is not, typically, to provide compensation for a loss inflicted by an external event. Instead, the indemnity is a contractual device that is intended to limit or exclude the indemnified party's liability to the indemnifier on the basis stated by the scope of the indemnity. Thus, indemnities in this form may have more in common with other exclusionary measures, such as exclusion or limitation clauses, or promises not to sue.

[8–2] Structure of chapter. The chapter begins by defining this form of indemnity. It is necessary to identify the person or class of persons against whose claims the indemnified party is to be protected. This feature distinguishes indemnities in the present form from indemnities against claims by or liabilities to third parties. The chapter then considers the nature of the promise of indemnity, and the manner in which it may be performed and enforced.

Classification

[8–3] Definition. An indemnity against claims by or liabilities to the indemnifier is a promise of indemnity by which the indemnifier engages to protect the indemnified party against a loss arising from:

(1) an actual liability of the indemnified party to the indemnifier; or
(2) the indemnifier's assertion of such a liability, regardless of whether that liability actually exists.

As with the definition of an indemnity against claims by or liabilities to third parties, this definition applies to a discrete aspect of an indemnity with a broader scope. Thus, where an indemnity covers claims by or liabilities to anyone – the indemnifier or third parties – the principles discussed in this chapter can be applied to the indemnity insofar as it operates in relation to the indemnifier.[1]

[1] cf *Farstad Supply AS v Enviroco Ltd (The Far Service)* [2010] UKSC 18; [2010] 2 Lloyd's Rep 387, [59] (Lord Mance).

[8–4] Identification of the claimant. The scope of the indemnity may expressly refer to claims by or liabilities to the indemnifier. Such drafting is common in agreements to settle disputes. Many indemnity clauses, however, simply refer to claims or liabilities, without specifying the class of persons by whom the claims are made or to whom the liabilities are owed. A threshold question is whether such an indemnity covers only claims by or liabilities to third parties or whether, alternatively or additionally, it covers claims by or liabilities to the indemnifier. This is a matter of construction.[2]

The authorities on the whole tend to favour the construction that the indemnity applies only to claims by third parties.[3] In *Great Western Railway Co v J Durnford and Son Ltd*,[4] the defendant gave the claimant permission to use a portable gangway that overhung the defendant's railway, the claimant in return promising to indemnify the defendant against 'all claims and demands or liability whatsoever . . . arising out of or in connection with the existence or user of the said gangway'. It was held that the defendant could not rely on the clause to defeat the claimant's claim against it for damage to the claimant's property. Considering the nature of the parties' arrangement, Viscount Sumner explained that 'abundant content' for the indemnity could be found by applying it to liabilities to third parties, so that it was not necessary to extend it to liabilities inter partes.[5] Legal technique was another consideration. If the commercial objective was to bar claims by the claimant, there were other, more direct methods of achieving that result.[6] A further consideration, not mentioned by Viscount Sumner, may be the traditional scepticism towards clauses that purport to exempt a party from the consequences of its own wrong, such as negligence. It is, perhaps, easier to conceive of fault-free liabilities to third parties than to the indemnifier.

Viscount Sumner's analysis coincides with views expressed in some decisions of the High Court of Australia.[7] In *Australian Coastal Shipping Commission v PV 'Wyuna'*,[8] Kitto J noted the 'aptness' of the term 'indemnify' to indicate claims by third parties. In *Sunbird Plaza Pty Ltd v Maloney*,[9] Mason CJ described an indemnity as a promise that the promisor 'will keep the promisee harmless against loss as a result of entering into a transaction with a third party'. In *Andar Transport Pty Ltd v Brambles Ltd*,[10] Gleeson CJ, McHugh, Gummow, Hayne and Heydon JJ remarked that guarantees and indemnities are both 'designed to satisfy a liability owed by someone other than the guarantor or indemnifier to a third person'. Similarly, in *Salmon River Logging Co Ltd v Burt Bros*,[11] a decision of the Supreme Court of Canada, Rand J said:

---

[2] *Westina Corp Pty Ltd v BGC Contracting Pty Ltd* [2009] WASCA 213; (2009) 41 WAR 263, [67] (Buss JA).

[3] In addition to the cases discussed in the text, see, eg, *The Carlton* [1931] P 186 (P); *The Lindenhall* [1945] P 8 (CA); *Stent Foundations Ltd v MJ Gleeson Group plc* [2001] BLR 134 (QB), [17]; *Concord Trust v The Law Debenture Trust Corp plc* [2004] EWHC 1216 (Ch), [56] (this point not considered on appeal: *Concord Trust v The Law Debenture Trust Corp plc* [2004] EWCA Civ 1001); *Ilion Technology Corp v Johannink* [2006] NZHC 27, [131]; *Westina Corp Pty Ltd v BGC Contracting Pty Ltd* [2009] WASCA 213; (2009) 41 WAR 263, [67]–[69], [76] (Buss JA).

[4] *Great Western Railway Co v J Durnford and Son Ltd* (1928) 44 TLR 415 (HL).

[5] *Great Western Railway Co v J Durnford and Son Ltd* (1928) 44 TLR 415 (HL), 416.

[6] *Great Western Railway Co v J Durnford and Son Ltd* (1928) 44 TLR 415 (HL), 416.

[7] cf *Qantas Airways Ltd v Aravco Ltd* (1996) 185 CLR 43, where it seems to have been accepted that the indemnity clause covered claims by third parties and by the indemnifier.

[8] *Australian Coastal Shipping Commission v PV 'Wyuna'* (1964) 111 CLR 303, 309.

[9] *Sunbird Plaza Pty Ltd v Maloney* (1988) 166 CLR 245, 254.

[10] *Andar Transport Pty Ltd v Brambles Ltd* [2004] HCA 28; (2004) 217 CLR 424, [23].

[11] *Salmon River Logging Co Ltd v Burt Bros* [1953] 2 SCR 117.

We do not 'indemnify and save harmless' from or against our own claims . . . [T]his familiar phrase must be given its well established meaning. To indemnify and save harmless is to protect one person against action in the nature of claims made or proceedings taken against him by a third person.[12]

This is the predominant construction, but it is not universally adopted. Various factors may support the inference that the indemnity is intended to apply to claims by or liabilities to the indemnifier. The commercial context and structure of the contract as a whole are relevant.[13] Another consideration is whether the claim or liability, as delimited by other elements in the scope of the indemnity, is likely to involve the indemnifier.[14]

[8–5] Commercial context and structure of contract. It is necessary to consider the commercial context, the nature of the contract and the relationship between the indemnity and other terms of the contract, particularly insurance or exclusion clauses. Labels applied to describe the indemnity clause may be relevant, as may be other acts or promises included in the indemnity clause, such as releases or promises not to sue.

A leading illustration is *Farstad Supply AS v Enviroco Ltd (The Far Service).*[15] The vessel under charter was damaged by fire. It was held that clause 33.5 of the charterparty excluded the charterer's liability to the owner for such damage. The clause provided that

the Owner shall defend, indemnify and hold harmless the Charterer . . . from and against any and all claims, demands, liabilities, proceedings and causes of action resulting from loss or damage in relation to the Vessel . . . including where such loss or damage is caused by, or contributed to, by the negligence of the Charterer.

A necessary step in that conclusion was that the indemnity applied to claims by or liabilities to the owner and not only third parties. Lord Clarke and Lord Mance, who delivered the leading judgments, considered that the words 'indemnify' and 'hold harmless' could refer to claims between the parties, as well as claims by third parties.[16] There were several contextual factors. Clause 33 was entitled 'EXCEPTIONS / INDEMNITIES'. The expression 'defend, indemnify and hold harmless' was used repeatedly throughout the clause, including in places where the only sensible interpretation was that there was an exclusion of liability. The contractual scheme in clause 33 indicated that the owner was expected to insure against all risk of loss to its own property. On that basis, it would have made little sense for the owner to indemnify the charterer against claims by third parties while leaving the charterer liable to a direct claim by the owner.

[8–6] Indemnifier likely to be claimant. The scope of the indemnity may be defined in such a way that a claim or liability that is within scope is likely to involve the indemnifier. If such claims or liabilities could form a significant part of the subject-matter of the indemnity, the inference may be that the parties intended them to be covered. In *Westerngeco Ltd*

---

[12] *Salmon River Logging Co Ltd v Burt Bros* [1953] 2 SCR 117, 120 and *cf* 121–22 (Kellock and Locke JJ).
[13] See [8–5].
[14] See [8–6].
[15] *Farstad Supply AS v Enviroco Ltd (The Far Service)* [2010] UKSC 18; [2010] 2 Lloyd's Rep 387. See also *Dyck v Manitoba Snowmobile Association Inc* [1985] 1 SCR 589 (indemnity clause on contestant's entry form referred to as a 'waiver of claim'); *Qantas Airways Ltd v Aravco Ltd* (1996) 185 CLR 43 (clause expressed to be release and indemnity).
[16] *Farstad Supply AS v Enviroco Ltd (The Far Service)* [2010] UKSC 18; [2010] 2 Lloyd's Rep 387, [24]–[27] (Lord Clarke), [57] (Lord Mance).

v ATP Oil & Gas (UK) Ltd,[17] for example, a gas company promised to indemnify a contractor against the contractor's group's 'liability under this Contract' exceeding a certain
amount. It was held that the clause did not protect the contractor against a substantial
claim by a third party for damage to property. The expression 'liability under this Contract'
clearly referred to liability to the contractual counterparty, the gas company.

The same construction may apply where a professional indemnifies a client against costs
or charges which may include charges for the professional's services;[18] or where, following
the dissolution of a marriage, one former spouse indemnifies the other against claims or
liabilities for maintenance of their children.[19] Alternatively, the indemnity may refer to
claims or liabilities for loss of or damage to the indemnifier's property,[20] or for injury to, or
the death of, the indemnifier.[21]

Nature of Indemnity

[8–7] **Purpose of indemnity.** Indemnities against claims by or liabilities to the indemnifier
have been described as 'curious' and 'slightly absurd'.[22] The ultimate object of such drafting is usually to exclude or limit the indemnified party's liability to the indemnifier on the
basis stated by the scope of the indemnity. If the indemnity extends to cover the indemnified party's costs of defence, it can serve as a stronger deterrent to action than an exclusion
or limitation clause framed in similar terms. Not only is the indemnifier's action barred if
the loss is within scope, but the indemnifier may be liable for costs on a basis that is more
favourable to the indemnified party than the usual.[23]

Where the indemnity applies to claims by or liabilities to the indemnifier and others
who are related to the indemnifier but not parties to the contract (for example, members of
the indemnifier's corporate group), the indemnity may be an approximate solution to the
privity problem associated with holding non-parties to an exclusion or limitation clause.

[8–8] **Nature of indemnity.** An indemnity against claims by or liabilities to the indemnifier can be effective to bar the indemnifier's action against the indemnified party. Various
explanations have been offered for why this is so, including the following:

(1) The promise of indemnity is construed in one of the usual ways, but operates in a
manner that provides a defence to the indemnifier's action.

(2) The promise of indemnity is tantamount to, or carries with it, a promise not to sue the
indemnified party.

---

[17] *Westerngeco Ltd v ATP Oil & Gas (UK) Ltd* [2006] EWHC 1164 (Comm); [2006] 2 Lloyd's Rep 535.
[18] *Hill v Allen* (1837) 2 M & W 283; 150 ER 763; *Connop v Levy* (1848) 11 QB 769; 16 ER 662; *Re Brampton and Longtown Railway Co; Shaw's Claim* (1875) LR 10 Ch App 177, 180–81 (Lord Cairns LC).
[19] *Rodgers v Rodgers* [1970] 1 NSWR 666 (SC); *In the Marriage of Burge* (1985) 10 Fam LR 514 (Fam CA).
[20] *Deepak Fertilisers and Petrochemicals Corp v ICI Chemicals & Polymers Ltd* [1999] 1 Lloyd's Rep 387 (CA);
Farstad Supply AS v Enviroco Ltd (The Far Service) [2010] UKSC 18; [2010] 2 Lloyd's Rep 387. cf *Powell Equipment
Co Ltd v Lac Seul Land and Lumber Co Ltd* [1967] 1 OR 103 (CA), 125 (Laskin JA) (dissenting). Contrast *Stent
Foundations Ltd v MJ Gleeson Group plc* [2001] BLR 134 (QB), [13] (clause potentially covering claims by bailor of
property in possession of indemnifier).
[21] *Dyck v Manitoba Snowmobile Association Inc* [1985] 1 SCR 589.
[22] *Equuscorp Pty Ltd v Glengallan Investments Pty Ltd* [2006] QCA 194, [12] (McPherson JA), [91] (Jerrard JA).
[23] See [4–78].

(3) The promise of indemnity is, in substance, an exclusion clause.
(4) The promise of indemnity is, in substance, a release or agreement for release.

[8–9] Indemnity has one of its usual senses. The traditional analysis of a promise to indemnify against claims by or liabilities to the indemnifier is that it confers upon the indemnified party a defence for the avoidance of circuity of action.[24] This describes the effect of the indemnity but does not reveal its essential nature. The defence can be justified on either of the two usual constructions, namely, prevention of loss or compensation for loss. It is, therefore, strictly unnecessary to choose between them, though the preventive construction appears to be more apt. It is the construction usually applied to indemnities against claims by or liabilities to third parties.[25] It is also consistent with the analogy sometimes drawn with a promise not to sue: the indemnifier promises not to harm the indemnified party, rather than to compensate for harm once inflicted.

[8–10] Promise not to sue. Another view is that a promise to indemnify against claims by or liabilities to the indemnifier is equivalent to, or imports, a promise by the indemnifier not to sue the indemnified party.[26] In *Equuscorp Pty Ltd v Glengallan Investments Pty Ltd*,[27] the terms of a contract provided that C would make three specified payments in relation to certain investment loans; that no further payments would be made by C 'beyond the above'; and that A and B would indemnify C against claims or demands by A, B or others for amounts exceeding the specified total. McPherson JA considered that the indemnity was analogous to a promise by A and B not to sue C for an amount above the specified limit.[28]

A similar approach was adopted in *Deepak Fertilisers and Petrochemicals Corp v ICI Chemicals & Polymers Ltd.*[29] Under clause 10.10.2 of the contract, Deepak promised to indemnify and hold Davy harmless against liability for loss of or damage to Deepak's property. Clause 10.10.3 extended the benefit of clause 10.10.2 to ICI as if it were Davy, though ICI was not a party to the contract. It was not disputed that clause 10.10.2 barred action by Deepak against Davy for losses that were within scope.[30] There remained a question as to the effect of clause 10.10.3 on Deepak's action against ICI. It was held that the indemnity contained an implied promise by Deepak not to sue ICI. Stuart-Smith LJ explained that such a term would meet 'any or all of the well known tests for implication of terms'.[31]

[8–11] Exclusion or limitation of liability. Another construction is that the promise of indemnity creates no executory obligation. It is, instead, a direct exclusion or limitation of the indemnified party's liability as defined by the scope of the indemnity.[32] In the leading

---

[24] See [8–15].
[25] See [6–9].
[26] Contrast *MRT Performance Pty Ltd v Mastro Motors Inc* [2005] NSWSC 316, [40]–[42]; *Equuscorp Pty Ltd v Glengallan Investments Pty Ltd* [2006] QCA 194, [91] (Jerrard JA).
[27] *Equuscorp Pty Ltd v Glengallan Investments Pty Ltd* [2006] QCA 194.
[28] *Equuscorp Pty Ltd v Glengallan Investments Pty Ltd* [2006] QCA 194, [12], but contrast [91] (Jerrard JA).
[29] *Deepak Fertilisers and Petrochemicals Corp v ICI Chemicals & Polymers Ltd* [1999] 1 Lloyd's Rep 387 (CA).
[30] *Deepak Fertilisers and Petrochemicals Corp v ICI Chemicals & Polymers Ltd* [1998] 2 Lloyd's Rep 139 (QB), 157.
[31] *Deepak Fertilisers and Petrochemicals Corp v ICI Chemicals & Polymers Ltd* [1999] 1 Lloyd's Rep 387 (CA), 401.
[32] See, eg, *Powell Equipment Co Ltd v Lac Seul Land and Lumber Co Ltd* [1967] 1 OR 103 (CA), 125 (Laskin JA) (dissenting); *Farstad Supply AS v Enviroco Ltd (The Far Service)* [2010] UKSC 18; [2010] 2 Lloyd's Rep 387.

decision, *Farstad Supply AS v Enviroco Ltd (The Far Service)*,[33] Lord Clarke attached significance to the phrase 'hold harmless' as indicating an exclusion of liability. That phrase is not decisive: it is commonly used as a synonym for 'indemnify'.[34]

The result is essentially the same as that arrived at upon the circuity of action analysis, in that the indemnified party cannot be held liable to the indemnifier. The underlying mechanism is, however, different. Where it functions as an exclusion or limitation clause, the indemnity may extinguish or qualify another primary obligation of the indemnified party,[35] or simply provide a direct defence to the indemnifier's action. The circuity of action analysis, in contrast, assumes an existing liability of the indemnified party that may be met by a countervailing claim under the indemnity.

[8–12] Release. A fourth construction is that the promise of indemnity constitutes an immediate release of the indemnifier's present rights, or an agreement to release the indemnifier's future rights, against the indemnified party.[36] In *Equuscorp Pty Ltd v Glengallan Investments Pty Ltd*,[37] a document under consideration contained several provisions, one of which was a promise by A and B to indemnify C against any claims or demands by A, B or others in excess of a certain amount. The point was only incidental, but the High Court of Australia asked rhetorically whether the document might have been a release.[38]

Another example is *Rodgers v Rodgers*.[39] The wife promised to indemnify the husband against any claims for maintenance of their child exceeding the provisions already made by court order. The wife later applied for increased maintenance. Selby J said: 'despite the fact that it is framed as an indemnity . . . it is, in essence, a renunciation of the petitioner's right to claim an order for the maintenance of the child'.[40]

In the absence of a distinct provision for release,[41] there seems to be little to commend this construction; a fortiori, where the subject-matter of the contract is executory in nature. It may be more accurate to say that an unqualified indemnity is equivalent in effect to a release or agreement for release, because it provides the indemnified party with a defence *in limine*. Later in his judgment in *Rodgers*, Selby J said that the indemnity 'in effect' involved a renunciation of the wife's rights.[42] McPherson JA made a similar point in *Equuscorp Pty Ltd v Glengallan Investments Pty Ltd*,[43] with reference to the tentative remarks of the High Court in that case. This perspective is also consistent with Viscount Sumner's analysis of the indemnity in issue in *Great Western Railway Co v J Durnford and Son Ltd*.[44] The indemnity was not a matter of defence, per se, though it might have provided the basis for a counterclaim by the indemnified party.

---

[33] *Farstad Supply AS v Enviroco Ltd (The Far Service)* [2010] UKSC 18; [2010] 2 Lloyd's Rep 387, [25]. As to other factors in that case, see [8–5].

[34] A point acknowledged by Lord Clarke: *Farstad Supply AS v Enviroco Ltd (The Far Service)* [2010] UKSC 18; [2010] 2 Lloyd's Rep 387, [26]–[27]. See generally W Courtney, 'Indemnities, Exclusions and Contribution' [2011] *Lloyd's Maritime and Commercial Law Quarterly* 339.

[35] *cf Hill v Allen* (1837) 2 M & W 283, 285; 150 ER 763, 764 (Parke B).

[36] See generally *Westina Corp Pty Ltd v BGC Contracting Pty Ltd* [2009] WASCA 213; (2009) 41 WAR 263, [51] (Buss JA).

[37] *Equuscorp Pty Ltd v Glengallan Investments Pty Ltd* [2004] HCA 55; (2004) 218 CLR 471.

[38] *Equuscorp Pty Ltd v Glengallan Investments Pty Ltd* [2004] HCA 55; (2004) 218 CLR 471, [30].

[39] *Rodgers v Rodgers* [1970] 1 NSWR 666 (SC). See also *In the Marriage of Burge* (1985) 10 Fam LR 514 (Fam CA).

[40] *Rodgers v Rodgers* [1970] 1 NSWR 666 (SC), 672.

[41] As existed in *Qantas Airways Ltd v Aravco Ltd* (1996) 185 CLR 43.

[42] *Rodgers v Rodgers* [1970] 1 NSWR 666 (SC), 672.

[43] *Equuscorp Pty Ltd v Glengallan Investments Pty Ltd* [2006] QCA 194, [12]–[13].

[44] *Great Western Railway Co v J Durnford and Son Ltd* (1928) 44 TLR 415 (HL), 416. See further [8–15].

Method of Indemnification

[8–13] General. Two of the four constructions considered above, namely, exclusion and release, can be omitted from consideration as they essentially involve no executory obligation on the part of the indemnifier. The remaining two constructions do raise the issue of performance but, in this context, that issue is trite or unreal.[45] This is because the indemnified party in practice invokes the indemnity as a defensive measure.

If the promise of indemnity is construed to be equivalent to, or as importing, a promise by the indemnifier not to sue the indemnified party, then it is performed by the indemnifier refraining from action. If the promise of indemnity is given one of the usual constructions, the method of performance will depend upon whether it is preventive or compensatory in nature. For a preventive indemnity, the indemnifier can abandon a claim against the indemnified party, or refrain from enforcing a judgment. For a compensatory indemnity, the indemnifier can perform by repaying to the indemnified party the amount of any judgment recovered against it.

Enforcement

[8–14] Exculpation. The object of enforcement is, generally, to exculpate the indemnified party. The manner in which that object is achieved depends on the construction of the promise of indemnity. In the simplest case, the indemnity is construed to be an outright exclusion or release of liability. This provides a direct defence to the indemnifier's claim.[46] Alternatively, the indemnity may provide the basis of a defence for the avoidance of circuity of action, or for an order to stay the proceedings by the indemnifier.

[8–15] Defence for the avoidance of circuity of action. A promise of indemnity that covers the entirety of the indemnifier's claim against the indemnified party can provide the indemnified party with a defence for the avoidance of circuity of action.[47] The defence is founded on the equality and reciprocity of the claimant's and defendant's claims against each other. Upon the claimant succeeding against the defendant, the defendant would be entitled to recover back from the claimant the same amount by a subsequent action.[48]

---

[45] *cf Farstad Supply AS v Enviroco Ltd (The Far Service)* [2010] UKSC 18; [2010] 2 Lloyd's Rep 387, [59] (Lord Mance).

[46] See, eg, *Farstad Supply AS v Enviroco Ltd (The Far Service)* [2010] UKSC 18; [2010] 2 Lloyd's Rep 387.

[47] *Carr v Stephens* (1829) 9 B & C 758; 109 ER 281; *Connop v Levy* (1848) 11 QB 769; 16 ER 662 (both decisions cited in *Eastern Extension Australasia & China Telegraph Co Ltd v Federal Commissioner of Taxation* (1923) 33 CLR 426, 441 (Isaacs and Rich JJ)); *Bayne v Blake* (1906) 4 CLR 1, 16 (Griffith CJ) (revd without reference to this point: *Blake v Bayne* (1908) 6 CLR 179 PC); *Re Brampton and Longtown Railway Co; Shaw's Claim* (1875) LR 10 Ch App 177, 180–81 (Lord Cairns LC); *Durham Fancy Goods Ltd v Michael Jackson (Fancy Goods) Ltd* [1968] 3 WLR 225 (QB), 230; *Farstad Supply AS v Enviroco Ltd (The Far Service)* [2010] UKSC 18; [2010] 2 Lloyd's Rep 387, [30]–[31] (Lord Clarke), [59] (Lord Mance).

[48] *Walmesley v Cooper* (1839) 11 Ad & E 216; 113 ER 398; *Eastern Extension Australasia & China Telegraph Co Ltd v Federal Commissioner of Taxation* (1923) 33 CLR 426, 441 (Isaacs and Rich JJ); *Aktieselskabet Ocean v B Harding and Sons Ltd* [1928] 2 KB 371 (CA), 385 (Scrutton LJ); *The Kafiristan* [1937] P 63 (CA), 69 (Bucknill J); *Woodside Petroleum Development Pty Ltd v H&R – E&W Pty Ltd* (1999) 20 WAR 380 (FC), 402 (Ipp J).

Applied to an indemnity, the present defendant (the indemnified party) would have an action against the present claimant (the indemnifier) to recoup the amount of the judgment recovered by the claimant.

The defence can arise on either of the two usual constructions of a promise of indemnity. If the indemnity is construed as a promise to prevent loss to the indemnified party, the indemnified party's subsequent action would be one for damages for breach of the indemnity.[49] The breach occurs when the indemnified party pays the indemnifier to satisfy the judgment.[50] The amount of the indemnified party's loss is the sum paid. A compensatory construction produces essentially the same result. The indemnifier becomes liable to compensate the indemnified party for its loss sustained in paying the judgment in favour of the indemnifier. The indemnified party can recover that amount in a later action, either for damages for breach of the indemnity or, perhaps, for a sum payable under contract.

For similar reasons, at common law an absolute covenant not to sue was treated in effect as a release for the avoidance of circuity of action, and could be pleaded as a bar to the claimant's claim.[51] Thus, the defence would also be available where the indemnity is construed as, or as importing, a promise by the indemnifier not to sue the indemnified party.

Some of Viscount Sumner's remarks in *Great Western Railway Co v J Durnford and Son Ltd*[52] require further explanation in this regard. Considering the defendant's argument that the indemnity applied to claims inter partes, Viscount Sumner said that the indemnity was not a matter of defence, but of counterclaim.[53] This was a criticism of the manner in which the trial judge and the majority of the Court of Appeal had approached the issue. The trial judge's approach, which was not challenged by the majority on appeal, was to consider whether the indemnity on its proper construction was a release, in the strict sense, of the defendant's liability to the claimant. Viscount Sumner's point was that the promise of indemnity was a primary obligation that assumed an existing liability in respect of which the indemnity might be exercised.[54] This is entirely consistent with a defence based on the avoidance of circuity of action.[55]

[8–16] Limitations of defence. The defence is not available in all situations. The indemnifier's claim may comprise some losses that are within scope and some that are beyond scope. Alternatively, the indemnity may be subject to a minimum or maximum monetary limit. Assume, for example, that the indemnity protects only against claims to the extent they exceed a certain amount, £x, and that the indemnifier brings an action for larger sum, £y. The indemnified party's loss under the indemnity appears to be £$y - x$, and not £y as is necessary for the defence to apply. The defence does not assist where third parties are involved, as in *Deepak Fertilisers and Petrochemicals Corp v ICI Chemicals & Polymers Ltd.*[56]

---

[49] *Equuscorp Pty Ltd v Glengallan Investments Pty Ltd* [2006] QCA 194, [12] (McPherson JA).

[50] There might, technically, be other breaches if the indemnified party paid legal costs during the course of proceedings: see [6–24].

[51] *Ford v Beech* (1848) 11 QB 852, 871; 116 ER 693, 700; *McDermott v Black* (1940) 63 CLR 161, 176 (Starke J), 186–87 (Dixon J). See generally E Bullen and SM Leake, *Precedents of Pleadings in Personal Actions in the Superior Courts of Common Law*, 3rd edn (London, Stevens and Sons, 1868), 558–59, 670.

[52] *Great Western Railway Co v J Durnford and Son Ltd* (1928) 44 TLR 415 (HL).

[53] *Great Western Railway Co v J Durnford and Son Ltd* (1928) 44 TLR 415 (HL), 416. But *cf Bayne v Blake* (1906) 4 CLR 1, 16 (Griffith CJ) (revd without reference to this point: *Blake v Bayne* (1908) 6 CLR 179 (PC)).

[54] See also *J Durnford and Son Ltd v Great Western Railway Co* (1927) 43 TLR 679 (CA), 680 (Sargant LJ).

[55] *cf Eastern Extension Australasia & China Telegraph Co Ltd v Federal Commissioner of Taxation* (1923) 33 CLR 426, 438 (Knox CJ, Gavan Duffy and Starke JJ).

[56] *Deepak Fertilisers and Petrochemicals Corp v ICI Chemicals & Polymers Ltd* [1999] 1 Lloyd's Rep 387 (CA). See [8–10].

It will be recalled that Deepak promised to indemnify Davy and ICI against liabilities to Deepak, but that ICI was not a party to the contract. Deepak sued Davy and ICI, and ICI claimed in turn against Davy. There was no question of circuity of action between Deepak and ICI because there was no mutuality in their respective claims; nor was the case decided on the basis of a tripartite circuity from Deepak to ICI to Davy to Deepak.[57]

[8–17] Stay of proceedings by indemnifier. Before the Judicature Act reforms, a promise not to sue or a release, if given for valuable consideration, could be given effect in equity by way of an injunction restraining the claimant's action from proceeding in another court on the contrary basis.[58] That procedure, insofar as it concerned common injunctions to restrain proceedings at law, was abolished when the administration of law and equity was unified.[59] Such matters became grounds for defence or a stay of proceedings in the same court.[60]

This jurisdiction may provide the indemnified party with an alternative means of protection in circumstances where it is not possible to raise a defence based on circuity of action. It has been invoked for actions by the indemnifier against third parties where there has been an express or implied promise not to sue in addition to a promise to indemnify.[61] In *Deepak Fertilisers and Petrochemicals Corp v ICI Chemicals & Polymers Ltd,*[62] Deepak's promise to indemnify ICI against liabilities to Deepak was held to include by implication a promise by Deepak not to sue ICI. Although ICI was not a party to the contract, Davy, as the contracting party, could enforce that promise for the benefit of ICI and, indirectly, itself. Davy had a sufficient interest in enforcement because ICI's claim for indemnity against Davy was a consequence of Deepak's claim against ICI; furthermore, ICI's claim was not obviously bad. The English Court of Appeal ordered a stay of Deepak's proceedings against ICI under section 49(3) of the (then) Supreme Court Act 1981.

---

[57] cf *Aktieselskabet Ocean v B Harding and Sons Ltd* [1928] 2 KB 371 (CA), 384–85 (Scrutton LJ).
[58] See generally *Webb v Hewitt* (1857) 3 K & J 438; 69 ER 1181; *McDermott v Black* (1940) 63 CLR 161, 176–77 (Starke J), 187 (Dixon J).
[59] By Judicature Act 1873, s 24(5).
[60] See now Senior Courts Act 1981, ss 49(2), 49(3).
[61] See also [7–55].
[62] *Deepak Fertilisers and Petrochemicals Corp v ICI Chemicals & Polymers Ltd* [1999] 1 Lloyd's Rep 387 (CA).

9

Non-Performance by a Third Party

Introduction

[9–1] **Purpose of chapter.** This chapter is concerned with promises of indemnity against loss sustained by the indemnified party in a transaction with a third party. The loss is the indemnified party's failure to obtain a particular return in the transaction. The expectation of the return is usually based, directly or indirectly, on a contract between the indemnified party and the third party. The particular return may be satisfactory performance of the contract by the third party, or the achievement of an outcome that may be hoped for, but which is not promised by the third party.

Indemnities in this form are commonly used in banking or financial transactions. They may appear in 'recourse' agreements, entered into in conjunction with a principal agreement for hire-purchase or lease of chattels. They may also be used in place of, or to supplement, promises of guarantee. The distinction between a guarantee and this form of indemnity is notoriously elusive.

[9–2] **Structure of chapter.** The chapter begins with a definition of an indemnity against loss from third party non-performance. Indemnities in this form are compared with guarantees and performance bonds. The nature of the promise to indemnify is then examined. Turning to proof of loss within scope, two features of this form of indemnity require attention. Identifying the point at which loss materialises may be difficult because the loss derives from the non-occurrence of an event, namely, receipt of the expected return. Another issue parallels that which arises for indemnities against claims by or liabilities to third parties: can the indemnified party rely on a judgment against the third party, in order to establish loss as against the indemnifier? The method of indemnification is also considered briefly.

The final part of the chapter is devoted to enforcement. The indemnifier occupies a position that is, in some respects, like that of a guarantor. Where circumstances affect the principal contract, it is necessary to consider their impact on the efficacy of the indemnity. The principal contract may be void or unenforceable, or it may be effective but then discharged by later events. Assuming that the indemnity still operates, enforcement also raises questions of the assessment of loss.

Classification

Definition

[9–3] **Definition.** The expression 'indemnity against third party non-performance' is used to describe a promise of indemnity that possesses the following qualities.

(1) The scope of the indemnity covers a loss that may be sustained by the indemnified party in connection with a transaction, of an executory nature, with a third party.
(2) The transaction is, typically, embodied in an enforceable contract between the indemnified party and the third party, though it need not be so limited.
(3) The loss referred to in (1) is the failure of the indemnified party to obtain a particular return from the transaction.
(4) The particular return relates to the third party's fulfilment of the transaction. The expectation may be, for example:

    (a) that the third party will perform its obligations to the indemnified party; or
    (b) that the third party will (although under no legal obligation to do so) perform the transaction in a certain way or achieve a result that is beneficial to the indemnified party.

The first and third elements indicate that this definition is not mutually incompatible with other forms of indemnity. Where the scope of an indemnity is expressed more broadly, it may be regarded as an indemnity against third party non-performance to the extent that it fulfils the criteria described above.

All elements refer to a transaction. This encompasses obligations arising from contract and from other sources. It is, however, not limited to legally enforceable obligations. An indemnity against third party non-performance may be used in place of a guarantee for the very reason that the underlying obligation of the debtor to the indemnified creditor may be, or is, void or unenforceable. Nonetheless, the 'transaction' between the debtor and creditor provides the basis of the expectation of a particular return. For similar reasons, the description of this form of indemnity is cast in terms of 'non-performance' by a third party rather than 'breach' or 'default'. The third party's default is often the reason for the indemnified party not obtaining a particular return, but the benefit of the transaction could be lost by other forms of non-performance not amounting to default.

The third and fourth elements describe the loss as the failure to obtain a particular return expected from the transaction. This is the principal concern of this chapter, though the indemnified party may suffer other losses from the transaction with the third party. Such losses include consequential losses incurred in enforcing rights against the third party. Alternatively, the third party's non-performance may expose the indemnified party to liability to another.[1] So, for example, where A indemnifies the buyer, B, against breach by the seller, C, under a contract for the sale of goods, C's breach may expose B to liability to a sub-buyer, D. Likewise, where A indemnifies a sub-lessor, B, against default by the sub-lessee, C, in paying rent or performing the covenants in the sub-lease, C's default may expose B to liability to the superior landlord, D. If such liabilities are within scope, the

---

[1] *cf* [9–9].

indemnity can, to that extent, be treated as an indemnity against liabilities to other parties.[2]

[9–4] Other terms. For convenience and familiarity, several terms used in this chapter are borrowed from the guarantee context. The indemnified party may also be described as the 'creditor' in the transaction. This is the person to whom the relevant obligations are, or are intended to be, owed, and who is to benefit from fulfilment of the transaction. The term 'debtor' has a corresponding meaning; the debtor is often not a party to the contract of indemnity. These terms are apt to describe obligations to pay money but they should be understood in this chapter as applying generally to other types of obligation. They are also used even where there is, strictly, no legally enforceable obligation of the debtor to the creditor.

The terms 'principal obligations' or 'principal contract' are used to describe the obligations of the debtor to the creditor, which are the subject of the indemnity. The indemnity is, in a general sense, ancillary or accessory to the main transaction. The terms are not intended to invoke the technical distinction, which is sometimes drawn, between a primary obligation and a collateral or secondary obligation in the nature of a guarantee.[3]

Illustrations

[9–5] Identification of the activating event or circumstances. There are many variations that meet the definition of an indemnity against third party non-performance. Three basic forms that commonly appear are as follows.

(1) Indemnities that are expressed to apply to loss arising due to the debtor's breach or default in relation to the indemnified creditor.

(2) Indemnities that refer, additionally or alternatively, to loss due to non-performance or unenforceability of the principal contract.

For these two forms of indemnity, the particular return expected from the transaction is generally fixed by reference to the performance specified by the principal contract.

(3) Indemnities that are expressed to cover loss by reference to a state of affairs that is not the subject of any promise by the debtor. The loss may be, for example, the indemnified creditor's failure to receive a nominated benefit which the debtor could elect to provide, though it has not undertaken to do so.

[9–6] Indemnity against breach or default. In a typical case, the indemnifier promises to indemnify the creditor against loss arising from the debtor's breach of a contract with the creditor. Such promises most closely resemble guarantees because they are solely engaged by the debtor's default in performing obligations to the creditor. Even so, the promise may retain its distinct character as an indemnity. In *Anglomar Shipping Co Ltd v Swan Hunter Shipbuilders Ltd (The London Lion)*,[4] there was a shipbuilding contract and a collateral contract under which the parent company of the shipbuilder promised to indemnify the buyer against 'all losses damages expenses or otherwise which you may incur by reason of any

---

[2] See generally ch 6.
[3] See [9–12].
[4] *Anglomar Shipping Co Ltd v Swan Hunter Shipbuilders Ltd (The London Lion)* [1980] 2 Lloyd's Rep 456 (CA).

such default by [the shipbuilder] in performing and observing its obligations under the said Contract'. The effect of that drafting was that the respective liabilities of the shipbuilder and the parent company to the buyer were not co-extensive. The parent company could be liable under the indemnity for the buyer's loss even though, in respect of the same default, the shipbuilder could rely on an exclusion or limitation clause in the shipbuilding contract.

[9–7] Indemnity against non-performance or unenforceable contract. This form of indemnity is commonly used in connection with leases, or loans or other credit facilities. The clause may refer to non-performance or unenforceability of the principal contract in addition, or as an alternative, to breach or default by the debtor. So, for example, in *McGuinness v Norwich and Peterborough Building Society*,[5] clause 2.4 of the guarantee provided:

> As a separate obligation you agree to make good (in full) any losses or expenses that we may incur if the Borrower fails to pay any money owed to us, or fails to satisfy any other liabilities to us, or if we are unable to enforce any of the Borrower's obligations to us or they are not legally binding on the borrower (whatever the reason).

The indemnity may still apply even though the debtor's failure to perform does not constitute a breach of contract. This characteristic may be important where it is contemplated that the principal contract is or might be void or unenforceable, or where the debtor, without default, has been discharged from performance of the principal contract.

[9–8] Indemnity based on uncovenanted state of affairs. Indemnities in this form can be found in decisions on recourse agreements associated with hire-purchase contracts. In *Goulston Discount Co Ltd v Clark*,[6] for example, a recourse agreement between a motor dealer and finance company provided that the dealer would indemnify the finance company against any loss suffered 'by reason of the fact that the hirer under the said agreement for any cause whatsoever does not pay the amounts which he would if he completed his agreement by exercising the option to purchase'. The recourse agreement went on to define loss as 'the total amount the hirer would have had to pay to acquire title to the goods under the hire-purchase agreement', together with the finance company's expenses, less payments received. Thus, the particular return under the indemnity was fixed by reference to an event – the purchase of the motor vehicle – that was not promised by the hirer. The definition also avoided reference to the hirer's liability for breach of the hire-purchase agreement. This was significant in the circumstances, because the finance company was able to obtain under the indemnity an amount that was substantially greater than the sum recoverable from the hirer.[7]

[9–9] Indemnity against liability related to non-performance. Under this type of indemnity, the *indemnified party* agrees to become responsible to the creditor in respect of the debtor's performance, in return for the promise of indemnity. The operation of the indemnity does, in a sense, depend on default by the debtor. But the indemnity is in substance

---

[5] *McGuinness v Norwich and Peterborough Building Society* [2011] EWCA Civ 1286; [2012] 2 All ER (Comm) 265.
[6] *Goulston Discount Co Ltd v Clark* [1967] 2 QB 493 (CA). See also *Yeoman Credit Ltd v Latter* [1961] 1 WLR 828 (CA); *Bowmaker (Commercial) Ltd v Smith* [1965] 1 WLR 855 (CA); *Direct Acceptance Finance Ltd v Cumberland Furnishing Pty Ltd* [1965] NSWR 1504 (FC).
[7] Contrast *Western Credit Ltd v Alberry* [1964] 1 WLR 945 (CA) (recourse agreement in form of guarantee).

concerned with the indemnified party's liability to the creditor, not loss due to the debtor's failure to render performance to the indemnified party.[8] It is an indemnity against liability.

A simple tripartite example is an express or implied counter-indemnity from a debtor to a person who assumes liability to the creditor in relation to the debtor's performance.[9] That assumption of liability may occur by way of a guarantee,[10] indemnity[11] or perform-ance bond[12] to the creditor. There are also quadripartite situations, in which the indemni-fier is a person other than the principal debtor.[13] In *Thomas v Cook*,[14] a bond of indemnity was given by three parties, two of whom joined the bond only as guarantors. An indemnity from one of the co-guarantors to the other against the liability on the bond was held to be outside section 4 of the Statute of Frauds 1677. Although that liability would be enlivened by a default by the principal obligor, it was not a promise by the former co-guarantor to answer to the creditor for that default.[15] A more recent illustration is *Total Oil Products (Australia) Pty Ltd v Robinson*.[16] B, the purchaser of the business of a company, C, and associated land, provided a limited guarantee of C's indebtedness to a bank. In return, A, the company's shareholders and directors, promised to indemnify B against loss sustained if B was called upon as guarantor to pay the bank following C's default. A's promise was held to be an indemnity and not a guarantee. As Asprey JA explained:[17]

> There was no party other than [A] responsible to [B] for the payment of that 'loss' . . . [T]here was no secondary liability in respect of that obligation which was entered into in the expectation that [C] would not be able to meet its indebtedness to the . . . bank.

Comparison with Similar Legal Relationships

Guarantees

[9–10] **General.** The distinction between a guarantee and an indemnity against third party non-performance is surprisingly difficult to articulate, despite being well-trodden ground.

---

[8] *cf* [9–15].

[9] An analogous situation is where the continuing partners in a partnership agree with a departing partner to be solely responsible for the partnership debts and to indemnify the departing partner against them: see, eg, *Rouse v Bradford Banking Co Ltd* [1894] AC 586 (HL); *Bradford v Gammon* [1925] Ch 132 (Ch).

[10] See also [2–24] (implied indemnity to guarantor).

[11] *cf MMI General Insurance Ltd v Copeland* [2000] NSWSC 317. See also JC Phillips, *The Modern Contract of Guarantee*, 2nd English edn (London, Sweet & Maxwell, 2010), 741–42, paras 12-23–12-25.

[12] Such arrangements are usually express. As to implied indemnities, see *IIG Capital LLC v Van Der Merwe* [2008] EWCA Civ 542; [2008] 2 Lloyd's Rep 187, [25]–[27] (Waller LJ) and *cf North Shore Ventures Ltd v Anstead Holdings Inc* [2011] EWCA Civ 230; [2012] Ch 31, [65]–[66] (Tomlinson LJ).

[13] *Thomas v Cook* (1828) 8 B & C 728; 108 ER 1213; *Hodgson v Hodgson* (1837) 2 Keen 704; 48 ER 800; *Wooldridge v Norris* (1868) LR 6 Eq 410; *Wildes v Dudlow* (1874) LR 19 Eq 198; *Total Oil Products (Australia) Pty Ltd v Robinson* [1970] 1 NSWR 701 (CA); *Argo Caribbean Group Ltd v Lewis* [1976] 2 Lloyd's Rep 289 (CA); *General Surety & Guarantee Co Ltd v Francis Parker Ltd* (1977) 6 BLR 16 (QB); *Agnes & Jennie Mining Co Ltd v Zen* (1982) 38 BCLR 385 (CA). *cf* the more complex arrangements in *Ibrahim v Barclays Bank plc* [2012] EWCA Civ 640; [2013] Ch 400, [7].

[14] *Thomas v Cook* (1828) 8 B & C 728; 108 ER 1213.

[15] Another interpretation of the case is that, as the co-guarantor was also liable, it was not a promise to answer for the default of *another* person: EC Arnold, 'Indemnity Contracts and the Statute of Frauds' (1925) 9 *Minnesota Law Review* 401, 404–05.

[16] *Total Oil Products (Australia) Pty Ltd v Robinson* [1970] 1 NSWR 701 (CA).

[17] *Total Oil Products (Australia) Pty Ltd v Robinson* [1970] 1 NSWR 701 (CA), 704.

In *Yeoman Credit Ltd v Latter*,[18] Harman LJ described the distinction as a 'most barren controversy' which had 'raised many hair-splitting distinctions of exactly that kind which brings the law into hatred, ridicule and contempt'. The distinction is usually made for one of two reasons. First, there is the statutory requirement of writing, imposed by section 4 of the Statute of Frauds 1677. Secondly, a recognised incident or characteristic of a contract of guarantee may be relied upon by one of the parties. Guarantees are associated with the principle of co-extensiveness and are subject to principles governing the discharge of the guarantor in certain circumstances. A promise of indemnity is a different juristic construct and does not possess all of the same characteristics.

Harman LJ's criticism may be well directed at the statutory requirement of writing.[19] There is, however, substance in the distinction as it relates to recognised characteristics of promises of guarantee or indemnity.[20] Its significance is lessened in practice owing to modern drafting techniques, which often purport to exclude the discharge rules applicable to guarantees, and combine a promise of guarantee and a promise of indemnity in the same instrument. Furthermore, it has repeatedly been emphasised that the task of the court is to construe the particular document before it. The parties are free to arrive at whatever agreement they please and a contract should not be forced into a particular category, so as then to impose upon it the recognised incidents of a contract of that type.[21] Accordingly, there are arrangements that, although performing a function similar to indemnities or guarantees, cannot be classified as either.[22] The possibility of a promise that is a hybrid of a guarantee and indemnity has also been acknowledged.[23]

[9–11] Comparison of definitions. Indemnity is a more general concept than guarantee. Thus, a contract of guarantee has been described as a type of contract of indemnity, in the broad sense that the promisor undertakes to protect the creditor against loss in its transaction with the debtor.[24] In *Yeoman Credit Ltd v Latter*,[25] Holroyd Pearce LJ observed that the object of the clause there in issue was to ensure that the claimant recovered, with profit, the money that it had expended in the transaction. He continued: 'that ultimate object is shared by guarantee and indemnity alike. It is the method by which that object is attained which decides the class to which the document belongs'.[26]

A more specific formulation is necessary. A guarantee may be described as a collateral contract to answer for the debt, default or miscarriage of another who is, or is to become, liable to the person to whom the guarantee is given.[27] Two common forms are: (1) a promise to

---

[18] *Yeoman Credit Ltd v Latter* [1961] 1 WLR 828 (CA), 835.

[19] cf *Actionstrength Ltd v International Glass Engineering IN.GLEN SpA* [2003] UKHL 17; [2003] 2 AC 541, [6]–[7] (Lord Bingham), [19]–[20] (Lord Hoffmann).

[20] *Scottish & Newcastle plc v Raguz* [2003] EWCA Civ 1070; [2004] L & TR 11, [8] (Morritt VC).

[21] *Moschi v Lep Air Services Ltd* [1973] AC 331 (HL), 344 (Lord Reid); *Ankar Pty Ltd v National Westminster Finance (Australia) Ltd* (1987) 162 CLR 549, 571 (Deane J); *Alfred McAlpine Construction Ltd v Unex Corp Ltd* (1994) 70 BLR 26 (CA), 33 (Evans LJ).

[22] See [9–24], [9–25] (performance bonds).

[23] *General Surety & Guarantee Co Ltd v Francis Parker Ltd* (1977) 6 BLR 16 (QB), 21.

[24] *Commercial Bank of Australia Ltd v Colonial Finance, Mortgage, Investment and Guarantee Corp Ltd* (1906) 4 CLR 57, 68 (O'Connor J); *Yeoman Credit Ltd v Latter* [1961] 1 WLR 828 (CA), 830 (Holroyd Pearce LJ); *Pitts v Jones* [2007] EWCA Civ 1301; [2008] QB 706, [21] (Smith LJ); *Bofinger v Kingsway Group Ltd* [2009] HCA 44; (2009) 239 CLR 269, [7]; *Vossloh AG v Alpha Trains (UK) Ltd* [2010] EWHC 2443 (Ch); [2011] 2 All ER (Comm) 307, [25].

[25] *Yeoman Credit Ltd v Latter* [1961] 1 WLR 828 (CA).

[26] *Yeoman Credit Ltd v Latter* [1961] 1 WLR 828 (CA), 831.

[27] *Re Conley* [1938] 2 All ER 127 (CA), 130–31 (Greene MR); *Jowitt v Callaghan* (1938) 38 SR (NSW) 512 (FC), 516–17 (Jordan CJ); *Sunbird Plaza Pty Ltd v Maloney* (1988) 166 CLR 245, 254 (Mason CJ).

ensure that the debtor will perform its obligations; and (2) a conditional promise that the guarantor will perform if the debtor does not.[28] In contrast, an indemnity is a promise to protect the indemnified party – the creditor – against loss in the transaction with the debtor. There is, however, a parallel between these two common types of guarantee and the two common constructions of an indemnity.

Consider a promise by A to indemnify B against C's default, where the relevant loss to B is the failure to receive the promised performance from C. If the indemnity is construed as a promise by A to prevent loss to B, and the circumstances are such that B will realise a loss immediately upon C's default,[29] then the indemnity effectively requires A to avert C's default. The promise is not easily distinguished in effect from a promise by A that C will perform,[30] one of the common types of guarantee. Alternatively, the indemnity may be construed as a promise by A to compensate B for loss from C's default. Where C's obligation is to pay money to B, then B is likely to suffer a loss at least equal to the sum not paid by C. The indemnity may, in effect, require A to pay B the specified amount if C does not. This resembles the other common type of guarantee.

[9–12] Essential difference between guarantee and indemnity. Guarantees and indemnities are often distinguished by emphasising the 'collateral' or 'secondary'[31] liability of a guarantor compared to the 'original',[32] 'primary'[33] or 'ultimate'[34] liability of an indemnifier. Alternatively, it is said that the liability of an indemnifier, unlike that of a guarantor, is independent of, or has no reference to, the debtor's liability.[35] Such statements indicate that the guarantor's obligation is related to that of the debtor in a way that an indemnifier's obligation is not. The difficulty lies in identifying the nature of that relationship.

At a theoretical level, the distinction lies in the essential concern of each promise. A guarantee is, fundamentally, concerned with responsibility for the debtor's performance of a legal obligation to the creditor. For that reason the guarantor's obligation is, in general, dependent upon the obligation of the debtor. The central concern of an indemnity is not, strictly, the debtor's performance or non-performance of a legal obligation. It is the loss to the creditor that results from the debtor's failure to perform in the transaction. Such non-performance (whether or not it amounts to a default) is simply an activating event like any other specified in the scope of an indemnity. It is one of the elements that demarcates recoverable losses from other losses. From that perspective, it can be seen that the promise of indemnity does not depend on any legally effective obligation of the debtor. The indemnity

---

[28] *Moschi v Lep Air Services Ltd* [1973] AC 331 (HL), 344–45 (Lord Reid), *cf* 348–49 (Lord Diplock); *Hyundai Heavy Industries Co Ltd v Papadopoulos* [1980] 1 WLR 1129 (HL), 1150–51 (Lord Fraser); *Sunbird Plaza Pty Ltd v Maloney* (1988) 166 CLR 245, 256 (Mason CJ). *cf Trafalgar House Construction (Regions) Ltd v General Surety & Guarantee Co Ltd* [1996] AC 199 (HL), 205 (Lord Jauncey).

[29] This is not always the case: see [9–29].

[30] *cf McGuinness v Norwich and Peterborough Building Society* [2011] EWCA Civ 1286; [2012] 2 All ER (Comm) 265, [8], [59] (Patten LJ).

[31] *Lakeman v Mountstephen* (1874) LR 7 HL 17, 24 (Lord Selborne).

[32] *Harburg India Rubber Comb Co v Martin* [1902] 1 KB 778 (CA), 785 (Vaughan Williams LJ).

[33] *Yeoman Credit Ltd v Latter* [1961] 1 WLR 828 (CA), 834 (Holroyd Pearce LJ); *Argo Caribbean Group Ltd v Lewis* [1976] 2 Lloyd's Rep 289 (CA), 296; *Citicorp Australia Ltd v Hendry* (1985) 4 NSWLR 1 (SC), 15 (Clarke J); *Re Taylor, ex p Century 21 Real Estate Corp* (1995) 130 ALR 723 (FCA), 727–28; *Associated British Ports v Ferryways NV* [2009] EWCA Civ 189; [2009] 1 Lloyd's Rep 595, [1] (Kay LJ).

[34] *Sunbird Plaza Pty Ltd v Maloney* (1988) 166 CLR 245, 254 (Mason CJ).

[35] *Harburg India Rubber Comb Co v Martin* [1902] 1 KB 778 (CA), 785 (Vaughan Williams LJ); *Clipper Maritime Ltd v Shirlstar Container Transport Ltd (The Anemone)* [1987] 1 Lloyd's Rep 546 (QB), 555; *Scottish & Newcastle plc v Raguz* [2003] EWCA Civ 1070; [2004] L & TR 11, [8] (Morritt VC); *Vossloh AG v Alpha Trains (UK) Ltd* [2010] EWHC 2443 (Ch); [2011] 2 All ER (Comm) 307, [25]–[26].

is valid in principle, though its *operation* may be dependent upon the debtor's obligation. An indemnity expressed to apply to 'breach' by the debtor, or the debtor's failure to pay 'money due', for example, presumes that the debtor is under a legal obligation to perform. If there is no such obligation, there may be no relevant loss to the creditor within the scope of the indemnity.

[9–13] **Approach to classification.** Whether a promise is one of indemnity or guarantee is ultimately determined by construction.[36] The classification is a matter of substance not form.[37] The description applied by the parties to their contract is a relevant consideration but not conclusive.[38] A document that is labelled as a 'guarantee' or that uses the terms 'guarantee' or 'guarantor' may be an indemnity.[39] Conversely, a document that is labelled as an 'indemnity' or uses the term 'indemnify' may still be a guarantee.[40]

The promise can sometimes be classified simply as a matter of definition, because it lacks a characteristic essential to a guarantee but not an indemnity, or vice versa. In other cases, a more sophisticated approach is required. A common technique is to compare the effect of the promise in various circumstances with the incidents typically expected of a promise of indemnity or guarantee.

[9–14] **Reliance on cases on the statutory requirement of writing.** Much consideration of the distinction between guarantees and indemnities has occurred in relation to the application of section 4 of the Statute of Frauds 1677 or derivative provisions in other jurisdictions. That distinction has been used as a shorthand way of indicating whether a particular arrangement falls within the section: if it is a 'guarantee', it does; if it is an 'indemnity', it does not.[41] It is not necessary here to consider all of the cases in detail. It suffices to note that they must be used cautiously as guides to determine the nature of a particular promise. The scope of the statute does not coincide exactly with the distinction between a promise of guarantee and a promise of indemnity.

Although a guarantee can be described as a promise to answer for a debt, default or miscarriage of another person, not all guarantees are within the statute.[42] Exceptions are made, for example, for some transactions in which the guarantor is concerned to relieve property

---

[36] *Moschi v Lep Air Services Ltd* [1973] AC 331 (HL), 349 (Lord Diplock); *Re Taylor, ex p Century 21 Real Estate Corp* (1995) 130 ALR 723 (FCA), 726–27; *Associated British Ports v Ferryways NV* [2009] EWCA Civ 189; [2009] 1 Lloyd's Rep 595, [9], (Kay LJ); *McIntosh v Linke Nominees Pty Ltd* [2008] QCA 275, [25] (Muir JA); *Vossloh AG v Alpha Trains (UK) Ltd* [2010] EWHC 2443 (Ch); [2011] 2 All ER (Comm) 307, [20], [27].

[37] *Harburg India Rubber Comb Co v Martin* [1902] 1 KB 778 (CA), 784 (Vaughan Williams LJ); *Actionstrength Ltd v International Glass Engineering IN.GLEN SpA* [2001] EWCA Civ 1477; [2002] 1 WLR 566, [13], [21] (Simon Brown LJ).

[38] *Western Credit Ltd v Alberry* [1964] 1 WLR 945 (CA), 949 (Davies LJ); *Total Oil Products (Australia) Pty Ltd v Robinson* [1970] 1 NSWR 701 (CA), 703 (Asprey JA); *Moschi v Lep Air Services Ltd* [1973] AC 331 (HL), 349 (Lord Diplock); *Housing Guarantee Fund Ltd v Johnson* (1995) V Conv R 54-524 (FC), 66,227 (JD Phillips J); *McIntosh v Linke Nominees Pty Ltd* [2008] QCA 275, [25] (Muir JA).

[39] *Muhammad Issa El Sheikh Ahmad v Ali* [1947] AC 414 (PC), 426; *Pao On v Lau Yiu Long* [1980] AC 614 (PC), 621–22; *Alfred McAlpine Construction Ltd v Unex Corp Ltd* (1994) 70 BLR 26 (CA), 33 (Evans LJ), 41 (Glidewell LJ).

[40] *Unity Finance Ltd v Woodcock* [1963] 1 WLR 455 (CA); *Western Credit Ltd v Alberry* [1964] 1 WLR 945 (CA); *Stadium Finance Co Ltd v Helm* (1965) 109 SJ 471 (CA); *Re Taylor, ex p Century 21 Real Estate Corp* (1995) 130 ALR 723 (FCA), 727–28.

[41] *Sutton & Co v Grey* [1894] 1 QB 285 (CA), 287–88 (Lord Esher MR); *Sunbird Plaza Pty Ltd v Maloney* (1988) 166 CLR 245, 254 (Mason CJ); *Pitts v Jones* [2007] EWCA Civ 1301; [2008] QB 706, [21] (Smith LJ); *Associated British Ports v Ferryways NV* [2009] EWCA Civ 189; [2009] 1 Lloyd's Rep 595, [1] (Kay LJ). *cf Harburg India Rubber Comb Co v Martin* [1902] 1 KB 778 (CA), 784–85 (Vaughan Williams LJ). See further [5–4].

[42] For a detailed discussion, see Phillips, *The Modern Contract of Guarantee* (n 11), 108–14, paras 3-29–3-43.

in which it has a legal or equitable interest from some claim or liability;[43] or for transactions whose central object is not to guarantee the debtor's obligations to the creditor.[44] The object of the transaction is distinct from the means by which that object is accomplished. The application of this criterion plainly does not indicate whether the essential promise is one of indemnity or guarantee. On rare occasions, promises of indemnity have been held to be within the section.[45] It has also been said in this context that all guarantees are, in a sense, contracts of indemnity.[46] From that perspective, the relevant distinction is not between a contract of guarantee or indemnity, but between different types of contracts of 'indemnity'.

Finally, the classifications of guarantee or indemnity are not exhaustive of all possibilities. A promise may be outside the statute and yet not an indemnity, as in the case of a promise to the debtor to pay the debt due to the creditor.[47]

[9–15] Arrangement of obligations. A point of distinction may be the promisee's position in the arrangement of obligations that are the subject of the promise. The essence of a guarantee is a promise by the guarantor, A, to the creditor, B, in respect of some obligation C owes, or is to owe, to B. In other cases, A promises to protect B against a liability to C, the liability arising upon the default of A or another, D, in performing some obligation owed to C.[48] B is a debtor to C, not a creditor of C. Even where D is involved, A's promise concerns D's performance to C, not B. A's promise is not a guarantee in either respect.

This distinction does not assist, however, where the pattern of obligations is the same as that for guarantees, namely, where A promises to indemnify B against C's default in performing obligations owed to B.

[9–16] Whether promise activated by default. The promise will generally not be a guarantee if the promisor is liable even without default by the debtor.[49] In *Guild & Co v Conrad*,[50] the defendant orally promised to indemnify the claimant against liability as acceptor on certain bills of exchange drawn by another firm. Lindley LJ said, of the promise in question: 'if it was a promise to pay if the Demerara firm did not pay, then it is void under the Statute of Frauds as not being in writing. But if, on the other hand, it was a promise to put the plaintiff in funds in any event, then it is not such a promise as is within the Statute of Frauds'.[51] The promise was held to be of the latter kind. The same point can be seen in hire-purchase cases where the amount of the indemnity is fixed by reference to the hirer's exercise of the option to purchase the goods. A hirer, of course, commits no breach by failing to do so.

---

[43] *Fitzgerald v Dressler* (1859) 7 CBNS 374; 141 ER 861; *Harburg India Rubber Comb Co v Martin* [1902] 1 KB 778 (CA), 784 (Vaughan Williams LJ), 791 (Stirling LJ), 792–93 (Cozens-Hardy LJ); *Marginson v Ian Potter & Co* (1976) 136 CLR 161.

[44] *Sutton & Co v Grey* [1894] 1 QB 285 (CA), 288 (Lord Esher MR), 291 (Kay LJ); *Harburg India Rubber Comb Co v Martin* [1902] 1 KB 778 (CA), 786–87 (Vaughan Williams LJ); *Pitts v Jones* [2007] EWCA Civ 1301; [2008] QB 706, [32], [38] (Smith LJ).

[45] See further [5–6].

[46] *Harburg India Rubber Comb Co v Martin* [1902] 1 KB 778 (CA), 784–85 (Vaughan Williams LJ); *Pitts v Jones* [2007] EWCA Civ 1301; [2008] QB 706, [21] (Smith LJ).

[47] *Eastwood v Kenyon* (1840) 11 Ad & E 438; 113 ER 482.

[48] See [9–9], [5–5].

[49] *Yeoman Credit Ltd v Latter* [1961] 1 WLR 828 (CA), 832–33 (Holroyd Pearce LJ); *Unity Finance Ltd v Woodcock* [1963] 1 WLR 455 (CA), 461 (Lord Denning MR) (pro tanto); *Direct Acceptance Finance Ltd v Cumberland Furnishing Pty Ltd* [1965] NSWR 1504 (FC), 1508–09 (Walsh J).

[50] *Guild & Co v Conrad* [1894] 2 QB 885 (CA).

[51] *Guild & Co v Conrad* [1894] 2 QB 885 (CA), 892.

More difficult is the situation where the promise expressly refers to default by the debtor. This factor influenced the classification of a clause in *Re Taylor, ex p Century 21 Real Estate Corp.*[52] At issue was the construction of a document that purported to provide a guarantee and indemnity in respect of a borrower's obligations under a promissory note. Clause 1 of the document contained an unconditional guarantee. In clause 2, expressed as a 'separate and severable covenant', the promisors agreed to indemnify the lender against damages and losses arising as a consequence of the borrower failing to discharge its obligations under the promissory note. Burchett J was inclined to construe clause 2 as a guarantee. He remarked:[53]

> [t]he word 'indemnify' is used, but the obligation is only to attach in the event of a failure by [the borrower] to discharge its obligations. This looks very like the language of a collateral contract to answer for the default of another.

A promise should not, however, be classified as a guarantee rather than an indemnity only because it is activated by the debtor's default. Other considerations are relevant, such as whether the promisor's liability upon the debtor's default is co-extensive with that of the debtor. Moreover, the practice of incorporating distinct promises of guarantee and indemnity in the same document is well established.

[9–17] Difference in extent of liability. Where the extent of the promisor's liability to the creditor differs from that of the debtor, this counts against classification of the promise as a guarantee.[54] This reflects a *modus tollens* logical inference, based on the premise that the principle of co-extensiveness applies to guarantees.[55] In contrast, no such principle applies generally to indemnities.[56]

The debtor may not be liable to the creditor because the principal transaction is void or unenforceable. If, generally, this has the consequence that a guarantee would also be ineffective, the purpose of the arrangement might be upheld by characterising the promise as an indemnity.[57] Thus, in *Yeoman Credit Ltd v Latter*,[58] Holroyd Pearce LJ referred to the fact that the debtor was an infant and that it would have been unlikely for the parties to guarantee obligations under a contract that was void by statute. Alternatively, the principal contract may be valid and enforceable, but the debtor and promisor liable to the creditor for different amounts in different circumstances. In *Anglomar Shipping Co Ltd v Swan Hunter Shipbuilders Ltd (The London Lion)*,[59] the buyer of the vessel was secured against loss from the shipbuilder's breach of contract, even where the shipbuilder could have relied upon an exclusion or limitation clause in that contract. In *Goulston Discount Co Ltd v*

---

[52] *Re Taylor, ex p Century 21 Real Estate Corp* (1995) 130 ALR 723 (FCA).

[53] *Re Taylor, ex p Century 21 Real Estate Corp* (1995) 130 ALR 723 (FCA), 727–28.

[54] *Yeoman Credit Ltd v Latter* [1961] 1 WLR 828 (CA), 832–33 (Holroyd Pearce LJ), 836 (Harman LJ); *Western Credit Ltd v Alberry* [1964] 1 WLR 945 (CA), 952 (Russell LJ); *Direct Acceptance Finance Ltd v Cumberland Furnishing Pty Ltd* [1965] NSWR 1504 (FC), 1509–10 (Walsh J).

[55] But see *Hyundai Heavy Industries Co Ltd v Papadopoulos* [1980] 1 WLR 1129 (HL), 1137 (Viscount Dilhorne), 1144 (Lord Edmund-Davies), 1151–52 (Lord Fraser).

[56] In addition to the cases referred to in the text, see *Communities Economic Development Fund v Canadian Pickles Corp* [1991] 3 SCR 388, 413; *Vossloh AG v Alpha Trains (UK) Ltd* [2010] EWHC 2443 (Ch); [2011] 2 All ER (Comm) 307, [26]. But an indemnity is not *necessarily* different in extent: *Peters v NZHB Holdings Ltd* [2004] NZCA 245, [22]; *Carey Value Added SL v Grupo Urvasco SA* [2010] EWHC 1905 (Comm); [2011] 2 All ER (Comm) 140, [37] (express provision as to quantification under indemnity).

[57] See further [9–41].

[58] *Yeoman Credit Ltd v Latter* [1961] 1 WLR 828 (CA), 833, but contrast 837 (Davies LJ).

[59] *Anglomar Shipping Co Ltd v Swan Hunter Shipbuilders Ltd (The London Lion)* [1980] 2 Lloyd's Rep 456 (CA).

Clark,[60] the hirer's liability under the hire-purchase contract in the circumstances was less than half that of the dealer under the recourse agreement with the finance company. In each case, the promise was an indemnity.

[9–18] Promise to some of joint creditors. In *Re Hoyle*,[61] a partner, A, made a promise to be responsible for a debt owed by A's son to the firm, comprising A, B and C. It was held that there was a sufficient record of the promise to satisfy the statutory requirement of writing. An alternative basis for decision, endorsed by Bowen LJ and Lindley LJ, was that the promise was outside the statute because it was an indemnity, namely, a promise by A to indemnify B and C against his son's failure to pay the debt to the firm. The reason for construing A's promise as being made to B and C only, and not A, B and C as the firm, is clear enough: the latter would have been ineffective at law as a promise made to joint promisees including the promisor.[62] The reason given by Bowen LJ for construing the promise as an indemnity and not a guarantee appears to have turned on the technical point of the indivisibility of A, B and C as the proper creditors.[63] A's promise to B and C alone was not made to the creditor who could bring an action for the debt.

[9–19] Displacement of recognised incidents. Clauses that modify or displace the usual incidents of a guarantee are commonplace in modern contracts. One example is a clause that preserves the liability of the guarantor when it would otherwise be discharged at law by events such as a variation of the principal contract, or the creditor allowing time to the debtor. The presence of such clauses has sometimes been considered to support the conclusion that the promise is one of guarantee and not indemnity.[64] There are, usually, three elements to that reasoning. First, the quality or incident which is sought to be modified or displaced is one that applies to a guarantee. Secondly, the same quality or incident does not apply for an indemnity. Thirdly, the parties have intended to modify an underlying promise of guarantee. The final element may be inferred from the preceding two. That inference is, with respect, less than compelling. The first two elements can also be consistent with an intention to create a fundamentally different promise, such as an indemnity.[65]

Clement v Clement[66] illustrates the interplay between these elements. The defendant gave a letter to the claimants which, in terms, purported to guarantee payment of a pension by a company to the claimants. Part of the letter stated: 'For the purposes of this guarantee the liability of the Company shall not be affected by any restriction modification or variation of the sums covenanted to be paid by it'. The defendant argued that the letter was a guarantee,

[60] *Goulston Discount Co Ltd v Clark* [1967] 2 QB 493 (CA). cf *Yeoman Credit Ltd v Latter* [1961] 1 WLR 828 (CA), 832–33 (Holroyd Pearce LJ), 836 (Harman LJ).

[61] *Re Hoyle; Hoyle v Hoyle* [1893] 1 Ch 84 (CA).

[62] *De Tastet v Shaw* (1818) 1 B & Ald 664; 106 ER 244; *Ellis v Kerr* [1910] 1 Ch 529 (Ch). See now Law of Property Act 1925, s 82.

[63] *Re Hoyle; Hoyle v Hoyle* [1893] 1 Ch 84 (CA), 99.

[64] See, eg, *Western Credit Ltd v Alberry* [1964] 1 WLR 945 (CA), 950 (Davies LJ); *Stadium Finance Co Ltd v Helm* (1965) 109 SJ 471 (CA), 471 (Lord Denning MR); *Vossloh AG v Alpha Trains (UK) Ltd* [2010] EWHC 2443 (Ch); [2011] 2 All ER (Comm) 307, [27]. cf *Trafalgar House Construction (Regions) Ltd v General Surety & Guarantee Co Ltd* [1996] AC 199 (HL), 205–06 (Lord Jauncey); *Gold Coast Ltd v Caja De Ahorros Del Mediterraneo* [2001] EWCA Civ 1806; [2002] 1 Lloyd's Rep 617, [25] (Tuckey LJ) (distinction between guarantee and performance bond). cf also *Associated British Ports v Ferryways NV* [2009] EWCA Civ 189; [2009] 1 Lloyd's Rep 595, [12] (Kay LJ) (absence of usual protective clause 'at best neutral').

[65] Such terms were present in the contracts of indemnity in *Goulston Discount Co Ltd v Clark* [1967] 2 QB 493 (CA); *Wardley Australia Ltd v Western Australia* (1992) 175 CLR 514. See also *Vossloh AG v Alpha Trains (UK) Ltd* [2010] EWHC 2443 (Ch); [2011] 2 All ER (Comm) 307, [27].

[66] *Clement v Clement* (CA, 20 October 1995).

pointing to that provision as evidence of an attempt to displace the usual rule about variation of the principal obligations. The English Court of Appeal rejected the argument, Peter Gibson LJ observing that the sentence referred to the liability of the company as principal and not the liability of the defendant as 'guarantor'. In context, the sentence reinforced the point that the defendant was liable to make up a shortfall in payments where the company's liability as principal was reduced or ceased to exist. The promise contained in the letter was, in substance, an indemnity.

[9–20] Indemnities and guarantees in the same document. It is common drafting practice for a single document to contain promises of guarantee and indemnity. The indemnity may cover much of the same ground as the guarantee,[67] or it may be expressed to apply only where it is contemplated that the guarantee might become ineffective. It is well established that the two promises can co-exist while retaining their distinct identity.[68] It is a matter of construction to determine whether there are two independent promises or only a single promise of one or the other kind. In the latter case, the various references to 'guarantee' or 'indemnity' must be reconciled.

In *Western Credit Ltd v Alberry*,[69] a collateral undertaking by a third party was indorsed upon a hire-purchase agreement. The undertaking was labelled 'Guarantee'. The third party undertook to 'guarantee' payments and performance by the hirer under the agreement and, later in the same clause, to 'indemnify' the finance company against loss sustained as a result of any act, default or negligence of the hirer. The undertaking concluded with a further reference to 'guarantee'. It was held that the undertaking was a guarantee only; the word 'indemnify' was descriptive of the guarantor's liability where the debtor defaulted.

[9–21] Effect of 'principal debtor' clauses. A contract of guarantee, whether or not it also includes a separate promise of indemnity, may contain a clause stating that the guarantor is to be treated as a 'principal debtor' or 'primary obligor'. The intention is usually to ensure that the guarantor remains liable in circumstances where the guarantor might otherwise be discharged at law.[70] The effect of a principal debtor clause depends on the construction of the particular contract,[71] but such a clause, of itself, generally does not convert a guarantee into an indemnity.[72]

---

[67] See, eg, *McGuinness v Norwich and Peterborough Building Society* [2011] EWCA Civ 1286; [2012] 2 All ER (Comm) 265, [59] (Patten LJ).

[68] *Citicorp Australia Ltd v Hendry* (1985) 4 NSWLR 1 (CA), 20 (Clarke J), 41 (Priestley JA); *Brick and Pipe Industries Ltd v Occidental Life Nominees Pty Ltd* [1992] 2 VR 279 (FC), 370; *Sandtara Pty Ltd v Abigroup Ltd* (1996) 42 NSWLR 491 (CA), 499 (Cole JA); *Turner v Leda Commercial Properties Pty Ltd* [2002] ACTCA 8; (2002) 171 FLR 245, [30], [34]; *McIntosh v Linke Nominees Pty Ltd* [2008] QCA 275, [25] (Muir JA); *McGuinness v Norwich and Peterborough Building Society* [2011] EWCA Civ 1286; [2012] 2 All ER (Comm) 265, [56], [59] (Patten LJ).

[69] *Western Credit Ltd v Alberry* [1964] 1 WLR 945 (CA). See also *Stadium Finance Co Ltd v Helm* (1965) 109 SJ 471 (CA); *Re Taylor, ex p Century 21 Real Estate Corp* (1995) 130 ALR 723 (FCA).

[70] Phillips (n 11), 44, para 1-104.

[71] See, eg, *General Produce Co v United Bank Ltd* [1979] 2 Lloyd's Rep 255 (QB), 259; *MS Fashions Ltd v Bank of Credit and Commerce International SA (in liq)* [1993] Ch 425 (CA), 447 (Dillon LJ); *Re Taylor, ex p Century 21 Real Estate Corp* (1995) 130 ALR 723 (FCA), 730; *Valstar v Silversmith* [2009] NSWCA 80, [44]–[46] (Sackville AJA); *McGuinness v Norwich and Peterborough Building Society* [2011] EWCA Civ 1286; [2012] 2 All ER (Comm) 265, [66] (Patten LJ); *CIMC Raffles Offshore (Singapore) Ltd v Schahin Holding SA* [2013] EWCA Civ 644, [59] (Sir Bernard Rix).

[72] *Heald v O'Connor* [1971] 1 WLR 497 (QB), 503; *General Produce Co v United Bank Ltd* [1979] 2 Lloyd's Rep 255 (QB), 259; *PT Jaya Sumpiles Indonesia v Kristle Trading Ltd* [2009] SGCA 20; [2009] 3 SLR(R) 689, [52], [57];

Performance Bonds[73]

[9–22] **Definition.** A performance bond, also known as a 'performance guarantee', 'demand bond' or 'demand guarantee', is a contractual arrangement that can be described broadly in the following terms. The issuer of the bond, generally a financial institution, promises to pay to another party, upon a certain event, a sum up to the specified limit. The bond is associated with a principal contract and is issued at the request of one of the parties to that contract, or a related entity. The party entitled to payment under the bond, the beneficiary, is generally the counterparty to the principal contract. The principal contract often relates to shipbuilding, construction or an international sale of goods.

   One function of a performance bond is to provide security for payments that are, or may become, due to the beneficiary in connection with the principal contract. Another function may be to provide a prompt and readily accessible means of payment.[74] In the latter respect, performance bonds have been likened to promissory notes payable upon demand[75] or irrevocable letters of credit,[76] or regarded as equivalent to cash.[77]

[9–23] **Enforcement.** There is considerable variation among bonds,[78] and the effect of a particular bond is always a matter of construction. Performance bonds are, in general, independent of the principal contract. Thus, the beneficiary can usually call for payment without having to establish that the other party has breached or is liable under the principal contract, or that the beneficiary has suffered a loss of the amount claimed.[79] At one end of the spectrum, the obligation to pay is activated by a simple demand by the beneficiary that complies with any notification requirements of the bond. Further along the spectrum are bonds that provide for payment upon a demand that includes an assertion of default. This may, for example, take the form of a written statement by the beneficiary identifying the counterparty's default, perhaps accompanied by a supporting certificate from a third party. Both types of bond are unconditional in the sense that the beneficiary can establish its entitlement to payment by making a demand and tendering any necessary documents. The issuer may only refuse payment in exceptional circumstances, such as fraud.[80]

Carey Value Added SL v Grupo Urvasco SA [2010] EWHC 1905 (Comm); [2011] 2 All ER (Comm) 140, [22]; *CIMC Raffles Offshore (Singapore) Ltd v Schahin Holding SA* [2013] EWCA Civ 644, [30] (Sir Bernard Rix). cf *McGuinness v Norwich and Peterborough Building Society* [2011] EWCA Civ 1286; [2012] 2 All ER (Comm) 265, [66]–[67] (Patten LJ).

   [73] A full treatment of the topic is beyond the scope of this book. For more detail, see Phillips (n 11), ch 13; G Andrews and R Millett, *Law of Guarantees*, 6th edn (London, Sweet & Maxwell, 2011), ch 16.

   [74] *Cargill International SA v Bangladesh Sugar and Food Industries Corp* [1998] 1 WLR 461 (CA), 468–69 (Potter LJ); *Lucas Stuart Pty Ltd v Hemmes Hermitage Pty Ltd* [2010] NSWCA 283, [39]–[40] (Macfarlan JA).

   [75] *Edward Owen Engineering Ltd v Barclays Bank International Ltd* [1978] QB 159 (CA), 170 (Lord Denning MR).

   [76] *Edward Owen Engineering Ltd v Barclays Bank International Ltd* [1978] QB 159 (CA), 171 (Lord Denning MR); *Intraco Ltd v Notis Shipping Corp of Liberia (The Bhoja Trader)* [1981] 2 Lloyd's Rep 256 (CA), 257 (Donaldson LJ); *Gold Coast Ltd v Caja De Ahorros Del Mediterraneo* [2001] EWCA Civ 1806; [2002] 1 Lloyd's Rep 617, [10] (Tuckey LJ); *Marubeni Hong Kong and South China Ltd v Ministry of Finance of Mongolia* [2005] EWCA Civ 395; [2005] 1 WLR 2497, [23] (Carnwath LJ).

   [77] *Wood Hall Ltd v Pipeline Authority* (1979) 141 CLR 443, 457–58 (Stephen J); *Intraco Ltd v Notis Shipping Corp of Liberia (The Bhoja Trader)* [1981] 2 Lloyd's Rep 256 (CA), 257 (Donaldson LJ).

   [78] See, eg, *Vossloh AG v Alpha Trains (UK) Ltd* [2010] EWHC 2443 (Ch); [2011] 2 All ER (Comm) 307, [34].

   [79] *Edward Owen Engineering Ltd v Barclays Bank International Ltd* [1978] QB 159 (CA); *Wood Hall Ltd v Pipeline Authority* (1979) 141 CLR 443; *Esal (Commodities) Ltd v Oriental Credit Ltd* [1985] 2 Lloyd's Rep 546 (CA), 549 (Ackner LJ); *Clough Engineering Ltd v Oil & Natural Gas Corp Ltd* [2008] FCAFC 136; (2008) 249 ALR 458, [75]–[76].

   [80] As to other bases for restraining payment, see *Potton Homes Ltd v Coleman Contractors Ltd* (1984) 28 BLR 19 (CA), 28 (Eveleigh LJ) (failure of consideration); *Bachmann Pty Ltd v BHP Power New Zealand Ltd* [1998] VSCA

At the other end of the spectrum are bonds whose terms require the beneficiary to establish that the counterparty is actually liable to the beneficiary. The liability may be to pay a sum fixed by the principal contract or to pay damages for breach of that contract. Such a feature favours the bond being construed as a true guarantee.

[9–24] Comparison of bond and true guarantee. A question that sometimes arises is whether the bond establishes a primary and independent liability, or whether it is a 'true' guarantee, that is, a collateral agreement by the issuer to answer to the beneficiary for the counterparty's default under the principal contract. Factors relevant to characterisation include:

(1) the description applied to the bond and the parties to it (though this is not conclusive);[81]
(2) the status of the issuer of the bond: where the instrument is issued outside the banking context, there is a presumption against it being unconditional and independent of the principal contract;[82]
(3) whether the bond contains clauses purporting to displace the usual incidents of a contract of guarantee (such as the discharge of the guarantor by certain events);[83]
(4) whether the terms expressly or by implication provide that the issuer's obligation to pay is conditional upon the beneficiary establishing an actual default or liability of the counterparty;[84] and
(5) in relation to (4) – whether the bond provides that certain documentation is conclusive evidence of liability of the counterparty.[85] It is, however, possible for an instrument with such a clause to be a true guarantee, albeit one that is easily enforced by the beneficiary.[86]

The fourth factor can be problematic because bonds commonly refer to non-performance by the counterparty as the reason for the beneficiary's claim on the bond. Such references

---

40; [1999] 1 VR 420, [28] (Brooking JA); *Clough Engineering Ltd v Oil & Natural Gas Corp Ltd* [2008] FCAFC 136; (2008) 249 ALR 458, [77]–[78]; *Lucas Stuart Pty Ltd v Hemmes Hermitage Pty Ltd* [2010] NSWCA 283 (limitations in principal contract).

[81] *Gold Coast Ltd v Caja De Ahorros Del Mediterraneo* [2001] EWCA Civ 1806; [2002] 1 Lloyd's Rep 617, [21] (Tuckey LJ); *IIG Capital LLC v Van Der Merwe* [2008] EWCA Civ 542; [2008] 2 Lloyd's Rep 187, [7] (Waller LJ); *Marubeni Hong Kong and South China Ltd v Ministry of Finance of Mongolia* [2005] EWCA Civ 395; [2005] 1 WLR 2497, [30] (Carnwath LJ); *Vossloh AG v Alpha Trains (UK) Ltd* [2010] EWHC 2443 (Ch); [2011] 2 All ER (Comm) 307, [20].

[82] *Marubeni Hong Kong and South China Ltd v Ministry of Finance of Mongolia* [2005] EWCA Civ 395; [2005] 1 WLR 2497, [28], [30] (Carnwath LJ); *IIG Capital LLC v Van Der Merwe* [2008] EWCA Civ 542; [2008] 2 Lloyd's Rep 187, [8]–[9], [30]–[32] (Waller LJ).

[83] *Trafalgar House Construction (Regions) Ltd v General Surety & Guarantee Co Ltd* [1996] AC 199 (HL), 205 (Lord Jauncey); *Gold Coast Ltd v Caja De Ahorros Del Mediterraneo* [2001] EWCA Civ 1806; [2002] 1 Lloyd's Rep 617, [25] (Tuckey LJ); *IIG Capital LLC v Van Der Merwe* [2008] EWCA Civ 542; [2008] 2 Lloyd's Rep 187, [30] (Waller LJ).

[84] *IE Contractors Ltd v Lloyds Bank plc* [1990] 2 Lloyd's Rep 496 (CA), 499–500 (Staughton LJ); *Trafalgar House Construction (Regions) Ltd v General Surety & Guarantee Co Ltd* [1996] AC 199 (HL), 206–07 (Lord Jauncey); *Marubeni Hong Kong and South China Ltd v Ministry of Finance of Mongolia* [2005] EWCA Civ 395; [2005] 1 WLR 2497, [31]–[32] (Carnwath LJ); *Meritz Fire and Marine Insurance Co Ltd v Jan de Nul NV* [2010] EWHC 3362 (Comm); [2011] 1 All ER (Comm) 1049, [70] (affd *Meritz Fire and Marine Insurance Co Ltd v Jan de Nul NV* [2011] EWCA Civ 827; [2011] 2 Lloyd's Rep 379); *Wuhan Guoyu Logistics Group Co Ltd v Emporiki Bank of Greece SA* [2012] EWCA Civ 1629; [2013] 1 All ER (Comm) 1191.

[85] *Balfour Beatty Civil Engineering v Technical & General Guarantee Co Ltd* (1999) 68 Con LR 180 (CA); *IIG Capital LLC v Van Der Merwe* [2008] EWCA Civ 542; [2008] 2 Lloyd's Rep 187, [31]–[32] (Waller LJ).

[86] cf *Dobbs v National Bank of Australasia Ltd* (1935) 53 CLR 643, 651 (Rich, Dixon, Evatt and McTiernan JJ); *Bache & Co (London) Ltd v Banque Vernes et Commerciale de Paris SA* [1973] 2 Lloyd's Rep 437 (CA), 438 (Lord Denning MR).

are usually interpreted as describing the circumstances expected to give rise to the claim, rather than as limiting the beneficiary's right to payment. In *IE Contractors Ltd v Lloyds Bank plc*,[87] Staughton LJ referred to a 'bias or presumption in favour of the construction which holds a performance bond to be conditioned upon documents rather than facts. But I would not hold the presumption to be irrebuttable, if the meaning is plain'.

Where the issuer's liability on the bond is independent of the counterparty's liability under the principal contract, labels such as 'performance guarantee' or 'demand guarantee' are misnomers.[88]

[9–25] **Comparison of bond and indemnity.** A performance bond has been described as an especially stringent type of contract of indemnity.[89] This is misleading. Such instruments generally do not satisfy the definition of an indemnity against third party non-performance used in this chapter, nor the broader definition of indemnity used in this work.[90]

Bonds that are true guarantees can be excluded from consideration at the outset. This leaves unconditional bonds that operate as independent, primary obligations. There are two points of similarity with promises of indemnity. The nature of the issuer's obligation under the bond is to pay a sum to the beneficiary. This corresponds to the indemnifier's obligation under a promise of indemnity that is compensatory in nature. The issuer's obligation to pay does not depend upon actual default by the counterparty to the principal contract. This same quality may be shared by an indemnity against third party non-performance.

The fundamental difference between a bond and an indemnity relates to the element of loss to the promisee.[91] Protection against loss is the central concern of a promise of indemnity. It may be one of the objects of a performance bond, but it is not essential to the promise under the bond. An indemnified party is generally only entitled to obtain payment in respect of loss it has actually sustained. In contrast, a beneficiary under a performance bond may claim for a sum that does not correspond to its actual loss; the beneficiary may even obtain payment where there is no substantial loss from a default by the counterparty.[92]

Furthermore, the bond may be intended to secure payment of a sum that does not bear the character of a loss to the beneficiary. In *Wardens and Commonalty of the Mystery of Mercers of the City of London v New Hampshire Insurance Co*,[93] the bond was provided to the employer in relation to advance payments made under a construction contract. The

---

[87] *IE Contractors Ltd v Lloyds Bank plc* [1990] 2 Lloyd's Rep 496 (CA), 500. See also *Gold Coast Ltd v Caja De Ahorros Del Mediterraneo* [2001] EWCA Civ 1806; [2002] 1 Lloyd's Rep 617, [17]–[18] (Tuckey LJ); *Wuhan Guoyu Logistics Group Co Ltd v Emporiki Bank of Greece SA* [2012] EWCA Civ 1629; [2013] 1 All ER (Comm) 1191, [26]–[29] (Longmore LJ). cf *Marubeni Hong Kong and South China Ltd v Ministry of Finance of Mongolia* [2005] EWCA Civ 395; [2005] 1 WLR 2497, [27] (Carnwath LJ).

[88] *Wood Hall Ltd v Pipeline Authority* (1979) 141 CLR 443, 445 (Barwick CJ).

[89] *American Home Assurance Co v Hong Lam Marine Pte Ltd* [1999] SGCA 55; [1999] 2 SLR(R) 992, [41]; *Marubeni Hong Kong and South China Ltd v Ministry of Finance of Mongolia* [2005] EWCA Civ 395; [2005] 1 WLR 2497, [22] (Carnwath LJ); *Vossloh AG v Alpha Trains (UK) Ltd* [2010] EWHC 2443 (Ch); [2011] 2 All ER (Comm) 307, [28].

[90] See also *Carey Value Added SL v Grupo Urvasco SA* [2010] EWHC 1905 (Comm); [2011] 2 All ER (Comm) 140, [23].

[91] cf *Ibrahim v Barclays Bank plc* [2012] EWCA Civ 640; [2013] Ch 400, [63] (Tomlinson LJ) (letter of credit not an indemnity for same reason).

[92] See, eg, *Edward Owen Engineering Ltd v Barclays Bank International Ltd* [1978] QB 159 (CA); *Comdel Commodities Ltd v Siporex Trade SA* [1997] 1 Lloyd's Rep 424 (CA), 431 (Potter LJ); *Cargill International SA v Bangladesh Sugar and Food Industries Corp* [1998] 1 WLR 461 (CA).

[93] *Wardens and Commonalty of the Mystery of Mercers of the City of London v New Hampshire Insurance Co* [1992] 2 Lloyd's Rep 365 (CA).

bond was not satisfactorily drafted, though the fourth recital stated that the bond was 'given to save the [employer] harmless against any and all losses which may result from the failure of the Principal to faithfully employ for the purpose of the contract . . . all or any portion of the advance payments so made'. The issuer of the bond argued that it was a guarantee, so that it could rely on breaches by the employer as grounds for discharge from the obligation to pay; the employer contended that it was an indemnity.

The bond defied neat categorisation. It was essentially concerned with the return of advance payments not earned by the contractor in the performance of the works. All members of the English Court of Appeal agreed that it was not a guarantee of the contractor's performance under the construction contract. But nor was it an indemnity. As Scott LJ remarked: 'Who is to be indemnified and against what? The beneficiary of the bond is [the employer] but the nature of [the employer's] benefit thereunder is not an indemnity'.[94] The subject-matter of the bond was not the employer's loss due to the contractor's non-performance of the construction contract, nor, strictly, loss due to the contractor's failure to repay the sums advanced.

Two further points relate to payments received by the beneficiary. The beneficiary may be required to deal with the funds in accordance with the terms of the principal contract.[95] In contrast, an indemnified party is generally not obliged to apply funds received in respect of a loss in any particular manner.[96] There is also the potential for overpayment, where the beneficiary obtains more under the bond than it is, on a proper legal analysis, entitled to receive from the counterparty under the principal contract. There may subsequently be an accounting to determine the amount actually owing by the counterparty to the beneficiary, with the beneficiary repaying any excess to the counterparty.[97] This may be no more than a specific application of the first point, namely, that the principal contract contains an express or implied term to this effect. Ultimately, therefore, the beneficiary is compensated only for its actual loss. It appears that the issuer has no general right to recover directly from the beneficiary in respect of an overpayment.[98] The issuer can instead usually recover from the counterparty who requested the issue of the bond.[99] In contrast, if the promise were one of indemnity, it might be expected that the beneficiary's obligation to account for overpayments would be owed directly to the indemnifier – the issuer of the bond – rather than the counterparty to the principal contract.[100]

[94] *Wardens and Commonalty of the Mystery of Mercers of the City of London v New Hampshire Insurance Co* [1992] 2 Lloyd's Rep 365 (CA), 374.

[95] See, eg, *Australasian Conference Association Ltd v Mainline Constructions Pty Ltd (in liq)* (1978) 141 CLR 335, 350–53 (Gibbs ACJ); *Wood Hall Ltd v Pipeline Authority* (1979) 141 CLR 443, 453–54 (Gibbs J).

[96] *cf* [7–62].

[97] *Bache & Co (London) Ltd v Banque Vernes et Commerciale de Paris SA* [1973] 2 Lloyd's Rep 437 (CA), 440 (Lord Denning MR); *Comdel Commodities Ltd v Siporex Trade SA* [1997] 1 Lloyd's Rep 424 (CA), 431 (Potter LJ); *Cargill International SA v Bangladesh Sugar and Food Industries Corp* [1998] 1 WLR 461 (CA), 465 (Potter LJ), 471 (Staughton LJ); *Tradigrain SA v State Trading Corp of India* [2005] EWHC 2206 (Comm); [2006] 1 Lloyd's Rep 216, [26]; *Uzinterimpex JSC v Standard Bank plc* [2008] EWCA Civ 819; [2008] 2 Lloyd's Rep 456, [20]–[21] (Moore-Bick LJ).

[98] *Australasian Conference Association Ltd v Mainline Constructions Pty Ltd (in liq)* (1978) 141 CLR 335; *Uzinterimpex JSC v Standard Bank plc* [2008] EWCA Civ 819; [2008] 2 Lloyd's Rep 456, [20]–[21], [26] (Moore-Bick LJ). *cf IIG Capital LLC v Van Der Merwe* [2008] EWCA Civ 542; [2008] 2 Lloyd's Rep 187, [27] (Waller LJ) (right of subrogation).

[99] *cf Cargill International SA v Bangladesh Sugar and Food Industries Corp* [1996] 2 Lloyd's Rep 524 (QB), 530; *Tradigrain SA v State Trading Corp of India* [2005] EWHC 2206 (Comm); [2006] 1 Lloyd's Rep 216, [35]; *IIG Capital LLC v Van Der Merwe* [2008] EWCA Civ 542; [2008] 2 Lloyd's Rep 187, [27] (Waller LJ); *North Shore Ventures Ltd v Anstead Holdings Inc* [2011] EWCA Civ 230; [2012] Ch 31, [65]–[66] (Tomlinson LJ).

[100] See [4–37].

Nature of Indemnity

[9–26] Construction of indemnity promise. The nature of a promise to indemnify against loss from third party non-performance has received relatively little attention. The parties may expressly define the nature of the indemnity. Such provisions have tended to be compensatory, as where the indemnifier promises to pay a sum calculated by reference to a formula. Where the terms of the indemnity are neutral, there does not appear to be a clear and consistent preference for one of the two usual constructions – prevention or compensation – over the other.

A parallel can be drawn between these constructions and the two common constructions of a guarantee.[101] An indemnity that is preventive in nature may be similar in effect to a guarantor's promise to ensure the debtor's performance; likewise, a compensatory indemnity and a guarantor's conditional promise to pay if the debtor does not. The former construction of a guarantee has traditionally been favoured, but it was criticised as 'fictitious and quite unrealistic' by Mason CJ in *Sunbird Plaza Pty Ltd v Maloney*.[102] Mason CJ explained: 'Rarely do guarantors have control of, or a capacity to influence, the principal debtor such that they would willingly assume an obligation to ensure that he performs his primary obligation'.[103] If that criticism is accepted for guarantees, the same could be said for some indemnities against third party non-performance that are preventive in character. It does not follow, however, that the indemnity must be given a preventive construction merely because the indemnifier exerts control or influence over the debtor. In *Kylsilver Pty Ltd v One Australia Pty Ltd*,[104] where the indemnifiers were the directors of the debtor company, Hamilton J described an indemnity as an undertaking 'to pay the promisee only in respect of actual losses suffered by the promisee'.[105]

[9–27] Preventive construction. *McGuinness v Norwich and Peterborough Building Society*[106] exemplifies a preventive construction. McGuinness was guarantor for a loan made by the building society. Under clause 2.2, McGuinness 'guarantee[d] that all money and liabilities owing . . . will be paid and satisfied when due'. Under clause 2.4, which was stated to be a separate obligation, McGuinness agreed 'to make good (in full)' the building society's losses or expenses if the borrower failed to pay, or if the obligations in the principal contract were not enforceable against the borrower.[107] The borrower defaulted. The building society issued a statutory demand against McGuinness, which was not satisfied. The building society then petitioned for bankruptcy. The amount of the borrower's liability was not in dispute, but McGuinness resisted the petition on the ground that his liability to the building society was not for a liquidated sum as required by section 267(2)(b) of the Insolvency Act 1986.

---

[101] See [9–11].
[102] *Sunbird Plaza Pty Ltd v Maloney* (1988) 166 CLR 245.
[103] *Sunbird Plaza Pty Ltd v Maloney* (1988) 166 CLR 245, 255–56.
[104] *Kylsilver Pty Ltd v One Australia Pty Ltd* [2001] NSWSC 611.
[105] *Kylsilver Pty Ltd v One Australia Pty Ltd* [2001] NSWSC 611, [4]. See also *Royscot Commercial Leasing Ltd v Ismail* (CA, 29 April 1993) as discussed at [9–28].
[106] *McGuinness v Norwich and Peterborough Building Society* [2011] EWCA Civ 1286; [2012] 2 All ER (Comm) 265.
[107] The full clause appears at [9–7].

Patten LJ, who delivered the leading judgment, concluded that the guarantee in clause 2.2 was in the nature of a conditional promise to pay if the borrower did not. The building society's claim under that clause was for a liquidated sum and thus sufficient to sustain the petition for bankruptcy. Reliance on the indemnity in clause 2.4 would not have availed the building society because such a claim was for unliquidated damages. On this point, Patten LJ referred to Lord Goff's analysis from *Firma C-Trade SA v Newcastle Protection and Indemnity Association (The Fanti) (No 2)*,[108] that the indemnifier promises to prevent the indemnified party from suffering loss within the scope of the indemnity.

[9–28] Compensatory construction. The compensatory nature of the indemnity is often made clear by the terms in which the promise is expressed. The clause may, for example, state that the indemnifier will pay for loss on the specified basis following a demand by the indemnified party.[109] An indemnity promise may receive a compensatory construction even when expressed in neutral terms. In *Royscot Commercial Leasing Ltd v Ismail*,[110] the director of the lessee company entered into a separate indemnity agreement with the lessor. The director promised 'to indemnify' the lessor upon demand against all loss, damage, costs and expenses that it might sustain in connection with the lease. It was held that the lessor's claim for loss under the indemnity was as for a 'debt', and thus not subject to principles of mitigation of damage. It is implicit in that conclusion that the promise of indemnity was compensatory in nature, and that the terms of the indemnity, in conjunction with those in the lease, were sufficiently detailed to liquidate the loss. The decision is best understood as turning on the construction of the particular agreement, rather than as establishing any general rule in this respect.[111]

Establishing Loss

Existence of Loss

[9–29] Identification of loss. Identifying loss under an indemnity against third party non-performance presents two complications, one a matter of characterisation and the other a matter of timing. It is, perhaps, for this reason that the point is often addressed expressly in the contract. The only general rule that can be stated is that the time at which a loss occurs depends upon the terms of the contract and the factual circumstances.

The indemnified creditor's loss can often be characterised as the failure to obtain a particular return from the transaction. A typical example is the debtor's non-payment of money due according to the terms of the principal contract. This type of loss is the focus of

---

[108] *Firma C-Trade SA v Newcastle Protection and Indemnity Association (The Fanti) (No 2)* [1991] 2 AC 1 (HL), 35–36.

[109] See, eg, *Yeoman Credit Ltd v Latter* [1961] 1 WLR 828 (CA); *Direct Acceptance Finance Ltd v Cumberland Furnishing Pty Ltd* [1965] NSWR 1504 (FC); *Wardley Australia Ltd v Western Australia* (1992) 175 CLR 514. See further [2–21].

[110] *Royscot Commercial Leasing Ltd v Ismail* (CA, 29 April 1993). cf *Sandtara Pty Ltd v Abigroup Ltd* (1996) 42 NSWLR 491 (CA), 499 (Cole JA) (indemnity an obligation 'to pay to the landlord loss suffered' due to lessee's non-performance); *Kylsilver Pty Ltd v One Australia Pty Ltd* [2001] NSWSC 611, [4] (indemnity an undertaking 'to pay the promisee only in respect of actual losses suffered by the promisee').

[111] See also [5–42].

this chapter. There may also be other losses that are consequential in nature. These include costs or expenses incurred in enforcing rights against the debtor, and liabilities to others incurred as a result of the debtor's failure to perform.[112]

The other complication, that of timing, arises because the creditor's loss is attributable to the non-occurrence of an event or the failure of an expected state of affairs. It does not necessarily follow that actual loss must crystallise upon such non-occurrence or failure. Where loss arises because the principal contract is inherently ineffective, it might be that the creditor sustains loss: when it purports to enter the contract; or when it fails to receive performance from the debtor at the time fixed by the terms of the (ineffective) contract; or when some external factor renders the loss definite. Similarly, where the principal contract is effective, the creditor's loss may not coincide with the debtor's failure to perform at the appointed time.[113] Actual loss may be suffered at some later point, when the debtor's non-performance has been sufficiently definite or enduring.

[9–30] **Use of formula.** Loss under the indemnity may be expressly defined by a formula. The existence and extent of loss is then determined by applying the formula to the circumstances. Formulae are common in contracts of indemnity associated with chattels leases and hire-purchase agreements.[114] In *Goulston Discount Co Ltd v Clark*,[115] for example, loss under the indemnity to the finance company was defined as 'the difference between the total amount the hirer would have had to pay to acquire title to the goods under the hire-purchase agreement, plus [the finance company's] expenses, less payments received by [the finance company]'. The date of loss was defined to be the date of notice to the indemnifier after termination of the hire-purchase agreement.

The definition of loss in this manner is unusual in one respect. For most forms of indemnity, the implicit assumption is that the indemnified party begins unharmed at the time of contract, but may then suffer loss as a result of some later event. A definition like that used in *Goulston* has the effect that there is a substantial, albeit inchoate, loss upon entry into the contract, with subsequent events generally reducing that loss.

[9–31] **Loss recoverable immediately upon default.** The terms of the indemnity may indicate that the loss arises and is recoverable immediately upon default by the debtor. In *Kylsilver Pty Ltd v One Australia Pty Ltd*,[116] there was an indemnity to the vendor in respect of the purchaser's performance under six separate contracts for the sale of land. The vendor sued on the indemnity for the balance of the deposits owing under the contracts. Hamilton J considered that the indemnity would have become enlivened once the moneys had become due and payable by the purchaser to the vendor.[117] This followed from the language of the clause, which referred to 'all losses . . . or other moneys which . . . may become due and payable by the Purchaser to the Vendor and have not been paid by the Purchaser to the Vendor'.

---

[112] See [9–3].
[113] The same is true for indemnities against breach of contract by the indemnifier: see [10–25].
[114] See, eg, *Yeoman Credit Ltd v Latter* [1961] 1 WLR 828 (CA); *Bowmaker (Commercial) Ltd v Smith* [1965] 1 WLR 855 (CA); *Goulston Discount Co Ltd v Clark* [1967] 2 QB 493 (CA); *Royscot Commercial Leasing Ltd v Ismail* (CA, 29 April 1993). cf *Unity Finance Ltd v Woodcock* [1963] 1 WLR 455 (CA).
[115] *Goulston Discount Co Ltd v Clark* [1967] 2 QB 493 (CA).
[116] *Kylsilver Pty Ltd v One Australia Pty Ltd* [2001] NSWSC 611.
[117] *Kylsilver Pty Ltd v One Australia Pty Ltd* [2001] NSWSC 611, [4]. In the circumstances, however, the moneys claimed by the vendor were not within the scope of the indemnity: see [9–48].

[9–32] Where performance not received within reasonable time. The terms of the indemnity in *Chief Commissioner of State Revenue v Reliance Financial Services Pty Ltd*[118] were not so explicit. Receivers were appointed to a company and the appointing parties provided the receivers with an indemnity in relation to their services. The indemnity covered moneys payable to the receivers by way of remuneration for their work, 'to the extent that the same shall not have been otherwise recovered from the assets' of the company. The receivers had rendered an invoice for their services and recovered nothing from the company. Assets of the company had been liquidated and the proceeds paid into court, but the various claims on that fund had not been determined at the time of the proceedings.

One issue was whether the receivers could establish a loss under the indemnity, in relation to their unpaid fees, while there remained the possibility of recovery against the fund in court. White J noted that the indemnity referred to fees which 'shall not have been' recovered, rather than fees which could not be recovered. He determined that 30 days was a reasonable time for payment after the receivers had rendered their invoice. That time having expired, the receivers were entitled to claim the unpaid fees as a loss under the indemnity.

[9–33] Where clear that performance will not be received. A creditor does not necessarily lose the expected benefit of the debtor's performance merely because the debtor does not perform at the appointed time. In its claim under the indemnity, the creditor may also have to establish that, to a sufficient degree of certainty, performance in whole or in part will not be forthcoming in the future.[119] The point is illustrated by *Montagu Stanley & Co v JC Solomon Ltd*.[120] The defendant introduced clients to the claimants, who were brokers on the stock exchange, on terms that the defendant was to share half the commission and to indemnify the claimants against half of 'any loss sustained . . . in connection with such business'. One client ran up large debts to the claimants and later executed a deed of assignment of his property for the benefit of his creditors. The creditors were to be paid in full or, in the case of a deficiency, in proportion to their respective claims on the debtor.

The claimants then claimed under the indemnity for half of the amount owing to them by the client, but their claim failed. Without a more specific reference point than 'loss sustained', the claimants had to establish that they had suffered a definite, present loss from the client. A loss did not arise immediately upon the client failing to pay his debts when due. Greer LJ said bluntly: 'That seems to me to be unarguable. Many debtors fail to pay on the due date, but it cannot be said that the money not then paid is lost money'.[121] The client's execution of the deed of assignment was not sufficient to sustain the claimants' claim, either. The amount (if any) that the claimants would receive under that deed was still uncertain at the time of their action to enforce the indemnity.

[9–34] Exhaustion of rights against debtor. The terms of the indemnity may expressly require the creditor to exhaust its rights against the debtor before claiming on the indemnity.[122] By that point, no further performance or compensation will be forthcoming from

---

[118] *Chief Commissioner of State Revenue v Reliance Financial Services Pty Ltd* [2006] NSWSC 1017.

[119] cf *Wardley Australia Ltd v Western Australia* (1992) 175 CLR 514, 532–33 (Mason CJ, Dawson, Gaudron and McHugh JJ).

[120] *Montagu Stanley & Co v JC Solomon Ltd* [1932] 2 KB 287 (CA).

[121] *Montagu Stanley & Co v JC Solomon Ltd* [1932] 2 KB 287 (CA), 291.

[122] See, eg, *Wardley Australia Ltd v Western Australia* (1992) 175 CLR 514; *Grenfell Securities Ltd v Midland Montagu Securities Pty Ltd* [2010] NSWSC 529, [14]–[15]. cf *James v Commonwealth Bank of Australia* (1992) 37 FCR 445 (FCA), 451–52 ('first recourse' against insurance or other indemnity). In the absence of an express provision, there is no general requirement to do so: see [5–15].

the debtor. The creditor has sustained a definite loss which is, in general terms, the difference between the expected return and the performance actually received from the debtor. In *Wardley Australia Ltd v Western Australia*,[123] the State of Western Australia promised to indemnify the lending bank in relation to borrowings by a private company under a bills facility. The terms of the indemnity provided that the State would, on demand, pay to the bank its 'net loss' due to the borrower's failure to satisfy the liability under the facility. Before making a claim on the indemnity, the bank was required to 'proceed to the fullest extent of its rights against [the borrower] . . . to obtain payment out of the assets of [the borrower]'. The terms of the indemnity also contemplated that the bank would prove in the liquidation of the borrower. The bank's net loss was only ascertained once the bank had received a final distribution in the liquidation.

Proof of Loss of Indemnified Party

[9–35] **General.** The debtor's liability to the indemnified creditor may be determined by some process in which the debtor and creditor, but not the indemnifier, participate: for example, by litigation culminating in judgment, by arbitration concluded by an award, or by a settlement agreement. The question is whether the creditor may, as against the indemnifier, rely on the judgment, award or settlement to establish the amount of its loss under the indemnity. A similar question has been the subject of some controversy for indemnities against claims by or liabilities to third parties.[124]

There is, at the outset, a significant obstacle to any general rule of conclusiveness for indemnities against third party non-performance. The principle of co-extensiveness applies to guarantees; thus, the measure of the debtor's liability to the creditor is, subject to any contrary terms in the guarantee, also the measure of the guarantor's. In the case of an indemnity against claims by or liabilities to third parties, the measure of indemnity is, in general, the amount of the indemnified party's liability. Co-extensiveness is not an inherent characteristic of indemnities against third party non-performance.[125] The basis of the debtor's liability to the creditor may inform the assessment of loss within the scope of the indemnity, but whether it does so is ultimately a matter of construction.[126] Where the measure of indemnity is not fixed by reference to the debtor's liability to the creditor, then a binding determination between the latter two parties may simply be irrelevant.

[9–36] **Judgment or arbitral award generally not binding.** The basic position appears to be the same as that for guarantees[127] and indemnities against claims by or liabilities to third parties.[128] A judgment or arbitral award in favour of the creditor against the debtor is not binding on, nor conclusive evidence of liability against, an indemnifier who was not party

---

[123] *Wardley Australia Ltd v Western Australia* (1992) 175 CLR 514.
[124] See [6–37]–[6–46].
[125] See [9–17].
[126] See [9–50], [9–52]–[9–53].
[127] *Ex p Young; re Kitchin* (1881) 17 Ch D 668 (CA); *Begley v Attorney-General (NSW)* (1910) 11 CLR 432; *Bruns v Colocotronis (The Vasso)* [1979] 2 Lloyd's Rep 412 (QB); *PT Jaya Sumpiles Indonesia v Kristle Trading Ltd* [2009] SGCA 20; [2009] 3 SLR(R) 689, [49]; *Rust Consulting Ltd v PB Ltd* [2010] EWHC 3243 (TCC); [2011] 1 All ER (Comm) 951, [45]. See generally Phillips (n 11), 343–44, paras 5-142–5-144; Andrews and Millett, *Law of Guarantees* (n 73), 355–59, para 7-035.
[128] See [6–37], [6–38].

to the proceedings, nor a privy of one of the parties. The same applies to a settlement concluded between the creditor and debtor.

The terms of the indemnity may expressly provide otherwise.[129] In *Alfred McAlpine Construction Ltd v Unex Corp Ltd*,[130] disputes arose in relation to a construction project and the contractor sought to enforce an indemnity from the parent company of the employer. The issue was whether the contractor's action on the indemnity could proceed while arbitration between the contractor and the employer under the main contract was pending. The proposition that the indemnifier's liability was not determined by arbitration between the contractor and employer was accepted as a starting point. There was a division of opinion, however, over the effect of a further proviso in the contract of indemnity. The proviso stated that the indemnifier 'shall not be under any greater liability to the Contractor than the Employer would have been liable in contract pursuant to the express terms of the Contract'. The terms of the main contract contained an arbitration clause.

Evans LJ considered that the proviso did not take the indemnity outside the general principle, at least where arbitration between the employer and contractor had not been concluded. Glidewell LJ went further and held that the proviso partly displaced the general principle. The limit of liability under the indemnity was fixed by whatever was found to be due from the employer to the contractor in the arbitration. It was, however, still open to the indemnifier to argue that the employer was not liable to the contractor at all, or was liable for a lesser sum.

[9–37] No special rule for judgments. According to a special rule said to apply to indemnities against claims by or liabilities to third parties, a judgment against the indemnified party may be conclusive evidence of its liability as against the indemnifier.[131] The rule derives from the nature of an indemnity of that kind. Even if the rule is sound in principle, it is doubtful that it extends by analogy to indemnities against third party non-performance.

Under an indemnity against claims by or liabilities to third parties, the indemnified party's liability represents a potential loss. When the underlying liability is recognised by and merged in the judgment, the liability created by the judgment itself becomes, as a practical matter, the source of potential loss to the indemnified party. As between the indemnifier and indemnified party, a controversy over whether the indemnified party was actually liable to the third party is, fundamentally, a dispute about whether the loss is within the scope of the indemnity. The policy foundation of the special rule is that the indemnified party should not be exposed to loss but left unprotected against it owing to conflicting determinations of liability.[132] Even so, the indemnifier can still dispute whether the circumstances in other respects fall within the scope of the indemnity.

The relationship between the judgment and loss is different where there is an indemnity against third party non-performance. The creditor's loss due to the debtor's failure to perform already exists as a matter of fact. A judgment in favour of the creditor merely recognises that loss; it does not lead to loss to the creditor. There is no specific concern that the creditor as the indemnified party is exposed without protection. The concern is a more

---

[129] *Rust Consulting Ltd v PB Ltd* [2010] EWHC 3243 (TCC); [2011] 1 All ER (Comm) 951, [45]. *cf Compania Sudamericana De Fletes SA v African Continental Bank Ltd (The Rosarino)* [1973] 1 Lloyd's Rep 21 (QB) (guarantee covering arbitral award).

[130] *Alfred McAlpine Construction Ltd v Unex Corp Ltd* (1994) 70 BLR 26 (CA).

[131] See [6–39]–[6–42].

[132] *Parker v Lewis* (1873) LR 8 Ch App 1035, 1059 (Mellish LJ).

general one, namely, the potential for inconsistency between the judgments for the creditor against the debtor and the indemnifier respectively.

[9–38] **Estoppel.** The indemnifier may be estopped from denying a liability recognised by a judgment, arbitral award, or settlement to which the indemnified party is a party. Most decisions have concerned indemnities against claims by or liabilities to third parties.[133] In that context, three factors have been emphasised: the indemnifier's awareness of the claim against the indemnified party; the indemnifier's positive involvement in the management of the claim; or, conversely, the indemnifier's failure to direct or assume responsibility for the defence of the claim when the opportunity arose. For indemnities against third party non-performance, that first factor must be transposed to refer to the claim by the indemnified creditor against the debtor. The second factor can be altered to apply vis-à-vis the debtor. Even with that adjustment, the last factor seems to have limited relevance for this type of indemnity.

In *Canon Australia Pty Ltd v Patton*,[134] Basten JA drew upon some of those liability indemnity decisions to suggest that an estoppel might arise where a guarantor controlled the debtor company,[135] or where the guarantor had notice of the demand against the debtor.[136] Similarly, Akenhead J in *Rust Consulting Ltd v PB Ltd*[137] drew no distinction between guarantees or different forms of indemnity. Without prescribing specific elements necessary for an estoppel, Akenhead J accepted that notice to the guarantor or indemnifier, coupled with the 'active participation of the guarantor or indemnifier in the proceedings' could assist in establishing an estoppel.[138]

Method of Indemnification

[9–39] **Method of indemnification.** The available modes of performance depend upon the construction of the promise of indemnity. A compensatory indemnity is performed by the indemnifier paying the indemnified creditor the amount of the loss ascertained in accordance with the terms of the indemnity. It is immaterial whether the debtor's principal obligations, which are the subject of the indemnity, are to pay money to the creditor. The indemnity is concerned with loss from the debtor's non-performance, not with substitution of performance.

A preventive construction offers wider possibilities. It is necessary to consider the time at which the creditor will sustain loss due to the debtor's failure to perform. This fixes the latest time for performance of the indemnity. If, for example, the loss will crystallise immediately upon the debtor's default or other non-performance, then the indemnifier effectively must act to ensure that the debtor performs. Another point concerns the possibility of substituted

---

[133] See [6–43]–[6–46].

[134] *Canon Australia Pty Ltd v Patton* [2007] NSWCA 246; (2007) 244 ALR 759.

[135] *cf Thomas v Balanced Securities Ltd* [2011] QCA 258; [2012] 2 Qd R 482, [40], [47]–[49] (White JA) (abuse of process).

[136] *Canon Australia Pty Ltd v Patton* [2007] NSWCA 246; (2007) 244 ALR 759, [8] but *cf* [68] (Campbell JA) (expressly refraining from deciding correctness of that proposition).

[137] *Rust Consulting Ltd v PB Ltd* [2010] EWHC 3243 (TCC); [2011] 1 All ER (Comm) 951.

[138] *Rust Consulting Ltd v PB Ltd* [2010] EWHC 3243 (TCC); [2011] 1 All ER (Comm) 951, [45]. See [6–43].

performance as a mode of performance of the indemnity. That is, the indemnifier performs the indemnity by rendering the debtor's performance to the creditor. Whether substituted performance is available as a mode of performance will depend upon the commercial context, particularly the nature of the debtor's principal obligations to the creditor. If the debtor's obligations are simply to pay money to the creditor, there seems to be no general reason why the indemnifier could not perform the indemnity by paying the creditor the sum due from the debtor.

Beyond this, it is more doubtful whether substituted performance is acceptable. Where, for example, an employer obtains an indemnity in relation to the builder's performance under a construction contract, it seems unlikely that the employer has bargained for the work to be completed by the indemnifier or its delegate. Instead, the indemnity serves as a security for the builder's performance. It allows the employer to recover its loss due to the builder's default on the basis provided in the indemnity clause. One instance in which substituted performance might be contemplated is where the indemnifier becomes liable to the creditor for the same performance as the debtor, as may occur in some novation arrangements. So, for example, A, as the incoming party to a novated contract, may assume responsibility for performance of the whole contract and agree to indemnify the remaining party, B, against any loss from breaches by the outgoing party, C, occurring before the novation.

Enforcement

The Status of the Principal Contract

[9–40] **Relationship between indemnity and principal contract.** This form of indemnity is, by definition, associated with the debtor's actual or supposed obligations to the indemnified creditor, even though it is not dependent upon those obligations in the same sense as a guarantee. As most cases concern obligations in a contract or purported contract between the debtor and creditor, the terminology of a principal contract will be used for convenience. It follows from this association that the extent of the indemnifier's liability under the indemnity can be affected by the status of the principal contract. The following section considers, in particular, the effect of invalidity, performance and discharge of the principal contract. The operation of the indemnity can also be affected by other changes in the relative legal positions of the debtor and creditor. Those parties might, for example, vary the principal contract, or the creditor might release the debtor from the obligations under contract. Such concerns arise generally for different forms of indemnity and are considered elsewhere.[139]

Principal Contract is Inherently Ineffective

[9–41] **Where contract void or unenforceable against the debtor.** The general rule for guarantees, in the absence of terms to the contrary, is that the guarantee is ineffective if

---

[139] See [5–20]–[5–29].

the principal contract is void.[140] This is a particular application of the principle of co-extensiveness. That principle does not generally apply to promises of indemnity.[141] An indemnity may, therefore, be valid and effective where the principal contract is void or unenforceable. Whether the indemnity continues to protect against loss in those circumstances is a matter of construction.[142] This approach has been applied where the principal contract is void for lack of capacity of the debtor;[143] where the debtor is not bound as principal because the agent lacked authority;[144] and where the principal contract fails to materialise due to the non-fulfilment of a condition precedent[145] or because the creditor fails to accept an offer.[146]

The usual reason for an indemnity being inoperative is that the scope of the indemnity is predicated on a subsisting, enforceable obligation of the debtor to the creditor. In *McIntosh v Linke Nominees Pty Ltd*,[147] a company director purported to enter a settlement deed on behalf of the company and also in a personal capacity. The company was not bound because the director lacked authority. At issue was whether the director's guarantee and indemnity in respect of the company's payment obligations under the deed could still be enforced. The indemnity was expressed to be against 'any failure by the Company to pay the settlement sum or any part thereof'. It was held that the indemnity presupposed a legally enforceable obligation of the company. The words 'failure by the Company to pay' meant non-compliance with a legal obligation to pay and not non-payment as a matter of fact. The indemnity was ineffective in the circumstances.

[9–42] Illegality. The principal contract or part of it may be illegal in the sense that it is prohibited by statute or is otherwise contrary to public policy. Where such illegality renders the principal contract or relevant part void against the debtor, it follows from the co-extensiveness principle that a guarantee will, in general, be equally ineffective.[148] The promise of indemnity is not necessarily so limited.[149] Whether the indemnity remains operative depends on further considerations. These include whether the indemnity is also affected by illegality, or, if not, whether the loss sustained by the creditor in relation to the principal contract is within the scope of the indemnity.[150]

---

[140] See generally Phillips (n 11), 348–51, paras 5-153–5-161; Andrews and Millett (n 73), 297–306, paras 6-018–6-025. Where the principal contract is merely unenforceable, the efficacy of the guarantee may depend on the reason for that unenforceability: *cf* Phillips (n 11), 353–55, paras 5-167–5-171; Andrews and Millett, *Law of Guarantees* (n 73), 306–07, paras 6-026–6-027.

[141] See [9–17].

[142] *Communities Economic Development Fund v Canadian Pickles Corp* [1991] 3 SCR 388, 413–14; *Conister Trust Ltd v John Hardman & Co* [2008] EWCA Civ 841, [76]–[77] (Lawrence Collins LJ); *McIntosh v Linke Nominees Pty Ltd* [2008] QCA 275, [29] (Muir JA), [46] (Douglas J).

[143] *Yeoman Credit Ltd v Latter* [1961] 1 WLR 828 (CA). See also *Garrard v James* [1925] Ch 616 (Ch) as considered in *Jowitt v Callaghan* (1938) 38 SR (NSW) 512 (FC), 518 (Jordan CJ); *Heald v O'Connor* [1971] 1 WLR 497 (QB), 506. *cf* J Steyn, 'Guarantees: the Co-Extensiveness Principle' (1974) 90 *Law Quarterly Review* 246, 249–51.

[144] *McIntosh v Linke Nominees Pty Ltd* [2008] QCA 275.

[145] *Bentworth Finance Ltd v Lubert* [1968] 1 QB 680 (CA), 685–86 (Lord Denning MR).

[146] *ICTA Investments Pty Ltd v GE Commercial Corp (Australia) Pty Ltd* [2006] NSWCA 290, [55] (Hodgson JA).

[147] *McIntosh v Linke Nominees Pty Ltd* [2008] QCA 275 (special leave to appeal refused: *McIntosh v Linke Nominees Pty Ltd* [2009] HCASL 59).

[148] *Heald v O'Connor* [1971] 1 WLR 497 (QB). *cf Citicorp Australia Ltd v Hendry* (1985) 4 NSWLR 1 (CA), 40 (Priestley JA) (penalty clause). See generally Phillips (n 11), 348–49, paras 5-154–5-156; Andrews and Millett, *Law of Guarantees* (n 73), 298–99, para 6-019.

[149] *cf Heald v O'Connor* [1971] 1 WLR 497 (QB), 502, 506.

[150] See, eg, *Unity Finance Ltd v Woodcock* [1963] 1 WLR 455 (CA), 463 (Davies LJ) (illegal repossession of vehicle by owner releasing hirer from liability under hire-purchase contract). *cf* the explanation of that case given in *Goulston Discount Co Ltd v Clark* [1967] 2 QB 493 (CA), 497–98 (Lord Denning MR).

The indemnity may be affected by illegality directly or indirectly. It may be affected directly where, for example, the statute that prohibits the principal contract also prohibits the indemnity. The indemnity may be affected indirectly where it is sufficiently closely associated with the principal contract to be considered 'tainted' by, or otherwise inseverable from, the illegality affecting the principal contract. *Cameo Motors Ltd v Portland Holdings Ltd*[151] appears to be the closest illustration. A hire-purchase contract for a motor vehicle was illegal owing to non-compliance with a statutory requirement of writing. The motor dealer also entered into a recourse agreement with the finance company. The agreement provided for an assignment, by way of mortgage, of the dealer's rights under the hire-purchase agreement and of the dealer's title to and interest in the vehicle. Under clause 1, the dealer promised to pay upon demand the balance owing under the hire-purchase agreement. By clause 2, the dealer promised that the hirer would 'punctually pay observe keep and perform all and singular his obligations under the said agreement'. The hirer defaulted and the finance company claimed against the dealer.

Richmond J held that clause 2 of the recourse agreement was ineffective because the principal contract was void. This did not necessarily invalidate clause 1, which was not a guarantee. Richmond J further held that the assignment element of the recourse agreement was so closely associated with the subject-matter of the illegal hire-purchase contract that it was tainted by that illegality. Clause 1 could not be severed from that part of the recourse agreement; it was, then, not necessary to determine whether clause 1 was also independently affected by illegality. The decision was reversed on appeal. The recourse agreement escaped the taint of illegality because it was subsequent to and sufficiently distinct from the hire-purchase agreement, and the finance company did not have knowledge of the illegality.[152]

[9–43] **Penalty clauses in principal contract.** The creditor may seek to be indemnified in respect of an amount payable by the debtor under an agreed damages clause in the principal contract. For present purposes, two assumptions must be made: that the clause is, in the circumstances, applicable;[153] and that the clause imposes a penalty. Although the indemnity is independent of the principal contract, such amounts might still be irrecoverable from the indemnifier.

Citicorp Australia Ltd v Hendry[154] is the leading decision. Certain acceleration clauses in chattels leases were penalties, but the lessor claimed the same amount under a separate guarantee and indemnity agreement. The indemnity in clause 9 stated that: 'notwithstanding that the whole or any part of the moneys hereinbefore described as "the Moneys Hereby Secured" are or may be irrecoverable . . . from the debtor', each of the guarantors would indemnify the lessor 'in respect of such moneys and . . . pay to the lessor on demand a sum equal to the amount of such moneys'. The capitalised expression was defined to include amounts 'owing or payable to' the lessor by the lessee.

Clarke J dismissed the lessor's claim under clause 9 on three grounds.[155] The first ground was that allowing recovery under the indemnity would indirectly enforce the penalty clauses

---

[151] *Cameo Motors Ltd v Portland Holdings Ltd* [1965] NZLR 109 (SC).

[152] *Portland Holdings Ltd v Cameo Motors Ltd* [1966] NZLR 571 (CA).

[153] Contrast *British Glanzstoff Manufacturing Co Ltd v General Accident, Fire and Life Assurance Corp Ltd* 1912 SC 591 (IH) (affd *British Glanzstoff Manufacturing Co Ltd v General Accident, Fire and Life Assurance Corp Ltd* [1913] AC 143 (HL)).

[154] *Citicorp Australia Ltd v Hendry* (1985) 4 NSWLR 1 (CA). cf *Azimut-Benetti SpA v Healey* [2010] EWHC 2234 (Comm); [2011] 1 Lloyd's Rep 473, [24].

[155] *Citicorp Australia Ltd v Hendry* (1985) 4 NSWLR 1 (SC), 21.

in the leases. This was contrary to public policy. The second ground was that the penalty clauses were unenforceable ab initio and so there was no amount owing to the lessor by the lessee. As a matter of construction, the sums claimed did not fall within the definition of 'Moneys Hereby Secured' referenced in cl 9. The third ground was that the essential nature of a promise of indemnity was to protect only against actual loss. The amount of the lessor's actual loss was not determined by the penal clause. On appeal, Priestley JA upheld Clarke J's decision on the second ground and reserved his opinion on the correctness of the first ground.[156]

The first ground is problematic. It is not easily reconciled with decisions on hire-purchase contracts, which recognise that the owner can recover under the indemnity for the loss of the bargain even when that loss is not recoverable from the hirer.[157] A point of distinction, albeit rather technical, may be that such clauses have typically been expressed in terms independent of the hirer's liability to pay damages under the hire-purchase contract. Clarke J's third ground might be sustained on the basis of construction, if it is sufficiently clear that the parties' intention is to provide no more than an indemnity.[158]

Principal Contract is Effective but Subsequently Discharged

[9–44] Extent of indemnity is a matter of construction. The principal contract may be inherently effective and then discharged in whole or in part by subsequent events. Such events include: performance by the debtor; termination by one of the parties for the other's breach;[159] frustration;[160] a court order relieving the debtor from a liability under the principal contract;[161] or a liquidator of the debtor company disclaiming the principal contract pursuant to a statutory procedure.[162] An important question is whether the promise of indemnity protects the creditor against loss from the debtor's non-performance, even though discharge has relieved the debtor of the obligation to perform.

In broad terms, the answer depends on the construction of the indemnity. The approach is simpler than that applicable for guarantees. There is no theoretical difficulty in accepting that the indemnifier may be liable where the debtor is not. The nature of a guarantee – as a promise to ensure the debtor's performance, or as a conditional promise to perform if the debtor does not – may affect the guarantor's liability for obligations of the debtor that were to arise after the principal contract was discharged.[163] A difference in the nature of the indemnity promise – as preventive or compensatory – does not affect the indemnifier's liability in the same way. The question is whether the creditor, as the indemnified party, has sustained a loss within the scope of the indemnity.

[9–45] Discharge by performance by the debtor. The question of loss under the indemnity usually does not arise where the debtor's obligations under the principal contract have been discharged by proper performance. The creditor has obtained the return to which it

---

[156] *Citicorp Australia Ltd v Hendry* (1985) 4 NSWLR 1 (CA), 41.
[157] See [9–46].
[158] See [9–51].
[159] See [9–46], [9–47].
[160] See, eg, *Goulston Discount Co Ltd v Sims* (1967) 111 SJ 682 (CA).
[161] See, eg, *Kylsilver Pty Ltd v One Australia Pty Ltd* [2001] NSWSC 611 (order for return of deposits defeating any further action for balance of deposits outstanding).
[162] See [9–48].
[163] See, eg, *Moschi v Lep Air Services Ltd* [1973] AC 331 (HL).

was entitled from the transaction.[164] The exception is where the indemnity adopts, as the measure of the return from the transaction, a state of affairs beyond that promised by the debtor in the principal contract. In that event, even if the debtor performs lawfully, the creditor may still recover under the indemnity for the loss of the supra-contractual benefit.[165]

[9–46] Discharge by creditor for breach or repudiation by debtor. Where the creditor terminates the principal contract for the debtor's breach or repudiation, its claim for loss under the indemnity may include loss accrued prior to termination[166] and also loss of the benefit of future performance by the debtor.[167] In the latter respect, the distinction made at general law between termination for a non-serious breach pursuant to an express contractual right, and termination for a serious breach or repudiation in reliance on a common law right, is not directly applicable. If there is an equivalent limitation, it must arise through construction of the scope of the indemnity.

The creditor is not necessarily debarred from recovering under the indemnity for the loss of the bargain where it terminates for a non-serious breach.[168] The creditor may, as a result, obtain more from the indemnifier than it can recover from the debtor as common law damages. In the leading example, *Goulston Discount Co Ltd v Clark*,[169] this result was dictated by the clear terms of the indemnity. The obligation to indemnify did not depend upon breach by the debtor, and loss was defined by reference to a particular return from the transaction, rather than by reference to the hirer's liability or the consequences of breach or termination. It may also follow that an indemnity framed in appropriate terms can provide a lessor with compensation for loss of the bargain when it re-enters after default by the lessee, even though such loss appears not to be recoverable from the lessee as damages under English law.[170]

[9–47] Discharge by debtor for breach or repudiation by creditor. Termination of the principal contract by the debtor for the creditor's breach or repudiation is far less common. Where the matter is not covered by an express provision,[171] there are at least two lines of analysis. The creditor's conduct may attract one of the generally recognised grounds for discharge of an indemnifier.[172] Alternatively, there may be an implied limitation to the scope of the indemnity to the creditor: the lost benefit of the debtor's future performance is excluded from scope where the debtor terminates the principal contract for a serious breach or repudiation by the creditor. It is commercially improbable that an indemnity is intended to protect the creditor absolutely, and irrespective of its disregard of the principal contract.

---

[164] *cf Western Credit Ltd v Alberry* [1964] 1 WLR 945 (CA), 950 (Davies LJ).

[165] See [9–8].

[166] See, eg, *Vickers v Stichtenoth Investments Pty Ltd* (1989) 52 SASR 90 (SC) (criticised on other grounds in *Reichman v Beveridge* [2006] EWCA Civ 1659; [2007] Bus LR 412, [32]–[33] (Lloyd LJ)).

[167] See, eg, *Goulston Discount Co Ltd v Clark* [1967] 2 QB 493 (CA); *Tebb v Filsee Pty Ltd* [2010] VSCA 311; (2010) 30 VR 473 (guarantee and indemnity).

[168] *cf* [9–48] (discharge by operation of law) and [10–55] (loss of bargain claims under indemnities against breach of contract by indemnifier).

[169] *Goulston Discount Co Ltd v Clark* [1967] 2 QB 493 (CA).

[170] *cf Reichman v Beveridge* [2006] EWCA Civ 1659; [2007] Bus LR 412, [26] (Lloyd LJ).

[171] *cf Treton Pty Ltd v HM Australia Holdings Pty Ltd* [2011] QSC 38, [39]–[40].

[172] See generally [5–20], [5–21].

In the Canadian case *Jens Hans Investments Co Ltd v Bridger*,[173] a director of the lessee company promised to indemnify the lessor against loss arising from any failure of the lessee to pay rent or perform the terms of the lease. The lessee's business was unsuccessful and the lessee made extensive attempts to sub-let part of the premises. The lessor persistently refused its consent, which was required under the terms of the lease. The lessee then terminated the lease for the lessor's breach by refusing consent. The lessee entered bankruptcy soon afterwards and the trustee in bankruptcy again disclaimed the lease. The indemnifier was held to be absolutely discharged because the indemnified lessor's conduct had materially prejudiced the indemnifier's position.[174] In the alternative, it was held that the indemnifier's liability under the indemnity was limited to the lessor's losses up to the date at which the lessee terminated for the lessor's breach.[175]

[9–48] Discharge by operation of law. The debtor's obligations under the principal contract may be discharged by operation of common law[176] or by operation of statute, including by the exercise of a power conferred by statute.[177] An example of the latter is the power of a liquidator or trustee in bankruptcy to disclaim onerous property of the liquidating company or bankrupt debtor.[178] The basis upon which the principal contract is discharged will determine the extent of the discharge and whether it operates ab initio or prospectively only.

Where the basis of discharge is statutory, it is necessary to consider whether the statute also has the effect of discharging the indemnifier's obligations under the associated contract of indemnity.[179] Furthermore, in all cases, the loss sustained by the indemnified creditor as a consequence of the discharge must be within the scope of the indemnity.[180] Both points are illustrated by *Sandtara Pty Ltd v Abigroup Ltd*.[181] The lessor was provided with a combined guarantee and indemnity in respect of the lessee company's performance of its obligations under the lease. The lessee eventually entered liquidation and its liquidator disclaimed the lease. The lessor's claim for loss under the indemnity included an amount for the period between the date of disclaimer and the specified date of expiry of the lease. That amount was effectively calculated on a loss of bargain basis, namely, by reference to the difference between the agreed rent under the lease and the rent received or to be received by the lessor through re-letting the premises.

The New South Wales Court of Appeal held that the indemnity provided by clause 18.02 was still operative. That clause stated that the indemnity would 'continue and the [guarantor/

---

[173] *Jens Hans Investments Co Ltd v Bridger* [2002] BCSC 1230; (2002) 6 BCLR (4th) 346 (affd on the first ground mentioned in the text: *Jens Hans Investments Co Ltd v Bridger* [2004] BCCA 340; (2004) 29 BCLR (4th) 1).

[174] See [5–29].

[175] *Jens Hans Investments Co Ltd v Bridger* [2002] BCSC 1230; (2002) 6 BCLR (4th) 346, [46]–[48].

[176] See, eg, *Goulston Discount Co Ltd v Sims* (1967) 111 SJ 682 (CA) (frustration).

[177] See, eg, *Unity Finance Ltd v Woodcock* [1963] 1 WLR 455 (CA) (owner's contravention of statute discharging hirer from liability under hire-purchase contract); *Kylsilver Pty Ltd v One Australia Pty Ltd* [2001] NSWSC 611 (order for refund of deposits made under statutory provision substantially equivalent to Law of Property Act 1925, s 49(2)).

[178] Insolvency Act 1986, ss 178, 315. See, eg, *Clement v Clement* (CA, 20 October 1995); *Sandtara Pty Ltd v Abigroup Ltd* (1996) 42 NSWLR 491 (CA). See generally *Hindcastle Ltd v Barbara Attenborough Associates Ltd* [1997] AC 70 (HL) (guarantee).

[179] cf *Unity Finance Ltd v Woodcock* [1963] 1 WLR 455 (CA) as explained in *Goulston Discount Co Ltd v Clark* [1967] 2 QB 493 (CA), 497–98 (Lord Denning MR).

[180] See, eg, *Unity Finance Ltd v Woodcock* [1963] 1 WLR 455 (CA), 463 (Davies LJ); *Kylsilver Pty Ltd v One Australia Pty Ltd* [2001] NSWSC 611, [6].

[181] *Sandtara Pty Ltd v Abigroup Ltd* (1996) 42 NSWLR 491 (CA).

indemnifier] shall remain liable to the Landlord under this indemnity . . . notwithstanding that the Tenant . . . may be wound up . . . and notwithstanding that the guarantee hereby given may for any reason whatsoever be unenforceable'. This was apt to cover the situation that had arisen. The loss was, therefore, within the scope of the indemnity.

The Court also concluded that, as a matter of statutory construction, the liquidator's disclaimer did not discharge the liability of the guarantor/indemnifier to the lessor.[182] The applicable provision, section 568(3) of the Corporations Law,[183] stated that the disclaimer did not 'except so far as is necessary for the purpose of releasing the company and the property of the company from liability, affect the rights or liabilities of any other person'. The disclaimer did, however, relieve the lessee from any obligation to indemnify the guarantor/indemnifier in respect of that liability to the lessor.[184] In place of the right to indemnity from the lessee, the guarantor/indemnifier acquired by statute a right to prove in the liquidation of the lessee.[185]

Enforcement after Loss

Accrual of Right to Enforce Indemnity

[9–49] Demands and the effect of 'principal debtor' clauses. Indemnities against third party non-performance are commonly expressed in terms of a promise to indemnify upon demand. An express requirement for a demand by the creditor upon the indemnifier will be given effect.[186] The creditor's right to make a demand may itself be conditioned upon an event or the existence of a state of affairs.[187] In the absence of an express provision, a demand by the creditor upon the indemnifier is generally not a condition precedent to enforcement. In these respects, an indemnity against third party non-performance is similar to a guarantee.[188]

Where this form of indemnity is combined with a guarantee, the contract may also contain a clause stating that the guarantor/indemnifier is to be treated as the 'principal debtor'. The effects of such clauses vary, though the usual objective is to preserve liability under the guarantee in circumstances where it would otherwise be discharged.[189] One view is that such a clause may also obviate a requirement for a demand upon the guarantor expressed elsewhere in the contract.[190] This is said to follow from the general proposi-

---

[182] Although the Court relied principally on the indemnity obligation, the liability under the guarantee obligation could also have survived: *Sandtara Pty Ltd v Abigroup Ltd* (1996) 42 NSWLR 491 (CA), 503 (Cole JA). See also *Hindcastle Ltd v Barbara Attenborough Associates Ltd* [1997] AC 70 (HL), 87–88 (Lord Nicholls), but *cf* 89 (liability ends if landlord retakes possession of premises).

[183] See now Corporations Act 2001 (Cth), s 568D(1). See also Insolvency Act 1986, ss 178(4), 315(3).

[184] *Sandtara Pty Ltd v Abigroup Ltd* (1996) 42 NSWLR 491 (CA), 503 (Cole JA). See also *Hindcastle Ltd v Barbara Attenborough Associates Ltd* [1997] AC 70 (HL), 88 (Lord Nicholls).

[185] See now Corporations Act 2001 (Cth), s 568D(2). See also Insolvency Act 1986, ss 178(6), 315(5).

[186] See [5–13].

[187] See, eg, *Direct Acceptance Finance Ltd v Cumberland Furnishing Pty Ltd* [1965] NSWR 1504 (FC) (debtor's account unsatisfactory in creditor's opinion); *Wardley Australia Ltd v Western Australia* (1992) 175 CLR 514 (rights against debtor exhausted).

[188] As to guarantees, see Phillips (n 11), 611–15, paras 10-118–10-126; Andrews and Millett, *Law of Guarantees* (n 73), 318–25, paras 7-005–7-007.

[189] See also [9–21].

[190] See, eg, *Esso Petroleum Co Ltd v Alstonbridge Properties Ltd* [1975] 1 WLR 1474 (Ch), 1483; *MS Fashions Ltd v Bank of Credit and Commerce International SA (in liq)* [1993] Ch 425 (CA), 436 (Hoffmann LJ) and on appeal 447 (Dillon LJ); *Emhill Pty Ltd v Bonsoc Pty Ltd* [2001] VSC 179, [18]–[26]; *TS&S Global Ltd v Fithian-Franks*

tion that the creditor need not make a demand upon the debtor before enforcing the principal liability.

As the indemnifier's liability is primary and independent of the debtor's, a 'principal debtor' clause makes little sense when applied to an indemnity. Particularly confusing are attempts to transplant the above reasoning to indemnities, to conclude that a principal debtor clause overrides a requirement stated elsewhere in the contract for a demand by the indemnified party upon the indemnifier. Which clause is to prevail is, in any event, a matter of construction. In *Australia and New Zealand Banking Group Ltd v Coutts*,[191] a director of the debtor company executed an instrument containing a guarantee (clause 4) and indemnity (clause 5) in favour of the creditor bank. The guarantee and indemnity were expressed to be independent of and additional to each other. Under clause 7, the director agreed that the creditor could 'enforce its rights under the indemnity against me as principal debtor'. Clause 11 provided that the director was obliged to pay sums owing under the instrument immediately upon a written demand by the creditor. Conti J held that clause 7 did not override or provide an alternative procedure to the requirement of a demand imposed by clause 11.[192] Thus, the creditor's right to enforce the indemnity in respect of certain amounts claimed did not arise until it made a written demand to that effect.

Assessment of Loss

[9–50] General principles. It is difficult to formulate specific propositions because the assessment of loss is highly sensitive to context. Some guiding principles can be stated in general terms.

(1) The creditor's loss under the indemnity may be assessed on a basis different from that applicable to the creditor's claim against the debtor under the principal contract. Instances include where:

    (a) the indemnity uses a formula that states a basis of liability different from that under the principal contract;[193]

    (b) the indemnity applies even though the debtor has excluded liability to the creditor under the principal contract;[194]

    (c) the indemnity covers the creditor's failure to receive a benefit that goes beyond the performance promised by the debtor under the principal contract;[195]

    (d) the indemnity covers the loss of the bargain due to premature discharge of the contract in circumstances where the creditor could not recover such loss from the debtor;[196] and

---

[2007] EWHC 1401 (Ch); [2008] 1 BCLC 277, [26]–[29]. Contrast *Re Taylor, ex p Century 21 Real Estate Corp* (1995) 130 ALR 723 (FCA), 729–30; *McGuinness v Norwich and Peterborough Building Society* [2011] EWCA Civ 1286; [2012] 2 All ER (Comm) 265, [65]–[66] (Patten LJ).

[191] *Australia and New Zealand Banking Group Ltd v Coutts* [2003] FCA 968; (2003) 201 ALR 728. *cf Benson-Brown v Smith* [1999] VSC 208, [147]–[152].

[192] *Australia and New Zealand Banking Group Ltd v Coutts* [2003] FCA 968; (2003) 201 ALR 728, [35].

[193] See [9–30], [9–51].

[194] *Anglomar Shipping Co Ltd v Swan Hunter Shipbuilders Ltd (The London Lion)* [1980] 2 Lloyd's Rep 456 (CA).

[195] See [9–8].

[196] See, eg, *Goulston Discount Co Ltd v Clark* [1967] 2 QB 493 (CA) (termination for non-serious breach); *Goulston Discount Co Ltd v Sims* (1967) 111 SJ 682 (CA) (frustration); *Treton Pty Ltd v HM Australia Holdings Pty Ltd* [2011] QSC 38, [39]–[41], [51]–[52] (possible termination by debtor for creditor's non-compliance with statute) (affd on another point *HM Australia Holdings Pty Ltd v Treton Pty Ltd* [2011] QCA 382).

(e) the indemnity covers a type of loss (such as legal costs of proceedings to enforce the principal contract or indemnity[197]) not ordinarily recoverable as common law damages from the debtor.

(2) Such instances are often determined by express terms of the contract of indemnity.

(3) The extent of the indemnifier's liability to the creditor is not, however, necessarily different from that of the debtor under the principal contract. There are instances where the assessment of loss under the indemnity is, as a matter of construction, informed by the principles governing the debtor's liability to the creditor. Thus, the principal contract may influence the scope of the indemnity or the application of a measure of loss under the indemnity.[198]

(4) The approach in (3) tends to be adopted as a matter of intuition or inference, in the absence of more specific provisions as to the assessment of loss. This may reflect a commercial perspective that the indemnity functions as a security for the debtor's performance by providing an alternative, though substantially equivalent, source of recovery for loss.

[9–51] Effect of inaccurate formula. The formula used to assess loss under an indemnity may be inaccurate, in the sense that it does not on any reasonable view correctly measure the actual loss suffered by the indemnified party in the circumstances. If the formula is contained in the principal contract and merely referenced in the indemnity, then it might be attacked indirectly on the basis that it imposes a penalty upon the debtor for breach of the contract with the creditor.[199] Where the formula appears in the contract of indemnity but not the principal contract, it would not be subject to challenge under the traditional scope of the penalty rules.[200]

It may, however, be possible through construction to override the formula to the extent that it fails to measure actual loss. It must be sufficiently clear that the parties intended the principle of indemnity to prevail. In *Goulston Discount Co Ltd v Sims*,[201] there was a hire-purchase contract for a motor vehicle and an associated indemnity agreement between the motor dealer and the finance company. Loss under the indemnity was defined to be the total amount the hirer would have had to pay to acquire the vehicle under contract, plus expenses, less payments received by the finance company. This formula did not account for the finance company's accelerated receipt, under the indemnity, of the future instalments due under the hire-purchase contract. The formula did not, therefore, represent the finance company's actual loss. The difference was not insignificant in the circumstances, because the hire-purchase contract had been discharged about 18 months short of the agreed term. It was held that the promise to indemnify was paramount, so that the finance company was required to give credit for that benefit in calculating its loss under the indemnity.

---

[197] See, eg, *Abigroup Ltd v Sandtara Pty Ltd* [2002] NSWCA 45. See generally [4–75].

[198] See [9–52], [9–53].

[199] See [9–43].

[200] cf *Export Credits Guarantee Department v Universal Oil Products Co* [1983] 1 WLR 399 (HL).

[201] *Goulston Discount Co Ltd v Sims* (1967) 111 SJ 682 (CA). See also *Citicorp Australia Ltd v Hendry* (1985) 4 NSWLR 1 (CA), 21 (Clarke J).

[9–52] **Scope of indemnity affected by principal contract.** The scope of the indemnity may explicitly incorporate a basis of liability under the principal contract.[202] In the absence of an express provision, qualifications to scope may be inferred by reference to the principles governing the creditor's claim against the debtor. So, for example, the creditor might not recover under the indemnity for loss of the bargain where the debtor terminates the principal contract for the creditor's serious breach or repudiation.[203]

Another example is the expectation that the indemnified party act reasonably in incurring losses under the indemnity. The expectation can be explained as an implied limitation to the scope of the indemnity, which is applied generally as a matter of construction.[204] In some Australian indemnity decisions concerning leases, the expectation of reasonable conduct by the lessor has been rationalised on a different basis, namely, that principles of mitigation apply to the lessee's default under the lease.[205] That approach achieves practically the same result though there is a distinct difference in perspective. On the former view, the limitation transcends the principal contract; it applies between the indemnifier and indemnified party as a general incident of their agreement for indemnity. On the latter view, the limitation is drawn from the principal contract that is the subject of the indemnity. The indemnifier cannot rely on principles of mitigation as a matter of law because it is not the defaulting party under the principal contract. Rather, those principles are embodied implicitly within the scope of the indemnity as a matter of construction.

A more difficult question arises where there is no such parallel. The effect of the general limitation of reasonableness under the indemnity is not so clear, for example, in circumstances where the creditor could, as against the debtor, invoke the principle from *White and Carter (Councils) Ltd v McGregor.*[206]

[9–53] **Measure of loss affected by principal contract.** In some circumstances, the creditor's loss under the indemnity may be measured in the same way as its loss under the principal contract. This may be made explicit by the terms of indemnity,[207] or it may be inferred by reference to the nature of the debtor's liability to the creditor under the principal contract. In one case, the indemnified lessors terminated for the lessee's repudiation and re-entered.[208] The measure of the loss of bargain was the same as that which would have applied under Australian[209] law in a claim for damages against the lessee. Thus, the lessors

---

[202] See, eg, *Unity Finance Ltd v Woodcock* [1963] 1 WLR 455 (CA), 463 (Davies LJ); *Citicorp Australia Ltd v Hendry* (1985) 4 NSWLR 1 (CA), 40–41 (Priestley JA); *Royscot Commercial Leasing Ltd v Ismail* (CA, 29 April 1993); *Kylsilver Pty Ltd v One Australia Pty Ltd* [2001] NSWSC 611; *Carey Value Added SL v Grupo Urvasco SA* [2010] EWHC 1905 (Comm); [2011] 2 All ER (Comm) 140, [37].

[203] See [9–47].

[204] See [4–30].

[205] *Vickers v Stichtenoth Investments Pty Ltd* (1989) 52 SASR 90 (SC) (criticised in *Reichman v Beveridge* [2006] EWCA Civ 1659; [2007] Bus LR 412, [32]–[33] (Lloyd LJ)); *Tebb v Filsee Pty Ltd* [2010] VSCA 311; (2010) 30 VR 473 (combined guarantee and indemnity). *cf* also *Wenkart v Pitman* (1998) 46 NSWLR 502 (CA), 520–24 (Powell JA) (mitigation by lessor after disclaimer by liquidator of lessee).

[206] *White and Carter (Councils) Ltd v McGregor* [1962] AC 413 (HL).

[207] See, eg, *Carey Value Added SL v Grupo Urvasco SA* [2010] EWHC 1905 (Comm); [2011] 2 All ER (Comm) 140, [37].

[208] *Tebb v Filsee Pty Ltd* [2010] VSCA 311; (2010) 30 VR 473 (combined guarantee and indemnity). *cf Sandtara Pty Ltd v Abigroup Ltd* (1996) 42 NSWLR 491 (CA) (claim including loss of bargain after disclaimer by liquidator of lessee).

[209] *Lamson Store Service Co Ltd v Russell Wilkins & Sons Ltd* (1906) 4 CLR 672, 684 (Griffith CJ); *Progressive Mailing House Pty Ltd v Tabali Pty Ltd* (1985) 157 CLR 17, 47 (Brennan J); *Gumland Property Holdings Pty Ltd v Duffy Bros Fruit Market (Campbelltown) Pty Ltd* [2008] HCA 10; (2008) 234 CLR 237, [55]. Contrast *Reichman v Beveridge* [2006] EWCA Civ 1659; [2007] Bus LR 412.

recovered the difference between the rent which would have been payable over the remainder of the term, and the amount received by re-letting the premises during that same period. In another case, the indemnified vendor's loss from the purchaser's failure to complete a contract for the sale of land was measured under the indemnity by the difference between the contract price and market price for the land at the date for completion.[210]

Enforcement before Loss

[9–54] **Whether indemnity enforceable in respect of potential loss.** The equitable jurisdiction specifically to enforce indemnities has developed in relation to indemnities against claims by or liabilities to third parties.[211] There appears to be no decision in which an indemnity against third party non-performance has been specifically enforced; equally, there appears to be no decision expressly rejecting that possibility. For the following reasons, it seems that specific enforcement is inapt or, at best, has a very limited role, for indemnities in this form.

Starting from basic principles, specific enforcement is only available where the indemnity is preventive in nature. Some indemnities against third party non-performance must, therefore, be excluded on this basis. An indemnity against claims by or liabilities to third parties is specifically enforced in relation to monetary liabilities of the indemnified party. A similar limitation might be applied to an indemnity against third party non-performance. Accordingly, relief would be available only where the primary obligation of the debtor is to pay money to the creditor, or where the creditor claims for a potential loss in money terms following the debtor's failure to perform.

Loss to the indemnified party must be sufficiently imminent to justify an order for specific enforcement. In relation to indemnities against claims by or liabilities to third parties, this generally requires a definite, presently accrued and enforceable liability of the indemnified party to the third party.[212] Furthermore, the amount of the liability should be ascertained or readily ascertainable. The former requirement might be transposed to a condition that the debtor is (or would be, but for the ineffectiveness of the principal contract) under a definite, presently accrued and enforceable liability to the indemnified creditor. The latter requirement is problematic. If the creditor's loss is still characterised as potential and not actual, then this is likely to be because there is some element of contingency involved. For example, it may still be possible that the creditor will receive some or all of the performance from the debtor in the future. That same element of contingency makes it difficult to fix the amount of the potential loss. The circumstances that allow the loss to be ascertained with sufficient certainty may, at the same time, convert the potential loss into an actual loss.

The obvious form of relief would be an order that the indemnifier pay to the indemnified creditor the amount of the potential loss. There is, therefore, a risk of over-compensation if the actual loss turns out to be less than expected. Techniques that might be used to avoid over-compensation where an indemnity against liabilities is specifically enforced – for example, payment to the third party, or an undertaking to pass on the funds to the third party – cannot be transferred directly to this context.

---

[210] *Treton Pty Ltd v HM Australia Holdings Pty Ltd* [2011] QSC 38, [40], [51]–[52]. Strictly, loss of bargain damages would not have been available at general law under the relevant hypothetical circumstances, which were that the purchaser had rightfully terminated the contract.

[211] See [5–68], [7–18]–[7–19].

[212] See generally [7–24].

10

Breach of Contract by the Indemnifier

Introduction

[10–1] **Purpose of chapter.** This chapter considers the nature and effect of promises of indemnity against the consequences of the indemnifier's breach of a contract with the indemnified party. Separate treatment is justified because of the well-established legal principles governing the assessment of damages for breach of contract. Much of the chapter is devoted to examining the relationship between these principles and the protection provided by the promise of indemnity.[1]

The case law on indemnities against breach is less developed than that for other types of indemnity. The relevant principles do not appear to be materially different from the general principles outlined earlier, though it can be hard to find specific illustrations. Some of the old decisions must also be approached with caution as they bear the imprint of procedural and substantive rules which have long since been discarded.

[10–2] **Structure of chapter.** The chapter begins by defining a promise of indemnity against breach and considering its various forms. The nature of the indemnity promise is considered next. This section examines a construction peculiar to this form of indemnity, namely, that the promise may attach to the secondary obligation to pay compensation for breach of contract, rather than stand as a separate primary obligation. The chapter then briefly reviews methods of indemnification before moving to the enforcement of indemnities against breach. There are three significant issues. The first is whether an indemnity against breach supplements or displaces the indemnified party's common law right to damages for breach of contract. The second is the extent to which, if at all, common law damages principles or concepts affect recovery for actual loss under an indemnity against breach. The third is whether specific enforcement is available or even necessary.

Classification

[10–3] **Definition.** The expression 'indemnity against breach' is used to describe a promise of indemnity against the consequences of a breach by the indemnifier of a contract with the indemnified party. That is, the event that activates the indemnity is the indemnifier's breach of contract. This definition refers to the 'consequences' of a breach of contract. An indemnity against breach need not, and generally will not, cover all possible consequences

---

[1] See also JW Carter and W Courtney, 'Indemnities Against Breach of Contract as Agreed Damages Clauses' [2012] *Journal of Business Law* 555.

of that breach. Equally, the scope of an indemnity may cover losses from breach of contract and losses from other events. To the extent that the indemnity protects against the former, it can be regarded as an indemnity against breach.

The scope of the indemnity may include losses that can be described as inter partes or 'personal' losses, in the sense that the losses do not relate to third parties. The loss may be, for example, the indemnified party's failure to obtain the expected benefit of the indemnifier's contractual performance. Alternatively, potential loss may arise from a liability to a third party that has been incurred as a result of the indemnifier's breach of contract. In that situation, the indemnity could be characterised as an indemnity against breach, or as an indemnity against claims by or liabilities to third parties, which happens to have been activated by a breach of contract. The better view is that this distinction is not significant because the same principles apply on either characterisation.

Express Indemnities

[10–4] **Indemnity against 'breach'.** In this form, the indemnifier promises to indemnify against its 'breach' or against its 'non-performance' of the contract. Breach of contract is an event leading to or an occasion for loss:[2] the indemnifier's breach may, but will not necessarily, cause loss to the indemnified party. Accordingly, an indemnity against 'breach' is directed to loss arising as a consequence of breach. In *County and District Properties Ltd v C Jenner & Sons Ltd*,[3] various sub-contractors promised to indemnify the main contractor against 'any breach non-observance or non-performance' of a sub-contract and also against 'any act or omission' of a sub-contractor which involved the main contractor in liability to the employer under the main contract. Swanwick J explained that 'an indemnity against a breach, or an act, or an omission, can only be an indemnity against the harmful consequences that may flow from it'.[4]

[10–5] **Indemnity against consequences of breach.** A common form of drafting relates a type of loss or potential loss to the indemnifier's breach of contract using a causal or connective descriptor. So, a clause may refer to claims, liabilities, or losses 'caused by',[5] 'contributed to by',[6] 'on account of',[7] 'as a consequence of',[8] 'arising as a result of',[9] or 'arising from'[10] a breach, default and so forth.

[10–6] **Indemnity against claims presupposing breach.** *Link Investments Pty Ltd v Zaraba Pty Ltd*[11] illustrates another form of indemnity against breach. In a contract for the sale of land, the purchaser warranted, by clause 3.1(a), that it had not been introduced to the property by an agent other than its own agent 'in circumstances which could give rise to a

---

[2] cf *Alfred McAlpine Construction Ltd v Panatown Ltd* [2001] 1 AC 518, 534 (Lord Clyde).
[3] *County and District Properties Ltd v C Jenner & Sons Ltd* [1976] 2 Lloyd's Rep 728 (QB). cf *White Industries Qld Pty Ltd v Hennessey Glass & Aluminium Systems Pty Ltd* [1999] 1 Qd R 210 (CA).
[4] *County and District Properties Ltd v C Jenner & Sons Ltd* [1976] 2 Lloyd's Rep 728 (QB), 735.
[5] *De Santo v Munduna Investments Ltd (in liq)* (1981) 12 ATR 517 (NSWCA).
[6] *Andar Transport Pty Ltd v Brambles Ltd* [2004] HCA 28; (2004) 217 CLR 424.
[7] See the covenants implied by Law of Property Act 1925, s 77(1)(C); Land Registration Act 1925, s 24(1)(b) (now repealed in relation to leases granted on or after 1 January 1996).
[8] *GEC Alsthom Australia Ltd v City of Sunshine* (FCA, 20 February 1996).
[9] *F&D Normoyle Pty Ltd v Transfield Pty Ltd* [2005] NSWCA 193; (2005) 63 NSWLR 502.
[10] *Kingston v Francis* [2001] EWCA Civ 1711.
[11] *Link Investments Pty Ltd v Zaraba Pty Ltd* [2001] NSWCA 14.

claim against the vendor for commission'. In clause 3.1(b), the purchaser promised to indemnify the vendor against 'any claim' in clause 3.1(a). It was held that 'any claim' meant any well-founded claim by an agent entitled to commission.[12] That construction effectively treated clause 3.1(b) as an indemnity against breach of clause 3.1(a). If the claim was bad, then the vendor would not have established a breach by the purchaser of the warranty in clause 3.1(a). If the claim was good, the purchaser would have been in breach of clause 3.1(a) and the indemnity in clause 3.1(b) would have applied.

[10–7] **Whether promise to perform is merely promise to indemnify.** Consider a contract between A and B in which A promises to perform and observe B's obligations to C. There may also be a further promise by A to indemnify B against those obligations, or to indemnify B against breach or non-performance of those obligations. For present purposes, nothing turns on a distinction between the two forms of indemnity.[13] A question that sometimes arises is whether A's promise to perform and observe B's obligations retains its distinct character, or whether it is, in essence, only a promise of indemnity against A's failure to do so. On the latter construction, A does not breach its contract with B merely because it fails to perform and observe B's obligations to C. The indemnity is activated by A's non-performance or non-observance but it is not an indemnity against A's breach of contract.

The approach has not been wholly consistent. A's promise to perform B's obligations to C may be construed to be just that,[14] but in other cases, as only a promise to indemnify B against A's non-performance.[15] Again, promises to perform B's obligations and to indemnify may be construed as two distinct promises,[16] or in composite, as only a promise to indemnify. Situations in which the promise to perform has been construed only as a promise to indemnify against non-performance include: (1) where B assigns to A its interest as lessee in a lease, with A promising to pay the rent and perform and observe the covenants in the lease and to indemnify B against them;[17] (2) where B transfers to A a freehold land, with A covenanting to perform and observe covenants affecting the land;[18] and (3) where B effects a transfer to A of the equity of redemption in a property, with A covenanting to pay the sums or perform the obligations secured by the mortgage and to indemnify B against the same.[19]

Harris v Boots, Cash Chemists (Southern) Ltd[20] is in the first category. The lessee assigned the residue of a lease, with the assignee promising to pay the rent, perform and observe the

---

[12] See generally [6–36].

[13] *cf Gooch v Clutterbuck* [1899] 2 QB 148 (CA), 153 (Vaughan Williams LJ).

[14] *Butler Estates Co Ltd v Bean* [1942] 1 KB 1 (CA). See 'Note' (1942) 58 *Law Quarterly Review* 25.

[15] In a third group of cases, A's promise to perform provides the basis for implying an additional indemnity from A to B against A's breach: see [10–11].

[16] See, eg, *Saward v Anstey* (1825) 2 Bing 519; 130 ER 406; *Carr v Roberts* (1833) 5 B & Ad 78; 110 ER 721; *Smith v Howell* (1851) 6 Ex 730; 155 ER 739; *Hodgson v Wood* (1863) 2 H & C 649; 159 ER 269; *Official Assignee v Jarvis* [1923] NZLR 1009 (CA).

[17] *Harris v Boots, Cash Chemists (Southern) Ltd* [1904] 2 Ch 376 (Ch); *Re Poole and Clarke's Contract* [1904] 2 Ch 173 (CA), 177 (Vaughan Williams LJ); *Scottish & Newcastle plc v Raguz* [2003] EWCA Civ 1070, [12] (Morritt VC). *cf Re Perkins; Poyser v Beyfus* [1898] 2 Ch 182 (CA), 187 (North J), 189–90 (Lindley MR). Contrast *Butler Estates Co Ltd v Bean* [1942] 1 KB 1 (CA).

[18] *Re Poole and Clarke's Contract* [1904] 2 Ch 173 (CA); *Reckitt v Cody* [1920] 2 Ch 452 (Ch). *cf Ridgewood Properties Group Ltd v Valero Energy Ltd* [2013] EWHC 98 (Ch); [2013] 3 WLR 327, [68]–[74] (transfer of various freehold and leasehold interests).

[19] *Goldsmid-Montefiore v Cavendish Land Co* (Bennett J, 19 December 1940) noted in *Butler Estates Co Ltd v Bean* [1942] 1 KB 1 (CA). Contrast *Official Assignee v Jarvis* [1923] NZLR 1009 (CA).

[20] *Harris v Boots, Cash Chemists (Southern) Ltd* [1904] 2 Ch 376 (Ch).

covenants in the lease and to indemnify the lessee against all claims and demands on account of the same. The assignee disregarded a negative covenant in the lease that prohibited alterations to the premises without the landlord's approval. At issue was whether the lessee could enforce the assignee's observance of the negative covenant and so compel the assignee to restore the premises. Warrington J held that the assignee's promises amounted to a promise of indemnity only and so refused to grant an injunction.

[10–8] **Rationale for construction.** The rationale in the cases considered above[21] is that the indemnified party has no apparent interest in receiving performance per se. The promise to perform and observe the indemnified party's obligations merely reinforces that the object is to keep the indemnified party harmless against the consequences of non-performance.[22] Accordingly, this construction was not adopted in *Ayling v Wade*.[23] The lessee of premises sub-let part of them. A term of the sub-lease was that the lessee/sub-lessor would pay the rent and observe the covenants in the head lease and indemnify the sub-lessee against the same. The premises fell out of repair and the sub-lessee was forced temporarily to close his business conducted on the premises. The sub-lessee then claimed damages from the lessee/sub-lessor for failing to observe the corresponding covenant in the head lease. The English Court of Appeal rejected the argument that the lessee/sub-lessor's covenants in the sub-lease amounted only to a single promise of indemnity, which was intended to protect the sub-lessee against forfeiture by the head lessor. The sub-lessee was concerned with the lessee/sub-lessor's compliance with the substance of the covenants in the head lease.

[10–9] **Losses or liabilities that may or may not arise from breach.** The scope of the indemnity may cover losses or liabilities arising in a variety of ways, only some of which constitute a breach of contract by the indemnifier. A typical example is the indemnity given by a contractor and expressed to apply generally to losses or liabilities incurred in connection with the works, or the performance of the services under contract.[24] The scope may be deliberately so framed because some of the anticipated losses or liabilities do not necessarily depend on the indemnifier's breach of contract. One such situation is where the indemnifier and the employer/customer are both held liable in negligence for injury to a third party. Alternatively, the indemnifying contractor may accept responsibility for losses or liabilities of the employer that are caused by the contractor's negligence or that of its sub-contractors. Such drafting is common in construction contracts.

Similarly, the usual form of indemnity from the charterer to the owner of the vessel under a time charterparty is stated in terms of the master's compliance with the charterer's orders, or signature of bills of lading. Depending upon the circumstances, a loss to the owner might be recoverable under the indemnity or, in the alternative, as damages for the

---

[21] See [10–7].

[22] *Ayling v Wade* [1961] 2 QB 228 (CA), 233–34 (Danckwerts LJ); *Easyair Ltd v Opal Telecom Ltd* [2009] EWHC 339 (Ch), [37].

[23] *Ayling v Wade* [1961] 2 QB 228 (CA). See also *West London Railway Co v London and North Western Railway Co* (1853) 11 CB 327, 351–52; 138 ER 499, 509 (Parke B).

[24] *Furness Shipbuilding Co Ltd v London and North Eastern Railway Co* (1934) 50 TLR 257 (HL); *Smith v South Wales Switchgear Co Ltd* [1978] 1 WLR 165 (HL); *EE Caledonia Ltd v Orbit Valve Co Europe* [1994] 1 WLR 1515 (CA); *Qantas Airways Ltd v Aravco Ltd* (1996) 185 CLR 43; *Erect Safe Scaffolding (Australia) Pty Ltd v Sutton* [2008] NSWCA 114; (2008) 72 NSWLR 1. See further [4–20], [4–21].

charterer's breach.[25] Other examples include: where breach is listed among other trigger events, such as an act, omission, neglect or default;[26] where the indemnity applies to a 'breach or alleged breach' of a contract;[27] and where the indemnity operates retrospectively, so as to include liability for breaches that occurred before the indemnifier assumed responsibility for ongoing performance.[28]

Implied Indemnities

[10–10] **Implied indemnities against breach.** Indemnities exclusively directed to the consequences of breach by the indemnifier are rarely implied into contracts. It has been said on several occasions that a contractual promise to perform an act is distinct from a promise to indemnify against the consequences of not doing it.[29] There is already a remedy at law – damages – that covers substantially the same ground as an indemnity against breach. As a matter of factual implication, an indemnity is rarely obvious or necessary to give business efficacy to the contract.[30] Likewise, it is rarely necessary or reasonable to imply by law such a potent term.

[10–11] **Assumption of responsibility for another's obligations.** An exception emerged from a series of cases, most of which concerned sub-leases or assignments of leases or sub-leases, where the superior landlord claimed against an intermediate party who, in turn, claimed against the sub-lessee or an assignee.[31] Those cases, perhaps, went no further than to acknowledge an exceptional application of principles of causation or remoteness, which allowed the promisee to recover damages for certain losses on a more generous (indemnity) measure. Nonetheless, the reasoning came to be rationalised in terms of an inferred or implied indemnity against breach.[32]

The implication was expressly recognised by Brett LJ in *Hornby v Cardwell*.[33] A lease of premises contained covenants to keep in repair, paint and leave in repair. The lessee later sub-let the premises, the sub-lease being 'subject in all respects to the terms of the existing lease'. The lessor sued the lessee for breach of the covenants in the lease. The lessee joined

---

[25] *Moel Tryvan Ship Co Ltd v Krüger & Co Ltd* [1907] 1 KB 809 (CA) and on appeal *Krüger & Co Ltd v Moel Tryvan Ship Co Ltd* [1907] AC 272 (HL); *Dawson Line Ltd v Adler AG* [1932] 1 KB 433 (CA), 438–39 (Scrutton LJ); *Telfair Shipping Corp v Inersea Carriers SA (The Caroline P)* [1985] 1 WLR 553 (QB), 568. *cf ENE Kos 1 Ltd v Petroleo Brasileiro SA (The Kos) (No 2)* [2012] UKSC 17; [2012] 2 WLR 976 (termination for non-serious breach).

[26] *Andar Transport Pty Ltd v Brambles Ltd* [2004] HCA 28; (2004) 217 CLR 424.

[27] *Codemasters Software Co Ltd v Automobile Club de L'Ouest* [2009] EWHC 2361 (Ch); [2010] FSR 12.

[28] *Gooch v Clutterbuck* [1899] 2 QB 148 (CA); *Safeway Food Stores Ltd v Property Growth Assurance Co Ltd* [1999] EWCA Civ 1531.

[29] *Birmingham and District Land Co v London and North Western Railway Co* (1886) 34 Ch D 261 (CA), 266 (Chitty J), 276–77 (Fry LJ); *Hammond & Co v Bussey* (1888) 20 QBD 79 (CA), 97 (Bowen LJ), 101 (Fry LJ); *Newman v McNicol* (1938) 38 SR (NSW) 609 (SC), 626; *Nederlandsch-Amerikaansche Stoomvaart Maatschappij NV v Royal Mail Lines Ltd (The Nieuw Amsterdam)* [1958] 1 Lloyd's Rep 412 (QB), 421.

[30] *County and District Properties Ltd v C Jenner & Sons Ltd* [1976] 2 Lloyd's Rep 728 (QB), 739; *TAL Structural Engineers Pty Ltd v Vaughan Constructions Pty Ltd* [1989] VR 545 (FC), 558 (Kaye J), 565 (Ormiston J). *cf Triad Shipping Co v Stellar Chartering & Brokerage Inc (The Island Archon)* [1994] 2 Lloyd's Rep 227 (CA), 237 (Evans LJ).

[31] See, eg, *Burnett v Lynch* (1826) 5 B & C 589, 610; 108 ER 220, 227 (Littledale J); *Penley v Watts* (1841) 7 M & W 601; 151 ER 907; *Walker v Hatton* (1842) 10 M & W 249; 152 ER 462; *Logan v Hall* (1847) 4 CB 598; 136 ER 642 (but *cf* 625; 653 (Maule J)).

[32] *cf* JW Smith, *A Selection of Leading Cases* (JS Willes and HS Keating eds, 4th edn, London, William Maxwell, 1856), 127.

[33] *Hornby v Cardwell* (1881) 8 QBD 329 (CA).

the sub-lessee as a third party, claiming the amount of the dilapidations for which the lessee was liable to the lessor, together with the lessor's costs in the principal action paid by the lessee and the lessee's own costs in that action. According to Brett LJ, whether the sub-lessee could be held liable for those costs depended on whether the sub-lessee had undertaken to indemnify the lessee. The implied indemnity, Brett LJ explained, 'seems to arise whenever two contracts are made, and the second contract contains a stipulation to do the very thing which is undertaken to be done by the first'.[34] On this basis, the costs were recoverable.

[10–12] **Subsequent developments.** In *Hornby v Cardwell*,[35] Brett LJ appears to have resorted to an indemnity to overcome the then-prevailing view that the lessee could not recover the legal costs from the sub-lessee as damages under *Hadley v Baxendale*.[36] That view was later exploded in *Hammond & Co v Bussey*.[37] The English Court of Appeal confronted an argument that costs could be recovered under a contract of indemnity but not as damages for breach of contract under *Hadley v Baxendale*. Brett LJ, now Lord Esher MR, acknowledged that in previous decisions he had referred to an implied contract to indemnify. He continued: 'I do not feel sure . . . that the obligation implied by the law under such circumstances as those with which we are now dealing might not be correctly expressed by that formula; but I purposely abstain from so deciding'.[38]

Fry LJ still entertained doubts whether 'an implied contract of indemnity can be raised in the case of a contract to do a particular thing, where the minds of the parties in contracting are directed not to the breach but to the performance of the contract'.[39] Fry LJ had expressed the same sentiment earlier in *Birmingham and District Land Co v London and North Western Railway Co*,[40] but had distinguished 'identical contracts where the second contract is entered into with a knowledge of the first'. Bowen LJ doubted 'whether out of the contract to do a particular thing, you can extract a contract, if that is not done, to do something else'.[41] But Bowen LJ also referred to his own judgment from *Birmingham* for support. In that judgment he had expressed general concurrence with Cotton LJ's analysis of several cases including *Hornby*. In *Birmingham*, Cotton LJ reiterated the view he had intimated in *Hornby*, namely, that the implied indemnity in *Hornby* was a genuine one.

Brett LJ's principle from *Hornby* has been applied or referred to without disapproval on several occasions.[42] A plausible argument could be made for treating the principle nowadays as a particular application of the second limb of *Hadley v Baxendale*,[43] but the better view seems to be that this is a genuine instance of an indemnity against breach.

---

[34] *Hornby v Cardwell* (1881) 8 QBD 329 (CA), 337. *cf* 333 (Jessel MR) and 339 (Cotton LJ) ('in no way dissent[ing]' on the point).

[35] *Hornby v Cardwell* (1881) 8 QBD 329 (CA).

[36] *Hadley v Baxendale* (1854) 9 Ex 341; 156 ER 145. See, eg, *Baxendale v London, Chatham and Dover Railway Co* (1873) LR 10 Ex 35, esp 44 (Quain J); *Fisher v Val de Travers Asphalte Co* (1876) 1 CPD 511. As to the position pre-*Hadley*, see [10–44].

[37] *Hammond & Co v Bussey* (1888) 20 QBD 79 (CA).

[38] *Hammond & Co v Bussey* (1888) 20 QBD 79 (CA), 90 (perhaps alluding to *Grébert-Borgnis v Nugent* (1885) 15 QBD 85 (CA), 90 though the remarks could apply mutatis mutandis to *Hornby v Cardwell* (1881) 8 QBD 329 (CA), 337).

[39] *Hammond & Co v Bussey* (1888) 20 QBD 79 (CA), 101.

[40] *Birmingham and District Land Co v London and North Western Railway Co* (1886) 34 Ch D 261 (CA), 277.

[41] *Hammond & Co v Bussey* (1888) 20 QBD 79 (CA), 97.

[42] *Pontifex v Foord* (1884) 12 QBD 152 (DC); 155–56 (Pollock B); *Travers v Richardson* (1920) 20 SR (NSW) 367 (SC), 371; *McColl's Wholesale Pty Ltd v State Bank of New South Wales* [1984] 3 NSWLR 365 (SC), 377; *Sears Properties Netherlands BV v Coal Pension Properties Ltd* 2001 SLT 761 (OH), 766.

[43] *cf Clare v Dobson* [1911] 1 KB 35 (KB), 41.

[10–13] **Basis for implication.** If the implied indemnity is to be recognised, it must stand as a limited exception to the general proposition that a promise to perform does not import a promise to indemnify against breach. The rationale for implying an indemnity from A to B against A's breach is that A and B have intended to effect, between themselves, a transfer to A of responsibility for B's obligations to a third party, C. From C's perspective, of course, the arrangement is *res inter alios acta.* The appropriate doctrinal basis for implication is not clear. It is perhaps best explained on an ad hoc basis, either as an implication in fact, in the strict sense, or as an inference drawn from the express terms of the contracts and the surrounding circumstances.[44]

Three relevant factors can be identified. The first concerns the configuration of obligations. A must promise B to perform B's obligations to a third party, C, or promise to perform the same obligations for B. B's obligations to C are generally found in a contract that already exists at the time of A's contract with B.

The second factor is that the obligations assumed by A must be the same in nature as those owed by B to C. So, for example, a shipowner's obligation to the charterer to ensure that the vessel is seaworthy is not the same as the charterer's obligation under a bill of lading for carriage of the goods. Accordingly, the charterer has no implied right to indemnity against the shipowner merely because unseaworthiness of the vessel renders the charterer liable for damage to the goods.[45] Even where the obligations are identical in nature, the substance must be the same. An obligation upon a lessee, B, to insure property with no beneficiary other than B under the policy may not be the same, in substance, as an obligation upon a sub-lessee, A, to insure only for A. That is because the obligation to insure may be regarded only as a means of ensuring the solvency of that particular party for losses arising due to its default under the lease; or because certain events may allow a claim on B's policy but not A's, or vice versa.[46] Similarly, the old cases show that if a lessee took premises, covenanting to keep them in repair, and sub-let the premises, the sub-lessee also undertaking to keep them in repair, the two obligations were usually not regarded as identical in substance. The extent of the obligation to repair was determined by reference to the state of the premises at the time of the relevant demise; when the sub-lessee took possession some time after the lessee, it could not be assumed that the premises were in the same condition.[47] There was, therefore, no implied indemnity.

The third consideration is that the arrangement between A and B must possess the character of a transfer to A of B's responsibility to C, that is, relief from the obligation or liability to C. It is not enough that B relies on A to perform so that B can fulfil its contract with C. Consider a case where A sells goods to B, warranting that they possess a particular quality or correspond with a certain description, and B reproduces that assurance when on-selling those goods to C; alternatively, B relies on the warranty and supplies the goods to C to meet commitments under a prior contract. In such a case there is generally no implied indemnity from A to B against A's breach.[48] Likewise, a head contractor is not entitled to an

---

[44] *cf TAL Structural Engineers Pty Ltd v Vaughan Constructions Pty Ltd* [1989] VR 545 (FC), 558 (Kaye J), 565 (Ormiston J).

[45] *Speller & Co v Bristol Steam Navigation Co* (1884) 13 QBD 96 (CA).

[46] *Logan v Hall* (1847) 4 CB 598, 613, 622–23, 625; 136 ER 642, 648, 652, 653 (Maule J).

[47] *Penley v Watts* (1841) 7 M & W 601, 608–09; 151 ER 907, 910–11 (Parke B); *Walker v Hatton* (1842) 10 M & W 249, 258; 152 ER 462, 466 (Parke B); *Logan v Hall* (1847) 4 CB 598; 136 ER 642; *Pontifex v Foord* (1884) 12 QBD 152 (DC), 156 (Pollock B).

[48] *Hammond & Co v Bussey* (1888) 20 QBD 79 (CA), 90–91 (Lord Esher MR), 97 (Bowen LJ), 101 (Fry LJ); *Westpac Banking Corp v P&O Containers Ltd* (1991) 102 ALR 239 (FCA), 242; *Total Liban SA v Vitol Energy SA* [2001] QB 643 (QB).

implied indemnity from a sub-contractor merely because default in the performance of the sub-contracted work may render the head contractor liable to the employer.[49]

[10–14] **Analogous situations.** The assumption or transfer of responsibility is a characteristic found in other situations in which indemnities have been implied into existing contracts, or contracts of indemnity have been inferred from the surrounding circumstances. So, for example, where B transfers to A shares in a company, C, the inference usually drawn is that A is to be responsible for any calls on those shares pending registration of the transfer. B is, accordingly, entitled to an indemnity from A against such liability.[50] In the cases on accommodation bills of exchange, the acceptor, B, is primarily liable to the holder, C, but as between B and the drawer, A, it is intended that A be ultimately liable.[51] Likewise, if B upon A's request gives a guarantee to C of A's debts, either party can be held liable to C but, as between A and B, A is to be ultimately liable. Thus, a contract by A to indemnify B against the liability to C may be inferred.[52] A similar point can be made about liabilities to third parties, C, incurred by an agent, B, in the course of performing its duties on the principal's, A's, behalf.[53]

There is also a parallel between the implied indemnity cases and those that concern the construction of an express promise by A to perform B's obligations to C.[54] In some circumstances, a promise in that form is construed only as a promise by A to indemnify B against liability to C arising from A's non-performance. Even where A's promise to perform is coupled with an express indemnity from A to B, the two promises may be construed together to be no more than an indemnity from A to B. In both situations, this construction of the promise to perform draws upon two inferences from the circumstances. The first is that B has no direct interest in performance by A. The second is that the identity of A's obligations to B and B's obligations to C indicates that A was to hold B harmless against B's obligations to C. A feature that distinguishes these cases from the implied indemnity cases is that A's promise to indemnify is express, even if it derives from the construction of other express terms of the contract. A more subtle distinction is that there is no primary obligation upon A to perform B's obligations to C. In contrast, in the implied indemnity cases, the primary obligation to perform remains and the indemnity supplements that obligation.

Nature of Indemnity

[10–15] **Different constructions of the promise of indemnity.** In theory, either of the two usual constructions of an indemnity promise – to prevent loss or to compensate for loss –

---

[49] *County and District Properties Ltd v C Jenner & Sons Ltd* [1976] 2 Lloyd's Rep 728 (QB). *cf TAL Structural Engineers Pty Ltd v Vaughan Constructions Pty Ltd* [1989] VR 545 (FC) (no implied indemnity against liability to injured third party); *Comorex Ltd v Costelloe Tunnelling (London) Ltd* 1995 SLT 1217 (OH) (indemnity not incorporated by reference to main contract).

[50] See generally [6–11].

[51] *Coles Myer Finance Ltd v Commissioner of Taxation* (1992) 176 CLR 640, 657–58 (Mason CJ, Brennan, Dawson, Toohey and Gaudron JJ).

[52] See generally [2–24].

[53] See generally [2–23].

[54] See [10–7].

might apply. There is another possible construction that is peculiar to an indemnity against breach. It is that the promise of indemnity is not a primary obligation but, instead, represents an agreement by the parties as to the basis upon which damages are payable for the indemnifier's breach of some other term of the contract. That is, the indemnity is the source of, or modifies, the secondary obligation to pay compensation for breach of contract. This will be described as the agreed damages construction.

On the whole, the cases favour the preventive construction, with limited support for the compensatory and agreed damages constructions. There may be little difference in practice among the constructions where the indemnified party claims for an actual loss from breach. On any of these constructions, recovery for actual loss is determined by the scope of the indemnity. The choice of construction may, however, affect matters such as whether specific enforcement is available and whether the indemnified party retains a common law right to damages that is independent of the right to indemnity.

Prevention of Loss from Breach

[10–16] Instances of construction. On this construction, the promise of indemnity is a distinct primary obligation to avoid loss to the indemnified party from the indemnifier's breach of contract. The manner in which actions on indemnities against breach were pleaded and analysed in the old cases tends to conform to this construction. It has also been acknowledged that an indemnity against breach may be specifically enforced in relation to liabilities to third parties arising from breach.[55] Specific enforcement is only available where the promise of indemnity is preventive in nature. A further consideration, which is consistent with a preventive construction though not decisive, is that the right to indemnity may be regarded as additional to and independent of the indemnified party's common law right to damages for breach.

[10–17] Historical perspective. The old cases bear the influences of the forms of action and pre-*Hadley v Baxendale*[56] understandings of remoteness of damage. Nonetheless, it emerges clearly enough that a promise of indemnity against breach was often regarded as an obligation distinct from the obligation to pay damages for breach of another term of the contract.[57] An indemnified claimant might aver breach of the relevant term and, further, breach by failing to indemnify against breach of that term. Breach of the indemnity occurred when the claimant was damnified by some event.

In *Smith v Howell*,[58] for example, the claimant, who was the assignee of a sub-lease, made a further assignment to the defendant. The defendant undertook to pay the rent, perform the covenants, and save harmless and indemnify the claimant against default. The defendant defaulted in paying rent and performing repairs and this precipitated a series of actions between superior parties, culminating in an action by the claimant against the defendant. The claimant claimed as damages a sum comprising: (1) an amount for the rent not paid;

---

[55] See [10–61].
[56] *Hadley v Baxendale* (1854) 9 Ex 341; 156 ER 145.
[57] See, eg, *Saward v Anstey* (1825) 2 Bing 519; 130 ER 406; *Carr v Roberts* (1833) 5 B & Ad 78; 110 ER 721; *Groom v Bluck* (1841) 2 Man & G 567; 133 ER 873; *Smith v Howell* (1851) 6 Ex 730; 155 ER 739; *Hodgson v Wood* (1863) 2 H & C 649; 159 ER 269. cf *Taylor v Young* (1820) 3 B & Ald 521; 106 ER 752 (distinct breaches pleaded but indemnity apparently qualifying damages payable).
[58] *Smith v Howell* (1851) 6 Ex 730; 155 ER 739.

(2) an amount for the repairs not performed; (3) an amount for costs incurred in an earlier action by the holder of the reversionary interest in the lease against the sub-lessee; (4) an amount for costs incurred by the now claimant unsuccessfully defending an action by the sub-lessee. In the case presented for the claimant, items (1) and (2) were attributed to the defendant's breaches of the covenants to pay rent and repair the premises respectively; items (3) and (4) were assigned to the defendant's breach of the covenant to indemnify the claimant against breach. The basis of the latter breach was that the claimant was damnified by the action or judgment against him. That view was accepted by the Court of Exchequer.[59]

In *Groom v Bluck*,[60] the defendant purchased a business from the claimant and another, and promised, inter alia, to pay the rent and taxes on the associated premises, and to indemnify and save them harmless against loss sustained by non-payment. Some of their goods, which were on the premises, were distrained for rent and taxes not paid by the defendant. Maule J explained that the claimant was damnified by the seizure, so as to render the defendant liable under the indemnity.[61]

Compensation for Loss from Breach

[10–18] **Instances of construction.** There are relatively few clear examples of this construction.[62] Bowen LJ appears to have adopted it in *Hammond & Co v Bussey*,[63] in the course of addressing the argument that legal costs were recoverable under an indemnity but not as ordinary damages for breach of contract. If there was a special agreement as to costs, then, he said, 'the question whether they can be treated as damages . . . does not arise. They are the subject-matter of the contract itself, and the case is like that of any other contract to pay a sum of money'.[64]

[10–19] **Limitations of construction.** This construction cannot explain the availability of specific enforcement of the indemnity in relation to liabilities to third parties. This does not mean that the possibility of a compensatory construction must be entirely discounted. It does suggest, however, that the construction would be unusual where the scope of the indemnity covers liabilities to third parties. The construction would, similarly, be inappropriate where an indemnity against breach is implied on the basis of a transfer of responsibility. The purpose of such an arrangement, to which the indemnity gives effect, is to relieve the indemnified party of its obligations to the third party.[65]

The compensatory construction might also be criticised for redundancy. A primary obligation to pay compensation for loss from breach substantially replicates the secondary obligation that is implied by law. Moreover, if unnecessary replication is generally a reason against implying an indemnity against breach, then that reason applies a fortiori where the

---

[59] As to the correctness of this view, see [10–26]–[10–27].
[60] *Groom v Bluck* (1841) 2 Man & G 567; 133 ER 873.
[61] See also *Groom v Bluck* (1841) 2 Man & G 567, 572; 133 ER 873, 875 (argument of counsel associating seizure of goods with breach of indemnity).
[62] See, eg, *Bovis Lend Lease Ltd v RD Fire Protection Ltd* [2003] EWHC 939 (TCC); (2003) 89 Con LR 169, [64]. This construction appears to be implicit in *Codemasters Software Co Ltd v Automobile Club de L'Ouest (No 2)* [2009] EWHC 3194 (Ch); [2010] FSR 13, [31]–[32]. cf also *Nederlandsch-Amerikaansche Stoomvaart Maatschappij NV v Royal Mail Lines Ltd (The Nieuw Amsterdam)* [1958] 1 Lloyd's Rep 412 (QB).
[63] *Hammond & Co v Bussey* (1888) 20 QBD 79 (CA).
[64] *Hammond & Co v Bussey* (1888) 20 QBD 79 (CA), 97.
[65] See [10–13].

indemnity promise is compensatory in nature. There are, of course, potential differences: compensation may be assessed on a different basis, or the indemnified party's right of action may accrue at a different time. But from that perspective, the agreed damages construction can usually provide a simpler and more direct route to the same result. The principal advantage of the compensatory construction over the agreed damages construction is that it affords a simple explanation of why the right to indemnity against breach can be additional and alternative to the common law right to damages.

An Agreement on Damages[66]

[10–20] Indemnity is a secondary obligation. A third construction is that the promise of indemnity against breach is not a primary obligation at all; rather, it represents an agreement that the indemnifier will pay damages for its breach of contract on the specified (indemnity) basis. The indemnity could be regarded as the consensual foundation of a secondary obligation to pay compensation,[67] or as modifying the secondary obligation to pay compensation that is implied by law. Conceptually, the former view is more coherent and elegant, though it is not necessary here to choose between them.

[10–21] Distinction between indemnity and damages. A distinction has sometimes been drawn between claims for 'indemnity' and claims for 'damages', in applying limitations statutes[68] or procedural rules concerning the joinder of other parties.[69] The decision most often cited is *Birmingham and District Land Co v London and North Western Railway Co*.[70] Bowen LJ said:[71]

> [A] right to damages . . . is not a right to indemnity as such. It is the converse of such a right. A right to indemnity as such is given by the original bargain between the parties. The right to damages is given in consequence of the breach of the original contract between the parties. It is an incident which the law attaches to the breach of a contract, and is not a provision of the contract itself.

Fry LJ said:[72]

> A breach of contract gives rise, or may give rise, to a right to damages, but those damages are not the subject of the contract. They arise from the breach of the contract, and therefore they are in no sense the subject of the contract itself . . . Therefore the right to such damages is not a right to indemnity, although when you come to ascertain what the measure of damages is, it may be that indemnity will properly express that measure of damages.

The issue in *Birmingham* was whether a claim for damages for breach of contract was a claim for 'indemnity' under the applicable third party procedure rules. It was held that the

---

[66] See Carter and Courtney, 'Indemnities Against Breach of Contract as Agreed Damages Clauses' (n 1).

[67] *cf C Czarnikow Ltd v Koufos* [1966] 2 QB 695 (CA), 731 (Diplock LJ).

[68] *McLaren Maycroft & Co v Fletcher Development Co Ltd* [1973] 2 NZLR 100 (CA), 116–17 (Richmond J).

[69] *Speller & Co v Bristol Steam Navigation Co* (1884) 13 QBD 96 (CA); *Marten v Whale* [1917] 1 KB 544 (KB), 551; *Westpac Banking Corp v P&O Containers Ltd* (1991) 102 ALR 239 (FCA), 242. *cf Johnston v Salvage Association* (1887) 19 QBD 458 (CA) (suing and labouring clause).

[70] *Birmingham and District Land Co v London and North Western Railway Co* (1886) 34 Ch D 261 (CA). The decision was cited with general approval in *Eastern Shipping Co Ltd v Quah Beng Kee* [1924] AC 177 (PC), 183.

[71] *Birmingham and District Land Co v London and North Western Railway Co* (1886) 34 Ch D 261 (CA), 274–75.

[72] *Birmingham and District Land Co v London and North Western Railway Co* (1886) 34 Ch D 261 (CA), 276.

rules required the claim to be for an indemnity in the strict sense. A claim for damages for breach of contract did not qualify even though the measure of damage might provide full compensation for loss. The court was not considering an express or implied promise to indemnify against breach. *Birmingham* has since been cited with approval in several cases concerning indemnities against breach.[73] In those cases, the point has been that an indemnity against breach will rarely be implied because the promisee already has a common law right to damages for breach. The distinction between 'indemnity' and 'damages' drawn in *Birmingham* and accepted in subsequent decisions does not directly bear on, nor necessarily preclude, the agreed damages construction.

[10–22] Instances of construction. A leading illustration is *Burkard & Co Ltd v Wahlen.*[74] A contract for the sale of tin clippings stated that

> you [*sc* the sellers] must keep us [*sc* the buyer] indemnified if you should not fulfil your contract, and our buyers on the other side succeed in a claim against us, when you will have to pay whatever we shall have to pay to satisfy our friends on the other side.

The sellers defaulted in delivery and the buyer claimed damages according to the usual measure, namely, the difference between the market price and the contract price. The claim failed. The Full Court of the Supreme Court of New South Wales held that the indemnity was a 'self-elected measure of damages' that 'entirely displaced' the usual measure of damages for non-delivery.[75] The decision was upheld by majority on appeal to the High Court of Australia.

Another example is *Petre v Duncombe.*[76] The recitals in a deed between a debtor and guarantor stated that the debtor had agreed 'to indemnify' the guarantor against liability to the creditor. By other terms of the deed, the debtor covenanted to make the relevant payments to the creditor and transferred to the guarantor certain property as security. The guarantor was entitled to use the property to 'indemnify and protect himself' against any losses incurred by reason of his position as surety. The guarantor answered for the debtor's defaults over an extended period, and then claimed the sums paid and interest as damages for the debtor's breach of the covenant to pay the creditor. Whether the guarantor could recover for interest was a matter of dispute because, by the time *Petre* was decided, the common law had firmed in its opposition to the award of interest as damages. Erle J distinguished other cases which denied recovery of interest on the ground that the express terms of the contracts had not indicated that the parties had bargained for interest. Erle J remarked that the guarantor had been 'damnified' by losing interest and that the award of damages 'ought to indemnify' him.[77] The parties had, essentially, adopted an indemnity measure of loss for breach of the covenant to pay the creditor.

[10–23] Analogous situations. Although not expressly described as indemnities, some agreed damages clauses that rely upon variables are, in effect, attempts to secure for the

---

[73] *Nederlandsch-Amerikaansche Stoomvaart Maatschappij NV v Royal Mail Lines Ltd (The Nieuw Amsterdam)* [1958] 1 Lloyd's Rep 412 (QB); *County and District Properties Ltd v C Jenner & Sons Ltd* [1976] 2 Lloyd's Rep 728 (QB); *TAL Structural Engineers Pty Ltd v Vaughan Constructions Pty Ltd* [1989] VR 545 (FC). *cf Total Liban SA v Vitol Energy SA* [2001] QB 643 (QB), 660 (whether usual damnification rule for indemnities should be applied to claim for common law damages).

[74] *Burkard & Co Ltd v Wahlen* (1928) 41 CLR 508.

[75] *Burkard & Co Ltd v Wahlen* (1928) 28 SR (NSW) 607 (FC), 611.

[76] *Petre v Duncombe* (1851) 20 LJQB 242.

[77] *Petre v Duncombe* (1851) 20 LJQB 242, 244.

promisee an indemnity against loss. Agreements for the lease of chattels often contain detailed provisions for calculating the lessor's loss. In *AMEV-UDC Finance Ltd v Austin*,[78] Mason and Wilson JJ referred to a lessor recovering its 'actual loss' arising from early termination of the lease under a 'correctly drawn indemnity provision'. Another example is a provision in a contract for the sale of land which, in the event of the purchaser's default, confers upon the vendor the power to resell the property and recover as 'liquidated damages' any deficiency in the sale price, together with expenses incidental to the resale.[79] Where the property is resold, the effect of the provision is essentially the same as if the purchaser had indemnified the vendor.

A parallel can also be drawn with indemnity insurance. A claim for a total loss under a valued policy has been described as one for 'liquidated' damages.[80] The reason for applying that description to a claim for a total, but not partial,[81] loss seems to be this: if the insured can establish a total loss, the amount payable is simply the value stated in the policy, whereas if the loss is only partial, there must be a binding ascertainment of the extent of the loss before the amount payable can be computed. This does not mean that the insured's claim for a partial loss is at large. The loss must still fall within the terms of the policy. The policy embodies an agreement as to the value of the insured subject-matter and the valuation of the loss proceeds on that basis.[82]

[10–24] **Limitations of construction.** There are two principal difficulties with the agreed damages construction. It is not easily reconciled with those cases that acknowledge the availability of specific enforcement of the indemnity in relation to liabilities to third parties. An indemnifier cannot be compelled to perform a non-existent primary obligation to indemnify. This construction may, therefore, have more relevance where the indemnity covers losses inter partes or 'personal' losses of the indemnified party.

An agreed damages clause generally displaces the promisee's common law right to damages for loss arising from the breach that activates the clause. If the same view were taken of an indemnity against breach, it would appear to follow that the indemnified party is restricted to claiming damages on the basis defined by the indemnity. There are, however, decisions that accept that the right to indemnity and the common law right to damages are alternatives.[83] Not all of those decisions can be explained on the ground that the indemnity is limited to particular breaches or particular aspects of a single breach.

Establishing Loss

[10–25] **Occurrence of loss.** The time at which loss occurs under the indemnity depends on the construction of the contract and the nature of the loss. The indemnified party does

---

[78] *AMEV-UDC Finance Ltd v Austin* (1986) 162 CLR 170, 194.

[79] See, eg, *Ockenden v Henly* (1858) 1 EB & E 485; 120 ER 590; *Howe v Smith* (1884) 27 Ch D 89 (CA); *Griffiths v Vezey* [1906] 1 Ch 796 (Ch); *Cooper v Ungar* (1958) 100 CLR 510.

[80] *Irving v Manning* (1847) 1 HLC 287, 307; 9 ER 766, 775; *Alexander v Ajax Insurance Co Ltd* [1956] VLR 436 (SC), 445–46 (Sholl J).

[81] *Castelli v Boddington* (1852) 1 El & Bl 66; 118 ER 361; *Luckie v Bushby* (1853) 13 CB 864; 138 ER 1443.

[82] See, eg, Marine Insurance Act 1906, s 27(3); *Elcock v Thomson* [1949] 2 KB 755 (KB); *British Traders' Insurance Co Ltd v Monson* (1964) 111 CLR 86, 93 (Kitto, Taylor and Owen JJ).

[83] See [10–33].

not necessarily sustain a loss merely because the indemnifier breaches the contract, nor do all losses coincide with the occurrence of breach.[84] There has been some conflict in the treatment of liabilities to third parties that arise from the indemnifier's breach. The usual rule for indemnities against claims by or liabilities to third parties differs from the usual rule applied to claims for damages for breach of contract. The former rule, which is a default rule of construction, is that the indemnified party is damnified not by the liability itself but by payment to discharge the liability.[85] By way of contrast, the rule applicable to claims for common law damages is that the promisee can recover for a definite liability to a third party even though it has not yet paid that third party.[86]

[10–26] No damnification until payment of liability. *County and District Properties Ltd v C Jenner & Sons Ltd*[87] illustrates the usual rule applied to indemnities. The main contractor was sued by the employer for defects in the works; the contractor in turn claimed on indemnities given by various sub-contractors. The action against the main contractor was brought within six years of practical completion of the works, but the contractor did not join the sub-contractors until more than six years after that date. Assuming that the sub-contractors' breaches, if any, had occurred before practical completion, the question was whether the contractor's actions against the sub-contractors were barred by the limitations statute. Swanwick J accepted that the contractor could not enforce the indemnities in respect of an actual loss until it paid the employer. The contractor might have sought specific enforcement in respect of a potential loss when its liability to the employer had been established, for example, by judgment.[88] On either basis, the contractor's actions on the indemnities were within time, though an ordinary action for damages for breach of contract would not have been.

[10–27] Damnification before payment of liability. The clearest and most significant decision is *Smith v Howell*,[89] where the claimant's claim under the indemnity succeeded even though he had not paid the legal costs that were the subject of his claim. *Collinge v Heywood*[90] was raised by the defendant but distinguished by the Court of Exchequer. The point of distinction seems to have been that the indemnified party in *Collinge* paid the

---

[84] See, eg, *County and District Properties Ltd v C Jenner & Sons Ltd* [1976] 2 Lloyd's Rep 728 (QB); *City of London v Reeve & Co Ltd* [2000] EWHC 138 (TCC); [2000] BLR 211; *Zaccardi v Caunt* [2008] NSWCA 202, [34] (Campbell JA). cf *ENE Kos 1 Ltd v Petroleo Brasileiro SA (The Kos) (No 2)* [2012] UKSC 17; [2012] 2 WLR 976 (loss sustained after termination for breach).

[85] See [6–23].

[86] *Randall v Raper* (1858) EB & E 84; 120 ER 438; *Total Liban SA v Vitol Energy SA* [2001] QB 643 (QB). cf *Household Machines Ltd v Cosmos Exporters Ltd* [1947] 1 KB 217 (KB); *Trans Trust SPRL v Danubian Trading Co Ltd* [1952] 2 QB 297 (CA), 303 (Somervell LJ), 307 (Denning LJ); *Deeny v Gooda Walker Ltd (in liq)* [1995] 1 WLR 1206 (QB), 1213–14 (where liability to third party is uncertain); *Biffa Waste Services Ltd v Maschinenfabrik Ernst Hese GmbH* [2008] EWHC 2210 (TCC); [2009] PNLR 5, [79]–[81] (no recovery where obvious that liability would not be paid).

[87] *County and District Properties Ltd v C Jenner & Sons Ltd* [1976] 2 Lloyd's Rep 728 (QB). See also *Taylor v Young* (1820) 3 B & Ald 521; 106 ER 752; *City of London v Reeve & Co Ltd* [2000] EWHC 138 (TCC); [2000] BLR 211, [26]–[35]; *Zaccardi v Caunt* [2008] NSWCA 202, [34] (Campbell JA) (citing *Collinge v Heywood* (1839) 9 Ad & E 634; 112 ER 1352).

[88] *County and District Properties Ltd v C Jenner & Sons Ltd* [1976] 2 Lloyd's Rep 728 (QB), 734–36.

[89] *Smith v Howell* (1851) 6 Ex 730; 155 ER 739 (see [10–17]). cf *White Industries Qld Pty Ltd v Hennessey Glass & Aluminium Systems Pty Ltd* [1999] 1 Qd R 210 (CA), 226–27 (Derrington J); *Bovis Lend Lease Ltd v RD Fire Protection Ltd* [2003] EWHC 939 (TCC); (2003) 89 Con LR 169, [65]; *Carillion JM Ltd v Phi Group Ltd* [2011] EWHC 1379 (TCC), [156]–[159].

[90] *Collinge v Heywood* (1839) 9 Ad & E 634; 112 ER 1352. See [2–8].

sums voluntarily, whereas the claimant in *Smith* had been sued and held liable by judgment. Thus, Alderson B accepted *Collinge* as correct but explained that the claimant in *Smith* was damnified by the action against him. It is not clear whether Alderson B meant the commencement or conclusion of that action. Pratt B said that the defendant became liable under the indemnity when the demand was actually made against the claimant. Martin B said that the defendant became responsible for the costs 'the moment the plaintiff became liable for them'.[91] Even so, the usual rule for indemnities does not distinguish between incurring a liability and being sued in respect of that liability: neither event damnifies the indemnified party. The decision in *Smith* on this point is, therefore, unusual. It is not clear whether indemnities against breach were thought to be an exception to the general rule.[92]

Method of Indemnification

[10–28] **Method dependent on construction.** The method of indemnification depends on the construction of the promise of indemnity. The compensatory and agreed damages constructions can be addressed shortly. On either construction, the indemnifier performs by paying the indemnified party compensation for loss on the basis specified in the indemnity clause. The difference between them is that, for the former, payment is made in performance of a primary obligation whereas for the latter, it is made in performance of a secondary obligation that is activated by the indemnifier's breach of contract.

The preventive construction requires further consideration. An obvious method by which the indemnifier can save the indemnified party harmless against loss from breach is to avoid breach itself, that is, to perform the contract. But the indemnity is something more than a superfluous promise to perform the other terms of the contract. Where the nature of the loss is such that it occurs immediately upon breach, further performance of the indemnity as a primary obligation is largely irrelevant. Where the loss does not coincide with breach, there remains the possibility of indemnification at some point between the occurrence of breach and the occurrence of loss from breach. Some consequential losses are caused by events over which the indemnifier has no real control; to this extent, the notion of performing the indemnity is rather artificial. Performance of the indemnity has most significance for claims by or liabilities to third parties that have arisen due to the indemnifier's breach of contract. In this context, the indemnifier performs by intervening and relieving the indemnified party of the claim or liability before the latter is compelled to pay the third party.[93]

Thus, in practice, the indemnifier is not always truly expected to play an active role in preventing loss to the indemnified party following breach of contract. The indemnity is not performed as a primary obligation. Instead, the indemnified party enforces the secondary obligation to pay damages for breach of the agreement to indemnify against breach of another term of the contract. As with the compensatory and agreed damages construc-

---

[91] *Smith v Howell* (1851) 6 Ex 730, 739; 155 ER 739, 743.

[92] In argument, counsel for the claimant relied on several cases where the damages claim was for breach of an obligation other than an indemnity: see *Smith v Howell* (1851) 6 Ex 730, 733–34; 155 ER 739, 740–41.

[93] Assuming that, in accordance with the usual rule, the indemnified party is damnified by payment but not before: see [10–26].

tions, the indemnity establishes the basis for assessing loss from breach of that other term of the contract.

Enforcement

Relationship between Right to Indemnity and Right to Damages

[10–29] **Nature of relationship.** An indemnified party potentially enjoys two rights to recover for its loss from the indemnifier's breach of contract: a right to enforce the indemnity and a common law right to damages. The latter right is the counterpart of the indemnifier's secondary obligation, implied by law, to pay compensation for its failure to perform a primary contractual obligation. It does not follow that the indemnified party can always exercise both rights in respect of a particular loss. One reason is that, in the circumstances, the particular loss may engage one of the rights but not the other. The loss may be recoverable as common law damages but excluded from the scope of the indemnity, or vice versa.[94] Alternatively, there may be a compensable loss at common law but no actual loss under the indemnity, as where the indemnifier breaches a contract to pay a creditor of the indemnified party, but the indemnified party itself makes no payment to discharge that liability.

Factual complications aside, it is necessary to determine the relationship between the two rights and their respective spheres of operation. There are several possibilities.

(1) *The right to indemnity is exhaustive.* The indemnified party may claim for loss under the indemnity but its common law right to damages is entirely displaced.

(2) *The right to indemnity is supplementary.* Both rights exist and the indemnified party may exercise those rights in respect of *different* losses: that is, the indemnified party may claim some losses as common law damages and others under the indemnity. Situations in which the indemnity operates exclusively on a limited basis – for example, in respect of only certain breaches, or certain losses from breach – may be included in this category.

(3) *The right to indemnity is concurrent.* The indemnified party may exercise either of the rights in relation to loss, and may seek to enforce both rights in respect of the *same* loss. The two rights can operate concurrently in relation to a particular loss without being co-extensive in all respects.

[10–30] **Relationship determined by construction.** The relationship between the right to indemnity and the common law right to damages is a matter of construction of the contract. An express statement that the indemnity is exclusive of, or additional to, other rights or remedies for breach will be given effect.[95] Where there is no express provision, the parties' intention must be inferred. There are, in general, two competing considerations. There is the principle of construction that favours the preservation of common law rights and

---

[94] *cf ENE Kos 1 Ltd v Petroleo Brasileiro SA (The Kos) (No 2)* [2012] UKSC 17; [2012] 2 WLR 976 (indemnified loss arising after termination for non-serious breach).

[95] See, eg, *Leighton Contractors Pty Ltd v Mohamad* [2001] NSWCA 453, [69]–[72]; *Man Nutzfahrzeuge AG v Freightliner Ltd* [2005] EWHC 2347 (Comm), [182]–[187]; *cf Seadrill Management Services Ltd v OAO Gazprom (The Ekha)* [2009] EWHC 1530 (Comm); [2010] 1 Lloyd's Rep 543, [186]–[187].

remedies. Clear words are necessary to rebut the presumption that a contracting party does not intend to abandon its rights or remedies for breach of contract arising by operation of law.[96] The contrary perspective is that it is commercially unrealistic to say that the parties, who have agreed on indemnity, intended to provide the indemnified party with a choice between two rights of action for compensation in respect of the same loss from breach. The object is to provide the indemnified party with a single right – to enforce the indemnity – in place of the right to damages; a fortiori, where the indemnity clause is the subject of extensive drafting.

[10–31] Indemnity is exhaustive. An indemnity against breach may entirely displace the indemnified party's common law right to damages. This consequence may be expressly provided for in the contract[97] or it may be inferred. *GEC Alsthom Australia Ltd v City of Sunshine*[98] is an example of the latter. A project to exploit a gas field was governed by a set of interdependent transaction documents, one of which was described as a deed of indemnity. In that deed the Council promised to indemnify GEC against any failure to perform its obligations under several of the agreements. The Council breached one of those agreements by failing to ensure the specified minimum gas supply. It was held that the indemnity exclusively governed GEC's right to recover losses from breach. That conclusion was significant because certain losses were excluded from the scope of the indemnity. To that extent, the indemnity in effect operated as an exclusion clause.[99]

[10–32] Indemnity is supplementary. This approach appears in the old cases. A common pleading practice seems to have been to attribute ordinary losses to breach of the relevant term, and extraordinary losses to the indemnity.[100] A similar approach can be found in some more recent cases.[101] Another possibility is that the indemnity is exclusive within a limited sphere of operation, but that the common law right to damages remains for losses outside that domain.[102]

In *Burkard & Co Ltd v Wahlen*,[103] the High Court of Australia held by majority that the indemnity against breach, which covered the buyer's liability to a third party, displaced the usual measure of damages for the sellers' non-delivery of goods. At first glance, the case appears to be an instance of an exhaustive indemnity. The sellers conceded, however, that the buyer was entitled to recover for its lost commission as intermediary on the sale of the goods to the third party.[104] The commission was referred to in the sale contract but was not

---

[96] *Modern Engineering (Bristol) Ltd v Gilbert-Ash (Northern) Ltd* [1974] AC 689 (HL), 717 (Lord Diplock); *Stocznia Gdanska SA v Latvian Shipping Co* [1998] 1 WLR 574 (HL), 585 (Lord Goff); *Concut Pty Ltd v Worrell* [2000] HCA 64; (2000) 176 ALR 693, [23] (Gleeson CJ, Gaudron and Gummow JJ).

[97] See n 95.

[98] *GEC Alsthom Australia Ltd v City of Sunshine* (FCA, 20 February 1996).

[99] See also [10–39].

[100] See, eg, *Groom v Bluck* (1841) 2 Man & G 567; 133 ER 873; *Smith v Howell* (1851) 6 Ex 730; 155 ER 739; *Hodgson v Wood* (1863) 2 H & C 649; 159 ER 269. *Carr v Roberts* (1833) 5 B & Ad 78; 110 ER 721 might also be explained on this basis.

[101] *UPM Kymmene Corp v BWG Ltd* [1999] IEHC 178, [71]; *McGrath Corp Pty Ltd v Ryan* [2010] QSC 101, [28]–[30].

[102] See, eg, *Burkard & Co Ltd v Wahlen* (1928) 41 CLR 508; *Seadrill Management Services Ltd v OAO Gazprom (The Ekha)* [2009] EWHC 1530 (Comm); [2010] 1 Lloyd's Rep 543, [186]–[187] (affd *Seadrill Management Services Ltd v OAO Gazprom (The Ekha)* [2010] EWCA Civ 691; [2011] 1 All ER (Comm) 1079, [32] (Moore-Bick LJ)).

[103] *Burkard & Co Ltd v Wahlen* (1928) 41 CLR 508.

[104] *Burkard & Co Ltd v Wahlen* (1928) 28 SR (NSW) 607 (FC), 613.

within the scope of the indemnity. Assuming the sellers' concession to be correct, the indemnity displaced the buyer's right to damages for one head of loss, but supplemented the buyer's right to damages on another.

[10–33] Indemnity is concurrent. An implied indemnity against breach appears to co-exist with the common law right to damages.[105] Concurrent operation may also be inferred where the promise of indemnity is express. This construction tends to be assumed rather than justified.[106] It may rest on a tacit application of the presumption in favour of common law rights and remedies for breach of contract. Another perspective may be that the promise of indemnity is an independent primary obligation that operates across a range of activating events.[107] That the event happens to be a breach of contract and attracts other consequences is incidental.

Although the right to indemnity and the common law right to damages may be exercised concurrently, the indemnified party cannot recover more than once for the same loss. In that respect, it must elect between remedies for breach of contract.[108]

[10–34] Indemnity is redundant. On rare occasions an indemnity against breach serves no useful purpose. It makes no difference, then, whether the indemnity is supplementary or concurrent in effect. It may be deduced that the indemnity is not exhaustive, so that the common law right to damages remains. In the unusual case of *Saward v Anstey*,[109] A covenanted with B to pay certain annuities to C and to indemnify B on account of the same. A failed to pay the annuities in circumstances where B was not, and could not be, personally liable to C. B was nonetheless entitled to maintain an action for A's breach of the covenant to pay. Best CJ reasoned that if the indemnity controlled B's recovery for loss from A's breach, then B's inability to be damnified would render nugatory the covenant to pay.

Enforcement after Loss

Accrual of Right to Enforce Indemnity and Date of Assessment of Loss

[10–35] Enforcement depends on loss, not only breach. As a general rule, a claimant's cause of action for damages for breach of contract accrues upon breach.[110] Where the claimant claims actual loss under an indemnity, the terms of the indemnity govern. The analysis for indemnities against breach is essentially the same as that for indemnities in general.[111] The fundamental concern of the indemnity is loss from the activating event – breach – and not the event itself. Subject to contrary terms, the right to enforce the indemnity in respect

---

[105] *Telfair Shipping Corp v Inersea Carriers SA (The Caroline P)* [1985] 1 WLR 553 (QB), 568; *TAL Structural Engineers Pty Ltd v Vaughan Constructions Pty Ltd* [1989] VR 545 (FC), 558 (Kaye J).

[106] See, eg, *Twentieth Super Pace Nominees Pty Ltd v Australian Rail Track Corp Ltd (No 3)* [2007] VSC 84; *Shepherd Homes Ltd v Encia Remediation Ltd* [2007] EWHC 1710 (TCC), [750]; *Abraaj Investment Management Ltd v Bregawn Jersey Ltd* [2010] EWHC 630 (Comm), [24]; *Carillion JM Ltd v Phi Group Ltd* [2011] EWHC 1379 (TCC), [156]–[161]. *cf AMF International Ltd v Magnet Bowling Ltd* [1968] 1 WLR 1028 (QB), 1060 (right to damages for breach not displaced merely because indemnity not applicable).

[107] This may explain the approach in charterparty cases: see n 25.

[108] *Twentieth Super Pace Nominees Pty Ltd v Australian Rail Track Corp Ltd (No 3)* [2007] VSC 84.

[109] *Saward v Anstey* (1825) 2 Bing 519; 130 ER 406.

[110] *Battley v Faulkner* (1820) 3 B & Ald 288; 106 ER 668; *East India Co v Oditchurn Paul* (1849) 7 Moo PC 85; 13 ER 811.

[111] See [5–44]–[5–46].

of an actual loss from breach will usually arise when the loss occurs. That may be some time after breach of the other term of the contract.[112] A common instance is where the indemnified party incurs a liability to a third party as a result of the indemnifier's breach.

[10–36] Date at which loss is assessed. Damages for breach of contract are generally assessed by reference to the time of breach. The circumstances may, however, justify a departure from that rule, because the overriding concern is to award a sum that represents fair compensation for the claimant's loss.[113] In contrast, actual loss claimed under an indemnity against breach is assessed by reference to the time at which it occurs[114] or, perhaps, the time at which the indemnity itself is breached, if that is any different. This follows naturally from the point that the right to enforce an indemnity against breach in respect of actual loss usually accrues upon the occurrence of the loss, which may not coincide with breach of the other term.[115]

The effect of the difference in timing is highlighted by the claimant's (unsuccessful) argument in *Nederlandsch-Amerikaansche Stoomvaart Maatschappij NV v Royal Mail Lines Ltd (The Nieuw Amsterdam)*.[116] The claimant incurred losses in settling several third party claims that arose from the defendant's breach of contract. The payments were made in US dollars and the claimant sought judgment in English pounds. At issue was the date for conversion between the currencies. The date of settlement was substantially more favourable to the claimant than the date of breach, some 22 months earlier. To circumvent the general rule,[117] the claimant argued that there was an implied indemnity against breach of contract, and that the indemnity was breached when the defendant failed to reimburse the claimant for the amounts paid under the settlements. The claimant's argument ultimately failed at the first hurdle: there was no basis for implying such a term.

[10–37] Future losses from accrued breach of contract. Damages for breach of contract are generally assessed on a once-and-for-all basis.[118] The award may include an amount for prospective loss that has not been realised by the commencement, nor even the conclusion, of proceedings. In contrast, the general rule for indemnities discussed above[119] produces a different result. Leaving aside the matter of specific enforcement, the indemnity is enforced in relation to actual, not merely potential, loss.

Carillion JM Ltd v Phi Group Ltd[120] demonstrates the difference between the two general rules. The main contractor sued engineering consultants who had provided inadequate designs for part of the contract works. The consultants' indemnity to the contractor covered, inter alia, 'losses, demands, proceedings, damages, costs and expenses' incurred by reason of the consultants' breach of the consultancy agreement. The contractor had

---

[112] See [10–25]–[10–27].

[113] *Miliangos v George Frank (Textiles) Ltd* [1976] AC 443 (HL), 468 (Lord Wilberforce); *Johnson v Agnew* [1980] AC 367 (HL), 400–01 (Lord Wilberforce); *Golden Strait Corp v Nippon Yusen Kubishka Kaisha (The Golden Victory)* [2007] UKHL 12; [2007] 2 AC 353. See also *Wenham v Ella* (1972) 127 CLR 454, 473 (Gibbs J); *Johnson v Perez* (1988) 166 CLR 351, 355–56 (Mason CJ), 367 (Wilson, Toohey and Gaudron JJ), 380 (Deane J), 386 (Dawson J).

[114] *Bovis Lend Lease Ltd v RD Fire Protection Ltd* [2003] EWHC 939 (TCC); (2003) 89 Con LR 169, [64].

[115] See [10–35].

[116] *Nederlandsch-Amerikaansche Stoomvaart Maatschappij NV v Royal Mail Lines Ltd (The Nieuw Amsterdam)* [1958] 1 Lloyd's Rep 412 (QB).

[117] *cf Miliangos v George Frank (Textiles) Ltd* [1976] AC 443 (HL), 468 (Lord Wilberforce).

[118] *Conquer v Boot* [1928] 2 KB 336 (DC); *Bellgrove v Eldridge* (1954) 90 CLR 613, 620.

[119] See [10–35].

[120] *Carillion JM Ltd v Phi Group Ltd* [2011] EWHC 1379 (TCC). *cf Management Corp Strata Title Plan No 1933 v Liang Huat Aluminium Ltd* [2001] BLR 351 (Sing CA).

incurred costs in performing some remedial work by the time of trial, and additional costs and losses were expected for remedial work required in the future. Akenhead J accepted that the indemnity was not presently enforceable in relation to those future costs and losses.[121] One possible course was to declare the contractor's right to indemnity and to defer the assessment of loss until it had been incurred. Instead, to avoid expense and delay, Akenhead J decided to assess the prospective losses on the balance of probabilities according to ordinary damages principles, and to award an appropriate sum as damages for the established breaches of contract.

The applicability of the general rule for indemnities is not so clear where the contract is discharged by the indemnified party for the indemnifier's serious breach or repudiation of contract. In that instance, assuming the indemnity covers loss of the bargain, can the indemnified party recover immediately for the whole loss? A pragmatic approach might allow recovery subject to an appropriate discount for the accelerated receipt of the benefit. In contrast, a rigorous application of the general rule suggests that the loss may unfold over time as the promised performance is not received and alternative events crystallise the actual loss.[122]

[10–38] Losses from future breaches of contract. An indemnity against breach cannot be enforced unless and until there has been a breach of contract. It follows that the indemnified party cannot recover presently for anticipated losses from future breaches.[123]

Extent of Protection against Loss

[10–39] Scope of indemnity determines recoverable loss. Whether a loss from the indemnifier's breach is recoverable under the indemnity depends upon whether it is within scope. Subject to statute and considerations of public policy, the indemnity may cover a type of loss for which common law damages are not ordinarily available. One example is a loss that arises due to the indemnified party exercising a contractual right to terminate the contract for a non-serious breach by the indemnifier.[124] Legal costs incurred by the indemnified party in proceedings against the indemnifier following breach are another example. The usual rule is that a claimant cannot recover as damages from the defendant all or part of its costs incurred in a civil action against the defendant.[125] The award of costs in the proceedings between the parties is a matter for determination by the court in accordance with the applicable rules. In contrast, it appears that the indemnified party's legal costs may be the subject of the indemnity, and are recoverable if the legal proceedings are sufficiently connected to the indemnifier's breach of contract.[126]

---

[121] *Carillion JM Ltd v Phi Group Ltd* [2011] EWHC 1379 (TCC), [160]. *cf* the analysis of the contractor's liability to the employer ([157]–[159]).

[122] *cf K/S Preston Street v Santander (UK) plc* [2012] EWHC 1633 (Ch), [27]–[34] (claim by indemnified lender for future losses where indemnifier redeemed loan early, though not in breach of contract).

[123] *Re Perkins; Poyser v Beyfus* [1898] 2 Ch 182 (CA), 190 (Lindley MR).

[124] See [10–55].

[125] *Cockburn v Edwards* (1881) 18 Ch D 449 (CA); *Anderson v Bowles* (1951) 84 CLR 310, 323–24 (Dixon CJ, Williams, Fullagar and Kitto JJ); *Lonrho plc v Fayed (No 5)* [1993] 1 WLR 1489 (CA); *Penn v Bristol & West Building Society* [1997] 1 WLR 1356 (CA), 1364–65 (Waller LJ); *Gray v Sirtex Medical Ltd* [2011] FCAFC 40; (2011) 193 FCR 1, [15]–[16]. See generally H McGregor, *McGregor on Damages*, 18th edn (London, Sweet & Maxwell, 2009), 712–13, para 17-003.

[126] *Leda Holdings Pty Ltd v Oraka Pty Ltd* (1999) ANZ Conv R 622 (FCA), 627; *Ringrow Pty Ltd v BP Australia Pty Ltd* [2006] FCA 1446; *Twentieth Super Pace Nominees Pty Ltd v Australian Rail Track Corp Ltd (No 3)* [2007] VSC 84; *McGrath Corp Pty Ltd v Ryan* [2010] QSC 101, [30]. Whether such costs are within scope is a matter of construction: see [4–75].

Conversely, the terms of the indemnity may exclude or limit protection for loss for which damages would ordinarily be available. In *Burkard & Co Ltd v Wahlen*,[127] the indemnity precluded recovery according to the usual measure for non-delivery of goods. In *GEC Alsthom Australia Ltd v City of Sunshine*,[128] 'consequential loss' was excluded from the scope of the indemnity against breach. That expression was held to eliminate loss arising from the indemnified party's inability to use its plant or other capital for purposes 'not directly contemplated' by the transaction documents for the project. The Victorian Court of Appeal in a later case[129] equated that construction with an exclusion of losses of the kind within the second limb of *Hadley v Baxendale*.[130]

[10–40] Default construction rules. It is difficult to identify default construction rules for determining the scope of an indemnity against breach. There are distinctly different approaches, which start from mutually opposing premises. One approach favours the indemnity being parallel or co-extensive in its operation. The indemnifier's contractual obligations are the subject-matter of the indemnity, and so the extent of the indemnity should follow, or be informed by, the extent of the indemnifier's liability for common law damages. Thus, where the parties' intention on a point has not been made clear, the inference may be that common law damages principles are imported by construction. The opposing approach gives more emphasis to the distinct character of a promise of indemnity. The indemnity would be otiose if it merely replicated the indemnified party's common law right to damages for breach. The term 'indemnity' might also connote complete protection against loss from an event, untrammelled by some of the limitations associated with common law damages.

The difference in approach will not necessarily dictate a difference in result. Either approach might be expected to cover ordinary losses from breach. Some limitations generally applicable to indemnities are similar in effect to aspects of common law damages principles. An indemnified party is generally expected to act reasonably in incurring losses under the indemnity. This limitation resembles the aspect of mitigation that debars the promisee from recovering for loss it could reasonably have avoided. Thus, where the indemnified party unreasonably incurs loss from the indemnifier's breach, it could be denied recovery on either approach: because it contravenes the limitation applied to indemnities in general, or because principles of mitigation are imported by construction into the scope of the indemnity,[131] and the loss would be excluded by those principles.

Causation

[10–41] Express provision. Where the causal or connective relationship between the activating event and the loss is expressly stated in the scope of the indemnity, the extent of protection is determined by that relationship.[132] The activating event may be identified as

---

[127] *Burkard & Co Ltd v Wahlen* (1928) 41 CLR 508. See [10–22].

[128] *GEC Alsthom Australia Ltd v City of Sunshine* (FCA, 20 February 1996). See [10–31].

[129] *Environmental Systems Pty Ltd v Peerless Holdings Ltd* [2008] VSCA 26; (2008) 19 VR 358, [85]–[87] (Nettle JA). But see *Caledonia North Sea Ltd v British Telecommunications plc (The Piper Alpha)* [2002] UKHL 4; [2002] 1 Lloyd's Rep 553, [99]–[100] (Lord Hoffmann).

[130] *Hadley v Baxendale* (1854) 9 Ex 341; 156 ER 145.

[131] See, eg, *Codemasters Software Co Ltd v Automobile Club de L'Ouest (No 2)* [2009] EWHC 3194 (Ch); [2010] FSR 13, [35], [39].

[132] *Bradstreets British Ltd v Mitchell* [1933] Ch 190 (Ch), 207; *Leda Holdings Pty Ltd v Oraka Pty Ltd* (1999) ANZ Conv R 622 (FCA), 626–27; *Kingston v Francis* [2001] EWCA Civ 1711, [21]–[24] (Sir Martin Nourse), [29] (Rix LJ).

'breach' but, in accordance with the definition adopted in this chapter, it can also be described in more general terms. Common law principles of causation do not directly affect the claim to enforce the indemnity, but similar concepts may be applied by analogy.

The facts in *Bradstreets British Ltd v Mitchell*[133] bear some resemblance to those of the well-known decision *Weld-Blundell v Stephens*.[134] The claimant was engaged to provide confidential reports on a company. The terms of the engagement, as relevant, were that the subscriber would not disclose the information provided and that the subscriber would indemnify the claimant against any loss or damage suffered or incurred 'directly or indirectly' from a breach of the terms of the engagement. The claimant furnished a report to a subscriber, it was communicated to solicitors acting for the company that was the subject of the report, and that company sued the claimant for libel. Luxmoore J held that the subscriber had breached the contract but that the claimant's claim on the indemnity failed for lack of causation. The claimant's liability for libel was created by its own act and did not arise 'directly or indirectly' from the subscriber's breach of contract. The result accords with *Weld-Blundell* though, arguably, the reasoning did not adequately account for two considerations specific to the indemnity: first, the inclusion of the word 'indirectly';[135] secondly, that the indemnity by its terms was concerned with a loss to the claimant and not merely with the incurring of liability. The loss would have occurred upon payment by the claimant and, in that regard, the subscriber's breach in fact led to the claimant being compelled to pay the company.[136]

[10–42] No express provision. The indemnity may be implied or it may be expressed tersely to apply 'against breach' or 'against' certain obligations of the indemnified party. For an implied indemnity, the causal or connective relationship will depend on the nature of the indemnity and the basis upon which it is implied. Where an express indemnity omits the causal or connective element, the cases provide little guidance. In *County and District Properties Ltd v C Jenner & Sons Ltd*,[137] Swanwick J said that an indemnity 'against breach' covered the 'harmful consequences that may flow from it'. A more general perspective can be found in *Total Transport Corp v Arcadia Petroleum Ltd (The Eurus)*.[138] Rix J remarked, in obiter, that where an indemnity 'tracks a contractual obligation' so that it is activated by a breach of contract, then 'one would expect that there should be no difference between the test of causation in the one case, indemnity, and the other, breach of contract'.[139] On that view common law principles of causation are, by default, imported into the scope of the indemnity through construction.

Remoteness

[10–43] Whether indemnity is antithetical to remoteness limitation. A controversial point has been whether a claim on an indemnity against breach is affected by the principle of remoteness of damage, or an equivalent limitation that is applied as a matter of construction

---

[133] *Bradstreets British Ltd v Mitchell* [1933] Ch 190 (Ch).
[134] *Weld-Blundell v Stephens* [1920] AC 956 (HL).
[135] *cf Weld-Blundell v Stephens* [1920] AC 956 (HL), 984 (Lord Sumner); *Mediterranean Freight Services Ltd v BP Oil International Ltd (The Fiona)* [1994] 2 Lloyd's Rep 506 (CA), 522 (Hoffmann LJ).
[136] *cf Weld-Blundell v Stephens* [1920] AC 956 (HL), 978, 981 (Lord Sumner).
[137] *County and District Properties Ltd v C Jenner & Sons Ltd* [1976] 2 Lloyd's Rep 728 (QB), 735.
[138] *Total Transport Corp v Arcadia Petroleum Ltd (The Eurus)* [1996] 2 Lloyd's Rep 408 (QB).
[139] *Total Transport Corp v Arcadia Petroleum Ltd (The Eurus)* [1996] 2 Lloyd's Rep 408 (QB), 432.

to the scope of the indemnity. The origin of the controversy may lie in the use of the term to suggest complete recovery for loss from an event. Of the three significant constraints on the recovery of damages for breach – causation, remoteness and mitigation – the term 'indemnity' is most often contrasted with remoteness. In a famous passage in *Victoria Laundry (Windsor) Ltd v Newman Industries Ltd*,[140] Asquith LJ said:

> It is well settled that the governing purpose of damages is to put the party whose rights have been violated in the same position, so far as money can do so, as if his rights had been observed: (*Sally Wertheim v Chicoutimi Pulp Company*). This purpose, if relentlessly pursued, would provide him with a complete indemnity for all loss de facto resulting from a particular breach, however improbable, however unpredictable.

Similarly, Staughton LJ in *Total Transport Corp v Arcadia Petroleum Ltd (The Eurus)*[141] remarked that

> the word 'indemnity' may refer to all loss suffered which is attributable to a specified cause, whether or not it was in the reasonable contemplation of the parties. There is precious little authority to support such a meaning, but I do not doubt that the word is often used in that sense.

[10–44] Historical perspective. A distinction between ordinary claims for damages for breach and claims under an indemnity against breach is apparent in old decisions. Many of them concerned sub-leases or assignments of leases or sub-leases. The promisor's breach of covenants relating to the demised premises caused the promisee (usually, the immediately preceding assignor or sub-lessor) to suffer a loss or incur an expense in connection with a third party (often, the next preceding assignor or superior landlord). Under the law prior to *Hadley v Baxendale*[142] and even for some time afterwards, such losses were often regarded as too remote. Costs incurred by a promisee in defending an action brought by a third party as a result of the promisor's breach were one example. Although there were authorities to the contrary,[143] the dominant view was that such costs were not usually recoverable because they were not the natural and necessary consequence of a breach.[144] In contrast, it came to be generally accepted that such costs were recoverable under an indemnity against breach, provided they were incurred reasonably.[145]

Logan v Hall[146] provides another illustration. The sub-lessees' breaches of covenants to repair and insure the premises led to the superior lessor re-entering and terminating the lease for the lessee's breaches of the corresponding covenants in the lease. The lessee claimed damages for the loss of his interest, measured by the difference between the rent payable by the sub-lessees to him and the rent payable by him to the lessor, over the term of the sub-lease. The claim was rejected. Coltman J said that it 'was an attempt on the part

---

[140] *Victoria Laundry (Windsor) Ltd v Newman Industries Ltd* [1949] 2 KB 528 (CA), 539.

[141] *Total Transport Corp v Arcadia Petroleum Ltd (The Eurus)* [1998] 1 Lloyd's Rep 351 (CA), 357.

[142] *Hadley v Baxendale* (1854) 9 Ex 341; 156 ER 145.

[143] See generally *Lewis v Peake* (1816) 7 Taunt 153; 129 ER 61; *Neale v Wyllie* (1824) 3 B & C 533; 107 ER 831; *Blyth v Smith* (1843) 5 Man & G 406; 134 ER 622.

[144] *Short v Kalloway* (1839) 11 Ad & E 28; 113 ER 322; *Penley v Watts* (1841) 7 M & W 601; 151 ER 907; *Walker v Hatton* (1842) 10 M & W 249; 152 ER 462. See also, after *Hadley*, *Baxendale v London, Chatham and Dover Railway Co* (1873) LR 10 Ex 35; *Fisher v Val de Travers Asphalte Co* (1876) 1 CPD 511.

[145] *Penley v Watts* (1841) 7 M & W 601; 151 ER 907; *Smith v Howell* (1851) 6 Ex 730; 155 ER 739; *Baxendale v London, Chatham and Dover Railway Co* (1873) LR 10 Ex 35, 44 (Quain J); *Hornby v Cardwell* (1881) 8 QBD 329 (CA), 337 (Brett LJ). *cf Walker v Hatton* (1842) 10 M & W 249, 259; 152 ER 462, 466 (Lord Abinger CB). See generally JD Mayne, *A Treatise on the Law of Damages* (London, H Sweet, 1856), 31–32 and see also [6–44]–[6–45].

[146] *Logan v Hall* (1847) 4 CB 598; 136 ER 642. See also *Groom v Bluck* (1841) 2 Man & G 567; 133 ER 873.

of the plaintiff to turn this into what it is not, viz. a covenant of indemnity'.[147] Although the sub-lessees had knowledge of the covenants in the lease, Coltman J inferred that they had only accepted a limited liability for breach; the lessee could have stipulated for an indemnity or for a right to re-enter to cure breaches. Maule J agreed that there was no indemnity. The sub-lessees were not liable for damages because the lessee's loss did not arise 'naturally and necessarily' from the sub-lessees' breach.

These old cases offer some insights for the modern law, though they are affected by a narrower and more rudimentary understanding of remoteness of damage. They show that an indemnity against breach can protect against losses beyond those that arise in the ordinary course of things, that is, under the first limb of *Hadley v Baxendale*. It is doubtful whether the decisions establish any general rule that the scope of an indemnity also extends beyond the boundary of the second limb of *Hadley v Baxendale*. Even so, there are more recent decisions that accept that some of the old cases remain good law, and that there may be a difference between recovery of damages and recovery under an indemnity.[148]

[10–45] Remoteness as a matter of law. Asquith LJ's famous statement in *Victoria Laundry (Windsor) Ltd v Newman Industries Ltd*[149] was directed to an ordinary breach of contract, not a breach of a promise to indemnify against breach of another term of the contract. Asquith LJ was making the point that, but for the rules on remoteness, a promisor could be liable for all loss caused by a breach of contract, no matter how improbable or unpredictable.

Provided that the loss is within scope, the compensatory and agreed damages constructions of the promise of indemnity do not raise any issue of remoteness as a matter of law. For a compensatory promise of indemnity, the loss accumulates within the scope of the indemnity. Remoteness is not relevant at this point,[150] but only later, if the indemnifier fails to pay the sum due under the indemnity. Similarly, remoteness is not relevant where the parties have adopted their own basis for the assessment of damages.[151] Remoteness is, potentially, an issue if the indemnity promise is preventive in nature. The general analysis of preventive indemnities provided earlier can be applied to indemnities against breach.[152] On that analysis, it is difficult to see remoteness imposing any effective limitation as a matter of law if the loss is otherwise within the scope of the indemnity.

[10–46] Remoteness as a matter of construction. [153] The better view is that if any remoteness limitation applies, then it does so through construction of the scope of the indemnity.[154] The

---

[147] *Logan v Hall* (1847) 4 CB 598, 624; 136 ER 642, 652.

[148] *cf Ebbetts v Conquest* [1895] 2 Ch 377 (CA), 382–83 (Lindley LJ) (point not considered on appeal: *Conquest v Ebbetts* [1896] AC 490 (HL)); *Clare v Dobson* [1911] 1 KB 35 (KB), 41–42.

[149] *Victoria Laundry (Windsor) Ltd v Newman Industries Ltd* [1949] 2 KB 528 (CA), 539.

[150] *cf Hammond & Co v Bussey* (1888) 20 QBD 79 (CA), 97 (Bowen LJ). See generally [5–52], [5–59].

[151] *Robophone Facilities Ltd v Blank* [1966] 1 WLR 1428 (CA), 1448 (Diplock LJ).

[152] See [5–62], [5–65].

[153] See generally [4–26]–[4–28].

[154] *Total Transport Corp v Arcadia Petroleum Ltd (The Eurus)* [1996] 2 Lloyd's Rep 408 (QB), 432; *Total Transport Corp v Arcadia Petroleum Ltd (The Eurus)* [1998] 1 Lloyd's Rep 351 (CA), 357 (Staughton LJ); *Ullises Shipping Corp v Fal Shipping Co Ltd (The Greek Fighter)* [2006] EWHC 1729 (Comm); [2006] Lloyd's Rep Plus 99, [302] (associating remoteness with causation); *ENE Kos 1 Ltd v Petroleo Brasileiro SA* [2009] EWHC 1843 (Comm); [2010] 1 Lloyd's Rep 87, [34]–[35]; *ENE Kos 1 Ltd v Petroleo Brasileiro SA* [2010] EWCA Civ 772; [2010] 2 Lloyd's Rep 409, [14] (Longmore LJ) (but see *ENE Kos 1 Ltd v Petroleo Brasileiro SA (The Kos) (No 2)* [2012] UKSC 17; [2012] 2 WLR 976, [10], [12] (Lord Sumption)).

parties may expressly agree to apply or to displace such a limitation.[155] Broad and general terms used to define the scope of the indemnity will not necessarily be construed literally, so as to exclude any limitation of remoteness. In *Total Transport Corp v Arcadia Petroleum Ltd (The Eurus)*,[156] for example, Rix J suggested that a reference to 'all consequences' of breach might be read as covering all consequences reasonably contemplated by the parties as a result of breach.

[10–47] Whether limitation of remoteness is presumed. The more difficult question is whether, in the absence of an express provision, a limitation of remoteness ought to be presumed for an indemnity against breach. Dicta of Rix J in *Total Transport Corp v Arcadia Petroleum Ltd (The Eurus)*[157] favour such a presumption. The charterer claimed for certain losses sustained due to the master's failure to comply with the charterer's instructions. To counter an argument about remoteness, the charterer relied upon clause 36 of the charter-party. The clause stated that the owner would be 'responsible for any time, costs, delays, or loss suffered by Charterers due to failure to comply fully with Charterers' voyage instructions'. The charterer's argument involved two propositions. First, clause 36 was an indemnity against breach. Secondly, under such an indemnity, the basic criterion for recovery was causation; there was no limitation of remoteness.

Rix J held that clause 36 was not an indemnity. In the alternative, Rix J suggested that a remoteness limitation would be presumed to apply to an indemnity against breach as a matter of construction.[158] This perspective may have been influenced by Rix J's view that a claim on an indemnity was not a claim for damages.[159] Although that is unorthodox, the conclusion that any remoteness limitation would be a matter of construction and not law should still be accepted as correct. The presumption itself was essentially one of co-extensiveness. Where an indemnity relates to contractual obligations and is activated by breach, the scope of the indemnifier's responsibility for loss should parallel that applicable under common law principles.

The presumption goes too far. The English Court of Appeal approached the matter differently. The question was whether cl 36 indicated that the charterer was to recover even though the loss from breach was not within the parties' reasonable contemplation. The answer was clearly negative. Staughton LJ accepted that the extent of responsibility under the indemnity was a matter of construction; he went on to deny that there was 'any fixed rule' that a claim under an indemnity was *not* subject to a limitation of remoteness.[160] Sir John Balcombe agreed in the result, but appeared to accept that a true indemnity would not be subject to a remoteness limitation. Later decisions referring to *The Eurus* have tentatively suggested that a remoteness limitation may apply in some circumstances. The

---

[155] See, eg, *Schenker & Co (Aust) Pty Ltd v Maplas Equipment and Services Pty Ltd* [1990] VR 834 (FC), 836 (express inclusion of losses whether or not foreseeable); *Mediterranean Freight Services Ltd v BP Oil International Ltd (The Fiona)* [1994] 2 Lloyd's Rep 506 (CA), 522 (Hoffmann LJ).

[156] *Total Transport Corp v Arcadia Petroleum Ltd (The Eurus)* [1996] 2 Lloyd's Rep 408 (QB), 424, 432. cf *Australian Coastal Shipping Commission v PV 'Wyuna'* (1964) 111 CLR 303, 309–10 (Kitto J). Contrast *ENE Kos 1 Ltd v Petroleo Brasiliero SA (The Kos) (No 2)* [2012] UKSC 17; [2012] 2 WLR 976, [10], [12] (Lord Sumption).

[157] *Total Transport Corp v Arcadia Petroleum Ltd (The Eurus)* [1996] 2 Lloyd's Rep 408 (QB).

[158] *Total Transport Corp v Arcadia Petroleum Ltd (The Eurus)* [1996] 2 Lloyd's Rep 408 (QB), 432.

[159] *Total Transport Corp v Arcadia Petroleum Ltd (The Eurus)* [1996] 2 Lloyd's Rep 408 (QB), 422.

[160] *Total Transport Corp v Arcadia Petroleum Ltd (The Eurus)* [1998] 1 Lloyd's Rep 351 (CA), 360–61.

limitation seems to rest on perceived commercial improbability, rather than any specific presumption concerning breach of contract.[161]

Other decisions proceed on the basis that no limitation of remoteness applies to an indemnity against breach. In *Zaccardi v Caunt*,[162] Campbell JA contrasted the effect of two terms in a purported contract for the sale of land: (1) a warranty that the purchaser of the property had not been introduced to the property or vendor by an agent; and (2) an indemnity from the purchaser to the vendor against claims by agents for commission arising out of any such introduction. Campbell JA remarked:[163]

> [D]amages for breach of the warranty would be measured in accordance with the rules in *Hadley v Baxendale* (1854) 9 Ex 341 at 354; 156 ER 145 at 151. By comparison, the amounts that can be recovered under an indemnity depend simply upon whether a loss that the person indemnified has suffered falls within the scope of the indemnity.

Another decision that may illustrate the same point, albeit implicitly, is *Kingston v Francis*.[164] B transferred to A certain land that was to become the site of a roadway, with A covenanting to construct the roadway and maintain it until it was taken over by a public authority. A also indemnified B against 'all actions costs claims and demands arising from any breach or non observance of the covenants'. B then conveyed nearby land to C, assigning to C the benefit of A's promise to construct and maintain the roadway. A later transferred to D the site of the roadway, with D covenanting with A to construct the roadway. The roadway was not constructed to the requisite standard. C did not, as assignee from B, sue A. Instead, in an entirely misconceived action, C sued B directly. That action was dismissed but B still claimed indemnity from A for certain losses incurred in connection with the action. A, in turn, claimed damages from D for breach of the undertaking to construct the roadway.

It was held that B could recover against A under the indemnity, and that A could recover damages from D for A's liability to B. The difference in approach is, however, instructive. B's claim under the indemnity succeeded on the simple basis that C's claim against B, although bad, was a claim 'arising from' A's breach and so within the scope of the indemnity.[165] Sir Martin Nourse and Rix LJ further noted that C's claim against B was within the reasonable contemplation of D. Rix LJ observed that the promise by D to construct the roadway was 'not supported by any indemnity . . . but nevertheless . . . [D] were clearly aware of [A]'s liability to [B] and therefore were aware of their own liability to compensate [A] for his liability to [B] in the case of a breach of covenant'.[166]

---

[161] *Ullises Shipping Corp v Fal Shipping Co Ltd (The Greek Fighter)* [2006] EWHC 1729 (Comm); [2006] Lloyd's Rep Plus 99, [302]; *Antiparos ENE v SK Shipping Co Ltd (The Antiparos)* [2008] EWHC 1139 (Comm); [2008] 2 Lloyd's Rep 237, [33]; *Maple Leaf Macro Volatility Master Fund v Rouvroy* [2009] EWHC 257 (Comm); [2009] 1 Lloyd's Rep 475, [259]; *ENE Kos 1 Ltd v Petroleo Brasileiro SA* [2009] EWHC 1843 (Comm); [2010] 1 Lloyd's Rep 87, [34]–[35]. cf *Parbulk AS v Kristen Marine SA* [2010] EWHC 900; [2011] 1 Lloyd's Rep 220, [25]. The remarks in the charterparty cases must be read in light of *ENE Kos 1 Ltd v Petroleo Brasileiro SA (The Kos) (No 2)* [2012] UKSC 17; [2012] 2 WLR 976, [10], [12] (Lord Sumption). See also [4–28].

[162] *Zaccardi v Caunt* [2008] NSWCA 202. See also *Bovis Lend Lease Ltd v RD Fire Protection Ltd* [2003] EWHC 939 (TCC); (2003) 89 Con LR 169, [65].

[163] *Zaccardi v Caunt* [2008] NSWCA 202, [33].

[164] *Kingston v Francis* [2001] EWCA Civ 1711.

[165] *Kingston v Francis* [2001] EWCA Civ 1711, [23] (Sir Martin Nourse), [29] (Rix LJ).

[166] *Kingston v Francis* [2001] EWCA Civ 1711, [30].

Mitigation

[10–48] Mitigation as a matter of construction. It has been suggested that mitigation principles do not apply as a matter of law to a claim under an indemnity against breach because the claim is not one for damages.[167] That characterisation of the claim is unorthodox. Even so, essentially the same result can be reached by accepting that the claim is for damages. The analysis already provided for preventive and compensatory promises of indemnity in general can be applied to indemnities against breach.[168] There remains the possibility of the agreed damages construction. Mitigation principles do not apply where the parties have themselves agreed the basis for the assessment of damages for breach of contract.[169] Thus, principles of mitigation do not, as a matter of law, affect recovery under that construction of the indemnity promise.

There are, instead, various characteristics of indemnities that are similar in effect to principles of mitigation of damage.[170] They can be explained on the basis of construction of the contract or, perhaps in some cases, as implied terms associated with the promise of indemnity. The characteristics apply to promises of indemnity against breach on any of the three suggested constructions.

[10–49] Comparison of mitigation principles and characteristics of indemnity. It is sufficient here to note some potential differences between principles of mitigation and the inherent characteristics of an indemnity as they might apply to the indemnifier's breach of contract.[171]

Under principles of mitigation, a loss reasonably sustained in an attempt to avoid loss from breach may be recoverable. For indemnities, the point tends to be approached as a matter of construction. It is doubtful that there is any general rule that the express scope of the indemnity extends further by implication to include losses incurred in a reasonable attempt to avoid other loss within scope. Implied coverage may, however, be recognised on a more specific and limited basis. Legal costs incurred by the indemnified party in the defence of an action by a third party are one example.

A further aspect of mitigation is that benefits accruing to the promisee as a result of breach must be taken into account in the overall calculation of loss. The comparable characteristic for an indemnity is found in the essential nature of the promise itself, namely, that the indemnified party should be exactly protected against loss. Benefits that diminish the loss and are not collateral are taken into account. It is not clear in principle that the two processes must always yield identical results.[172] In cases of mitigation, a controlling consideration is that the benefit must arise out of the breach. For indemnities, the relevant enquiry is into the nature of the benefit received and its effect on the indemnified loss. Benefits that are identified as diminishing an indemnified loss may not be the same as those that are identified as sufficiently connected with breach for the purposes of mitigation.

---

[167] *Total Transport Corp v Arcadia Petroleum Ltd (The Eurus)* [1996] 2 Lloyd's Rep 408 (QB), 422; *Codemasters Software Co Ltd v Automobile Club de L'Ouest (No 2)* [2009] EWHC 3194 (Ch); [2010] FSR 13, [32].

[168] See [5–59], [5–63], [5–65].

[169] *Abrahams v Performing Right Society Ltd* [1995] 1 ICR 1028 (CA).

[170] See [4–29]–[4–43].

[171] *cf* [10–40] (importation of common law principles into scope of indemnity through construction).

[172] *cf*, eg, *Jebsen v East and West India Dock Co* (1875) LR 10 CP 300, 305; *City Tailors Ltd v Evans* (1921) 126 LT 439 (CA); *Platt v London Underground Ltd* [2001] 2 EGLR 121 (Ch). *cf* also *ENE Kos 1 Ltd v Petroleo Brasileiro SA (The Kos) (No 2)* [2012] UKSC 17; [2012] 2 WLR 976 as discussed in W Courtney, 'Indemnities in Time Charterparties and the Effect of the Withdrawal of the Vessel' (2013) 30 *Journal of Contract Law* 243.

Another point of distinction concerns the right of subrogation. As the right derives from the nature of a promise of indemnity, it should exist also for an indemnity against breach. In contrast, a right of subrogation is not a general incident of the payment of damages for breach of contract. Even if the right exists by virtue of the indemnity, it is likely to be of relatively limited utility in practice. There must be another person liable to the indemnified party in respect of the loss. It would be futile for the indemnifier to be subrogated to a claim against itself. In any event, the indemnifier's payment of the loss, which would enliven the right of subrogation, simultaneously extinguishes that claim. That payment may, depending on the circumstances, also extinguish the indemnified party's rights against another person. In considering the effect of the indemnifier's payment on others' liabilities to the indemnified party, the indemnifier should not be able to take advantage of the indemnity to subordinate its degree of responsibility. That is, it should be recognised that the indemnifier's liability is in the nature of a liability for a wrong, and not simply in the nature of a liability as a contractual indemnifier.

Measure of Loss

[10–50] Basis of measurement of loss. The approach is necessarily general because much depends on the scope of the indemnity and the nature of the loss claimed in the circumstances. Whatever the particular construction of the promise of indemnity against breach, the object is essentially to protect the indemnified party against its own loss. Punishment of the indemnifier is incompatible with the concept of indemnity. A restitutionary or a gains-stripping perspective is also inappropriate.

There is an attractive simplicity in the view that an indemnity against breach is only concerned with real events that, as a matter of fact, leave the indemnified party worse off than before. Many of the reported cases concern claims for consequential losses of this nature. This approach would in some respects approximate a tortious measure of loss. Claims for loss on an expectation basis are also possible, and these introduce complications.

[10–51] Loss of covenanted benefits. Benefits to be obtained by the promisee through performance of the contract can be divided into two kinds.[173] Covenanted benefits are those that the promisor promised directly to provide by performance of the contract. The timely delivery of sound goods, or the completion of construction work in accordance with specifications, are common examples. Uncovenanted benefits are indirect; they are incidental benefits that the promisee will receive through performance of the contract, but are not expressly the subject of a contractual promise. An anticipated commission or profit on a sub-sale of goods is an example.

It appears that an indemnified party may, subject to the terms of the contract, recover for the loss of the covenanted benefit of performance.[174] Some cases concerning liabilities to third parties could be placed in the present category or in the consequential loss category. Assume that A promises B to pay C, a creditor, and to indemnify B against the liability; that A fails to pay C; and that B is then compelled to pay the amount of its liability to C. B's loss could be characterised as the lost benefit of discharge by A, or as the expenditure made by B as a consequence of A's breach. According to the usual rule as to damnification,

---

[173] H Lücke, 'Two Types of Expectation Interest in Contract Damages' (1989) 12 *University of New South Wales Law Journal* 98, 108.
[174] *Man Nutzfahrzeuge AG v Freightliner Ltd* [2005] EWHC 2347 (Comm), [135] (breach of warranty in share sale agreement).

the occurrence of loss under the indemnity is associated with B's payment and not A's breach.[175] For that reason, the consequential loss perspective may be more apt.

[10–52] Loss of uncovenanted benefits. The loss of an uncovenanted benefit can be regarded as a type of consequential loss. It is mentioned separately because it involves a lost gain, as opposed to an additional cost, expense or detriment, as is usual for consequential loss claims under indemnities. In principle, such loss may be the subject of an indemnity against breach, though the extent of protection is not necessarily unlimited.[176] In *Perpetual Trustees Australia Ltd v Schmidt (No 3)*[177] a loan contract and mortgage were set aside owing to unconscionable conduct by the mortgage originator, who acted on the lender's behalf. The originator's conduct also constituted a breach of its contract with the lender. The lender claimed, under an indemnity against breach, the amount of principal and interest to which it would have been entitled had the loan contract and mortgage been enforceable against the borrower. Its claim for interest was based on the rate for borrower default prescribed by the loan contract, which was two per cent, compounding, above the ordinary variable rate. It was held that the lender was restricted to simple interest at the ordinary variable rate. To allow the higher rate would, in effect, have treated the originator's promise of indemnity against breach as a promise to guarantee the borrower's performance under an enforceable loan contract.

[10–53] Conventional measures of loss. The lost benefit of performance may be measurable in different ways. Conventional measures of loss are recognised in various situations according to ordinary damages principles. The question is whether these are relevant to a claim under the indemnity.

It is sometimes said that the award of damages for breach of contract secures an indemnity for the claimant.[178] Nonetheless, there are many instances in which the conventional measure of loss does not correspond to the claimant's real loss in the circumstances.[179] Some conventional measures are based on hypotheses: for example, that upon the seller's breach the buyer would have gone into the available market and acquired substitute goods. It is not clear whether the emphasis on 'indemnity' means that these measures can be displaced in favour of considering actual events.[180] Nor is an indemnity against breach necessarily subject to a remoteness limitation. Whether a loss is too remote is, of course, a matter distinct from quantification, but in some instances the conventional measure of loss reflects an implicit assumption about remoteness. Under sale of goods legislation, the right to damages for non-delivery, non-acceptance and breach of warranty is expressed in terms of the first limb of *Hadley v Baxendale*,[181] and there are prima facie rules to measure loss on that basis.[182]

---

[175] See [10–26].

[176] *GEC Alsthom Australia Ltd v City of Sunshine* (FCA, 20 February 1996) (breach of warranty as to rate of gas supply: claim by indemnified purchaser for lost income); *Abraaj Investment Management Ltd v Bregawn Jersey Ltd* [2010] EWHC 630 (Comm), [22], [24] (breach by agent failing to use supplied funds to acquire artwork as instructed: loss of proceeds from expected onsale); *Perpetual Trustees Australia Ltd v Schmidt (No 3)* [2010] VSC 261.

[177] *Perpetual Trustees Australia Ltd v Schmidt (No 3)* [2010] VSC 261.

[178] *Addis v Gramophone Co Ltd* [1909] AC 488 (HL), 491 (Lord Loreburn LC); *Wertheim v Chicoutimi Pulp Co* [1911] AC 301 (PC), 307; *Banco de Portugal v Waterlow and Sons Ltd* [1932] AC 452 (HL), 512 (Lord Macmillan).

[179] *James Finlay & Co v Kwik Hoo Tong* [1929] 1 KB 400 (CA), 411 (Scrutton LJ).

[180] *cf K/S Preston Street v Santander (UK) plc* [2012] EWHC 1633 (Ch), [30]–[34] (claim for future losses where indemnifier redeemed loan early, though not in breach of contract).

[181] *Hadley v Baxendale* (1854) 9 Ex 341; 156 ER 145. The right to recover damages under the second limb is preserved: Sale of Goods Act 1979, s 54.

[182] Sale of Goods Act 1979, ss 51(2) and (3), 50(2) and (3), and 53(2) and (3) respectively.

For these reasons, conventional measures of loss may not be reliable guides for the assessment of loss under the indemnity.

[10–54] Illustrations. The conventional measure was recognised in *Man Nutzfahrzeuge AG v Freightliner Ltd.*[183] An agreement for the sale of shares in a company contained certain warranties and representations about the company, and also an indemnity against loss or damage from 'any breach or inaccuracy of any representation or warranty given by [the indemnifier] ... contained in this Agreement'. Moore-Bick LJ indicated that loss from a breach of warranty would principally be quantified under the indemnity by reference to the 'value of the promise' or contractual measure, that is, the difference between the value of the shares as warranted and their actual value.[184] The scope of the indemnity also covered losses beyond the conventional measure for breach of warranty.[185]

In other cases, the conventional measure does not apply.[186] In *Re Russell*,[187] Hampton and Russell held four sub-leases in relation to certain premises. Hampton assigned to Russell all of his interest in them, in return for Russell undertaking to pay the rent, perform the covenants in the sub-leases and indemnify against default. There were further assignments and, eventually, defaults in the payment of rent and the performance of repairs. A sub-lessor made claims on Hampton for dilapidations under two of the sub-leases. Instead of paying compensation for repairs, Hampton agreed to purchase the sub-lessor's interest in the premises. Through later dealings Hampton acquired other interests in the premises and then entered an agreement to sell the entirety of his interest to another. Hampton claimed against Russell under the indemnity for, inter alia, the failure to keep the premises in repair.

Kay J held that Hampton was entitled to succeed and ordered an inquiry into damages. It might be thought that this would take account of Hampton's original position as assignor and sub-lessee vis-à-vis the sub-lessor. The measure of loss would be the cost of repairs.[188] The English Court of Appeal adopted a different perspective. Explaining that Hampton was to be protected only against his actual loss, Fry LJ observed that the dilapidated condition of the premises would have been factored into the price when Hampton acquired various interests in the premises and again, later, when he sold the entirety of his interest to another.[189] Hampton was unable to show that, had the premises been in good repair, he would have made any greater net gain from those transactions.

[10–55] Contractual rights to terminate. At common law a distinction is drawn between discharge of the contract for the promisor's serious breach,[190] and discharge pursuant to a contractual right where the promisor's breach is not serious. In the former case, the promisee is entitled to be compensated for loss due to the premature termination of the contract. The loss usually claimed is the loss of the bargain, that is, the lost benefit of future performance by the promisor of its obligations under the contract. In the latter case, the promisee cannot recover for such losses.[191]

---

[183] *Man Nutzfahrzeuge AG v Freightliner Ltd* [2005] EWHC 2347 (Comm).
[184] *Man Nutzfahrzeuge AG v Freightliner Ltd* [2005] EWHC 2347 (Comm), [135].
[185] *Man Nutzfahrzeuge AG v Freightliner Ltd* [2005] EWHC 2347 (Comm), [190]. See further [10–56].
[186] *Re Russell; Russell v Shoolbred* (1883) 29 Ch D 254 (CA); *Burkard & Co Ltd v Wahlen* (1928) 41 CLR 508.
[187] *Re Russell; Russell v Shoolbred* (1883) 29 Ch D 254 (CA).
[188] *cf* McGregor, *McGregor on Damages* (n 125), 940–42, paras 23-073–23.077. Hampton claimed on this basis.
[189] *Re Russell; Russell v Shoolbred* (1883) 29 Ch D 254 (CA), 267.
[190] In the sense of a breach of condition or fundamental breach of an intermediate term.
[191] *Financings Ltd v Baldock* [1963] 2 QB 104 (CA); *Charterhouse Credit Co Ltd v Tolly* [1963] 2 QB 683 (CA); *Shevill v Builders Licensing Board* (1982) 149 CLR 620.

The same limitation does not necessarily apply to an indemnity against breach. This is implicit in the reasoning in *ENE Kos 1 Ltd v Petroleo Brasileiro SA (The Kos) (No 2)*.[192] The owner exercised a contractual right to withdraw the vessel for the charterer's non-payment of hire, and then sustained losses in discharging the cargo already aboard. The charterer's breach was not regarded as serious,[193] so there was no common law right to damages for the losses following termination. The owner succeeded in a claim under an indemnity in the usual form as found in time charterparties, on the basis that the charterer's orders to load cargo were an effective cause of the loss.

The point is essentially one of construction: did the parties intend to cover losses arising from the indemnified party's termination of the contract for the indemnifier's non-serious breach? It is not immediately evident that there should be a presumption in favour of coverage, though *The Kos* does seem to proceed on a similar basis. Other elements in the scope of the indemnity, particularly causation and the reasonableness limitation, might also be considered. Causation has been offered as an explanation for the common law rule.[194] It is not entirely satisfactory in that context and seems even less suited to indemnities, where the causal or connective factor may be expressed with varying degrees of stringency. The decision to terminate the contract can simply be regarded as one cause of the loss. The reasonableness limitation might seem more promising, though a similar perspective was cast off in the development of the present common law rule.[195] If the reasonableness limitation is to do something more than merely replicate the common law position, then the nature of the indemnifier's breach cannot be the sole criterion.

[10–56] **Reliance losses.** For present purposes, a reliance loss may be described as an expenditure or investment made by the promisee in reliance on the contract (whether in the course of performance or otherwise) which becomes wasted because of the promisor's breach of contract. Although not directly on point, *Man Nutzfahrzeuge AG v Freightliner Ltd*[196] suggests that such losses may be recoverable under an indemnity against breach. The indemnified party's claim for loss was based on the falsity of certain statements in an agreement, which were expressed to take effect as representations and warranties. It was held that the indemnified party was not restricted to a claim for breach of warranty according to the conventional measure; it could recover for losses incurred in entering the agreement in reliance on an inaccurate representation.[197] Moore-Bick LJ was, however, concerned to limit the scope of the indemnity by analogy with decisions on the scope of liability for negligent misrepresentation. The indemnity covered loss flowing from the inaccuracy of a particular representation, but not all loss consequential upon entry into the transaction.[198]

---

[192] *ENE Kos 1 Ltd v Petroleo Brasileiro SA (The Kos) (No 2)* [2012] UKSC 17; [2012] 2 WLR 976. See further [4–13].

[193] *cf Kuwait Rocks Co v AMN Bulkcarriers Inc (The Astra)* [2013] EWHC 865 (Comm); [2013] 2 All ER (Comm) 689.

[194] *Overstone Ltd v Shipway* [1962] 1 WLR 117 (CA), 123 (Holroyd Pearce LJ); *Financings Ltd v Baldock* [1963] 2 QB 104 (CA), 112 (Lord Denning MR); *Shevill v Builders Licensing Board* (1982) 149 CLR 620, 629 (Gibbs CJ), 638 (Wilson J); *AMEV-UDC Finance Ltd v Austin* (1986) 162 CLR 170, 186 (Mason and Wilson JJ).

[195] *cf Overstone Ltd v Shipway* [1962] 1 WLR 117 (CA), 123 (Holroyd Pearce LJ), 130 (Davies LJ); *Financings Ltd v Baldock* [1963] 2 QB 104 (CA), 113 (Lord Denning MR), 115–17 (Upjohn LJ), 122–23 (Diplock LJ).

[196] *Man Nutzfahrzeuge AG v Freightliner Ltd* [2005] EWHC 2347 (Comm). *cf* also *Codemasters Software Co Ltd v Automobile Club de L'Ouest (No 2)* [2009] EWHC 3194 (Ch); [2010] FSR 13, [2] (claim for lost profits abandoned in favour of claim for reimbursement of licence fees).

[197] *Man Nutzfahrzeuge AG v Freightliner Ltd* [2005] EWHC 2347 (Comm), [135], [141], [188]–[190].

[198] *Man Nutzfahrzeuge AG v Freightliner Ltd* [2005] EWHC 2347 (Comm), [193]–[197].

[10–57] Other consequential losses. Many cases involve claims for consequential losses. These are often sums paid by the indemnified party to discharge liabilities to third parties, or other costs or expenses incurred by the indemnified party in connection with claims by third parties. Subject to considerations of reasonableness, the measure of loss is generally taken to be the amount of the payment, cost or expense.[199]

Penalties

[10–58] Indemnity activated by breach. The possibility that an indemnity against breach may be a penalty has been countenanced in at least two cases[200] and, apparently, dismissed in another.[201] The penalty rules apply where the event that activates the allegedly penal obligation is a breach by the promisor of the contract with the promisee.[202] This is true of indemnities against breach, where the basis for applying the indemnity is a breach by the indemnifier of the contract with the indemnified party.

The penalty rules are commonly applied to clauses that fix a sum payable as damages for breach, but they are not limited in application only to such clauses. They extend to obligations to pay a sum determined according to a formula that includes variable elements, and to non-monetary obligations.[203] On that basis, the agreed damages construction of an indemnity against breach clearly falls within the ambit of the rules. If the promise of indemnity is a primary obligation it is, arguably, still subject to the rules. The essential object is to protect the indemnified party against loss caused by the indemnifier's breach of contract. The liability cast upon the indemnifier may differ in extent from that arising under common law principles. Enforcement of the indemnity in respect of actual loss[204] from breach leads ultimately to payment to the indemnified party of an amount for that loss.

[10–59] Indemnity activated by events other than breach. The indemnity may be framed so that it is activated by various events, only some of which constitute breaches by the indemnifier of the contract with the indemnified party. The application of the penalty rules to clauses that can be engaged by breach or other events has proven controversial. It appears that the rules will apply where, in the circumstances, the indemnity is activated by breach,[205] but not where the indemnity is activated by some other event.[206]

---

[199] *Groom v Bluck* (1841) 2 Man & G 567; 133 ER 873 (loss including loss of distrained property); *Smith v Howell* (1851) 6 Ex 730; 155 ER 739; *Howard v Lovegrove* (1870) LR 6 Exch 43; *Hornby v Cardwell* (1881) 8 QBD 329 (CA), 337 (Brett LJ); *Travers v Richardson* (1920) 20 SR (NSW) 367 (SC), 375. cf *Scottish & Newcastle plc v Raguz* [2008] UKHL 65; [2008] 1 WLR 2494.

[200] *Yes Home Loans Pty Ltd v AFIG Wholesale Pty Ltd* [2008] NSWSC 1017, [136]–[137]; *K/S Preston Street v Santander (UK) plc* [2012] EWHC 1633 (Ch), [15]. cf *Calcorp (Australia) Pty Ltd v 271 Collins Pty Ltd* [2010] VSCA 259, [25]–[30] (Nettle JA).

[201] *Total Transport Corp v Arcadia Petroleum Ltd (The Eurus)* [1996] 2 Lloyd's Rep 408 (QB), 422.

[202] *Dunlop Pneumatic Tyre Co Ltd v New Garage and Motor Co Ltd* [1915] AC 79 (HL); *Export Credits Guarantee Department v Universal Oil Products Co* [1983] 1 WLR 399 (HL); *Ringrow Pty Ltd v BP Australia Pty Ltd* [2005] HCA 71; (2005) 224 CLR 656, [10].

[203] *Jobson v Johnson* [1989] 1 WLR 1026 (CA); *Wollondilly Shire Council v Picton Power Lines Pty Ltd* (1994) 33 NSWLR 551 (CA); *Ringrow Pty Ltd v BP Australia Pty Ltd* [2005] HCA 71; (2005) 224 CLR 656.

[204] Specific enforcement for liabilities may produce a different result: see [10–62].

[205] cf *Cooden Engineering Co Ltd v Stanford* [1953] 1 QB 86 (CA).

[206] cf *Associated Distributors Ltd v Hall* [1938] 2 KB 83 (CA). This point was left unresolved in *Bridge v Campbell Discount Co Ltd* [1962] AC 600 (HL) but may have been settled by *Export Credits Guarantee Department v Universal Oil Products Co* [1983] 1 WLR 399 (HL).

An indemnity that cannot be activated by the indemnifier's breach of the contract with the indemnified party is, strictly, not an indemnity against breach as defined in this chapter. In any event, no question of penalties arises under English law.[207] In *Export Credits Guarantee Department v Universal Oil Products Co*,[208] Lord Roskill explained that the indemnity in issue in that case was not a penalty 'because it provided for payment of money upon the happening of a specified event other than a breach of a contractual duty owed by the contemplated payor to the contemplated payee'.[209] The amount was payable to the indemnified party following the indemnifier's breach of a contract with a *third party*. Similarly, the rules do not apply to an indemnity against breach by a third party of a contract with the indemnified party. This is recognised implicitly in the decisions on indemnities associated with hire-purchase contracts. A sum payable by the hirer upon breach or termination for breach of the hire-purchase contract is subject to the rules. Yet the rules are not applied to a separate contract to indemnify the owner against loss from the hirer's non-performance. This is so even where the owner recovers more from the indemnifier under the indemnity than it would be entitled to recover from the hirer as common law damages.[210]

In contrast to the English position, it has recently been established under Australian law that the ambit of the penalty rules extends beyond breach of contract.[211] The full impact of that development remains to be seen, though it clearly has the potential to affect indemnities that are activated by events other than breach.

[10–60] Basis for classification as penalty. The traditional test distinguishes between a sum payable as *in terrorem* of the party in breach, and a genuine pre-estimate of loss.[212] In more modern terms, the distinction is between a clause whose predominant function is to deter breach and one whose function is to compensate for loss from breach.[213] The obvious ground on which an indemnity might be challenged as penal concerns the magnitude of the sum payable to the indemnified party. The benchmark for comparison is the amount recoverable as common law damages.[214] The mere fact that a clause may provide for a sum exceeding that recoverable as common law damages does not necessarily render that clause a penalty. Furthermore, even if this is true of an indemnity against breach, the indemnity by its nature still provides only for the recovery of the indemnified party's actual loss. It is unlikely that the amount will be extravagant or out of all proportion when compared to the amount recoverable as common law damages. As Mason and Wilson JJ observed in *AMEV-UDC Finance Ltd v Austin*:[215]

---

[207] See, eg, *K/S Preston Street v Santander (UK) plc* [2012] EWHC 1633 (Ch), [15].
[208] *Export Credits Guarantee Department v Universal Oil Products Co* [1983] 1 WLR 399 (HL).
[209] *Export Credits Guarantee Department v Universal Oil Products Co* [1983] 1 WLR 399 (HL), 402.
[210] See [9–46].
[211] *Andrews v Australia and New Zealand Banking Group Ltd* [2012] HCA 30; (2012) 247 CLR 205.
[212] *Dunlop Pneumatic Tyre Co Ltd v New Garage and Motor Co Ltd* [1915] AC 79 (HL), 86 (Lord Dunedin).
[213] *Lordsvale Finance plc v Bank of Zambia* [1996] QB 752 (QB), 762.
[214] *Robophone Facilities Ltd v Blank* [1966] 1 WLR 1428 (CA), 1446–47 (Diplock LJ); *Citicorp Australia Ltd v Hendry* (1985) 4 NSWLR 1 (CA), 29–30 (Mahoney JA); *Lombard North Central plc v Butterworth* [1987] QB 527 (CA), 537 (Mustill LJ); *Ringrow Pty Ltd v BP Australia Pty Ltd* [2005] HCA 71; (2005) 224 CLR 656, [21].
[215] *AMEV-UDC Finance Ltd v Austin* (1986) 162 CLR 170, 193. See also *Robophone Facilities Ltd v Blank* [1966] 1 WLR 1428 (CA), 1448 (Diplock LJ); *Export Credits Guarantee Department v Universal Oil Products Co* [1983] 1 WLR 399 (HL), 403 (Lord Roskill) (respondents 'not . . . seeking to recover more than their actual loss as compensation by way of damages for breach of a contract').

Penalty clauses are not, generally speaking, so expressed as to entitle the plaintiff to recover his actual loss. Instead they prescribe the payment of a sum which is exorbitant or a sum to be ascertained by reference to a formula which is not an acceptable pre-estimate of damage.

It is possible to conceive of unusual situations in which the indemnity might be penal. The clause may define loss according to a formula that produces a patently inaccurate and inflated amount.[216] Alternatively, the indemnity may cover substantial losses for which damages are not ordinarily recoverable. It may, for example, be problematic under English law[217] for an indemnity to purport to cover the indemnified party's loss of the bargain after its exercise of a contractual right to terminate for a non-serious breach by the indemnifier.[218] In other circumstances, it might be argued that the indemnity is penal in effect if it extends to the costs of proceedings (on an indemnity basis) against the indemnifier for trifling breaches of contract.

Enforcement before Loss

[10–61] Availability of specific enforcement. The basis for specific enforcement appears to be the same as for other forms of indemnity against claims by or liabilities to third parties. In *Travers v Richardson*,[219] in the context of an implied indemnity against breach, Street CJ accepted the principles generally applicable to specific enforcement as being relevant to the case before him. Furthermore, the right to enforce an indemnity in the event of the indemnifier's breach of contract has been said to arise upon, or at least no earlier than, the time at which the indemnified party's liability to the third party is established or ascertained.[220] That is consistent with the usual requirement of a definite, presently accrued liability as a precondition of specific enforcement.

Specific enforcement is available where the promise of indemnity against breach is preventive in nature. It is not available upon the compensatory or agreed damages constructions.

[10–62] Form of specific enforcement. Specific enforcement of an indemnity against breach does not necessarily entail specific performance of the entire contract or an associated contract.[221] In *Travers v Richardson*,[222] the indemnifier agreed with the indemnified party to assume the indemnified party's rights and liabilities as buyer under a contract for the sale of goods by instalments. Street CJ dismissed the argument that enforcement of the indemnity, in relation to those liabilities, was tantamount to ordering specific performance of an executory contract for the sale of unascertained goods.[223] The indemnifier could perform the indemnity in any manner that kept the indemnified party harmless against claims by the seller under the sale contract.

---

[216] cf *Goulston Discount Co Ltd v Sims* (1967) 111 SJ 682 (CA). See [9–51].

[217] In Australia, contrast *AMEV-UDC Finance Ltd v Austin* (1986) 162 CLR 170, 194 (Mason and Wilson JJ); *Esanda Finance Corp Ltd v Plessnig* (1989) 166 CLR 131.

[218] A point not considered in *ENE Kos 1 Ltd v Petroleo Brasileiro SA (The Kos) (No 2)* [2012] UKSC 17; [2012] 2 WLR 976 (see [10–55]). 'Non-serious' is used in contradistinction to 'serious' as in n 190.

[219] *Travers v Richardson* (1920) 20 SR (NSW) 367 (SC), 370–71.

[220] *County and District Properties Ltd v C Jenner & Sons Ltd* [1976] 2 Lloyd's Rep 728 (QB), 734–36; *Telfair Shipping Corp v Inersea Carriers SA (The Caroline P)* [1985] 1 WLR 553 (QB), 568–69; *City of London v Reeve & Co Ltd* [2000] EWHC 138 (TCC); [2000] BLR 211, [34]–[35]. cf *Carillion JM Ltd v Phi Group Ltd* [2011] EWHC 1379 (TCC), [157]–[159].

[221] See [7–19].

[222] *Travers v Richardson* (1920) 20 SR (NSW) 367 (SC).

[223] *Travers v Richardson* (1920) 20 SR (NSW) 367 (SC), 370.

Performance of the indemnity may, however, coincide with performance of other terms of the contract or an associated contract. In *Travers v Richardson*, an obvious mode of performance of the indemnity would have been for the indemnifier to accept and pay for deliveries as required by the sale contract. That would have discharged the indemnified party's obligations as buyer under that contract, and also the indemnifier's obligations to the indemnified party under the second contract. The same point was made in *McMahon v Ambrose*,[224] in relation to a deed of assignment of a lease containing the usual covenants on the part of the assignee to pay the rent, perform the covenants in the lease, and indemnify the assignor against default. With reference to *McIntosh v Dalwood (No 4)*,[225] McGarvie J said that the assignor would have a right, which could be specifically enforced, to compel the assignee to pay the rent to the landlord.[226]

[10–63] **Utility of specific enforcement.** The utility of specific enforcement is affected by two considerations: first, the default rule as to damnification under an indemnity, and secondly, whether the indemnified party can also exercise a common law right to damages for breach. The default rule as to damnification is that the existence of a claim by or liability to a third party is not, of itself, a loss; rather, the loss is sustained generally when the indemnified party pays the third party to satisfy the claim or liability. The better view is that this rule applies also to indemnities against breach insofar as they concern claims by or liabilities to third parties.[227] There are, however, cases that appear to accept that a sufficiently definite liability of the indemnified party constitutes a loss.[228] On the latter view specific enforcement is largely, if not entirely, redundant. The indemnified party can obtain payment to itself by enforcing the indemnity as for an actual loss. Moreover, there is a conceptual difficulty in compelling performance of a promise to prevent loss to the indemnified party when that loss has already occurred.

If the default rule as to damnification applies, it becomes necessary to consider the relationship between the right to indemnity and the common law right to damages for breach. Specific enforcement has a significant role to play where the right to indemnity is the only right available to the indemnified party in the circumstances. The position may be different where the indemnified party can exercise both the right to indemnity and its common law right to damages in relation to the liability. The common law rule permits a promisee to recover damages for a liability, even before it makes payment, provided the liability is sufficiently definite.[229] That requirement does not appear to be any more stringent than the corresponding precondition for specific enforcement of the indemnity. Thus, there may be no practical advantage in seeking specific enforcement in comparison with a straightforward claim for damages for breach of contract.

---

[224] *McMahon v Ambrose* [1987] VR 817 (FC).
[225] *McIntosh v Dalwood (No 4)* (1930) 30 SR (NSW) 415 (FC).
[226] *McMahon v Ambrose* [1987] VR 817 (FC), 825.
[227] See [10–25], [10–26].
[228] See [10–27].
[229] *Randall v Raper* (1858) EB & E 84; 120 ER 438; *Total Liban SA v Vitol Energy SA* [2001] QB 643 (QB). cf *Household Machines Ltd v Cosmos Exporters Ltd* [1947] 1 KB 217 (KB); *Trans Trust SPRL v Danubian Trading Co Ltd* [1952] 2 QB 297 (CA), 303 (Somervell LJ), 307 (Denning LJ); *Deeny v Gooda Walker Ltd (in liq)* [1995] 1 WLR 1206 (QB), 1213–14 (where liability to third party is uncertain); *Biffa Waste Services Ltd v Maschinenfabrik Ernst Hese GmbH* [2008] EWHC 2210 (TCC); [2009] PNLR 5, [79]–[81] (no recovery where obvious that liability would not be paid).

Index